Real Estate Finance

Real Estate Finance

HENRY E. HOAGLAND, Ph.D.
Late Professor Emeritus of Business Finance
College of Administrative Science
The Ohio State University
Former Member, Federal Home Loan Bank Board

LEO D. STONE, M.B.A., J.D.
Professor Emeritus of Business Finance
College of Administrative Science
The Ohio State University
Certified Public Accountant; Chartered Financial Analyst;
   Member of the Ohio Bar

WILLIAM B. BRUEGGEMAN, Ph.D.
Associate Professor of Business Finance, Real Estate, and
   Urban Analysis
College of Administrative Science
The Ohio State University
Real Estate Consultant

 Sixth Edition   1977

RICHARD D. IRWIN, INC.   Homewood, Illinois   60430
Irwin-Dorsey Limited   Georgetown, Ontario   L7G 4B3

Sixth Edition

4 5 6 7 8 9 0 Q 5 4 3 2 1 0 9 8

ISBN 0-256-01930-4
Library of Congress Catalog Card No. 76–49321

Printed in the United States of America

Preface

This edition represents a major effort to preserve the values inherent in the Fifth Edition yet to give the new text a significant thrust into the area of decision making in the financing of real estate. Whereas the major strength of previous editions was probably the depth and extent of treatment of institutional aspects of the financing process, an equally great contribution of this edition may be in the development of student or professional skills in dealing with problem situations related to the textual discussion. Two major additions to this revision should assist in the attainment of this objective.

First, a whole new section has been incorporated to deal with risk and return analysis and financing techniques. This section, designated Part Two, presents instruction in the use of basic analytic tools, particularly in the applications of the various compound interest tables. A set of the tables is included in the Appendix. Other chapters deal with the computation of effective borrowing costs under varying mortgage payment patterns, loan risk analysis and underwriting of residential and income-producing properties, and development and construction lending patterns and techniques.

Second, at the end of all chapters a selection of cases has been included to invite students to deal realistically with problems suggested by the subject matter. Where solutions of financial problems are involved, a model is typically included in the text of the chapter. In this way, the student derives the reinforcing benefit of operational analysis and application of appropriate techniques.

This new edition also includes three other major parts, whose subject matter is detailed in the table of contents. These are Part One, describing the legal characteristics and financial implications of the use of the principal instruments involved in financing real estate; Part Three, dealing with the total mortgage market, and specifically with the major institutional sources of funds; and Part Four, "Government and Real Estate Finance," which summarizes the principal FHA and VA programs; the functions of the Federal National Mortgage Association, the Government National Mortgage Association, and the Federal Home Loan Mortgage Corporation in the secondary mortgage market; and the Farmers Home Administration as an aid to rural economic interests and housing.

This edition is designed for both academic and professional use. Its goal is not only to provide a basic orientation in commonly used instruments and institutional structures and policies, but also to develop problem-solving capabilities in all areas of general discussion.

The authors responsible for this revision want to express their appreciation to their reviewers for many helpful comments and constructive suggestions. In particular, they are grateful to William M. Shenkel of the University of Georgia and Stephen D. Messner and T. Gregory Morton of the University of Connecticut at Storrs. They also especially acknowledge their great debt to the late Henry E. Hoagland, who wrote the first edition of this text and set the tone of the editions that have followed. He was a distinguished pioneer in real estate education. His absence is deeply felt.

January 1977   LEO D. STONE
                                                 WILLIAM B. BRUEGGEMAN

Contents

part two
Risk and Return Analysis and Financing Techniques

part three
Sources of Real Estate Credit

rience. Mortgage Loan Department. Loan Correspondents. Home-Office Operations. Ownership versus Lending. Private Placements.

Introduction

The practice of financing real estate dates back to the earliest history of man. The durability and immobility of land have always made it an ideal security to support credit extension. Before World War I and the Great Depression of the 1930s, however, mortgage debt financing tended to carry an evil connotation: it should be extinguished at the earliest opportunity.

Since the mid-1930s and particularly after World War II, real estate credit has been accepted as a moral and often necessary means of achieving the goal of home ownership. The criterion for becoming a buyer of housing today relates to a person's ability to carry the financing, not the extent of his or her savings. Similar principles have applied in the financing of commercial and industrial properties to support our population demands.

In addition to sheer growth in volume of activity, dynamic changes in policies, techniques, and institutional patterns during the late 1960s and early 1970s have made the area of real estate financing hard to fathom and even more difficult to describe. The recent historically high interest rates sent shock waves throughout the institutional structures and management, causing new attitudes toward old policies. This was particularly noteworthy in the areas of interest rates and equity participations, development of secondary markets, and deeper involvement of the federal government in subsidized housing, particularly for persons with low and moderate incomes. These trends have occasioned new consideration of variable interest rates, arrangements whereby equity participations are granted institutional providers of funds, privatization of the Federal National Mortgage Association and its move toward establishing a secondary market for conventional mortgages, establishment of tandem relationships between the Federal Mortgage Association and the Government National Mortgage Association, and the launching of the Federal Home Loan Mortgage Corporation as an auxiliary agency in the secondary market. Scarcities of funds in thrift institutions, brought on by extensive disintermediation by the public, encouraged extensive growth of real estate investment trusts and new forms of syndications as additional means of public participation in real estate finance. Then, most recently, the disastrous impacts of the economic recession on developers, real estate investment trusts, commercial banks, and others have left their traumatic marks. These trends are taken into account, and the development and characteristics of the new business forms are discussed in this edition.

When one of the blind men in a Hindu fable sought to describe an elephant, he said the beast is like a rope. This man had felt only its tail. Another, who had stroked its ear, thought the elephant to be like a fan.

So students who read real estate finance topics tend to become lost in a maze of individual bits of information. The purpose of this text is to isolate and deal with the major problems in a discrete order.

Thus it is that Part One discusses the instruments of real estate finance and characteristic legal problems created by their use. In this part of the text, the discussion is particularly detailed and comprehensive, to develop an awareness of the dangers of a little knowledge, a sense of the great variety and flexibility of financing tools, and an appreciation of the need for professional expertise to operate in the field.

Part Two reviews the many analytic factors involved in the financing and investment decision-making process, together with the most commonly-used specialized varieties of financing techniques. The purpose of this discussion is to advance the reader's technical abilities to participate in the decision-making process in such matters as borrowing or lending, owning or leasing, evaluating sources of funds, and many others.

Part Three, in order, considers the significance of savings and loan associations, mutual savings and commercial banks, life insurance companies, real estate investment trusts, syndicates, and mortgage bankers as sources of funds. Some history of each institution has been considered essential to an understanding of its position as a source of funds today—to give a perspective of its philosophy and predilections. Beyond that, discussion of the general nature and limitations of its operations is designed to give a sense of its potentiality as a source of funds.

Part Four seeks to put in their place the expanding roles of the federal government in its various approaches to assistance in the financing of real estate. Particularly because of the magnitude of the housing programs and the importance of the federal support of secondary mortgage markets, financial terms and practices in all markets are affected by government action.

part one

Instruments Used in
Real Estate Finance:
Legal and Financial
Considerations

1

Legal Nature of Real Estate Mortgages

Definition of Mortgage

A standard law treatise on mortgages says: "A real estate mortgage is a lien on an interest in the land, created by a formal agreement, by a transfer of such interest, to secure the payment of money or the performance of some other act."[1] In the model "Power of Sale Mortgage Foreclosure Act," promulgated by the National Conference on Uniform State Laws in 1940, a mortgage is defined as "any form of instrument whereby a lien is created upon real estate or whereby title to real estate is reserved or conveyed as security for the payment of a debt or other obligation." As will be noted from both of the above definitions, the essential point is their application to an interest in real estate in the form of an agreement which establishes a lien against the particular interest in question.

Interests Covered

Because "interest in real estate" covers a wide variety of possibilities, "mortgage" must be considered equally broad in its applications. In general we are accustomed to think of the mortgage in relation to fee ownership. In addition it may cover any interest in real estate that is a proper subject of sale, grant, or assignment. This means that rents, dower interests, an estate for years, the rights of a remainderman, reversion rights, life estates, the interest of an heir or devisee (subject to the debts of the decedent), an option in a lease, improvements apart from the land,

---

[1] H. T. Tiffany, *A Treatise on the Modern Law of Real Property* (Chicago: Callaghan & Co., 1939), p. 912. Treatise is updated to current years by supplements.

and so forth, are proper bases for mortgages so far as legal theory is concerned. Whether, as a matter of sound business judgment, mortgagees would be willing to lend money against each of the above-named interests is quite another question.

In addition, mortgages are used to protect obligations that are more or less independent of the property mortgaged. For example, a mortgage on a home may be used to protect a line of credit to be used for business purposes; to assure the payment of an annuity; to guarantee an agreement by A to support B during the latter's lifetime; to make sure that some contract will be fufilled; and so forth.

Background of Legal Theory

Legal theories frequently represent the accumulation of experiences— some of which are in conflict with one another—which may start by accident rather than by intent. One accidental experience produces results which are sufficiently satisfactory to warrant its repetition by intent. Continued repetition crystallizes the practices into what we come to recognize as law. Because the law is never final in its implications until it has been accepted by the courts, we are accustomed to place much emphasis upon court interpretations. Those situations which have been adjudicated tend to give color to future thinking, even after new conditions seem to dictate entirely new approaches in our processes of analysis. Because of this, much of our legal theory is based upon a process of accretion. We are much more prone to add to what we already have than to substitute the new for the old.

Nowhere in our body of law does the past intrude into the present and threaten to influence our future thinking more than in the field of real estate law. This is an inevitable result of the maner in which real estate law has evolved. While progress is being made toward clarification of real estate legal theory and simplification of business practices governed by it, the wheels of legal machinery grind exceedingly slowly— or so thinks the layman.

Recently, some breakthroughs have been achieved. In the interest of expanding the secondary markets for conventionally originated mortgages, the Federal National Mortgage Association and the Federal Home Loan Mortgage Corporation have joined forces to develop a standard mortgage form which is now in use.

Objectives of Uniform Mortgage Law

National conferences have been held over many years in the quest to achieve greater uniformity in mortgage practices in the country. There remains a great divergence.

The objectives sought in most attempts to draft a uniform mortgage law include the following: (1) to prevent unconscionable deficiency judgments; (2) to encourage high percentage loans, thus spreading the advantages of homeownership; (3) to extend leniency to unfortunate mortgagors without jeopardizing too severely the legitimate interests of the mortgagee; (4) to find ways of reducing the cost of mortgage money by making mortgages more marketable; (5) to reduce foreclosure costs, which are really a part of the cost of mortgage money; and (6) to reduce the costs of drafting and recording mortgages.

Every mortgagee, under whatever theory in operation, is concerned with the following:* (1) He wants to be assured that he has a proper lien and that he will retain it until the obligation to him has been met. (2) He wants to be able to realize as much as possible in the disposal of the security which protects his claim, should a default occur. (3) He wants to have the right to elect the time of asking that the security be disposed of, subject to confirmation by a court of equity. (4) In order to protect his rights, he wants the privilege of bidding at the foreclosure sale. (5) Finally, he would like to get control of the property if default occurs, to prevent waste and to make sure that its income-producing capacities will be used to best advantage to apply against his claims.

Title Theory

The title theory of mortgages is one of our heritages from England. Under it, the title to the land rests with the mortgagee. Those who adhere to it take the mortgage deed seriously enough to conclude that title and the right of possession actually pass from the mortgagor to the mortgagee at the time the mortgage is executed. Even if the mortgagor retains physical possession of the land, he does so at the sufferance of the mortgagee, who can dispossess the mortgagor at any time. Since the mortgagor is not admitted to own any estate in the land so long as it is mortgaged to another, he can be dispossessed by that other even without notice. Since the real owner is the mortgagee, he is obligated to observe and to be held liable for all covenants that run with the land.

Under this theory, the mortgagor, by virtue of the terms of the mortgage, retains the right to revest title in himself and thereby regain the right of possession if he should meet his obligations to the mortgagee on the due day. Thanks to the equity of redemption, this right of revesting title and of securing lawful possession is extended beyond the due date of the mortgage to the time of foreclosure sale of the land which secured it.

---

* In this and similar passages throughout this book, the male pronoun "he" applies to both men and women.

In the United States this theory, in the states where it still prevails, has been subjected to several modifications. From the standpoint of the mortgagee, his liability to observe the covenants that run with the land has been largely abandoned. The mortgagor, meantime, has been given more protection by the provision that so long as he abides by the terms of the mortgage he cannot be dispossessed. It is only when he defaults in his obligations that possession of the land may be passed to the mortgagee.

Lien Theory

This theory developed somewhat later than the title theory. Its use has now become the prevalent one in this country. It prevails in all states west of the Mississippi except Arkansas and Missouri. In addition, some of the older states east of the Mississippi have adopted it. The lien theory adheres more directly than the title theory to the idea that the mortgage merely provides security to protect the obligations that are due the mortgagee. It grants neither title nor the right of possession to the mortgagee. Indeed, even after a default by the mortgagor, the latter can retain possession of the land unless he voluntarily surrenders it in accordance with the terms of the mortgage.

The exceptions to the above rule apply in those cases where a court may decree that the mortgagor shall turn possession over to a receiver, pending the completion of arrangements for a foreclosure sale of the security behind the mortgage. Since not all states recognize the need or desirability of receivers for this purpose, the mortgagor may retain possession until dispossessed as a result of the sale.

The differences between these two theories may be material, even though they finally lead to the same destination. The right of the mortgagee in title-theory states to take possession of his property upon default by the one who has been using it seems logical enough and is so recognized in some state laws. Likewise, the denial of the right of possession except with the consent of the mortgagor in lien-theory states is also consistent with the basic idea that the mortgagee is not yet the owner of the real property and therefore should be denied possession of it until its ownership is determined as the result of a foreclosure sale.

Defeasance Clause

The clause in the mortgage which gives the mortgagor the right to redeem his property upon the payment of his obligations to the mortgagee is known as the defeasance clause. This clause is a double-edged instrument. On the one hand it says "Pay and you get your property back." But it also says "Fail to pay and you lose your property and any rights therein."

This clause is usually made a part of the mortgage, even though it frequently takes the form of an afterthought added at the end of a document which reads quite differently. It may assume the character of a separate instrument, with no mention of it within the body of the mortgage. If a separate instrument is used for this purpose, the protection of all concerned is best served if mortgage and defeasance instrument are treated as one document, even to the extent of having them recorded at the same time. To serve purposes which are not always in the best interest of all concerned, they are sometimes kept separate.

Equity of Redemption

At common law, the defeasible fee of a mortgagee became absolute if payment was not made by the law day. The necessity for strict compliance with the exact terms of the defeasance clause frequently worked hardship upon hard-pressed mortgagors. In response to complaints about the inequity of rigid requirements of this clause, equity courts came to view the subject from the point of view of fairness to all concerned. Out of this grew the equity of redemption, which says that equitable principles rather than technical rules should govern whenever the mortgagor is unable to live up to the letter of the contract.

The result of the substitution of equity for rigid rules was an extension of time for redemption, this extension to be fixed by chancery. Hence the name "equity of redemption." Early decrees for this purpose fixed the time to which the equity of redemption must conform. Only after this time extension expired and the mortgagor failed to meet his obligations did the mortgagee obtain an unqualified title. In fact, courts of equity became overzealous in recognizing the equity of redemption. This position radically limited the effectiveness of the mortgage as a security instrument until the courts developed the decree of foreclosure, whereby a forfeiture of the equity of redemption could be declared under appropriate conditions.

In this exercise of this equity of redemption, the mortgagor possesses the absolute right to recover the property mortgaged upon the payment of all obligations due the mortgagee, plus all costs and expenses incurred in connection with the foreclosure suit and sale. This right may be exercised at any time before the actual confirmation of sale. It applies regardless of the form of foreclosure action.

The mortgagee is given the right to foreclose upon a breach of contract by the mortgagor. As a reciprocal right, the mortgagor may redeem his property upon meeting his obligation. The equity of redemption constitutes an estate in the land. The mortgagor may not be estopped from exercising it; nor may he be bargained out of it except upon fair terms. By agreement, the parties at interest may extend the time for redemption. This will not affect the rights of intervening interests who also possess the right of redemption—for example, those of a junior mortgagee. Any purchaser of the equity of redemption has the same rights under it as the mortgagor.

Who Share in Equity of Redemption Not only the mortgagor but others possess rights to the equity of redemption. Those who share in these rights include holders of dower and curtesy interests and all junior lienors. This is another reason for joining all of these interests in foreclosure suits. If they or any of them are not joined, any foreclosure decree does not affect their interests. If they are joined, they must be given their day in court. Failure to protect their interests on such occasion will result in having such interests cut off by the foreclosure decree. Since the interests of all such claimants are of the same nature as that of the mortgagor, they must be protected in the same way—pay up or lose. Any party who shares in the equity of redemption with the mortgagor may protect his interests by meeting the obligations of those whose claims are superior to his own. On occasion this can be accomplished by compromise or by agreement to keep the prior claim alive.

Statutory Redemption Distinguished The equity of redemption is a right confirmed by a court of equity. It ceases when the property is sold at foreclosure sale. In about half of the states there is, in addition, a legal right to redeem, granted mortgagors by statute, which becomes effective at the time of foreclosure sale and runs for varying periods of time thereafter. The longest period permitted is two years. Statutory redemption is a right granted to the owner having an equity of redemption before foreclosure and to all junior lienholders, including judgment creditors. Usually the law provides one period of time for the mortgagor, with a succeeding period for junior lienors. The amount required for redemption covers the sale price, interest to the date of redemption, and expenses. At the expiration of the time permitted for statutory redemption, this right too is cut off.

Meantime the purchaser possesses what may be termed only nascent title. He may not even receive a deed as evidence of his interest, but only a certificate of purchase. His chances of losing his title by redemption by a claimant protected by statutory redemption depend upon a combination of circumstances. Near the top of the list of such circumstances is the price he paid for the property at foreclosure sale. If he paid approximately all the property is worth, his chances of losing the property are certainly less than if he paid much less than it is worth on the open market or than it may become worth during the period when the statutory redemption is effective.

Minimum Contents of Mortgage

Whether a printed form of mortgage instrument is used or an attorney draws up a special form, certain subjects must always be included. These are:

1. Appropriate identification of the mortgagor and mortgagee.
2. Proper description of the liened property.
3. Covenants of seizin and warranty.
4. Provision for release of dower by the mortgagor.

The proper names of both mortgagor and mortgagee should be used with great care. If possible, the mortgagor should use the same form of name by which he is known as the lawful owner of the property. In case there has been a change of name since the property was acquired, either through marriage or otherwise, this fact should be shown in the records to avoid future confusion. Likewise the proper and correct name of the mortgagee is important, whether an individual or a corporation is involved.

In like manner the description of the property which serves as security for the loan should be the legal description as recorded in the public records. While this is not an absolute requirement, it can save future confusion. In any event, the property must be described in such terms that there can be no reasonable doubt about its identification. The mortgagee is usually given the right to transfer his interests to his heirs and assigns (successors and assigns in the event that the mortgagee is a corporation).

As a practical matter, the covenant of seizin and warranty may give the mortgagee paper protection against the mortgagor, but no substantial protection in case the mortgagee depends too much upon this clause. For example, such a clause commonly reads as follows: "The mortgagor covenants that he is lawfully seized of the above described premises in fee simple, and has good right to bargain and sell the same; and that the same are free from all encumbrances whatsoever; and that he will warrant and defend said premises, with all the appurtenances thereto belonging, against all lawful claims or demands." A breach of this covenant by a financially irresponsible mortgagor might result in a worthless judgment in favor of the mortgagee and against the mortgagor. Nevertheless, it is well to include this clause and then to determine the seizin part of it by an independent check of the records. If this is done, the warranty part assumes less importance. However, an occasion in which the covenant of seizin and warranty may become important arises when the mortgagor later acquires a title of which he was not seized when he executed the mortgage on the property. By his covenant he is estopped from denying the full effect of his mortgage grant as a conveyance, and the subsequently acquired title inures to the benefit of the mortgagee.

The dower clause should be observed if the mortgagor is married. If not, the mortgage should show his unmarried status. This too should be checked for the protection of the mortgagee. Execution and acknowledgment should carefully follow the established practices in the state in which the property is located.

Mortgage Forms

The best assurance that a mortgage conforms to the laws of the state to which it applies, and that it represents the type of lien it purports to be, is to have it drafted or at least inspected by a competent attorney thoroughly familiar with the laws and court decisions of the state on the subject of real estate encumbrances. This may become expensive. Such a mortgage may easily contain three to four thousand words. As an alternative, printed mortgage forms are available which can be used to establish real estate liens. The short form is sometimes opposed because it omits some of the covenants which are considered essential for the protection of the mortgagee. The long form spells out these covenants in terms that are more or less common to all such mortgages. Why not have these covenants incorporated into the statutes? Then let each mortgage, by the use of the word or phrase, include each of such statutory covenants as are agreed upon by the mortgagor and the mortgagee. Such a practice would not eliminate the need for a legal counsel. But it would reduce his duties and, presumably, his charges, without causing undue risk of those whom he serves. Several states have taken statutory measures to simplify and clarify mortgage forms.

Other Important Clauses

As a part of the total loan agreement there are several important protective provisions for one or the other party in common use. These include:

1. Acceleration clause.
2. Escalator clause.
3. Variable rate mortgage provisions.
4. Subordination clause.
5. Insurance clauses.
6. Prepayment privilege.

Acceleration Clause Most modern mortgages contain an acceleration clause. In effect this permits the mortgagee, in case of default by the mortgagor, to declare the full amount of the obligation due and payable immediately. In other words, even though the terms of the mortgage give the mortgagor 20 years within which to amortize the principal amount of the loan, in monthly installments or otherwise, the acceleration clause in the mortgage gives the mortgagee the right to demand payment of the full amount of the debt should the mortgagor fail to meet a specified small number of payments. Although legally any default will authorize the holder to make use of the acceleration clause, this is rarely done on default in a single payment. Most holders seek to avoid foreclosure and a forbearance of 60 to 90 days is common.

Also, it should be remembered that the acceleration clause merely represents an option available to the mortgagee. He may use it or not as he sees fit. Whether or not he exercises his rights under it usually depends upon a combination of factors, including his estimate of the amount of cushion of value left in the property to protect his lien, the circumstances which resulted in the default, the attitude and intentions of the mortgagor, the state of the real estate market, the presence and amount of junior liens, and a variety of other conditions. As a general rule, the mortgagee would prefer to help the mortgagor solve his financial problems rather than to take advantage of the first opportunity to exercise his option under an acceleration clause.

Sleeper Clause. There is another type of acceleration clause, no longer in common use, that has been given the not too complimentary name of "sleeper" clause. This is a clause that permits acceleration at the expiration of some period of time, say three years, even though the mortgagor is not in default. Since the average mortgagor does not read the fine print carefully, or does not grasp its significance, he is not aware of the authority of the holder to accelerate the debt and demand payment in full. Later, at a most inconvenient time, he may awake in dismay to the acceleration of the full debt when he has promptly met all of his obligations. Such a clause is outlawed by the regulations of the Federal Housing Administration and the Veterans Administration, but it may still be found in conventional loan mortgages.

This type of acceleration clause is wholly unrelated to the paying habits of the mortgagor. He may meet every payment on an installment mortgage on the due date or even in advance. Resting in the confidence that so long as he keeps up this record he will have 20 years in which to amortize his debt, he may be rudely shocked at the expiration of only 3 years to find in his mail a demand from the mortgagee to pay the balance due under the mortgage within 30 days.

Such shocks usually come in pairs. The first one tells him that he has obligated himself, in signing the mortgage, to permit the mortgagee—

at his option—to declare the full amount of the unpaid balance of the debt due and payable at any time after two years from the date of execution of the mortgage, regardless of the payment record of the mortgagor. The second shock hits the mortgagor when he learns that his ability to refinance his loan is greatly restricted at the time the mortgagee sees fit to exercise his option under an acceleration clause of this type. Such an option would be used only in a tight money market, when the mortgagee can use the money to better advantage than to leave it tied up in the mortgage.

Nor does it always follow that only Shylocks take advantage of the sleeper type of acceleration clause. Sometimes a hard-pressed mortgagee turns reluctantly to such a clause as a means of extricating himself from a tight spot; he, too, is being pressed by those who have a right to call upon him for liquid funds when he is short of cash. Generally speaking, however, it appears clear that the inexperienced mortgagor needs freedom from this type of acceleration clause more often than the experienced mortgagee needs its protection. It is not difficult to find valid reasons why this type of mortgage is looked upon with distinct disfavor by progressive mortgage lenders as well as experienced and informed borrowers.

One use of the sleeper type of acceleration clause is perhaps less defensible than the desire for liquidity in a tight money market. If the mortgage is executed at a time when competition favors the borrower, a sleeper acceleration clause may operate to his disadvantage when the wheel of fortune turns in favor of lenders who are willing to recast the loan on much less favorable terms. For example, the mortgagee may exercise his option under this clause, call the loan, and then make a new loan at a higher interest rate, for a shorter period of time, and with other features less favorable to the mortgagor. This assumes that the borrower has no alternative source of funds—an assumption that would frequently hold good in a tight money market—more or less without regard to his equity in the property and his credit standing.

Acceleration upon Transfer. Still another type of acceleration clause included in some mortgages gives the mortgagee the right to declare the unpaid balance of the debt due and payable in case the mortgagor sells his property to someone not acceptable to the mortgagee. Even the FHA at one time included in one mortgage form the following clause: "If there shall be any change in the ownership of the premises covered hereby without the consent of the Grantee, the entire principal and all accrued interest shall become due and payable at the election of the Grantee, and foreclosure proceedings may be instituted thereon." The justification for such a clause is that since the mortgagee takes pains to measure the moral hazard of the borrower before he makes the loan originally, he should have the same opportunity to examine and evaluate the moral hazard of any person who assumes the mortgage.

Absence of Acceleration Clause. Failure to include any acceleration clause in a mortgage means that a default occurs only in the part of the debt that is matured and unpaid. The remainder of the debt cannot be said to be in default because it is not yet due. Consequently the mortgagee may find that he is permitted to sue only for the matured and unpaid part of the debt. This would suggest a succession of suits as additional installments of the debt fall due, if they remain unpaid. Under these circumstances an appeal to a court of equity would probably result in a decree of foreclosure and sale, subject to the unmatured part of the debt.

Some statutes come to the rescue of the mortgagee at this point, permitting him to bring foreclosure suit, involving the entire amount of the debt to date but omitting any consideration of unmatured interest. Public policy as represented in such statutes assumes that the mortgagee would rather realize his principal and accrued interest at the time of foreclosure sale than to wait until unmatured interest has accrued.

Escalator Clause A mortgage provision that has been little used in this country until its recent revival with the rapidly rising interest rates is called an escalator clause. This provision gives the mortgagee, at his option, the right to raise the interest rate on the loan at any time after a specified interval, or upon the occurring of a certain condition, regardless of the debt-paying experience of the mortgagor.

One of the paradoxes of real estate finance is the use of the escalator clause against mortgagors in default. For example, the mortgage may be written to provide for 7 percent interest but with a proviso that, in case of default in two successive installment payments, the rate shall be increased, at the option of the mortgagee, to 8 percent. While it is recognized that this is a penalty clause to prevent default, nevertheless it seems a bit odd to tell the mortgagor, "If you can't pay 7 percent we shall charge you 8 percent."

The opposite policy is sometimes written into a mortgage in order to reach the same goal as does the escalator clause. The mortgage may be written at a rate of 8 percent. Then the borrower is told, "So long as you make regular payments without default, we will charge you only 7 percent. In other words, we will allow you a bonus of 1 percent for living up to your contract." Or this kind of clause may provide in addition that, while the mortgagee reserves the right to charge the contract rate of 8 percent at some future time, he will not make the change during the first two (or three) years and then only after notice of the change of 30 to 90 days. The psychological effect upon the borrower of starting with a bonus which may later be eliminated, instead of assessing a penalty, seems to favor the substitute plan.

Variable Rate Mortgage Plans When the mortgage interest rate may be raised or lowered over the life of the loan in accord with the variation of some other financial rate, the borrower has what is known as a variable interest rate mortgage. Commonly used reference series are the Federal Reserve discount rate, the prime rate for bank borrowers, the Federal Home Loan Bank Board series of effective mortgage rates, a bond rate, or some other indicator of current money costs. Often upper and lower limits are also established by the rate variation formula.

From the lender's point of view, variable rate mortgages add considerable attractiveness to long-term lending at times of rapid shifts in capital market money rates. By this plan, the mortgage achieves increased flexibility in portfolio earnings. Furthermore, with interest rates subject to adjustment the mortgage more nearly retains its par value in the secondary market in times of rising money costs.

Along with these advantages, the lender must accept certain drawbacks. The flexible interest rate injects an element of uncertainty into cash flow projections that affect the valuation process and marketability of the mortgage. If the mortgage interest rate is changed, it should be clear whether the monthly debt-service payments will be raised or lowered without changing the maturity date, or the monthly payments held constant and the maturity date altered. A second problem for the lender created by variable interest rates arises out of increased uncertainty of gross earnings on his loan portfolio. In a period of declining interest rates, coverage of dividends or interest costs on savings accounts or time deposits may be jeopardized. There are also obvious problems in loan servicing and customer relations associated with every change in rate.

So long as both fixed and variable rate options are open, the borrower will avoid variable plans in periods of low interest rates and surplus available funds, but will seek them out when the opposite condition of high interest rates and tight money exists. The lender will move in the opposite direction. The only way to avoid this counteractive expression of preferences would be for variable mortgage plans to become universally adopted to the exclusion of fixed rate plans.

Subordination Clause   In the disposal of unimproved land, a variety of practices are followed. In one that is frequently used, the seller transfers title, taking back a purchase-money first mortgage as part payment for the land. Since such a sale is likely to be to a builder who needs a construction loan to finance the improvements which he plans to place on the land, it follows that such a loan must be given priority over the purchase-money mortgage. The well-informed subdivider is not likely to accept a second mortgage which permits just any first lien to take precedence over it. In such a case, an unscrupulous purchaser might take advantage of the seller and simply borrow money with the land as security for a first mortgage which would have priority over the purchase-money second mortgage.

The more common practice would be to make the purchase-money mortgage a first mortgage in form but include a subordination clause which agrees that it shall become a junior lien if and when a construction loan is obtained for the purpose of financing the structure to be built upon the land. As a result, the original first lien purchase-money mortgage becomes a junior lien. This the subdivision company seller willingly agrees to because it will be to its advantage in selling additional building sites to encourage all the construction possible in its locality. The average individual who owns a building site for sale can ill afford to run the risk of selling it in the manner indicated here.

Insurance Clauses Every mortgage should (and most of them do) contain provisions for insurance of the property as protection to both mortgagor and mortgagee. The exact nature of the insurance varies with geography, the nature of the property, and the experience of the parties. Fire insurance is standard. Extended coverage is commonly used. Rent insurance and other less well-known types are not as generally needed.

Mortgage Clause. The "mortgage clause" is commonly included as a rider in insurance policies against properties that are mortgaged. Under it, both mortgagor and mortgagee are protected, "as their respective interests may appear." This usually means that the interest of the mortgagee is taken care of first, with the remainder applicable to the interest of the mortgagor. Incidentally, the application of this division may not be as simple as it appears. Depending upon a variety of factors, including the age of the building, the neighborhood in which it is located, and the extent of the damage by fire or otherwise, the major interest of the mortgagee may be to use the proceeds of insurance to liquidate his claims. Meantime, the mortgagor may prefer to use such proceeds to repair or rebuild the damaged structure.

The mortgage should require the mortgagor to keep the property insured (the forms of insurance should be specified, although sometimes they are left to be determined from time to time by the mortgagee) and to give the mortgagee the right to insure if the mortgagor does not, adding the cost of insurance to the claims of the mortgagee. In addition, the latter has the independent right to carry such insurance on the property as he sees fit. He is never permitted to collect more than the amount of his interest. Also, standard policies protect the rights of the mortgagee, regardless of the defenses that may be set up against the mortgagor. Even where the mortgage makes no mention of insurance, the mortgagee has the right to purchase insurance on his own account for an amount not in excess of his mortgage claims. In such case he must bear the cost of such insurance.

Foreclosure Clause. The "foreclosure clause" should be reviewed to make sure what it means in relation to the rights of both the mortgagor and the mortgagee in case of foreclosure sale. In some cases, a foreclosure sale cuts off the mortgagor's equity of redemption so that he no longer has any interest in the property to be protected by insurance. Likewise, if the old mortgagee becomes the new owner, he no longer has an interest as mortgagee to be covered by insurance. The change in his status may cancel his part in the insurance policy. And certainly the old policy was not drawn in such manner that it will cover the interests of a completely new owner who acquires title at foreclosure sale. The purchaser at such sale should act promptly to make sure he has whatever insurance he needs to protect his interests in the property.

It is a common practice for the insurance policies to be kept by the mortgagee. By this means he is always in a better position to check on the kinds and amounts of insurance in force; whether or not the premiums have been paid; and whether the carriers are acceptable to the mortgagee according to the terms of the mortgage.

Prepayment Privilege   Mortgages are expected to prescribe the manner of the payment of the debt which they secure. If this is included only in the note or bond—which may not be reproduced in the body of the mortgage—the effect is the same as if such statement were made a part of the mortgage. By mutual agreement the debt may be paid and the mortgage released at any time before the maturity date. In the absence of mortgagee consent, the debtor has no right to insist upon payment before maturity. Even though the full amount of the debt—including full interest to the date of maturity—be tendered to the mortgagee, he is not bound to accept it before the due date of the mortgage.

Sometimes the mortgagor is embarrassed by the absence of a privilege to prepay. For example, suppose that the due date occurs three years in the future. Suppose also that, for some reason, it is necessary for the owner of the property to refinance it immediately. He may not insist upon clearing the record of its existing mortgage, either to make a new mortgage possible or to be able to sell the property free and clear to a buyer who will take it no other way. Unless the mortgagee is willing to accept prepayment, he is in a position to drive a hard bargain in compensation for his consent to prepayment. The result of such bargaining is likely to be a penalty of some sort. It could be all or part of unearned interest to maturity or even more. While the mortgagee cannot insist upon more than principal and interest if he waits until maturity, as a penalty he may exact all that the traffic will bear. If there is no doubt about the adequacy of security, he is not likely to desire prepayment of the debt. Hence, the mortgagee whose consent to prepayment is sought is not running much risk to refuse the request except on his own terms.

In recent years most mortgages, on residential properties in particular, have included prepayment clauses. Some are unqualified in character, giving the debtor the right to prepay any or all of the debt at any time.

Some provide that prepayment must take place at the time any regular installment of the debt is due. Some provide limited prepayment privileges—e.g., not to exceed 20 percent of the principal amount of the debt in one calendar year. Others set a preliminary period of time within which prepayment privileges may not apply. For example, it may be stipulated that no prepayment will be accepted during the first two years after the execution of the mortgage.

In some mortgages, prepayment penalties are fixed in the instrument. The mortgagee may reserve the right to extract a penalty of three months' interest in case the mortgage is redeemed within three years. Since this is an option, the mortgagee may not see fit to take advantage of it. Or the mortgage may provide that, if it is redeemed from the proceeds of another mortgage to a different mortgagee, a penalty for prepayment may apply. Regardless of penalty clauses in mortgages, their use frequently depends upon competitive conditions at the time prepayment is planned.

The exercise of prepayment privileges by a mortgagor may seriously interrupt investment plans of a mortgagee. The latter thinks that he has made a long-term investment. If the term is shortened abruptly, it seems fair to compensate him in some manner for his loss of income while he is seeking another satisfactory outlet for his funds.

Probably most mortgagees would prefer not to grant prepayment privileges to their borrowers. As a rule, however, under the pressure of governmental agencies and the practices of competitors, the tendency in recent years has been in the direction of granting prepayment privileges. It is not at all clear that such privileges always work to the disadvantage of lenders. Corporate bonds commonly recognize the right of a mortgagee to prepayment compensation by providing for a call premium in case the debt is paid off before maturity. In general, this premium is largest when the bonds have been outstanding only a short time. It is reduced periodically thereafter until it disappears entirely as the bonds approach maturity.

Note or Bond

A mortgage is usually accompanied by a note or "bond" which deals with the features of the debt secured by the mortgage. This note may be written separately or may be made a part of the mortgage. If written separately, it may be copied into the mortgage. In either event the note is the primary obligation of the mortgagor. The mortgage merely represents the security to protect the noteholder in case of default. If the lender were sufficiently confident that the borrower would always be able to meet his obligations, no mortgage would be necessary. The note constitutes all the evidence of the debt that is needed.

In fact, in case of default the mortgagee may elect to disregard the mortgage and sue on the note. The judgment awarded him as the result of the suit on the note may be attached to other property owned by the mortgagor which, through sale, may enable the mortgagee to recover the amount of his claims more readily than if he foreclosed his mortgage. Should the mortgagee elect to do so, he may take double-barreled action against the mortgagor simultaneously. He may bring suit in a court of law praying for relief on the note and at the same time enforce his foreclosure rights in a court of equity. Unless one of these suits results in a decision which completely satisfies his claim, the other is not affected. Since, however, such simultaneous suits are not likely to produce either more speedy or more complete results than one of them, simultaneous suits are seldom resorted to.

Just as a debt could be evidenced without a mortgage, so is it possible to have a mortgage without a note. The mortgagee could agree to leave the mortgagor free from any form of personal liability. Such an arrangement would not affect the validity of the mortgage. If the mortgagor undertakes no personal liability, the mortgagee must look to the security alone to provide the means of satisfying his claims. In such case, he would be in no different position than if he failed to ask for a deficiency judgment or if he failed to pursue his rights under it if a judgment were rendered in his favor.

Because of recent practices, it is recommended that the note not only be a separate instrument from the mortgage but that its terms be omitted from the mortgage. Reference to the note in such terms as to identify it without stating its terms is sufficient to fix the mortgage as its security. By this means the rate of interest, the terms of repayment, and so forth, are not made matters of record. A common form of reference to the note in the mortgage mentions a "certain promissory note of even date herewith in the principal sum of (amount here filled in) with interest from date at the rate therein specified." Consequently, competitors of the mortgagee who might take advantage of the knowledge they could gain from the record for raiding purposes are denied this privilege.

Discharge of Debt Cancels Lien

Since the mortgage lien is currently considered to be merely security for an obligation, it necessarily follows that any discharge of the debt will cancel the lien of the mortgage. Whether the debt be paid in cash, by a valid check, by accumulation of rents collected by the mortgagee in possession, by the proceeds of an insurance policy, by an offset of counterclaims, or in any other lawful manner, the effect is the same.

Even forgiveness of the obligation by the mortgagee or any part of it in consideration for meeting the remainder will constitute a termination of the lien. Acceptance of less than the full amount obligated will not necessarily result in a cancellation of the lien unless the mortgagee is willing voluntarily to grant a release to the mortgagor. Obviously the latter should always insist upon a release in such form that it may be used to cancel the lien of record. In exceptional cases it may be necessary for the mortgagor to resort to court action to obtain a release of the mortgage.

In lien states a satisfaction piece is sufficient to clear the record. This merely directs the county clerk or registrar to indicate on the record of the mortgage that the lien no longer applies against the property. It should be drawn with sufficient care to make sure that the description of the property, the amount of the loan, the names of the mortgagor and the mortgagee, and the date and place of the recorded mortgage are all properly included. Meanwhile, if there has been an assignment of the mortgage, this fact should be recited in the satisfaction piece. Whether the satisfaction piece is tendered voluntarily by the mortgagee or is issued by a court of equity, the effect is the same. In title states, the cancellation of a mortgage lien is usually dependent upon whether the debt secured by the mortgage was paid before or after default. Payment of the debt in accordance with the terms of the note terminates the right of the mortgagee and an unencumbered title remains in the mortgagor, when entry is made of record, without a reconveyance or other act on the part of the mortgagee. Payment of the debt after maturity or other default, on the other hand, has generally been held not to restore title in the mortgagor, since an absolute title passed to the mortgagee upon defaut. In such cases, the mortgagor must secure a reconveyance of title—from the mortgagee if voluntarily given or from a court of equity if not voluntarily given. In some title states, however, payment has the effect of continuing title in the name of the mortgagor whether made before or after default.

Canceled Mortgage Dead A mortgage which has been canceled, followed by the recording of a satisfaction piece or a reconveyance of title, cannot be revived. As long as the mortgage is kept alive its lien may be extended beyond its stated maturity by agreement between the mortgagor and the mortgagee. In such case it is not necessary for the extension agreement to be spread upon the record. As long as the original mortgage remains on the record it serves notice to all and sundry that it is there to protect the unpaid claims of the mortgagee. But once the lien of the mortgage is discharged, a new instrument is required to protect new or different claims of the mortgagee. This is a frequent reason why a mortgagee has a nominee purchase his mortgage. He may thereby employ the subterfuge of keeping the mortgage alive after actual payment of the obligation instead of having its cancellation tell the true story of what has happened.

Forms of Notice

To protect the mortgage lienholder against the claims of subsequent creditors of the mortgagor, proper notice should be given of the lienholder's prior claim. This notice may take the form of:

1. Recording into a public record.
2. Some form of actual notice.
3. Mortgagee in possession.

Recording of Mortgages   Public records provide opportunities for the protection of holders of estates in real property and, at the same time, place upon them obligations to make use of them. By recording a mortgage we simply mean having it copied by a public official into a public record kept for that purpose. Indexes and cross-indexes are used for convenience in the use of the records and are usually considered to be a part of the record. The first recording act in the United States was passed in Massachusetts Bay Colony in 1634. Other colonies soon followed the example of Massachusetts.

Records are usually kept in the county (or township in some states) where the property is located. If the property is located in more than one county, a record should be made in the proper public office in each county concerned. Before the mortgage is made a part of the record it must be "admitted to record." By this is meant that all formalities peculiar to the locality must be observed. These peculiarities attain significance for anyone who is required to search the records to discover the quality of title to a piece of real estate. Unless the searcher knows what to look for and where to find it, he may waste much time and still fail to reach his goal.

A mortgage record is expected to speak for itself. If errors appear in it, they can be corrected. If the errors result from the carelessness of the recording agents, they can be corrected without too much trouble. But if the errors appearing in the record are also in the documents recorded, changes can be made only as the result of a suit to reform the record.

Because time is of the essence in settling disputes where priorities of liens are concerned, it becomes a matter of very great importance to have the time of acceptance for record show not only the day but the exact hour and minute. It should be noted that the time that governs is not the time of spreading the mortgage upon the records. Instead it is the day, hour, and minute that shows the act of accepting the mortgage for record. This means that anyone searching the records should include in his search mortgages accepted for record but not yet recorded.

When a property is transferred from one party to another with new financing involved in the transaction, the new deed is usually filed as of one instant of time, a senior mortgage as of a couple of minutes later, and a second mortgage, if any, as still later, in order to show the proper order of claims. For purchase-money mortgages, however, the deed and the mortgage should be filed for record simultaneously. The record should show no gap between them.

Purpose of Recording   As between the mortgagor and the mortgagee, recording is usually not necessary. Recording is not essential to the validity of a mortgage unless the statutes of the state require it. For example, in Maryland a mortgage must be filed within six months of its execution or it is not a valid lien.

The act of recording creates no rights that did not exist before. But it does give notice of their existence. And it does put all other parties in a position where they are obligated to search the record or take the consequences of their negligence. In other words, a recorded mortgage protects its holder by giving him priority over the subsequent acts of the mortgagor. In general the priority of successive liens is determined by the time of accepting them for record.

Since records are available for those entitled to make use of them, failure to take advantage of the opportunities offered may result in loss to the mortgagee. In most states junior lienors of record without notice of the existence of a senior mortgage may acquire priority of lien over an unrecorded senior mortgage. Likewise, judgments, which are statutory liens upon property that the debtor presently owns or may later acquire title to, may take precedence over unrecorded mortgages. Even subsequent recordation of an antecedent mortgage lien will not affect the order of priority.

Not all equitable mortgages are recorded. In some cases they are not intended to be recorded as mortgages because they appear to be something else. Even what is presumed to be a regular mortgage may lose the effect of the mortgage as such. Suppose that a regular mortgage deed is spread upon the record, omitting the defeasance clause which takes the form of a separate instrument and is not recorded. An unscrupulous mortgagee could sell the property to a bona fide purchaser for value without notice of the defeasance clause, since it is not a part of the record. In this case the purchaser would have unencumbered title to the property, leaving the mortgagor with an unsecured claim against the mortgagee.

Other Forms of Notice   Since the purpose of recording a mortgage is essentially to put on notice all those having a possible interest in the property that it already has a lien against it, other forms of notice may accomplish the same purpose. This means that an unrecorded mortgage would maintain its priority over all subsequent lienors if they knew of its existence and effect. Whenever the mortgagee knows of possible complications arising from his failure to have his mortgage recorded, he can counteract this failure by letting others know about his lien.

Even though the mortgagee takes no positive action to warn others of his lien, one form of notice is usually considered adequate where it obtains. Interested parties are usually put on notice to ascertain the nature of the interest held by the party in possession of the property. The mortgagee would seldom be in possession. Since the mortgagor would usually possess the property and even occupy it, he could easily deceive others about the absence of an unrecorded mortgage, should he care to do so. In inducing another party to grant a loan with mortgage security, he might become involved in later trouble even though a much needed loan would serve a present purpose.

QUESTIONS

1. Compare the early mortgages with those generally in use today. In what principal respects do they differ?
2. What advantages may be gained through adoption of a uniform mortgage law? What difficulties are created by the adoption of such a law?
3. What theory of mortgages do you favor—the title theory, the lien theory, or a modified position? Why?
4. What parties share in the equity of redemption and what rights does it give them?
5. What are the relative advantages and disadvantages of borrowing on a real estate mortgage in a state where the mortgagor has a right to redeem for a statutory period after foreclosure?
6. How important is the covenant of seizin and warranty in a mortgage instrument?
7. What purpose is served by an acceleration clause in a note?
8. What is a "sleeper" clause as related to acceleration provisions in a mortgage note? Is this type of clause defensible? Why or why not?
9. What is an escalator clause and how is it distinguished from a clause creating a variable mortgage rate?
10. What is the purpose of each of the following:
    a.   Subordination clause.
    b.   Insurance clause.
    c.   Prepayment clause.
11. What are the advantages and disadvantages of variable mortgage rate plans from the point of view of (a) the lender; (b) the borrower; and (c) the public interest?
12. What is the effect of recording a mortgage on notice requirements to third parties?

13.   What are the holder's alternative courses of action available in event of default on a mortgage note?

CASE PROBLEMS

1.   Smith mortgaged his real estate to Jones. Jones has not recorded the mortgage. To what extent is it valid?

2.   A holds the legal title to Brownacre. B holds A's note and an unrecorded mortgage on Brownacre. Under his mortgage rights, B has gained possession of Brownacre upon default in payments due on the note. A assigns his title to C, who lives in another state and has never seen the land. What are C's rights?

3.   Black borrowed from Green and gave him a note and mortgage on his office building. As further security, Black then executed a deed conveying title to the building to Green and delivered it to the First National Bank to be held in escrow with instructions for delivery to Green in case Black should default in his mortgage payments. Black defaulted and the deed was delivered to Green. Black then sought to cure his default on the basis of his rights under the equity of redemption. May he do so?

2

Kinds and Special Forms
of Mortgages

Three Kinds of Mortgages

There are essentially three kinds of mortgages in common use:

1. Those between individuals that take the legal form.
2. Equitable mortgages that are treated similarly to legal mortgages by judicial construction although they take the form of different documentation.
3. Collective mortgages.

First, when the term "mortgage" is used, it is generally assumed that it means the kind of financial instrument discussed in the preceding chapter. As such it is presumed to constitute the first private lien against the real estate which is used to secure it. Public claims—such as tax liens— take precedence over first or prior lien mortgages. By statutory exception, federal income tax liens are only effective against subsequent lienors after notice has been filed by the District Director of Internal Revenue. Whenever mortgages are not given first private lien status, they are usually designated in such manner as to indicate their junior position. Such mortgages are discussed in Chapter 4.

Second, there are equitable mortgages, frequently given too little attention even by those whose business interests involve first mortgages. For this reason they are defined with some care in this chapter.

Third, what may be classed as "collective" mortgages are commonly known as mortgage bonds. They are collective in the sense that instead of a single mortgagee there may be many beneficial owners of one mortgage. The nature of such bonds is discussed briefly in this chapter.

Equitable Mortgages   In addition to regular mortgages which are readily identifiable as such, common practice sanctions the use of a variety of financial arrangements which are really mortgages even though they carry some other label. These are called equitable mortgages. A few examples will suffice to indicate possibilities in this direction.

Absolute Conveyance of Title. What appears to be an outright conveyance of title to a property by the use of a deed may be construed to be a mortgage if the parties to the deed intended it to be merely security for a debt. Even though no written evidence of the debt exists, parol evidence, if it be clear, convincing and unequivocal, will be sufficient to determine the true character of the transaction. Even presumedly innocent purchasers of the property in question may not rely solely upon the record of sale rather than the mortgage against the property if they have notice of the facts. This apparent transfer of title is usually construed to be an equitable mortgage instead.

Likewise, a sale of property with an option to repurchase may be construed to be an equitable mortgage. If it is a bona fide sale, the option must be exercised according to the terms of the option, including its date of expiration. Otherwise, the rights of the seller to repurchase cease to exist. On the other hand, if the option to repurchase can be held to be a mortgage in fact if not in form, the seller can exercise the option any time before foreclosure sale becomes effective. In case of doubt, a court of equity may resolve a dispute concerning the facts in favor of the seller of the property and construe the sale as a mortgage.

A third example is provided by the circumstances which result in an advance of funds to purchase property which is to become the security for a regular mortgage. While this is not a common practice, it occurs occasionally. For some reason it may not be feasible for the cancellation of one mortgage to take place simultaneously with the placing of a new one. Hence, a friend of the purchaser may advance the money, knowing that his loan will soon be secured by a regular mortgage, the terms of which have no doubt been subject to previous discussion and agreement. Until this regular mortgage becomes effective, the creditor has an equitable mortgage against the property.

Vendor's Lien. Another form of equitable mortgage is the vendor's (or grantor's) lien. When a trusting vendor transfers title to property in return for only part of the payment agreed upon, the property in question is considered to be an implied security for the payment of the remainder of the purchase price. At best, this is an unsatisfactory method of transferring title, since an innocent third party who may not know of the unpaid balance, if it does not show on the record, may acquire title to the property free of the vendor's lien.

For his own protection the vendor may do one of two things: (1) He may take back a purchase-money mortgage even though it is to remain in effect only a short time. (2) He may recite in the deed that there is an unpaid remainder which the vendor proposes to protect. Such a recital will be notice to all of the presence of an equitable mortgage. The purchase-money mortgage and, where recognized by statute at least, the second form of protection will give the vendor priority over both dower interests and judgment liens.

Vendee's Lien. Whenever a purchaser of real estate advances any part of the purchase money before he receives title to the property, he does so on his faith in the integrity of the seller. Should the seller or vendor violate this confidence and fail to convey title according to the terms of the sale contract, the vendee would have an equitable mortgage against the property. The right is enforceable in equity in the same manner that vendors' liens are enforceable. This situation may arise when a purchaser of real estate signs a preliminary contract and shows his good faith by the tender of a binder check for a part of the purchase price. In case the vendor keeps the binder payment but fails to consummate the deal according to its terms, the vendee would have an equitable mortgage claim against the property.

Land contracts upon which payments have been made may also be construed to be in the nature of equitable mortgages. They are discussed in Chapter 5.

Debts of Decedent. Debts of a decedent constitute a lien against whatever property he may possess at the time of his death. These are again in the nature of equitable mortgages. They follow the property, but the purchaser of such property is not bound to assume personal responsibility for their payment if he does not care to do so. He may be asked to assume them as a part of the bargain when the purchase of the property is arranged. The purchaser usually cannot claim that he did not have notice of such debts, since the records of the estate will be a necessary part of public records which should be searched before purchase is consummated. Difficulties may arise, however, where additional estate tax assessments are made by governmental authorities upon audit of tax returns long after the property has passed to a new purchaser. The purchaser's examination of the records of the estate should take contingent liabilities fully into account.

Priority of Equitable Mortgage. Depending upon the circumstances in each particular case, an equitable mortgage may or may not enjoy high priority. Liens of record at the time an equitable mortgage is established would normally take precedence. Generally speaking, however, an equitable mortgage will enjoy priority over unsecured creditors. Vendors' liens and long-term land contracts are now commonly accepted for record.

Collective Mortgages—Real Estate Bonds In following this discussion of real estate bonds, the reader should not be confused by the subject of notes or "bonds" which evidence the primary form of obligation behind a real estate mortgage. As pointed out earlier in this text, the mortgagor is expected to execute a promissory note which is sometimes called a bond. Then he pledges the real estate as security to insure the payment of his note. When we speak of real estate bonds at this time, we have quite a different meaning in mind. Real estate bonds constitute a series of notes. For example, if the amount to be borrowed is $500,000, instead of issuing one note for that amount the mortgagor, through the use of a deed of trust, will perhaps mortgage the property to a trustee. Against this are issued perhaps 300 bonds each carrying a face value of $500, and 350 bonds each carrying a face value of $1,000. Bonds of less than $500 have been used occasionally but are not very popular because of the high cost of floating them. The costs of engraving, accounting, and so on, are as much for a $100 bond as for a $1,000 bond. By the use of bonds a broad market for participation in real estate financing is tapped.

Students of corporation finance will recognize that corporate bonds issued for whatever purpose are commonly secured by a mortgage on corporate real estate and equipment. The characteristics of mortgage bonds described herein are generally applicable to such bonds. Of particular concern to students of real estate, however, are bonds used in real estate finance, or real estate bonds.

The use of real estate bonds has had an interesting history. In the early days of financing even larger properties, dependence rested almost entirely upon single mortgages. Then a recognition of a sizable market for participation in this type of financing among small investors resulted in the development of real estate bonds. During the decade of the 1920s in particular, this form of financing was very popular. Indeed, it was so popular that it overreached itself and many investors lost heavily on purchases of real estate bonds. The common use of leasehold bonds, whose exact character was not generally understood by those who bought them, added to the losses when the dark days of the 1930 depression brought with them wholesale defaults of such bond issues.

The popularity lost by real estate bonds in the 1930s did not recover until the late 1960s and early 1970s. Several factors account for this. One is undoubtedly the recollections of those who lost heavily on their purchase. Another is the decline of demand for new money for this type of real estate mortgage financing. Relatively few new office and hotel/motel buildings were constructed between the early 1930s and the late 1950s. It was not until the early 1960s that the construction of such properties took a substantial upturn. During the early years of the resurgence, particularly, financing for construction of this type was mainly provided by mortgages privately placed with large institutional investors, especially insurance companies. At that time, the participation of the small investor in such a venture was likely to be limited to subordinated debentures.

In the late 1960s, however, real estate investment trusts specializing in mortgage portfolios became a significant factor in construction loan financing.[1] A number of these trusts utilized bonds secured by mortgages to varying degrees, many as debentures looking to the mortgage asset base for credit support, as a basic part of their capital structure. Such bonds were often issued with privileges of convertibility into equity shares or with warrants attached. By 1975, the real estate bond investor's experience had come full cycle. In the rigors of a deep recession, with wholesale defaults on mortgages in the real estate investment trust portfolios, the trusts stood hard-pressed to meet their obligations to their short-term creditors and over the longer term the bond obligations looked risky. In depressed markets, such bonds commanded extremely high yields and the attached privileges had purely nominal value.

Description of Bonds   The form of the definitive bond is included as a part of the indenture for purposes of identification. The subjects covered are as follows: (1) amount of bond issue, both currently offered for sale and reserved for future offer, including conditions necessary before future bonds may be offered; (2) maturity date and interest rate; (3) option to redeem outstanding bonds, with dates and call premiums; (4) call dates and premiums for sinking-fund purposes; (5) conditions for making changes in indenture, and vote of bondholders needed to sanction such changes; (6) negotiability and registration of individual bonds; (7) acceleration in case of default; (8) immunity of shareholders from personal liability on the bonds; (9) corporate seal and signatures of officers. Then follows the form of coupon attached to the bond, the form of the trustee's authentication, and the form of registration of the bonds.

Security for Real Estate Bonds   Since real estate bonds are essentially notes backed by real estate values, the trustee is interested in measuring the security which protects the bondholders. Since the latter have little capacity of performing this service for themselves, the trustee is expected to protect bond purchasers by taking an interest in the nature of the security behind their investments. Two elements of safety are sought:

1.   Since the property is a going concern, its income potential takes first place. A rule of thumb ratio calls for income twice as great as the amount needed to meet obligations. This rule may be said to be based upon the principle of discounted optimism. On the theory that the optimism may visualize a situation twice as favorable as it really is, if it is discounted 50 percent it is still safe.

On the other hand, if leasehold bonds are issued in such amounts that the expected income is less than the demands against it, the results are bound to cause trouble. For example, suppose that net income from

---

[1] See further treatment of real estate investment trusts, Chapter 18.

a property available for bond payments at the peak of prosperity, with high rents and a low vacancy ratio, is only $12,000 as against bond interest and retirement allowances of $10,000. A small increase in the vacancy ratio or a slight decline in rent levels can easily result in a net income less than is required to meet bond interest and amortization commitments.

2. In addition to the going concern value of the property, based upon its income potential, those interested in real estate bonds must consider also the liquidation value of the property. While this is determined in part by the income potential, it is based upon other variables as well. It is conceivable that a speculative use of a given property might produce a net income of $15,000, while any other use might earn only $6,000 net. In case the latter contingency becomes effective, the question arises, "What will the property then be worth?" In case this amount is $100,000 or less, it would not be safe to issue $100,000 of bonds against an earning capacity of $15,000 even though this would show a bond interest ratio of more than two times.

It follows, therefore, that, in appraising the soundness of real estate bond issues, both the liquidation value of the property in case of default on the bond issue, and the income potential of the property from the standpoint of its use by a going concern, are important. Of the two, the long-range income potential is more significant. Since the use of property gives its value, the net return made possible by this use is the basis for the valuation placed upon the property. Vacant property has only potential use. Care should be exercised in the use of pro forma income statements which assume the presence of unrealized income, gross and net. Much more reliable is the income statement based upon actual experience, which takes into account all probable charges against the gross income before arriving at a net figure.

Parties to Bond Issue   As in all other bond issues, usually three parties are concerned: the issuing corporation, the trustee, and the bondholder. The contents of a typical deed of trust or indenture of a first mortgage bond issue are briefly summarized in the paragraphs that follow. First, the borrowing corporation and the trustee are carefully identified. Next in order is the recitation of the authority of the borrowing corporation to borrow money and to issue bonds as evidence of such indebtedness.

The Bond Indenture   The bond indenture describes the security behind the bond issue under several captions. These include legal, as well as physical, descriptions of buildings and other tangible property. Intangibles, such as patents, copyrights, trademarks, licenses, and good will, are also incorporated as security.

The definitions section of the indenture includes numerous formal definitions of such terms as "trustee," "bond," "outstanding," "current assets," "current liabilities," "funded indebtedness," and "net income." Under the subject of the particular covenants to which the company subscribes appear the following items: to pay all debts as they come due; to maintain the corporate existence of the obligor and preserve its rights; to conduct the business in an efficient and proper manner; to restrict dividends so long as the bonds are outstanding; to give no prior liens, except that purchase-money mortgages may be issued for an amount not to exceed a fixed percentage of the cost of fixed assets acquired thereby; to restrict subsidiary operations according to a detailed formula set forth in the indenture; not to guarantee obligations of other corporations; not to make loans to officers, directors, or stockholders; to restrict compensation of officers and directors according to terms of the indenture; to render proper accounting; to keep specified amounts of insurance; and to restrict expansion programs to a relationship to net assets as set forth in the indenture.

Sinking-fund provisions of real estate bond issues usually give the issuing company considerable leeway. The required deposit may be a low minimum, such as 2 percent of the original amount of the bond issue annually. Additional deposits will normally be related to annual net corporate income, with a maximum regardless of the net earnings. In lieu of cash, the mortgagor may deposit bonds of this issue, or any combination of cash or bonds. When it is advantageous to do so, the trustee may use sinking-fund cash to retire the bonds.

Default on Bonds   When a default occurs, either the trustee or the holders of the contractually required percentage of the outstanding bonds may file notice with the borrower that the bonds are due and payable immediately. If the borrower makes up all defaults at any time before a judgment shall be entered in favor of the bondholder, the default shall be considered cured and the trustee may rescind the declaration of default. In the meantime, upon a declaration of default, the trustee may enter the property, exclude the borrower from possession, and manage the property as if it were owned by the trustee. The trustee may sell the estate, as an entirety or in such parcels as the trustee and the holders of a majority of the bonds may determine. As an alternative, the trustee may foreclose the indenture or use any other remedy available to it to protect the interest of the bondholders.

The indenture provides that, should any part of the security be taken over by the exercise of eminent domain or otherwise, the proceeds shall be paid to the trustee for the benefit of bondholders. However, should the borrower wish to use these funds to acquire new land or to construct buildings, it may do so. Meantime, the trustee has the right to contest any award and may charge to the borrower any costs incurred in such contest. In case such proceeds are not used for the purchase of land or the construction of buildings to be used in the business, they may be used by the trustee to redeem bonds outstanding. In such case the pattern of bond redemption set forth elsewhere in the indenture shall be followed.

The Trustee The trustee assumes no responsibility for any statements of facts contained in the indenture. It makes no representation concerning the validity or the sufficiency of the indenture or of any bonds or coupons, or as to the security afforded by the indenture. It assumes no responsibility for the application by the borrower of the proceeds of the bond issue. If the trustee acts in good faith on any matter affecting the interests of the bondholders, it may not be held responsible for any mistakes due to forgery of documents, and so forth. In case of doubt about the ownership of a bond, the trustee need not act until it has been reasonably satisfied.

The borrower pays the compensation and expenses of the trustee. The claims of the trustee take priority over the claims of the bondholders. It is not presumed to have notice of any default under the bond indenture unless and until it has been so notified in writing by the holders of the required percentage of the outstanding bonds. The trustee may buy and sell bonds and be dealt with in the same manner as any other bondholder. The trustee may resign at any time or may be removed at the request of the holders of a majority of outstanding bonds.

Other Special Forms of Real Estate Securities

Within the framework of the real estate mortgage, special designations are applied to instruments containing particular provisions. The instruments considered in this chapter include:

1. Mortgage for future advances, or "open-end" mortgage.
2. Participation mortgage.
3. Purchase-money mortgage.
4. Packaged mortgage.
5. Budget mortgage.
6. Blanket mortgage.
7. Balloon mortgage.
8. Deed of trust.

Mortgage for Future Advances Since a mortgage provides security to protect an obligation, this obligation may take the form of an executory contract as well as a debt already in existence. While it is expected that a mortgage will always state the total amount of the debt it is expected to secure, this amount may be in the nature of a forecast of total debt incurred in installments. In other words, a mortgage may cover future as well as current advances. For example, a mortgage may be so written that it will protect several successive loans under a general line of credit extended by the mortgagee to the mortgagor. In case the total amount cannot be forecasted with accuracy, at least the general nature of the advances or loans must be apparent from the wording of the mortgage.

From one of the mortgagor covenants of a mortgage form in common use, the following quotation indicates the intent of the mortgagor and the mortgagee on this subject:

That the mortgagee or legal holder of this mortgage may make future advancements for the repair, restoration and improvement of said buildings, and that the amount of funds so advanced may be added to the then unpaid balance on said loan and bear interest as provided by the terms of the original note, and shall be secured by and subject to all of the terms of this mortgage deed.

One excellent illustration of a mortgage for future advances (sometimes called an open or open-end mortgage) takes the form of construction loans. Here the borrower arranges in advance with a mortgagee for a total amount—usually definitely stated in the mortgage—which will be advanced under the mortgage to meet the part of the costs of construction which the owner of the property does not expect to meet from his own capital funds. As the structure progresses, the mortgagor has the right to call upon the mortgagee for successive advances on the loan.

The timing and amounts of these advances follow various patterns. If a residence is being financed, one pattern follows a rule of thumb plan which reads somewhat as follows: One third is advanced when the house is under roof. Presumably the builder's capital or his credit or unsecured short-term loans will take care of his bills up to this point. He may use the proceeds of the first advance to meet his obligations to short-term creditors presently owed. A second third may be advanced when the house is plastered. This does not imply that the plastering cost alone will justify this second advance. Rather, other work has been in progress, including plumbing, painting, and so on. The final third is advanced when the house is completed and ready for occupancy. Sometimes a small portion of this final advance is held back for a time to meet the obligations of materialmen, laborers, or others who have not been paid by the builder.

Some lenders on construction loans hold back a portion of the loan commitment when the mortgagor is a speculative builder. The amount held back may be as much as 20 percent. It may be released only when the loan has been assumed by an owner-occupant. The occupancy of the property by the owner is presumed to add security to the loan.

A variation of this plan calls for four payments instead of three:

(1) the first payment when the building is enclosed; (2) the second when the interior rough work is completed and the building is ready for plastering; (3) a third when wood trim has been applied; and (4) the fourth and final payment when the building is completed and ready for occupancy.

Still other variations follow a variety of practices. One calls for advances at such stages as: installation of the foundation; construction of superstructure floor by floor; completion of roof; plastering; installation of trim; and so forth. In more informal disbursements, the practice is to avoid a fixed pattern but to make advances to the builder as he needs cash, provided the inspector knows the builder well and feels that the lender is well protected by the progress of the building plus the lot value. This kind of disbursement procedure is not recommended because it is too personal in character.

A second kind of pattern of advances requires the builder to submit all bills for material, from subcontractors in particular, to the mortgagee. These bills may be paid directly by the latter and charged against the construction loan. This plan is most often resorted to in periods of economic uncertainty or in cases where the mortgagee is not too sure of the financial status of the mortgagor.

A third pattern, applicable particularly to more pretentious structures, sets up a definite schedule of advances which is related to the progress of the work. While the mortgagee should make frequent enough inspections to keep himself informed of the progress of construction—under either plan of advances—he is likely to be best informed when a definite schedule of advances is stipulated.

Intervening Liens. One problem that is always faced by a mortgagee when the mortgage provides for future advances has to do with the priority of intervening liens. Suppose, for example, that a construction mortgage has been duly executed and recorded, and a first advance has been made. Suppose also that, before a second advance is due, a junior lien of some kind is filed against the property. If now a second advance is made under the original mortgage, does it take precedence over the intervening junior lien? Here again there is considerable confusion because of a variety of court decisions, some of which conflict with others made under similar conditions.

A general rule seems to sanction the idea that if the mortgage contract makes the future advances obligatory if stipulated conditions are met by the mortgagor, then the mortgagee may make the future advances regardless of the existence of intervening liens. This rule seems to govern even though the obligatory nature of the advances is not spelled out in the mortgage but is dependent upon a definite oral agreement. When the mortgage mentions future advances, however, junior lienors are at least on notice of the probable superior lien of the senior mortgagee.

The junior lienor may still wish to pursue the subject further to try to determine if a contract for future advances actually exists.

Where there is no definite contract requiring the mortgagee to make future advances, court decisions may follow at least two paths. One leads to the conclusion that the mortgagee is protected in the priority of his future advances, even though he does not take the trouble to search the record for intervening liens. However, if he has notice outside of the record that such junior liens exist, he is bound by their priority over his future advances. This seems to be the prevailing rule. The other path leads to a different conclusion. In a minority of cases, the courts hold that, before discretionary future advances are made by the mortgagee, he must search the record and be bound by any intervening liens that he finds there. The unsatisfactory nature of the answers available in considering the question at issue places both mortgagee and mortgagor at a distinct disadvantage. For example, suppose that a mortgagor borrows $8,000 and gives a first mortgage to secure his debt. Suppose that by regular and uninterrupted payments he has reduced the amount of his indebtedness to $5,000. Suppose that he now needs to borrow $1,000 for repairs to his house or for any other purpose. Can the mortgagee make this advance safely without a search of the records for intervening liens? Because of his past satisfactory experience with the borrower, he might like very much to make the advance and add it to the unpaid balance of the loan. But if he must first search the record for intervening liens, he can hardly afford to render this service without charging the borrower for it.

Then, if he finds intervening liens which he must observe, he may be compelled to refuse the request of the borrower, thereby possibly reducing the value of his security because the owner cannot finance needed repairs. Nor can the lender recast the loan, adding to a new mortgage the amount needed by the mortgagor. In this case he has incurred an expense which he must pass along to the borrower without rendering him an acceptable service. Numerous state legislatures have seen fit to clarify, in particular, the uncertain status of optional future advances. There is a tendency to set a firm upper limit to such advances, as for example, $3,000 in Rhode Island and $3,500 in Maryland.

Some mortgagees rely primarily upon their past experience with the mortgagor, obtain from him an affidavit to the effect that there are no intervening liens, and disregard the record. They testify that the risk they run under such conditions is not great. Meantime, if his past experience with the mortgagor has been unsatisfactory, the mortgagee would probably not wish to make an additional advance, regardless of the existence or absence of intervening liens.

Other Uses of Open-End Mortgage. The open-end mortgage is generally desirable from the standpoint of both borrowers and lenders.

Under present payment plans, a mortgage is commonly amortized over an extended period of time. Under an open-end mortgage, the mortgagor can maintain or improve his mortgaged property, often his home, by borrowing from his original lender within the terms of his original mortgage. Repayment of the additional borrowing can be amortized by a relatively small addition, if any, to the monthly payments required under the mortgage. Compared with personal loans or even FHA loans for modernization, which must be repaid in a relatively short time, borrowing under an original open-end mortgage is often decidedly advantageous. The borrowing costs where repairs and improvements are financed by a loan secured by a second mortgage are also relatively high. The advantage of the open-end mortgage to the lender is readily appreciated if a comparison is made of the relative security values of a property which is well maintained or improved and one which is allowed to deteriorate.

Use of the open-end mortgage is not limited to application of the newly borrowed funds to improving the mortgaged property. Increasing the lien under such a mortgage can also provide economical financing of other unusual family obligations, such as purchase of a new car, medical care, or education for the children.

What is particularly desired in an open-end mortgage is to secure future advances without running the risk of making such advances junior to intervening liens. In recent years several states have passed legislation pointing in this direction. Among these states are Connecticut, Louisiana, Maryland, Massachusetts, Missouri, New Jersey, New Hampshire, North Dakota, and Vermont.

Second Mortgages for Future Advances. In the absence of such legislation, numerous questions are left unanswered. One answer given to financial institutions by conservative lawyers is the use of second mortgages to evidence future advances. For example, suppose that a mortgagor executed an original mortgage for $8,000. Suppose also that this mortgage has been amortized down to $4,500. An additional advance of $2,000 is desired, for any purpose that may suit the needs of the borrower. The mortgagee secures from the borrower and his spouse signatures to a second mortgage for the added advance. If a short check of the record—covering the period since the original loan was granted —finds no intervening liens, the money is disbursed to the borrower. Should there be an intervening lien—say, for $250—the second mortgage could then be rewritten for $2,250, and $250 could be held in escrow by the lending institutions until this intervening lien has been canceled.

Where such a plan is followed, the amount of the advance will be added to the balance on the books of the lender. The monthly payments may or may not be increased. The period of amortization will probably be extended to take care of the additional repayments. The sum of the first mortgage balance and the second mortgage will probably not exceed the original amount of the first mortgage. Since a second mortgage is being used, this total might be larger than the original amount. The time necessary to amortize the two mortgages will not be longer than the period for which the lender is authorized to make real estate loans. This is necessarily so, since the new payment program will amortize the remainder of the first loan balance as well as the second mortgage over the remaining time necessary to pay off both loans.

This plan meets the needs of many borrowers and is a source of new business for lending institutions. The short check of the record may be inexpensive except for very small advances desired. For example, such a record check would cost as much for a $100 advance as for one for $3,000. The interest rate may or may not be increased. That will depend upon the cost of money at the time of the new advance. Indeed, costs might differ for the two loans. The original loan might continue to carry a 7 percent rate while the second mortgage might be written for 9 percent.

Participation Mortgage   One plan of real estate finance which formerly had considerable favor in the eastern section of the country, particularly during the decade of the 1920s, is the participation mortgage. In effect, this was a form of trust. The *res*, or trust property, consisted of one large mortgage or a collection of smaller mortgages. If the latter, considerable leeway was given the trustee in permitting substitutions of collateral as the small individual mortgages were paid off. The money needed to finance the collateral held by the trustee was obtained by selling what amounted to certificates of beneficial interest in the total collateral. These participation certificates possessed some, but not all, of the characteristics of mortgage bonds issued by a corporation.

Both lack of capital and lack of experience recommend the use of mortgage-participation certificates as an alternative to the direct purchase of mortgages. The investor may have only a limited amount of money that he can use for this purpose. He may be able to buy a participation certificate for $1,000, whereas he probably could not invest this amount either directly or indirectly in a single mortgage. Even though his investable surplus is sufficient to cover the amount of a single mortgage, his lack of experience might cause him to hesitate to take the risk involved. By buying a certificate of beneficial interest in a block of mortgages, his risk is spread instead of concentrated. In addition, he should have the benefit of expert and experienced management to manage his investment for him.

In recent years, institutional lenders have been acquiring interests in mortgage participations as a convenient means of expanding loan portfolios, particularly on an extraterritorial basis. The Government

National Mortgage Association (GNMA) will guarantee securities backed by pools of federally underwritten mortgages in order to tap the public market for funds to finance more real estate acquisition and development. This practice is discussed in depth in Chapter 21.

Purchase-Money Mortgage   Any mortgage given by the vendee to secure the payment of all or a part of the purchase price of the land is called a purchase-money mortgage. As such it must be differentiated from mortgages given to secure a loan from a third party for the purchase of the land. It has been said that a purchase-money mortgage carries the highest priority that an equity court can consider. If it is executed simultaneously with the deed which conveys title to the property, it takes precedence over judgments, other mortgages, liens, and all other debts of the mortgagor. If the mortgagor should anticipate a purchase of land by placing a mortgage against it before the deed and purchase-money mortgage are executed, the latter would take precedence over the former even though the former were made a matter of record first. The recorded mortgage could have no effect until the mortgagor obtained title to the land. By the time he did so, it would be encumbered by the purchase-money mortgage.

While the purchase-money mortgage need not be designated as such to give it priority, its time of execution is governing. If, for example, a deed were executed some time before the purchase-money mortgage, intervening liens could take priority over such a mortgage if they were filed after the deed was executed but before the mortgage was placed upon the record. The purchase-money mortgage should be filed simultaneously with the deed to avoid any question about intervening liens.

Purchase-money mortgages retain their priority even when written in the name of a third party at the request of the vendor of the real estate. It is not necessary for the spouse of the mortgagor to sign the mortgage. This is true even when the mortgagee becomes a third person. This third person may even provide the funds with which to purchase the property. For the protection of the mortgagee, it is well to state in the mortgage that the mortgage is accepted as a part of the purchase price of the property. A purchase-money mortgage can represent either a senior or a junior lien against the property used as security.

Packaged Mortgage   The growing popularity of practices of selling in one package not only the land and the structure erected thereupon, but all the fixtures needed for comfortable living, makes necessary a reexamination of what is meant by "fixtures." Tradition has included in the meaning of this term three concepts, each of which is capable of flexibility of definition: (1) A fixture must be annexed to and made a part of the real estate. (2) It must be appropriate to the part of the real estate to which it is attached. (3) It must be intended by the party making the annexation that it shall become and remain a part of the real estate. All that remains is to determine the meaning of "annexation," "appropriate," and "intention."

In times past our ancestors heated water in a kettle on a stove in order that members of the family could take their Saturday night bath in the family tub. No one considered either kettle or tub as real estate. They were not annexed to the real estate. Modern practice does annex the bathtub as a part of the bathroom fixtures and annexes the automatic water heater as a part of the permanent plumbing fixtures of the house. We find both of these fixtures appropriate to their uses. We also find that the person responsible for their installation intended them to serve the purposes for which they are now used.

Currently we are wondering why kitchen ranges, refrigerators, garbage disposal units, kitchen cabinets (not necessarily built in), ventilating fans, and even air-conditioning units, television sets, and home-freezer units should not be considered as attached to the real estate. To be sure, the method of attachment may be by a pipe coupling, an electric plug, or a few screws instead of by nails or bolts and nuts, but they are, nevertheless, attached. They are certainly appropriate to the uses to which they are being put. And their sale as a part of the house that is being sold indicates the intent of the person who installed them. In one combination or another they are needed for comfortable living.

Yet we hesitate to include some of the facilities mentioned above when we mortgage real estate for fear that they will be adjudged to be chattels instead of real estate fixtures. If the court finds them to be the former, the mortgagee may discover that his security is worth somewhat less than he thought it was.

Some brave souls undertake to sanction the financing of these articles needed for comfortable living as a part of the security for the real estate mortgage by enumerating, immediately following the land description in the mortgage, the things that are sought to be included, but about which there may be some doubt as to legal coverage. This enumeration is then followed by a declaration that such articles "are and shall be deemed to be fixtures" and are to be considered in all respects as a part of the real estate which serves as security for the mortgage. This is a brave declaration which attempts to settle legal difficulties by a sort of manifesto. However, the courts may still decide that all or some of the articles enumerated are still chattels and therefore not a proper subject for inclusion in a real estate mortgage. Therefore, their removal and sale would not affect the interests of the real estate mortgagee.

Arguments in Favor of Packaged Mortgages.   At least six arguments are advanced in favor of the use of packaged mortgages. These are in addition to the selling argument of the builder who presents a house equipped with those appliances needed for comfortable living. From the purely financing point of view, the arguments in favor of packaged mortgages are: (1) The homeowner deals with one lender only. He need not worry about a variety of monthly payments to cover parts of the same property. (2) Payments for the home equipment are distributed over a longer repayment period. Instead of allowing a few months or, at most, a few years for purchasing the refrigerator and other household equipment, their financing covers essentially the same period of time as the financing of the house. (3) The interest rate on the mortgage loan, which in this case covers equipment also, is always lower than the carrying charges on installment sales. (4) The payments may be made uniform throughout the life of the loan. As an alternative, where several items of household equipment are purchased on the installment plan, the monthly payments required will be very heavy for several months or a few years. In some cases a middle position is agreed upon with the monthly payments on the packaged mortgage somewhat larger for the first 10 years of the mortgage term. Even then they would be less than under installment purchases. (5) Since the cost of the equipment is merged with the cost of the house, the amount of the down payment attributable to equipment alone is less than if the equipment were purchased separately. (6) The mortgagee can better control the total amount of monthly payments by the mortgagor.

Budget Mortgage Another concession to the need to tailor monthly mortgage payments to the debt-paying capacity of the mortgagor is the "budget" mortgage. The connotation of this term is that the monthly payment made to the lender includes sufficient amounts, in addition to principal amortization and interest, to meet premium payments for required insurance coverage and real estate taxes. The stability of the required payment covering these principal housing expenditures tends to normalize the borrower's budget. By the same token, the lender has the use of the funds held in escrow as they build up to meet the periodic payments to the insuror and the taxing authorities. In some instances, payment schedules may be adjusted for seasonality of income flow or some predictable irregularity in the debt-paying ability of the borrower that might throw the mortgage into default if not taken into account.

Blanket Mortgage As the name suggests, a blanket mortgage covers several pieces of real estate as security. Several sets of circumstances give rise to its use. Subdividers sometimes give a blanket mortgage as part payment for acreage. As each lot is sold, it is released from this mortgage by agreement with the mortgagee according to a schedule of release credits. Normally the amount of cash required to be paid to the mortgagee would be considerably more than the ratio of the number of lots to the amount of the mortgage. For example, if 500 lots are covered by a $100,000 mortgage, it might require a payment of $400 instead of $200 to obtain a release of one lot from the mortgage.

Sometimes an owner of various pieces of real estate needs to borrow more than any one property can produce by the use of a mortgage. Several properties are included as security for a blanket mortgage. As lump-sum payments, agreed upon in advance or at the time of payments, are made on the unpaid balance of the debt, one by one the properties are released from the mortgage.

A third practice commonly used by some mortgagees follows a pattern like this: A wishes to purchase B's unencumbered property for $20,000. A hopes to dispose of his own property, presently mortgaged for $5,000 and priced at $15,000. Instead of making sure of the sale of his own property first, he contracts to buy B's property, putting up $5,000 in cash and offering both properties as security for a blanket loan of $20,000. The new mortgagee pays off the mortgage on A's property and has a first lien on both. The proceeds from the sale of A's property are applied to the blanket mortgage, securing a release of A's property so that it may be sold to C. The remainder of the debt is then owed by A against the property formerly owned by B as security.

Corporate mortgages are frequently of a blanket character. In addition to specific property named in the mortgage as security, arrangements such as "after-acquired" property clauses and "general" mortgages carry the blanket connotation.

Balloon Mortgage   Although it has long been used to some extent, the balloon mortgage has had a resurgence of popularity within the last few years. A balloon mortgage is one that provides for regular amortization payments with a final payment substantially higher than the periodic payments. The effect of this requirement of a large final payment is to accelerate the maturity and to create a need for refinancing at a date ahead of that which would result if total amortization were permitted at the regular rate.

Recent high interest rates have pressed borrowers beyond their capacity to amortize a loan over, say, 15 to 20 years. This may be the maximum period for which the lender will be willing to set his loan. The lender, however, may be willing to accept a monthly payment to include the interest plus an amortization amount based on a 30-year maturity. He may then provide that the note becomes due and payable in the amount of the unpaid balance at the end of 15 years. Thus, the borrower has substantially lower amortization payments over the 15 years, but he is faced with a substantial balloon payment at the end of the 15th year. He hopes, of course, that he can refinance under satisfactory terms, but there is a chance that he cannot.

Deed of Trust   One of the differences in detail mentioned in the preceding chapter makes use of a deed of trust instead of the regular mortgage. For example, in several states the borrower ordinarily conveys title to a trustee to be held in trust so long as his rights are alive. The conveyance is by a deed absolute, but the transfer is accompanied by a trust agreement, either as a part of the deed or in addition to it, setting forth the terms of the security arrangement and giving the trustee a power of sale in event of default. The deed of trust is commonly used in California, Colorado, District of Columbia, Delaware, Mississippi, Missouri, Tennessee, Texas, Virginia, and West Virginia. Deeds of trust are not extensively used in other states because their courts have held that any conveyance of real estate given to secure a debt is a mortgage, irrespective of the form of the instrument used. In some jurisdictions, like California, both the mortgage and the deed of trust are used.

Where the deed of trust is used, the trustee is authorized, in case of default, to foreclose the mortgagor's equity by a sale of the property at public auction, after proper advertisement. He must account to both parties for the proceeds of the sale. Each is entitled to his share as his interest may appear, after expenses of the sale, including compensation of the trustee, have been met. Since the mortgagor has never actually relinquished his title, but only the power of sale in case of his default, the purchaser must look to the mortgagor for title.

Deed of Trust and Mortgage Compared. The deed of trust is such a mixture of trust and mortgage law in concept that anyone using it should act under the counsel of a local real estate lawyer. In general, however, the legal rules surrounding the creation and evidence of the debt in the form of a note, rights of the borrower left in possession, legal description of the property, creation of a valid lien on after-acquired property, and recording are the same for both mortgages and deeds of trust. Similarly, a property subject to a deed of trust may be sold subject to the deed of trust either with or without an assumption of the debt by the purchaser. The assignment of the lender's rights is similar to assignment of a mortgagee's interest except that an assignment under a deed of trust need never be recorded. The original recording of the trust deed gives notice of the lien on the real estate, and only the trustee can release this lien by an appropriate act of reconveyance. In event of failure or refusal of a trustee to execute a reconveyance when the borrower repays his debt, the trustee may be forced to act by legal process. In fact, the trustee can be removed and a successor appointed by the noteholder without recourse to court or execution of a conveyance if the trust deed provides for such action.

In California, where deeds of trust and mortgages are used side by side, several distinctions are made between the two instruments. Whereas a mortgage may be discharged by a simple acknowledgment of satisfaction on the record, a reconveyance of title is considered necessary to extinguish a deed of trust. Under a deed of trust, an assignee of a creditor cannot sell the security property because his assignor did not have the power of sale to transfer; only the trustee has this power. Where a mortgage is used, however, if it contains a power of sale, the assignee of the note can himself exercise the power of sale if he has the assignment acknowledged and recorded.

Deeds of trust are necessarily used in connection with corporate mortgages. They have been so used in this country since the corporate mortgage first came into use more than a century ago.

QUESTIONS

1. What are the three principal kinds of mortgages and how are they basically different in derivation?

2. Would you recognize an equitable mortgage by the form of the instrument on which it is based? Why or why not?

3. What is a vendor's lien? How may a vendor protect it?

4. Review briefly the financial history of real estate bonds.

5. What protective covenants would you expect to find in the bond indenture?

6. What are the responsibilities of the trustee to the holders of real estate mortgage bonds?

7. What dangers to mortgage bondholders lie in the fact that their lien security is in trusteeship?

8. How may eminent domain proceedings or other forms of involuntary conversion of mortgaged property affect the underlying security, and how should the bond indenture deal with these possibilities?

9. As a real estate bondholder, what protection would you expect to find in the sinking-fund provisions of the bond indenture?

10. Under what conditions does a real estate bond qualify as a sound investment?

11. Recently a considerable portion of long-term real estate financing has been done by subordinated debentures. What are the advantages of this form (a) to the borrower and (b) to the investor? What are the disadvantages?

12. What problems do subsequent lienholders create for first mortgagees holding open-end mortgages permitting future advances? What precautions may be taken to maintain the highest priority?

13. What are the common practices for making advances under construction loans and for policing the loans after advances have been made?

14. What is a purchase-money mortgage and how is it different in effect from a mortgage given to secure a loan from a third party for the purchase of land?

15. Is it essential that a mortgagor's wife sign a release of dower on a purchase-money mortgage? Why or why not?

16. If mortgages usually establish priority by the time at which they

are recorded, what purpose is fulfilled by the use of subordination clauses in the mortgage instrument?

   17. Identify each of the following:

      a. Participation mortgage.

      b. Packaged mortgage.

      c. Budget mortgage.

      d. Balloon mortgage.

   18. How does a deed of trust differ from a mortgage?

CASE PROBLEMS

   1. Jones bought land from Smith with funds provided by Hancock. Hancock advanced the funds on Jones's oral promise to give him a mortgage on the land once he acquired the title. Jones then refused to execute a mortgage in favor of Hancock. What is Hancock's position?

   2. X Corporation had mortgage bonds outstanding with an after-acquired property clause providing for the extension of the mortgage lien to all real property subsequently acquired. X Corporation bought a real estate parcel from Y, giving back a purchase-money mortgage. Which lien has priority?

   3. *a.* Sedgewick arranged for an open-end mortgage loan from the Second National Bank in amounts up to $50,000. The loan was closed and Sedgewick drew down $30,000 initially. Three months later he drew the remaining $20,000. What is the position of the bank with regard to the possibility of intervening liens?

      b. Assume there was no definite agreement for future advances between Sedgewick and the bank at the time the initial $30,000 loan was closed. Would your answer be different?

3

Mortgage Default
and Adjustments

Two major kinds of events take place when a mortgage loan is repaid in a manner other than by full compliance with the contemplated plan of repayment. A default may occur or adjustments in the terms or changes in the parties may take place which raise new legal and financial problems. Part 1 of this chapter deals with the problems of default and Part 2 considers special questions raised by the introduction of mortgage adjustments.

PART 1: MORTGAGE DEFAULT

What Constitutes Default

An ordinary dictionary definition of a "default" is "a failure to fulfill a contract, agreement, or duty, especially a financial obligation." From this it follows that a default in a mortgage contract can result from any breach of the contract. The most common is the failure to meet an installment of the interest or principal payments. But failure to pay taxes or insurance premiums when due may also result in a default which may precipitate a foreclosure action. Indeed, some mortgages make specific stipulations to this effect. Even a failure to keep the security in repair may constitute a technical default. We speak of this as a technical default because it would seldom result in an actual foreclosure sale. It might be difficult for the mortgagee to prove that the repair clause in the mortgage had been broken unless the property showed definite evidence of the effects of waste.

From another point of view, default is defined first in the breach of the letter of the contract and then in the attitude of the mortgagee. By this is meant that, even though there is a breach of contract, the mortgagee may see fit to ignore it or to postpone action in doing something about it. In case of default accompanied by abandonment, the probabilities are that the mortgagee will act quickly to protect his interests against vandalism, neglect, and waste. If, on the other hand, the mortgagor is a man of good character, has generally met his obligations promptly in the past, wishes to retain his interest in the property, and is only temporarily unable to meet his obligations, a default is not likely to be declared by the mortgagee for an indefinite period.

A form of default definition reads as follows:

It is agreed that time is of the essence of this contract and that in the event of default in payment of any monthly installment or any part thereof for a period of sixty days after the same is due and payable as herein provided, or in the event of failure to pay when due all the premiums and renewals on the insurance policies on said real estate, and to pay when due all the taxes, assessments or other charges that may be levied, assessed or charged by any public authority on said real estate or the interest of this Association in said real estate or the interest of this Association in this note, or in the event of a breach of any covenant or condition in the mortgage given to secure this note, then the whole of the principal and accrued interest on this note, shall at the option of the holder hereof become immediately due and payable without demand or notice, and the undersigned do hereby specifically waive such demand or notice, and the filing of any action on this note shall be deemed to be an exercise of said option. Any failure to exercise said option shall not constitute a waiver of the right to exercise the same at any other time.

Foreclosure

When we speak commonly of "mortgage foreclosure" we are using language loosely. What is really foreclosed is the mortgagor's equity of redemption. When the equity of redemption merely takes the position that a mortgagor in default should have more time in which to meet his obligations, this could become unfair to the mortgagee unless some provision is made to limit the amount of time at the disposal of the mortgagor. Hence, as an offset to the equity of redemption, the mortgagee was given the right to foreclose it or cut it off.

In practice, most mortgagees are not anxious to take property from mortgagors. The Federal Housing Administration and Veterans Administration, for example, have established policies of forebearance in the enforcement of mortgages serviced in their behalf. Mortgagees prefer to collect the amounts owed them and are likely to be lenient and patient when circumstances warrant it. Seldom does the mortgagee insist upon the exact letter of his contract. Nor does he rush into court to insist upon his full pound of flesh. But after patience and leniency have been extended to delinquent mortgagors, eventually a settlement seems necessary. Then foreclosure proceedings are started. Incidentally, it is interesting to see how frequently a delinquent mortgagor gets off the delinquent list by paying up past-due obligations as soon as foreclosure proceedings are started.

Strict Foreclosure   It is still possible in some instances to follow the rule of strict foreclosure. In other words, in such cases the mortgagee may ask that the mortgagor's right of redemption be completely cut off and that unqualified title be vested in the mortgagee. If this is done, the mortgagor loses all rights in the property if he does not redeem it before foreclosure becomes effective. After the equity court gives the mortgagor one last chance to meet his obligations, he is thereafter barred from troubling the mortgagee about the property mortgaged—if he fails to make good. However, the court may not relieve him of his obligations. He may still be held for any part of his obligations that cannot be satisfied by the forfeiture of his claims against the property.

In general, however, the strict foreclosure rule is not favored. In most cases, legislation has eliminated it, at least in theory. In specific cases, an equity court may permit its application if it finds that undue injury will not result.

Alternatives to Strict Foreclosure   In the absence of the right of strict foreclosure, the mortgagee possesses two types of remedies to protect his interests in case of default by the mortgagor: (1) He may sue in a law court on the debt, obtain judgment, and execute the judgment against the property of the mortgagor. (2) He may bring a foreclosure suit in a court of equity, following the form of strict foreclosure, but ending in a decree of foreclosure and sale. Since these choices are open to the mortgagee in some states, he must determine from the facts in the case which route to follow.

If he elects to sue on the debt, any intervening liens entered between the date of execution of the mortgage and the date of judgment on the debt must be taken into account. They cannot be frozen out, as they could be under foreclosure sale. On the other hand, a judgment against the debtor can be executed against any property owned by him. For this reason it may be advantageous in some cases for the mortgagee to sue on the debt rather than foreclose if he is given a choice.

The prevailing procedure in this country is a resort to a court of equity looking toward a decree of foreclosure and sale of the security. In many states this method of procedure is mandatory in all cases where the plaintiff resorts to a court of equity. While these are really two separate steps—foreclosure and sale—they are commonly treated as one.

Sale of Property   Even though the mortgagor who defaults in his obligations and thereby faces foreclosure of his equity of redemption is unable to take advantage of his time extension, he is currently considered to have rights which should be protected in ways never contemplated in early mortgages. He is presumed to have an equity which can be realized only in the marketplace. Hence, currently, equity courts called upon to grant the mortgagee the right of foreclosure accompany their decision with a decree of sale to determine whether or not there is anything left for the mortgagor. Where a sale is decided upon, this of course represents a departure from the strict foreclosure rule.

If such sale realizes a price high enough to meet the expenses of the sale and the claims of the mortgagee and still leave a balance, this balance goes to the mortgagor. The demands of other claimants will be considered later. While foreclosure of the mortgagor's equity of redemption and sale of the property may be undertaken in two separate actions, at the present time they usually go together in practice.

In determining the amounts to be accounted for at a foreclosure sale, it must be remembered that the mortgage secures not only the principal amount of the debt but all lawful interest as well. The interest to be accounted for includes not only all amounts unpaid up to the time of foreclosure but all amounts accruing after default up to the date of the decree of sale.

The advertising of the sale, the place where it takes place, and the method of sale by a county sheriff, a referee, an auctioneer, or a master are all matters that are governed by local practice. While details differ, the results are approximately the same in all localities.

Fixing a Price. Mortgage foreclosure sale emanates from the assumption that a public auction is a satisfactory way to realize the best possible price in selling property. Hence, in some jurisdictions, the highest bidder gets the property irrespective of its cost, the amount of liens against it, or any other consideration. The mortgagee is usually the successful bidder. He can use his claims as a medium of exchange in the purchase—except for costs which must be paid in cash. Others must pay cash for their purchases, unless the successful bidder can arrange with the mortgagee to keep his lien alive. As a consequence, frequently only the mortgagee makes any serious bid for the property. In some states his right to bid is protected by statute, while in others the court of equity recognizes this method of protecting the mortgagee's interests. In the absence of either statutory permission or approval by the equity court, a mortgagee who buys the security for his claims may run some risk. However, this issue is academic, since it is inconceivable that a court of equity would refuse to grant the mortgagee the right to protect his interests in this manner.

In a few states an upset price is fixed in advance of the sale. By this is meant that an appraisal by agents of the court fixes a value for the property that must be reached in the bidding or the court will refuse to confirm the sale. This is not a common practice. In any event, the court of equity is expected to determine that the price realized at the foreclosure sale is adequate before it is confirmed. But adequacy is a flexible concept. Even though the court may have some doubt about it, it may question whether a subsequent sale would produce a price as high as the highest one offered at the first sale.

Nevertheless, a judicial sale may be a poor method of realizing the true value of the property. Recognizing this, the court must exercise its best judgment in viewing the offers made for the property at the foreclosure sale. Hence, while every offer made by a prospective purchaser is irrevocable and may not be withdrawn, the court is not bound to accept any offer made. At the outset the court may condition its confirmation by providing, for example, that the price paid must be sufficient to pay all expenses of the sale and the debts of the mortgagor.

It would be quite difficult for the court to fix the price that the property must bring at the foreclosure sale. On the one hand, the court is interested in doing justice to the mortgagor. Since a deficiency judgment may be decreed in case the mortgagee is not completely satisfied from the proceeds of the sale, the lower the price, the larger the deficiency judgment. On the other hand, the mortgagee's rights must be protected also. If the court should attempt to insist upon too high a price, no sale would be effected, and hence the mortgagee would receive no satisfaction of his claims.

Nature of Title at Foreclosure Sale. The purchaser of property at a foreclosure sale is, in effect, the purchaser of the rights of the mortgagor whose interests are cut off by the sale. Even though the sale is conducted under court procedure, the court makes no representation concerning the nature of the title. Certainly there is no implication that a title passed by a court carries any suggestion of full warranty. Any defects that may have been applicable to the title as it was held by the mortgagor will continue with the title as it passes to the purchaser at foreclosure sale. If a junior lienor's interests have been omitted in the suit for foreclosure, his claims will not be cut off by such suit. As long as lienor claims are not satisfied, the purchaser, instead of acquiring a fee simple unencumbered, stands in the position of a mortgagee in possession of his security.

The obvious conclusion to be drawn from this analysis is that any prospective purchaser at a foreclosure sale should have the record of the title to the property thoroughly searched before he bids for it. He should know exactly the nature of the title which he may be able to secure. Relying on the assumption that the title was properly searched before the mortgagee accepted a lien upon the property may not be a safe practice.

Parties to Foreclosure Suit When the holder of a senior mortgage brings suit to foreclose the equity of redemption, he must join in the suit all who share the mortgagor's interest. These include not only junior mortgage holders but judgment creditors, a purchaser at an execution sale, and a trustee in bankruptcy, if any. Failure to include all of these might improve their position with the foreclosure of the senior lien. For example, should the senior mortgagee become the successful bidder at the foreclosure sale, and should a junior lienor of record be not joined in the suit, it is possible that, when the senior mortgagee takes title to the land, the junior mortgagee may acquire the position of a senior lienor. To make sure of the avoidance of this possibility, every foreclosure action should be preceded by a careful search of the record to discover all junior lien claimants who should be joined in the foreclosure suit.

Should any junior lienor think that he has an equity to protect, he has the right to purchase the property at a foreclosure sale, paying off or otherwise providing for the interests of the claimants whose liens are superior to his. It is not uncommon for a senior claimant to agree in advance upon the method of settlement of his claims. This may include an agreement to renew the senior mortgagee's claims, either with or without a reduction in their amount.

The purchaser at the foreclosure sale takes over the property free of the lien of the mortgage being foreclosed, but also free of all holders of junior liens who have been joined in the foreclosure action. If the senior mortgage holder or a third party purchases the property at a foreclosure sale, all such junior liens are of no further force or effect. If, however, the mortgagor purchases the property at such sale, all liens against it will remain alive; except, of course, such liens as may have been satisfied from the proceeds of the sale. There is one exception to this rule. If the mortgagor borrowed the money with which to purchase the property, the lender comes in ahead of the liens wiped out by the sale.

If a junior lienholder brings suit for foreclosure, he should not join the senior lienholder in the suit. Instead, he should sue subject to the senior lien. By this means he is not obligated to pay off the senior lienholder. He may prefer to keep the senior mortgage alive. The holder of the senior lien may join the action voluntarily, and sometimes does so to make sure that his interests are fully protected. He may wish to have determined by the court the amount due him to be assumed by the purchaser. Or, should there be any question about the order of priority of his lien, he may join the foreclosure action to have this question answered. Again he may have a side agreement with the junior lienor to continue his mortgage unchanged in amount. In case the junior mortgage holder plans to buy the property at the foreclosure sale, he may prefer to pay off the senior lien as well. This must be done with the consent of the lienholder if he is not a party to the suit. This practice represents a redemption of the senior mortgage and follows the English maxim of "Redeem up, but foreclose down." In other words, redeem claims superior to your own, but wipe out, by the process of foreclosure, those that are inferior.

When separate suits are brought contemporaneously by both a senior and a junior lienor, they should be joined in a single action. The consequences of separate suits would be the same as those following a single suit.

Holders of junior liens which are destroyed in a foreclosure action are entitled to have the surplus of sale price over senior mortgage claims applied to their claims. If there is no surplus, then they are entitled to a judgment for the full amount of their claims. From that time on, they are merely general, unsecured creditors of the mortgagor, unless the latter should own other real estate to which such judgments would attach.

Taxes in Default

Payment of taxes is an obligation of the mortgagor. As such, taxes constitute a prior lien against the security. Transfers of title always take into account accrued but unpaid taxes. Mortgages commonly contain tax clauses giving the mortgagee the right to pay taxes not paid regularly by the mortgagor. The amounts so paid are then added to the claims of the mortgagee. While the lien of taxes gives tax-collecting authorities the right to foreclose in case of default, such right is seldom exercised on first or even second default. Instead, the taxing authority may pursue an alternative policy of selling tax liens from time to time. Since they constitute superior liens prior to the claims of mortgagees if the taxing authorities have observed statutory procedure, and since they customarily carry high effective rates of interest, the mortgagee may prefer to save the accumulation of high interest as a prior claim by paying delinquent taxes and adding them to his claims.

If foreclosure becomes necessary, the mortgagee includes all taxes paid by him. Usually at the time of a foreclosure sale the purchaser is expected to pay all delinquent taxes, thus making the tax status of the property current.

Tax Sales In the preceding section we discussed the relation of delinquent taxes and mortgages. Where there is no mortgage against the property or where the mortgagee does not act to protect his interests against tax liens, it is expected that, sooner or later, pressure will be brought by taxing authorities to collect delinquent taxes. In effect, if not in form, the procedure followed is intended to parallel that in the foreclosure of mortgages. The time interval between the date of delinquency and the sale date varies from 20 days to 18 months. At the time of sale the purchaser receives a tax certificate, which is then subject to redemption in nearly all states. The period of redemption is usually two or three years. If the property is not redeemed by the delinquent taxpayer within this period, the purchaser at the tax sale is then entitled to receive a deed to the property.

In the absence of bidders at a tax sale—as might occur in periods of depression or in the sale of inexpensive vacant land—the property usually reverts to the state, the county, or some other local governmental unit. Such reversions do not in all cases enrich the new owner or provide the means of meeting delinquent tax obligations. Either the property may be practically worthless, as the complete absence of private bidders suggests, or the governmental unit may neglect to take steps to realize the best price that can be obtained from its disposition. States and local units are notoriously careless in their housekeeping habits in this area.

Tax Titles   Tax titles are usually looked upon as weak evidences of ownership. The interest of the tax collector is to find someone willing and able to pay taxes for someone else in return for a claim against the property. The collector is not greatly concerned about passing good title. There is no suggestion of warranty. In addition to any defects in title irrespective of delinquent taxes, the unconcern of the tax collector may in turn result in added clouds on the title. Among the latter the following may occur: (1) Because of inaccurate description of the property or incorrect records of ownership, the notice of sale may be defective. (2) The property owner may have been denied his day in court. (3) The line of authority for the sale may not be clear. (4) Irregularities and carelessness, even in minor procedural matters, may give rise to an invalidation of the tax sale.

All of these depend in part upon the recuperative powers of the delinquent taxpayer. If he has lost interest in the property, or if he lacks the financial resources to protect his interests, he may interpose no objections that will interfere with the plans of the purchaser at the tax sale. Nevertheless, the risk is great enough to suggest caution and due attention even to minor details before purchasing tax liens.

Sale of property which has reverted to the state or some other governmental unit involves fewer complications than sale of tax liens with a tax deed to follow. Because of this, it appears that much confusion could be avoided if the governmental unit would follow a procedure that includes these steps: (1) retain tax liens until the end of the redemption period; (2) foreclose unredeemed liens; (3) sell titles to lands so acquired, giving good title therefor.

Effect of Foreclosure on Junior Lienors

If a senior mortgage holder brings foreclosure suit and joins junior claimants in the suit, the question arises, "What happens to the claims of those cut off by the foreclosure sale?" As indicated above, any surplus remaining, after satisfying the costs of foreclosure and the claims of the senior lienor, is distributed according to the priority rights of junior claims. Sometimes the distribution of this surplus is not as simple as it sounds. Frequent disputes concerning the order of priority require action by a court of equity to establish the order of settlement.

Where there is no surplus, or where it is insufficient to meet all claims, the holders of such claims still maintain their rights to pursue the mortgagor on whatever personal obligation he has incurred in establishing their interests. This legal right may or may not result in satisfaction of claims to their holders. It may acquire only nuisance value to rise up and plague the mortgagor at some future time should he ever recover his economic status sufficiently to make pursuit of claims against him worthwhile.

Unrecorded Liens on Foreclosure

It has been pointed out that the mortgagor's interest in mortgaged property is essentially limited to his equity of redemption. While the purchaser at a foreclosure sale is expected to acquire only the mortgagor's interest, he may acquire more than this if he makes the purchase without notice of latent equities. He might even acquire the property free of a mortgage if the mortgage is not recorded. In any event, his equity of redemption usually gives him the right to redeem an underlying mortgage, whether or not it is on record and whether or not he assumes it at the time of purchase.

As pointed out above, the purchaser should cause a thorough search of the record to discover the condition of the title. Having done so, he is entitled to rely upon the record to disclose the existence of any liens against the property, unless he has other forms of notice of such liens.

Deficiency Judgment

While a sale of the mortgaged property may result in a surplus to which the mortgagor is entitled, it may, on the contrary, be consummated at a price that fails to satisfy the claims of the mortgagee. Since equity courts have arrived at the conclusion that the mortgagor is entitled to the surplus, they have followed this with the correlative decision that any deficit should constitute a continuing claim by the mortgagee against the mortgagor. This is known as a deficiency judgment. Since all mortgages involve one or more specific properties—which must be accurately described in the mortgage—the mortgagee must look to such property to provide primary security for his claim.

Deficiency judgments are unsecured claims—unless the mortgagor owns other real estate—and take their place alongside other debts of the mortgagor. Unlike the mortgage from which such judgment springs, the latter gives the holder no right of preference against any of the non-real estate assets of the debtor. Hence, the value of deficiency judgments is always open to serious question. This is true in part because of the ways by which they can be avoided or defeated.

One paradox of deficiency judgments is that they tend to protect dishonest mortgagors against which they are filed. By this is meant that while an honest debtor will frequently strive to discharge them, even at the expense of self-denial for himself and those dependent upon him, the presence of a deficiency judgment may not interfere with the spending habits of debtors whose consciences are callous to them. Since such judgments could be attached only to real estate which the debtor holds or may acquire in the future, the dishonest debtor may see to it that he does not acquire any future real estate interests; or if he does so, he will be careful to have the titles recorded in names other than his own.

In some quarters there is considerable sentiment in favor of legislation to abolish deficiency judgments altogether, leaving the mortgagee with only the property to protect his claims. Several states strictly limit the applicability of deficiency judgments.

It should be noted that a deficiency judgment is always entered against the person of the mortgagor or his successor. Hence, it cannot be entered unless he is personally served as a part of the proceedings for foreclosure and sale.

Significance of Possession

A little thought will show the significance of the right of possession after default but before a foreclosure sale. If the mortgagor is in lawful possession, he is not accountable to the mortgagee for either the disposition of the proceeds of the mortgage or the income which he may derive from the property while he possesses it. Even where it is evident that the security is inadequate to protect the obligations due the mortgagee, this rule is not relaxed. An honest mortgagor may continue to enjoy normal income until he is dispossessed lawfully as the result of a foreclosure sale. A dishonest or, shall we say, a resourceful mortgagor can find means of increasing normal income substantially, perhaps at the expense of the mortgagee. Such mortgagors are called "milkers."

Hence, the only way for the mortgagee to protect his interest adequately is to obtain possession and, through it, control over the property and its potential income. If he can get possession, he can better protect the property against waste. Even though waste committed by the mortgagor while in possession may decrease the value of the security and correspondingly increase the amount of the deficiency judgment, this may not result in collection by the holder of the judgment of amounts to offset the effects of the waste.

Even rent clauses and other types of income clauses in mortgages are not adequate substitutes for possession. If the mortgagor feels that he has little at stake in his equity of redemption, he may lose interest in collecting the income which he has agreed in the mortgage to turn over to the mortgagee. Or income may be so difficult to define that it disappears entirely. It may not be in the nature of rent, but of net income from business operations. If the mortgagor's financial affairs are in such condition that it is impossible for him to keep up the contractual payments on his mortgage, his ability to produce any net income from his business may have reached the vanishing point. To be sure, adverse economic conditions rather than inherent managerial weakness may be at the base of his troubles. Even this explanation fails to produce anything to credit to the amounts due the mortgagee. Or a junior lienor may be more agile than the holder of the senior mortgage and may secure the right to collect rents which he may apply toward the liquidation of his own claims.

For these and other less obvious reasons, the significance of possession becomes quite apparent. In the end, the law and court decisions may decree that both title and lien theories reach the same destination. The mortgaged property is sold, and the proceeds are applied to the satisfaction of the obligations owed the mortgagee. If these obligations are not completely liquidated, the mortgagor will be liable under a deficiency judgment. Until actual foreclosure sale is consummated, the mortgage continues to be a security device.

Meantime, unrecoverable wastes may occur, and income may flow into channels which lead away from the mortgagee's interests rather than toward them. Deficiency judgments may be in perfect legal form, but also may be perfectly worthless in the recovery of funds that might have been diverted to the mortgagee had he been in possession pending foreclosure sale of the mortgaged property. In some instances the rent assignment clause in a mortgage is so drawn that, in effect, it virtually gives the mortgagee possession of the property upon default and until the foreclosure sale is confirmed.

While the mortgagee is in possession, he may find it necessary or desirable to spend money for repairs or improvements on the property. Subsequently, he may be called upon to demonstrate that these expenditures were needed to protect his interests. Even though he benefits therefrom, there will be little difficulty in adding such costs to the previous claims of the mortgagee. But if the expenditures merely cause the property to look better, he may have difficulty in recovering such expenditures.

However, the mortgagee in possession is required to render an account annually to the equity court, showing the amount of his receipts from the operation of the property and their disposition. In general, these receipts must be applied first to expenses of operation—including necessary repairs, then to interest accruals, and finally to a reduction in the principal balance. This requirement for an annual reduction in the principal balance is called an "annual rest." Its purpose is to prevent the mortgagee from having free use indefinitely of funds collected from the use of the property.

Other Remedies for Default

In addition to the remedies previously discussed, there may be other appropriate courses of action: These include:

1. Receivership.
2. Power of sale.
3. Foreclosure of deeds of trust.
4. Foreclosure by entry.

Receivership Frequently a mortgage contains a clause which permits the mortgagee to have a receiver appointed to protect his interests in case of a default. Even though the statute makes no specific provision for the appointment of a receiver, it may result from an agreement written into the mortgage or may be agreed upon at the time of default. The receivership should be looked upon merely as an interim device for temporary control pending the consummation of a foreclosure sale. As such, it takes the place of a mortgagee in possession. While it is preferable to have a disinterested, impartial person appointed as a receiver, the mortgagor may serve in this capacity if the mortgagee consents.

Where a receiver is appointed, he is recognized as the direct representative of the mortgagee. He is not expected to represent all creditors of the mortgagor. Even when the mortgagee has the right to ask for the appointment of a receiver, he may not see fit to exercise it. The most common motives for the use of receivers are the desire to conserve already inadequate security and the fear of waste which may cause the security to depreciate in value before a foreclosure sale can be arranged. "Waste" means any condition that results directly in a diminution in the value of the property. It may be due to intentional destructive tactics or to neglect of needed repairs. A serious hole in the roof may be just as injurious as acts of vandalism. Sometimes, also, the relationship between mortgagor and mortgagee may play its part. If the former should show any indication of resisting the plans of the latter, a receiver may be used to take possession away from the mortgagor.

If the property over which the receiver assumes jurisdiction happens to be the mortgagor's home, the receiver may not ask the mortgagor to vacate the property immediately. Instead, he may determine reasonable rent for it and give the mortgagor the privilege of continuing to occupy the property, pending foreclosure sale, as long as he pays the rent asked of him. In general, there is a tendency to permit the mortgagor in default to occupy his home until the foreclosure sale takes place.

When the right of the mortgagee to have a receiver appointed is written into the mortgage instrument, the mortgagee sees to it that the right is as inclusive as possible. One such clause reads in part as follows:

In the event of any breach of the terms or conditions of this mortgage or the note which this mortgage secures, the holder of this mortage shall be entitled to the appointment of a receiver of the rents, issues, and profits of said premises, without regard to the value of the mortgaged premises as security for the amount due, or the solvency of any person or persons liable for the payment of the amount due, and without notice to any party, and in the event of any such default herein described, such rents and profits are hereby assigned to the holder of this mortgage as further security for the payment of said indebtedness.

Power of Sale   As a substitute for a foreclosure sale, the statutes of about a third of the states permit the use of the power of sale, provided it is written into the mortgage. A power of sale is a provision permitting the lender, in the event of the borrower's default, to sell the mortgaged premises after merely giving statutory notices. Even though the procedure of satisfying a mortgagee's claims is supposed to be faster and more economical where the power of sale is exercised, the use of this practice is not always followed, even in the states that have legislated on the subject. Some state statutes prohibit its use. A few undertake to regulate the manner of its use. Where the deed of trust is in use, the power of sale must be exercised by the trustee. One reason it is not always used is that whenever questions arise that do not produce the same answers for both mortgagor and mortgagee, resort must be had to a court of equity. Then follows foreclosure sale as described above. One question about which there may be a disagreement is the exact amount of the indebtedness. Questions even may arise concerning the fairness of the manner in which the sale is conducted.

Another complication in the use of the power of sale arises when the mortgagee may wish to buy the property. In the absence of statutory permission, the mortgagee may not purchase the property either directly or indirectly. If the mortgagee prefers to bid on the property at its sale, he should follow the foreclosure route.

While the mortgagee may dispose of his interest in a mortgage at private sale, the power of sale must be exercised only in public, and the successful bidder must pay cash. Proceeds of the sale go first to pay the expenses of the sale, then to apply on the claims of the senior mortgagee. Any surplus is applied successively to the claims of junior lienors, then to the mortgagor. If there is a deficiency instead of a surplus, the mortgagee is entitled to bring suit for a deficiency judgment.

The notice of the sale must state the total amount claimed by the mortgagee. Unless the statute so requires, no special notice need be sent to holders of junior liens. They are supposed to look out for their own interests. The mortgagor, on the other hand, is entitled to special notice of the sale. This is so because a power of sale may not cut off or impair his equity of redemption. This is his right up to the time of the actual sale of the property.

The purchaser under power of sale acquires the same kind of title that would be available to him where foreclosure proceedings are used. He merely succeeds to the type of interest which the mortgagor held. In effect, he receives only a special warranty deed.

Some laws tend to abolish deficiency judgments where power of sale is used. In other cases the statutes place limits upon the amount of deficiency judgments by providing that such judgment may not be greater than the difference between the amount claimed by the mortgagee and the fair value of the property, instead of the amount realized at the sale. The burden of proof for establishing the fair value usually rests upon the mortgagee.

First by emergency statutes during the depression of the 1930s and later by permanent statutes, some states—including New York—have taken the position that a mortgagee may not take advantage of a depressed real estate market, use his power of sale to dispose of the property at a price that represents less than its long-term value, and saddle the mortgagor with a correspondingly large deficiency judgment. The mortgagee may not even anticipate such a situation and use a waiver of this mandatory law which he requires the mortgagor to sign at the time the mortgage is executed.

Sometimes mortgagees use the foreclosure sale in preference to the power of sale because they fear that questions may be raised about the marketability of the title if the land is sold under power of sale. Such questions are predicated upon the existence of some irregularity in connection with the sale that might result in its nullification. The same doubts are not usually present when title passes as a result of a foreclosure sale.

Foreclosure of Deeds of Trust   It has generally been held that when money is raised with a deed of trust given as security the creditor cannot bring a foreclosure action. Instead, he relies upon the trustee to exercise the powers conferred directly by the trust instrument. In California, however, the trustee has a statutory option to foreclose by suit and decree. Foreclosure is also commonly available, without the necessity of a statute, when judicial aid is required to determine parties' rights, as where it is necessary to have an accounting, adjust setoffs, ascertain the amount due in event of dispute, or establish whether the debt is really in default. Sometimes there are junior liens and their relative priorities are unclear. In such cases the trustee may sue to foreclose. Once the matter has been brought within the jurisdiction of the court the property may then be sold by an officer of the court, as in foreclosure proceedings, rather than by the trustee.

A right of redemption exists after a mortgage foreclosure sale, but not after a trustee's sale under a deed of trust. If the holder of the deed, however, elects to foreclose it in the same manner as a mortgage, the debtor has the same rights of redemption as though a mortgage had been executed in the beginning. In the event that a receivership becomes necessary, properly drawn trust deeds usually give more protection than mortgages. This is true because under an ordinary mortgage the receiver cannot acquire possession until foreclosure and then he must return the property to the mortgagor after the foreclosure sale until the redemption period runs. On the other hand, where a trust deed is used, the receiver may take possession under its terms and retain it until the property is turned over permanently to the purchaser at the sale.

Foreclosure by Entry   In several New England states foreclosure by peaceful entry is permitted, provided all formalities are observed. These include the requirement that the entry must be without the opposition of the mortgagor. If it is opposed, resort must be had to judicial proceedings, which means that it soon develops into a foreclosure sale. The entry must be made in the presence of witnesses who can testify to its peaceable nature. And a certificate of entry reciting the action taken by the mortgagee must be properly recorded. Even where foreclosure by entry is used, the mortgagor is protected by a right of recovery of the difference if the security is more valuable than the debt. In addition, the mortgagor enjoys the statutory right of redemption where foreclosure by entry is used. The statutes allow a period varying from one to three years after entry before the right of redemption is cut off.

Also, in some New England states the mortgagee may foreclose by writ of entry. This kind of action partakes of some of the characteristics of equity proceedings. After the amount of the debt is judicially determined, the mortgagor in default is given a definite period of time within which to meet his obligations. If he fails, or is unable to take advantage of this opportunity, the mortgagee is put in possession of the property.

He then occupies the same position as if he had foreclosed by peaceable entry as described in the preceding paragraph.

Under both of these plans of foreclosure the mortgagor is allowed a statutory right of redemption varying from one to three years. A long period of redemption may interfere with the plans of the mortgagee in disposing of the property. For this reason foreclosure sales are frequently resorted to even though foreclosure by peaceable entry or by writ of entry is available to the mortgagee.

PART 2: MORTGAGE ADJUSTMENTS

Need for Mortgage Adjustments

As pointed out previously, mortgage contracts are so drawn as to indicate definite penalties to follow any breach therein. Our most heart-rending melodramas would have lost much of their appeal except for their recitals of the dire consequences which follow a failure to keep up mortgage payments on the old homestead. Nevertheless, experience testifies that, in spite of provisions for prompt action in case of a default in mortgage payments, many such commitments are not met in strict accordance with the letter of the contract. Instead, whenever mortgagors get into financial trouble and are unable to meet their obligations, adjustments rather than demands for the proverbial pound of flesh are likely to follow. Some of these adjustments best meet the needs of the mortgagee, to be sure. Others are accepted at times when strict adherence to the letter of the contract would give the holder of the mortgage a financial advantage. Various types of mortgage adjustments are discussed in the pages that follow. These adjustments include:

1. Voluntary conveyance.
2. Assumption.
3. Purchase of the mortgage by the grantor.
4. Assignment.
5. Extension agreement.
6. Release.
7. Recasting of terms.

Voluntary Conveyance

On the theory that the mortgagor is a free agent, he may sell his equity to the mortgagee at any time after the mortgage becomes effective. Such sale must be conditioned upon the appearance of a new form of consideration—not present before—and complete freedom from fraud or duress. Because there are so many ways of taking advantage of a distressed mortgagor and of freezing out those with junior claims against him, the burden of proof governing the absence of fraud or duress usually rests upon the mortgagee.

For example, suppose that the mortgagor is unable to meet his obligations and faces foreclosure of his equity. In perfect good faith and to save time, trouble, and expense, the mortgagee may make or accept a proposal to take title from the mortgagor upon paying a nominal sum to the latter for his equity. Suppose also that shortly thereafter the former mortgagor's fortunes improve; or suppose that depressed real estate values recover sharply. The former mortgagee may face a suit for recovery on the ground that he used duress to wrest title from the mortgagor. He might have difficulty in proving his honest intentions and in demonstrating that, at the time of the purchase, he paid the fair value of the mortgagor's equity. At that time the property might have possessed little or no value over and above the amount of the mortgage.

Where such voluntary conveyances are used, the common practice in lien states would include a warranty deed from mortgagor to mortgagee. A quitclaim deed would probably suffice in title states. In either event the mortgagor should insist upon a satisfaction piece to make sure that he is no longer bound under his note and mortgage. Otherwise, he may find that he has sacrificed his equity and still is under financial obligation to the mortgagee.

In addition to the legal questions involved in voluntary conveyances, the mortgagee frequently faces very practical financial issues as well. If there are junior liens outstanding, they are not wiped out by a voluntary conveyance. Indeed, their holders may be in a better position than before if the title to the property passes into stronger hands. Unless in some manner these junior liens may be lifted from the property in question—possibly by agreement with their holders to transfer them to other property owned by the mortgagor or even on occasion to cancel them—the mortgagee may find it necessary to foreclose instead of taking a voluntary conveyance. By this means he has a lawful method of becoming free from the liens of the junior claimants.

Assumption of Mortgage

It has been pointed out that a mortgage is essentially security for a personal debt. The mortgagor is expected to sign a note which accompanies or becomes a part of the mortgage. By agreement, it is possible for the mortgagor to obtain release from his personal obligation after he assumes it; or if the mortgagee consents, he may be relieved of such obligation at the time the mortgage is executed. This would be an unusual type of agreement for the mortgagee to become a party to, but it would be one that would find sanction at law because it is a matter of voluntary agreement, resulting in a contract.

When the mortgagor transfers his rights to another, the question arises, "Does the grantee undertake to relieve the mortgagor of his personal obligation?" If this is the intention of both parties, the assumption of the obligation by the grantee may accomplish the purpose. The deed, after reciting the nature of the mortgage which encumbers the property, will contain a clause to the effect that the grantee assumes and agrees to pay the amount of the obligations owed to the mortgagee, as part consideration of the conveyance of title. Where an assumption is undertaken by the grantee, it should be couched in such language that there should be no doubt about his intent.

An assumption agreement takes the form of a contract of indemnity. It undertakes to shift the responsibility for the payment of the debt from the shoulders of the grantor to those of the grantee. Thereafter the grantor stands in the position of surety for the payment of the debt. However, such an arrangement binds only the parties to it—the grantor and the grantee. Since the mortgagee is not ordinarily a party to such an agreement, he is not bound by it. As a consequence, he may still hold the original mortgagor and every grantee in the chain of title who has assumed the personal obligation of the debt. He may see fit to release the original mortgagor and any subsequent grantee. Occasionally questions are raised about the ability of the mortgagee to reach back of any nonassuming grantees. Some courts seem to take the position that non-assumption interrupts the right of the mortgagee to hold all assuming grantees in the chain of title.

In case the mortgagee undertakes to hold all grantees who assume personal responsibility for the debt, he should make sure that they are joined in any suit for foreclosure. If they are so joined, any deficiency judgment may bind grantees who have disposed of their interest in the property years before. If one of these is financially responsible, the mortgagee may collect from him even though he has not owned the property covered by the mortgage for some time. Or the mortgagee may see fit to let his judgments stand on the record without pursuing his remedies under it. In this case, it continues to be a lien upon all real estate owned by all assuming grantees until it is released of record or expires by limitation.

During the intervening years until the statute of limitations runs out, any transfer of property by any assuming grantee will be complicated, because a new grantee will not usually be willing to take title encumbered by the lien of a deficiency judgment arising out of a foreclosure sale affecting another property. Consequently, sooner or later some grantee will probably move to cancel the deficiency judgment by agreeing with the holder to pay it off.

Any such grantee who pays off a deficiency judgment would then have recourse against any predecessor assuming grantee, and of course against the original mortgagor as well, unless he has already been released by the mortgagee. There are occasions when a transfer of title is conditioned upon the securing of a release of the grantor by the mortgagee.

Release of Grantor from Assumed Debt

Should the security appear to provide ample protection for the mortgagee, or should the grantee's financial standing be adequate, the mortgagee may see fit to release the grantor from the burden of an assumed mortgage. If he does so, there may be questions raised about his release of antecedent grantors, including the original mortgagor. In any event the mortgagee is not likely to weaken unduly his capacity to collect the debt. In the absence of a release from the mortgagee when a mortgaged property is transferred, there is always one sure way for the grantor to obtain release from an assumed mortgage—that is, to sell the property free and clear of all encumbrances, letting the grantee do his own financing. Even this proposal is based upon two assumptions: (1) that the mortgage contains a prepayment clause, permitting the grantor to pay off at his discretion; and (2) that the grantee has access to funds that will permit him to refinance the mortgage.

Sometimes even where there is no provision for prepayment, the grantor may still prefer to get the grantee to do his own financing, provided that the grantor can prepay the loan without too great a penalty. If the grantee will accept a loan from the same mortgagee, there may be little or no penalty. In such case, the old mortgage may be continued with a release granted to the grantor. In many instances, particularly in a tight money market, it is not convenient for the grantee to refinance the mortgage. In such case it is futile for the grantor to insist upon selling the property free and clear. The grantee may be willing but unable to purchase on those terms.

"Subject to" In contrast to the assumption of the personal obligation to pay the debt, the grantee may refuse to accept this responsibility. In this case he takes title "subject to" the mortgage. So long as he thinks it will be to his advantage—assuming his continuing financial ability—he will keep up payments on the mortgage and observe its other covenants. Under normal conditions, if he purchased the property at a fair price, it will be to his advantage to avoid default on the mortgage as the best means of protecting his own equity.

But should the grantee reach the conclusion that it will no longer be to his advantage to make further payments, or should be become financially unable to do so, he may default in his payments. By so doing, he runs the risk of losing whatever equity he has in the property. He cannot be held personally liable for the debt. The mortgagor and all subsequent assuming grantees are still personally liable and may be held for any deficiency judgment.

It is not ordinarily to the advantage of the grantor to sell property subject to the mortgage. He would much prefer that a responsible grantee assume it instead. But there are occasions when the most advantageous sale can be made subject to the mortgage. Indeed, in some situations the only buyer insists upon such an arrangement. If the mortgagor is about to default and expects to lose his property anyhow, he loses little by finding some prospective purchaser willing to take a chance on the recovery of the value of the property in question. Milkers frequently take title subject to the mortgage.

In case of a gift of property encumbered by a mortgage, the donee takes the property subject to the mortgage. Since he does not acquire the property as the result of a contract, he is not required to make any commitment that would bind him personally to pay the debt. Again this rule is subject to exceptions. If the gift is conditioned upon the willingness of the donee to assume personal responsibility for the debt of the donor that is secured by the mortgage, then, of course, the donee assumes the mortgage rather than takes title subject to it.

Purchase of Mortgage by Grantor

Not all defaults result in foreclosure actions. Sometimes the mortgagee will approach a financially responsible grantor—or the original mortgagor—for the purpose of giving him a chance to take action that does not involve a foreclosure suit and resulting deficiency judgment. By demonstrating to him that the present grantee has defaulted and that a foreclosure is imminent, he may induce the grantor to follow an alternative course for the purpose of protecting his own interests. One course open to him is to purchase the mortgage—perhaps through a nominee—thus keeping the mortgage alive. By this means he may preserve his right of indemnity against the grantee. By temporizing, through a reduction of installments or otherwise, he may hold the mortgage until the grantee recovers his financial health or until depressed real estate values are improved.

The purchaser may find it to his advantage to secure a voluntary conveyance from the grantee at the same time he purchases the mortgage. Or he may secure an agreement to repossess the property—leaving the question of ultimate title unsettled until a later date. Of course, if he should purchase the mortgage and secure a voluntary conveyance from the grantee without giving a satisfaction piece in return, he could in effect own the property and still hold the right of indemnity against the grantee should his nominee foreclose the mortgage. Since the grantee faces foreclosure and deficiency judgment anyhow, he would probably be no worse off if he followed the plan outlined above.

It is possible for the grantee to purchase a mortgage at its maturity rather than to repay the amount it represents. Instead of asking the mortgagee for a satisfaction piece in return for the amount due, he could request an assignment instead. This might give him some advantage if the property is sold, but it would not provide for him any sort of contract of indemnity such as the mortgagor or a previous grantee could secure by a similar purchase. Generally speaking, if the grantee pays off a mortgage, it is expected that the mortgage will become merged with the title.

Assignment of Mortgages

Since a mortgage is considered to be an asset owned by its holder, it follows that he may dispose of it as he would any other asset. The person who acquires it should make sure that he succeeds to the rights of the original mortgagee. This process is known as an assignment. In the absence of an agreement to the contrary, the right of assignment does not require the consent of the mortgagor. Presumably his rights and obligations are not affected. He merely owes the assignee instead of the assignor.

The assignee will do well to record his assignment at the earliest possible moment. Otherwise, he may find that his newly acquired asset has diminished in value. Conceivably the original mortgagee could practice double assignment. If he first assigns his mortgage to A who fails to record the assignment, and subsequently to B, who promptly records his assignment, as between A and B the latter's rights would prevail. A would have a claim against the assignor, but not against the property.

Estoppel Certificates   In order to make sure that an agreement reached in the assignment of a mortgage states exact facts, estoppel certificates are sometimes used to prevent subsequent representations about a different set of facts. For example, if A is about to purchase from B a mortgage on property owned by C, A would be better protected if he obtained a written statement from C, showng the unpaid balance of the mortgage. Otherwise, representations made by B might be intentionally or unintentionally erroneous. Or a verbal statement by C might later be denied and C might produce evidence to show that the amount owed by him is less than A thought it was. The estoppel certificate protects the purchaser of the mortgage.

Estoppel certificates as such are not usually secured from the assignor, since the form of assignment commonly used includes a recital by the assignor giving the amount due on the mortgage. It is frequently desirable to obtain an estoppel certificate from the holder of a junior mortgage when a senior mortgage is being assigned. This prevents future disagreements about the amount of debt based on the claims of the junior mortgagee at the time of assignment of the senior lien.

Extension Agreements

Occasionally, at the maturity of a mortgage or in anticipation of it, the mortgagor may seek permission from the mortgagee to extend it for a succeeding period of time. In responding to such a request the mortgagee may need to pursue several lines of inquiry before arriving at a conclusion. Certainly he should know the condition of the security. Has it been reasonably well maintained, or does it show the effects of waste and neglect? He should determine the existence of intervening liens and their effect upon an extension agreement. Should there be no intervening liens, he has nothing to worry about from this source. But if any exist, will the extension of an existing mortgage which has matured amount to a cancellation of the old mortgage and the making of a new one? If so, will this advance the priority of intervening liens? In most cases the answer to these questions is probably in the negative.

What about the surety status of grantees in the chain of title who have assumed the mortgage? Will an extension of time for the payment of the debt secured by the mortgage terminate such sureties? The best way for the mortgagee to protect himself against the possibilities implied in these questions is to secure the consent of such sureties to the extension. As parties to it they can have no grounds for opposing it. But if they are not made parties, and particularly if changes in the terms of the mortgage through the extension agreement tend to increase the obligations for which the sureties are expected to be bound, then care should be exercised that those sureties who refuse to sign the agreement may not be released by the extension agreement. Perhaps the threat of foreclosure and the placing of a deficiency judgment on the record against them may be used to force an agreement to make them parties to the extension.

The exact nature of an extension agreement depends upon the bargaining position of mortgagor and mortgagee. Since the use of extension agreements is limited to term loans, it is probable that the original loan has not been greatly reduced. If the mortgagor can refinance the loan on more favorable terms, he will probably not apply for an extension agreement. This will suggest that, in most cases, the mortgagee occupies a more favorable position than the mortgagor in dictating terms of the extension agreement. As a consequence, he may eliminate some clauses in the original mortgage, such as prepayment privileges, which favored the mortgagor. He may make changes that favor the mortgagee, such as an increase in the interest rate. The changes made will perhaps be tempered by his ability to secure approval of the extension agreement by previous grantees whom he wishes to hold along with the present grantee. Frequently the latter has no choice but to accept whatever terms are offered to him. The previous grantees may protest and make the granting of the extension agreement uncertain because of their unwillingness to accept harsher terms than they had once been held to.

Alternative to Extension Agreement   As an alternative to an extension agreement, the mortgagee may agree informally to a temporary extension, without making any changes in the record. If the mortgagor is unable to meet all of the obligations of the mortgage payments, these too may be waived, in whole or in part. For example, the fact that the question of such an agreement is raised is probably proof that the mortgagor cannot pay the matured principal of the loan. Therefore, some informal arrangement may be made to permit him to retain possession of the property in return for meeting monthly payments which may or may not include principal installments. In general, if such an informal agreement is reached, the amounts demanded will be adjusted to the payment capacities of the borrower.

The use of such an alternative to a definite extension agreement may serve the temporary needs of both mortgagor and mortgagee. If the latter feels that the security amply protects his lien, he can afford to be lenient in helping the mortgagor to adjust his financial arrangements during a difficult period. If the mortgagor also feels that he has a real equity in the property, he will wish to protect it if at all possible.

Release of Mortgage

The impact of mortgages may be released by various practices—intentional and otherwise. We have just indicated that intermediate grantees who refuse to sign extension agreements may be released from their liabilities under a mortgage if the mortgagee nevertheless persists in granting an extension of time to the assuming grantee. If the mortgagee voluntarily releases the grantee who has assumed the debt, that act probably releases all grantors as well. Since they stand merely in the position of sureties, the mortgagee must exhaust his claims against the assuming grantee before he can proceed against the sureties. If the mortgagee settles with the grantee for less than the whole debt and thereby releases him from the mortgage, this act releases all grantors as well. Whether the mortgagee collects a part of the debt from the assuming grantee or none at all, if he refuses to bring action on the amount owed he cannot thereafter bring action against any of those who act as sureties on the debt.

Partial releases are of quite a different character. They are quite common. If the mortgage is secured by more than one parcel, the time may come when the owner desires the release of one parcel, either for the purposes of sale or otherwise. The same principle applies when collateral other than real estate is put up to help secure the loan. When the debt is reduced sufficiently to justify the release of this added collateral, a formal release will usually be granted by the mortgagee. The amount of reduction required for this purpose may be written into the mortgage at the time it is executed. Or, if the mortgage covers only one parcel, a sale of a portion of it—provided the remainder is not unduly decreased in value as a result of the sale—will usually be permitted by a release of the lien of the mortgage upon the portion sold. It should be noted, however, that where the debt has also been secured by intermediate grantees who stand in the position of sureties, a release of the lien on any part of the real estate described in the mortgage, or of any collateral security, without the consent of the sureties will immediately discharge them from their whole obligation unless a partial release has been provided for in the mortgage instrument.

Recasting of Mortgages

Once a mortgage is executed and placed on record, its form may change substantially before it is redeemed. It may be recast for any one of several reasons. Although the mortgage may contain no provision for future advances, they may be made nevertheless by mutual agreement of mortgagor and mortgagee. If there are no intervening liens, nothing further is required than to change the amount of the obligations that the mortgage secures. The result may be recorded only on the books of the mortgagee without changing the record of the mortgage. If the original note and mortgage call for a lesser amount than the unpaid principal plus the advances, a change in the mortgage may be required to give the mortgagee full protection.

If a patient mortgagee permits the amount of the debt to increase because of delinquency, this too may call for a recasting of the mortgage. Again the subjects of intervening liens and of total debt must be considered. Or should multiple properties be offered as security for the original mortgage, any request for release of any of the original security from the lien of the mortgage must take into account possible changes in the mortgage.

Where a monthly payment direct reduction loan plan is used, with a level monthly payment throughout the life of the mortgage, the time will come when the unpaid balance is but a fraction of the original loan. At that time the mortgagor may request a recasting of the mortgage to provide for a reduction in the interest rate or in the monthly payments, or both. Possessed of a seasoned mortgage and a favorable experience with the mortgagor, the mortgagee is not likely to brush aside such a request. He would probably reduce the monthly payments gladly, since that enables him to keep a good investment for a longer period of time. He may agree to some reduction in the rate of interest more reluctantly. But if the mortgage contains prepayment privileges, he will probably lose it through refinancing by a competitor unless he makes reasonable concessions to the mortgagor. Again, rather than lose the investment he will probably prefer the change in interest rates. A windfall into the lap of a mortgagor may enable him to make a substantial reduction in his real estate loan and to justify an immediate request for a recasting of his mortgage as outlined above.

Recasting of mortgages to admit interests not present at the time the mortgages were executed is sometimes necessary. For example, the mortgage may make no provision for an easement of a public utility company which requires access to the rear of the site covered by the mortgage. Since the installation of the services of the utility will add to rather than subtract from the value of the security, the mortgagee will usually be glad to approve the change. Nevertheless it will require a recasting of the mortgage to the extent indicated.

Power of Attorney

In many business transactions it is common for one party to authorize another to act for him without any formal written instrument being required for this purpose. But in authorizing most acts that involve decisions concerning real estate rights, such authorization must be in writing. This writing is commonly known as a power of attorney. The principal who gives the power may be anyone, including a corporation, competent to execute real estate instruments. The agent who receives the power can be any natural and competent person or may be a corporation such as a bank or trust company. When used in connection with transactions involving real estate finance, the power given the agent should be set forth specifically in the instrument. A power of attorney should be made a matter of record so that the signature on the mortgage, for example, of someone other than the owner of the property may not cloud the title. Powers of attorney are subject to revocation by the principal and are generally terminated as a matter of law upon his death or insanity. Such a power does not terminate upon the death or insanity of the principal, however, when his agent, or attorney in fact, has a "power coupled with an interest," as where there has been such a transfer of title, or legal or equitable interest, in property to the attorney in fact that he can exercise the power in his own name.

QUESTIONS

1.   What is meant by "strict foreclosure" and what alternatives are there to such action?

2.   What special procedures are necessary to determine a proper bid for property available through a tax sale?

3.   Why is it that some state statutes prohibit the use of a power of sale written into the terms of a mortgage?

4.   What advantages may be gained by providing for the appointment of a receiver in event of default by the borrower on a mortgage loan?

5.   How valuable to the mortgagee is the right to obtain a deficiency judgment?

6.   Should the deficiency judgment be abolished? Why or why not?

7.   May a foreclosure sale sometimes be desirable even though the mortgagee would prefer a voluntary deed? Why?

8.   What special advantages does a mortgagee have in bidding at the foreclosure sale incident to his own proceedings? Is this arrangement fair?

9.   When a mortgagor assigns his property and his obligations under his note and mortgage on the property to another, how is the mortgagee affected?

10.   How may a mortgagor obtain a release from liability on a note and mortgage on real estate when the obligations under such note and mortgage have been assumed by another?

11.   What dangers are encountered by mortgagees and unreleased mortgagors when property is sold "subject to" a mortgage?

12.   What is an estoppel certificate and why is it necessary?

13.   In general, how may the surety status of a grantee in the chain of title, who has assumed the mortgage, be affected by an extension of the existing mortgage?

14.   How is a partial release used in a mortgage?

CASE PROBLEMS

1.   Mortgagor owns a property. A holds a first mortgage against it and B holds a second mortgage. Mortgagor defaults on his mortgage payments. A forecloses without joining B in the action? The property is sold at the foreclosure sale to C. What are B's rights?

2.   In case 1 above, what would your answer be if B's lien were not recorded?

3.   The Guardian Insurance Company holds a note from X and a first mortgage on a real estate parcel owned by X to secure it. X sold his property to Y and Y assumed the mortgage. The insurance company did not give X a release from his debt. Subsequently, Y missed required payments and the note became overdue. After some negotiating, the insurance company extended the note payment date and restructured the loan at a higher rate of interest. What is X's position at this stage of the transaction?

4.   Green held a mortgage against the real property of Grey. Green assigned his mortgage to Brown, who did not record the assignment. Green died. His executor, ignorant of the assignment, brought foreclosure proceedings at which the property was sold to Black. What is Black's position?

4

Junior Mortgages and Special Security Forms

PART 1: JUNIOR MORTGAGES

Dependence upon Junior Financing

Prospective purchasers of real estate, particularly purchasers of homes, have always been short of capital with which to make substantial down payments. The use of high percentage loans in recent years does not indicate a change in capital accumulations by most people. Instead, it represents a change of pattern in the means used to meet their needs. When lower percentage loans were the order of the day—as represented both in the lending policies of financial institutions and in the laws which regulated their operations—there was still the need for bridging the gap between a 60 percent loan and an inadequate down payment. This gap could be bridged in any one of several ways. One way that was not admitted to be such a bridge was to make the appraisal of the property so high that the loan was in reality for at least 80 percent of the cost of the property instead of the presumed 60 percent.

The other bridge, labeled as such, was a resort to a junior mortgage. As at first commonly used, it was a stopgap rather than a complete answer to a perplexing problem. If the property sold for $10,000, with a $6,000 first mortgage against it, and the purchaser had only $2,000 cash to make a down payment, someone came along with the missing $2,000 in return for a short-term second or junior mortgage. Short-sightedness induced both borrower and junior mortgagee to become parties to such a transaction, without either of them stopping to seek an answer to the question, "What will happen when the short-term junior mortgage matures?" Unlike the short-term senior mortgages used earlier, junior

72

mortgages were never expected to be subject to automatic renewal year after year.

Junior Mortgages

In simple real estate financing transactions, such as those involving single residences, the character of the mortgage structure is easily defined. The senior or prior mortgage is usually called a first mortgage. All others are given the class name of junior mortgages. In any particular situation, there may be one or more junior mortgages or none at all. One junior lien, usually called a second mortgage, is sometimes used to bridge the gap between the price of the property and the sum of the first mortgage and the amount of money available to the purchaser to use as a down payment.

Traditionally, second mortgages are short term and carry a higher rate of interest than first mortgages. They frequently cause trouble for mortgagors who are unable to pay them off at their early maturity date. Such mortgagors are then at the mercy of the holder of such paper, who may consent to renew the mortgage for another short term in consideration for the payment of a stiff renewal fee. While the mortgagor is struggling to reduce his first mortgage balance, he is faced with successive heavy renewal charges and high interest rates for junior mortgages.

In other cases, second mortgages may run for somewhat longer periods of time—perhaps as long as five years. Since there is no "business" of second mortgage lending that is organized into financial institutions, the pattern of lending depends in every case upon local conditions and the demands of those individuals who are willing to take the risks that accompany this type of lending. Where second mortgages represent the advance of money needed to bridge the gap between the amount of the purchase price of the property and the sum of the amount of equity funds of the purchaser and the amount available on a first mortgage, the mortgagee who advances the money and takes a second mortgage as security is likely to be an experienced, shrewd person who takes pains to protect his own interests. At the same time he does make possible the purchase of property that would otherwise not be placed at the disposal of a purchaser who cannot finance the purchase otherwise. If, on the other hand, the second mortgage is a purchase-money mortgage needed to enable the seller to dispose of property that he might otherwise be required to hold longer than he wishes, the terms of the second mortgage may be somewhat more to the liking of the purchaser.

The second mortgage reads like a first mortgage, except that it is expected to make reference to and accept the priority of the first mortgage. Unless the mortgagor is careful in writing the second mortgage, he may elevate the priority of the second mortgage to that of a senior lien upon the event of redemption of the first mortgage.

The best way for the mortgagor to protect himself against this contingency is to include, in the second mortgage instrument, a waiver clause committing the holder of the second mortgage to waive its priority, not only over an existing first mortgage, but over any succeeding first mortgage written for an amount not in excess of the amount of the existing first mortgage. This is commonly known as the "lifting clause," since it permits the mortgagor to lift the first mortgage and replace it with another one without disturbing the junior status of the second mortgage. For the protection of the holder of the latter, the lifting clause should contain the limitation that the new first mortgage shall not be for a greater amount than the one it replaces, carried at the time the second mortgage was executed.

Other junior liens, subsequent in priority to second mortgages, are sometimes used. For example, suppose that a contractor purchases a building site, financing it through a first mortgage containing a waiver clause in favor of a construction mortgage. With the execution of the latter, the earlier first mortgage becomes a second mortgage. Suppose that the sum of these two is $20,000. Suppose also that a purchaser of the property at $28,000 has only $4,000 for a down payment. The contractor may see fit to accept the $4,000 in cash, take back a purchase-money third mortgage for $4,000, and sell the property to the purchaser who assumes the first and second mortgages. That means a pretty heavy load of junior mortgage financing for the purchaser to carry.

Junior mortgages are highly speculative. Those who find it advantageous to take them in financing real estate sales are frequently forced to dispose of them promptly in order to free their limited capital for other uses. The sale of junior mortgages at discounts ranging as high as 50 percent is not unusual. The purchaser may be a casual buyer or one who finds trafficking in this kind of paper profitable. For one with capital, courage, and foresight, junior mortgages offer acceptable speculations.

Not all junior mortgages carry the same degree of risk. Some alert speculators are so well acquainted with the territory in which they operate and are such keen students of real estate trends that they are able to minimize their risks by making their commitments on a highly selective basis. Not only must they know the neighborhoods in which the properties on which they are willing to purchase mortgages are located, but they must be good judges of human nature. In one case the mortgagor may have such a low moral hazard that he can be depended upon to make good on a junior mortgage, regardless of the value of the property securing it.

Junior Mortgage Discounts   Because of the greater risks accepted by those who hold junior mortgages, it is expected that they shall bear rates of interest commensurate with the nature of the risks assumed. Laws against usury, if applied strictly, would interfere with some of the practices surrounding the use of junior mortgages. These laws are frequently circumvented by discount operations. For example, suppose that a single residence valued at $20,000 carries a first mortgage of $13,000. Suppose also that a prospective purchaser has only $4,000 available as a down payment. In order for the vendor to realize the additional $3,000 required to complete the price of $20,000, it may be necessary for him to take a second mortgage for $3,500 or even $4,000. He will then hope to sell this second mortgage for at least $3,000. The discount enjoyed by the purchaser will enhance the effective interest rate which he realizes on his investment.

This does not mean that two prices will be quoted for the property, one for cash and the other involving a second mortgage. As a matter of fact, if the seller hopes to realize $20,000 from the sale, he will probably ask more. He will then consider offers submitted upon the basis of financing arrangements, among other considerations. While the purchaser of such a property may not realize it, he will probably pay several hundred dollars more for it if a second mortgage is used as a part of the purchase price.

In the sale of highly speculative real estate in active markets, second mortgages may serve little purpose other than to create future trouble for the mortgagor. For example, the first mortgage may be large enough to cover the real costs of land and improvements. The down payment may pay a reasonable profit to the seller and the sales costs. The second mortgage is so speculative that if nothing is ever realized upon it the seller has not really suffered a loss from holding it. Nevertheless, its existence places a burden upon the mortgagor and his assigns. It may be very difficult meantime for the holder of such a second mortgage to obtain an advantage from it.

The discount on junior mortgages will usually continue to apply even after the senior mortgage has been written down to a point where the property might easily be financed with a single mortgage. This the mortgagor may not know. If he does not, he will probably continue to pay heavy discounts to obtain renewals of the junior financing. For example, suppose that a property costing $20,000 is financed with a $12,000 first mortgage, a $4,000 second mortgage, and $4,000 cash. Suppose that the income of the mortgagor is just sufficient to enable him to meet his obligations on both mortgages, pay his taxes, maintain his property in good condition, and pay the normal living expenses of himself and his family. In due time his savings, amounting to $4,000, are represented in the amortization of the first lien to $8,000.

At this point it should be possible to increase the first mortgage back to the original $12,000, using the increase to pay off the junior mortgage. Both the mortgagor and the holder of the senior mortgage would be better protected if this were done, assuming that the mortgagor is dependable and can carry a $12,000 lien on his property comfortably. Any circumstance that would make a renewal of the second mortgage difficult might eventually jeopardize the position of the holder of the first lien.

The latter is not likely to take the initiative in absorbing the second mortgage into an increased first lien. If the mortgagor does not know of the possibility so that he can take the initiative, he may go on year after year renewing the second mortgage. If his payments on the first mortgage are on a standard level basis, he never gets any relief here to permit him to accumulate funds to pay off the junior lien. His equity is increasing but his liquid resources are not.

Different Use of Discount   Sometimes discounts on junior mortgages are used in ways different from those mentioned above. Suppose that A sells his property to B, reluctantly taking back a purchase-money junior mortgage for $2,000. Suppose that B is not financially responsible and has difficulty in keeping up his payments. Since he is unable to meet the mortgage principal at its maturity date, it is informally extended. In other words, A does not press for payment for fear that he will have the property back on his hands when he has no use for it any longer.

Along comes C, who is willing to take over the property from B and to assume the first mortgage, provided that something can be done to reduce the second mortgage. A might be very glad to discount the mortgage 50 percent in order to get $1,000 cash and to be relieved of the worry of trying to make occasional collections from B. Or if C is a shrewd bargainer and is known to meet his financial obligations promptly and without fail, A might even be talked into canceling $1,000 of his second mortgage in return for the assumption of the other $1,000 by C. If he does so, it should be the second $1,000 that is canceled rather than the first. By this is meant that A might agree to cancel the entire mortgage after $1,000 has been paid on the principal. If he merely cancels $1,000 of the $2,000 mortgage, title to the property might again get into the hands of someone who is no more capable of meeting his obligations than B was. While C is still bound on his mortgage assumption, he may have lost his financial responsibility, moved out of the jurisdiction of the mortgage, and so forth.

Market for Junior Mortgages   Because of the relatively high return on second mortgage paper, speculative-minded investors sometimes favor commitments in this field of real estate finance. Most financial institutions which are regulated in the interest of those who supply their funds are prohibited by law from accepting junior mortgages as primary security for their advances, or from their purchase. Occasionally a second mortgage is taken as supplemental security to bolster weak security behind a senior lien or one that subsequently may become weak. This leaves the purchase of second mortgages almost entirely in the hands of individuals. Trafficking in them is no game for an amateur to play. The chances for loss are great. Even where losses are not suffered, this field of real estate finance grows much worry and uncertainty.

The successful speculator in junior mortgages must know much more than the legal details about the drawing up and assignment of mortgages. This phase is important and its neglect may be serious. But he must also be a close student of the market in which he operates, possessing a knowledge of such subjects as population changes and trends, general business conditions and cyclical changes in them, and real estate values and how to determine them. He must be able to judge soundness of construction, the effects of depreciation and obsolescence, and a host of other things that may affect the quality of his commitment. As an apprenticeship for the art of junior mortgage financing, successful experience in senior mortgages is sometimes used. It seems axiomatic that one who cannot succeed in dealing with senior mortgages should not tackle the greater hazards of junior mortgage financing.

The U.S. Securities and Exchange Commission and certain state regulatory officials have expressed concern over promotional techniques whereby the investor is "assured" his fixed rate of interest on a "secured" investment. The trust deed business in California, for example, has burgeoned in recent years because of the unusual population growth and the general scarcity of funds for real estate loans. A recent study of a committee of the state legislature found cases in southern California developments where first trust deeds had been written for over $16,000 against houses which sold for less than $14,000. Needless to say, the underlying security for junior liens in such transactions could be nothing but pure blue sky.

Occasionally a first mortgage institution is induced to take over a second mortgage from a good customer such as a contractor. Suppose that contractor A holds a second mortgage for $3,000 on property he has sold to B. Suppose that institution C has agreed to grant a first mortgage on the same property. In case A would rather not bother with collections on his second mortgage, C may be willing to purchase the second from A under some such terms as the following: Instead of paying cash to A, C may give A credit on an account as supplemental security to protect C's investment in the second mortgage on B's property. When the second mortgage is paid off, the account will be released to A.

Such an arrangement may be advantageous to A because, generally speaking, a mortgagor will probably default in his payments less frequently if his mortgage is held by a financial institution than if it is held by an individual. In addition, A is relieved from collection and bookkeeping problems. It can be advantageous to C for two reasons. The interest rate on the second mortgage is high and C has pleased a good customer by buying the second mortgage.

In the illustration used, there is not likely to be too much question raised about C holding the second mortgage against B's property, because it already holds the first mortgage on the same property. It is usually to the advantage of the holder of the first mortgage to be in a position to check up on payments on a junior lien. Default on the latter may cause trouble for the former.

Senior and Junior Mortgages   The existence of a junior mortgage is never a matter of indifference to the senior mortgagee. Neither should be the gambling instincts of the mortgagor nor the buying habits of his spouse. While the lien of the first mortgage takes priority over that of the second mortgage, this becomes most important in times of crisis, when the mortgagor finds that he can no longer meet his obligations. What will normally please the first mortgagee most is an assurance that no such crisis will ever arise during the life of his mortgage. Therefore, anything that creates an undue drain upon the income of the mortgagor may work against the best interests of the first mortgagee. For this reason he cannot be indifferent to the existence of a second mortgage, the obligations of which may create a crisis in the financial affairs of the mortgagor.

Some real estate financial institutions even go so far as to hesitate to grant first mortgages if the mortgagor expects to depend upon a second mortgage to help him finance his property. Others study carefully the amount and nature of the proposed second mortgage to determine whether or not to place a first mortgage on the property. The Federal Housing Administration has definitely frowned upon the use of second mortgages in connection with first mortgages insured by it. As a general rule it has refused insurance where a second mortgage is used.

From the standpoint of the holder of the junior mortgage, he has a definite interest in the actions of the senior mortgagee. If the latter refuses to grant any leniency to the mortgagor in a period of reduced capacity to meet his obligations—regardless of the willingness of the junior mortgagee to grant a temporary moratorium—the senior lien may be foreclosed at a time when the junior mortgagee will be hesitant to buy the property to protect his own interests. It is always to the interests of the junior mortgagee to try to cooperate with the senior mortgagee. On occasion the holder of the junior mortgage may find it to his advantage to purchase the senior mortgage to avoid difficulty with its holder. A better alternative might be to work with the mortgagor to refinance the property with a new first mortgagee, on the basis of merging the two mortgages if possible.

Foreclosure of Junior Mortgage   The holder of a junior mortgage has the legal right to foreclose his mortgage whenever the mortgagor defaults in his obligations. The possession of this right and the decision to exercise it are two quite different concepts. If the default occurs at a time when the junior mortgagee thinks the property is not worth more than the unpaid principal of the senior lien, foreclosure would produce nothing more valuable than a deficiency judgment. Meantime, if the mortgagor is keeping up his payments on his senior lien—or has made arrangements satisfactory to its holder—and if taxes are current, the holder of the junior lien may find it most advantageous to mark time, hoping for a recovery in real estate values, in the fortunes of the mortgagor, or both. He may even agree with the mortgagor, in writing if necessary, not to press his claims for a specified period of time.

If, however, the junior mortgagee thinks the property is worth more than the unpaid principal of the senior lien, particularly if he doubts the capacity of the mortgagor to improve his debt-paying ability, he may take steps to protect his interests before they become more involved. There are several possibilities open to him. He may buy out the interests of the mortgagor for a nominal sum, perhaps through a dummy purchaser, in order to keep his own mortgage alive. In such case he hopes to dispose of the property soon to a purchaser who can carry the obligations against it.

He may bargain with the mortgagor directly, agreeing to accept a voluntary conveyance in lieu of a foreclosure suit and a subsequent deficiency judgment. In such case he would probably cancel his junior mortgage, merging his claims into the title to the property. His acceptance of a deed from the mortgagor would probably be conditioned by the absence of any other junior liens of record and by his confidence that the mortgagor would not later claim duress in passing title to the property should real estate values stage an early recovery. In accepting a voluntary conveyance he may take title subject to the first mortgage if he hesitates to assume it. Even where there are subsequent junior liens of record, their holders might not think too highly of their value and might be willing to cancel them for a nominal sum. If this is less than foreclosure costs, the mortgagee may see fit to accept a voluntary conveyance of title.

Should there be any doubt about either of these matters, the junior mortgagee might find it advantageous to bring foreclosure suit, joining all subsequent junior lienors in the suit. If foreclosure is resorted to, the interests of the senior mortgagee must be taken into account. Several alternatives are open to the junior mortgagee. He may sue only the mortgagor and the subsequent lienholders, leaving the senior mortgage undisturbed unless its holder decides to enter foreclosure suit also. He may pay off the senior mortgage, with the consent of its holder if that is necessary. He may bargain with the latter to let his first mortgage stand undisturbed or to take back a new mortgage if the senior mortgagee is a party to the foreclosure suit.

In bargaining with the holder of the first mortgage, there must result a meeting of the minds. Depending upon a variety of factors, the holder of the first mortgage may be willing to accept a lower interest rate, some reduction in principal, or an easing up of payment requirements; or he may make other concessions to the new titleholder. He may insist upon much harsher terms in the new mortgage as his price for granting it. His estimate of the current and prospective value of the property and of the debt-paying capacities of the former holder of the junior lien will color his judgment on these issues.

Indeed, there are occasions when, if the senior mortgage as well as the junior is in default, the holder of the former will approach the holder of the latter to work out a plan by which the latter may take title to the property, even though the junior lienholder thinks he has no equity in it. Suppose for some reason that the holder of the senior lien does not wish to take title to the property. He may offer such terms to a financially responsible holder of a second mortgage as to create an equity where none existed. He may not only be willing to compromise his own claims, but agree to advance additional funds for the purpose of rehabilitating the property to make it more salable or rentable. Such an arrangement may well work to the advantage of both parties to it.

Merging of Mortgages   For the better protection of the mortgagor, junior mortgages should be long-term amortized instruments of real estate finance. Sometimes an arrangement is made with the holder of the first mortgage that he will serve as collection agent for the owner of the second mortgage. Suppose that the first mortgage is for $18,000 and the second for $6,000. In this case the mortgagor may make monthly payments to the first mortgagee as if he had a single mortgage for $24,000. Various plans are used in crediting these payments. Under one, all payments of principal installments may be applied against the unpaid balance of the first mortgage, until it has been reduced to $12,000. Meantime, the holder of the second mortgage would be credited with interest only. When the first mortgage is written down to $12,000, its holder may agree to recast his loan, writing it up again to $18,000, thereby releasing funds to redeem the second mortgage.

This practice of merging two mortgages is not too commonly used but it has possibilities. Until the time comes to merge the two, the first mortgagee not only has the advantage of more rapid amortization of his claims, but he has the added protection of an interest of the junior lienholder that will not be lightly cast aside. While the first mortgage is being amortized, its holder has an opportunity to become acquainted with the debt-paying capacities of the mortgagor. By the time the debt is written down from $18,000 to $12,000, the former should know the latter well enough to determine whether or not to increase the first mortgage indebtedness. The mortgagor certainly has a better deal than if he faced periodical renewals of junior financing. And the second mortgagee who can wait for his money probably stands a better chance of being paid in full in cash.

Redemption Clause   While the holder of a second or junior mortgage would normally be much pleased to have his loan paid off, there are occasions when he might prefer to have his mortgage instead of the money. Suppose that the term of the second mortgage is three years. The holder is not obligated to accept payment until the maturity date of his mortgage. Suppose also that the mortgagor has a good opportunity to refinance the property, merging the second mortgage with the senior lien. Without the consent of the holder of the junior lien, the mortgagor might not be able to take advantage of this opportunity.

The best way to be assured of having such an opportunity is to include in the second mortgage a redemption or prepayment clause. A common method of expressing such a clause is to state that "on or before" the maturity date of the mortgage, the amount of the mortgage may be paid and the mortgage canceled, at the option of the mortgagor. In the absence of some kind of redemption or call clause, the holder of the second mortgage might exact a heavy penalty as the price of accepting payment on the mortgage before it matures. Because of the junior position of the second mortgage and the uncertainties surrounding its collectibility, it is ordinarily not difficult to include a prepayment clause in a second mortgage. What is said here about a second mortgage would apply with equal if not greater force to third and subsequent mortgages.

Hierarchy of Mortgages   In contrast to the fairly simple mortgage structure which characterizes the financing of single-family residences, the hierarchy of mortgages sometimes used in the financing of corporations requires the services of a Philadelphia lawyer and two assistants to decipher. Not only are there second and third mortgages outstanding under that name, but frequently several layers of mortgage liens are so designated that the names given them confuse rather than enlighten the casual investor who may be attracted to them. This is particularly true in the financing of railroads and public utilities, where existing corporations may be the result of combinations or of a combination of combinations of corporations which had various types of mortgages outstanding at the time of merger or consolidation. When such combinations take place, the existing mortgage indebtedness is usually assumed and remains outstanding. By the time the new corporations execute some mortgages on their own account, complications can easily develop which require a careful study of wordy legal documents to decipher.

Even names are sometimes deceptive without being intentionally so. An owner of a single residence who uses a first mortgage seldom does anything to raise a question about the legal nature of this type of lien. On the other hand, corporation A might combine with corporation B to form corporation X, which assumes first and second mortgages against real estate owned previously by A and B separately. If now X issues its own first mortgage, with the same real estate as security, this mortgage constitutes a third rather than a first lien as its name implies.

Or suppose that corporation C, with a first mortgage against its real estate, gets into financial difficulty and is forced to raise new money. Suppose also that its only method of doing so is by the issuance of a senior mortgage. But there is already a senior mortgage outstanding. With the reluctant consent of the mortgagees, their claims may be subordinated to those of the new mortgagee whose mortgage is given the title of "prior lien mortgage." By this means the "first" mortgage, by subordination, becomes a junior lien. Meantime the wording of the "first" mortgage may not be changed. On its face it still carries the impression that it constitutes a senior lien. Sometimes the bonds issued under this mortgage are stamped to show the change in status indicated above. This is not always done. In other ways corporations frequently build up complex hierarchies of mortgages.

Later Discussion of Junior Liens   In subsequent chapters of this text, further discussion of junior liens will be pursued. This is especially true in the chapters on syndication, long-term leases, and sale and leaseback. Because of the importance of these subjects, it seems best to discuss them separately, rather than to include in the chapter on junior liens all of the material that is relevant to the subject.

PART 2: SPECIAL SECURITY FORMS

Subjects covered in this part of Chapter 4 include security forms that do not fall into the pattern of the real estate mortgage. These forms are:

1. Mechanics' liens.
2. Ground rents.
3. Fee ownership certificates.
4. Options.

Mechanics' Liens

Mechanics' liens are frequently misunderstood by those who are in a position to gain from their use. Many of our statutes represent modifications in practices formerly governed by common law or by equity.

Mechanics' liens have no such heritage. They are distinctly creatures of statute, with no background of antecedent policies. The first mechanic's lien law was passed in Maryland in 1791 as a means of attracting needed building labor. In effect, such a law gives certain types of creditors a preferential claim over other creditors of a debtor who owns real estate. These protected in this manner include the creditors who provide materials for structures which become a part of the real estate; the workmen who perform the labor of building the structure; the contractors who take responsibility for seeing that proper use is made of the materials and the labor; and even the subcontractors who have no immediate and direct responsibility to the owner of the property, but serve him indirectly through their relationship with general contractors. As a matter of practice, the owner customarily deals only with the general contractor. He probably could not identify any others protected by mechanics' liens. Yet, in three fourths of the states, any amounts paid by the owner to the general contractor could conceivably be collected a second time under mechanics' liens.

At the outset it must be recognized that a mechanic's lien, if filed in proper order, constitutes a lien against real estate. It is not automatic in operation, but must be foreclosed like any other lien to ensure final satisfaction, so far as the court of equity can ensure it. Also, the mere fact that material has been supplied or that labor has been performed does not fulfill the requirements of a mechanic's lien. There is no lien until notice of it is properly filed and recorded in the appropriate public office.

Because of the confusion arising from some statutes that have not been too carefully drawn, many conflicts result from their interpretation. Generally speaking, priorities of liens are expected to be determined by the order in which they are filed. This is not universally true. In some cases the first overt acts undertaken in the performance of the contract may determine the order of priority. Here is a fruitful source of confusion that should be clarified by more explicit statutes. The time for filing mechanics' liens varies from 30 days to six months after the work has been performed or the material has been delivered.

Mechanics' Liens and Mortgages   Conflicts between mechanics' liens and mortgages concerning their priority arise quite frequently. Not all of them can be resolved amicably, and one party or another is often forced to resort to court action to get the issue settled. Nevertheless, there are some principles which have common application to the question at issue. One is that purchase-money mortgages normally enjoy priority over mechanics' liens. This naturally follows from the fact that title and purchase-money mortgage are generally created simultaneously. In other words, the grantee takes the title encumbered by a purchase-money mortgage. Hence his first opportunity to incur an obligation that would give rise to a mechanic's lien would take place after the purchase-money mortgage has been executed. If its holder is diligent in protecting his interests, he will see that his mortgage is placed on record at the same instant of time that the grantee's title finds its way into the records.

Likewise, ordinary mortgages against improved property that are on record before the delivery of materials or the performance of work on the structure would take precedence over mechanics' liens. Even though some recent laws tend to give protection to holders of mechanics' liens by giving them priority over existing mortgages, this principle has not acquired much support as yet.

Most of the conflicts arise out of the simultaneous appearance of mechanics' liens and construction loans. The latter are presumed to provide much of the funds needed to pay for materials and to compensate labor used in the construction of a building which is to constitute the chief security for the construction loan. Since, by definition, the building does not exist before the material is delivered and the work is performed, confusion over the priority of construction mortgage liens and mechanics' liens may easily arise. In general, the weight of opinion favors priority to the construction mortgage which is made a part of the record prior to the filing of mechanics' liens. Even this preference is subject to disputes on occasion because of the cloudy character of the statutes mentioned above. If the mechanics' lien is interpreted as becoming effective at the time work on the project begins instead of at the time of filing the lien, this might readily cause confusion if work has begun before the construction mortgage is filed, even though such lien is placed upon the record before the mechanics' lien is recorded. Indeed, mechanics' liens have been known to attach under any of the following sets of circumstances: at the time the contract for materials or labor is agreed upon; at the time the first materials are delivered or the first labor is performed; when the construction is started; on the date of filing the lien; or on the date the owner is notified that the lien has been filed.

Because of possible confusion arising from the above situation, some mortgagees insist that no materials be delivered to the site and that no work be performed on the structure until the construction mortgage has been filed. If work has been started, affidavits are sometimes required from all who may be protected by mechanics' liens, showing that all such work has been paid for, before the construction mortgage will be executed. In extreme cases, materials delivered to the site have been taken back to their source, excavations have been filled, and the building site has been restored to its original condition. After all bills incurred up to that time have been paid and receipts have been obtained, the construction mortgage is then placed on record to give it priority, and the work of construction starts over again.

Other complications resulting in conflicts between mechanics' liens and mortgages arise even after questions are submitted to the courts for answers. In some cases a theory is prevalent to the effect that mechanics' liens should take precedence even over prior lien mortgages to the extent of the value added to the property by the improvement which gave rise to the mechanics' lien. Under this theory, if the foreclosure sale produces an amount insufficient to satisfy the claims of the mortgagee and the holders of the mechanics' liens, then the mortgagee is entitled only to the part of the proceeds that the ratio of the value of the property before the improvements represents in comparison with the value after the improvements have been made. For example, suppose that the mortgagee's claim is $6,000, the mechanics' liens amount to $2,000, the proceeds of the sale amount to only $6,000, and the value of the property before the improvements, $8,000; then the mortgagee would be entitled only to $4,800 instead of $6,000.

In still other cases the mechanics' lienholders are entitled to priority up to the full amount that has been added by the improvements. In the above illustration the mechanics' lienholders would get $2,000 and the mortgagee only $4,000, in spite of his supposed prior lien of $6,000. This principle is known as the severability doctrine, which undertakes to separate improvements cost as a special basis for preference.

Discharge of Mechanics' Liens Seldom does a mechanic's lien progress to the point of actual foreclosure. If foreclosure is resorted to, it may be instituted any time after the lien has been recorded and must be started within the time limit established by law. The procedure to sell the land to satisfy the mechanic's lien follows the same path as is followed in a mortgage foreclosure sale. Other forms of discharge and cancellations are more common. Some liens may be withdrawn because they were filed in error. Others may be canceled by court order if the defendant against whose property they were filed can prove that the amounts claimed are not applicable to this property. Many are either paid in full or compromised and the record is cleared. Pending court action to settle disputes, arrangements are sometimes made to lift the lien from property A and apply it to property B owned by the same party in order to facilitate the disposal of property A. Sometimes the defendant deposits with the court money or its equivalent in order to shift the lien to this asset. Again the purpose is to facilitate the sale or further financing of the property against which the lien was first placed.

Where the mortgagor acknowledges the debt, he may be willing to exchange some other form of assurance of repayment for the lien. For example, he may give the lienholder a note in return for the release of the lien. He should make sure that the lienholder is willing to go through with this kind of arrangement. Acceptance of the note by the lienholder might not necessarily induce him to release his mechanic's lien.

Some mechanics' liens are filed for protective purposes only. For example, if the financial affairs of a property owner are considerably involved, those eligible to file mechanics' liens may elect to do so merely to establish the security for their claims. As soon as the owner of the property straightens out his financial tangles, he may be able to pay off all lienholders, thus discharging their liens. Occasionally nuisance liens are filed. Their disposal may cost the property owner time, or money, or both.

Occasionally mechanics' liens are discharged because their holders fail to pursue their rights within the time allotted to them for this purpose. The time for foreclosing mechanic's liens varies from 60 days to six years, with one year most common.

Ground Rents

The two principal forms of ground rents originated in Baltimore, Maryland, and in Pennsylvania. These two forms will be discussed in order and current extensions of the ground rent form will then be considered.

Baltimore Ground Rents   In Maryland, particularly in the city of Baltimore, a system of financing real estate has been used since colonial days under the general name of "ground rents." At the outset, what amounted to perpetual leases were granted on vacant lands to be used for building construction. While the actual term of the lease might have been only 99 years, it was renewable in perpetuity. The lessor retained title to the land and granted its use, under conditions stipulated in the lease, to the lessee in return for an annual rental. Since in the early use of ground rents there was no provision for giving the lessee the right to acquire title by purchasing the fee, he could obtain the cancellation of an irredeemable lease only by the process of bargaining the title away from the lessor. Even where redemption rights were given the lessee in the lease contract, they expired by limitation in case they were not exercised within the time fixed in such contract.

In general it appears that the lessor was better acquainted with ground rents than the lessee, and for that reason the lease contract was likely to favor the former rather than the latter. Consequently, the right to purchase the fee was not commonly included. Eventually public policy decreed that irredeemable ground rents were undesirable. Through a succession of laws, beginning in 1884, Maryland determined that all subsequent leases for as long as 15 years should be considered to contain an option for the lessee to purchase the fee at a sum not larger than the capitalization of the ground rent at 6 percent. All ground rent leases executed subsequent to 1884 have been considered to be redeemable.

Pennsylvania Ground Rents In Pennsylvania a somewhat different system of ground rents developed in the early days. While the effect is the same as under the Baltimore irredeemable ground rents, the form is different. In Pennsylvania the title passed to the vendee in return for an agreement to pay a perpetual rent. Under both systems the result is the same as if the grantor had taken a perpetual mortgage on the land equal to its value. In some cases the vendee was permitted, during a specified period of time, to obtain a release from and discharge of the obligation to pay an annual rent, upon payment of a stipulated sum which amounted to the capitalization of the rent. If this privilege was not exercised within the time specified, the rent became perpetual and the arrangement irredeemable. It was still subject to subsequent cancellation through bargaining. As in Maryland, the Pennsylvania legislature in 1885 passed a law prohibiting the execution of irredeemable ground rents in the future.

Financing Construction under Ground Rents. Although in both Maryland and Pennsylvania ground rents have been extensively redeemed, financial institutions have been accustomed to finance the construction of buildings where ground rents are used. Mortgages used for this purpose are really leasehold mortgages with the ground rent contract acting as a prior lien. Nevertheless, in those areas where this method of financing has been employed for many years, there is no hesitancy to take leasehold mortgages. Since the ground rent contracts are assignable, in case a mortgage on the structure is foreclosed the mortgagee may succeed to the position of the mortgagor with respect to his rights and obligations under the ground rent plan. The mortgagee then has a property to be disposed of subject to the ground rent.

Current Uses of Residential Ground Rents Except in Maryland and parts of Pennsylvania, ground rents have been little used in this country. Several reasons account for this. In the newer sections of the United States, early land grants passed title more easily than in the two states where ground rents were more common. Other methods of financing construction also developed in the newer areas. While some settlers in these newer sections from Baltimore and Philadelphia tried out ground rents in their new home communities, no real financial pattern developed from these sporadic uses. In recent years, however, net ground leases have been adapted to an increasing extent to single-family dwellings in new developments, particularly in Hawaii and California.[1]

Developers save the most desirable sites for leasing, and thereby overcome initial unfavorable reactions to leasing as opposed to buying the underlying land. Usually the owner of the leased land does not do the

---

[1] William M. Shenkel, "Residential Net Ground Leases," *Journal of Property Management,* vol. 29, no. 4 (March–April 1964), pp. 180–93.

subdividing or housing construction. Rather, he grants a "master lease" to a subdivider who makes the improvements, such as streets and sewers. The subdivider may then either build a house on the lot or sell it. In either case, the cost of the improvements will be added on to the price of the house or to the cost of the lease. Many landowners have incorporated a hedge against inflation in the lease terms. They have required that the lease rentals shall be renegotiated halfway through the primary term of the lease. For example, leases at Laguna-Niguel subdivision in California require that ground rents be adjusted after 3 years to compensate for changes in the U.S. government cost-of-living index during the interim period.

Leaseholds are eligible for FHA insurance if the term is for 50 years or not less than 99 years for renewable leases. The Veterans Administration will guarantee leasehold loans if the primary term of the lease is at least 14 years beyond the maturity date of the loans. Leasehold loans are permissible under national banking regulations provided the lease extends at least 10 years beyond the loan maturity date. Federally chartered savings and loan associations may take liens on leaseholds with a primary period of, or renewable for, at least 10 years beyond the terminal date of the loan. Insurance companies may also take leasehold loans according to the laws of the states governing investment policies.

Besides the obvious advantage to the purchaser of avoiding lot costs at time of purchase, it has also been pointed out that restrictive covenants and a continuing repair and maintenance obligation in the lease do much to forestall depreciation and obsolescence.[2] The interest of the developer extends beyond the sale. On the other hand, the inherent disadvantages to this form of tenancy in the purchaser's eyes lies in the emotional appeal and sense of independence, without a terminal date, that is associated with homeownership.

Fee Ownership Certificates

One method of financing income property that has some vogue in some parts of the country is the fee ownership certificate. The holders occupy the position of common stockholders, except that they usually have all the risks of, but do not enjoy the gains that might accrue to, the speculative holders of common stock. Perhaps an illustration taken from actual experience will make clear the true nature of such certificates. Suppose that an apartment house is financed by the use of as large a

---

[2] A full consideration of residential lease covenants is contained in William M. Shenkel, *An Analysis of Long Term Residential Leases*. A report prepared for the Bureau of Indian Affairs, Department of Interior, March 1963 (second printing).

mortgage as it will stand—say $350,000. Suppose also that the promoter decides that he can sell 2,000 units of fee ownership certificates at $100 each, provided that he can show a return of 8 percent upon them. By the use of a lease to a company organized for the purpose, he receives a contract for a fixed rent of $16,000 per annum. The lessee agrees to pay all carrying charges, including the payments on the mortgage. The lessor then sells fee ownership certificates representing an undivided interest in an indivisible fee. He retains a management contract in addition to the profit he made on the deal. If conditions are favorable, the "common stockholders" will receive their 8 percent return on their investment. If they are too favorable, the lessee will probably exercise a purchase option reserved in the fee ownership certificates and buy them back at the option price of $105. But if future conditions should fail to justify the rent, the lessee will probably give up and leave the fee ownership certificate owners holding the bag, getting what rent they can and dividing net earnings among themselves if any are available. In other words, fee ownership certificates suffer from the weaknesses, but do not enjoy the strength, of common stock. An additional weakness has created difficulties in financing through fee ownership certificates. As certificate holders have moved to inaccessible places, or encountered domestic difficulties, the redemption by the lessee of all of the certificates to recapture the full title of the property becomes a near impossibility. Some certificate holders or persons entitled to dower and curtesy rights cannot be found, or may be located in remote places anywhere in the world. The current tendency is to issue subordinated debentures instead of fee ownership certificates and to retain the title in comparable situations.

Options

Another commonly used form for obtaining control of real property is the "option." Options may be "to purchase" or "to sell." By definition, a purchase option is the right to acquire property interests from another until a certain cut-off date at an agreed price and terms. This right is supported by a valuable consideration (often called a "premium") paid by the option holder, or "optionee," to the owner of the property, who for the duration of the option becomes the "optioner." Under an option to sell, the property owner, as the option holder, has the right to require the party granting the option to buy his property under the option terms, or he may decline to sell. In either case, if the option holder does not exercise the option, he forfeits the consideration provided for it.

The purchase option is more generally used. Its great value as a financing tool lies in its effectiveness in stabilizing terms in a negotiation until the optionee can conduct further exploration and discovery in regard to the feasibility of his project. For example, a $500 option premium may support an option to buy $200,000 worth of potential development land for a time, subject to elimination of contingencies regarding zoning, drainage, access, availability of public amenities, and the like.

Options have also been useful in limited cases for purposes of income tax conservation. The tax advantage gained in the use of options usually lies in the fact that under appropriate circumstances profits from real estate transactions may be classified as "capital gains" and, if long-term, taxed at a lower rate than is applied to ordinary income.

Capital gains are realized from the sale of capital assets only. With regard to real estate, all assets are defined as capital assets except those held primarily for resale, or those used in the trade or business. Capital gains may be classified as long-term and may receive favorable tax treatment if the taxpayer's holding period is of sufficient duration. An option to buy or sell real estate follows the same asset classification (capital asset or not) as the subject matter of the option.

It may thus be an advantage to sell an option held for over a year instead of the property for which it may be exercised.[3] If it is exercised and the property is sold immediately, the gain or loss is short-term. If the option is sold instead and exercised by the buyer, the transaction is long-term and taxable to the seller in a manner consistent with the classification of the subject property. If the option relates to:

1.   Capital assets, such as investment real estate, there is a capital gain or loss. Losses, however, from the sale of capital assets held for personal use as opposed to production of income are not deductible.

2.   Ordinary assets, as property held for resale by a dealer, there is an ordinary gain or loss.

3.   Assets used in the trade or business (like rentals), there is a capital gain or an ordinary loss. This unusual treatment is granted under Section 1231 of the Internal Revenue Code, which provides that if gains on the sale or exchange of real or depreciable property used in a trade or business exceed the losses, the gains and losses may be treated as long-term gains or losses. If the losses exceed the gains, however, the net loss may be treated as ordinary loss deductible in full from ordinary income.

This comment is not intended to present an exhaustive tax treatment of the subject of options. It is given merely to indicate potentials in the tax area. The overriding value of the option lies in its unique attractiveness for buying time to permit correct decision-making processes.

---

[3] For tax years beginning in 1977, the holding period to qualify for long-term capital gain or loss treatment is more than 9 months. For tax years beginning in 1978 and thereafter, the holding period must be over a year to qualify for long-term treatment.

QUESTIONS

1. What is the difference between a claim secured by a promissory note and a lien?

2. Recently, there has been a marked increase in the use of junior liens in areas of extensive real estate development. Specifically, how do these liens arise?

3. If you were considering purchase of a junior lien, how might your investigation differ from that which you would make if the lien were of first priority?

4. Why do many real estate financial institutions hesitate to grant first mortgages to a mortgagor who expects to depend upon a second mortgage to help him finance his property?

5. What alternatives are available to a junior mortgage lienholder in event of default by the mortgagor in connection with the senior mortgage?

6. Under what circumstances may a junior real estate lien have value even though there is no apparent equity in the property above the claim of the senior mortgage?

7. May anyone besides a mechanic obtain a mechanic's lien?

8. In what ways are mechanics' liens discharged?

9. A ground rent contract is an obligation of the lessee to make future payments. How may this contract take on substantial value to the lessee as a property for assignment to another?

10. What are fee ownership certificates? What are the advantages and disadvantages of this form of financing (*a*) from the point of view of the company issuing the certificate and (*b*) from the point of view of the investor?

11. What is an option and how is it used? How may it be used to obtain tax advantages?

CASE PROBLEMS

1. Interview a local lender and determine how construction lenders in your area guard against mechanics' liens.

2. Under the Maryland "ground rents" system, a lease for as long as 15 years is considered redeemable and the lessee is permitted to purchase the fee for a sum not larger than the capitalization of the annual ground rent at 6 percent. What would be the maximum purchase price of a lot whose annual rental was $720.

3. *a.* Green is considering buying a new house for his residence and acquires an option to buy a certain house at a fixed price. Although the property goes up in value, Green decides that he does not want the house and sells the option for more than he paid for it. What is the nature of his gain? How would the holding period of the option affect the taxability of the gain?

b. A dealer in industrial property acquires an option to buy an industrial site. The option was good for 13 months, but he allowed it to expire without exercising it. What is the nature of the loss of the price paid for the option? Why?

5

Land Contracts

Meaning

One form of real estate finance that has been commonly used over the years is the land contract. In some respects it has been treated like an unwanted stepchild, in spite of its usefulness. The term "land contract" is more frequently used in real estate offices than among members of the legal profession. There it is recognized—if at all—under a variety of aliases including "real estate contract," "installment sales contract," "agreement to convey," and "contract for deed." From one point of view, the latter term is well chosen. The land contract is accurately described as a contract for a deed. But the implications of that concept are not always properly observed.

Perhaps one of the reasons this form of financing has been somewhat neglected is that, in many cases, the members of the legal profession have little part in its use. They may take a major part in its aftermath but frequently are bypassed when the contract is signed.

Informality Surrounding Use

The above statement suggests that the drafting of land contracts is too often left to laypersons. This is true. The circumstances surrounding the drawing up of land contracts are exceedingly informal. Both vendor and vendee approach the subject with a lack of attention to details that is absent in transactions involving much less responsibility on the part of all concerned. In his eagerness to economize, the vendee may consider the services of an attorney to represent his interests an unnecessary cost.

Under the land contract, the vendor retains the title in his name. So far as the deed record shows, he is still the owner of the property.

But the land contract or contract for deed is supposed to tie the hands of the vendor in future transfers of title to make sure that he or his assigns must transfer it finally to the vendee or his heirs or assigns.

The land contract may be used as a substitute for either a vendor's lien or a purchase-money mortgage. Like the former, it is often a fragile type of evidence of the vendee's equity and would normally not be preferred for a long period of time over the purchase-money mortgage, if the latter is available. In states, however, that have long redemption periods during which the vendee has the right to possession and to collection of rents even though in default, sellers of land may refuse to give a deed and take back a mortgage until a very substantial part of the purchase price has been paid.

Uses   In general, land contracts are used when:

1. The buyer does not qualify for long-term mortgage credit.
2. The property is ineligible for mortgage credit from institutions.
3. Mortgage money is unavailable, as in rural areas.

In some circumstances, contract terms are more liberal than mortgage terms. For this reason, land contracts are used extensively (1) in the sale of vacant lots under exceedingly liberal credit arrangements with the vendor and (2) in the sale of improved property in which the purchaser usually has only a small amount for a down payment and depends upon his future income, often from the property itself, rather than his capital accumulations to liquidate his obligations to the vendor.

Sale of Vacant Lots   In the sale of vacant lots where the purchaser makes a small down payment—frequently no more than enough to cover the salesman's commission—land contracts find common use. Since the default ratio in such sales has been exceedingly high, it is difficult to visualize any other form of financing that is equally practical. Certainly it would not be expected that the development company which sells the lot on a very small down payment should transfer its title to the purchaser and take back a purchase-money mortgage to account for the remainder of the purchase price. Much of its activities would involve foreclosure suits under such circumstances, because of the frequent defaults by purchasers of vacant lots.

Partly because of these defaults, land contracts used by development companies are so drawn that they place major emphasis upon the protection of the vendor. The printed forms used in such cases contain the information required to fit the lots being sold and require but few items to be filled in at the time of sale. Purchasers who buy the lots put implicit trust in the seller and almost never even think about asking a member of the legal profession to inspect the contract to determine whether or not it protects their interests.

Sale of Improved Property   As in the case of the sale of vacant lots, with improved property acquired with only a small down payment or none at all, the vendor can scarcely afford to give a deed and take back a purchase money mortgage in light of the cost of recovery of the property in event of failure of the purchaser to meet his obligations. Defaults in this use of land contracts often take place but they are not nearly as common as with the sale of vacant lots.

The type of improved property—frequently for residential use—which becomes subject to sale under a land contract frequently possesses some major disability that makes its disposal in the ordinary way difficult. The neighborhood may be questionable, the structure may be old, the arrangement of the rooms may leave something to be desired, the market for the property may be sluggish, and so forth. This element of major disability may not necessarily be present, but it frequently is. Any type of property can use the land contract should the vendor and vendee agree. But where disabilities are present, the seller must seek a purchaser whose amount of available capital is so small that he cannot be too choosy in his purchase. Likewise, the purchaser must seek a seller who is attracted by only a small down payment or none at all.

A number of investors have used the land contract-low down payment combination as a means of acquiring control of large amounts of income property (largely residential) with little capital. During the post-World War II period until the late 1960s and early 1970s, a period of general housing scarcity, the consistency of rental incomes produced excellent opportunities for rapid estate building. The deals were structured so that the income streams from the property supported the financing and maintenance requirements. Interest costs and depreciation allowances largely negated the taxability of the income, thus providing a tax-sheltered, highly leveraged investment. At the same time, with strong inflationary forces acting on the total property value, the investor found his depreciation more than offset by inflation. The recent serious recession has seriously impaired many investment programs of this nature and, of course, has cast doubt on the advisability of such thinly financed future ventures, certainly unless the investor has iron-clad escape clauses in his contract to cover unexpected adversity.

Essentials of Land Contracts

Because of the informality surrounding the use of land contracts and, as a result, the frequent failure to give attention to matters that might later create headaches for both vendor and vendee, a major portion of the remainder of this chapter will deal with the essentials of land contracts required to protect both parties. The subjects discussed represent actual practices where more than ordinary attention is given to essential details of the contents of land contracts.

Vendor and Vendee   Assuming that the property which is to be the subject of the land contract is owned by one person, several questions arise about signatures to the contract on his account. Is it sufficient for him to sign for himself, or should his spouse sign also? Since it is a contract for deed, the latter to be delivered when the requirements of the land contract have been fulfilled, it is always safest to have the spouse sign also. Her failure to do so might give her a valid excuse for refusing to release her dower interest when it comes time to transfer title by deed. So far as the intent of the vendor is concerned, his signature alone could indicate that.

Shall the purchaser be indicated in the land contract as the vendee, or shall the contract indicate that he and his spouse are to be considered as joint tenants, with the right of holding the title later in the two names rather than one? Without undertaking at this time to answer this question, let us state that it at least merits greater consideration than it usually receives. If only one name is to be indicated as the vendee, shall the spouse sign the contract along with the vendee? Again caution would recommend both signatures. While the spouse probably has no dower interest in a land contract, one never knows what a court of equity might decide on a subject not too well defined in either law or equity. It is freely admitted that there appears to be less reason for the spouse of the vendee to sign than for the spouse of the vendor to sign. If nothing else is gained, however, the signature of the former is likely to impress her more with the seriousness of the obligation the vendee is undertaking.

Description of Property   Inclusion of the legal description of the property avoids complications. Since this kind of description must later appear in the deed at the time title passes, it is better to start with it in the land contract. In the absence of this type of description, the property must be so described that its identification is certain without too much expense or difficulty. It is never sufficient to attempt to describe a property by street number alone. In addition to complications that may arise even at the date of sale, street numbers are sometimes changed. This may create additional unnecessary complications that are easily avoided at the outset.

Existing Mortgage   Should there be a mortgage of record against the property at the time the land contract is drawn up, it will of course give its holder a prior lien over the contract. Likewise, a subsequent mortgage of record without notice of the existence of the land contract would normally take precedence over the contract. Either one of two policies may be followed in making payments to the mortgagee under an antecedent mortgage: (1) The vendor may continue to make the payments, perhaps using the land contract installments for this purpose. (2) The vendee may agree to make the payments directly to the mortgagee. Perhaps the vendee will assume the mortgage, thereby accepting personal responsibility for it.

In any event, the mortgage should be accurately described in the land contract with sufficient particularity to make sure that the vendee understands its terms. While, for his own protection, he should have the record of the mortgage carefully studied by someone acquainted with such matters, this is seldom done. The amount of the mortgage, its due date, the method and manner of payments, and so on, should all be set forth in the land contract; or at least by reference to the record they should be made a part of the contract. In order to make sure of his own protection in regard to the amount of the unpaid balance of the debt, the vendee should secure from the mortgagee a statement of such balance, together with a statement of any unpaid installments and any other pertinent information that will help the vendee see the whole picture. Such information should be calculated as of the date of the contract.

In case the vendor expects to continue to make the payments on the mortgage, the contract should give the vendee the right to pay directly any amounts due or that may become due in the future but may not be paid on time by the vendor. Any payments so made should apply on the debt of the vendee to the vendor. Since the mortgage represents a lien prior to that of the vendee, any default by the vendor that could result in a foreclosure sale could thereby jeopardize the position of the vendee.

The vendee should also be given the similar right to pay taxes, insurance premiums, or other obligations of the vendor if his neglect to pay these as they fall due could interfere with the rights of the vendee. In all such cases the amounts so paid should be credited against the debt of the vendee.

Insurance Clause   Upon taking over possession of the property, the vendee acquires an interest in any insurance on it. It will be to the interest of the vendor to require the vendee to pay the cost of this type of protection. While it is common practice to state in the contract that the "insurance now in force shall be continued," this hardly gives the vendee a very intelligent picture of the amount of protection from this quarter. In case the vendor is not insurance-minded, he may be carrying insufficient coverage. Of course the vendee can check with the carrier to learn the kinds and amounts being currently carried. In addition, he may wish to add to the amount or provide other types of insurance protection at his own expense.

At the time the contract is signed, insurance carriers should be notified so that they can add the vendee to their policies, to be indemnified along with the vendor in case of loss, "as their interests may appear." If the carrier is not notified of the change in ownership of the property, it may refuse to pay for the loss if it occurs. Incidentally, these interests not only are separate, but they may be in conflict in case of serious loss covered by insurance. Since the vendor usually dictates the terms of the land contract, he will probably provide that in case of destruction or serious damage to the structure he shall have the option to apply the insurance proceeds to the liquidation of the unpaid balance of the debt or to the replacement or repair of the building. If the former policy is followed, any surplus will go to the vendee. If the latter policy is chosen, arrangements must be made to make up any deficit of repair or replacement expenditures over the amount of insurance recovery.

Rights of Tenants   Land contracts should spell out in detail the rights of tenants in possession of any part of the property. In addition, the vendee should check with the tenant to find out if the term of his lease, the amount of rent for which he is obligated—including a statement of prepayments or delinquencies—and all other pertinent facts conform to the representations made by the vendor. The latter might not be dishonest. Even though honest, he can be mistaken. There may even be conflicts of interests between tenant and landlord which should be resolved before the vendee becomes a party to them or has his interests affected by them.

Upon investigation the vendee may decide that he would be well advised not to go through with his part of the land contract, if he finds that the rights of the tenants would interfere too seriously with his own plans. It is always better to discover these rights before, rather than after, the contract is signed. If any tenant rights are to be bought off, this is better taken care of before, rather than after, the contract is executed. Even though the tenant's rights have expired, the time and expense of dispossessing him are factors to be taken into account.

If the tenant is not in possession of the property and the vendee has no notice of his rights, he is not bound by them. The tenant in such case would still have recourse against the vendor, but he could not lawfully interfere with the interests of the vendee.

Payments under Land Contract   Even the questions arising concerning the payments to be made under the land contract by the vendee to the vendor cannot be simply stated as so many dollars per month, with nothing further said about them. The time and place of making such payments should be carefully defined. The down payment may have been made in the office of a real estate broker, in the directors' room of a local bank, and so forth. It is probable that future payments are not expected to be made at the same place. The rate of interest should be stated specifically, including any change of rate that may be contemplated during the life of the contract.

The contract should outline in detail just what the payments cover. If the monthly payments include interest, this should be stated. If, in addition, they include something for taxes, insurance, and so on, this too should be specifically stated. The contract should leave no doubt about the time and manner of distributing the ingredients of monthly installments. For example, is interest to be credited monthly or semiannually? Will the tax payments be held by the vendor as a trustee, or will they be credited against the unpaid balance of the principal each month and then added again to the principal each half year as the taxes are paid by the vendor?

What about prepayments? Is the vendee permitted to make prepayments as his resources permit? If so, at what times and in what amounts? No doubt the vendor will ordinarily be glad to encourage prepayments in order to increase his security. Nevertheless, the details concerning them should be included in the land contract in clear form, so that all parties will understand them. Will prepayments provide a cushion against possible future defaults? If so, in just what manner will they operate? These questions can and should be answered in the contract at the time it is executed.

Mortgage Clause   Whether or not there is a mortgage against the property at the time the land contract is executed, it is customary to provide that the vendor shall be permitted to mortgage the property for an amount not to exceed his equity. In such case the mortgage is given priority over the land contract. This provision enables the vendor to get at least part of his money out of the property should he care to do so. Presumably the interests of the vendee would not be adversely affected even in case of default on the mortgage by the vendor, since the rate of interest and terms of repayment on the mortgage are not likely to be more burdensome than those on the land contract.

However, if the contract does contain a mortgage clause, it should be couched in such terms that there can be no grounds for future disputes about its meaning. So far as possible, all features of the mortgage should be detailed in the contract. Since the interest rate which will govern such financing a few years hence cannot be accurately forecast at the time the contract is executed, it is sufficient to provide that the rate shall be that amount obtainable in the market at the time the mortgage is sought. Care should be exercised to prevent placing ahead of the vendee's interest any mortgage terms that would be unusually difficult for him to meet should the vendor default on the mortgage.

If care is exercised in drafting the mortgage clause in the land contract, and if later the vendor gets into trouble because he has failed to observe the requirements of the contract, the vendee should not be made to suffer. For example, suppose that the contract contains a prepayment clause giving the vendee the right to make advance payments as he sees fit. Suppose also that subsequently the vendor takes out a mortgage which gives him no prepayment privilege. He might easily find himself in a position where the amount of the outstanding mortgage exceeds his equity in the property, constituting a violation of his contract. If he gives prepayment privileges to the vendee, he should make sure that he receives prepayment privileges in his mortgage.

Another type of mortgage clause is frequently made a part of land contracts. The vendor may agree that when the amount of the indebtedness to him has been reduced a stipulated amount—say 25 percent—he will deed the property to the vendee and take back a purchase-money mortgage for the remainder. This clause may be inserted both as a means of providing a continuing investment for the vendor and as a further assurance to the vendee that he can obtain title to the property upon reaching a stipulated goal. The form of this clause should leave the vendee in a position to accept this option if he sees fit or to arrange some other alternative plan of financing instead. He might even prefer to continue the land contract, even though he has the right to have title transferred to his name.

If this type of mortgage provision is inserted in the land contract, its terms should be in such detail that there can at least be no doubt about the nature of the mortgage to be written at a future date. It is probable that the vendor—as an inducement to the purchase of the property—would agree at the time of executing a contract upon mortgage terms somewhat more liberal than could be obtained in the open market. Such liberality should not be nullified at a later time by giving the vendor an opportunity to hide behind indefinite or vague terms in the mortgage clause.

Provision for Deed As noted above, the vendee looks forward to the time when he will hold title to the property purchased under a land contract. The contract should definitely stipulate the conditions under which deed will be available to the vendee and the kind of deed to be used. Presumably it will be a full warranty deed. If so, the contract should so state. If not, the nature of the deed to be used should be set forth without equivocation.

It is not sufficient for the vendee to take the word of the vendor that a deed will be forthcoming. Before signing the contract, the vendee should make sure, as the result of a proper search of title, of the exact nature of the vendor's interest in the property. In other words, the vendee wants assurance that the vendor has good title. If he has not, he cannot pass it on to the vendee. Then the vendee should be protected against interests which refuse to join the vendor in passing title. For example, it is elementary that the spouse should sign the contract, thereby committing herself to sign away her dower interest when the proper time comes. Her refusal to do so might make it impossible for the vendor to pass good title to the property. Suppose that a life estate in the property exists in the name of someone other than the vendor and his spouse. In such a case the owner of this estate also should sign the contract or in some other manner should indicate his willingness to release his life estate at the time the deed is called for.

Since the vendor may see fit to dispose of his interests in the land contract before title to the land passes to the vendee, the latter is properly concerned with several features of the vendor's assignment of his interests. In the first place, he wants to make sure that the assignee understands the exact nature of the contract and that no new interpretation will be placed upon its provisions.

Then he is concerned with another question which may be very vital to his interests: Will his deed, if and when he is entitled to receive it, be signed by the original vendor, or can an assignee be substituted for him? If the latter is permissible, a second question follows: Would it be possible for the vendor to pass title to a grantee, known to be financially irresponsible, by the use of a special warranty deed which gets the grantor out from under any responsibility for the character of the title? If so, even though the vendee under the contract receives a full warranty deed from the assignee, he does not get the full warranty deed which he thought he was to get when he executed the contract.

While the vendor should not be restricted in his disposal of his interest, it should be stated in the contract that both the vendor and his assigns must give a full warranty deed in passing their interests along to someone else. To protect the assigns of the vendee, provision should be made in the contract that the deed may pass either to the vendee or to his assigns. While it is generally assumed that a deed shall be accompanied by an abstract of title brought down to date—or whatever substitute is common in the community—this should be definitely stated in the contract.

Restrictions upon Assignment by Vendee   There are occasions when the vendor prefers to place restrictions upon the right of the vendee to assign his interests in a land contract. For example, suppose that the vendor knows about the thrifty habits and the housekeeping ability of the vendees. He may be willing to sell them a piece of property because he feels sure that they will take good care of it and will make every effort to live up to their contract obligations. At the same time the vendor might be quite unwilling to sell the property, under the same terms and conditions, to a specific friend of the vendee. What is to prevent the vendee from assigning his interest in the land contract to this friend? Perhaps he signed the contract in the first instance for this purpose; or perhaps such an assignment is an afterthought and is planned without knowledge that the vendor distrusts the new vendee.

The vendor, at the time the contract is executed, can restrict the negotiability of the vendee's interests by the insertion of a clause providing that the vendee may not assign such interests without the consent of the vendor. In the event of a dispute over the application of such a clause to a specific case, the courts would probably look to the reasonableness of the vendor's refusal to approve an assignment as the basis for a decision. It is not probable that the vendor could use his veto power, without justification, to the financial injury of the vendee.

In any event the right of prepayment clause would undoubtedly protect the vendee against prejudicial vetoes by the vendor if the property could be financed in any other manner. Refusal of the vendor to sanction a proposed assignment could be nullified by paying him the amount of the unpaid balance of the debt, thereby canceling his interest in the property.

Failure to Pass Title   As stated above, unless the vendee makes sure of using all precautions to protect his interest at the time he executes the contract, he may find that, when the time comes to secure title, the vendor is unable to transfer title to him. For example, his wife may not release her dower interest. Unless she has agreed to this in effect at the time she signed the land contract, she cannot be forced to do so. The vendor may find that he cannot secure the release of a life estate; there may be an indestructible contingent remainderman's interest; and so forth. Consequently, the vendor cannot give the vendee a good merchantable title. Since he cannot perform his part of the contract, a suit for specific performance is fruitless.

Here is another place where the vendee needs competent legal advice to know his interests and the best manner of protecting them. Otherwise he may be "bought off" by the vendor at a price that is too low. Since he cannot sue for specific performance, he can bring action for damages. He should be able to recover whatever he has paid on the principal of the debt and the cost of improvements made with the consent of the vendor, and perhaps also an amount representing any increase in value that the property has enjoyed since his execution of the contract.

Since land contracts frequently contain penalty clauses against default by the vendee, it would not be amiss to include a stipulation to the effect that, in case of default by the vendor, a penalty of a stipulated amount shall be paid by him to the vendee. In the absence of such a provision in the contract, his chances of collecting a penalty through court action are not good.

Improvements Directed by Vendee   The land contract usually provides that no major improvements or physical changes will be made in the property without the consent of the vendor. The reason for such a provision is obvious. Before the vendee has built up a substantial equity in the property, he might wish to make major changes which would please his peculiar tastes but might not be acceptable to a subsequent purchaser, in case the vendee defaults on his contract. Even the removal of trees and shrubs might result in a decrease in the value of the property. Therefore, any major change should be subject to a veto by the vendor, at least until the vendee has built up a substantial equity.

Should this clause be omitted from the contract or should it be violated by the vendee, the cost of any improvements directed by the vendee could not be assessed against the interest of the vendor without his authorization. As a consequence, a mechanic's lien would attach to the interest of the vendee only. In case the vendee's interest was later forfeited before the mechanic's lien had been attached, no lien would continue. The person filing the mechanic's lien must thereafter look to the vendee for satisfaction. In case the vendee directs and the vendor authorizes the improvement, the whole property could be held as security for any mechanics' liens that might be properly filed subject, of course, to prior liens.

Recording of Land Contracts   State laws provide for the recording of conveyances of land and instruments affecting title. Land contracts generally are considered instruments affecting title and are consequently admissible to record. Recording land contracts is not essential to their validity; it merely gives notice of their existence to third parties.

In some cases the contract contains a stipulation that it shall not be recorded. This is included at the instance of the vendor who receives only a small down payment or none at all. If such a contract is recorded and there is an early default, clearing the record may take time and involve expense to the vendor. Even so, such a contract is occasionally recorded, in violation of its terms. This does not invalidate the contract. It may subject the vendee to a suit for damages if the vendor suffers loss by being unable immediately to effect a sale to another buyer who refuses to take title with the cloud of the recorded contract against it, and who is unwilling to wait upon the purchase until the record can be cleared Probably such a right of suit for damages would seldom be exercised.

On the other hand, failure to record land contracts against vacant lots because of small down payments affords the vendor a particularly good opportunity to take advantage of the vendee, should he care to do so. The complete absence of possession by the vendee, or of any evidence of it, makes it easy for the dishonest vendor to sell the land and deliver good title to a third party, even though the vendee be not in default.

If, however, the vendee makes a substantial down payment, or as he builds up an equity with subsequent payments, he may feel safer if his contract is recorded. Under either of these sets of circumstances, the recording of the contract should meet with little opposition from the vendor. However, immediate and continued possession of the property by the vendee will normally serve as a satisfactory substitute for a record of the contract. All parties who might wish to acquire a lien prior to the claims of the vendee are put on notice to determine by what right the vendee occupies the property. Physical possession is not necessary to protect the rights of the vendee if sufficient evidence of possession exists to warrant a further inquiry by other parties.

Judgments and Land Contracts Since judgments against a debtor become a lien against any real estate held in his name from the instant of entry of the judgments upon the record, the vendee of a land contract should make sure that there are no unsatisfied judgments on the record at the time the contract is executed. If there are, they probably have preference over the land contract. As to judgments filed after the contract becomes effective, it appears that the vendee is not chargeable with notice of such entry. Consequently, he runs little risk by continuing to make his payments to the vendor. The judgment creditors can best reach the vendor's interest in these payments through court action. Through garnishment or equity proceedings, judgment holders could probably secure a diversion of such payments to a liquidation of their claims.

Complications sometimes result in conflicts between land contracts and mechanics' liens. Because mechanics generally have from 30 days to 6 months in which to file their liens, the vendee should inspect the property before signing a land contract, to determine if there is any evidence that work has recently been done or material delivered that might give rise to a mechanic's lien. If so, receipts from those who did the work or supplied the materials might be a necessary precaution against prior claims. In case the vendee finds that he is responsible for mechanics' liens that were not accounted for in the contract, he may pay them, obtain a discharge of the liens from the record, and take credit for his payments on the debt. If he is not personally responsible for them, he can disregard them, since his claims would precede theirs.

Default and Foreclosure

Because of the frequency with which land contracts are not completely executed in accordance with their provisions, consideration of what happens in event of default and foreclosure is particularly important. Courts in the application of principles of equity will often interpret provisions of land contracts in a manner somewhat at variance from what the contract would seem to provide.

Default by Vendee Because of the informality surrounding the execution of land contracts, the inexperience of the vendee, and the common absence of legal counsel to advise him, the vendee frequently interprets the contract to be a kind of option. He assumes that, if he decides to default on his contract, all he needs to do is forfeit his rights under it and walk away from it. He may find that conditions established by his signature on the contract are not quite this simple. To be sure most land contracts specifically provide that—at the option of the vendor—a default by the vendee may result in the forfeiture of the rights of the latter. In addition, the vendor reserves the right to retain as liquidated damages any amounts paid by the vendee, including any improvements to the property made by him.

The vendor may not see fit to exercise this option. If he thinks the unpaid portion of the debt exceeds the value of the property, and if he thinks the vendee is financially responsible, he may insist that the contract be lived up to. As an alternative, he may insist upon a cash settlement as the price of releasing the vendee from his contract. Depending upon the vendee's experience and the nature of advice available to him, the amount of cash demanded may not bear too definite a relationship to the amount of loss presumably suffered by the vendor.

If the vendee has had experience with such questions or if he has competent legal advice, he may decide not to forfeit any equity he may have in the property without a struggle. Even though he has technically violated the contract by defaulting in his payments, he may insist upon retention of possession of the property and may actively resist any effort on the part of the vendor to dispossess him. He too may do a little bargaining and agree to vacate and release the vendor only upon consideration that the vendor pay him a substantial sum of money —perhaps the amount by which the vendee has reduced the principal amount of the debt.

While negotiations are in progress, the vendee continues in possession of the property. Depending upon a combination of circumstances, including the pulse of the real estate market, the attitude of the vendee toward committing waste, and the forecast of a favorable or unfavorable decision in a court of equity, the vendor may be willing to pay a persistent vendee in default something to purchase a release from the contract. Perhaps the amount paid may even be considered by the vendor as a price of ridding himself of a nuisance. Even without such nuisance payment, something may be paid even though the vendor expects to suffer a loss, if he thinks that the vendee is financially irresponsible.

Loss of Payments under Land Contracts   Under a long-term land contract, regular payments over a considerable period of time may have reduced the original indebtedness substantially. Since it is customary to stipulate in the contract that, in case of a default on the part of the vendee, all payments made may be retained by the vendor in lieu of liquidated damages, on the face of it appearances seem to indicate that a default might nullify all the equity the vendee has built up in the property. Because courts of equity, if appealed to, may construe a land contract as an equitable mortgage, it is not clear what rights the vendee may possess in relation to payments already made.

It does not appear fair that he should be permitted to ask for the repayment of any amounts paid to the vendor. Why not give him an equity of redemption similar to that given the mortgagor? At least he should be permitted to find a means of protecting his equity even after a technical default. Giving him an equity of redemption would probably carry with it an obligation covered by a deficiency judgment, if any applies.

Foreclosure Sale   Failing to dispossess a vendee in default, either by a request for observance of the forfeiture clause in the land contract or by an offer of compensation for release from the contract, the vendor may pursue his rights in a court of equity. Since the law on the subject is not well defined, the equity court may render any one of several decisions. It may grant the vendor the relief he prays for, decree that the forfeiture clause in the contract be made effective, and dispossess the vendee from the property. It may even render judgment against the vendee for any installments in default.

As an alternative, it may determine that the vendee still has an equity in the property which he is entitled to recover by continued occupancy of the property for a period of time—fixed in the decree—sufficient to absorb or live up this equity. In other words, without any additional payment, the court may grant the vendee what amounts to free rent for a determined period of time. At the end of that period the vendor is entitled to recover possession of the property unless a new agreement is reached with the vendee in the meantime.

As a second alternative, the court of equity may decree that the land contract is in effect an equitable mortgage. As such it must be foreclosed like other mortgages to determine what disposition shall be made of the proceeds of the sale. Where such an alternative is followed, the procedure from then on follows the path taken by mortgage foreclosure and sale of the security, discussed elsewhere in this text. In general, courts of equity tend to protect the interests of the vendee in default so long as there appear to be reasonable grounds in his favor.

Strict Foreclosure of Land Contracts   In some cases the rule of strict foreclosure is applied to land contracts. In other words, even after default a court of equity may fix a time within which the purchaser under a land contract may pay up his indebtedness to the vendor if he can find an alternative method of financing the deal. Failing to finance the property within the time fixed by the court may be followed by a complete loss of equity by the vendee, leaving the vendor with undisputed and unqualified title to the property. Except in times of extremely tight money, the vendee who is entitled to financial assistance will probably be able to find it. If his equity is so thin that no one will be willing to take the risks involved in assisting him, even a foreclosure sale would result in no recovery for him. If, on the other hand, he has a substantial equity in the property and cannot find someone willing to finance him he should be able to find a purchaser for his equity, enabling him to enjoy some recovery of previous outlays. If he fails to make use of either of these possibilities, strict foreclosure may follow.

Lease and Option Contracts

One form of land contract that is even more informal than the forms just discussed is the lease and purchase option contract. The conditions of its use may follow a pattern of this nature. Suppose that A owns an inexpensive property in a neighborhood that is on the decline. Suppose that his efforts to sell it have met with complete failure. Suppose also that he would prefer to sell it rather than rent it. He may be able to combine renting it with an option to purchase. B may find that the property meets his needs. He would like to purchase it but has nothing to use as a down payment. Meantime he requires a place for his family to live in.

Landlord and tenant arrive at an agreement which contains these elements: First the tenant is permitted to use the property for a specified period of time—e.g., one year—at a rental that represents fair rent to both parties. At the end of the period, if he has faithfully met his obligations to the landlord, he may exercise his option to buy the property at a price that should have been agreed upon at the time the arrangement was set up. The exercise of the option may or may not require any additional down payment in cash—probably not. The tenant now becomes a vendee and the landlord a vendor under a land contract. Subsequent developments follow the pattern already outlined in this chapter. The monthly payments, which may not be substantially increased, if at all, are applied as installments on a debt rather than as rent.

As already indicated, this kind of deal is likely to be quite informal at the time it is made. It may not even be in writing. As a matter of fact, neither party may feel that he is bound by it. The saving clause for the landlord is contained in the interpretation he wishes to put upon the manner in which the tenant has met his obligations as a tenant. Even though the tenant pays the rent promptly, the landlord may contend that he has neglected other obligations, such as the proper care of the property. The tenant, by definition, has an option that he may ignore as he sees fit. If, however, both landlord and tenant are satisfied with the original deal, the lease may readily ripen into a land contract. Conceivably it could bypass the contract stage and become an outright sale, with passage of title at the end of the lease if the tenant can finance the transfer.

Because so many uncertainties and possibilities are involved in such an arrangement, it does not appear that the tenant will find it desirable to incur the expense necessary to secure legal counsel to protect all his rights at the time the deal is made. Even should an unscrupulous landlord deny his option to purchase, the tenant has at least had use of the property at its fair rental value. The chief loss he has suffered is the possibility of making an alternative deal for another property that is no longer available to him at the end of his lease period.

Combined with this type of contract is an arrangement that frequently works to the advantage of both vendor and vendee. The arrangement described below could of course be a part of any land contract, but it is particularly applicable here. By definition the structure is probably not modern. It may even need major repairs, such as a new roof or a new paint job. The vendee has little opportunity to add to his monthly cash payments, but he may have some time which he can devote to repairs and improvements to the property.

So the land contract sets up a schedule of allowances which may cumulate to a sizable "sweat" equity. For example, the vendor may agree to allow $180 for the labor of reroofing the house, $275 for the labor of giving it two coats of paint, and so on. Meantime, the vendee agrees that the materials required for these jobs shall add $400 to the debt against the property. The results please both parties. The property becomes more valuable than it was before the repairs and improvements were made. The added value benefits the vendor because the security for his claims is now proportionately higher than his added investment. The vendee benefits because he has a greater equity in a better property. Even though the vendee is not a skilled building craftsman, he can probably do many things about the place with his own labor. Perhaps he can obtain the assistance of a more experienced friend on a trade-work basis. The vendor is likely to have greater experience than the vendee and will find it to his advantage to advise and assist the latter in making his contributions of time and labor.

Market for Land Contracts

In general, the market for land contracts is limited to their sale to individuals acquainted with this type of real estate financing. They know the nature of the risks involved and usually are financially able to bear them. Occasionally a financial institution, such as a savings and loan association, buys them. In such case precautions are taken to protect the purchaser against loss. For example, suppose that a property owner disposes of his real estate at a price of $20,000, accepts a down payment of $1,500, and takes back a land contract for $18,500. If he is sufficiently anxious to raise cash, he may make a deal somewhat as follows: He may sell his contract to a financial institution—with or without a discount—and agree to keep $5,000 on deposit with the purchaser as supplemental security. Usually when the contract balance is written down to $12,000 or when the vendee under the contract is able to finance his property by some other means, the deposit will be released and the vendor permitted to obtain unrestricted possession of the net selling price of his property.

Taxation of Installment Sales

Because the land contract is often used in connection with a low down payment, it is appropriate to consider a special method of federal income tax reporting that may be elected by the seller in connection with installment sales. This method relieves the seller of paying tax on income he has not yet collected. He includes in his gross income only that portion of each collection that constitutes profit.

Income from installment sales is determined by using a gross profit percentage. This percentage is the ratio of the total profit to the contract price. Thus, if the contract price is $10,000 and the gain on the sale is $2,500, the gross profit percentage is 25 percent. Under this condition, 25 percent of each payment collected on the sale is includible as taxable gross income in the year of collection. The percentage, once determined, never changes. In this way, taxable income is spread over a number of years.

To qualify for use of this method, the seller must agree to take two or more payments in two or more tax years. Furthermore, not more than 30 percent of the selling price may be collected in the year of sale. In transactions exceeding $3,000, special attention must be paid to the "unstated interest" rule.[1] Unstated interest occurs when a sales contract makes no provision for payment of interest on the unpaid balance or, if interest is specified, it provides for a rate less than 6 percent per annum simple interest. In this case, interest will be imputed at 7 percent compounded semiannually. The amount of imputed interest for the entire payment period is deducted from the sale price of the property, since interest is deemed to be a cost of financing and not a part of the purchase price to the buyer. The newly computed sale price, reduced by the amount of interest imputed in the note, may be too low to permit the seller to qualify for the installment method because his down payment may exceed 30 percent of the new figure.

Example On February 1, 1977, Harry Carey sells a building site for

---

[1] Internal Revenue Code, Sec. 483, as amended.

$14,200, of which $4,200 is received and the remaining $10,000 is to be received in annual payments of $2,500, plus interest at 3 percent annually. Since the stated interest rate is less than 6 percent, a 7 percent rate is imputed. A table of the present value of $1 at 7 percent compounded semiannually, which is used in the computation, is shown below:[2]

Number of Months Deferred		
More Than	*But Not More Than*	*Factor*
0	6	1.00000
6	9	0.96618
9	15	0.93351
15	21	0.90194
21	27	0.87144
27	33	0.84197
33	39	0.81350
39	45	0.78599
45	51	0.75941
51	57	0.73373
57	63	0.70892

Computation of the unstated interest is performed as follows:

(1) Date of Payment	*(2)* Amount of Payment (Principal + Interest)	*(3)* Number of Months Deferred	*(4)* Present Value of $1 Payable at End of Period	*(5)* Present Value of Payment (Col. 2 × Col. 4)
Feb. 1, 1978	$ 2,800	12	0.93351	$2,613.83
Feb. 1, 1979	2,725	24	0.87144	2,374.67
Feb. 1, 1980	2,650	36	0.81350	2,155.78
Feb. 1, 1981	2,575	48	0.75941	1,955.48
Totals	$10,750			$9,099.76

The sum of the principal payments due under the contract ($10,000) less the present value of such payments plus interest payments due under the contract ($9,099.76) equals the unstated interest ($900.24). This interest income is allocated over the collection period in proportion to the principal reduction received.

---

[2] The concept of the time value of money is explained in detail in Chapter 8.

Because of the interest element imputed in the $10,000 balance owing on the selling price at the time of closing, the selling price is reduced by $900.24 for purposes of computing the 30 percent limitation on a down payment to qualify a sale for deferred tax treatment. In this case, the selling price becomes ($14,200 − $900.24) $13,299.76. The down payment of $4,200 is in excess of 30 percent of the newly computed sale price. Thus, the sale cannot be taxed as a deferred payment sale although, nominally, the down payment was less than 30 percent of the sale price.

Structuring transactions to qualify for installment sale treatment is a highly technical task. Tax counsel should participate in such arrangements.

QUESTIONS

1. What is a land contract?
2. What other terms are commonly used synonymously with "land contract"?
3. What dangers are attendant upon the use of land contracts by lay-persons without professional assistance?
4. Under what circumstances are land contracts commonly used?
5. When a vendee on a land contract acquires property subject to a mortgage which was placed on the property by the vendor, what precautions should the vendee take with regard to future borrowing by the vendor where the property may be used as security?
6. What provisions should be made for a deed where property is purchased under a land contract? Might an escrow arrangement be established to the advantage of the vendee?
7. What alternative remedies does a seller under a land contract have in event of default in payment of the purchase price by the buyer?
8. What problems arise when a purchaser under a land contract wishes to make major improvements to the premises?
9. Under what circumstances may a lease and purchase option contract be advantageous?
10. What are the advantages and disadvantages to the use of land contracts as a means of achieving control over large amounts of investment real estate?

CASE PROBLEMS

1. Vendee X installed new plumbing fixtures in a building which he is buying under a land contract. No provision was made in the contract regarding improvements, and Vendor Y did not consent. Plumber Z made the improvements. What right, if any, does Z have to enforce a mechanics' lien?
2. B entered into a land contract to purchase real estate from S. The

purchase price was to be paid over a 10-year period by monthly amortization. At the end of five years, B defaulted, failing to make his required payments. The contract provided that in event of default for a period of 30 days the seller could declare a forfeiture under the contract and repossess the property. If the courts should consider the land contract an equitable mortgage, what might be the rights of B and S?

3. A sound property in an older neighborhood can be bought on a land contract. It is a 12-unit apartment building that has the following estimated income and expenses:

Income
7 five-room apartments @ $40 per week	$280
5 four-room apartments @ $35 per week	175
Rental income per week	$455
Annualized ($455 × 52)	$23,660
Less: Vacancy allowance	1,660
Estimated effective gross rental	$22,000

Expenses
Utilities	$5,000	
Insurance	500	
Real estate taxes	1,500	
Maintenance—furniture and fixtures	1,500	
Maintenance—other	1,000	
Management	1,000	10,500
Estimated net cash receipts before financing		$11,500

a. Assuming the purchase price is $90,000 compute the net cash flow in relation to the cash investment required for the first year of ownership under the following conditions (disregarding depreciation and income taxes):[*]

	Condition A	Condition B
Down payment of investor	$ 7,000	$15,000
Land contract @ 9% annual interest	83,000	75,000
Annual payment required on contract	9,500	8,000

b. In further analysis, compute taxable income to the investor assuming a depreciation charge of $4,500 annually and an effective income tax rate of 35 percent.

c. Under both conditions *a* and *b*, what would be the investor's yield for the first year (1) on an accounting statement basis and (2) in terms of cash flow after taxes? Consider the impacts of the following on this kind of financing: (1) size of down payment; (2) tax shelter; (3) inflation; (4) kinds of risk.

4. Jones sold a property to Smith for $20,000. His tax basis for the property at time of sale was $16,000. His contract of sale specified that he

---

[*] Net cash flow is equal to net cash receipts before financing minus payment on land contract.

was to receive $5,900 down and $4,700 a year for three years, plus simple interest computed annually at 6 percent.

a.   May Jones use the installment method of federal income tax reporting? How much gain should be reported in the year of the sale?

b.   How would the transaction be treated if the interest rate payable on the unpaid balance of the contract had been 3 percent?

6

Financing Long-Term Leases

Meaning of "Lease"

A lease represents a commitment by one party—called "the lessor"—to turn over to another party—called the "lessee"—the use of real estate in return for rent or other consideration. In general, there are two broad classes of leases. The short-term lease leaves the financing and the management in the hands of the lessor. He is expected to supply not only the use of real estate but the necessary services required to make the real estate usable, such as janitor and elevator services. Even though such an arrangement between lessor and lessee might continue indefinitely, this type of lease is considered short term. Since such a lease presents no problems of financing that are peculiar to the fact that real estate uses are subject to rental payments, we shall not be concerned in this chapter with short-term lease financing.

The other type of lease, usually covering a longer period of time than the one just described (though actually it might be for a shorter period) is a type of real estate transaction in which the lessee takes over the management and frequently the financing of the property. The lessor gives up to the lessee the operation and maintenance of the property. The rent paid represents a net return upon the investment, unless it includes in addition an amount needed to pay taxes in case the lessee does not assume them also. If a building already exists on the site leased, it will probably be purchased by the lessee. Or it may be obsolete or inadequate for the purposes of the lessee. In either case the building will be demolished and will be replaced by a building constructed for and financed by the lessee. Where the lessee constructs and finances the building, its ownership and disposition at the termination of the lease should be specified in the lease.

Complex Nature of Long-Term Leases

One of the subjects that give rise to conflicts of interests between real estate brokers and attorneys is: Who should take responsibility for drawing up long-term leases? Lawyers contend that they know best how to protect the interests of all parties concerned because there are so many possibilities for error unless all legal angles are properly explored. Few would dispute the existence of many possible legal complications. On the other hand, real estate brokers contend that most of the questions to be settled in drafting long-term leases involve business practices with which the lawyer may not be fully acquainted. Some years ago the National Association of Real Estate Boards canvassed its members who dealt in long-term leases to determine what questions were encountered in lease negotiations. The results of the study showed that there were 350 such questions, which could be grouped into 44 convenient classes. Probably others would now be added if the study were repeated.

The answer to the controversy mentioned above seems quite obvious. Long-term leases are so important to both lessor and lessee that both real estate brokers and lawyers should be asked to make their contributions to the drafting process. Even though divided responsibility may produce further controversy, the interests involved are too important to risk giving the drafting responsibility to one not acquainted with all angles of the subject.

Provisions of Long-Term Leases

In addition to giving the identity of the property and of the parties to the lease, the long-term lease should deal with the following: (1) The subject of improvements has many facets. If the lessee takes over the existing improvements, by purchase or otherwise, maintenance, replacement in case of fire or other cause of damage, erection of new improvements by lessee, ownership of improvements at the expiration or earlier termination of the lease, and so on—all need careful definition in the lease. (2) Then, of course, rents and their payment; insurance —kinds and amounts; purchase options; renewal privileges; rights of the parties in case of forfeiture of lease by lessee; condemnation proceedings—total or partial—and their consequences for both parties; taxes, present and future—all should be carefully spelled out in the lease so that there can be no reasonable grounds for disagreement later.

Rentals on Long-Term Leases

Flat rentals—sometimes called fixed—are agreed upon in advance to pay the same amount each year for the life of the lease. A succession of flat rentals for predetermined periods of time receives the name "graded or step-up rentals." For example, the rent may be $4,000 a year for the first 5 years, $5,000 a year for the next 10 years, and $6,000 annually thereafter. Conceivably the succeeding periods could carry step-down instead of step-up rentals. In case there is doubt in the beginning about the amount to be charged for succeeding periods, the rent for the first period only may be fixed in the lease.

For later periods, the standards for rent escalation may be set by reappraisal or by index. Under the reappraisal method, an adjusted rental is established on the basis of the new valuation of the property. When an index method is used for the adjustment, the question always arises concerning the appropriateness of the index. The U.S. Bureau of Labor Statistics Consumer Price Index ("cost-of-living" index) is commonly used. A wholesale price or a cost of construction index tends to have greater sensitivity and might be a more representative measure. The implicit price deflator published by the Department of Commerce in the *Survey of Current Business* has much to commend it. This is the index that is divided into the gross national product in current dollars to convert it to constant dollars. It is designed to correct for the effect of inflation (or deflation) in the prices of all goods and services. Use of such an index tends to treat the parties to the lease as if prices are generally stable.[1]

In any case, limits to the amount of change for any one adjustment period are usually contained in the terms. For times when fair rentals or other interpretations of the lease provisions can not be resolved by the parties, the properly drafted lease provides for arbitration.

The rental provisions sometimes stipulate for a percentage participation in the tenant's revenues in addition to a fixed rental amount. This participation may be quoted in terms of gross or net revenues and it may start from the first dollar or after the tenant has realized a certain amount free of participation. Percentage participations are generally associated with tenants whose rentals support the financing of leasehold improvements.

Advantages to Lessor

The lessor may prefer to lease his property for a long term rather than sell it. The possible advantages that may accrue to the lessor are:

[1] See further William M. Shenkel, "The Case for Index Leases," *Journal of Property Management,* July/August 1975, pp. 156–61.

(1) The amount of the principal is fixed for the term of the lease. (2) The lessee assumes most of the responsibilities of managing the property. (3) All new capital expenditures, such as the cost of the erection of a building, are borne by the lessee. (4) The rate of return is presumably fixed for the life of the lease. This is subject to limitations that will be discussed below. (5) By leasing the property instead of selling it, the lessor may save taxes. His income is spread over a long period of time as against a larger capital gains tax in case of sale.

Another type of advantage presumably accruing to the lessor is the improvement in his position from the investment in the building by the lessee. A vacant site, having only potential use, is a more speculative holding than the same site after it has been improved by a suitable structure. This added investment by the lessee not only provides the basis for a return to the lessor, but it assures the latter that the return will not be defaulted by the lessee except under the most dire circumstances. Since a default in the rental payment may result in the forfeiture of the building to the lessor, the lessee will not permit such a default if he can possibly avoid it.

The lessor may prefer to continue his investment in the real estate as against the acquisition of cash for which he has no satisfactory alternative use immediately. The lessor may also feel that, by leasing his property, he is, in effect, receiving a higher price for it than if he sold it.

Advantages to Lessee

When a lessee prefers to hire the use of property owned by another instead of buying it, he hopes to gain the following advantages: (1) His capital investment is reduced, thereby making his funds available for other uses. (2) In case his capital is limited, the lease makes unnecessary the large loan that would be required to finance the purchase of the property. (3) The speculative advantages which may result in an increase in the use value of the property may accrue to the advantage of the lessee who pays a flat rental during its life. If the rent is $6,000 a year for the life of the lease and later becomes worth $10,000 a year, the lessee gets the advantage.

On the other hand, the owner may insist upon a sale even though the lessee might prefer a long-term lease. In such a case perhaps both interests can be served by finding a third party willing to buy the property provided the long-term lease is consummated. Or the same results could be attained if the original parties entered into the lease, and subsequently the lessor disposed of his fee underlying the lease. He might be able to realize a higher price after the new building is completed. Particularly is this true if he effects the sale through the use of land trust certificates, described later in this chapter. Of course, if he insists upon a sale rather than a lease, he is on safer ground to follow the first practice suggested above.

Long-Term Lease Covering Land Only

Often, long-term leases cover land values only. The lessee is then expected to build a building on the site or replace one already in existence. All construction arrangements should be anticipated in the lease. The rent on such long-term leases is usually net to the lessor, with the lessee obligated to pay taxes, maintenance costs, and so on. As assurance that a building arranged for in the lease will be built, the lessor frequently requires a bond for his protection until the building is erected. All improvements to the land revert to the lessor at the expiration or other termination of the lease, in the absence of arrangements to the contrary.

Financing the Leasehold

The right of the tenant to use the property during the term of the lease is called his leasehold. Irrespective of the value of any improvements that he may add to the property, this right may acquire value. In some instances the value has been very large. For example, suppose that a site was leased for 99 years, renewable forever, at $6,000 per year, at a time when this rent measured the current value of the land use. Suppose that through a shift of business districts or otherwise, the rental that could be obtained from this site increased to $50,000 per year. The owner of the lease would enjoy a profit of $44,000 per year in perpetuity, should this new value continue. The present value of this annuity of $44,000 per year would measure the value of the leasehold as such. In case of a reappraisal rental arrangement, to be applied at intervals throughout the life of the lease, the lessor rather than the lessee would enjoy the fruits of any increment in value that might accrue. Hence the leasehold as such would never acquire any substantial value.

In addition to whatever value the leasehold acquires, the lessee usually owns the building erected upon the site, so long as he meets his obligations to the lessor. He may have purchased the building originally from the lessor or, more commonly, he may have caused it to be erected at his expense. In either event, it requires financing. To obtain the funds for this purpose it has been customary for the lessee to issue a leasehold mortgage. Although the mortgage constitutes a first lien on the leasehold and the building, the value of this lien may be obscure to the uninitiated. Underlying this lien is the land lease requiring that the lessee meet his obligations to the land lessor. Should the lessee default in meeting these obligations, the leasehold mortgage may become worthless.

Because of the junior position of the holder of the leasehold mortgage, he will insist upon various protections. Since his resources are necessary to finance the building, the erection of which adds needed protection to the interests of the lessor, he looks to the latter for protection in turn. He wants to be sure of ample notice before action to cancel a lease on account of a breach by the lessee. The mortgagee may elect to succeed to the position of the lessee in such case by keeping up rental payments and by meeting other obligations to the lessor. He much prefers to finance a building under a lease where any increments of land value accrue to the benefit of the lessee instead of the lessor. Reappraisal leaseholds are very difficult to finance for this reason.

The mortgagee also prefers that the lease include a purchase option at a price not too greatly in excess of the value of the land at the time the mortgage is executed. An option at a fantastic price is no option at all. One at a reasonable price enables the lessee, or if necessary the mortgagee, to purchase the fee as a measure of protection at a future time. The lessor's desire to retain this investment in the property may be tempered by the necessity for granting a purchase option as the price of enabling the lessee to secure the financial assistance required to construct the building. As noted above, the lessor's interest is better protected by the presence of the building. The lessee will be well advised to make sure that the terms of the lease will enable him to finance the building before he signs the lease.

In addition to a purchase option, a renewal option is favored by mortgagees. This is particularly true if the lease is about to expire. The shorter the term of the lease, the less likelihood of financing the leasehold. For example, if the lease has only two years to run to maturity, no mortgagee would advance to the lessee more than he was sure of realizing during two years by subtracting from the assured net return from the use of the property all rents, taxes, and other carrying charges for which the lessee is obligated. If there is a renewal clause, it extends the potential life of the lease, unless its terms are unacceptable.

Joining Lessor in Financing Building

Because it is not always easy to secure leasehold financing necessary to pay the cost of constructing an expensive building on a vacant site, particularly in a financial market that is not accustomed to the use of mortgages against leaseholds, it has become increasingly common for the lessee to enlist the cooperation of the lessor in financing the construction. If the lessor is willing to let the mortgage cover the value of the land as well as that of the building, funds from an institutional lender become much more readily available.

This type of financing is accomplished by means of an arrangement whereby the land owner agrees to subordinate his interest in the land to that of the lender's mortgage. The arrangement is called a "subordinated ground lease," or, sometimes, a "subordinated fee." Although the land owner does not sign the note to the lender, in event of foreclosure, by virtue of his subordination of his underlying fee interest, the owner forfeits his interest in the property to the lender. From the standpoint of the lender, this structuring of the priorities provides the equivalent of a fee ownership security and therefore an unimpaired basis for a loan.

For obvious reasons, land owners have long shied away from such subordinations. After all, why should the owner risk the loss of his property for the benefit of the lessee-developer? In the last few years, however, it has become apparent that both the lessee-developer and the lessor-owner may benefit from a subordination. More lenders are interested in having an unimpaired lien on the fee for reasons of legality or policy, and most are more generous in their loan appraisals. The developer can, therefore, more nearly optimize his project and respond to the lessor-owner by paying him higher land rentals, likely including a participation in revenues generated above certain minimum levels. Furthermore, it has been made more apparent to the land owner that if he were to develop the project on his own (assuming that he had the expertise) he would have to put up the land in any case, becoming personally liable for the debts of the venture. Under the leasing arrangement, the owner's maximum exposure is the loss of the land.

Problems in Financing the Underlying Fee

There is a recognized conflict of interest between financing the leasehold and improvements thereon and financing the fee underlying the leasehold. Any protections which the lessor sacrifices in making the lease may be necessarily yielded as a condition to securing the signature of the lessee; but, at the same time, such sacrifices may decrease the value of the interest of the lessor. Should the lessor subsequently find it necessary or desirable to finance his fee in any manner, the terms of the lease will be carefully scrutinized by the party furnishing the finances. For example, a reappraisal lease or even one that provides for a graded rental would normally be more favorable to the interests of the lessor than would one calling for level payments throughout the life of the lease. On the other hand, where the land value is declining rather than increasing, flat rentals might be preferred by the lessor if they reflect at least current land values. This would be exceptional. In like manner purchase options are not always favored by those who finance the fee.

The fee underlying the lease can be financed in either of two ways. Under a favorable lease to a responsible tenant, the value of the fee is determined by the terms of the lease and by the level of interest rates in the financial markets. The latter may become very important. Omitting any speculative advantages which the fee owner may enjoy, a fee worth $100,000 when its rent would be capitalized at 8 percent would drop to $80,000 if the capitalization rate became 10 percent. Of course, one factor which helps to determine the capitalization rate is the credit rating of the lessee.

Like any other real estate interest, the fee underlying a long-term lease can be mortgaged. This mortgage, as a lien upon the senior interest in the real estate, constitutes a prior claim which takes precedence over the lease and consequently over leasehold mortgages or bonds. As an alternative to a mortgage, the fee owner may assign his interests to any purchaser. The assignee would necessarily take title subject to any claims against the fee of which he has notice. Presumably he would have notice of both the long-term lease and of any mortgage against it. Since the fee involves less risk than the leasehold, it follows that financing the fee is much easier than financing the leasehold. In many instances, rates of return upon fees underlying leaseholds are comparable to rates of return upon government bonds.

Financing Subleases

A long-term sublease is sometimes financed in a manner similar to that described above for long-term leases. So far as the mortgagee is concerned, his interest is primarily in some questions that would call for answers if he became interested in financing a long-term lease. The difference between financing leases and financing subleases is important and may become the governing factor. In financing the lease, the mortgagee is interested in measuring the difference between the value of the land and building on the one hand and the capitalized rent to the owner on the other. In financing subleases, the latter element would be replaced by the capitalized rent paid to the sublessor instead of to the owner.

The term "sandwich" lease arises out of the case where lessee A subleases to party B. A is then sandwiched between the property owner and B. The value of A's lease is the present value of the excess of his rent claim from B over his rent obligation to the owner. Thus, if A leases from the owner for $5,000 annually and subleases to B for $12,000 annually, the net leasehold income to A is $7,000. If the correct capitalization rate for this investment in light of all the risks and conditions is 10 percent, the leasehold is worth ($7,000 ÷ 0.10) $70,000.

Valuation of Leaseholds The crucial part of the lending decision where a leasehold is the basis of security lies in its appraisal value. This value is largely dependent upon the type of lease, the correctness of appraisal techniques, and the prevailing costs of money in the capital markets.

Types of Leases In appraising commercial property for lending purposes, the type of lease used is a matter of prime importance to the lender. Of the many types in use, the most common only will be mentioned here. In the net lease the tenant contracts to pay all operating expenses, taxes, and insurance. A modification of this form places the burden of taxes and insurance upon the lessor. At the other extreme, some percentage leases provide for a fixed minimum rent regardless of the amount of business done, while others have no such minimum.

The appraiser must study the type of lease used in order to determine what stabilized income to expect. In the net lease to a financially responsible tenant, the amount to be expected is most easily calculated, particularly if the rent is fixed for the life of the lease. Even where it is graded, the amount is easily ascertainable if the steps are definitely set forth in the lease as to both time and amount of rent changes. While the net lease may hold down the income accruing to the holder of the equity, it probably best suits the needs of the lender on a mortgage against the property. Next to this type, the lender will probably prefer the percentage lease with a minimum guarantee.

Leasehold Formulas Brokerage of leaseholds is not as simple as some think. On the contrary, the longer the term of the lease and the greater the amount involved, the greater the need for specialized knowledge on the part of leasehold brokers. The lessee acquires an interest that declines in value as the termination of the lease is approached. Meantime the lessor gives up rights that may increase in value without a corresponding increase in payment to him. The broker should not only be capable of evaluating the lease at the time it is made, but he should be able to advise both lessor and lessee about their future commitments. These involve principles concerned with sinking-fund amortization, straight-line amortization, the Inwood coefficient, the Hoskold premise, the Babcock premise, and so on. The technical nature of these formulas precludes their discussion in a treatise of this kind. The broker who deals in long-term leases should be familiar with them.

Such knowledge may lead to profitable business for the broker. For example, under what circumstances would it be to the advantage of the lessor under a long-term lease to sell the fee to the lessee? And under what conditions will the lessee be well advised to merge the fee with the lease? The income tax status of each may help to find answers to these questions. The broker who can calculate the relative advantages of either sales or purchases of fees underlying long-term leases can frequently develop for himself quite desirable business deals.

Present Value of Future Rentals In calculating the value of long-term leaseholds, the element of interest must be taken into account. For example, suppose that a well-secured leasehold agreement provides for an annual payment of $12,000 per year to the owner of the lease. Let us assume that the factors of management and risk hazard are negligible and that the nonliquidity factor is not heavily weighted. Such a lease might well be calculated on a basis of 8 percent interest. If the lease runs for 15 years, the owner may think that his lease is worth $180,000 because he expects to receive $12,000 per year for 15 years from it. But discounted at 8 percent interest compounded monthly, the present value of the lease would be only $104,640. Whether the owner would be willing to sell the lease for the lower amount would depend upon numerous factors, including his need for cash. A common measure of the usefulness of cash to him is the owner's opportunity cost of funds; that is, his anticipated rate of return on alternative investment opportunities of comparable risk. If the leasehold return should compare favorably, he might prefer to retain his investment for the full life of the lease. Again, the tax considerations would enter into his calculations. The use of present value tables is discussed in detail in Chapter 8.

Legal Problems in Establishing and Terminating Leases

Numerous conflicts have arisen in establishing priorities between lessees' and mortgagees' rights to a property. These will be discussed in succeeding sections. The considerations involved in lease termination will also be considered.

Leases and Mortgages One question which sometimes complicates real estate finance is: When a mortgage is defaulted and the mortgagee takes steps to protect his interests, which takes precedence—the mortgage or a lease on the property which constitutes the security for the mortgage? The answer to this question appears to be quite simple. If the lease was in existence at the time the mortgage was executed, the mortgagee in possession must respect the tenant's rights. If the lease is favorable from the standpoint of the mortgagee or the prospective future owner of the property, the tenant is not likely to be disturbed so long as he meets his obligations. In case he defaults, action will probably be taken against him to bring him into line. But if the lease favors the lessee, the mortgagee is not permitted to cancel it without the approval of the tenant.

So far we have assumed that the mortgagee has notice of the prior rights of the lease as against the mortgage. This notice may take the form of a recorded lease or recognize that the lessee or his successor is in possession at the time the mortgage is executed. Complications may arise if the lease is not recorded and if the lessee is not currently exercising his rights of physical possession.

Leases that become effective subsequent to the execution and recording of a mortgage enjoy no such priority. In case of a default on the part of the mortgagor, the mortgagee in possession may alter the terms of the lease and offer the new terms as the condition upon which the lessee may retain use of the property. If the lessee refuses to accept such new terms, he forfeits whatever rights he may have enjoyed up to the time they are offered him. In addition, he may be required to pay again any rents that he may have paid in advance to the mortgagor. It is frequently to the advantage of the lessee whose lease postdates a mortgage to make a satisfactory settlement concerning a new lease with the mortgagee. Any agreement so reached binds the mortgagee as well as the tenant. And since the mortgagee is likely to become the owner of the property after the foreclosure sale, the future may be better taken care of for the tenant. Failure to arrive at a satisfactory settlement leaves the tenant in a position where he may be dispossessed at the will of the mortgagee.

Mortgage Waiver in Favor of Lease   Even where the mortgage exists against the property at the time the lease is executed, it is to the advantage of the lessee to secure a waiver from the mortgagee giving the former the right to retain possession of the land even though the property were to be sold under foreclosure of the mortgage. If such a waiver is obtained, the position of the lessee is protected as long as he meets his obligations under the lease. On the assumption that the lease calls for payments equal to reasonable rent on the property, the mortgagee's position could easily be improved by the lease. If he acquires the active interest of a financially responsible lessee to add to that of the lessor, his chances of obtaining satisfaction on his mortgage should be enhanced. Even if the mortgagor defaults and the mortgagee is forced to buy the property at foreclosure sale, he still has the lessee bound to a lease which the latter will protect, if he can do so, as long as he thinks he has an equity in it. Even should the mortgagee who becomes the owner of the property prefer to dispose of it, his chances of doing so are enhanced if it has a favorable lease against it.

One advantage might be enjoyed by a mortgagee who refuses to waive the priority of his mortgage in favor of a subsequently placed lease. If he thinks that a financially weak mortgagor, with title to vacant property which is, temporarily at least, a liability instead of an asset, may be forced to default on his mortgage, he may prefer to wait until he takes over title by foreclosure before disposing of the use of the property. In such case he may elect not to waive the priority of his mortgage in favor of a long-term lease.

Recording of Long-Term Leases   Not all states provide for recording of long-term leases. One reason for this omission is the failure to agree upon the nature of a lease. In some states it is looked upon as a real estate interest and is recorded as such. In others it is looked upon as personal property. In the latter states recordation of leases along with deeds and mortgages is not looked upon with favor. Indeed, in some states there is doubt whether a long-term lease is real estate or personal property. To play safe, some leases are recorded as both. Where the lessee occupies the property, there is less concern about recordation, since possession is notice that may not be ignored by parties with a possible financial interest that may come into conflict with that of the lessee.

Termination of Long-Term Leases   Some long-term leases run only for a specified number of years. No provision is made for any successive use of the property by the lessee. In the absence of any agreement to the contrary, the lessor would acquire whatever improvements the lessee had made during the life of the lease. In anticipation of this situation, the lessee would make no additional improvements and might even neglect repairs to buildings during the last years of the lease. There would be no incentive to spend money for the benefit of the lessor. Consequently, the improvements that the latter might acquire at the termination of the lease could be quite obsolete and valueless.

Lease renewal or fee purchase options encourage the lessee to maintain and even further to improve the structures. In the absence of such options, some years before the expiration date of the lease, the lessee may negotiate for a new lease to run for a new period of time. If successful in these negotiations, he can then safely proceed with improvement programs. At the opposite swing of the pendulum, the lessor may be given an option to purchase, at the expiration of the lease, any remaining improvements which may have been added by the lessee. The price to be paid for such improvements may be reached by agreement or by arbitration.

Leasehold Bonds

Leasehold bonds can sometimes be floated successfully where a leasehold mortgage to a single mortgagee might be impossible. Two reasons account for this difference: (1) Bonds sold to numerous purchasers spread the risk inherent in junior financing operations. (2) Resort to many suppliers of funds makes it possible to finance larger properties than might otherwise be feasible. This situation tends to favor leasehold bonds issued against properties large enough to absorb the costs of investigation, engraving of bonds, sales expense, and underwriting commissions, in contrast with smaller business properties which cannot afford such costs.

Speculation in Real Estate Equities

Shrewd speculators who have unusual success in purchasing real estate equities on business properties can frequently earn a high return upon their money. If the property in question is outside an established business district, there is probably considerable uncertainty about its future stability. The chances for loss in a period of decreased demand for goods and services are great. In periods like the mid-1970s, equities in such properties are entirely wiped out if the equity holder is unable or unwilling to keep up payments on his mortgage. If the property is carried in the name of a corporation with no other assets, the real owner can avoid personal liability for the mortgage debt. If this plan is followed, however, the lender will advance a smaller percentage of value in making a loan.

A financially responsible owner who is successful in selecting real estate for purchase, and who is not faced with early difficulties in collecting rents, can earn high returns upon his own investment by trading on his equity. For example, suppose that a store building in a new neighborhood, with an investment of $100,000, is leased to net 11 percent. Suppose that a 60 percent loan at 9 percent has been obtained with the property as security. This will allow a 14 percent return upon the equity. The computation is as follows:

$100,000 @ 0.11 ....$11,000
less $60,000 (loan) @ 0.09 5,400

Return on equity ....$ 5,600
$5,600 ÷ $40,000 (equity) 0.14

In slightly more than seven years the owner of the equity will have recovered his entire investment if the loan against the property is a straight loan; it will take him a bit longer if it is an amortized loan. Meantime, any increase in rent that can be collected as the new neighborhood is stabilized accrues to the benefit of the equity holder. This increase would become greatest under percentage leases as the business of the tenants grows.

Competition for loans in established commercial and industrial districts will permit a slightly lower rate of interest on mortgages. But confidence of equity purchasers in such districts will enable them to purchase equities at much lower rates of return. As a result, the chances for high returns on equities and for loss of principal invested in them are much less in established business districts than in surrounding, less well-defined areas.

Lending institutions are much more likely to be interested in making loans against commercial real estate when the borrower can show that the property has been leased to financially responsible tenants. Such leases are looked upon by lenders as supplemental security for their loans. The equity owner in commercial property is always a speculator to some extent. The lending institution tries to avoid sharing his speculative losses, since it is generally permitted to share his speculative gains only in a very limited way at most.

PART 2: LAND TRUST CERTIFICATES

Meaning

One method of financing long-term leases that has had considerable vogue in some sections of the country, particularly during the decade of the 1920s, is the use of land trust certificates. This plan of financing did not originate at that time. It is simply an application of the much older idea of the Massachusetts trust. In effect it provides for the owner-ship of a parcel of land by a number of owners, each of whom owns one or more land trust certificates. Other names used to designate such certificates of ownership are fee ownership certificates, certificates of equitable ownership, participation certificates, and ground rent certificates. The latter should not be confused with Baltimore or Pennsylvania ground rents.

The manner in which such certificates are used follows a pattern somewhat as follows: The owner of a business site leases it to a finan-cially responsible tenant. The latter agrees to build a suitable building on the site. Let us assume that the annual net rental is to be $17,000 a year. If $1,000 is sufficient to pay the fee for managing the project in the interest of the owners of the site, $16,000 remains to pay for the use of the land. Capitalized at 8 percent, the indicated value of the site is $200,000. With the lease to a financially responsible tenant as security, the owner then proceeds to sell the site, vesting legal title in a managing trustee. Equitable title will rest with the owners of the land trust certificates. These certificates typically might have a face value of $1,000 each and pay an annual return of $80.

Land trust certificates have been used also where the owner of the land and the building decides to use money for some other use by selling its land, leasing it back, and returning ownership of the building. The same process will be followed as if the seller of the land and the lessee were two different parties.

Legal Nature of Land Trust Certificates

If the land trust certificate holders are the unequivocal and unconditional owners of the site, there appears to be no question of the nature of such certificates, in the eyes of the law. As often happens in such cases, courts reach decisions on such questions in answer to a suit brought for another purpose. In the leading case on the subject of the nature of land trust certificates,[2] the question raised was the right of a state to levy a tax on land trust certificates. In seeking an answer to this question, the Supreme Court of the United States found that land trust certificates evidence an interest in land. Therefore they are not taxable as personal property. If the land is located beyond the borders of the state which levies the tax, the tax levied by the state will not apply because one state may not tax land or interests in land situated beyond its borders. If the land is located within the state which levies the tax, such levy must be in a uniform manner according to the value of the property taxes. Since the tax in question did not follow this rule, it was declared to be unconstitutional. Three justices dissented from this opinion. The important part of the decision, from the standpoint of real estate finance, is the finding by the Supreme Court of the United States that land trust certificates evidence ownership in land and are not personal property.

Land Trust as Mortgage   One question that has caused considerable confusion in the consideration of the legal nature of land trust certificates involves the inclusion in the lease of the right of the lessee to purchase (or to repurchase) the land. In the leading case covering this phase of the subject the Lazarus Company of Columbus, Ohio, had sold the site on which its department store was situated to a local bank as legal owner.[3] The Lazarus Company leased back the site for a period of 99 years. Meantime the beneficial interest in the land was sold to land trust certificate holders with the local bank serving as trustee.

In addition to the payments under the contract for the use of the land, the Lazarus Company retained an option to repurchase the fee at stipulated scheduled prices throughout the life of the lease. This option was subsequently exercised. Meantime the company claimed the right, for federal income tax purposes, to deduct a depreciation charge sufficient to amortize the cost of the building in 40 years. Without discussing the prices at which the Lazarus Company could repurchase the land, the Supreme Court of the United States addressed itself to the depreciation charge. In discussing the findings of the Board of Tax Appeals, which had reversed the decision of the Commissioner of In-

[2] *Senior* v. *Braden,* 55 Sup. Ct. 800, 295 U.S. 422.

[3] *Helvering* v. *F. & R. Lazarus & Co.,* 60 Sup. Ct. 209, 308 U.S. 252.

ternal Revenue, the court upheld the depreciation charge in the following language:

We think the Board justifiably concluded from its findings that the transaction between the taxpayer and the trustee bank, in written form a transfer of ownership with a lease-back, was actually a loan secured by the property involved. General recognition has been given the established doctrine that a court of equity will treat a deed, absolute in form, as a mortgage, when it is executed as security for a loan of money.

Highlights of Lease A review of numerous leases using land trust certificates in recent years reveals a more or less common pattern of their contents. In addition to the identification of the lessor and lessee and a description of the property involved, the following highlights are significant: (1) The term for which the lease is to run, subject to earlier cancellation by exercise of a purchase option by the lessee, is stated. (2) The amount of annual rental to be paid and the manner of its distribution are stipulated. (3) A depreciation fund is frequently established, to consist of an annual deposit of a stipulated part of the net earnings of the lessee with the lessor. While the deposits into this fund are dependent upon earnings, minimums are usually established for each year of the lease. Both the percentage of earnings and the minimums are frequently stepped up at intervals during the life of the lease. Maximum payments may also be stipulated in the lease, to be observed at the option of the lessee. He is permitted to make any payments in excess of requirements that he may see fit. In lieu of depositing cash, an equivalent amount of land trust certificates, as measured by face value, may be used by the lessee for this purpose. (4) Amounts in the depreciation fund may be invested in U.S. government bonds; or in land trust certificates of the issue involved, upon approval of the price to be paid therefor by the lessor and the lessee. (5) If the certificates are made callable in the land trust indenture, the lessor agrees to call enough from time to time to absorb such of the depreciation fund as shall be requested by the lessee. Call prices are fixed, usually on a declining basis at intervals during the early life of the leases. After 10 years or so the call price remains stationary at only a nominal premium. (6) Purchase options are commonly included in leases where land trust certificates are used. They are exercisable by the lessee on short notice—30 days being common—at step-down prices fixed in the lease. The price provides the amount needed to pay the call price of the land trust certificates. In addition, there may be minor debits and credits to be adjusted in case the lessee exercises his purchase option.

Financing the Building Where land trust certificates are used to finance the site, they become the senior lien against the entire property. The building can be financed with leasehold bonds, debenture bonds, equity funds, or any combination of these types of securities. In any event, the financing of the building will place the contributors of the funds needed for this purpose in the position of junior claimants.

Rental Trust Certificates

A financing device similar to land trust certificates has been given the name "rental trust certificates." The legal ownership of leases and subleases is vested in a trustee. Against such ownership, certificates of beneficial interest are sold, usually in denominations of $500 or $1,000. They represent fractional parts in an undivided estate in the leases and subleases. The trustee collects all rents due under the leases and sub-leases. Quarterly payments are made to the holders of the rental trust certificates. Payments up to a certain percent a year are considered to be a return on the investment. Any payments over this amount are considered to represent amortization of the investment. Before making any distribution, the trustee deducts from the rentals received any expenses incurred by him, plus his own fees. Rental trust certificates simply represent a means of distributing the ownership of leases and subleases among a sizable number of people.

QUESTIONS

1. What are the usual distinctions between long-term and short-term leases?
2. What principal advantages may a property owner hope to gain by becoming a lessor on a long-term lease? What are the disadvantages?
3. What principal advantages may a long-term lessee hope to gain by becoming a tenant as opposed to buying a land site outright? What are the disadvantages?
4. What are flat rentals? Step-up rentals? Percentage leases?
5. What limitations do rental escalation clauses impose on tenants who might desire to utilize leasehold values as security to finance property improvements?
6. What is a sandwich lease and how does it derive value? May it become a vehicle for speculation?
7. What principles are utilized to calculate the value of a long-term leasehold?
8. If you were a lending officer of a financial institution, what principal conditions and provisions would you expect to find present before you would accept a long-term lease as security for a loan to the lessor?
9. Should a long-term lessor require bond to ensure that the lessee will complete his undertaking to construct a building on a land parcel?
10. What are land trust certificates and what purposes do they serve in financing real estate?
11. What are rental trust certificates and why may they be used?

CASE PROBLEMS

1. A is a tenant-in-possession under a long-term lease. The lease is not recorded. B is a mortgagee whose instrument is recorded. The mortgage lien was placed on the property while A was in possession. Does B hold subject to the terms of A's unrecorded lease?

2. White and Black are investors. White holds leasehold mortgage bonds whose proceeds were used to finance an office building on the land parcel. Black holds land trust certificates. Who has the senior lien?

3. Brown has leased land from Green for 50 years at $3,000 annually. He has constructed a warehouse building on the site at a cost of $100,000. He estimates the life of the building at 50 years with no salvage value.

    a. Assuming his only costs are land rentals and depreciation, how much must Brown earn in warehouse rentals if he expects to earn 10% on his initial investment?

    b. If he earns a net rental income of $25,000 applicable to these factors during the first year and this income may reasonably be expected to continue, what would be a reasonable asking price for his leasehold interest should he choose to put it up for sale?

4. The High Stick Hockey Club sold its sports arena to Hughes Howard for $4 million. Mr. Howard paid $1 million in cash and gave a $3 million mortgage at 9% interest per annum. The annual payment on the mortgage was agreed to be $306,000, all excess over interest to be applied in reduction of the mortgage obligation. The club then leased back the arena for 25 years at a net annual rental of $440,000. Mr. Howard then sold the underlying land to a religious foundation for $800,000 cash and leased it back from the foundation for $80,000 per year. The arena is estimated to have a 25-year life and Mr. Howard expects to be taxed on his net income at an overall 50% rate.

    a. What is Mr. Howard's cash flow before income tax?°

    b. Compute the effects of the transaction on Mr. Howard's taxes for the first year.

    c. Evaluate the deal for Mr. Howard.

° "Cash flow" is equal to the annual rental income reduced by annual payments for ground rents and mortgage financing.

7

Validation of Title

Evolution of Assurance of Good Title

In the evolution of assurance of good title upon which real estate finance must be based, several significant steps can be traced. In some instances even today, title passes with no assurance of the validity of title other than the trust placed by the purchaser in the seller. To save expense, deeds are occasionally accepted without reference to the records. A series of old deeds, showing an unbroken chain of title for a long period of time, may accompany the new deed and may be accepted by the grantee as sufficient evidence of title, particularly if the grantor is a well-known citizen whose word is usually trusted. This course is not recommended. The few dollars saved may be poor compensation for much larger losses that may be suffered, perhaps through no intent of the grantor.

In earlier periods of our history and even in rural communities today, the above course of action may be supplemented by a more or less careful search of the records by a local lawyer who may have some acquaintance with the recording processes in his community. As a matter of fact, even though he is a general practitioner rather than a specialist in real estate law, he may be able to render satisfactory service because of his acquaintance with the peculiarities of the recording system and with the parties involved in the real estate transaction. The results of his researches may be stated orally to his client; may be included in a letter to him; or may be couched in the phrases peculiar to the more formal title "opinion." Where the grantee acts upon the recommendations of his lawyer, he substitutes his trust in him for his former trust in the vendor. For the small fee charged, the lawyer cannot be expected to be held responsible for errors in judgment, if any. Gross negligence on his part or willful intent to take advantage of his client are proper grounds for damage suits.

If the attorney discussed above should "abstract" from the record the salient points upon which he bases his opinion and should pass these along to his client as evidence to support his conclusions, he might well call his report an abstract and title opinion. As this abstracting process became more formal, it not only summarized some parts of the record but copied verbatim some other parts. Thus was born the abstract system which forms the basis of title opinions in many sections of the country. Abstracts are never official documents enjoying the importance attributed to legislation and court decisions. Instead, they represent some presumably competent individual's concept of what parts of the records are significant in searching title to real estate.

Abstracts go back to the earliest records available, presumably at least to those which recorded the earliest grant from the government to an individual owner. One noteworthy abstract started out somewhat as follows: "Assuming the title in the name of John F. Jones under date of August 17, 1870, to be valid," and so forth. The courthouse had burned and with it all land records preceding this date. From the date of earliest land records, abstracts attempt to include all actions of importance that may affect the quality of title to the land in question. In addition to identifying maps, abstracts deal with deeds, mortgages, releases, taxes, leases, judgments and other liens, wills, pending suits, and a variety of other items that may cover 40 or more categories.

The development of the abstract system tended to separate record search and title examination. Abstract companies and young attorneys are assigned the duty of continuing an abstract once it has been developed. Normally the abstract is passed along with the deed to the grantee. When he in turn becomes a grantor, he is responsible for having the abstract brought down to date by the use of tail sheets that deal with anything that affects the title to the property since the abstract was last continued. When this service has been performed, the abstract is then turned over to the attorney for the new grantee, who bases his opinion of title upon his examination of the abstract. Again he advises his client—orally, by letter, or by a more formal opinion—of his conclusions. His opinion may recite specific items that lead him to question the validity of title or that he thinks his client should know about, even though he concludes that the title is merchantable. As before, the attorney who passes upon title is not expected to guarantee its quality.

The next stage in the evolution of assurance of title makes use of the certificate of title, a little-used plan in most sections of the country today. This is a form of title opinion by which the author may again combine the search of the records with a statement of his conclusions based thereon. The searcher may use the abstract or he may bypass it. In any event he issues to his client a statement in the form of certificate of title, the legal status of which is not always clearly defined. Is a certificate any different from an opinion? Does the author assume any different responsibility when he says, "I certify"? Partly because of the uncertainty surrounding this issue, the certificate is not commonly used.

Title Insurance

The insurance of title to interests in real property encompasses a unique combination of characteristics: (1) liability is assumed only after evaluation of the risk; but (2) the protection is against events that, with certain exceptions, have taken place before the policy was written; and (3) the coverage continues without recurring premiums as long as ownership is retained by the insured or his heirs. When the certificate takes the form of a guarantee of title, something new has been added. Companies organized and operating solely for this purpose, or in combination with other financial functions, make a business of indemnifying their policyholders against losses that may develop as a result of defective titles. Some are simply title guarantee companies; others combine title guarantee with banking or trust functions; still others combine title guarantee with mortgage operations. Geography plays a part in these combinations. Title and trust companies are probably most common.

Title insurance is based upon several considerations. The records may be incomplete or defective. While they are expected to speak for themselves, the courts may cause them to speak a language that is not understood by even the experienced searcher. Title insurance affords a means of warning or protecting against risks of acquiring a defective land title either by pointing out the defect and excepting it or by insuring against the potential loss. The title insurance business originated in the United States in the last century. Title insurance is now being used extensively throughout the United States.

Torrens System

Under the Torrens system, the state supervises and arranges for an assurance of title. In effect, the state undertakes two obligations: (1) upon application, to determine the character of title of a specific property, at the expense of the applicant; (2) by a system similar to title insurance, to guarantee the character of title insofar as the resources in the insurance reserve are sufficient for that purpose. In Hawaii no reserve has been established, but the general credit of the state is pledged to protect against loss. Twenty states have had legislation permitting use of the Torrens system, but 8 states have since repealed it, leaving only 12 with registration statutes still on their books. Only Hawaii, Illinois, Massachusetts, and Minnesota make substantial use of it. The other states in which use is permitted are Colorado, Georgia, New York, North Carolina, Ohio, Oregon, Virginia, and Washington.

The major purpose of the Torrens system is to create and to maintain a merchantable title to land. Before such a title is created, any adverse claims must first be determined and dealt with. In defense of his plan Torrens stated that his purpose was to "simplify, quicken, and cheapen the transfer of real estate and to render titles safe and indefeasible." Specific advantages claimed for the Torrens system include: (1) It substitutes the greater certainty of an official adjudication of title for the uncertainty of unofficial examinations and opinions. (2) It cheapens the cost of title transfer by avoiding the necessity for repeated examination of title whenever a title is transferred. (3) It speeds up the process of title transfer. (4) It avoids the increasing accumulation of title evidence over the years which makes future determination of titles increasingly more difficult and expensive.

Most of the arguments against its use are really against its introduction. The inconvenience and expense of initial registration are cited. Further, it is pointed out that permission of the court must be obtained to remove property from the system once it is registered, and the court must issue an order directing registration of heirs and devisees in case of descent. A major weakness has been the failure of government to provide adequate assurance funds to back up registered titles. This objection could be overcome once a system was under way sufficiently to build a fund large enough to cover the risk to the registrant of title defects not dealt with by registration.

The Torrens law has been in successful operation in Cook County (Chicago), Illinois, since 1897. Registration of titles requires about three months and costs about $50, to cover filing of application, examination of title, publication, and issuance of the first certificate of title. To this cost must be added the payment of $1/10$ of 1 percent of the value of the land to be paid to the indemnity fund and to defray abstract charges. Since 1897, the total charges against the fund on account of errors have averaged only about 3 percent of the payments into the fund. The cost of transfer of registration, after the original issuance of the certificate of title, is a nominal set fee irrespective of the value of the property.

Without title registration, reliance must be placed on attorneys' opinions and title insurance for protection from losses because of defective titles. It is apparent that strong vested interests find great advantage in continuation of this mode. These interests have exerted such forces that the movement toward title registration has subsided.

Origin of Abstract Companies

Most law offices, except those which specialize in other phases of the law, render service to those interested in real estate transactions. Occasionally a lawyer becomes so much interested in the field of real estate that he specializes in it. He may even decide to substitute the business of real estate abstracting for the general practice of law. This is one way in which real estate abstract companies are established. Some abstract companies, in turn, find it advantageous to become agents for title insurance companies. They may even operate as a dual type of business—doing abstract work for those wishing it and adding title insurance for those who prefer it. In time the agent may become a principal, organizing his own title insurance company instead of depending upon an underwriter to assume the risks of the business.

Meantime, lawyers are supposed to be jealous of both abstract companies and title insurance companies, where the business of serving real estate clients is involved. If the abstract companies or the title insurance companies take business that otherwise is sought by lawyers, the cause for the jealousy is apparent. On the other hand, it does not necessarily follow that the lawyer is bypassed in closing real estate transactions. Instead, he may still be included as the adviser to parties to a real estate transaction, with the specialized part of the work, which he may be glad to be rid of, being taken care of outside of his office.

In some instances, title insurance companies not only make use of local attorneys in searching the records and in other ways, but they encourage the latter to close their own deals and bring their opinions of title to the title insurance companies for insurance. Where the insurance company has an approved list of attorneys, such procedure minimizes the work of the company. In the other cases, the preliminary work is all done by the title insurance company, on order of an attorney who then proceeds to close the transaction, thereby avoiding details of title search which he may not care to deal with.

Nature of Abstract

Recorded instruments constitute the basic evidence of title to real estate. The records are official and are treated as such. An abstract, on the other hand, is not an official document. It may be a full and complete copy of every pertinent record, or it may be a short form or synopsis type, often called a "bobtailed" abstract. Its purpose is to furnish all the material information contained in the original documents and records from which it is compiled, so that they may be studied as completely as if the originals were under inspection. The abstract should show the inception and foundation of the title, together with its devolution to the date of examination. The abstract should document the incidents of the land, its divisions and subdivisions, all adverse claims and titles, liens or charges, and every other matter of record that may affect the title. Although an abstracter is not required to go beyond the record, he may do so if he becomes aware of an item that may have a bearing on the quality of the title.

Abstracts usually include reference to the source of the original title from the government. City and town plats are usually included if such are in existence. All legal actions pending that may affect the title should be noted. Easements and restrictions are carefully noted, since they run with the land. Likewise, zoning and other regulatory ordinances governing the use and occupancy of the real estate and the improvements permitted to be placed upon the land are important parts of abstracts. The status of taxes is always important.

An abstracter—whether a firm specializing in such activities or a lawyer who takes on abstract work incidentally—is responsible only for an accurate portrayal of original documents and records affecting title. Any mistakes in recording or in indexing legal documents will be carried into the abstract without identifying them as mistakes. The abstract makes no pretense of disclosing hidden title hazards. Among the latter may be one or more of the following: (1) forged deeds in the chain of title; (2) deeds by minors or other incompetents; (3) deeds by grantors who represent themselves as single persons when in fact they are married; (4) claims of unknown or forgotten heirs; (5) mistakes in recording legal documents; (6) falsification of records; (7) errors in indexing of records; (8) birth or adoption of a child after a will is made; (9) deeds delivered after death of grantor; (10) impersonation of true owners of land by others not having title to it; and so forth.

When abstracts were first used, they were made by public officers who had charge of the records. In a dozen or so states it is still the law that, when called upon to do so and when compensated according to a schedule of fees, the public official will check the records for specific findings requested of him. Public records are open to the public. Their use by outsiders is not subject to a charge by the public official who is not called upon to make a search of any part of the records.

Legal Definition of Abstract   The Supreme Court of Illinois has defined an abstract as follows:[1]

In a legal sense, a summary or epitome of the parts relied on as evidence of title and it must contain a note of all conveyances, transfers or other facts relied on as evidence of the claimant's title, together with all such facts appearing on record as may impair the title. It should contain a full

---

[1] 244 Ill. 363, 91 N.E. 475, 135 Am. St. Rep. 342.

summary of all grants, conveyances, wills and all records and judicial proceedings whereby the title is in any way affected and all encumbrances and liens of record and show whether they have been released or not.

Lack of Uniformity   In many areas there is a lack of uniformity in the practices of abstracters. In general, there are no standard requirements which govern the operations of those who profess to be expert in making or in continuing abstracts. Trade associations have done much to raise standards; but, unfortunately, those who need the benefits of trade association contacts most are those who expose themselves to the practices of others least frequently. Some abstracters have little investment in plant and depend entirely upon the use of public records when their services are sought. Even here they may not be too careful or too wise in the use of information available to them. Such abstracters are sometimes known in the trade as "curbstoners." Others have a great deal invested in what are known in the trade as "title plants." These consist of tract indices, miscellaneous indices, suit and judgment dockets, plats, maps, takeoffs, and photostatic, photographic, and microfilm equipment. The results of abstracts vary widely, owing to differences in the experience, care, and ingenuity of those who do the work.

Some degree of uniformity has been introduced by some state associations of title companies. One of the most ambitious efforts in this direction took the form of a booklet issued by the Wisconsin Association, entitled *Suggestions of What an Abstract of Title Should Contain.* According to its author, the secretary of the Wisconsin Association, this booklet was the outgrowth of recommendations made by the Home Owners Loan Corporation (HOLC) and the Federal Land Bank. These, together with certain large insurance companies, preferred uniform abstracts to suit their own needs. The impetus given by these agencies led the abstracters of Wisconsin to see the advantages of greater uniformity in abstracts for all users. Some other states have followed the example of Wisconsin in encouraging greater uniformity through the trade associations in their area.

In some states abstracters are licensed and bonded. The license requirements may include an examination, to make sure that the applicant has an adequate set of records and is equipped to make a daily takeoff of new material from the records. Where licensing procedure is first used, it customarily includes the usual "grandfather clause," which blankets in those already engaged in the abstract business. In many states there are no license laws for abstracters. Many abstracters hesitate to sponsor license laws for fear they might include too much regulation of their business by public agencies.

Short-Term Abstracts   In some cases a practice of using what has come to be known as "short-term" abstracts has sprung up. Suppose, for example, that a plot of ground is being subdivided and that the abstract of title up to the time of subdivision has been so carefully drawn that no attorney or other local interested party will question the title. The abstracts of the lots into which the plot is subdivided begin with the date of the subdivision. Therefore they are called short-term abstracts. They may even serve all local needs quite acceptably. Outside agencies, such as out-of-state insurance companies which may later be called upon to finance a property located in the subdivision, may refuse to base their decisions upon such short-term abstracts. The cost of revising the abstract or of adding to it at a later date may be considerable.

Abstracter's Certificate   At the end of the abstract there should be the certificate of the abstracter, showing the nature of his work, the records searched, and the contents of the abstract. If the abstract does not purport to cover some records, that fact should be stated unequivocally. For example, if the certificate states that the records of the county treasurer, the county clerk, the county recorder, and the clerk of the local courts only have been searched, then any loss occasioned by the failure to include any records from the federal court could not be assessed against the abstracter. However, the certificate of the abstracter cannot protect him if it is couched in vague or obscure language. If he certifies that his searches have revealed no encumbrances, this will be interpreted to mean that there are no encumbrances against the property whose title is at stake.

A typical abstract certificate reads as follows:

We hereby certify that the foregoing Abstract of Title, consisting of 116 sections, was collated by us from the records of Franklin County Ohio: and we believe the same contains every instrument of record in said County, in any way affecting the premises described at title page, as shown by the respective indexes to said records.

Legal Opinion of Title

A lawyer studies abstracts for the purpose of arriving at an expert opinion of the character of the title. In his study of a specific abstract, the lawyer is generally limited to the evidence presented in the abstract. If it has been carefully compiled and recently brought down to date, any further study of the primary records would disclose no new evidence about the title so far as the records are concerned. The lawyer who renders an opinion about a real estate title is not asked to insure the title. The fee he is paid for examining it will not warrant his assumption of this risk. Based upon his study of the abstract and/or the record, the opinion he gives is his best judgment concerning the character of the title.

The lawyer cannot be expected to take responsibility for any defect in title not disclosed by the records. Any responsibility borne by the lawyer is based upon proof of his negligence or of his lack of professional skill. Either would be difficult to prove. There is always room for honest differences of opinion among competent lawyers on such questions as interpretations of wills and probable outcome of litigation affecting land titles.

Any defects disclosed by the records are likely to be flagged by most lawyers. As a class, lawyers are inclined to be conservative, technical, conscious of criticism resulting from their own errors, and observers of form and precedent. Consequently, in studying the record, they are apt to be attracted by evidence that raises questions about the character of the title. Even in exceptional cases involving negligence or lack of professional skill, the consequences may not show up until it is too late to do anything about it. The lawyer may be dead or unable to make good on any judgment rendered against him.

Scope of Real Estate Law for Title Examination Purposes   One skilled in corporation law or the law of domestic relations is not necessarily qualified to pass upon questions involving title to real estate. Real estate law is technical in many respects. But the lawyer who examines an abstract for the purpose of determining the quality of a real estate title may and frequently does encounter questions involving corporation law, bankruptcy, divorce court proceedings, and many other phases of law. On all questions of this nature the abstracter must first decide what is important and significant to be included in the abstract. Then the examining attorney must pass upon the sufficiency and the validity of the actions taken in various types of legal proceedings, many of which affect the field of technical real estate law only indirectly. That is one reason that five lawyers examining the same abstract may find five different sets of objections to the title of the real estate in question. Each in turn may object to something which his predecessor examiners have approved or at least have not raised objections against.

Defects in Records   Titles may be defective in many ways. Shortcomings may include: defects in execution; defective descriptions; tax liens and judgments; encumbrances not covered by escrow instructions; and miscellaneous errors, including potential mechanics' liens and defective proceedings of various types. Any one of these defects may carry with it a potential liability of the warrantor of the title for large dollar amounts.

Meaning of Title Insurance

Title insurance does all that both a carefully drawn abstract and a well-considered opinion by a competent lawyer are expected to do. In addition, it adds the principle of insurance to the above services and undertakes to spread the risk of unseen hazards among all who benefit from it. It must start with careful analysis of the records. The plant of the commercial title company may be even more complete than the public records. Then there must be skilled technicians to examine all evidence of the title to determine its character. If the conclusions warrant, the title company will back up its opinion about the title to a given piece of property by assuming the risk that is not disclosed in the records or in its own files.

What title insurance is supposed to add to the abstract system and the opinion of skilled lawyers may be classified as follows: (1) definite contract liability to the premium payer; (2) ample resources to back up this liability; (3) reserves sufficient to meet losses; (4) supervision by an agency of the state in which the title insurance company operates; (5) protection to the policyholder against financial losses that may show up at any future time because of title defects of any kind, disclosed or hidden.

Types of Title Insurance Policies

There are two types of title insurance policies in common use. The first type guarantees that the title is good. The second type also insures the title to be marketable. In other words, it can be used to force an unwilling purchaser to accept the title, because it is guaranteed. While the owner's policy does not ordinarily cover the interests of the purchaser, the insurance of title in the name of the owner reduces the probabilities of loss by litigation. The owner's policy is purchased with a single premium which purports to protect the owner and his heirs forever. There is no statute of limitations that outlaws the life of the policy.

The most commonly used title policy forms were developed by the American Land Title Association (ALTA). There are two forms of owners' policies: ALTA Form A–1970 and ALTA Form B–1970. Form A insures a good title but does not insure marketability. Form B insures both a good and marketable title. Thus, Form A might not give adequate coverage to a buyer where the seller acquired title by adverse possession, for example, and did not establish it by court record; or where a defective deed in the sellers chain of title needs reformation. Form B is customarily used, although in some states, including Florida, Indiana, and Illinois, Form A is the more common policy issued. New York, Texas, and a few other states require special forms.[2]

---

[2] William A. Thau, "Protecting the Real Estate Buyer's Title," *Real Estate Review,* vol. 3, no. 4 (Winter 1974), pp. 71–83. See also Marvin C. Bowling, Jr., "The ALTA Loan Policy—Have You Read Paragraph 3(a)?" *The Mortgage Banker,* vol. 34, no. 5 (February 1974), pp. 28–33.

The mortgagee policy insures the status of the lien and the mortgage. Since the interest of the mortgagee in the land is terminated when his money has been repaid, the mortgagee policy expires when the mortgage is paid off or canceled. If, as a result of foreclosure, the mortgagee becomes the owner of the real estate, the mortgagee policy becomes an owner's policy as of the date of change of title. Because the mortgagee policy is expected to run for a shorter period of time than an owner's policy, it is usually somewhat cheaper.

The risk rate for owners' policies is commonly $3.50 per $1,000 up to $50,000 and becomes progressively lower as the insured amount increases. For amounts over $15,000,000, the rate is $1.25 per $1,000. Mortgage premiums run $2.50 per $1,000 up to $50,000 and become as low as $1 per $1,000 on amounts in excess of $15,000,000. The minimum premium on an owner's policy is $10 and on a mortgage policy, $7.50. These rates prevail in about half the states. In other states and areas special rates apply. These rates are often under the surveillance of the state insurance commission. They tend to be somewhat higher in areas where the loss experience has been bad. Premiums charged are for insurance only and do not cover examination cost, record search, abstract, or closing expenses. In some localities reissues of title insurance policies on the same property, but to different policyholders, are reduced to 50 or 75 percent of the original premium.

It is customary to write two policies on the same property. For example, if A purchases a property for $10,000, he will probably want a title insurance policy for that amount. If he mortgages his property for $5,000 to B, a separate policy for $5,000 will be written to protect B's interest. If the insurance company should pay a loss claim to the mortgagee for his $5,000 interest, the owner's policy would normally be reduced by this amount.

Where an owner's policy and a mortgage policy covering the same property are issued simultaneously there is some saving in premium. The rates applicable to the owner's policy are the regular owner's rates, but the premium for the mortgage policy is generally a nominal amount, often $7.50, for an insurance coverage not in excess of the owner's policy.

A third type of policy, less common than the other two, should be mentioned. The leasehold policy is written in favor of the lessee to protect his interest in the property during the term of his lease.

Full Coverage Demanded   Title insurance companies usually demand that the policy covering the title to a parcel of real estate be written for the full value of the property, in case the owner's policy is used; or for the full amount of the mortgage, in a mortgagee's policy. The reason for insistence upon full coverage is quite obvious. For example, suppose that an owner of a $50,000 property requested a title insurance policy for only $10,000. It is quite probable that any losses that might be suffered would fall within the $10,000. Consequently, the insurance company would, in effect, be giving 100 percent protection but would be collecting a risk premium on only 20 percent of the value of the property.

Extra Fees   In general, title insurance companies will not insure a title unless they think it is good. Therefore they do not make a practice of charging extra fees to cover unusual hazards. If unusual hazards are present, they must be cleared up before the title will be insured. There are occasional exceptions to this rule. Tax titles are not liked by many insurance companies. When they are presented for insurance, sometimes an extra fee is charged. Likewise, temporary hazards are sometimes compensated for by extra fees. For example, during depressions, many voluntary deeds are given to save foreclosure costs and resulting deficiency judgments. Since there is always a question as to whether a court of equity may frown upon such deeds at a subsequent time, an extra and unmeasurable hazard is created which is sometimes the occasion for an extra fee. Other extra hazards may result from any one of several causes. For example, an unreleased though presumably paid mortgage may cause future trouble.

Expansion of Coverage   In areas where title insurance is commonly used, there appears to be developing a tendency to look to the title insurance policy to protect the purchaser of or the lender against real estate from any hazards that might in any manner affect the character of the title. As a result, title insurance in such cases tends to become indemnity insurance as well. The specific hazards which may be covered by such expanded coverage include the following:

1. Loss resulting from mechanics' liens.
2. Loss resulting from violations—present or prospective—of covenants or conditions that limit the use to which the real estate may be put. Included among these covenants and conditions are:
    a. Those which govern the type and cost of improvements.
    b. Those which prohibit the manufacture or sale of intoxicating liquors.
    c. Setback limitations.
3. Loss resulting from improvement encroachments.
4. Loss resulting from the presence and use of easements, which use might result in damage to buildings, trees, shrubbery, and so on.
5. Loss resulting from rights of tenants holding property under unrecorded leases, including rent prepayments.

Lenders rather than owners are responsible for the tendency toward expansion of coverage of title insurance policies. This is an outgrowth of the increased marketability of real estate mortgages. If a lender in one section of the country purchases a mortgage on real estate located in a different section, it is natural to expect the lender to seek all possible protection against future potential losses; hence the urge to expand the liabilities placed upon the title company.

Meeting Added Hazards In cases where the expanded coverage of title insurance policies—by the use of riders covering the added risks discussed in the preceding section—creates added burdens for the title insurance companies, means are sometimes used to minimize the risks. For example, to protect against losses resulting from mechanics' liens, the title insurance company may take over some of the functions of the lender. It may insist upon paying out the funds provided by the lender. In this manner it can follow prudent practices in making sure that all bills are paid to the proper people, thus avoiding the possibility of losses resulting from mechanics' liens. In such case the title insurance company would assume the responsibility of checking all subcontract bids against the plans and specifications to make sure that the money supplied by the lender, plus the equity funds provided by the owner, will be sufficient to pay all costs of construction. Such service takes the title insurance company far afield from the business of strict title insurance but helps to get business that might otherwise go to competitors.

To protect title insurance companies against possible losses due to reversions, various plans are followed. One plan that has gained some popularity is to require the mortgagor to deed his property to a trustee who in turn leases it to the mortgagor. The lease contains a cancellation clause which may become effective immediately upon the violation of any of the lease terms, such as prohibition against the manufacture or sale of intoxicating liquor. By invoking such a cancellation clause, the trustee could effectively prevent loss to the title insurance company. The lease would bind not only the original mortgagor but all grantees who hold under him.

Exceptions Since the title insurance policy is a contract between the insurer and the insured, it may contain such terms and conditions as are agreed upon between the contracting parties. Consequently, any exceptions become matters of great importance. They should be plainly stated in such manner as to make them clear to all concerned. Among the exceptions most commonly found in title insurance policies are: (1) the rights of tenants or others in possession of the property, which are not matters of record and which are not ordinarily found in the plant of the insurance company; (2) any questions which may arise on account of easements, party walls, encroachments, and those that might be disclosed by a survey of the property whose title is insured; (3) laws, government acts, or regulations, including zoning ordinances, restrictions governing use and occupancy of the property, and so on;

(4) current taxes and assessments; (5) unrecorded liens; and (6) special conditions which may apply to a particular title and be written into the policy insuring it.

While there is a tendency to standardize title insurance policies, exceptions are frequently subject to bargaining and adjustment. If the insurance company thinks it runs little risk in so doing, it may agree to eliminate some restriction or exception to which the prospective policyholder makes strenuous objection. In other cases, a survey of the property as a condition of insurance will usually result in the elimination of the survey exception.

Binder of Commitment   A prospective purchaser of a parcel of real estate may wish to make sure of his status as owner if and when he consummates the purchase. Until he becomes the owner he cannot have the title insured in his name. Likewise, a mortgagee who is approached to make a loan with the real estate as security prefers to know his status before he agrees to make the loan. In either case a binder (called a commitment in some areas) is used to recite the title insurance company's findings concerning the character of the title to the date of the binder. The binder also recites the acts which must be performed and the requirements which must be met before the title insurance policy can be written. When all necessary instruments have been drawn and recorded, the policy will become effective, assuming that no new complications have arisen to create doubts about the character of the title. Usually the time during which the binder takes the place of the policy is short. In unusual cases, such as a delay caused by inability to close a deal because one grantor cannot be easily and quickly located, the time may be longer.

If there are defects in the title which the insurance company insists must be cured before a title policy will be written, they will usually be noted in the binder. In other words, the binder states that the specified defects must be cured and that, when they are so taken care of, the policy will be executed.

Losses under Title Insurance   In effect, title insurance consists of two parts: (1) a determination of ascertainable facts about the character of the title before insurance is granted and a willingness to stand behind such determination; and (2) a wager against the happening of an unascertainable event—beyond the control of the insurer and the insured—which will have an adverse effect upon the title. The primary purpose of the insurance company is so to conduct its investigations that no serious question can be left unanswered under the first heading outlined above. This does not mean that absolute perfection of title is insisted upon as a prerequisite to its insurance. Minor irregularities that are not likely to cause serious difficulty are frequently overlooked. If the latter were to be corrected by the insured before title was accepted for insurance, much business would be lost because the insured would conclude that, if a title must first be perfected in all details, it probably would not need to be insured.

The initial impulse is to consider losses and loss adjustment expenses of title insurance companies quite low when related to premium income. Their reasonableness will become more apparent, however, when the full character of the business is taken into account. For example, a survey by the ALTA Research Committee taken among its membership showed losses and loss adjustment expenses for the years 1968 through 1974 averaging 4.8 percent of premium income. However, total pretax operating results for these years averaged only 11.4 percent of gross operating income. By comparison, for the year 1974, 425 industrial companies reported in Standard & Poor's *Analysis Handbook* showed pretax operating profits averaging 15.4 percent.[3]

The title insurance business deals with risk elimination as well as with risk assumption. The noninsurance services rendered by title insurance companies greatly outweigh the insurance function. If the preliminary work is properly done, the actual insurance underwriting involves a relatively slight chance of liability. The preliminary work, however, is time-consuming and costly. Many writers in the field have likened title insurance to a service with a warranty. The rate charged, therefore, must not be related solely to the risk assumed, but also to the cost of services rendered.

Experience has taught the management of title insurance companies that certain conditions are conducive to a higher loss ratio. For example, examinations made by other than full-time company specialists are usually less reliable. Losses are most frequent during the early years of the policy, since the passage of time seasons the title. Periods of economic distress and accompanying declines in real estate prices prompt more attempts by buyers to escape the bonds of executory contracts by challenging the title; under the same conditions of economic stress, recoveries on mortgage policies are substantially less. The most common cause of loss is negligence on the part of employees or agents making the title examination. Most losses result from failure to discover unpaid taxes, restrictive covenants, easements, and judgments. There have been practically no losses because of an unmarketable title.

Most title insurers take an optimistic attitude toward their loss expectancy. In fact, some companies maintain no reserves at all. As will be noted later, several states have not seen fit to impose reserve requirements. The impact of this policy is somewhat lightened, however, by the practice of reinsurance, which is common in the business where

---

[3] John E. Jensen, "Rising Expenses Affect Land Title Industry," *Title News,* December 1975, p. 7.

risks are substantial. Some companies, for example, reinsure all risks in excess of $25,000.

In general, direct costs which are charged to losses include the following:

1. Those caused by oversight or negligence on the part of the employees of the insurance company, or by mistakes in the company's records. Among the subjects of such losses are taxes and special assessments overlooked or underestimated, followed in order by prior mortgages, judgments, mechanics' liens, and easements.

2. Losses resulting from borderline cases where there may not be a valid claim should it be carried into the courts. Nevertheless, the title insurance company may find it desirable to pay some such claims as a means of building and maintaining goodwill.

Indirect costs arise from the defense, at the expense of the title insurance company, of attacks upon insured titles. Some of these may be brought with honest intent, while others are simply nuisance suits. If it appears that a company will settle one of the latter rather than pursue it in the courts, this company may find that it becomes the victim of numerous suits of this kind.

In a sense, most of the expense of a title insurance company is incurred as an offset against losses. The establishment, improvement, and maintenance of a plant all serve the purpose of minimizing losses. By having access to a complete and dependable record, presumably the insurer can determine better the nature of the risk assumed in any specific case. Without its investment in its plant, more of its decisions would become gambles rather than fact-finding operations. In other words, title insurance is not looked upon as a form of casualty insurance. When a company issues a title policy, it does so in the firm belief that, while the character of the title does not make it letter-perfect, it cannot be subject to successful attack. Only the unknowable—the part not covered by the records or the plant of the insurer—is looked upon as a chance-taking procedure. To the extent that examiners and others are made loss conscious, losses should be minimized.

Abstract versus Title Insurance   In attempting to compare the time it takes to determine the quality of a real estate title by the abstract system with what it takes under the title insurance system, a wide variety of practices is encountered. If no abstract exists, a record of title down to date must be compiled in either event. The more complete records normally kept by title insurance companies should favor them, so far as the time element is concerned. Furthermore, the title insurance company probably has more personnel capable of putting together the material needed. In case an abstract already exists, the process of continuation should again favor the title insurance company, so far as time taken to arrive at a decision concerning the quality of title is concerned. If the records of the plant are reasonably complete, a decision should be reached quickly.

While the abstracter also may have a set of records to work from, his continuation of an abstract is only the first step in the process of determining title. Once the abstract is continued, it is turned over to an examiner who may not be able to give it immediate attention. Time is lost which would probably not be consumed by the insurance company. Then the practices of the examiner must be taken into account. If he insists upon reexamining all the abstract—from the first transfer of title from the government down to date—he will probably consume more time than the insurance company will use in reaching a decision about the title. The latter will probably use as a starting point the date of the latest previous insurance policy.

On the other hand, if the examiner of the abstract also takes for granted that the latest previous examination was complete and accurate, he may pay attention only to the tail sheets, thus economizing time in his examination. By this means it is possible for an abstract to be continued and to be examined within about the same time limit as that used by the title insurance company.

Influence of Large Investors   The trend toward nationalizing the market for real estate mortgages has had its effect upon the increasing demand for real estate title insurance. Any absentee owner of a mortgage prefers to play safe by asking that titles to real estate on which he holds titles be insured. Large institutional investors recognize that the greatest risk assumed in the acquisition of federally underwritten real estate mortgages may be in the mortgagor's title. Government insurance is conditioned upon the ultimate ability of the approved mortgagee to offer, in exchange for the government debentures for which the law provides, a foreclosed title satisfactory to the FHA. This condition, in effect, requires of investors in FHA mortgages that they have positive assurance of a good and marketable title, for anything less may result in the nullification of the government insurance upon which the investors depend for protection in event of the mortgagor's delinquency. In general, only with title insurance does the investor have positive protection against financial loss because of unmarketability of titles and indemnification for losses in event the FHA declines to accept titles for causes which can be amply covered in an insurance policy. Investing in mortgages without title insurance protection involves an assumption that the mortgagee, or his assignee, will be able to obtain government debentures in exchange for foreclosed properties; but, too late, the investor may discover that his assumption is false. For these reasons, most corporate investors regard federally underwritten loans as safer when the title is insured. The secondary market for these loans, therefore, is also a primary title insurance market. Life insurance companies, savings banks, savings and loan associations, and commercial banks almost always require title insurance in these circumstances. A similar practice is followed by the federal agencies that are active in the secondary market. Although neither the FHA nor the VA insists upon title insurance as a prerequisite to federal underwriting of mortgages, even small institutional lenders, including local banks and savings and loan associations, may require title insurance if they contemplate resale of a mortgage in the national market. While abstracts may satisfy local needs, title insurance will probably produce a more ready sale should the holder of the mortgage wish to dispose of it later.

Government Regulation of Title Insurance Companies   Experiences of the 1930s took a heavy toll of title insurance companies along with many others. Relative freedom from regulation by governmental authorities was a contributing factor. In recent years, however, in the wake of the *South-Eastern Underwriters* case, which held that insurance transactions across state lines were subject to federal regulation, the states have greatly extended their interest in all insurance companies.[4] This was motivated by the expressed congressional policy that regulation of insurance companies at the state level is in the public interest, but that if the states do not meet their responsibilities in this regard, the Congress will fill the void.[5] The state legislation has had several major effects beyond forestalling federal entry into the field. Many of the provisions are directed at assuring the financial ability of the insurance companies to meet loss claims. Several states require title insurers to fund reserves with a state agency as a condition of doing business. Restrictions on investments and minimum reserve and capital requirements are imposed in some cases. Some states require reinsurance under certain conditions. In some instances, the state statute may have the effect of preserving monopolistic advantages. These advantages have been preserved by requiring extremely high deposits with the state to do business in a certain area (as a minimum of $50,000 to operate in Cook County, Illinois), or by limiting the type of business which may be done (possibly excluding business in any other form of insurance), or by setting high minimum standards for the title plant. As to rate regulations, most statutes simply require that rates be reasonable and nondiscriminatory. Rate schedules and policy forms must generally be filed with the state insurance commission and are subject to commission disapproval.

Title insurance companies generally must file annual reports with their state regulatory agency and are subject to audit. Texas and New York, in particular, carry out extensive audit programs for title insurers. Other states generally have not been concerned to any major degree about the compliance of title insurance companies.

---

[4] *United States* v. *South-Eastern Underwriters Association,* 322 U.S. 533 (1944).
[5] Public Law No. 15 (79th Cong., 1st sess., approved March 9, 1945).

The present situation suggests that there may be substantial dangers in uncritical reliance on the ability of all title insurance companies to meet their full liabilities. One danger lies in the fact that state policies governing the deposit of funds with the state or providing for the establishment of company reserves are generally without any actuarial basis. As previously stated in connection with the discussion of loss experience, many companies carry no reserve for the payment of loss claims. The "Model Title Insurance Code" developed in the mid-1960s by the American Land Title Association prescribed for reserves in considerable detail. Since that time, several states have established codes for the regulation of title insurance where none previously existed and other states have revised existing statutory provisions. Deposit requirements now vary from none whatever to up to 40 percent of aggregate capital. The statutes generally also require unearned premium reserves, ranging from as high as 10 percent to as low as 3 percent of the premium charge for the policy. By common practice, the unearned premium reserve is maintained for 20 years, with a 5 percent recovery to income each year. Experience has shown, however, that as much as 80 percent of losses on title insurance usually occur during the first five years the policy is in existence. This suggests that the bulk of the premiums are earned during the first five years, and some states, like California, have set their reserve adjustment policies to take this into account.[6] With considerable irregularity in the regulation of company reserve requirements and the lackadaisical attitude toward audit and other forms of supervision which is evident in many states, the possibility that some companies may find themselves in difficulty at a later date must be the concern of any purchaser of title insurance. Since the insurance cannot be better than the insurer, consideration of the financial status of the title insurance company is indicated as a proper procedure for any purchaser of this kind of protection.

Surveys

One important feature of real estate financing that is frequently overlooked is the need for an accurate survey of the property to be financed. Before a mortgage loan is disbursed, it may be desirable to make sure that it is protected by the right property as security. Surveys serve other purposes also. For example, should a request for a partial release of security be presented at any time, a survey will show whether the remaining security is what it is supposed to be. Easements can scarcely be granted safely without a survey. Finally, if the mortgage should for any reason become involved in court proceedings, a survey is almost essential before decisions can be relied upon.

---

[6] William H. Deatly, "Solvency Aspects of Title Insurance Regulation," *Title News*, June 1969, pp. 25–30.

Errors sometimes discovered by surveys include the following: (1) The building which affords the chief security for the mortgage loan may not even be located on the land described in the title. It may be on an adjoining lot instead. (2) Buildings, particularly garages, encroach upon adjacent lots and even upon alleys and streets. (3) Buildings on adjacent lots encroach upon the land described in the title to the property being financed. (4) There may be a material surplus or deficiency of land or its measurements as described in the title. (5) While the building may be located on the proper lot, it may be so situated as to violate setback lines prescribed in the title. (6) Easements may be improperly located or improperly used. (7) Conveyances may not properly describe the property intended to be used as security for the mortgage loan.

Once a proper survey is conducted by a competent engineer or surveyor and a map is submitted by him as evidence of his findings, the next step is to determine what, if anything, is to be done about his findings. If no irregularities are found and if the survey conforms in all respects to the title to the land, so much the better. If inconsequential irregularities are found, they may be disregarded by the lending institution. In some cases it may be best to insist upon corrections before mortgage funds are disbursed. Finally, in some instances, admittedly small in number, the findings of the survey may cause the lending institution to refuse to make the loan.

Surveys of commercial and industrial real estate which is offered as security for mortgage loans are generally more imperative than surveys of residential property. This is true for two reasons. In the first place, much greater amounts of money are usually involved, so that the risk of a mistake is correspondingly greater. In the second place, much more of the land area—even up to 100 percent—is covered by the building. As a result, encroachments upon adjoining property are much more common. Where encroachment consists only of use for flower beds, hedges, and so forth, corrections are easily made. Even secondary buildings such as garages can be moved if necessary. But the encroachment of a major building is much more serious. It cannot be moved if it covers 100 percent plus of the land area it is expected to occupy. Its owner may be forced to purchase the "plus" area, perhaps at a holdup price.

Use of Escrow

"By escrow" is meant the use of an impartial third person to represent all parties to a contract in such manner that the contract will be observed without deviation. Escrow can be used with many types of business relations. In the field of real estate it is primarily concerned with closing of title transfers, or placing of mortgages, or both. If the first of these two only is present, the term commonly used to describe the use of the third party is "deed and money escrow." If the second only is present, the term used is "moneylender's escrow."

In the latter case, the mortgagor deposits with the escrow agent the mortgage, properly executed in the name of the mortgagee. The mortgagee deposits with the same agent the money to be lent to the mortgagor. When this agent has satisfied himself that the mortgage represents a valid first lien and that the mortgagee's check is good, he disburses the money according to his instructions and directs that the mortgage, after it is recorded, shall be turned over to the mortgagee. In like manner the use of escrow could serve holders of junior liens as well as those of senior liens. It is particularly desirable to use escrow when the new mortgage produces the means of paying off an existing mortgage, mechanics' liens, a judgment, an accumulation of taxes and assessments, or any other kind of encumbrance against the property.

In the above cases escrow involves only two parties—the mortgagor and the mortgagee. It could involve any number. For example, when A sells property to B, B may see fit to finance his purchase by a loan from C, which he uses to pay off a mortgage due D. In such a case one escrow agent can well represent all four parties, receiving from each the money or legal papers which he should contribute and delivering to each whatever he is entitled to receive in closing the sale and financing the property.

In what is commonly spoken of as a "profit" escrow, it is possible for a real estate operator to make a profit for himself without the investment of his own funds. Suppose, for example, that A contracts to purchase property from B and in turn makes a deal to sell the same property to C at a higher price. By the use of a double escrow, B obtains the price due him, C obtains title to and possession of the property, and A takes his profit without the investment of his own funds. Indeed he can take his profit without having his name appear upon a deed either as grantee or as grantor.

In some cases several properties may be included in a profit escrow, each of which is finally deeded to a different ultimate purchaser. Existing mortgages may be paid off and new ones placed against the properties. Regardless of the complications involved in such deals, escrow arrangements can be made to cover them without confusion and to work to the satisfaction of all parties concerned. These are commonly known as concurrent escrows.

The escrow agent, or escrow holder as he is sometimes called, is supposed to be not only an impartial third party but one experienced in handling arrangements of the kind that require his services. In fulfilling his obligations to both parties to a real estate transaction, he should know what to look for and where to find it in the records. Sometimes it is contended that when an escrow agent is used, there is less likelihood that one party or the other can upset a deal by refusing to see it to a conclusion. In practice, however, the use of escrow is surrounded by about the same amount of mutual confidence as any other arrangement for closing real estate deals. Escrow is not a substitute for honesty or a complete meeting of minds. These are presumed to be present in the use of escrow agents. The use of elaborate escrow contracts, sometimes in printed form, which are signed by both parties, does not invalidate what is said above. Nevertheless, escrow is supposed to establish some relationships that are more difficult to break than if escrow arrangements are not used. For example, an escrow in mortgage financing gives the assurance to a borrower that he can get the agreed-upon loan if the title to his property is good.

Probate Escrows When an owner of real estate dies, his property passes to the devisees named in his will—or to his heirs, in case the owner dies without leaving a will. In any event, the probate of the estate takes time and involves expenses such as the payment of the debts of the decedent and of estate and inheritance taxes. In case the will is contested, or in case other complications delay the settlement of the estate, a good market for the disposal of the real estate may be missed. Through the use of escrow, the property may be sold immediately, with the proceeds held by the escrow agent until the estate is closed and all obligations have been met. The remainder is then distributed to those entitled to receive it. The purchaser of the property is protected against taxes, expenses, or the consequences of a will contest. Meantime, if it appears that the final settlement of the estate may be deferred for a year or more, it may be desirable for the court to authorize the escrow agent to invest the funds held by him in a manner to provide safety and liquidity and at the same time to produce some return.

QUESTIONS

1. What is an abstract of title?
2. How does an attorney's opinion or certificate that a title is good, based on review of an abstract, differ in effect from title insurance?
3. What is the Torrens system, and why is it not more widely used?
4. What is the legal responsibility of an attorney for an opinion which he has rendered stating that he considered the title good and unencumbered when it later appears that the title was defective when the opinion was given?
5. In what ways does title insurance render benefits which are not available to a person relying solely on the abstract system and an attorney's opinion?
6. What types of title insurance policies are in common use?

7.   What difference do you see between insurance that the title is "good" and that it is "good and marketable"?

8.   What is the loss experience of title insurance companies? How does it differ from that of most insurance companies?

9.   How has nationalizing the market for real estate mortgages affected the title insurance business?

10.   Do you see any dangers in the manner in which title insurance companies are presently regulated by state authorities? Do you have any suggestions for improvement?

CASE PROBLEMS

1.   *a.*   Smithers was married in the Hawaiian Islands during World War II. In 1948 he acquired land in a stateside jurisdiction that requires release of dower rights upon disposition of real property. He did not disclose his marriage, although it remained intact, and he sold the land in 1970 without release of dower to Bumstead. Bumstead has now sold the property to you. Evaluate the relative advantages of an attorney's review of the abstract and title insurance.

  b.   Develop as many fact patterns as you can under which an attorney's opinion might give you less protection as a buyer or lender than title insurance.

2.   Assume that you as an owner receive a title insurance policy with typical coverage. Give three examples in which you might not be protected by the insurance.

3.   Create three examples whereby an escrow agent may be utilized as a means of protecting the parties to a real estate transaction.

part two
Risk and Return Analysis and Financing Techniques

8

The Interest Factor
in Financing

Financing the purchase of real estate usually involves borrowing on a long- or short-term basis. Since amounts borrowed are usually large in relation to prices paid for real estate, financing costs are usually significant in amount and weigh heavily in the decision to buy property. Because financing costs are important in borrowing decisions, individuals involved in real estate finance must understand how these costs are computed and how various provisions in loan agreements affect financing costs and mortgage payments. Familiarity with the "mathematics of finance" is essential in understanding simple mortgage payment calculations, how loan provisions affect financing costs, and how borrowing decisions affect investment returns.

This chapter provides an introduction to the mathematics of finance. It forms a basis for concepts discussed in financing single family and income producing properties and in funding construction and development projects. These topics are included in chapters immediately following. Although the subject matter of mathematics sometimes appears burdensome and difficult, this chapter and the succeeding one will provide a fundamental approach to problem solving. From the concrete applications and illustrations in these chapters, the necessity of an understanding of these subjects will become readily apparent to anyone who seeks to achieve professional levels of competency in the field of real estate finance.

Compound Interest

Understanding the process of compounding in finance requires the knowledge of only a few basic formulas. At the root of these formulas is the most elementary relationship: simple compounding. For example, if an individual makes a bank deposit of $10,000 that pays an annual rate of 6 percent interest *compounded monthy*, what will be the value of the deposit at the end of one year?[1] In examining this problem, one should be aware that any compounding problem has *four* basic components. These are:

1. An initial deposit, payment, or investment of money.
2. An interest rate.
3. Time.
4. Value at some specified future period.

In our problem, the deposit is $10,000, interest is at an annual rate of 6 percent compounded monthly, time is one year (12 months), and value at the end of the year is what we would like to know. We have then, four components, three of which are known and one for which a solution is desired.

Compound Value   In the preceding problem, we would like to determine what value will exist at the end of one year if a *single* deposit or payment of $10,000 is made at the beginning of the year and the deposit balance earns a 6 percent rate of interest compounded monthly. To find the solution some terminology must be introduced:

P_0 = deposit or principal at the beginning of the year
i = annual interest rate
I = dollar amount of interest earned during a period
P_n = principal at the end of n periods
n = number of periods

In this problem then, P_0 = $10,000, i = 6 percent, n = 12 months, and P_n or the value after one year is what we would like to know.

If we first determine how much interest is earned in a one month period and in each succeeding month, the investment value at the end of one year can be determined. This can be done by examining the following relationship:

$$P_1 = P_0 + I_1$$

or the principal, P_1 at the end of month *one* (the reason for the small subscript 1) equals the deposit made at the beginning of month one P_0, plus interest, I_1, earned in the first period. Since P_0 = $10,000, by determining I_1, the ending value P_1 will be known. Since we are compounding monthly, P_1 is easily determined to be $10,050 which is shown in Exhibit 8–1.

---

[1] Throughout this chapter and the remainder of the text, monthly compounding is used. This is because in real estate finance payments or receipts on loans, investments, etc., usually occur monthly.

EXHIBIT 8–1
Compound Interest Calculation
for One Month

$$P_0 \times i/12 = I_1$$
$$\$10,000 \times 0.06/12 = I_1$$
$$\$10,000 \times 0.005 = I_1$$
$$\$50 = I_1$$

Value at the end of one month (P_1) is equal to:

$$P_0 + I_1 = P_1$$
$$\$10,000 + \$50 = P_1$$
$$\$10,050 = P_1$$

or value at the end of one month (P_1) is equal to:

$$P_0 (1 + i/12) = P_1$$
$$\$10,000 (1 + 0.005) = P_1$$
$$\$10,000 (1.005) = P_1$$
$$\$10,050 = P_1$$

Multiple Periods   To find the value at the end of two months, P_2, the *compounding process* can be continued by taking P_1 and making it the deposit at the beginning of the second month and compounding again as shown in Exhibit 8–2. From Exhibit 8–2 it can be seen that

EXHIBIT 8–2
Compound Interest Calculation
for Two Months

$$P_1 \times 0.06/12 = I_2$$
$$\$10,050 \times 0.005 = \$50.25$$

and

$$P_1 + I_2 = P_2$$
$$\$10,050 + \$50.25 = P_2$$
$$\$10,100.25 = P_2$$

$10,100.25 has been accumulated at the end of the second month. Note that in period two, not only is interest earned on the original deposit of $10,000, but interest is also earned on interest of $50, which was earned in period one. Hence in period two "interest on interest" is earned. This is really the *essential* ingredient in understanding the compounding process.

From the computation in Exhibit 8–2 it should be pointed out that P_2 can also be determined directly from P_0 as follows:

$$P_2 = P_0 (1 + i/12) (1 + i/12)$$
$$P_2 = P_0 (1 + i/12)^2$$

in our problem then:

$$P_2 = \$10,000 \ (1 + 0.005)^2$$
$$P_2 = \$10,000 \ (1.010025)$$
$$P_2 = \$10,100.25$$

From this computation, P_2 is determined to be $10,100.25, which is equal to the result obtained in Exhibit 8–2. Being able to compute P_2 directly from P_0 is a very important relationship because it means that the ending principal, or value for a deposit left to compound for any number of periods, can be determined directly from P_0 by simple multiplication. For example, in our problem the value at the end of three months would be determined as follows:

$$P_3 = P_0 \ (1 + i/12) \ (1 + i/12) \ (1 + i/12)$$
$$P_3 = P_0 \ (1 + i/12)^3$$

Therefore, if we want to determine the compound value of a deposit after any number of months (n), we can find the solution with the *general formula for monthly compound interest* which is:

$$P_n = P_0 \ (1 + i/12)^n$$

Since we want to know the ending value of a $10,000 deposit compounded monthly at an annual rate of 6 percent after one year, by using the general formula for compound interest we have:

$$P_{12} = \$10,000 \ (1 + 0.06/12)^{12}$$

Use of Compound Interest Tables   Finding a solution to a compounding problem involving 12 periods is very awkward because of the amount of multiplication involved. To provide a shortcut for finding solutions to compound interest problems such as the one we are concerned with in our example, a series of *interest factors* has been developed in tables in the Appendix to this book. These interest factors are contained in column 1 titled: *Compound Value of $1*, for every interest rate contained in the Appendix. Essentially, these interest factors enable us to make a simple multiplication to find answers to compounding problems.

To familiarize the student with the use of these tables, interest factors (now referred to as *IF*) for the Compound Value (*CV*) of $1, for various interest rates, are shown in Exhibit 8–3. These factors have been taken directly from column (1) in each table for respective interest rates contained in the Appendix.

In our problem we want to determine the ending value of a $10,000 deposit compounded monthly at an annual rate of 6 percent after 12 months. Looking down the 6 percent column in Exhibit 8–3 to the row corresponding to 12 months, we find the interest factor 1.06168. This interest factor when multiplied by $10,000 gives us the solution to our problem:

EXHIBIT 8–3
Compound Value of $1 (column 1, Appendix)

				Rate		
Month	*4%*	*5%*	*6%*	*7%*	*8%*	*9%*
1	1.00333	1.00417	1.00500	1.00583	1.00667	1.00750
2	1.00668	1.00835	1.01003	1.01170	1.01338	1.01506
3	1.01003	1.01255	1.01508	1.01760	1.02013	1.02267
4	1.01340	1.01677	1.02015	1.02354	1.02693	1.03034
5	1.01678	1.02101	1.02525	1.02951	1.03378	1.03807
6	1.02017	1.02526	1.03038	1.03551	1.04067	1.04585
7	1.02357	1.02953	1.03553	1.04155	1.04761	1.05370
8	1.02698	1.03382	1.04071	1.04763	1.05459	1.06160
9	1.03040	1.03813	1.04591	1.05374	1.06163	1.06956
10	1.03384	1.04246	1.05114	1.05989	1.06870	1.07758
11	1.03728	1.04680	1.05640	1.06607	1.07583	1.08566
12	1.04074	1.05116	*1.06168*	1.07229	1.08300	1.09381
24	1.08314	1.10494	1.12716	1.14981	1.17289	1.19641
36	1.12727	1.16147	1.19668	1.23293	1.27024	1.30865
48	1.17320	1.22090	1.27049	1.32205	1.37567	1.43141

$$\$10,000 \ (IF, \ CV \ of \ \$1, \ 6\%, \ 12 \ mos.) = P_{12}$$
$$\$10,000 \ (1.06168) = \$10,616.80$$

The interest factor for the compound value of $1, at 6% for 12 months, (*IF, CV* of $1, 6%, 12 months), is 1.06168, which is the same result we would obtain if we expanded $(1 + 0.06/12)^{12}$ by multiplying. In other words:

$$(IF, \ CV \ of \ \$1, \ 6\%, \ 12 \ mos.) = (1 + 0.06/12)^{12} = 1.06168$$

The interest factors in column 1 in the tables in the Appendix allow us to find a solution to any compounding problem as long as we know the deposit (P), the interest rate (i), and the number of periods (n) over which the compounding is to occur.

Question:　What would be the value of $5,000 deposited for a period of two years, when compounded monthly at an annual rate of 8%?

Solution:　$5,000 (*IF, CV* of $1, 8%, 2 yrs.) = P_{24}
$$\$5,000 \times 1.17289 = P_{24}$$
$$\$5,864.45 = P_{24}$$

Present Value

In the previous section on compounding, we were concerned with determining the value of a sum at some point in the *future*. That is, we considered the case where a deposit had been made and compounded into the *future* to yield some unknown *future value*.

In this section we are interested in the problem of knowing the future cash receipts for an investment and trying to determine how much should be paid for the investment at *present.* That is, we take the future dollar returns to be earned and, given a desired rate of interest, we determine how much should be paid for the investment today; i.e., we determine the investment's *present value.* This concept lays the cornerstone for calculating mortgage payments, determining the effective cost of mortgage loans, and finding investment and appraised values, all of which are very important procedures in real estate finance.

A Graphic Illustration of Present Value   An example of how discounting becomes an important concept in financing can be seen from the following problem. Suppose an individual is considering an investment that promises a cash return of $10,618.80 at the end of one year. This investment, in the investor's evaluation, should return an annual rate (yield) of 6 percent compounded monthly. The question to be considered here is how much should be offered or paid today, if $10,616.80 is to be received at the end of the year *and* the investor requires an annual 6 percent return on the amount invested?

The problem can be seen more clearly by comparing it to the problem of finding the compound value of $1 discussed in the first part of this chapter. In that discussion we were concerned with finding the *future value* of a $10,000 deposit compounded monthly at 6 percent for one year. This comparison is depicted in Exhibit 8–4.

EXHIBIT 8–4
Comparison of Compound Value and Present Value

	Month	
	1 2 3 4 5 6 7 8 9 10 11 12	
Compounding at 6% ....$10,000———————————————		Compound →value (?)
Discounting Present at 6% ....value (?)←———————————————		$10,616.80

Note from Exhibit 8–4 that, when *compounding,* we are concerned with determining the *future value* of an investment. With *discounting,* we are concerned with just the *opposite* concept, that is, what *present value* or price should be paid *today* for a particular investment, assuming a specific interest rate is to be earned.

Since we know from the preceding section that $10,000 compounded monthly at an annual rate of 6 percent yields $10,616.80 at the end of one year, $10,000 would be the *present value* of such an investment. However, had we not done the compounding problem in the preceding section, how would we know that $10,000 equals the present value of the investment? Let us again examine the compounding problem we considered in the previous section. To determine compound value, recall the general equation for compound interest:

$$P_n = P_0 (1 + i/12)^n$$

In our present value problem P_0 becomes the unknown because P_n, or the value to be received at the end of 12 months ($n = 12$), is $10,616.80. Since the interest rate (i) is known to be 6 percent, P_0 is the only value which is not known. P_0, the present value or amount we should pay for the investment today, can be easily determined by rearranging terms in the above compounding formula as follows:

$$P_n = P_0 (1 + i/12)^n$$
$$P_0 = P_n \div (1 + i/12)^n$$
$$P_0 = P_n \times \frac{1}{(1 + i/12)^n}$$

In our problem then, we can directly determine P_0 by substituting the known values into the above expression as follows:

$$P_0 = P_n \times \frac{1}{(1 + i/12)^n}$$
$$P_0 = \$10,616.80 \times \frac{1}{(1 + 0.06/12)^{12}}$$
$$P_0 = \$10,616.80 \times \frac{1}{1.06168}$$
$$P_0 = \$10,616.80 \times 0.94191 \text{ (rounded)}$$
$$\text{Present value} = P_0 = \$10,000$$

Note that the procedure used in solving for the present value is simply to multiply the ending value, P_n by 1 divided by $(1 + i/12)^n$. We know from the previous section on compounding that in our problem $(1 + i/12)^n$ is $(1 + 0.06/12)^{12}$ or (*IF, CV* of $1, 6%, 12 mos.) which equals 1.06168. After dividing 1.06168 into 1, the factor 0.94191 results. This last result is important in present value analysis because it shows the relationship between compound value and present value.

Since we have seen from Exhibit 8–4 that the *discounting process* is an opposite process from compounding, to find the present value of any investment is simply to compound in reverse sense. This is done in our problem by taking the inverse of the interest factor for the compound value of $1 at 6 percent, $1 \div 1.06168$, or 0.94191, and multiplying it by the *ending value* of our investment to find the *present value of*

the investment. We can now say that $10,616.80 received at the end of
one year, when discounted by 6 percent, has a present value of $10,000.
Alternatively, if an investment is offered which promises $10,616.80
to us after one year and we want to earn a 6 percent return on our
investment, we should not pay more than $10,000 for the investment
(it is on the $10,000 present value that we earn the 6 percent interest).

Use of Present Value Tables   Since the discounting process is the
reverse of compounding, and the interest factor for discounting
$1 \div (1 + i/12)^n$ is simply the inverse of the interest factor for compounding, a series of interest factors has been developed that enables
us to solve directly for present value (PV) instead of having to multiply
out the term $(1 + i/12)^n$ and to divide it into 1. In fact, all of that
work has been done for us and compiled in column 3 in tables included
in the appendix titled: *Present Value of $1*. In other words, the term
$1 \div (1 + i/12)^n$ has been computed for given interest rates (i) and
periods (n) so that we do not have to make lengthy multiplications
each time we seek a solution to a present value problem. We will call
these interest factors $(IF, PV, \text{of } \$1, i\%, n \text{ mos.})$ Exhibit 8–5 contains

EXHIBIT 8–5
Present Value of $1 (column 3, Appendix)

Month	Rate					
	4%	5%	6%	7%	8%	9%
1	.99668	.99585	.99502	.99420	.99338	.99256
2	.99337	.99172	.99007	.98843	.98680	.98517
3	.99007	.98760	.98515	.98270	.98026	.97783
4	.98678	.98351	.98025	.97700	.97377	.97055
5	.98350	.97942	.97537	.97134	.96732	.96333
6	.98023	.97536	.97052	.96570	.96092	.95616
7	.97697	.97131	.96569	.96010	.95455	.94904
8	.97373	.96728	.96089	.95453	.94823	.94198
9	.97049	.96327	.95610	.94900	.94195	.93496
10	.96727	.95927	.95135	.94350	.93571	.92800
11	.96406	.95529	.94661	.93802	.92952	.92109
12	.96085	.95133	.94191	.93258	.92336	.91424
24	.92324	.90503	.88719	.86971	.85260	.83583
36	.88710	.86098	.83564	.81108	.78725	.76415
48	.85237	.81907	.78710	.75640	.72692	.69861

a sample of these *IF*s to be used for discounting, taken directly from
column 3 in tables for selected interest rates in the Appendix.

In our problem we want to know how much should be paid for a
$10,616.80 return received at the end of 12 months if an investor demands
a 6 percent return. The solution can be determined by going to the 6%

column in Exhibit 8–5, looking down to the row corresponding to 12 months, and obtaining the factor for discounting, 0.94191. We can now find the solution by performing a simple multiplication as follows:

$10,616.80 (*IF, PV* of $1, 6%, 12 mos.) = *PV*
$10,616.80 × 0.94191 = $10,000 (rounded)

Suppose our investor desired a 7 *percent* interest rate as an appropriate return, how much should be paid for the $10,618.80 receipt? By looking to the 7 percent column in Exhibit 8–5, it is seen that the *IF* for one year is 0.93258. Multiplying $10,616.80 × 0.93258 = $9,901, we find that $9,901 is the maximum amount that should be paid today to receive $10,616.80 at the end of one year if a 7 percent return on the investment is desired. (The investment amount, should we choose to make it, would be $9,901. It is on this amount that the 7 percent is earned.)

Question: How much should be paid *today* for a real estate investment which will return $5,000 three years from now, assuming an investor desires an 8 percent annual return compounded monthly?

Solution: $5,000 (*IF, PV* of $1, 8%, 36 mos.) = Present value
$5,000 (0.78725) = Present value
$3,936.25 = Present value

Compound Value of an Annuity The first section of this chapter dealt with finding the compound or ending value of a *single* deposit or payment made only once, at the beginning of a period. An equally relevant consideration involves a *series* of equal deposits or payments made at *equal intervals*. For example, assume deposits of $1,000 are made *each month* for a period of one year and interest is compounded at an annual rate of 5 percent on the monthly balance. What would be the value at the end of the year for series of deposits plus all compound interest?

In this case the problem involves *equal deposits* made at *equal time intervals*. This series of deposits or payments is defined as an *annuity*. Since we know how to find the answer to a problem in which only one deposit is made, it would be logical, and correct, to assume the same basic compounding process applies when dealing with annuities. Recalling the general formula for monthly compound interest, $P_n = P_o (1 + i/12)^n$, for the first $1,000 deposit the value can be found at the end of the first year by structuring the problem as in the section on compounding a single deposit. The value of the first $1,000 deposit earning interest at an annual rate of 5 percent compounded monthly can be found by multiplying $1,000 by the interest factor in column (1) corresponding to the row for 12 months in the 5 percent interest tables in the Appendix, or $1,000 (*IF, CV* of $1, 5%, 12 mos.) = $1,000 (1.05116) = $1,051.16. However, this is only a *partial solution* to the problem since we are dealing with an annuity, or a series of deposits which occur *monthly* during the year.

To compute the sum of all deposits made in each succeeding month, and to include compound interest on deposits only as they occur, the general formula for compound interest must be expanded as follows:

$$S_{.1} = P \ (1 + i/12)^n + P \ (1 + i/12)^{n-1} + P \ (1 + i/12)^{n-2} + \ldots P \ (1 + i/12)^1$$

In this expression, S_n is the compound value of an annuity,[2] or the sum of all deposits, P, compounded monthly at an annual rate (i) for (n) periods. The important thing to note in the expression, how-ever, is that each deposit is compounded only from the period in which it is deposited through period (n). In our example, since we are dealing with a series of $1,000 deposits made monthly over a 12-month period, the first $1,000 deposit would be compounded for 12 periods (n), the $1,000 deposit made at the beginning of the second month would be compounded for 11 periods ($n-1$), and so on until the last deposit, which would be compounded only once ($n-11$) since it is deposited at the be-ginning of the twelfth month.

To compute the value of these deposits, a solution like the one shown in Exhibit 8–6 could be constructed. Note that each $1,000 deposit is compounded from the *beginning* of the month in which the deposit was made to the end of the year. In other words, as shown in our expanded formula above, the deposit at the beginning of month one is com-pounded for 12 months, the deposit made at the beginning of the second month is compounded for 11 months, and so on. By carrying this process out one month at a time, the solution, or $12,330.02, is determined when the compounded amounts in the extreme right column are added.

Although the compound value of $1,000 per period, S_n, can be determined in the manner shown in Exhibit 8–6, careful examination of the compounding process reveals another, easier way to find the solu-tion. Note that the $1,000 deposit occurs monthly and never changes, that is, it is *constant*. When the deposits are *constant*, it is possible to sum all of the individual *IF*s for all periods shown in Exhibit 8–6. The total of the *IF*s is 12.33002. By multiplying $1,000 by 12.3302, a solution of $12,330.02 is obtained, as is shown in Exhibit 8–6 at the bottom of the right hand column.

Use of Compound Interest Tables for Annuities   Because the *IF*s

---

[2] Some other textbooks may refer to S_n as the sum of an annuity or the amount of $1 per period. The formula shown here is the formula for an annuity due which assumes all deposits are made at the beginning of the month.

EXHIBIT 8–6
Compound Value of $1,000 per Month at 5%

Month	Deposit		IF	Compound Value
1 ....$1,000 ×	(IF, 5%, 12 mos., Col. 1)°	= $1,000 ×	1.05116 =	$ 1,051.16
2 .... 1,000 ×	(IF, 5%, 11 mos., Col. 1)	= 1,000 ×	1.04680 =	1,046.80
3 .... 1,000 ×	(IF, 5%, 10 mos., Col. 1)	= 1,000 ×	1.04246 =	1,042.46
4 .... 1,000 ×	(IF, 5%, 9 mos., Col. 1)	= 1,000 ×	1.03813 =	1,038.13
5 .... 1,000 ×	(IF, 5%, 8 mos., Col. 1)	= 1,000 ×	1,03382 =	1,033.82
6 .... 1,000 ×	(IF, 5%, 7 mos., Col. 1)	= 1,000 ×	1.02953 =	1,029.53
7 .... 1,000 ×	(IF, 5%, 6 mos., Col. 1)	= 1,000 ×	1.02526 =	1,025.26
8 .... 1,000 ×	(IF, 5%, 5 mos., Col. 1)	= 1,000 ×	1.02101 =	1,021.01
9 .... 1,000 ×	(IF, 5%, 4 mos., Col. 1)	= 1,000 ×	1.01677 =	1,016.77
10 .... 1,000 ×	(IF, 5%, 3 mos., Col. 1)	= 1,000 ×	1.01255 =	1,012.55
11 .... 1,000 ×	(IF, 5%, 2 mos., Col. 1)	= 1,000 ×	1.00835 =	1,008.35
12 .... 1,000 ×	(IF, 5%, 1 mo., Col. 1)	= 1,000 ×	1.00417 =	1,004.17

Also: Compound value =   1,000 × 12.33002 = $12,330.02

° Column 1 of Appendix.

in Exhibit 8–6 can be added, a series of new interest factors has been developed for various interest rates in the Appendix, column 2, titled: *Compound Value of $1 per Month.* A sample of these *IFs*, now referred to as (*IF, CV* of $1 *per mo., i% n mos.*), has been taken for various interest rates directly from column 2 in the Appendix and compiled in Exhibit 8–7. The *IFs* in Exhibit 8–7 are simply the sum of the *IFs* in Exhibit 8–3 for any given number of months.[3]

In the problem at hand, to determine the compound value of $1,000 per month at 5 percent for one year, note that if we go to the 5% column in Exhibit 8–7 and obtain the *IF* which corresponds to one year we can find the solution to our problem as follows:

$$P \ (IF, CV \text{ of } \$1 \ per \ mo., i\%, n \text{ mos.}) = S_n$$
$$\$1,000 \ (IF, CV \text{ of } \$1 \ per \ mo., 5\%, 12 \text{ mos.}) = S_{12}$$
$$\$1,000 \times 12.33002 = S_{12}$$
$$\$12,330.02 = S_{12}$$

This solution, or $12,330.02, corresponds exactly to the long series of multiplications carried out in Exhibit 8–6.

Question: What would be the value of $800 deposited each month for two years and compounded at 8 percent interest?

---

[3] Recalling the expanded compound interest formula for an annuity, note that *IFs* are simply the sum of the interest components, $(1 + i/12)^n + (1 + i/12)^{n-1} \ldots + (1 + i/12)^1$ for a given interest rate (i) and period (n).

EXHIBIT 8-7

Compound Value of $1 per Month (column 2, Appendix)

Month	4%	5%	6%	7%	8%	9%
1	1.00333	1.00417	1.00500	1.00583	1.00667	1.00750
2	2.01001	2.01252	2.01503	2.01753	2.02004	2.02256
3	3.02004	3.02507	3.03010	3.03514	3.04018	3.04523
4	4.03344	4.04184	4.05025	4.05867	4.06711	4.07556
5	5.05022	5.06285	5.07550	5.08818	5.10089	5.11363
6	6.07039	6.08811	6.10588	6.12370	6.14157	6.15948
7	7.09396	7.11764	7.14141	7.16525	7.18918	7.21318
8	8.12094	8.15147	8.18212	8.21288	8.24377	8.27478
9	9.15134	9.18960	9.22803	9.26663	9.30540	9.34434
10	10.18518	10.23206	10.27917	10.32651	10.37410	10.42192
11	11.22246	11.27886	11.33556	11.39259	11.44993	11.50759
12	12.26321	12.33002	12.39724	12.46488	12.53293	12.60139
24	25.02603	25.29086	25.55912	25.83084	26.10608	26.38488
36	38.30883	38.91481	39.53279	40.16303	40.80580	41.46136
48	52.13280	53.23578	54.36832	55.53129	56.72558	57.95212

Solution: $800 $\times$ *(IF, CV of $1 per mo., 8%, 24 mos.)* $= S_{24}$

$800 $\times$ 26.10608 $= S_{24}$

$20,884.86 $= S_{24}$

Present Value of an Annuity   In the preceding section, our primary concern was to determine the compound value of an annuity, or constant payments received at equal time intervals. In this section we want to consider the *present value* of a *series* of monthly receipts as the investment produces income over time. Since an investor may have to consider a series of monthly income payments when trying to decide whether or not to invest, this is an important problem.

Recalling from the earlier section dealing with the present value of a single receipt, or ending value, P_n, we took the basic formula for compounding interest and rearranged it to determine the present value of an investment as follows:

$$P_n = P_0 (1 + i/12)^n$$
$$P_0 = P_n \div (1 + i/12)^n$$
$$\text{Present value} = P_0 = P_n \times \frac{1}{(1 + i/12)^n}$$

To consider the present value of an *annuity*, defined as A_n, we need only consider the sum of individual present values for all monthly receipts. This can be done by modifying the basic present value formula above as follows:

$$A_n = R \frac{1}{(1 + i/12)^1} + R \frac{1}{(1 + i/12)^2} \cdots + R \frac{1}{(1 + i/12)^n}$$

Note in this expression that each receipt, R, is discounted for the number of months corresponding to the time at which the funds are actually received. In other words, the first receipt would occur at the end of the first period and would be discounted only one period, or $R \times 1 \div (1 + i/12)^1$. The second receipt would be discounted for two periods, or $R \times 1 \div (1 + i/12)^2$, and so on.[4]

Assuming an individual is considering an investment which will provide a series of monthly cash receipts of $500 for a period of one year, and the investor desires a 6 percent return, how much should be paid for the investment today?

We can begin by considering the present value of the $500 receipt in month 1 as shown in Exhibit 8–8. Note that the present value of the $500 receipt is discounted for one month at 6 percent. This is true because the first month's income of $500 is not received until the *end* of the first period and our investor only wants to pay an amount today (present value) which will assure him of a 6 percent return on the amount he pays today. Therefore, by discounting this $500 receipt by the interest factor in column 3 for one month in the 6 percent tables in the Appendix, or 0.99502, the present value is $497.51.

Note that the second $500 income payment is received at the end of the second month. Therefore, it should be discounted for two months at 6 percent. Its present value is found by multiplying $500 by the interest factor in column 3 in the 6 percent tables for two months, or 0.99007, giving a present value of $495.04. This process can be continued for each receipt for the remaining ten months as shown in Exhibit 8–8. The present value of the entire series of $500 monthly income payments can be found by adding the series of receipts discounted each month in the far right column, which totals $5,809.47.

However, as also shown in Exhibit 8–8, since the $500 series of payments is *constant*, it is possible to *add* all interest factors to obtain one interest factor that can be multiplied by $500 to obtain the same present value.[5] The sum of all interest factors for 6 percent in Exhibit 8–8 is 11.61893. When 11.61893 is multiplied by $500, the present value, $5,809.47, found in the lengthy series of multiplications in Exhibit 8–8, is again determined.

Use of Present Value of an Annuity Tables   Because the interest

---

[4] The pattern of equal receipts occurring at the end of the month is called an ordinary annuity.

[5] Determining these interest factors amounts to adding the interest components $1 \div (1 + i/12)^1 + 1 \div (1 + i/12)^2 + \ldots 1 \div (1 + i/12)^n$ from the modified formula for the present value of an annuity, A_n, presented above.

EXHIBIT 8–8
Present Value of $500 per Month Discounted at 6%

Month	Receipt						Present Value
1	......$500 ×	(*IF*, 6%,	1 mo.,	Col. 3)°	= $500 ×	.99502 =	$ 497.51
2	...... 500 ×	(*IF*, 6%,	2 mos.,	Col. 3)	= 500 ×	.99007 =	495.04
3	...... 500 ×	(*IF*, 6%,	3 mos.,	Col. 3)	= 500 ×	.98515 =	492.58
4	...... 500 ×	(*IF*, 6%,	4 mos.,	Col. 3)	= 500 ×	.98025 =	490.13
5	...... 500 ×	(*IF*, 6%,	5 mos.,	Col. 3)	= 500 ×	.97537 =	487.69
6	...... 500 ×	(*IF*, 6%,	6 mos.,	Col. 3)	= 500 ×	.97052 =	485.26
7	...... 500 ×	(*IF*, 6%,	7 mos.,	Col. 3)	= 500 ×	.96569 =	482.84
8	...... 500 ×	(*IF*, 6%,	8 mos.,	Col. 3)	= 500 ×	.96089 =	480.44
9	...... 500 ×	(*IF*, 6%,	9 mos.,	Col. 3)	= 500 ×	.95610 =	478.05
10	...... 500 ×	(*IF*, 6%,	10 mos.,	Col. 3)	= 500 ×	.95135 =	475.68
11	...... 500 ×	(*IF*, 6%,	11 mos.,	Col. 3)	= 500 ×	.94661 =	473.30
12	...... 500 ×	(*IF*, 6%,	12 mos.,	Col. 3)	= 500 ×	.94191 =	470.95

Also: Present value = $500 × 11.61893 = $5,809.47

° Column 3 of the Appendix.

factors in Exhibit 8–8 may be summed, as long as the income payments are *equal* in amount and received at *equal* intervals, this combination obviously takes a lot of work out of problem-solving. The sums of *IF*s for various interest rates now referred to as (*IF*, *PV* of $1 *per mo.*, *i%, n* months) have been compiled in table form and are listed in column 4 titled: *Present Value of $1 per Month* in the tables in the Appendix.

To familiarize the student with discounting annuities, Exhibit 8–9 has

EXHIBIT 8–9
Present Value of $1 per Month (column 4, Appendix)

Month	Rate					
	4%	5%	6%	7%	8%	9%
1	0.99668	0.99585	0.99502	0.99420	0.99338	0.99256
2	1.99004	1.98757	1.98510	1.98263	1.98018	1.97772
3	2.98011	2.97517	2.97025	2.96534	2.96044	2.95556
4	3.96689	3.95868	3.95050	3.94234	3.93421	3.92611
5	4.95039	4.93810	4.92587	4.91368	4.90153	4.88944
6	5.93062	5.91346	5.89638	5.87938	5.86245	5.84560
7	6.90759	6.88478	6.86207	6.83948	6.81700	6.79464
8	7.88132	7.85206	7.82296	7.79402	7.76524	7.73661
9	8.85181	8.81533	8.77906	8.74302	8.70719	8.67158
10	9.81908	9.77460	9.73041	9.68651	9.64290	9.59958
11	10.78314	10.72989	10.67703	10.62454	10.57242	10.52067
12	11.74399	11.68122	*11.61893*	11.55712	11.49578	11.43491
24	23.02825	22.79390	22.56286	22.33510	22.11054	21.88914
36	33.87076	33.36570	32.87101	32.38646	31.91180	31.44680
48	44.28883	43.42295	42.58032	41.76020	40.96191	40.18478

been developed showing the *IF*s for the present value of $1 per period (annuity). These *IF*s were taken directly from column 4 in the tables contained in the Appendix for a sample of interest rates. In our problem then, we want to determine the present value of $500 received monthly for one year assuming a 6 percent rate of return is desired. How much should an investor pay for this total investment today and be assured of earning his desired return? We solve this problem by looking at Exhibit 8–9, finding the 6 percent column, and looking down the column until the *IF* in the row corresponding to 12 months is located. The *IF* is 11.61893. We can now solve the following:

$$\$500 \ (IF, \ PV \ of \ \$1 \ per \ mo., \ 6\%, \ 12 \ mos.) = A_n$$
$$\$500 \times 11.61893 = \$5,809.47$$

This solution corresponds to that obtained in Exhibit 8–8.

Question: An investor has an opportunity to invest in a rental property which will provide net cash returns of $400 *per month* for three years. The investor believes that an 8 percent return should be earned on this investment. How much should be paid for the rental property?

Solution: $$\$400 \times (IF, \ PV \ of \ \$1 \ per \ mo., \ 8\%, \ 36 \ mos.) = A_n$$
$$\$400 \ (31.91180) = \$12,764.72$$

No more than $12,764.72 should be paid for the investment property. If the investor pays $12,764.72, an 8% return will be earned on the investment.

Determining Yields on Investments

Up to now, this chapter has demonstrated how to determine future values in the case of compounding and present values in the case of discounting. These two topics are important in their own right. They have also provided tools for determining an equally important component used extensively in real estate financing, that is, calculating *rates of return* or *investment yields*. In other words, the concepts illustrated in the compounding and discounting processes can also be used to determine rates of return or yields on investments, mortgage loans, etc. These concepts must be mastered since procedures used here will form the basis for much of what follows in succeeding chapters.

In the prior sections of this chapter, we have concentrated on determining the *future value* of an investment made today when compounded at some *given* rate of interest, or the *present investment value* of a stream of cash returns received in the future when discounted at a *given* rate of interest. In this section we are concerned with knowing what an investment will cost today and what the future stream of cash returns will be, but not knowing what yield or rate of return is earned if the investment is made.

Yields on Single Receipts   To illustrate the yield concept, assume an investor has an opportunity to buy an unimproved one-acre lot for $7,470 today. The lot is expected to appreciate in value and will be worth $15,000 after seven years. What would be the *percentage rate of return* on the $7,470 investment in the property if it were made today, held for seven years, and sold for $15,000?

To solve for the unknown interest rate, we can formulate the problem as follows:

$$\$15,000 \times (IF, PV \text{ of } \$1, ?\%, 7 \text{ yrs.}) = \$7,470$$

In other words, we would like to know what interest rate can be substituted in the above expression for the unknown interest rate (?%) which will make the $15,000 return equal to the $7,470 investment outlay, or present value, today. The interest rate can be determined by first solving for the interest factor as follows:

$$\$15,000 \times (IF, PV \text{ of } \$1, ?\%, 7 \text{ yrs.}) = \$7,470$$
$$(IF, PV \text{ of } \$1, ?\%, 7 \text{ yrs.}) = \$7,470 \div \$15,000$$
$$(IF, PV \text{ of } \$1, ?\%, 7 \text{ yrs.}) = 0.498$$

From the above calculations the *interest factor* is 0.498, but we still do not know the *interest rate*. However we do know that the time period over which the investment is to appreciate in value is seven years. Since the *IF* is 0.498 and the term of investment is seven years, by consulting the interest tables in the Appendix, we can easily find the interest rate. Since the cash return of $15,000 is a *single receipt*, we need only to locate an *IF* for the present value of $1 equal to 0.498 in column 3 in the row corresponding to seven years for some interest rate. We begin the search for the interest rate by choosing an arbitrary interest rate, say 8 percent. Looking to the 8 percent table we see the *IF* in column 3 for seven years is 0.57227, which is larger than 0.498. Moving to the 9 percent table, the *IF* for seven years is 0.53385 which is lower than the *IF* at 8 percent and comes closer to the *IF* we are looking for. Continuing this "trial and error" process, by looking to the 10 percent table we see that the *IF* in column 3 for seven years is 0.49803, therefore the interest rate we desire is 10 percent.[6] We know this is the correct interest factor because $15,000 × 0.498 = $7,470. This proves that 10 percent is the true yield on this investment.

---

[6] Even though the interest factor we were seeking was 0.498 and the one selected was 0.49803, for all practical purposes the two *IF*s are close enough for a very accurate solution. When searching for an *IF* in column 3, if the first three decimal places are the same this is usually adequate in solving a problem. There will usually be some differences in *IF*s due to rounding which can be safely ignored past the third decimal place. When searching for an *IF* in column 4, usually the first two decimal places are adequate for most problems. The amount of error involved beyond two decimal places is usually small enough to be safely ignored.

What does this interest rate mean? It means that if the $7,470 investment is made today, then held for seven years and sold for $15,000, this would be equivalent to investing $7,470 today and letting it *compound monthly* at an annual rate of 10 percent. This fact can be determined with the following computation:

$$\$7,470 \times (IF, CV \text{ of } \$1, 10\%, 7 \text{ yrs.}) = P_{84}$$
$$\$7,470 \times 2.008 = \$15,000 \text{ (rounded)}$$

This calculation simply shows that $7,470 compounded monthly at an annual rate of 10 percent for seven years is $15,000. Hence, making this investment is equivalent to earning a rate of return of 10 percent. This rate of return is sometimes referred to as the *investment yield*, or as the *internal rate of return*.

The internal rate of return integrates the concepts of compounding and present value. It represents an interest rate equivalent for an alternative investment earning interest at some annual interest rate compounded monthly. In other words, if an investor is faced with making an investment in some income-producing venture, *regardless of how the cash returns are patterned*, the internal rate of return provides a guide or comparison for the investor. *It tells the investor what compound interest rate the return on an investment being considered is equivalent to.* In our example of the unimproved one-acre lot, the 10 percent yield or internal rate of return, is *equivalent* to making a deposit of $7,470 and allowing it to compound monthly at an annual interest rate of 10 percent for seven years. After seven years the investor would receive $15,000, which includes the original investment of $7,470 plus all compound interest. With the internal rate of return known, the investor can make an easier judgment as to whether or not the investment should be made. If the 10 percent return is adequate it will be made; if not, the investor should reject it.

The concepts of the internal rate of return or yield, present value, and compounding are indispensable tools that are continually used in real estate finance and investment. The reader should not venture beyond this section without firmly grasping the concepts explained. These concepts form the basis for the remainder of this chapter and the four chapters which follow.

Yields on Investment Annuities   The concepts just illustrated with a single receipt of cash (when the unimproved lot was sold) also apply to situations where a series of cash receipts is involved. Consequently, a yield or internal rate of return also can be computed on these types of investments. To illustrate, suppose an investor has the opportunity to make an investment of $22,000 and it is estimated that cash returns from this investment will be $1,000 *per month* for two years. How would the *yield* or *internal rate of return* be calculated on the investment?[7] The solution to this type of problem is actually easier than one might think. First, it should be noticed that cash returns in this problem constitute an *annuity,* that is, equal amounts of cash received in equal time intervals. To determine the yield on this investment, since cash payments are $1,000 per month, and the price of the investment is $22,000 (the $22,000 is the same as *PV* in our earlier discussion) with an investment period of two years, the problem may be solved as follows where the unknown is the interest rate (?%):

$$R \times (IF, PV \text{ of } \$1 \text{ per mo., } ?\%, 2 \text{ yrs.}) = A_n$$
$$\$1,000 \times (IF, PV \text{ of } \$1 \text{ per mo., } ?\%, 2 \text{ yrs.}) = \$22,000$$
$$(IF, PV \text{ of } \$1 \text{ per mo., } ?\% \ 2 \text{ yrs.}) = \$22,000 \div \$1,000$$
$$(IF, PV \text{ of } \$1 \text{ per mo., } ?\% \ 2 \text{ yrs.}) = 22.00$$

What has been done in the solution is simply to solve for an *IF* for the present value of $1 per month by dividing the monthly cash returns of $1,000 into the investment amount of $22,000. But we still do not know the yield or return on the investment. However, we do know that the *IF* is 22.00 and that the investment will provide monthly returns for *two years.* By looking at column 4, the present value of $1 per mo., in the tables in the Appendix for *two years,* or 24 months, the yield is easy to determine. We have to find an *IF* in *column 4* for *24 months* equal to 22.00 for some interest rate. This is a searching process that must be started again by picking an arbitrary rate, say 6 percent. At 6 percent, the *IF* in column 4 for two years is about 22.56 which is not close enough to 22.00. Looking at the 7 percent tables the *IF* for two years is 22.34 which means that the solution is closer to 22.00 as the interest rate selected is increased. When 8 percent is selected, the *IF* decreases to 22.11 which is closer, but still not close enough to the desired *IF* of 22.00. Finally, by trying 8½ percent, the *IF* in column 4 for two years is 21.99945, and if we "round off," it is effectively 22.00. We know this is the desired solution. The yield on this investment is effectively 8½ percent. We can "prove" this to ourselves by making the following calculation:

$$\$1,000 \times (PV \text{ of } \$1 \text{ per mo., } 8\tfrac{1}{2}\%, 2 \text{ yrs.}) = A_n$$
$$\$1,000 \times (22.00) = A_n$$
$$\$22,000 = A_n$$

---

[7] At this point the reader might be tempted to make the following calculation: $1,000 per month divided by $22,000 or $1,000/$22,000 = 4.5% for a "monthly" return, or perhaps $1,000 × 12 months or $12,000/$22,000 = 54.5%, for an "annual" return. Obviously both calculations are *incorrect* as far as the yield is concerned because (1) they do not consider that the $22,000 investment must also be recovered and (2) all $1,000 payments are treated equally as far as timing of receipt of the money is concerned. Clearly, $1,000 received in the first month is worth more to an investor than $1,000 received in succeeding months. Consequently, these calculations are not accurate. This demonstrates the importance of the method shown here.

This calculation shows that $1,000 discounted at 8½ percent gives a present value of $22,000. The emphasis here is that the present value does equal $22,000, which is also the amount invested. If it did not equal $22,000, we would know that the yield chosen for discounting is incorrect. *Consequently, when the present value computed is equal to the amount invested, this indicates that the correct interest rate has been chosen. The interest rate chosen for discounting is equal to the yield or internal rate of return on the investment.* We can now interpret our answer of 8½ percent as follows: if our investor will be satisfied with an 8½ percent interest return compounded monthly, the investment should be made. If a return *higher* than 8½ percent is expected, the investment should not be made.

The reader may think this is a tedious process to find solutions such as this one. However, after working the problems in the chapter and at the end of the chapter, it will be much easier to determine solutions and less time-consuming. In any event, the importance of this material cannot be overemphasized, as will become apparent in the next chapter.

Determining Yields on an Annuity and a Single Receipt Another problem in real estate financing involves calculating yields on the combination of *monthly receipts and* a *lump sum* or single receipt in the last month of the investment. For example, suppose an investor makes the following investment: $20,000, with monthly cash returns of $200 for 10 years and a large single receipt of $15,000 at the end of the tenth year. This is a common pattern of cash flow from an investment in a real estate partnership, where monthly cash returns may be constant and a lump sum receipt at the end of the tenth year may be realized from the sale of the real estate. How will the yield be calculated on such an investment?

The method for solving this problem combines the concepts used in finding the present value of an annuity *and* the present value of $1. The returns involve an *annuity* of $200 per month for ten years and a *single amount* or lump sum at the end of ten years of $15,000. When finding the yield, the *annuity* must be discounted using interest factors from *column 4* in the Appendix or the present value of $1 per month. The lump sum or *single payment* must be discounted using interest factors from *column 3*, or the present value of $1. The sum of both discounted present values *must* total $20,000 when the proper interest rate has been chosen.[8]

---

[8] Since we have both a series of payments and a lump sum receipt in this case, and since we must use IFs for the *PV* of $1 per month *and PV* of $1, we are precluded from solving for a single *IF* as was done in the cases of the single receipt and the annuity. We must complete the total present value by looking for *two* IFs from the *same* interest table, which when used to discount the annuity and lump sum, will equal the original investment amount.

Conceptually, what we want to know is what interest rate in the following expression will result in a computed present value equal to $20,000. To illustrate:

$$\$200 \times (IF, PV \text{ of } \$1 \text{ per mo., } ?\% \text{ 10 yrs.})$$
$$+ \ \$15,000 \times (IF, PV \text{ of } \$1, ?\% \text{ 10 yrs.}) = \$20,000$$

When the "correct" interest rate (?%) is found, the interest factors for that rate obtained from columns 3 and 4 when multiplied by the cash returns will result in a $PV = \$20,000$, which also equals the investment of $20,000.

A "trial and error" approach can be used by choosing an interest rate and the interest factors for that rate, then finding the present value. For example, if we choose an arbitrary interest rate, say 8 percent, and compute the present value, we can ascertain how close we are to the internal rate of return by comparing the computed present value with $20,000.

Discounting by 8 percent:
$$\$200 \times (IF, PV \text{ of } \$1 \text{ per mo., } 8\%, \text{ 10 yrs.})$$
$$+ \ \$15,000 \times (IF, PV \text{ of } \$1, 8\%, \text{ 10 yrs.}) = \text{Present value}$$

$$\$200 \times (82.42148) + \$15,000 \times (0.45052) = \$23,242$$

The present value computed when discounting with an 8 percent interest rate is $23,242, which is *greater* than the desired present value of $20,000. Any time the *computed* present value is *greater* than desired, the interest rate selected for discounting is *too low*. We can use "trial and error" again, this time increasing the interest rate, computing the present value again, and comparing the computed value with the desired value. This process should continue until the interest rate chosen makes the computed present value equal to the desired present value. To shorten this time-consuming process, it is sometimes possible to use an approximation procedure which enables us to come closer to the yield on the first "trial and error" attempt.

Approximation Procedure. First, by determining the *annual* cash flow from the investment, that is, $200 × 12 months, or $2,400 per year, a simple average annual return on the $20,000 investment is $2,400/20,000 or 12 percent. However, when an average return such as this is calculated, in order for it to be a true or exact rate of return, one of two conditions must exist. Either the entire investment balance, $20,000, must be returned at some future date, or the $2,400 per year must be received forever.[9] Since the cash returns in our case include only a $15,000 receipt at the end of the tenth year, which is obviously less

---

[9] These two facts can be proven mathematically.

than $20,000, the simple ratio of 12 percent *overstates* the actual yield. (If the payment in the tenth year were greater than $20,000, the simple average return would understate the actual yield.) Therefore, we know that we should begin searching for the actual yield by using interest rates *below* 12 percent. To begin the search for the yield on the $20,000 investment we begin with 11 percent.[10]

$200 × (*IF, PV* of $1 per mo., 11%, 120 mos.)
+ $15,000 × (*IF, PV* of $1, 11%, 120 mos.) = Present value (*PV*)

$200 × (72.59527) + $15,000 × (0.33454) = *PV*
$19,537 = *PV*

Note that the approximation works nicely since the present value is near $20.000.[11] However, since the computed present value of $19,537 is below $20,000, we know that the yield is yet to be found, since present value must *equal* the amount to be invested, $20,000.

Discounting by 10½ percent:
$200 × (74.10975) + $15,000 × (0.35154) = *PV*
$20,095 = *PV*

Discounting by 10¾ percent:
$200 × (73.34675) + $15,000 × (0.34294) = *PV*
$19,813 = *PV*

We know that the actual yield falls between 10½ percent and 10¾ percent, because the desired solution, $20,000, falls between $20,095 and $19,813.

Interpolation Procedure. Some investors or lenders may be satisfied with the solution determined between 10½ and 10¾ percent. However, most investors, and particularly lenders, prefer a more exact solution. Greater precision can be achieved through a procedure called *interpolation*. The interpolation procedure is demonstrated as follows:

1. Computed present values:
   PV at 10½%   = $20,095
   PV at 10¾%   =   19,813
   Difference: ¼% $ 282

2. Desired present value = $20,000

---

[10] Note that both the annuity and the lump sum are discounted by the *same* interest rate. The two amounts should always be discounted at the same *rate*, although the interest *factors* come from *different* columns.

[11] This approximation works adequately as long as the lump sum received at the end of the investment period is similar in amount to the original amount invested. If the lump sum is much larger than the original amount invested, the yield should be approximated by ignoring the annual cash flows, and computing the internal rate of return by considering the lump sum alone. This approximation will be closer to the actual rate, which can then be determined by "trial and error."

3. Difference between *highest* computed present value and *desired* present value:

    PV at 10½%   = $20,095
    Desired *PV*   = 20,000

    Difference $ 95

4. Ratio of difference in (3) to difference in (1) times difference in rates in (1) or:

    $$\$95/\$282 \times \text{¼\% or } 0.25\% = 0.08\%$$

5. Yield equals:
    10½% or 10.50% + 0.08% = 10.58%.

Therefore, a more exact yield on this investment is 10.58 percent.

QUESTIONS

1. What is the essential ingredient in understanding the compounding process?
2. Which set of interest factors is larger: *CV* of $1 or *CV* of $1 per month? Why?
3. How are the interest factors for the *CV* of $1 per month developed (column 2 of the Appendix)?
4. If you deposited $1,000 today and had the choice of having it compounded annually at 6 percent or compounded monthly at an annual rate of 6 percent, which would you choose? What compounding pattern is assumed in this text?
5. What does present value mean? How would it ever be used?
6. How are the interest factors for the *PV* of $1 per month developed (column 4 of the Appendix)?
7. The internal rate of return is an important concept in real estate finance. What is it? How would it ever be used?
8. Why is the internal rate of return more difficult to find when investment returns are made up of an annuity and a lump sum receipt?
9. What is interpolation? Why is it necessary?

CASE PROBLEMS

1. Investor A deposits $2,000 in a bank for a period of three years at 7 percent interest, compounded monthly. How much will investor A have at the end of three years?
2. Mr. George Smith makes an investment in XYZ Development Corporation which calls for a $100 monthly payment for five years. XYZ Development Corporation promises to compound interest monthly at 9 percent on the amount invested during the five-year period. How much will Mr. Smith's investment be worth after five years?

3.   Ms. Linda Goodwill is considering the following investment in a lot which has good development potential. She can buy the property today and hopes to sell it four years from now for $10,500. She also believes that 10 percent is a fair return on investment for holding the property for four years. The asking price for the lot is $8,000.

a.   Should she buy it?

b.   If the asking price were $7,000, should she buy it?

4.   An investor has an opportunity to invest in a development which promises to pay $200 per month for six years. The investor believes that based on the nature of the project, a return of 11 percent per year should be earned if the investment is made. How much should be paid for this investment today?

5.   Mr. Stanley can make an investment which yields the following returns: $200 monthly during the first year, $400 monthly during the second year and $700 per month during the third year. Assuming he desires a 12 percent return on investment, how much should be paid for the investment?

6.   An investment is available which yields $2,000 at the end of the year for the next three years. Assuming an investor desires a 10 percent return, how much should be paid for this investment?

7.   Mr. Blackwell is considering an investment which will provide the following returns: $500 at the end of year 1, $300 at the end of year 2, and $100 at the end of year 3. Assuming Mr. Blackwell desires a return of 10 percent, how much should he pay for this investment?

8.   An investment opportunity promises the following returns: $500 per month for five years and $10,000 at the end of the fifth year. Assuming an investor desires an 8 percent return on investment, how much should be paid for this opportunity?

9.   Mr. Crossbuck has an opportunity to invest $10,000 in a real estate partnership which will return $450 per month for two years. What would the internal rate of return or yield be if this investment were made by Mr. Crossbuck?

10.   An investor is considering the purchase of an unimproved lot which can be bought for $12,000. If purchased and held for five years, the investor believes it can be sold for $20,000. What would be the yield or internal rate of return on such an investment?

11.   A lender is considering whether to make the following loan. The amount to be loaned is $20,000 with the borrowers making monthly payments of $167.80 for 11 years and a single lump sum, or balloon, payment of $16,000 at the end of 11 years. What would the yield, or internal rate of return, be to the lender on an investment in such a loan?

12.   An investor is considering an investment which costs $12,060 and will return $200 per month for two years, then $300 per month for two more years and $400 per month during the last year the investment is held. What would be the yield on such an investment?

9

Mortgage Loans: Payment Patterns and Effective Borrowing Costs

In the previous chapter, concepts in compounding, discounting, and the procedure for determining yields were introduced as a foundation for what follows in this chapter and for much of the material in succeeding chapters. The major objective of this chapter is to illustrate payment patterns for various kinds of mortgage loans and to provide techniques for determining the effective cost of borrowing under varying conditions in loan agreements. Common practices found in real estate finance include charges such as loan discount or origination fees, prepayment penalties, prepaid interest, and variable interest rate provisions. In addition, various amortization, or loan repayment schedules can be agreed on by the borrower and lender to facilitate financing a particular real estate transaction. Since these provisions often affect the cost of borrowing, effective borrowing costs are stressed heavily in this chapter. Many provisions illustrated here are commonly encountered in real estate transactions and should be understood by individuals buying and financing property or by anyone providing counsel in the area.

Loan Payment Patterns—Fixed Interest Rate Loans

Many possible loan payment patterns may be agreed upon by a borrower and lender depending on the circumstances surrounding the real estate transaction being financed. It is safe to say, however, that three loan payment patterns dominate in practice: (1) the fully amortized loan; (2) the partially amortized loan; and (3) the demand loan. In this section we consider all three payment patterns in sequence.

Fully Amortized Mortgage Loans The most common loan payment pattern used in real estate finance is the fully amortized mortgage loan. This type of loan payment pattern is used extensively in financing single family residences and is also used in long-term mortgage lending on income-producing properties such as multi-family apartment complexes and shopping centers. The fully amortized loan payment pattern simply means that a level or constant monthly payment is calculated on an original loan amount, at a given rate of interest, for a given term. Each payment includes interest and some repayment of principal. At the end of the term of the mortgage loan, the original loan amount or principal is completely repaid and the lender has earned a fixed rate of interest on the monthly loan balance.

To illustrate how the loan payment calculation is made, assume that an individual wishes to purchase a property which costs $40,000. He or she would like to borrow $32,000 for a period of 30 years. After negotiating with ABC Savings and Loan Association, a loan commitment is obtained for $32,000 for 30 years at an interest rate of 9 percent. What will be the monthly mortgage payment on this loan, assuming it is to be fully amortized ("paid off") at the end of 30 years? Based on our knowledge of discounting annuities from the preceding chapter, the problem is really no more than finding the present value of an annuity and can be formulated as shown in Exhibit 9–1.

EXHIBIT 9–1
Determining Monthly Payments—Fully Amortized Mortgage

$$\text{Monthly payment} \times (IF, PV \text{ of } \$1 \text{ per mo., } 9\%, 30 \text{ yrs.}) = \$\ 32,000$$
$$\text{Monthly payment} \times 124.28186 = \$\ 32,000$$
$$\text{Monthly payment} = \frac{32,000}{124.28186}$$
$$or \qquad = 32,000 \times \frac{1}{124.28186}$$
$$or \qquad = 32,000 \times 0.00805$$
$$\text{Monthly payment} = \$257.60$$

From the point of view of the *lender* the loan represents an *investment* of $32,000 today (present value) on which an annual rate of 9 percent interest must be earned. What must the series of constant monthly payments (annuity) be to repay fully the $32,000 over the 30-year period and also to earn the lender an annual return of 9 percent compounded monthly? The monthly mortgage payments of $257.60, when discounted by the lender at 9 percent, yields a present value of $32,000 as shown in Exhibit 9–1. Consequently, monthly payments of $257.60 must be made to pay off the loan in 30 years and to earn the lender a 9 percent rate compounded monthly.

Returning to the calculation of the monthly mortgage payment in Exhibit 9–1, we should give particular attention to the following step in the solution:

$$\text{Monthly payment} = \frac{\$32,000}{124.28186}$$
$$= 32,000 \times (1 \div 124.28186)$$
$$= 32,000 \times 0.00805$$
$$= \$257.60$$

Note that dividing the *IF* 124.28186 into $32,000 is identical to multiplying $32,000 by (1 ÷ 124.28186) or 0.00805 (rounded). This simple fact enables us to simplify calculations of this kind considerably.

Mortgage Loan Constants   Since multiplying is always faster and more convenient than dividing, particularly when decimals are involved, a series of new interest factors, or *loan constants,* has been developed for various interest rates and loan maturities. These loan constants enable a simple multiplication to be made ($32,000 × 0.00805 = $257.60) to determine monthly mortgage payments, rather than the more awkward division ($32,000 ÷ 124.28186). The factor used for multiplication in our example, 0.00805, is the *loan constant* for 30 years at 9 percent. In the Appendix to this book, column 5 is titled: *Loan Constant* in all interest rate tables. Given an interest rate and term of a loan, one can find the appropriate loan constant by looking down column 5 and finding the factor in the row corresponding to the number of years for which the loan is to be made. The loan constant can then be multiplied by any beginning loan amount to obtain the monthly mortgage payment necessary to amortize the loan fully by the maturity date.

Exhibit 9–2 provides a sample of loan constants for various interest rates and loan maturities. Returning to our problem of finding the monthly mortgage payment for a $32,000 loan made at 9 percent for

EXHIBIT 9–2
Mortgage Loan Constants (column 5, Appendix)

Years	Months		Rate			
			7%	8%	9%	10%
5	(60)		.01980	.02028	.02076	.02125
10	(120)		.01161	.01213	.01267	.01322
15	(180)		.00899	.00956	.01014	.01075
20	(240)		.00775	.00836	.00900	.00965
25	(300)		.00707	.00772	.00839	.00909
30	(360)		.00665	.00734	.00805	.00878

30 years, by locating the 9 percent column and looking down until we find the row corresponding to 30 years, we see that the loan constant in that position is 0.00805. This constant multiplied by $32,000 results in a monthly mortgage payment of $257.60.

Analysis of Principal and Interest To examine this payment pattern in more detail, it should be obvious that the sum of all mortgage payments made over the 30-year (360 months) period is $257.60 × 360, or $92,736. This amount is far greater than the original loan of $32,000. Why are the total payments so much higher than the amount of the loan? The reason for this relationship is shown in Exhibit 9–3.

EXHIBIT 9–3
Loan Amortization Pattern, $32,000 Loan at 9 Percent Interest for 30 Years

Month	(1) Beginning Loan Balance	(2) Monthly Payment	(3) Interest (0.09/12 or 0.0075)	(4) Principal Reduction	(5) Ending Loan Balance
1	$32,000.00	$257.60	$240.00	$17.60	$31,982.40
2	31,982.40	257.60	239.87	17.73	31,964.67
3	31,964.67	257.60	239.74	17.86	31,946.81
4	31,946.81	257.60	239.60	18.00	31,928.81
5	31,928.81	257.60	239.47	18.13	31,910.68
6	31,910.68	257.60	239.33	18.27	31,892.41
358	761.33	257.60	5.71	251.89	509.44
359	509.44	257.60	3.82	253.78	255.68
360	255.68	257.60	1.92	255.68	–0–
Totals	—	$92,736	$60,736	$32,000	—

The pattern developed in Exhibit 9–3 shows in month 1 a beginning mortgage balance, or loan principal, of $32,000. The monthly payment, which was calculated to be $257.60, includes interest of $240.00 in the first month, determined by the beginning loan amount $32,000 multiplied by (0.09/12), or the annual rate of 9 percent divided by 12 months to obtain a monthly compound interest factor (0.0075). The difference between $257.60 (column 2) and $240.00 (column 3) gives the amount of loan amortization or principal reduction (column 4) of $17.60 during the first month. The beginning loan balance $32,000 less the principal reduction in the first month, $17.60, gives the balance at the end of the first month of $31,982.40, which provides the beginning balance for the interest calculation in the second month. This process continues through the 360th month, or end of the 30th year, when the loan balance diminishes to zero.

The initial, relatively low, principal reduction, shown in column 4 in Exhibit 9–3, results in a high portion of the early monthly payments being interest charges. Note that the ending loan balance after the first six monthly payments (column 5) is approximately $31,892.41; thus only $107.59 has been amortized from the original balance of $32,000 after six months. Interest paid during the same six-month period totals $1,438.01. The reason for such a high interest component in each monthly payment is that the lender earns an annual 9 percent return (0.0075 monthly) on the outstanding loan balance. Since the loan is being repaid over a 30-year period, obviously the loan balance is reduced only very slightly at first and monthly interest charges are correspondingly high. Exhibit 9–3 goes on to show that the pattern of high interest charges in the early years of the loan reverses as the loan begins to mature. Note that during the last three months of the loan, interest charges (column 3) fall off sharply and principal reduction increases (column 4).

Interest, Principal, and Loan Balance Illustrated   To illustrate the loan payment pattern over time, Exhibit 9–4 shows the relative proportions of interest and principal in each monthly mortgage payment over the 30-year term of the loan. Exhibit 9–5 shows the rate of decline in the loan balance over the same 30-year period. It becomes clear from Exhibit 9–4 that the relative share of interest as a percentage of the total monthly mortgage payment declines very slowly at first. Note in Exhibit 9–4 that halfway into the term of the mortgage, or after 15 years, interest still comprises approximately $190 of the $257.60 monthly payment. Exhibit 9–5 shows that after 15 years the loan balance is approximately $25,390. Mortgage payments of $46,368 ($257.60 × 180 months) have been made through the 15th year, with only $6,610 ($32,000 − $25,390) of the loan having been repaid at that point. This pattern reverses with time. Note in Exhibit 9–4 that after 25 years, interest comprises only $93 of the $257.60 monthly payment and the loan balance has declined sharply to $12,400 as shown in Exhibit 9–5.

Determining Loan Balances   A useful tool in mortgage lending is the ability to determine the balance on a fully amortized loan at any time. Most mortgage loans are repaid before they mature. In fact, even though most loans are made for terms of 25 or 30 years, statistics gathered on a national basis indicate that they are usually paid off anywhere from 8 to 12 years after they are made. Therefore it is very important to know what the loan balance will be at any point in time when financing real estate.

To illustrate, let us return to the previous example of the $32,000 mortgage loan made at 9 percent interest for a term of 30 years. After

EXHIBIT 9–4
Mortgage Payment Pattern

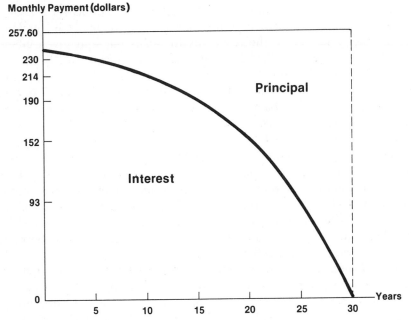

Monthly Payment (dollars)

Principal

Interest

Years

EXHIBIT 9–5
Loan Balance Pattern

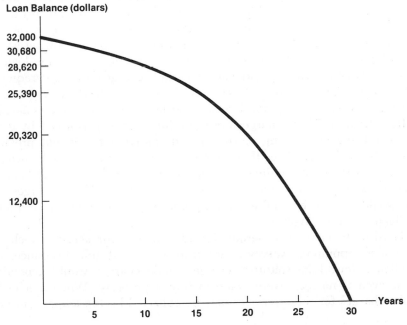

Loan Balance (dollars)

Years

10 years the borrower decides to sell the property and to buy another one. In order to do so, the existing loan must be paid off. How much will have to be repaid to the lender after 10 years? To answer this question a series of *loan balance factors* has been developed and included in the tables provided in the Appendix for loans made at given interest rates. Column 6 titled: *"Bal 25 Year Loan"* shows the loan balance as a percentage of the initial loan amount; for a loan with an *original 25-year term,* in each year after the loan is originated. Column 7 in these same tables shows loan balance factors in each year remaining on loans with an *original* term of *30 years.*

To determine how much loan principal our borrower must repay after 10 years, we go to column 7 in the 9 percent tables, since we are dealing with a 30-year loan, and look down until the row corresponding to 10 years (120 months) is found. The loan balance factor shown in that position is 0.8943. To determine the balance remaining on a $32,000, 30-year loan after 10 years, we multiply the loan balance factor, 0.8943, by $32,000 and the loan balance $28,618 is determined. The borrower must repay the lender $28,618 after 10 years.

Loan Closing Costs and Effective Borrowing Costs—Fully Amortized Loans Understanding loan closing costs is interesting and vital for professionals associated with the real estate industry. Closing costs are incurred in many types of real estate financing, including residential property, income property, construction, and land development loans. Closing costs can generally be placed in one of three categories: statutory costs, third-party charges, and additional finance charges. These categories are discussed more fully in Chapter 10; however, they are briefly reviewed here in order to point out their relationship to effective borrowing costs.

Statutory Costs and Third-Party Charges. When a mortgage loan is closed between borrower and lender, certain charges for legal requirements pertaining to transfer taxes, recording of the deed and mortgage, as well as other fees required by state and local law, are usually charged to the borrower. These charges are made for services performed by governmental agencies for the borrower and consequently do not provide income to the lender. Since these statutory charges do not provide income to the lender, they generally should not be included as additional finance charges as they do not affect the cost of borrowing. These charges by law would have to be paid even if a property were bought for cash and no financing was involved.

Third-party charges generally include charges for services such as legal fees, appraisals, surveys, pest inspection, and title insurance, to mention a few. Like statutory charges, these charges would generally occur even if no loan were made to buy a property. When a loan is made, charges for these services may be collected by the lender, but are in turn paid out to third parties, hence they do not constitute additional income to the lender. As such, they are not charges associated with financing the real estate being purchased.

Additional Finance Charges.   Another category of closing costs which does affect the cost of borrowing is additional finance charges levied by the lender. These charges constitute additional income to the lender and as a result must be included as a part of the cost of borrowing. Generally, lenders refer to these additional charges as *loan origination fees.* Such fees are intended to cover expenses incurred by the lender for processing loan applications, preparation of loan documentation and amortization schedules, obtaining credit reports, and other expenses which the lender feels should be recovered from the borrower. Sometimes these charges are itemized separately in the loan closing statement and sometimes they are grouped under the general category of loan origination fees.

Another item, which may be itemized separately or included in the over-all category of loan origination fees, is *loan discount.*[1] This charge also represents an additional finance charge but its sole purpose is to raise the yield on a mortgage loan. In the context of real estate lending, loan discounting amounts to a borrower and lender negotiating the terms of a loan based on a certain loan amount. The lender then discounts the loan by actually disbursing an amount of funds less than the contract loan amount to the borrower. Payments made by the borrower, however, are based on the contract amount of the loan. For example, assume a borrower and lender agree on a $40,000 loan at 8 percent interest for 20 years. The lender actually disburses $39,000 to the borrower by including a loan discount charge of $1,000. The borrower is required to repay $40,000 at 8 percent interest for 20 years. Since the borrower actually receives $39,000 but must repay $40,000 plus interest, it is clear that the effective borrowing cost to the buyer is greater than 8 percent.

Why do practices such as discounting exist, since any additional lending costs could be recovered by the lender by charging the borrower a higher interest rate which would be adequate to cover these costs? Many reasons for these practices have been advanced. One reason set forth by lenders is that mortgage rates tend to be somewhat "sticky" in upward and downward moves. This means that if the prevailing rate

---

[1] Lenders in some areas of the country refer to loan discount as "discount points" or simply "points." In conventional mortgage lending, the borrower usually pays this charge, which adds to financing costs. When FHA and VA mortgages are involved, however, the seller of the property pays the discount points. In this chapter we are concerned with conventional lending situations where the borrower pays the loan discount as a part of origination fees.

is 8 percent and market pressures push upward on rates, rather than one lender making a move to perhaps 8.25 percent, 8 percent may still be quoted as the loan rate but a higher origination fee (or loan discount if itemized separately) may be charged. This practice will be continued until the lender is sure that all competition is charging 8.25 percent. Although charging extra fees may amount to the same thing as charging an effective rate of 8.25 percent, lenders prefer this practice to increasing the interest rate. In this case it is obvious that a higher origination fee is used primarily to adjust the interest rate charged rather than to recover additional expenses associated with the loan.

Another reason for this practice may stem from the fact that conventional lenders compete with lenders making FHA-insured loans. Contract interest rates on FHA-insured loans are regulated by the Secretary of the Department of Housing and Urban Development. Changes in rates allowed on FHA-insured loans tend to lag behind those of conventional lenders (i.e., those lenders who make loans without FHA insurance). Consequently, when a borrower shops around for a mortgage loan, a rate may be quoted based on an FHA-insured loan, which is regulated, and it may well be lower than the market rate on conventional loans. So rather than quote a higher rate of interest, conventional lenders may quote the same rate as lenders making FHA-insured loans, and "make up the difference" between the current actual market rate and the regulated FHA rate by charging a loan discount or origination fee.[2]

Another reason for loan discount fees is that lenders believe that in this way they can better tailor their return on the loan to the risk they take. For example, some riskier loans may require more time and expense to process and control than others. Since this may not be fully anticipated by the lender when the loan application is made, an interest rate may be quoted on the loan with the understanding that any "extraordinary" charges will be passed on to the borrower with a higher origination or loan discount fee.

In any event, the practice of using loan origination and discount fees has historically prevailed throughout the lending industry. It is important to understand (1) that these charges increase borrowing costs, and (2) how to include them in computing effective borrowing costs on loan alternatives when financing any real estate transaction.

Origination Fees and Borrowing Costs. To illustrate loan origination fees and their effects on borrowing costs in more detail, consider the fol-

---

[2] It may appear that if this practice is followed by conventional lenders, a borrower will be better off with an FHA-insured mortgage because it usually carries a lower, regulated interest rate. This will not necessarily be true because a lender making FHA-insured loans also charges a discount fee, or "points," which must be paid by the seller of a property. Athough this fee is usually recovered by the seller of a property in the form of a higher selling price to the buyer, the lender will still quote the fixed FHA rate to the borrower (buyer).

lowing problem: A borrower is considering the purchase of a $50,000 property, and would like to finance it with a $40,000, fully amortized loan for 30 years. A lender is contacted who is willing to make the $40,000 loan at 8.5 percent interest for 30 years. The borrower inquires whether any loan origination fee will be charged. The lender indicates that an origination fee of 2¼ percent of the loan amount will be charged. What is the effective interest rate[3] on the loan?

We structure the problem by first determining the amount of the origination fee or 2.25% × $40,000 = $900. Second, we compute the monthly mortgage payments based on $40,000 for 30 years at 8.5 percent. The loan constant from column 5, for 30 years, in the 8.5 percent tables in the Appendix is 0.00769. The monthly mortgage payments will be $40,000 × 0.00769 or $307.60. Now we can determine the effect of the origination fee on the interest rate being charged as follows:

Amount actually loaned:
    Contractual loan amount $40,000
    Less: Origination fee   900
    Net cash disbursed $39,100

Amount to be repaid:
    Based on $40,000 contractual loan amount,
    $307.60 for 30 years.

In other words, the amount actually disbursed by the lender will be $39,100, but the repayment will be made on the basis of $40,000 plus interest at 8.5 percent, in the amount of $307.60 a month. Consequently, the lender earns a yield on the $39,100 actually disbursed, which must be greater than 8.5 percent. To solve for the effective interest cost on the loan we proceed as follows:

Monthly payment × (IF, PV of $1 per mo., ?%, 30 yrs.) = Amount disbursed
    $307.60 × (IF, PV of $1 per mo., ?%, 30 yrs.) − $39,100
        IF, PV of $1 per mo., ?%, 30 yrs. = $39,100 ÷ $307.60
        IF, PV of $1 per mo., ?%, 30 yrs. = 127.113

Using the procedure in the previous chapter, when solving for yields on investment *annuities,* this calculation results in an interest factor of 127.113.[4] We know that the loan will be outstanding for a period of 30 years. Therefore, to find the actual interest cost of this loan we want

---

[3] The effective interest rate referred to here is the effective cost to the borrower. However, the effective interest rate also means the internal rate of return or investment yield to the lender.

[4] Note that anytime a lump sum repayment is not included with an annuity, we can divide the monthly payment directly into the amount of funds disbursed and derive an interest factor, which reduces the effort involved in finding the interest rate. When lump sum payments occur, this division is not possible because two interest factors are involved, one for discounting the monthly payments and one for discounting the lump sum, hence the "trial and error" discounting approach must be used.

to locate an interest factor in column 4 for 30 years which equals 127.113 for some interest rate. A search for this interest rate leads us to column 4 in the 8.75 percent table, which shows an *IF* of 127.113 for 30 years. Consequently, we know that the effective interest cost being charged on this loan is 8.75 percent.[5] This is obviously higher than the 8.5 percent contract interest rate that will appear on the note accompanying the loan.

Truth-in-Lending Requirements and the Annual Percentage Rate. Because of problems involving loan discounts and the potential abuse by some lenders of charging high fees to unwary borrowers, Congress passed a federal Truth-in-Lending Act.[6] As a result of this legislation, the lender must disclose to the borrower the annual percentage rate being charged on the loan. Calculation of the annual percentage rate (*APR*) is made exactly in the manner as shown in the preceding example. The annual percentage rate in this case must be disclosed at closing to the borrower as 8.75 percent. The *APR*, then, does reflect origination fees, and treats them as additional income, or yield, to the lender regardless of what costs, if any, the fees are intended to cover.

Origination Fees and Early Repayment—Fully Amortized Loans An important result of origination fees and early loan payment must now be examined in terms of the effect on interest cost. In this section it will be shown that when origination fees are charged and the loan is paid off before maturity, the effective interest cost of the loan increases even further than when the loan runs for the full term.

To demonstrate this point, we again assume our borrower obtained the $40,000 loan at 8.5 percent for 30 years and was charged a $900 or 2.25 percent loan origination fee. At the end of five years, the borrower decides to sell the property. The loan balance must be repaid at the time the property is sold. What will be the effective interest cost on the loan as a result of both the origination fee and early loan repayment?

To determine the effective interest cost on the loan, we first find the outstanding loan balance after five years to be: 0.9549 (column 7, 5 yrs., 8.5% table in the Appendix) × $40,000 = $38,196. To solve for the yield to the lender (cost to the borrower) we proceed by finding the rate to discount the monthly payments of $307.60 and the lump sum payment of $38,196 by, so that the present value we compute equals $39,100, or the amount actually disbursed by the lender. To do this we proceed as follows:

---

[5] In this case if a lender wanted to know how much of a discount to charge to provide a yield of 8.75%, it would proceed by taking the *IF* in column 4 of the 8.75% table, 127.11 × $307.60 = $39,100, then by subtracting: $40,000 − $39,100 = $900. This amount, $900, would be the loan discount necessary to increase the yield to 8.75%. The $900 when divided by $40,000 gives the percentage amount of the loan discount, or 2.25%.

[6] See Regulation Z of the Federal Reserve Board, 12 C.F.R., Section 226.

$307.60 × (*IF, PV* of $1 per mo., ?%, 5 yrs.)
+ $38,196 × (*IF, PV* of $1, ?%, 5 yrs.) = $39,100

Since $307.60 × 12 = $3,691.20, we can approximate the actual yield by using the simple annual yield $3,691.20 ÷ $39,100 = 0.0944. We also know from Chapter 8, that because the lump sum payment $38,196 is less than the amount loaned $39,100, the simple yield of 0.0944 *overstates* the actual yield. By using our "trial and error" search to find the correct discount rate, we continue:

Discounting by 9.25 percent
$307.60 × (*IF, PV* of $1 per mo., 9.25%, 5 yrs.)
+ $38,196 × (*IF, PV* of $1,9.25%, 5 yrs.)   = *PV*

$307.60 × (47.89295) + $38,196 (0.63083)   = $38,827

Discounting by 9.0 percent
$307.60 × (*IF, PV* of $1 per mo., 9.0%, 5 yrs.)
+ $38,196 × (*IF, PV* of $1, 9.0%, 5 yrs.)   = *PV*

$307.60 × (48.17337) + $38,196 × (0.63870) = $39,214

From these two calculations, we see that when 9.25 percent is used for discounting, our solution is below the amount actually loaned, or $39,100, which means the 9.25 rate is too high. When 9 percent is tried, the solution is $39,214 which is over $39,100. We know the actual yield falls between 9 percent and 9.25 percent. By interpolating:

1. PV at 9.00% = $39,214
    PV at 9.25% =   38,827
    Difference 0.25% $ 387

2. Desired *PV* = $39,100

3. Difference between highest *PV* in 1 and desired *PV* in 2:
    $39,214 − $39,100 = $114

4. Interpolating:
    $114/$387 × .0025 = .00074
    and .09 + .00074   = .09074 or 9.074%

As a result of early repayment of the loan and the 2.25 percent discount charged at the time of closing, the lender earns an effective yield (borrower pays an effective interest cost) of about 9.074 percent. The reason for such a large increase over the 8.75 yield when the origination fee alone was considered, is that the amount actually disbursed is $39,100 and the amount being repaid is based on $40,000 over a 30-year period. However, the loan repayment occurs sooner, after five years. Therefore, the amount of the discount, $900, is paid to the lender within five years rather than 30 years, and is worth more.[7]

Another point to be made here is that the 9.074 yield is *not* reported as being the "annual percentage rate" required under the Truth-in-Lending Act. This is because neither the borrower nor lender knows for certain that the loan will be repaid ahead of schedule. Therefore, 8.75 will still be reported as the "annual percentage rate" and 8.5 will be the contract rate, although the actual yield to the lender in this case is 9.074 percent. It should be remembered that the "annual percentage rate" (APR) under Truth-in-Lending requirements never takes into account early repayment of loans. The APR calculation takes into account origination fees, but always assumes the loan is paid off at maturity.[8]

Prepayment Penalties—Fully Amortized Loans Another common provision in many mortgage loan agreements is a prepayment penalty if the loan is repaid before some specified time limit. The rationale for this penalty is that the lender has committed to extend funds for a specified time, 30 years in our present example. Early payment for the lender represents an unanticipated inflow of funds that may or may not be readily reinvested. Use of prepayment penalties is widespread in periods when mortgage rates are stable, or are expected to decline. This is true because lenders may have to reinvest in lower yielding opportunities. In recent years, however, with continued increases in mortgage interest rates, most lenders have been delighted when early payments occurred, as they have been able to loan funds out again at higher rates of interest.

The final problem to be considered with fully amortized loans is the effective mortgage loan yield (interest cost) when *both a loan discount fee and a prepayment penalty* are charged on the loan. This combination is used with considerable frequency in practice, consequently one should be familiar with the combined effect.

To illustrate, we consider both the effects of the 2.25 percent loan discount *and* a 2 percent prepayment penalty on the outstanding loan balance for the $40,000, 30-year loan with a contract interest rate of 8.5 percent used in the preceding section. We assume the loan is repaid early, at the end of five years, and would like to determine the effective interest cost to the borrower (yield to the lender). To solve for the

---

[7] It should also be pointed out that the longer the mortgage loan is outstanding the lower the effective interest cost is in this case. The effective interest cost, for example, could range from 9.072% if repaid after 5 years to 8.75% if repaid after 30 years. Hence the effective interest cost will vary depending on when the loan is repaid.

[8] It has also been suggested that lenders use origination fees rather than charge a higher interest rate when a loan is made because most loans are repaid early. By using origination fees, the effective yield to the lender will be higher; however, the APR will not reflect the higher yield if loan repayment occurs early. The borrower may not be aware of this possibility. Hence, one can see the importance of the methodology being presented here.

yield, mortgage funds actually disbursed in this case will be $40,000 less the origination fee of $900, or $39,100. Taking the loan discount fee into account, we want to find the discount rate which when used to discount the series of monthly payments of $307.60, plus the outstanding loan balance of $38,196 and the prepayment penalty of $764 (2% of $38,196) will result in a present value equal to the amount of funds actually disbursed, $39,100. This is done as follows:

$307.60 × (IF, PV of $1 per mo., ?%, 5 yrs.)
+ (38,196 + $764) × (IF, PV of $1, ?%, 5 yrs.) = $39,100

Using the simple yield approximation: ($307.60 × 12) ÷ 39,100, we again obtain 0.0944. We should also note that the lump sum composed of the outstanding loan balance and the prepayment penalty, $38,960, is very close to the $39,100 used in the simple yield calculation. Hence actual yield on the loan is only slightly overstated by the simple yield. Proceeding with the calculations:

Discounting by 9.25 percent:
$307.60 (47.89295) + $38,960 (0.63083) = PV
$14,732 + $24,577 = $39,309

Discounting by 9.5 percent:
.$307.60 (47.61482) + $38,960 (0.62305) = PV
$14,646 + $24,274 = $38,920

From calculations made at 9.25 and 9.50 percent, it can be seen that the desired present value of $39,100 falls between $39,309 and $38,920. Interpolating provides a closer approximation of 9.38 percent as the actual yield (cost) to the lender (borrower).

In this case the APR will be disclosed at 8.75, which reflects the loan discount only, not the prepayment penalty, and assumes the loan is repaid at the end of 30 years. The actual yield computed here is 9.38 percent which is a marked difference from both the loan contract rate of 8.5 percent and the disclosed APR of 8.75 percent.

Partially Amortized Loans Depending on the circumstances surrounding the nature of the real estate transaction, a partially amortized mortgage loan may be called for. This payment pattern works as follows: the loan contract specifies the loan amount, interest rate, and maturity as usual; however, the loan payment calculation is made by assuming a longer loan repayment schedule with the provision that the loan balance outstanding on the maturity date is to be repaid in a lump sum.

To illustrate the use of a partially amortized loan, assume that an individual owns a group of rental income properties with a total appraised value of $500,000. These properties are free and clear of debt. The owner is interested in acquiring some attractively located unimproved land that might be profitably developed over the next ten years. If the individual does not develop it, the land could be sold to another developer after it appreciates in value. To finance the acquisition of this land, which will cost $250,000, the buyer decides to borrow against the rental income properties, which are presently free of debt, by obtaining a mortgage loan. A lender is found willing to lend $250,000, or 50 percent of the appraised value of the rental properties, for 10 years. This coincides with the time that the borrower thinks it will take either to develop or to sell the land acquired for a gain.

Two conditions are encountered in this situation which make the use of a partially amortized loan possible. The first condition is that the borrower is borrowing only 50 percent of the value of the appraised value of the rental properties, thereby providing the lender with collateral value ($500,000) considerably over the loan amount ($250,000). Second, since the unimproved land will not provide any monthly income to help pay the mortgage loan, the income from the rental property being used as collateral must ultimately be used to make the mortgage payments. The borrower does not wish to use a large amount of income from the rental properties to pay off a mortgage loan on the undeveloped property; he may expect to develop or sell the undeveloped property in ten years at a large profit. Under such conditions, the borrower may be able to obtain a partially amortized mortgage loan from the lender. In this way, the expected cash inflow from the sale or development of the property will coincide with repaying the large loan balance due on the mortgage. To illustrate further, assume the lender agrees to lend $250,000 for 10 years; however, after negotiation with the borrower, the lender agrees to compute the monthly mortgage payments on the basis of a *25-year* amortization schedule with the unpaid balance of the loan due after 10 years. This unpaid balance is referred to as a balloon payment and the note evidencing the debt is referred to as a "balloon note" because of the large payment due to the lender at the end of ten years. Because of the added risk to the lender, who must estimate the ability of the borrower to make the large balloon payment after ten years, the interest rate on this loan will be 10 percent.

Payments on a Partially Amortized Loan. To analyze the effect of this type of financing we first consider the difference in mortgage payments between a fully amortized and the partially amortized loan.

Payments with 10-year maturity:
$250,000 × (loan constant, 10%, 10 yrs.) = Monthly payment
$250,000 × 0.01322 = $3,305

Payments under 25-year repayment schedule:
$250,000 × (loan constant, 10%, 25 yrs.) = Monthly payment
$250,000 × 0.00909 = $2,272.50

If the lender agrees to a 25-year schedule, the monthly payment will be reduced by $1,032.50 per month, or $12,390 per year, thereby easing the cash flow on the borrower during the years that the unimproved property is held. But since the loan payments are calculated on a 25-year basis, a sizable loan balance will remain outstanding after 10 years. This loan balance is found as if the loan were made for 25 years and repaid early (after 10 years). This is done by going to the 10 percent tables in the Appendix, and from column 6 dropping down to the row corresponding to 10 years. The loan balance factor at that point is 0.8456 which we convert to the actual loan balance by multiplying it by the original $250,000 loan amount. This results in a loan balance of $211,400 which is due after ten years.

Therefore, in this example, if the loan is granted, the borrower will pay $2,272.50 per month for ten years and make a balloon payment of $211,400 at the end of the tenth year. Since there is no origination fee or prepayment penalty in the transaction, the true interest cost (yield) on the loan is 10 percent.

Loan Origination Fees—Partially Amortized Loans As with fully amortized loans, origination fees are sometimes charged on partially amortized loans. Such charges serve to increase the effective loan yield to the lender, or interest cost to the borrower. To solve for the effective loan yield on a partially amortized loan when discount fees are charged, the procedure is virtually the same as solving for yields on fully amortized loans except that, by design, with partially amortized loans some outstanding loan balance must always be considered.

To illustrate the effect of these fees on effective yields for a partially amortized loan, we return to the example of the $250,000 loan on unimproved property, made for 10 years at 10 percent interest, with monthly payments computed on the basis of a 25-year loan amortization schedule. We now assume that the lender charges a 3.0 percent origination fee. What will be the effective yield on the loan if it is repaid after ten years?

Computing the yield in this case first requires that we determine the amount of funds actually disbursed by the lender. This is $250,000 less 3.0 percent, or $242,500. Recall from the previous example that the monthly payments computed on a 25-year basis were $2,272.50 and the outstanding loan balance at the end of 10 years was $211,400. The yield on the loan will be the interest rate which, after discounting the monthly payments and outstanding loan balance, provides a computed present value equal to the amount of funds actually disbursed, or $242,500. To solve the yield we proceed as follows:

$$\$2,272.50 \times (IF, PV \text{ of } \$1, \text{ per mo., } ?\%, 10 \text{ yrs.})$$
$$+ \$211,400 \times (IF, PV \text{ of } \$1, ?\%, 10 \text{ yrs.}) = \$242,500$$

Computing a simple annual yield, to begin our search for the effective yield, results in: ($2,272.50 × 12) ÷ $242,500 = 11.25 percent. Since the lump sum repayment of $211,400 is less than the amount actually loaned, this simple yield overstates the effective yield. By trial and error:

Discounting at 10.75 percent:
$2,272.50 × (73.34675) + $211,400 × (0.34294) = $239,178

Discounting by 10.50 percent:
$2,272.50 × (74.10975) + $211,400 × (0.35154) = $242,730

Since the desired present value or amount of funds actually disbursed, $242,500, falls between the present values computed at 10.75 and 10.50 percent, the effective yield lies between those two yields. Interpolation yields a more exact solution of 10.52 percent. The *APR* disclosed in this case would also be 10.52 percent. This yield is obviously higher than the contract rate of 10.0 percent.

Loan Origination Fees and Early Repayment—Partially Amortized Loans

The final example included in this section dealing with partially amortized loans considers the effect of early repayment on loan yields. Prepayment penalties could be included in a discussion of partially amortized loans; however, in practice these penalties are rarely employed. This is true because if a partially amortized loan is repaid early, it may very well be by reason of a decision by the borrower to develop a property before the loan maturity date. In many cases the same lender and borrower may be anticipating additional financing for development of the property. Since this possibility is anticipated when the loan is made, a prepayment penalty is difficult to justify. In addition, a borrower may not be at all pleased if a prepayment penalty is charged, particularly if the borrower must negotiate for more funds, perhaps with the same lender, to develop the property immediately after the balloon payment is made.

To illustrate the effects of loan origination fees and early repayment on partially amortized loans, we reconsider the $250,000 mortgage loan made on the developed rental income properties used to buy undeveloped land. In that case the term of the loan was 10 years, the interest rate was 10 percent and the repayment schedule used to determine monthly payments was 25 years. Assuming the lender charges a 3 percent loan discount fee and the loan is repaid at the end of five years, what will be the effective yield (cost) to the lender (borrower)?

To determine the yield in this case, we recall that the amount of funds actually disbursed by the lender was $242,500. The loan balance after five years is $235,400, determined by obtaining the loan balance factor in the 10 percent table (column 6) after five years or 0.9416 and multiplying it by the original loan amount of $250,000. Since the monthly payments are $2,272.50, the effective yield on this loan can be found by searching for the interest rate, which when used to discount the monthly and lump sum payments, results in a present value of $242,500. This is done as follows:

$$\$2,272.50 \times (IF, PV \text{ of } \$1 \text{ per mo., } ?\%, 5 \text{ yrs.})$$
$$+ \ \$235,400 \times (IF, PV \text{ of } \$1, ?\%, 5 \text{ yrs.}) = \$242,500$$

Using the simple average yield approximation $2,272.50 \times 12 = $27,270 per year, or a simple yield of $27,270 ÷ $242,500 = 11.25%. Since the $235,400 lump sum payment is less than the $242,500 disbursed, the simple yield again overstates the true yield.

Discounting by 11 percent:
$$\$2,272.50 \ (45.99303) + \$235,400 \ (0.57840) = PV$$
$$\$104,519 + \$136,155 = \$240,675$$

Discounting by 10¾ percent:
$$\$2,272.50 \ (46.25785) + \$235,400 \ (0.58561) = PV$$
$$\$105,121 + \$137,853 = \$242,974$$

The desired present value $242,500 falls between the present values calculated at 11 percent and 10.75 percent. Interpolating yields a solution closer to 10.80 percent. This compares with the contract rate of 10 percent and the *APR* of 10.52 computed when the discount alone was considered.

Demand Loans and Short-Term Real Estate Financing This section deals with payment patterns and yield determination on loans used under special circumstances when short-term borrowing is necessary. Circumstances that may require short-term financing include: interim borrowing by someone who has contracted to buy a new property while waiting to sell his present property, borrowing for minor property improvements that an owner wants to pay off in a short period of time, and borrowing on a short-term basis while waiting for a decline in long-term interest rates to refinance long-term. The reasons why a borrower may desire interim real estate financing are numerous. Successful professionals involved in real estate finance must be aware of a wide variety of financing patterns. Sometimes a combination of short-term and long-term financing techniques is required to complete a transaction.

Demand Loans—Interest-Only Monthly Payments Demand loans[9] differ greatly from fully amortized and partially amortized loans. With demand loans, in most cases no monthly amortization of loan principal is involved and the full amount of loan principal is repaid at maturity. Monthly payments are usually made on these loans but they are "interest-only" payments and generally do not include any repayment of loan principal. To illustrate the use of a demand loan, consider an individual

---

[9] The term "demand loan" arises from the fact that the loan is short-term in nature and may include a provision that the loan is callable or must be repaid to the lender on demand without notice.

who wants to borrow $10,000 for a period of one year to make an improvement on a property. A loan with a bank is negotiated at 9 percent interest with "interest-only" payments to be made monthly and full repayment of the $10,000 principal at the end of one year. How much will the monthly payment be? What will be the actual yield to the lender?

Since no amortization of principal occurs on this loan, the monthly payments are simply "interest only" and are calculated as: $10,000 × 0.09/12 = $75 per month. Therefore, 12 monthly payments of $75 plus one lump sum payment of $10,000 will be made at the end of the 12th month. The yield to the lender is effectively 9 percent. This is obvious since the full amount of the loan principal is outstanding for one year with no prepayment penalties or origination fees and interest is assessed at an annual rate of 9 percent compounded monthly.

Prepaid Interest—Demand Loans A practice peculiar to demand loans, which is frequently used by banks, is a requirement that all interest on term loans be prepaid when the loan funds are disbursed. Since all interest is prepaid, there are usually no monthly payments. Only one payment is made at the end of the loan period.

The practice of requiring interest to be prepaid is similar to charging an origination fee in terms of its effect on loan yield. To illustrate the use of prepaid interest, let us assume that the borrower in our previous $10,000, 9 percent, one-year loan example is required to prepay all interest. In other words, $10,000 × 0.09 = $900, or $75 × 12 months = $900, will be prepaid at closing. The actual amount disbursed will be $9,100 at closing and the amount repaid will be $10,000 at the end of the first year with no monthly payments between the two points in time. The effective yield in this case is found by discounting the lump sum repayment of $10,000 made at the end of the year by an interest rate such that the computed present value equals the amount actually disbursed, or $9,100. This can be done as follows:

$$\$10,000 \ (IF, PV \text{ of } \$1, ?\%, 12 \text{ mos.}) = \$9,100$$
$$(IF, PV \text{ of } \$1, ?\%, 12 \text{ mos.}) = \$9,100 \div 10,000$$
$$(IF, PV \text{ of } \$1, ?\%, 12 \text{ mos.}) = 0.9100$$

This computation results in an $IF = 0.9100$. Looking to column 3 in the 9.5 percent interest tables for one year an IF of 0.90971 is located. This IF when rounded is effectively 0.91. Hence the effective interest rate is 9.5 percent. The APR would also be disclosed as 9.5 percent. The yield on this loan is higher than the contract rate because interest ($900) is charged as though the borrower actually has the use of $10,000 during the year. In fact, the borrower has the use of $9,100 and is really paying interest of $900 on that amount, not $10,000.

As in previous examples, if the loan is repaid early, the yield increases sharply. For example, if it is repaid after six months, the yield increases to 19 percent or double the 9.5 percent yield computed for the full term on the loan. This can be seen as follows:

$10,000 (*IF, PV* of $1, ?%, 6 mos.) = $9,100
              (*IF, PV* of $1, ?%, 6 mos.) = $9,100 ÷ 10,000
              (*IF, PV* of $1, ?%, 6 mos.) = 0.91

Looking in the interest rate tables for an *IF* equal to 0.91 for 6 months in column 3, it can be verified that the 19 percent tables provide the *IF* we are seeking.

Note that a full year's interest payment of $900 has been collected in advance and the funds have been used for only six months. For this reason, when prepaid interest is charged on a loan, the borrower should always be aware of how early repayments are to be treated in the loan contract. If no reduction of interest is provided for when early repayment occurs, borrowing costs increase considerably.

Prepaid Interest, Monthly Principal Amortization—Demand Loans A variation sometimes encountered when prepaid interest is charged is a requirement by the lender that monthly payments providing pro rata reductions of loan principal be made. For example, in the case of our $10,000, 9 percent, one-year loan, in addition to the interest charges being prepaid, monthly payments of $833.33 ($10,000 ÷ 12) may be required, instead of the $10,000 payment after one year. In this case to compute the effective loan yield, the $833.33 monthly payments must be discounted by an interest rate which makes the calculated present value equal to $9,100, or the loan amount actually disbursed. Solving for the yield:

$833.33 (*IF, PV* of $1 per mo., ?%, 12 mos.) = $9,100
           (*IF, PV* of $1 per mo., ?%, 12 mos.) = $9,100 ÷ $833.33 = 10.9200

The interest factor in this case equals 10.9200. Looking to column 4 for 12 months for various interest rates, we find that the effective yield is between 17 and 18 percent, or 17.8 percent after interpolation. The yield in this case increases substantially because the simple interest calculation ($10,000 × 0.09 = $900) presupposes that the full $10,000 is repaid at the end of one year. In fact, when monthly payments of principal are required, the borrower pays full interest charges even though the full $10,000 is not available for use during the full year.

Both the *APR* and the effective yield in this case would be 17.8 percent and if state laws specifying usury rates are not violated, this type of loan can be made.[10] Obviously, if the loan is prepaid the effective yield will rise even higher.

---

[10] Many states, though not all, have enacted laws establishing the maximum rates that lenders may charge individuals. These laws are referred to as usury laws and violation can result in fines or imprisonment. Usually, these laws affect only lenders and individuals, not corporate borrowers.

"Add-On Interest"—Demand Loans The final type of demand loan and payment pattern to be considered is the "add-on interest" demand loan with monthly payments. This loan gets its name from the fact that simple annual interest is computed and "added on" to the amount loaned, then the resulting sum is divided by the number of months over which the loan is to be outstanding, to arrive at the monthly payment.

To illustrate the use of "add-on" interest in our example, simple annual interest is computed as 9 percent of $10,000, or $900. The $900 is then "added on" to the principal of $10,000 to arrive at $10,900 which is divided by 12 to arrive at monthly payments of $908.33. Although the contract rate of interest is 9 percent, the effective rate is computed by discounting the monthly series of payments, $908.33, by an appropriate interest rate until the present value computed is equal to the amount of funds disbursed, or $10,000. This can be seen as:

$908.33 (*IF*, *PV* of $1 per mo., ?%, 12 mos.) = $10,000
    (*IF*, *PV* of $1 per mo., ?%, 12 mos.) = $10,000 ÷ $908.33 = 11.0092

From column 3 in the interest rate tables, it can be determined that the interest factor 11.0092 for 12 months, falls between 16 and 17 percent. By interpolating, the actual yield is close to 16.2 percent. The reason why the effective interest rate is so much higher than the contract rate is that simple interest when expressed as an annual rate, will equal the effective yield only when both the full interest payment and the loan repayment are made at the end of the year. In this case the borrower does not have full use of the funds for one year because the loan amortization and interest payments are made during the year. But interest is computed ($10,000 × 0.09) as though the borrower had use of the funds for the full year.

Variable Interest Rate Mortgages

This chapter concludes with a discussion of mortgages that have an interest rate that varies in accordance with an index agreed upon in advance by borrower and lender. Hence the term *variable rate mortgages* (*VRMs*). Although these mortgages are not used as frequently as fixed rate mortgages, they are growing in importance in real estate financing.

The use *VRMs* has come about because many lenders have grown reluctant to lend at fixed interest rates for relatively long periods of time. Because of unanticipated sharp rises in prices (inflation) and interest rates after loans are made, lenders have been looking more and more to *VRMs*. Rates on *VRMs* are tied to some market index of interest rates, so that as prices and interest rates rise, income to the lender (cost to the borrower) increases automatically because the mortgage rate rises. This, in turn, provides additional funds to be loaned on new mortgages.

To illustrate the payment and yield characteristics of variable rate mortgages, we assume a borrower desires to purchase a $50,000 property and finances it with a $40,000 variable rate mortgage loan at 8 percent interest for 25 years. The lender and borrower agree that the interest rate will be tied to some external market interest rate index,[11] and can be adjusted at the end of each year, either up or down as the index warrants. They further agree that in no event can the interest rate on the mortgage be increased by more than a total 2.5 percent from the original 8 percent rate. Generally, there will be no discount, origination fees, or prepayment penalties associated with a variable rate mortgage, as there is little need for the lender to charge additional fees in light of the fact that the VRM will usually provide a current, competitive yield on the loan investment.[12]

To demonstrate what happens when the variable rate changes, we assume that the market index changes and the new variable rate at the end of the first year increases to 8.5 percent. What possibilities face the borrower at this point? This depends on whether or not the VRM agreement contains either one or both of the following options: (1) to increase the monthly mortgage payment or (2) to keep the mortgage payment constant and extend the maturity on the loan. In most cases, the only option open to borrowers will be option (1); that is, increased monthly payments. However, some VRMs do contain option (2) with the possibility of extending the maturity (usually only to 35 years), and it will also be considered here.

Increased Payment Option–VRMs. Looking to Exhibit 9–6, the procedure for determining new monthly loan payments is illustrated.

EXHIBIT 9–6
Determining New Monthly Payments on a Variable Interest Rate Mortgage Loan

Option 1—Increased monthly payments
 Original mortgage $40,000
 Interest rate 8%
 Terms 25 years
 Monthly payment: $40,000 × (loan constant, 8%, 25 yrs.)
$$= \$40,000 \times (0.00772) = \$308.80$$
 Change in VRM rate from 8%–8.5% end of year 1
 a. Determine—Loan Balance end of year 1
  Loan Bal. Factor, 8%, 25 yr. loan, end of 1 yr. × loan = Mortgage balance
$$0.9869 \times \$40,000 = \$39,476$$
 b. Determine—new monthly payments—end of year 1
  Loan Bal. end of year 1 × (loan constant, 8.5%, 24 yrs.) = New monthly payment
$$\$39,476 \times 0.00815 = \$321.73$$

---

[11] Such as the average yield of U.S. Treasury bills and AAA-rated corporate bonds.

[12] These provisions are fairly common with VRM's. The specific limits imposed on adjusting the rates (annually, semi-annually, etc.) and maximum increases in rates may differ.

The first step requires the determination of the loan balance based on the original mortgage terms of 8 percent for 25 years after the first year when the adjustment occurs. Then the new monthly payment can be computed by finding the new loan constant corresponding to an 8.5 percent mortgage loan for 24 years, or 0.00815. When multiplied by the loan balance of $39,476, the new monthly payment of $321.73 is determined. This payment is $12.93 per month higher than the original payment of $308.80. The $321.73 will be paid monthly for 24 years or until the next adjustment occurs. If an adjustment is necessary at the end of the second year, the new monthly payments will be based on the loan balance at that time. That balance will be the balance after one year on a $39,476 loan at 8.5 percent interest made for 24 years. These were the relevant terms in force at the end of year one. The new loan constant, based on the new variable rate, will be applied to that balance to compute the new monthly payment. This process will be repeated each time an adjustment in the interest rate is required until the loan is repaid.

Increased Maturity Option–VRMs. Should the mortgage contain the option to extend the loan maturity while keeping the monthly loan payment constant, the procedure for determining the new maturity period can be seen in Exhibit 9–7.

EXHIBIT 9–7
Determining the New Maturity on a Variable Interest Rate Mortgage Loan

a. Loan Balance end of year 1 (from Exhibit 9–6): $39,476
b. Original monthly payment (to be kept constant): $308.80
c. Determine new loan constant necessary to provide an 8.5% loan yield:

$$\frac{\$308.80}{\$39,476} = 0.00782$$

d. Number of years and months corresponding to a loan yield of 8.5% *and* a loan constant of 0.00782 (from Column 5, 8.5% tables):

Approximately 28 years

Since the borrower has the option to keep the $308.80 monthly payment the same while the mortgage rate has increased to 8.5 percent, it is clear that a greater number of monthly payments will be required for the lender to earn the increased yield. By dividing the loan balance at the end of the first year, $39,476, by the desired $308.80 constant monthly payments as shown in Exhibit 9–7, a new loan constant, 0.00782, is derived. The significance of this new loan constant is that since the new mortgage yield must be 8.5 percent, and the payment remains at $308.80, the new term of the loan can be found by using the loan constant.

The new maturity period can be ascertained by looking to the 8.5 percent table in the Appendix, locating column 5, and looking down the column until the loan constant closest to 0.00782 is found. The new maturity of the loan can then be determined by following the row in which the loan constant appears over to the column denoting years. Note that the loan constant closest to 0.00782 is the 0.00781 constant corresponding to 28 years. The new loan maturity will be slightly less than 28 years from the beginning of the second year.[13] Consequently, the borrower will pay $308.80 for approximately four extra years, from year 24 through year 28, if the variable rate increases to 8.5 percent.

Usually a provision limiting the maturity extension to 35 years is included in VRM loan contracts. After the maturity reaches 35 years, increased monthly payments are required. The reason for the 35-year limit is that should the interest rate move upward sharply in a short period of time, the maturity period could easily increase to 50 years and beyond. Most lenders would consider the future estimated collateral value of the property, plus the fact that the loan balance is declining too slowly, a great risk and would therefore demand a limit to the maturity extension to avoid it.

QUESTIONS

1. What are the major differences between fully amortized, partially amortized, and demand loans?

2. What does the term amortization mean?

3. Why are the monthly payments in the beginning months of a fully amortized mortgage loan comprised of a higher proportion of interest when compared to principal repayment?

4. What are loan closing costs? How can they be categorized? Which of the categories influence borrowing costs and why?

5. When a loan is repaid early, does this ever affect the effective interest cost to the borrower?

6. Why do lenders charge origination fees, especially loan discount fees?

7. What are the Truth-In-Lending Act and the annual percentage rate (APR)?

8. Does the annual percentage rate (APR) always equal the effective borrowing cost?

9. With respect to demand loans, differentiate between "interest only" and prepaid interest requirements. How might each type of payment pattern affect the cost of borrowing?

10. What is a variable rate mortgage? How does it work? What happens to a borrower's mortgage payment when the variable rate changes?

---

[13] A more exact solution can be gained by interpolating, or with a more detailed set of mortgage tables. The new loan maturity is about 27 years and 11 months in this case.

CASE PROBLEMS

1.   Ms. Alice Cooper makes a fully amortized mortgage loan for $40,000 at 9 percent interest for 25 years. What will be the monthly payment on the loan?

2.   Mr. John Brown made a 30 year mortgage loan 5 years ago for $20,000 at 7 percent interest. He would like to pay down the mortgage balance by $5,000.

   a.   Assuming he can reduce his monthly mortgage payments, what will the new mortgage payment be?

   b.   Assuming the loan maturity is shortened, what will the new loan maturity be?

3.   Mr. James Doe wants to buy a property for $60,000 and obtain an 80 percent loan for $48,000. A lender indicates that a $48,000 loan can be obtained for 25 years at 8 percent interest; however, a loan origination fee of $1,000 will also be necessary for Mr. Doe to obtain the loan.

   a.   How much will the lender actually disburse?

   b.   What is the effective interest cost to the borrower assuming that the mortgage is paid off after 25 years (full term)?

   c.   What is the annual percentage rate (*APR*) which the lender must disclose to the borrower?

   d.   If Mr. Doe pays off the loan after 5 years, what is the effective interest charge? Why is it different from the *APR* in *c?*

   e.   Assume the lender also imposes a prepayment penalty of 1.5 percent of the outstanding loan balance if the loan is repaid within eight years of closing. If Mr. Doe repays the loan after five years, what is the effective interest cost now? Why is it different from the *APR* in *c?*

4.   A lender is considering what terms should be allowed on a loan to Mr. Charles Good. Current market terms are 8 percent interest for 25 years, and the loan amount Mr. Good has requested is $30,000. The lender believes that extra credit analysis and careful loan control will have to be exercised in this case as Mr. Good has never borrowed such a large sum before. In addition, the lender expects that market rates will move upward very soon, perhaps even before the loan with Mr. Good is closed. To be on the safe side, the lender decides to extend a loan commitment to Mr. Good for $30,000 at 8 percent interest for 25 years; however, he wants to charge a loan origination fee to make the mortgage loan yield 8.25 percent. How much origination fee should be charged?

5.   Ms. Merry Whether of ABC Development Company would like to purchase some unimproved land for future development. Since lenders typically do not lend on unimproved land unless immediate development is planned, Ms. Whether will have to refinance some existing properties and use them as loan collateral. She desires a $50,000 loan on property with a $100,000 value, but would like a partially amortized loan repayment pattern with a balloon note after ten years, when she expects to sell the land for a profit or to refinance for development. The lender offers her a $50,000 loan with monthly payments based on a 25-year amortization schedule at 9 percent interest. However, the loan agreement specifies that the loan will be repaid after 10 years.

    a. Compute the monthly loan payment.

    b. How much will the balloon payment be after 10 years?

    c. If the lender also indicated that a loan origination fee of $775 would be charged, what would be the effective interest rate on this loan?

    d. Assuming the facts in *c* what would be the effective interest rate if the loan is repaid after 5 years. Would this rate be the same as the *APR?*

    6. A borrower makes a short-term demand loan for $2,000 at 9 percent for one year. Monthly, interest only, payments are to be made with the $2,000 principal due after one year.

    a. What will the monthly payments be on such a loan?

    b. What is the effective interest rate?

    7. A borrower makes a short-term demand loan for $5,000 at 10 percent for one year. All interest is to be prepaid at closing and principal is due after one year.

    a. What is the amount of prepaid interest?

    b. What is the effective interest rate on this loan?

    c. What is the effective interest rate if the loan is repaid after 10 months? Is it higher or lower than the *APR?*

    d. Assume that equal monthly payments are also required in addition to the prepaid interest and the loan is not repaid early. What is the effective interest rate now?

    8. Ms. Sally Swift makes a short-term loan for $3,000 at 9 percent for one year. The lender informs her that "add-on" interest will be charged and monthly payments will be equal to total principal and interest prorated over 12 months.

    a. What will the monthly payments be?

    b. What will the effective interest rate be? The *APR?*

    c. If the loan is prepaid early, what will the borrower want to be sure of?

    9. Mr. Robert Bedford makes a variable interest rate loan for $40,000 at 8½ percent for 25 years. One year later the index to which the mortgage rate is tied increases and the new interest rate is determined to be 9 percent.

    a. What will the new payments be beginning in year two? How much greater will the payment be?

    b. If the borrower has the option of keeping monthly payments constant, how much will the loan maturity increase?

10

Financing Residential Properties

Introduction

This chapter deals with the process of seeking long-term conventional mortgage financing for owner-occupied residential properties.[1] The topics included are not only intended to provide a description of steps one might pursue in obtaining financing, but also to provide insights into borrowing and lending risks. In addition, alternatives which commonly confront the borrower in deciding how much to borrow, given different interest rates and loan repayment patterns, are considered in detail. Finally, special financing considerations which frequently confront borrowers after closing, such as refinancing, selling on assumption, and using second mortgages, are included in the appendix to this chapter. Many concepts in this chapter form a basis for discussing the material in the next chapter, which deals with income-producing properties.

Basic Concepts in Loan Risk Analysis

Underwriting The process involved in evaluating a loan by assessing its risk before approval and closing is referred to as *underwriting*. This function is usually performed by a loan officer at a financial institution such as a savings and loan association, commercial bank, mutual savings bank, or mortgage banking company, where a borrower may seek funds. The loan officer performs this function based on an analysis of (1) a loan application submitted by the borrower and (2) the characteristics of the property. This analysis is made also in the context of a lending policy, or guidelines, which a particular institution specifies. In

---

[1] Practices relating to FHA and VA mortgages are considered in Chapter 20.

deciding whether a loan application should be accepted or rejected, the loan officer follows some fundamental concepts in loan risk analysis.

Evaluation of the Borrower   One major concern of the lender is the risk associated with the borrower himself. Since loan conditions require repayment in future periods, the lender must consider the borrower's ability to repay the loan based on present financial condition as well as probable future financial condition. In making the loan analysis the lender may require, as part of this application, basic information on the makeup of the household, a statement of present income, occupations of members of the household, a list of personal assets such as automobiles, savings, stocks, bonds, or life insurance in force, and approval by the applicant to obtain a credit report verifying any of the information in the application.

Borrower Income   As to borrower income, some general policy guidelines are commonly employed by lenders concerning how high income must be in relation to the loan amount sought and the borrower's ability to meet monthly mortgage payments. These guidelines are used as credit standards, which are applied to a credit applicant as a risk indicator. Since the primary concern of the lender is the risk that the borrower will default on the loan, both present and future income are used to gauge the ability of the borrower to repay the loan. Whether a borrower can make monthly payments while at the same time leaving enough "cushion," or excess income, to make normal consumption expenditures over the period of the loan is of primary importance to the lender. However, more emphasis is placed on the current financial status of the applicant as most loan defaults usually occur within three years from closing, due to the borrower's inability to make timely payments.

Commonly employed guidelines used to determine how high income should be in relation to monthly mortgage payments and property value have been developed through statistical studies that show historically what the average household in the United States spends on housing consumption.[2] These guidelines are as follows:

a.   Total monthly mortgage payments generally should not exceed 25 percent of the borrower's gross monthly income.

b.   Total monthly mortgage payments *plus* installment obligations should not exceed 35 percent of gross monthly income (where installment obligations are defined as obligations on which payments must be made for 10 consecutive months).

c.   The value of the dwelling purchased generally should be no more

[2] For a description of the underwriting process see Rod L. Reppe, "Why Residential Lenders Like Mortgage Guaranty Insurance," *Real Estate Review* (Fall 1973), pp. 58–61.

than approximately two and one half times the borrower's gross annual income.

d. The borrower's credit experience must be rated as good, per a credit report or investigation.

e. Job and income stability must be considered in light of mortgage payment and installment obligations.

f. Guidelines *a–f* must also be considered with respect to the borrower's existing assets in savings accounts, life insurance and other assets.

In implementing these guidelines, it should be kept in mind that they are *general statements of policy, not hard and steadfast rules.* Loan policy serves as a *guide* for evaluating many average households seeking credit; however, there may be circumstances peculiar to a particular borrower's financial condition that necessitate *exceptions* to the general policy.

Underwriting Standards—Illustrated   To illustrate the application of loan underwriting standards, if a borrower's income is presently $1,000 per month, or $12,000 per year, underwriting guidelines may indicate that the maximum monthly mortgage payment should not exceed $250, or 25 percent of monthly gross income, for this borrower. Total fixed installment payments, including monthly mortgage payment, should not exceed $350, or 35 percent of gross income. The value of the dwelling being financed should be in the general range of $30,000, or two and one half times annual gross income. Many lenders find that exceeding these limits for the "average" borrower may cause overextension of credit and eventual default on the mortgage loan.

It must be stressed that underwriting guidelines are intended for the average borrower, with average income and family size.[3] If an applicant has a higher than average income, a proportionally greater amount can generally be borrowed with no substantial increase in risk of default. This is true because, as income rises over the average, outlays for living essentials are easily made and more income can be used for discretionary purchases, saving, and investing. Additional housing generally becomes one of the discretionary purchases. On the other hand, if an applicant's income is below average, essential outlays for food, clothing, etc., usually take up a greater percentage of income. Hence any excess for saving is generally low and consequently the guidelines are more strictly enforced.

Problem Areas in Underwriting   Additional questions immediately arise concerning underwriting guidelines. To begin with, a definition

---

[3] By average, we mean households earning an average income with an average-size family, when compared to all households in the community representing a particular lending area.

of income is necessary. If we assume that there is only one employed individual in the household, this generally presents no problem; however, if there are two individuals employed, the question of what constitutes income arises. The general rule applied by the lender takes a long-run viewpoint, that is, whether both individuals will remain employed indefinitely, or at least until the income of one is sufficient to meet the monthly mortgage payments. This question often presents difficulty when the value of the property and the corresponding loan amount being requested are high in relation to the income of only one of the income earners. Obviously, a judgment by the lender as to the future stability of the joint incomes will have to be exercised. Generally, if both parties have been employed for several consecutive years, there is a greater likelihood of future income stability. Or, if the intent of one of the parties is to end employment after a given number of years, and this individual is presently employed in a professional activity that lends to employment stability, both incomes may be included for the time both expect to remain employed. An estimate may then be made as to what the primary worker's total income will be at the time the other party ceases employment.

Additional problems in defining or estimating future income arise with individuals whose incomes are strongly affected by general economic conditions. For example, some construction workers, commission salesmen, or individuals who earn a considerable portion of their income by working overtime fall into a category where seasonality or changing economic conditions cause fluctuations in income. Assessment of future income in these cases is sometimes difficult, as averages must be relied on over the year. The lender will look closely at the applicant's saving behavior and installment credit purchases, to determine how well the household budgets income over seasonal or cyclical periods when current income may be low.

Other Considerations   It goes without saying that qualitative considerations enter into any underwriting process dealing with the analysis of granting mortgage credit. An applicant's credit history, which can be obtained from a credit report, relating to installment buying, attitude toward prompt payment of obligations, and any past overextension of credit-buying resulting in default or delayed payments, will weigh heavily in the judgment of the loan officer. In addition, future installment buying is considered by the lender to the extent possible. For example, if the property being financed is a first purchase by the applicant, consideration of possible additional purchases for furnishings for the property and the ability of the borrower to carry both the mortgage payment and the installment note accompanying those purchases must be taken into account. Other anticipated purchases which are unrelated to the housing purchase, such as automobiles, must also be taken into account by the borrower. All of these purchases are considered by the lender in establishing the borrower's ability to carry the amount of mortgage credit being sought.

Other assets owned by the applicant also play an important role in the rating loan quality by the lender. The rating will be improved if the applicant has demonstrated a consistent ability to save as evidenced by savings accounts or investments in other property, ownership of life insurance (cash value), purchase of securities and the like, as well as the ability to carry the obligations associated with the acquisition of these assets. For example, an older applicant whose remaining life expectancy is less than the term of the mortgage being sought may be granted a loan with the desired maturity, even though it exceeds the years of life expectancy remaining, if adequate life insurance exists to pay off the mortgage loan in the event death occurs before the loan is repaid.

While income and credit capacity form much of the basis for risk analysis by the lender, recent federal regulations have limited the extent to which lenders may obtain information or make inferences concerning a loan applicant's background. Regulation B of the Federal Reserve Act provides guidelines that lenders must comply with when gathering information from potential borrowers. A summary of the major guidelines that must be followed by lenders is provided below:

a. The use of sex or marital status in a credit scoring system is prohibited.
b. Creditors may not inquire into birth control practices or into childbearing capabilities or intentions, or assume, from her age that an applicant or an applicant's spouse may drop out of the labor force due to childbearing and thus have an interruption of income.
c. A creditor may not discount part-time income but may examine the probable continuity of the applicant's job.
d. A creditor may ask and consider whether and to what extent an applicant's income is affected by obligations to make almony or child support or maintenance payments.
e. A creditor may ask to what extent an applicant is relying on alimony or child support or maintenance payments to repay the debt being insured; but the applicant must first be informed that no such disclosure is necessary if the applicant does not rely on such income to obtain the credit. Where the applicant chooses to rely on alimony, a creditor shall consider such payments as income to the extent the payments are likely to be made consistently.
f. A creditor shall not take into account the existence of a telephone listing in the name of an applicant in a credit scoring system or

other method of evaluating applications. A creditor may take into account the existence of a telephone in the applicant's home.

g. Upon the request of an applicant, creditor will be required to provide reasons for terminating or denying credit.

Evaluation of the Property   The second half of the underwriting process leading to acceptance or rejection of a loan request deals with the characteristics of the property being financed. These characteristics include the property's value and future trends in that value, which invariably include other characteristics such as property values in the neighborhood, local public services, property taxes, and location of the property within the neighborhood and its proximity to major work centers in the community.

Property Appraisals   Since the loan being applied for will be used to finance a residential property, the lender must make an estimate of the property's present value, as it will serve as collateral value for the loan in event the borrower defaults. This estimate of value is usually made of an experienced appraiser on the staff of the lending institution or by an independent fee appraiser.[4] In any event, the appraised value, and not necessarily the agreed sales price between the buyer and seller of a property, serves as the basis for the amount to be loaned.

Market Comparison Appraisals.   In making residential property valution estimates, one method of appraising commonly used is referred to as the "market comparison," or market, approach. It is an appraising technique which employs data compiled on comparable properties recently sold in the same area as the property being appraised. The sources of data used by the appraiser are usually recent sales prices known from previous appraisals. Other sources of data are real estate transfer documents, which are on file in the county courthouse and which indicate how much transfer tax or transfer fees were paid at the time comparable properties were sold. Since transfer fees or taxes in an area are usually proportional to the sales price paid by a buyer, the sales price is easily determined. For example, if the transfer fee charged in a particular county or state is one tenth of one percent (0.001) of the sales price, and the transfer fee shown on the transfer document is $33.00, then the price paid by the buyer was $33.00 ÷ 0.001, or $33,000.

Whether tax data from transfer documents or other sources of sales data for comparable properties are used in estimating value, the ap-

---

[4] An independent appraiser is generally an MAI (Member of the American Institute of Real Estate Appraisers) or an SRA (Member of the Society of Real Estate Appraisers). Independence here means that the appraiser has no vested interest in the transaction at hand, and therefore he can give an independent estimate of value.

praiser must be sure that the transactions used were made at arm's length between buyer and seller. Obviously, a sale between relatives would not be desirable for use as a comparable sale. In addition, when arriving at estimated value, adjustments must usually be made by the appraiser for minor differences in physical and locational characteristics between the property being appraised and comparable properties. These adjustments are necessary because normally no two properties are exactly alike; they differ in living area (square footage), lot size, age, condition, or location. After compiling all of the relevant comparable sales prices and adjustments, the appraiser reports an estimated property value.

Cost Appraisals. A second approach commonly used in appraising residential properties is the "cost" approach to valuation. When used by appraisers, this method basically takes into account the cost of the lot and the cost of physical components in the structure based on a detailed inventory. For new structures the cost approach is generally a reliable technique for value estimation. When the property being appraised is not new, the appraiser must estimate the current reproduction cost of the structure and deduct an estimated allowance for depreciation from the reproduction cost.[5] The cost approach is difficult to use in many cases. If no recent comparable properties have been sold, however, use of the comparable sales approach is precluded and reliance on the cost approach is necessary.

Residential Property Appraisals—Illustrated To provide more insight into what variables may be included in both the cost and market comparison approaches to appraising residential property, Exhibit 10–1 illustrates a standardized appraisal form presently used by many lenders.[6] Note that page 1 of Exhibit 10–1 requires a detailed description of neighborhood characteristics and physical components of the structure being appraised. In addition to the description, a qualitative judgment must be made by the appraiser as to the desirability of the neighborhood and condition of the structure with appropriate comments required as to undesirable neighborhood conditions and whether the unit is in need of structural repair.

Page 2 of Exhibit 10–1 contains the basic requirements necessary for completion of a cost approach and a market comparison approach to value. At the top of page 2 of Exhibit 10–1, the cost approach must

---

[5] For a description of various methods used in appraising residential property see Alfred A. Ring, *The Valuation of Real Estate,* 2d ed. (Englewood Cliffs, N.J.: Prentice-Hall, Inc., 1970).

[6] This form is a part of the required mortgage documentation for any lender desiring to sell mortgages in the secondary mortgage market to the Federal Home Loan Mortgage Corporation or the Federal National Mortgage Association. Both of these corporations are discussed in detail in Chapter 21.

EXHIBIT 10–1
Residential Appraisal Report

RESIDENTIAL APPRAISAL REPORT   File No.

To be completed by Lender	
Borrower/Client	Census Tract Map Reference
Property Address	
City	County State Zip Code
Legal Description	
Sale Price $ Date of Sale	Property Rights Appraised ☐ Fee ☐ Leasehold ☐ DeMinimis PUD(FNMA only ☐ Condo ☐ PUD)
Actual Real Estate Taxes $ (yr) Loan charges to be paid by seller $	Other sales concessions
Lender	Lender's Address
Occupant Appraiser	Instructions to Appraiser

NEIGHBORHOOD

				Good Avg. Fair Poor
Location	☐ Urban	☐ Suburban	☐ Rural	
Built Up	☐ Over 75%	☐ 25% to 75%	☐ Under 25%	Employment Stability ☐ ☐ ☐ ☐
Growth Rate ☐ Fully Dev.	☐ Rapid	☐ Steady	☐ Slow	Convenience to Employment ☐ ☐ ☐ ☐
Property Values	☐ Increasing	☐ Stable	☐ Declining	Convenience to Shopping ☐ ☐ ☐ ☐
Demand/Supply	☐ Shortage	☐ In Balance	☐ Over Supply	Convenience to Schools ☐ ☐ ☐ ☐
Marketing Time	☐ Under 3 Mos.	☐ 4–6 Mos.	☐ Over 6 Mos.	Quality of Schools ☐ ☐ ☐ ☐

Present Land Use ___% 1 Family ___% 2–4 Family ___% Apts. ___% Condo ___% Commercial   Recreational Facilities ☐ ☐ ☐ ☐
___% Industrial ___% Vacant ___%   Adequacy of Utilities ☐ ☐ ☐ ☐
Change in Present Land Use ☐ Not Likely ☐ Likely (*) ☐ Taking Place (*)   Property Compatibility ☐ ☐ ☐ ☐
(*) From _____ To _____   Protection from Detrimental Conditions ☐ ☐ ☐ ☐
Predominant Occupancy ☐ Owner ☐ Tenant ___% Vacant   Police and Fire Protection ☐ ☐ ☐ ☐
Single Family Price Range $_____ to $_____ Predominant Value $_____   General Appearance of Properties ☐ ☐ ☐ ☐
Single Family Age _____ yrs to _____ yrs Predominant Age _____ yrs   Appeal to Market ☐ ☐ ☐ ☐

Note: FHLMC/FNMA do not consider the racial composition of the neighborhood to be a relevant factor and it must not be considered in the appraisal.
Comments (including those factors adversely affecting marketability) _____

SITE

Dimensions _____ = _____ Sq. Ft. or Acres   ☐ Corner Lot
Zoning classification _____ Present improvements ☐ do ☐ do not conform to zoning regulations
Highest and best use: ☐ Present use ☐ Other (specify) _____

	Public	Other (Describe)	OFF SITE IMPROVEMENTS	Topo _____
Elec.	☐		Street Access: ☐ Public ☐ Private	Size _____
Gas	☐		Surface	Shape _____
Water	☐		Maintenance: ☐ Public ☐ Private	View _____
San.Sewer	☐		☐ Storm Sewer ☐ Curb/Gutter	Drainage _____

☐ Underground Elect. & Tel. ☐ Sidewalk ☐ Street Lights   Is the property located in a HUD identified Flood Hazard Area? ☐ No ☐ Yes
Comments (favorable or unfavorable including any apparent adverse easements, encroachments or other adverse conditions) _____

IMPROVEMENTS

☐ Existing (approx. yr. blt.) 19___ No. Units ___ Type (det, duplex, semi/det, etc.) Design (rambler, split level, etc.)   Exterior Walls
☐ Proposed ☐ Under Construction No. Stories ___

Roof Material	Gutters & Downspouts ☐ None	Window (Type):	Insulation ☐ None ☐ Floor
		☐ Storm Sash ☐ Screens ☐ Combination	☐ Ceiling ☐ Roof ☐ Walls

Foundation Walls	**BSMT** % Basement ☐ Floor Drain	Finished Ceiling _____
	☐ Outside Entrance ☐ Sump Pump	Finished Walls _____
☐ Crawl Space	☐ Concrete Floor ___% Finished	Finished Floor _____
☐ Slab on Grade	Evidence of: ☐ Dampness ☐ Termites ☐ Settlement	

Comments _____

ROOM LIST

Room List	Foyer	Living	Dining	Kitchen	Den	Family Rm.	Rec. Rm.	Bedrooms	No. Baths	Laundry	Other
Basement											
1st Level											
2nd Level											

Total ___ Rooms ___ Bedrooms ___ Baths in finished area above grade.

INTERIOR FINISH & EQUIPMENT

Kitchen Equipment: ☐ Refrigerator ☐ Range/Oven ☐ Disposal ☐ Dishwasher ☐ Fan/Hood ☐ Compactor ☐ Washer ☐ Dryer ☐
HEAT: Type ___ Fuel ___ Cond. ___ AIR COND: ☐ Central ☐ Other ___ ☐ Adequate ☐ Inadequate

				Good Avg. Fair Poor
Floors	☐ Hardwood	☐ Carpet Over ☐		
Walls	☐ Drywall	☐ Plaster ☐		Quality of Construction (Materials & Finish) ☐ ☐ ☐ ☐
Trim/Finish	☐ Good	☐ Average ☐ Fair ☐ Poor	**PROPERTY RATING**	Condition of Improvements ☐ ☐ ☐ ☐
Bath Floor	☐ Ceramic	☐		Rooms size and layout ☐ ☐ ☐ ☐
Bath Wainscot	☐ Ceramic	☐		Closets and Storage ☐ ☐ ☐ ☐

Special Features (including fireplaces): _____   Plumbing—adequacy and condition ☐ ☐ ☐ ☐
Electrical—adequacy and condition ☐ ☐ ☐ ☐
Kitchen Cabinets—adequacy and condition ☐ ☐ ☐ ☐
ATTIC: ☐ Yes ☐ No ☐ Stairway ☐ Drop-stair ☐ Scuttle ☐ Floored   Compatibility to Neighborhood ☐ ☐ ☐ ☐
Finished (Describe) _____ ☐ Heated   Overall Livability ☐ ☐ ☐ ☐
CAR STORAGE: ☐ Garage ☐ Built-in ☐ Attached ☐ Detached ☐ Car Port   Appeal and Marketability ☐ ☐ ☐ ☐
No. Cars ___ ☐ Adequate ☐ Inadequate Condition _____   Effective Age ___ Yrs. Est. Remaining Economic Life ___ Yrs.

PORCHES, PATIOS, POOL, FENCES, etc. (describe) _____

COMMENTS (including functional or physical inadequacies, repairs needed, modernization, etc.) _____

FHLMC Form 70 Rev. 9/75   ATTACH DESCRIPTIVE PHOTOGRAPHS OF SUBJECT PROPERTY AND STREET SCENE   FNMA Form 1004 Rev. 9/75

EXHIBIT 10–1 *(continued)*
Valuation Section

VALUATION SECTION

Purpose of Appraisal is to estimate Market Value as defined in Certification & Statement of Limiting Conditions (FHLMC Form 439/FNMA Form 1004B). If submitted for FNMA, the appraiser must attach (1) sketch or map showing location of subject, street names, distance from nearest intersection, and any detrimental conditions and (2) exterior building sketch of improvements showing dimensions.

COST APPROACH

Measurements		No. Stories	Sq. Ft.
x	x	=	
x	x	=	
x	x	=	
x	x	=	
x	x	=	
x	x	=	

Total Gross Living Area (List in Market Data Analysis below) _____

Comment on functional and economic obsolescence: _____

ESTIMATED REPRODUCTION COST — NEW — OF IMPROVEMENTS:

Dwelling _____ Sq. Ft. @ $ _____ = $ _____
_____ Sq. Ft. @ $ _____ = _____
Extras _____ = _____
_____ = _____
_____ = _____
Porches, Patios, etc. _____ = _____
Garage/Car Port _____ Sq. Ft. @ $ _____ = _____
Site Improvements (driveway, landscaping, etc.) = _____
Total Estimated Cost New . . . . . . = $ _____

Less | Physical | Functional | Economic
Depreciation $ _____ | $ _____ | $ _____ = $ (_____)
Depreciated value of improvements . . . . = $ _____
ESTIMATED LAND VALUE . . . . = $ _____
(If leasehold, show only leasehold value)

INDICATED VALUE BY COST APPROACH . . . $ _____

The undersigned has recited three recent sales of properties most similar and proximate to subject and has considered these in the market analysis. The description includes a dollar adjustment, reflecting market reaction to those items of significant variation between the subject and comparable properties. If a significant item in the comparable property is superior to, or more favorable than, the subject property, a minus (-) adjustment is made, thus reducing the indicated value of subject; if a significant item in the comparable is inferior to, or less favorable than, the subject property, a plus (+) adjustment is made, thus increasing the indicated value of the subject.

MARKET DATA ANALYSIS

ITEM	Subject Property	COMPARABLE NO. 1		COMPARABLE NO. 2		COMPARABLE NO. 3	
Address							
Proximity to Subj.							
Sales Price	$	$		$		$	
Price/Living area	$	$		$		$	
Data Source							
Date of Sale and Time Adjustment	DESCRIPTION	DESCRIPTION	+(−)$ Adjustment	DESCRIPTION	+(−)$ Adjustment	DESCRIPTION	+(−)$ Adjustment
Location							
Site/View							
Design and Appeal							
Quality of Const.							
Age							
Condition							
Living Area Room Count and Total	Total · B-rms · Baths	Total · B-rms · Baths		Total · B-rms · Baths		Total · B-rms · Baths	
Gross Living Area	Sq.Ft.	Sq.Ft.		Sq.Ft.		Sq.Ft.	
Basement & Bsmt. Finished Rooms							
Functional Utility							
Air Conditioning							
Garage/Car Port							
Porches, Patio, Pools, etc.							
Other (e.g. fireplaces, kitchen equip., heating, remodeling)							
Sales or Financing Concessions							
Net Adj. (Total)		☐ Plus; ☐ Minus $		☐ Plus; ☐ Minus $		☐ Plus; ☐ Minus $	
Indicated Value of Subject		$		$		$	

Comments on Market Data _____

INDICATED VALUE BY MARKET DATA APPROACH . . . . $ _____
INDICATED VALUE BY INCOME APPROACH (If applicable) Economic Market Rent $ _____ /Mo. x Gross Rent Multiplier _____ = $ _____
This appraisal is made ☐ "as is" ☐ subject to the repairs, alterations, or conditions listed below ☐ completion per plans and specifications.
Comments and Conditions of Appraisal: _____

Final Reconciliation: _____

This appraisal is based upon the above requirements, the certification, contingent and limiting conditions, and Market Value definition that are stated in
☐ FHLMC Form 439 (Rev. 9/75)/FNMA Form 1004B filed with client _____ 19 _____ ☐ attached.
If submitted for FNMA, the report has been prepared in compliance with FNMA form instructions.
I ESTIMATE THE MARKET VALUE, AS DEFINED, OF SUBJECT PROPERTY AS OF _____ 19 _____ to be $ _____

Appraiser(s) _____ Review Appraiser (If applicable) _____
☐ Did ☐ Did Not Physically Inspect Property

be determined by costing out the square-footage reproduction of the unit, then adding the value of amenities (such as air conditioning, carpeting, built-in equipment, etc.). From the reproduction value is subtracted an estimate of any depreciation due to physical deterioration, design or functional obsolescence, and economic obsolescence because of neighborhood deterioration (traffic, location of undesirable industries nearby, etc.). After amounts have been assigned to all of the categories, the remaining figure is the value estimated by use of the cost approach.

The middle portion of the second page of Exhibit 10–1 contains the data requirements for the market approach. Note that this appraisal form requires at least three properties comparable to the subject property to complete the appraisal. A detailed comparison of physical attributes for each comparable property, as well as its sale price and location, are included in the estimate of value for the subject property. The appraiser then judges whether increases or decreases in value should be made to the subject property when its attributes are compared with the market comparables, before arriving at a value using the market approach. Finally, the appraiser reconciles the value estimated using the cost approach and the value estimated using the market approach before making a best estimate of the value of the property.

Property Appraisal and Sale Price   It should also be pointed out that the sale price of a property agreed on between a buyer and seller may not always correspond to the lender's appraised value. For example, if a buyer and a seller agree on a price of $42,000 for a property and the appraised value obtained by the lender comes in at $40,000, the lender will generally use the $40,000 as the value on which the loan will be based, unless there is convincing evidence to change it.[7] In this case, the lender obviously thinks the buyer is overpaying for the property and, therefore, is unwilling to use the sale price as a basis for the loan. This concept is important because if the buyer is applying for a 90 percent loan, the lender may be willing to lend 90 percent of $40,000, or $36,000, with the buyer making a down payment of ($42,000 − $36,000) $6,000. If the property had been appraised at $42,000, the loan would be $37,800 and the down payment, $4,200. Consequently, the buyer will have to make a down payment $1,800 higher simply on the basis of the difference in appraisals.

Carried to an extreme, if the sale price agreed on were $50,000 and the lender based the 90 percent loan on the sale price, $45,000 would be loaned and the buyer would make a $5,000 down payment. If the

---

[7] An independent appraisal obtained by the buyer or seller may reveal an aspect of the property overlooked by the lender, and because of the oversight, the lender may be willing to change the estimate. However, if no independent appraisal is obtained by the buyer or seller, the lender's appraised value is likely to stand, regardless of what the buyer pays for the property.

buyer defaulted shortly thereafter and the loan was foreclosed, resulting in a sale for only $40,000, the lender would lose $5,000 and the buyer would lose the $5,000 down payment. The upshot of this analysis is that the lender wants to be sure that the appraised value is accurate, for if too large a loan is made as a result of a poor value estimate, the lender stands to lose in the event a buyer defaults on the loan.

Property Values over Time   A cardinal rule followed by lenders is that the value of a mortgaged property should never fall below the outstanding loan balance at any time during the life of the mortgage. In other words, the lender wants to be assured that the market value of the property will always be high enough to assure that the loan balance will be recovered in the event of default by the borrower. As has already been seen in Exhibit 9–2 in Chapter 9, the outstanding loan balance for a fully amortized loan declines over the loan period. This pattern is reproduced in Exhibit 10–2.

An important consideration in the mind of the underwriter is the possible pattern value that a given property will follow *over time*. Exhibit 10–2 depicts two hypothetical patterns that a property could follow. In the case of property value A, it is clear that the risk of loss for the lender in the event of default would be slight since the property is *appreciating* in value. The value pattern A is always higher than the loan balance in each period over the term of the loan. Because of the protection afforded to the lender by the rising property value,

EXHIBIT 10–2
Relationship between Property Value and Loan Balance
Dollars

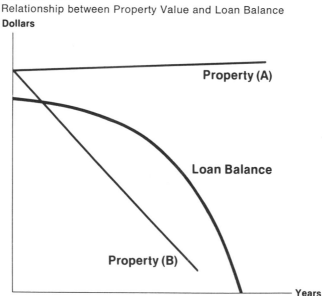

if the household's income is adequate, the loan would undoubtedly be granted.

In the case of pattern B shown in Exhibit 10–2, however, it is clear that since the property value is declining over time, the borrower would not extend the amount of credit being sought. Note that pattern B actually *falls below* the loan balance during the life of the loan. The lender could adjust the loan terms by lending substantially less, for a shorter time period, so that the loan balance curve would be lower in the first place and so that the loan would mature sooner. However, since the risk of value decline appears extremely great to the lender, chances are that the loan would not be made regardless of the amount and the terms.

Factors Influencing Property Value Trends. What factors influence property values over time? A number of influences must be considered by a lender when making this determination:

1. Income of households in the contiguous neighborhood.
2. Quality of public services delivered in the form of schools, police and fire protection, recreational facilities, road maintenance, water and sewer service; property taxes associated with provision of public services.
3. Location relative to major employment centers, shopping and other frequented activities.
4. External influences, including industrial plants, sewer plants, heavy traffic patterns, and other negative sources of pollution, noise, etc.
5. Positive external influences such as green areas, parks, and other amenities.

While this list does not exhaust all considerations, it covers the major categories investigated by lenders when evaluating property value trends. The first consideration listed, income of residents in the area, cannot be overemphasized. Income is the primary determinant of the demand for housing and what households spend on housing. This expenditure includes not only outlays for acquisition of housing but also expenditures for maintenance, repair, and improvements, and other housing services. Obviously, higher income households will demand more housing services than lower income households. Consequently, the level of maintenance, repair, etc., is strictly a function of income. The condition, and hence the value, of a property will reflect the outlays made on these services over time. Income of households in a given area also spills over into the demand for public services, particularly schools and educational services as listed in the second category above. Demand for these services also increases with income and reinforces the stability of property value in any given area.

Locational factors, such as distance to work, shopping, etc., obviously affect travel time and cost outlays by households. Higher income households are generally willing to pay a premium for good accessibility. Finally, other locational factors, such as proximity to negative external influences like air pollution, require higher maintenance expenditures. Consequently, it is easier for households living adjacent to these negative influences to allow property to decline than to keep it up. On the other hand, nearness to positive external influences, such as parks and green areas, generally acts as a catalyst for households to maintain housing quality.

Borrower Considerations in Financing

While the lender is concerned with both property and borrower characteristics when evaluating a loan, the borrower also has options to consider when making financial decisions. One question in the mind of the borrower is how much financing should be applied for. This question may be easily answered for buyers of residential property for the first time who have managed to save just enough for a minimum down payment. For many households, however, the question of how much to borrow must be considered in relation to other investments that may be undertaken with available funds. A second question deals with returns on yields that might be realized from an investment in housing due to possible appreciation in value, and how that return is affected by borrowing.

Housing serves two purposes for the borrower. The more obvious purpose is shelter and attendant amenities. A less obvious one is investment. Anyone familiar with real estate investment knows of the rapid price appreciation in housing that has occurred in recent years. The major causes of this increase have been rising incomes and inflationary pressures; hence, the homeowner has come to look on housing as an excellent inflation hedge with which to preserve the economic value of personal assets.[8] Consequently, when a borrower considers the purchase of a property, its investment dimensions should be considered as well as how much borrowing is desirable.

Analysis of Financing Alternatives In determining how much to borrow, the buyer of a property may be faced with several options. For example, assume a borrower is purchasing a property for $50,000 and faces two possible loan alternatives. One lender is willing to make an 80 percent loan, or $40,000, for 25 years at 8 percent interest. Another lender is willing to lend 90 percent, or $45,000, for 25 years, also at 8 percent. Since two lenders may view the risk of lending to a specific

---

[8] For a study of home ownership costs see John C. Weicher and John C. Simonson "Recent Trends in Housing Costs," *Journal of Economics and Business,* vol. 27, no. 2, Winter 1975, pp. 177–85.

borrower slightly differently, it may be possible for a borrower who shops around for the most competitive loan terms to obtain a slightly larger loan from one lender at the same rate as that quoted on a smaller loan from a different lender. Which alternative should be chosen?

To analyze this problem, emphasis should be placed on two basic concepts in borrowing: (1) the incremental cost of borrowing and (2) the rate of appreciation or depreciation in the asset being purchased. If a property has a present value of $50,000 and we assume that after one year the property increases 2 percent in value to $51,000, what would be the rate of equity appreciation under each borrowing alternative?

Exhibit 10–3 contains a comparison of increases in equity apprecia-

EXHIBIT 10–3
Comparison of Borrowing Alternatives

Alternative I—80% Loan
Price = $50,000
Amount borrowed = $40,000 at 8% for 25 years
Monthly payment = $40,000 × Loan Constant
$\qquad$ = $40,000 × 0.00772 = $308.80
Loan balance end of year 1 = $40,000 × Mortgage balance factor
$\qquad$ = $40,000 × 0.9869 = $39,476

Alternative II—90% Loan
Price = $50,000
Amount borrowed = $45,000 at 8% for 25 years
Monthly payment = $45,000 × 0.00772 = $347.40
Loan balance end of year 1 = $45,000 × 0.9869 = $44,410.50

Returns at Sale:

		Alternative I	Alternative II
Price	....	$51,000.00	$51,000.00
Less:	Mortgage balance	39,476.00	44,410.50
	Down payment	10,000.00	5,000.00
	Difference in		
	monthly payments		463.20[*]
Net return at sale:	...................$ 1,524.00	$ 1,126.30
	÷ Down payment $10,000.00	$ 5,000.00
	Percent appreciation ..	15.2	22.5

[*] $347.40 − $308.80 = $38.60 per month × 12 months = $463.20.

tion under both borrowing alternatives, based on the assumption that the property is sold after one year.[9] Since there is no rent or income involved, the analysis is confined only to gains that would be realized from appreciation in property value, plus any difference in interest costs between borrowing alternatives.

_____
[9] The property does not have to be sold after one year to demonstrate the concepts involved here. Any time period of ownership can be used to facilitate a comparison.

The basic information concerning the loan alternatives is provided at the top of Exhibit 10–2 and is used as input for comparing appreciation rates. Note that comparing equity appreciation under each alternative involves a simple analysis which begins with the sale price less the mortgage balance at the end of the first year for both loans, less the down payments made under each alternative. However, in order to make Alternative II strictly comparable with Alternative I, an adjustment must be made by taking into account the difference in monthly mortgage payments, which are higher under Alternative II. In looking at returns under both alternatives, we see that under Alternative I the rate of equity appreciation is 15.2 percent, compared to a 22.5 percent increase under Alternative II. Both rates are far in excess of the 2 percent appreciation in the price of the property. This relationship brings out a very basic principle in finance called *financial leverage*. It is borrowing funds to finance the purchase of an asset in order to earn a higher return on equity invested.

From a comparison of the two alternatives, it is very tempting to say that Alternative II with its 22.5 percent return is better than Alternative I, and that therefore a borrower should use as much leverage as possible in financing the purchase of a property. However, this statement is not always true. A more accurate choice among Alternatives I and II requires the introduction of the concept of the incremental cost of borrowing.

The Incremental Cost of Borrowing   To analyze our choice of alternatives, we must consider one additional difference between Alternatives I and II, namely, the difference in amounts borrowed. It would be easy to say that Alternative II should be chosen because it requires a smaller down payment and provides a much higher rate of equity appreciation when compared with Alternative I; therefore, it is very attractive from both aspects. But, does this mean that all borrowers would always choose Alternative II? If a borrower had $10,000 which could be used as a down payment, would Alternative II always be chosen since it requires only a $5,000 down payment and since it provides a higher rate of equity appreciation?

From the preceding analysis, it is clear that if Alternative II is chosen over Alternative I, $5,000 more will be borrowed and consequently a $5,000 smaller down payment is required. The critical issue now becomes: if Alternative II is selected, what will be done with the $5,000 saved with the lower down payment? We know the cost of acquiring the additional $5,000 is 8 percent; in other words, by choosing to put down $5,000 less, we have borrowed $5,000 more at 8 percent. Therefore, the *marginal or incremental cost of borrowing is 8 percent*. We can develop a simple decision rule from this marginal cost concept: as long as the $5,000 reduction in down payment can be invested in some other asset, equal in risk, at a yield *greater than 8 percent,* Alternative II will be the better choice.

A demonstration of this rule can be seen very easily in Exhibit 10–4, by assuming that an investment is undertaken at 8 percent for 25 years with the $5,000 lower down payment under Alternative II. The returns from this additional $5,000 investment are *combined* with returns from

EXHIBIT 10–4
Combined Returns under Borrowing Alternative II

A. Additional returns at 8% for 25 years on $5,000 additional investment:
    Monthly earnings:
    $5,000 × Loan constant 8%, 25 years
    $5,000 × 0.00772 = $ 38.60
    $\qquad\qquad\qquad\qquad$ × 12 months =

Yearly earnings: $463.20	
Additional earnings during year 1:	$ 463.20
Investment balance end of year 1: $5,000 × 0.9869°	4,934.50
Total returns from additional investment	$ 5,397.70
Less: Additional amount invested	5,000.00
Net returns from additional investment	$ 397.70
B. Net returns from Alternative II (Exhibit 10–3)	1,126.30
Net returns on combined investments	$ 1,524.00
C. Percent return on combined amounts invested:	
Net return on combined investment	$ 1,524.00
Combined investment	10,000.00
Percent on combined investment	15.2

° Balance, 25-year loan, 8%, after one year.

Alternative II in Exhibit 10–3. The outcome in Exhibit 10–4 shows that when returns from Alternative II are combined with returns from the additional $5,000 investment undertaken at 8 percent for 25 years, the rate of equity appreciation on combined investments is 15.2 percent, which is equal to the rate of appreciation on the $10,000 down payment under *Alternative I* shown in Exhibit 10–3.

The importance of the result now becomes apparent. Alternative II, or the $45,000 loan at 8 percent for 25 years, is superior to Alternative I, the $40,000 loan at 8 percent for 25 years, only if the difference in down payments ($5,000) can be reinvested at a rate greater than 8 percent.[10] If no alternative equal in risk exists yielding a return of 8

[10] Actually, the $5,000 does not have to be reinvested, as the borrower may prefer to spend it. For example, if a borrower decides to borrow $45,000 and to make a down payment of $5,000, the additional $5,000 borrowed still carries a marginal or incremental cost of 8 percent. This merely means that other goods and services on which he spends the rest of his income have a value or utility worth in excess of 8 percent per year to him now; consequently he prefers not to reduce his present spending level and is willing to borrow more.

percent or better, the borrower would be better off by borrowing $5,000 less, saving interest costs, and earning the 15.2 percent under Alternative I.

From the foregoing analysis some general rules emerge that govern how much down payment should be made in any situation. When properties are expected to appreciate in value, returns will always be greater when more leverage is used *only if* reductions in down payments can be reinvested at yields greater than the incremental cost of borrowing. Stated another way, if property values are expected to rise, financial leverage can be used to increase return only when reductions in equity brought about by increased borrowing can be used or reinvested at a rate which exceeds the marginal cost of borrowing.

The Incremental Cost of Borrowing—Further Considerations   It should be apparent that the incremental borrowing cost concept is extremely important when deciding how much should be borrowed to finance a given transaction. In the preceding section, the two alternatives considered were fairly straightforward with the only difference between them being the amount borrowed. In most cases financing alternatives under consideration will have *different* interest rates as the amount borrowed increases, and possibly *different* loan maturities. Financing alternatives with these characteristic differences are considered in this section.

Differences in Amounts Borrowed and Interest Rates.   To illustrate how changes in interest rates as well as differences in amounts borrowed affect incremental or marginal borrowing costs, we compare Alternative I, or a $40,000 loan for 25 years at 8 percent interest, to a new Alternative III, which is a $45,000 loan for 25 years at 8½ percent interest. The decision now faced is the same as before: when buying the $50,000 property which alternative will be better, Alternative I or Alternative III?

To answer this question, we need to make only two computations, one that provides an approximate rate of appreciation in equity and a second that provides the incremental borrowing cost. It should be recalled from Exhibit 10–3 that Alternative I provided an appreciation in equity of 15.2 percent, assuming that the property increased by 2 percent from $50,000 to $51,000 and was sold after one year. Exhibit 10–5 provides results under the provisions of Alternative III which, in addition to the $45,000 loan amount for 25 years carries a higher interest rate than Alternative I. Note that the computation in Exhibit 10–5 shows that the appreciation in equity under Alternative III is slightly over 18.1 percent for the first year when compared to 15.2 percent for Alternative I. This rate is still much higher than the rate shown for Alternative I. The question now becomes: should Alternative III be

EXHIBIT 10–5
Equity Appreciation Computation, Borrowing
Alternative III

Loan Information Alternative III:
Terms: $45,000, 8½%, 25 years
Monthly payment: $45,000 × 0.00805° = $362.25
Loan balance after 1 year: $44,455.50
Returns at Sale:
Price: $51,000.00
    Less: Mortgage balance 44,455.50
            Down payment 5,000.00
            Difference in monthly
                payments† 641.40
Net return ....$ 903.10
÷ Down payment 5,000.00
Percent return 18.1

° Loan constant, 8½%, 25 years.
† Monthly payment Alternative III ....$ 362.25
   Monthly payment Alternative I .... − 308.80
   Difference ....$ 53.45
   Difference × 12 ....$ 641.40

chosen over Alternative I? This depends on the incremental cost of borrowing associated with Alternative III.

It must be pointed out that when compared to Alternative I, the incremental borrowing cost under Alternative III is *not* 8½ percent. It is different when the additional $5,000 is borrowed, the interest rate of 8½ percent is applied on the full loan amount of $45,000. In other words, when compared to Alternative I, in order to obtain the increased loan amount of $5,000, the borrower must pay one half of a percent more on the first $40,000 plus 8½ percent on the next $5,000, when borrowing $45,000. To compute the incremental cost of borrowing, we need only to compare the difference in the amounts borrowed[11] and monthly payments over the term of both alternatives as follows:

	Amount Borrowed	Monthly Payments
Alternative III $45,000		$362.25
Alternative I 40,000		308.80
Difference ....$ 5,000		$ 53.45

Recalling from the previous chapter, in determining the yield (cost) for an annuity, we proceed as follows:

[11] It should be noted that if loan origination fees are charged, the amount borrowed under each alternative should be reduced. The monthly payments would, of course, remain the same. However, the incremental cost would change.

$53.45 \ (IF, PV \text{ of } \$1 \text{ per month, } ?\%, 25 \text{ years}) \ = \$5,000$
$(IF, PV \text{ of } \$1 \text{ per month, } ?\%, 25 \text{ years}) \ = \$5,000/\$53.45$
$(IF, PV \text{ of } \$1 \text{ per month, } ?\%, 25 \text{ years}) \ = 93.545$

Since the term is 25 years, we need only to find the *IF* in column 4 in the Appendix for the correct interest rate. A search of the table reveals that rate to be slightly less than 12.25 percent. In other words, the marginal cost of borrowing an additional $5,000 in this case is slightly less than 12.25 percent! Unless some other investment with equal risk can be found which provides a return at least as high as 12.25 percent per year, Alternative I should be chosen even though its equity appreciation rate is lower. Obviously, if an investment equal in risk can be found which yields a return greater than 12.25 percent per year, Alternative III should be chosen.

Incremental Borrowing Cost, Changes in Interest Rate and Maturity Considered. A common problem faced by borrowers involves not only a change in interest rates when the amount borrowed increases, but also a change in maturity. For example, in contrast to Alternative I, which provided a $40,000, 8 percent loan for 25 years, suppose a borrower is faced with the following Alternative IV: $45,000, 8¾ percent for 30 years. When compared to Alternative I, the loan amount, interest rate, and maturity period are different. How should these two alternatives be analyzed?

The basic procedure used in the preceding section should be employed. Exhibit 10–6 provides us with an idea of what the annual rate

---

EXHIBIT 10–6

Equity Appreciation Computation, Borrowing
Alternative IV

Loan Information Alternative IV:
Terms: $45,000, 8¾%, 30 years
Monthly payment: $45,000 × 0.00787* = $354.15
Loan balance after 1 year: $44,676
Returns at Sale:

Price:	.....	$51,000.00
Less:	Mortgage balance	44,676.00
	Down payment	5,000.00
	Difference in monthly payments (Alternative I versus IV)**	544.20
Net return	.....$	779.80
÷ Down payment		5,000.00
Percent return		15.6

  * Loan constant, 8.75%, 30 years.
  ** Monthly payment Alternative IV ....$ 354.15
  Monthly payment Alternative I .... − 308.80

  Difference ....$ 45.35
  Difference × 12 ....$ 544.20

in equity appreciation would be if our new Alternative IV is chosen. Based on the data provided, the rate of equity appreciation for Alternative IV is about 15.6 percent for the first year when compared to 15.2 percent in Alternative I. Should Alternative IV be chosen?

The incremental cost of borrowing an additional $5,000 for 30 years under Alternative IV is computed as follows:

	Amount Borrowed	*Monthly Payments*	*Loan Balance End of Year 1*
Alternative IV $45,000		$354.15	$44,676
Alternative I 40,000		308.80	39,476
Difference ....$ 5,000		$ 45.35	$ 5,200

It must be stressed that any time a loan comparison is made when loan maturities differ, not only must the difference in monthly payments be taken into account, but the difference in outstanding loan balances must be considered in the sale year. This is true because the periods over which the two loans are amortized differ. The difference in maturity affects the rate of loan amortization, which in turn affects the outstanding loan balance at any point in time. The computation of the incremental borrowing cost in our example can be completed as follows:

$$\$45.35 \ (IF, PV \ of \ \$1 \ per \ month, \ ?\%, \ year)$$
$$+ \ \$5,200.00 \ (IF, PV \ of \ \$1, \ ?\%, \ 1 \ year) = \$5,000$$

Discounting at 14.5 percent:
$$\$45.35 \ (11.10833) + \$5,200 \ (0.86577) = \$5,005.76$$

From the above calculation, we can see that the incremental borrowing cost for Alternative IV is approximately 14.5 percent. In other words, if we do not have an alternative investment with the same risk, which provides an annual return of at least 14.5 percent, we are better off choosing Alternative I.[12]

Tax Considerations—Borrower The final consideration by the borrower to be developed here deals with the effect of federal income taxes on personal financial leverage. One advantage that ownership of

---

[12] It must be pointed out that when the maturity periods on two loan alternatives differ, the marginal borrowing cost will change depending on how long the property is held before sale. In other words, if the property is held for five years, the incremental borrowing cost under alternative IV will be slightly lower. Hence when the maturity periods on two loan alternatives differ, a holding period for the property should be estimated, then the computation can be completed.

residential property affords a borrower lies in the deductibility of interest charges on mortgage loans in determining federal income tax liability. There is also an opportunity to defer capital gains tax in the event that a taxpayer's principal resident is sold and replaced with another.

To illustrate how federal income taxes provide an incentive to borrow and hence to use financial leverage, we consider Alternative I from the previous example for a borrower in a 35 percent tax bracket. Under Alternative I (Exhibit 10–3), $40,000 was borrowed for a period of 25 years at 8 percent interest. The effects of federal income tax on the financing cost of Alternative I can be seen as follows:

Annual mortgage payments: $308.80 × 12 = $ 3,705.60
Less: Principal reduction
   Initial mortgage balance $40,000
   Less: Mortgage balance year 1 39,476

Principal reduction .... − 524.00

Total interest payments year 1 ....$ 3,181.60

Total interest payments year 1 ....$ 3,181.60
× Marginal tax rate .... .35

Tax reduction due to mortgage interest ....$ 1,113.56

Monthly mortgage payment ....$ 308.80
Less: Tax reduction restated on a
       monthly basis ($1,113.56 ÷ 12)..   92.80

Average after-tax monthly payment ....$ 216.00

In this case, for a borrower in a 35 percent tax bracket, it can be seen that the effect of the $3,181.60 interest deduction is equivalent to a reduction in mortgage payments during the first year by an average of $92.80 per month, or from $308.80 to $216.00. This provision obviously reduces the cost of borrowing and adds to the incentive to utilize financial leverage.[13]

Capital Gains Tax Deferment   The ability to defer capital gains tax when a taxpayer's principal residence is sold is another consideration that affects the annual rate of equity appreciation under any financial alternative. For example, suppose that the $50,000 property in our example was held for four years and sold for $58,000. The difference between $50,000 and $58,000, or $8,000, represents a taxable capital gain. However, if the proceeds from the sale are reinvested in a time

---

[13] It should be pointed out that since the interest deductibility in tax determination reduces borrowing costs, it also reduces the marginal cost of borrowing and hence the reinvestment rates dealt with in the preceding section.

limit prescribed by the IRS Code, no capital gains tax must be paid.[14] In addition, if the owner of a residential property is over 65 years of age and chooses not to purchase another residential property, a reduction in capital gains tax is allowed. At this writing a special exclusion of $35,000 of the gain is allowed if the adjusted basis of a property is $35,000 or less. For properties with a selling price greater than $35,000, the gain on which tax must be paid is reduced by the ratio of $35,000 to the sales price. In the preceding example, the cost basis of the property is $50,000. Since is was sold for $58,000, the gain at sale is $58,000 − $50,000 or $8,000. However, because of the $35,000 exclusion rule, the taxpayer is allowed to reduce the $8,000 gain by the ratio $35,000 ÷ $58,000 or 60.3 percent. Hence, the capital gains tax will be paid on $3,176, or $8,000 less 60.3 percent.

The beneficial tax treatment affecting residential real estate obviously serves to increase even further the rate of equity appreciation for property owners. These tax advantages coupled with financial leverage and general inflation, have resulted in a tremendous incentive to purchase real estate in recent years.

Rating Loan Terms The initial loan application, completed by the borrower and submitted for evaluation by the lender, does not represent a binding contract. Normally it represents a mechanism to gather information concerning the loan, the borrower, and the property. After negotiation between the borrower and lender, if the loan application is approved, the lender will issue a *loan commitment*. The loan commitment is binding and details the loan amount and the terms on which the lender is willing to lend. The commitment usually carries an expiration date, setting the time by which the borrower must accept the terms of the loan offer or lose the commitment.

Borrowers may seek a loan commitment from many different lenders to ascertain what the most competitive terms are among them. The extent to which a borrower wants to utilize financial leverage is based on personal assets, incremental borrowing costs, rates of return on alternative investments available, and tax consideraions. All of these factors will influence the amount of loan applied for. The lender will be considering the borrower's income, credit standing, and ability to repay the loan, as well as the property characteristics, in judging how much should be loaned, for how long, and at what interest rate. The borrower

---

[14] As of this writing, the IRS Code specifies that proceeds from the sale of a taxpayer's residential property must be reinvested during a period ranging from 12 months before to 18 months after actual sale if the acquired property is newly constructed. In case the acquired property has been previously used, reinvestment of proceeds must occur 12 months prior to or after actual sale. For a concise treatment of tax regulations relating to real estate see J. O. McCoy, H. A. Olsen, C. H. Reed, R. W. Sandison and R. F. Wright, *Federal Taxes Affecting Real Estate* (Chicago: National Association of Realtors, 1970).

and lender ultimately agree on the amount of loan and terms of payment satisfactory to each.

Residential Real Estate Closings

After the loan commitment has been accepted by the buyer, the usual next step is for all interested parties to gather, execute, and exchange the documents necessary to make settlements and close or complete the transaction.[15] Generally, such closings are attended by (1) buyer and seller (perhaps each with legal counsel), (2) any real estate brokers involved, and (3) the settlement agent. The settlement agent is usually a representative of a title insurance company, if such insurance is being purchased, or a representative of the lender if no title insurance is purchased.[16] The purpose of the closing, then, is to make final settlement between buyer and seller of costs, fees, and prorations associated with the real estate transaction prior to the transfer of title.

To summarize the many sources, disbursements, charges, and credits associated with the closing, a "settlement" or "closing" statement is prepared by the settlement agent. This statement summarizes the expenses and fees to be paid by the buyer and seller, and it shows the amount of funds that the buyer must pay and the amount of funds that the seller will receive at closing. Before illustrating the closing statement, a summary of some of the costs associated with real estate closings is presented.

Fees and Expenses   Expenses associated with loan closings must be paid either by the buyer or the seller depending somewhat on custom in a particular lending area. There is no generally established practice in the area of expense settlement, and in many cases payment of any, or all, expenses is negotiated between buyer and seller. What follows is an identification of various expenses associated with real estate closings, followed by an illustration of a settlement statement.

Financing Costs   These charges, called loan origination fees, are generally paid to the lender and are made in connection with services performed by the lender when underwriting and approving the loan. Sometimes many of these services are performed by the lender without charge, depending on how competitive the market for mortgage loans is at the time. During periods when ample funds are available for lending, lenders may not charge for some services; when funds are scarce, however, lenders may charge for all services performed in connection with

---

[15] For an excellent discussion of loan closings and the Real Estate Settlement and Procedures Act of 1974, see Paul Barron, *Federal Regulation of Real Estate: The Real Estate Settlement and Procedures Act* (Boston: Warren, Gorman & Lamont, 1975).

[16] In many cases a real estate broker or an attorney for the buyer or seller may act as the settlement agent with a letter of instructions from the lender.

a loan. What follows is an extensive list of possible charges that may be made by the lender.

1. Loan application fee. Charge made for processing the borrower's loan application.
2. Credit report fee. Charge made for compilation of the borrower's credit statement.
3. Attorney's fees. For preparing loan documents—mortgage/note; also for examining title documents presented to the lender.
4. Property inspection and property appraisal fee required by the lender. (This does not include fees for appraisals desired by the buyer or seller. Those fees are usually paid directly by the buyer and seller outside of the closing.)
5. Fees for property survey/photos when required by the lender.
6. Fees for preparation of loan amortization schedule by the lender for the borrower.
7. Loan discount points. Additional charge paid to the lender to increase the loan yield (per discussion in the preceding chapter).

Prorations and Escrow Costs

Property Taxes, Prorations, and Escrow Accounts. Because the dates on which property taxes are due to a particular governmental unit rarely coincide with the loan closing date, a portion of the taxes that come due at the next collection date is paid by the seller at closing. In other words, the buyer pays taxes only from the date title to the property is transferred. For example, if a county collects taxes on January 1 and July 1 of each year, and the loan closing date is April 1, the seller should pay one half of the taxes (January through March), which will be due on July 1. A *proration of taxes* is usually made at closing by deducting the seller's share of taxes from the purchase price paid by the buyer. In this way the seller pays the buyer for taxes up until the closing date.

Depending on the loan to value ratio in the transaction, the lender may require that an *escrow account* be established into which is deposited prorated taxes from the seller, and into which the borrower pays a monthly share of property tax along with the monthly mortgage payment. These funds are accumulated until taxes are due; then a disbursement is made by the lender to pay the tax bill when due. This provision assures the lender that no tax liens will be established on the property as a result of the borrower's failure to pay property tax and it is usually required in cases where the loan to value ratio exceeds 80 percent.[17]

---

[17] When the loan to value ratio is less than 80 percent, the borrower often takes responsibility for payment of taxes when they become due. However, depending on the circumstances, a lender may require a property tax escrow for loans which are less than 80 percent of value.

Private Mortgage Insurance.   This insurance may be purchased by the borrower to reimburse the lender for any loss in the event of *loan default.* In conventional lending transactions this insurance is usually required by federal or state regulations on loans made in excess of 80 percent of value. Premiums are paid to a private insurer who in turn makes a settlement for any loss to the lender if the borrower defaults. Generally this insurance is taken out by the borrower for the number of years of amortization necessary to reduce the loan balance to 80 percent of value. For example, if an 85 percent loan is made initially, the term of insurance coverage would be equal to the number of years necessary to amortize the loan balance down by 5 percent.[18] The cost of such insurance can range from ¼ to 2¾ percent of the loan balance annually, depending on the excess over 80 percent borrowed and the maturity period of the loan. Premiums are usually added to the monthly mortgage payment and collected by the lender who makes the disbursement to the private insurer. For loans made at 80 percent of value or less, this insurance is usually not purchased.[19]

Hazard Insurance and Escrow Accounts.   Hazard insurance against property damage is required by the lender as a condition for making the loan and the mortgage usually carries a provision to that effect. For loans made in excess of 80 percent of value, however, the lender usually requires the establishment of an *escrow account* for pro rata payments made by the borrower toward the next annual premium due on the policy renewal date.[20] In other words, the lender collects monthly installments equal to one-twelfth of the annual premium, along with the mortgage payment, and credits the insurance payment to the borrower's escrow account. When the policy renewal date arrives, the lender then disburses the 12 monthly payments which have been accumulated to the property insurance company. In this way the lender is certain that the property is always insured against damage. This in turn insures the loan collateral.

Mortgage Cancellation Insurance.   Mortgage cancellation insurance

---

[18] In periods when housing values are rising, it may be in the borrower's best interest to have the property reappraised by the lender after a few years. If values have gone up high enough, since the outstanding loan balance has been amortized down somewhat, the loan-to-value ratio may have fallen to 80 percent or below and the mortgage insurance may be cancelled.

[19] Private insurance is applicable to conventional mortgage loans only, not to FHA-insured mortgage loans. FHA mortgage insurance is discussed in Chapter 20. For a brief discussion of private mortgage insurance policies, practices, and charges see: Rod L. Reppe, "Why Residential Lenders Like Mortgage Guaranty Insurance"; also, see Chapter 15.

[20] When loans are made for less than 80 percent of value, the borrower generally takes responsibility for making insurance payments. The lender usually requires no escrow account or monthly installments. At closing the borrower usually needs only to show evidence of an insurance binder or a statement from the insurance company that the property is insured.

is usually optional, depending on whether the borrower desires it. Essentially, it amounts to a declining term life insurance policy which is taken out at closing and runs for the term of the mortgage. Since, with a fully amortized mortgage, the outstanding loan balance declines as monthly payments are made, the insurance coverage also declines with the loan balance. In the event of the borrower's death, the insurance coverage is equal to the outstanding loan balance. The mortgage loan is repaid with insurance proceeds. Premiums are usually paid monthly, being added to the monthly mortgage payment. The lender than disburses those payments to the life insurance company. Although mortgage cancellation insurance is usually bought at the borrower's option, if the borrower's age is a critical factor in the lender's loan analysis, purchase of such insurance may be necessary to obtain the loan.

Title Costs   Title costs are charges for searching, abstracting, examining, insuring, or guaranteeing title.

Title Insurance, Lawyer's Title Opinion.   Premiums are charged by the title insurance company to search, abstract, and examine title to a property and to issue an insurance policy that indemnifies the buyer against loss arising from claims against the property. Attorneys may perform a similar service for a fee and render an opinion as to the validity of the title held by the seller and whether it is merchantable. Normally the full premium/fee for the insurance policy/abstract opinion is paid at closing. Depending on the policy of the lending institution and government regulations, either title insurance or an attorney's opnion is required as a condition for granting a loan.

Release Fees.   Release fees are associated with paying off outstanding liens, such as the seller's mortgage lien, mechanics' liens, etc., and for services rendered by third parties in negotiating and obtaining such releases.

Statutory Costs   Certain costs are imposed by a local or state government agency and must be paid before deeds can be recorded. These include:

1. *Recording fees.*   Fees paid for recording of the mortgage and note in the public records.
2. *Transfer tax.*   A tax usually imposed by the county on all real estate transfers.

Miscellaneous Costs

Prepaid Items.   Prepayments generally involve interest on the mortgage loan from the closing date to the time during the month when the borrower begins making regular mortgage payments. For example, if the closing date is January 20 and the borrower wants regular payments to begin on March 1, twelve days of interest will be prepaid at closing (January 20–January 31 inclusive). Regular monthly payments will begin on March 1 covering the loan balance outstanding during the month of February.

Attorney's Fee. When incurred by the buyer or seller, legal fees may be paid directly by each party outside of the closing or may be included in the closing.

Pest Inspection Certificate. A pest inspection may be made at the insistence of the lender or buyer. In some states, such as Florida, an inspection is required before title is transferred. The inspection fee may be paid directly or included in the closing settlement.

Real Estate Commission. When a seller of a property engages the service of a real estate agent to sell a property, the seller usually pays the commission for such service, generally at the closing.

The Real Estate Settlement and Procedures Act (RESPA) From the preceding discussion of settlement costs, it is apparent that with the many possible fees and disbursements involved in a residential real estate closing, the event can become a fairly complex undertaking. Because of the lack of buyer sophistication in real estate transactions and because of past abuses in the form of exorbitant closing and referral fees charged mainly to buyers, Congress passed Public Law 95–533, known as the Real Estate Settlement and Procedures Act of 1974 (which became effective June 20, 1975) and Public Law 94–205 (effective January 1976) which amended the 1974 Act. These laws established federal control over settlement and closing procedures in transactions involving the purchase of residential real estate. This control is clearly for consumer protection and its express purpose, as stated in Section 213 of the 1974 Act, is to effect certain changes that should result in:

1. More effective advance disclosure of settlement costs.
2. Elimination of kickbacks or unearned fees.
3. A reduction in the amount of escrow placed in accounts by homeowners.
4. Modernization of local land title records and information.

Coverage of the Act The act, as presently constituted, affects any residential purchase involving a federally related loan. By "federally related" is meant any financial institution accepting federal deposits, having federal deposit insurance, or making or dealing in federally insured mortgage loans. In essence, *virtually all residential real estate transactions are covered under this act.* However, mobile home loans, purchases of vacant land, home improvement loans, refinancing of existing loans, and the purchase of property with the intent to resell in the ordinary course of business generally do not fall under provisions of the act. RESPA does apply, though, to mortgage assumptions (sales subject to existing mortgages) and to refinancing if a change in the interest rate or other loan conditions is provided for by the lender, or if the lender charges an assumption or other fee in excess of fifty dollars to approve the transaction.

Requirements under the Act   Although RESPA includes many provisions, only those directly associated with the closing are covered here.[21] The essential aspects of RESPA fall into six areas which are used here to facilitate discussion. These areas are:

1. Consumer information.
2. Advance disclosure of settlement costs.
3. Title insurance placement.
4. Kickbacks and referral fees.
5. Use of a uniform settlement statement.
6. Advance inspection of uniform settlement statement.

Consumer Information.   Under provisions in RESPA, lenders are required to provide prospective borrowers with an information booklet containing information on estate closings and RESPA when a loan application is made. This booklet contains information provided by the U.S. Department of Housing and Urban Development. It provides a description of closing costs and contains various illustrations designed to inform a prospective buyer/borrower of the nature of the costs. It describes the function of the parties usually involved in a real estate transaction, as well as fees likely to be charged by lenders. It also provides information on the responsibility of all parties engaged in the closing under RESPA provisions.

Advance Disclosure of Settlement Costs.   At present the lender is required to provide to the borrower, at the time of application, good faith estimates of certain closing costs for which information is available. The lender must provide information on the basis of actual costs known at that time, or estimates based on past experience in the locality in which the property is located.

The estimates provided by the lender generally cover costs in the following categories: (a) title search; (b) title examination and opinion; (c) title insurance; (d) attorney's fee; (e) preparation of documents; (f) property survey; (g) credit report; (h) appraisal; (i) pest inspection; (j) notary fees; (k) loan closing service fee; and (l) recording fees and any transfer tax. These items carry fairly standard charges and are usually easy for a lender to estimate.

The lender is encouraged to provide information regarding a second group of costs when the application is made, but is not required to do so. This second group of costs include: (a) loan origination fees; (b) loan discounts; (c) mortgage insurance application fees; (d) assump-

---

[21] For a much more detailed treatment of RESPA see Paul Barron, *Federal Regulation of Real Estate.*

tion/refinancing fees; (*e*) mortgage insurance and hazard insurance premiums; and (*f*) any escrow deposits for hazard insurance, mortgage insurance, and real estate taxes. These costs vary somewhat with time and, depending on companies used by the borrower for insurance, etc., are more difficult for a lender to estimate at the time of application. However, these costs must eventually be estimated by the lender if the loan application is approved. As will be discussed below, this second group of costs, along with any necessary revisions in the good faith estimates on costs disclosed at the time of application, must be made available for inspection by the borrower one day before the loan is closed.

Title Insurance Placement.   Under RESPA, a seller may not require that a buyer use a specific title company as a condition of sale. This regulation is aimed primarily at developers who may have obtained a very favorable title insurance rate on undeveloped land, with the understanding that after development, buyers would be required to place the title insurance with the same company. This part of the act prohibits such requirements and insures the freedom of the buyer to place title insurance with any title company.

Prohibition of Kickbacks and Unearned Fees.   Under RESPA, no person can give or receive a kickback or fee as a result of a referral. If any person refers a buyer-borrower to any specific party involved in the closing (lender, title company, attorney, real estate broker, appraiser, etc.) and receives a fee for the referral, receipt of such a fee violates the act.[22] RESPA also prohibits fee-splitting by parties associated with the closing unless fees are paid for services actually performed. This latter part of RESPA has probably caused more confusion than any other provision of the act because of the vagueness of the term "services actually performed." However, the intent was to prohibit any circumvention of payments that would have been normally called referral fees by simply splitting fees.

Uniform Settlement Cost Statement.   Under RESPA provisions, a uniform settlement statement must be used by the settlement agent at closing. The responsibility for preparation of this statement lies with the lender and it must be delivered to the borrower and seller at closing. Other closing statements, such as a company form, can also be used for closing purposes, if desired, but the uniform statement must be completed.

This statement is uniform in the sense that the same form (shown in Exhibit 10–7) must be used in all loan closings covered under

---

[22] This simply means that a person must actually perform some service to earn a fee. For example, attorney's fees, cooperative real estate brokerage fees, and title company closing fees are paid for service performed. However, a referral by a real estate broker or lender to a title company, where a kickback, commission, etc., is paid by the title company, is prohibited.

EXHIBIT 10-7

A. U.S. DEPARTMENT OF HOUSING AND URBAN DEVELOPMENT DISCLOSURE/SETTLEMENT STATEMENT	B. TYPE OF LOAN	
	1. ☐ FHA 2. ☐ FMHA 3. ☐ CONV. UNINS.	
	4. ☐ VA 5. ☐ CONV. INS.	
	6. FILE NUMBER	7. LOAN NUMBER
If the Truth-in-Lending Act applies to this transaction, a Truth-in-Lending statement is attached as page 3 of this form.	8. MORTG. INS. CASE NO.	

C. NOTE: This form is furnished to you prior to settlement to give you information about your settlement costs, and again after settlement to show the actual costs you have paid. The present copy of the form is:

☐ ADVANCE DISCLOSURE OF COSTS. Some items are estimated, and are marked "(e)". Some amounts may change if the settlement is held on a date other than the date estimated below. The preparer of this form is not responsible for errors or changes in amounts furnished by others.

☒ STATEMENT OF ACTUAL COSTS. Amounts paid to and by the settlement agent are shown. Items marked "(p.o.c.)" were paid outside the closing; they are shown here for informational purposes and are not included in totals.

D. NAME OF BORROWER	E. SELLER	F. LENDER
George and Alice Smith 100 Dirt Road Anytown, U.S.A.	Ralph and Pearl Brown 200 Heavenly Drive Anytown, U.S.A.	ABC Savings and Loan Anytown, U.S.A.

G. PROPERTY LOCATION	H. SETTLEMENT AGENT	I. DATES	
200 Heavenly Drive Anytown, U.S.A.	Land Title Co.	LOAN COMMITMENT 1-10-77	ADVANCE DISCLOSURE 1-30-77
	PLACE OF SETTLEMENT 100 North Street Anytown, U.S.A.	SETTLEMENT 1-31-77	DATE OF PRORATIONS IF DIFFERENT FROM SETTLEMENT —

J. SUMMARY OF BORROWER'S TRANSACTION		K. SUMMARY OF SELLER'S TRANSACTION	
		400. GROSS AMOUNT DUE TO SELLER:	
100. GROSS AMOUNT DUE FROM BORROWER:		401. Contract sales price	50,000.00
101. Contract sales price	50,000.00	402. Personal property	—
102. Personal property	—	403.	
103. Settlement charges to borrower (from line 1400, Section L)	1,854.86	404.	
104.		Adjustments for items paid by seller in advance:	
105.		405. City/town taxes to	—
Adjustments for items paid by seller in advance:		406. County taxes to	—
106. City/town taxes to		407. Assessments to	—
107. County taxes to		408. to	
108. Assessments to		409. to	
109. to		410. to	
110. to		411. to	
111. to		**420. GROSS AMOUNT DUE TO SELLER**	50,000.00
112. to		NOTE: The following 500 and 600 series sections are not required to be completed when this form is used for advance disclosure of settlement costs prior to settlement.	
120. GROSS AMOUNT DUE FROM BORROWER:	51,854.86		
200. AMOUNTS PAID BY OR IN BEHALF OF BORROWER:		**500. REDUCTIONS IN AMOUNT DUE TO SELLER:**	
		501. Payoff of first mortgage loan	21,284.15
201. Deposit or earnest money	500.00	502. Payoff of second mortgage loan	—
202. Principal amount of new loan(s)	40,000.00	503. Settlement charges to seller (from line 1400, Section L)	3,135.00
203. Existing loan(s) taken subject to			
204.		504. Existing loan(s) taken subject to	—
205.		505.	—
Credits to borrower for items unpaid by seller:		506.	—
206. City/town taxes to		507.	—
207. County taxes 1-1-77 to 1-30-77	78.90	508.	—
208. Assessments to		509.	—
209. to		Credits to borrower for items unpaid by seller:	
210. to			
211. to		510. City/town taxes to	—
212. to		511. County taxes 1-1-77 to 1-30-77	78.90
220. TOTAL AMOUNTS PAID BY OR IN BEHALF OF BORROWER	40,578.90	512. Assessments to	—
		513. to	
300. CASH AT SETTLEMENT REQUIRED FROM OR PAYABLE TO BORROWER:		514. to	
		515. to	
301. Gross amount due from borrower (from line 120)	51,854.86	**520. TOTAL REDUCTIONS IN AMOUNT DUE TO SELLER:**	24,498.05
		600. CASH TO SELLER FROM SETTLEMENT:	
302. Less amounts paid by or in behalf of borrower (from line 220)	(40,578.90)	601. Gross amount due to seller (from line 420)	50,000.00
		602. Less total reductions in amount due to seller (from line 520)	(24,495.05)
303. CASH (☒ REQUIRED FROM) OR (☐ PAYABLE TO) BORROWER:	11,275.96	**603. CASH TO SELLER FROM SETTLEMENT**	25,501.95

HUD 1A REV 6-75 AS & AS (1323)   **LENDER COPY**   SPECIAL FORM OMB No. 63-R 1501

EXHIBIT 10-7 *(continued)*

L. SETTLEMENT CHARGES	PAID FROM BORROWER'S FUNDS	PAID FROM SELLER'S FUNDS
700. SALES/BROKER'S COMMISSION based on price $50,000.00 @ 6 %		
701. Total commission paid by seller Division of commission as follows: Anytown Realty Co.		3,000.00
702. $ to		
703. $ to		
704.		
800. ITEMS PAYABLE IN CONNECTION WITH LOAN.		
801. Loan Origination fee 1.5 %	800.00	
802. Loan Discount %		
803. Appraisal Fee to		
804. Credit Report to		
805. Lender's inspection fee		
806. Mortgage Insurance application fee to		
807. Assumption/refinancing fee		
808. Loan Application Fee		
809.		
810.		
811.		
900. ITEMS REQUIRED BY LENDER TO BE PAID IN ADVANCE.		
901. Interest from 1-31-77 to 2-1-77 @ $9.86 /day	9.86	
902. Mortgage insurance premium for mo. to		
903. Hazard insurance premium for yrs. to		
904. yrs. to		
905.		
1000. RESERVES DEPOSITED WITH LENDER FOR:		
1001. Hazard insurance mo. @ $ /mo.		
1002. Mortgage insurance mo. @ $ /mo.		
1003. City property taxes mo. @ $ /mo.		
1004. County property taxes 4 mo. @ $ 80 /mo.	320.00	
1005. Annual assessments mo. @ $ /mo.		
1006. mo. @ $ /mo.		
1007. mo. @ $ /mo.		
1008. mo. @ $ /mo.		
1100. TITLE CHARGES:		
1101. Settlement or closing fee to		10.00
1102. Abstract or title search to		
1103. Title examination to		
1104. Title insurance binder to		
1105. Document preparation to		
1106. Notary fees to		
1107. Attorney's Fees to *(includes above items No.:)*		
1108. Title insurance to *(includes above items No.: 1102, 1103, 1104, 1106)*	350.00	
1109. Lender's coverage $		
1110. Owner's coverage $		
1111.		
1112.		
1113.		
1200. GOVERNMENT RECORDING AND TRANSFER CHARGES		
1201. Recording fees: Deed $ 10 ; Mortgage $ 15 Releases $ 5	25.00	5.00
1202. City/county tax/stamps: Deed $ 1/2% ; Mortgage $	250.00	
1203. State tax/stamps: Deed $; Mortgage $		
1204.		
1300. ADDITIONAL SETTLEMENT CHARGES		
1301. Survey to		20.00
1302. Pest inspection to		
1303. Connie Counsel - Attorney		100.00
1304. Larry Lawyer - Attorney	100.00	
1305.		
1400. TOTAL SETTLEMENT CHARGES *(entered on lines 103 and 503, Sections J and K)*	1,854.86	3,135.00

The Undersigned Acknowledges Receipt of This Disclosure Settlement Statement and Agrees to the Correctness Thereof.

_____   _____
Buyer or Agent   Seller or Agent

NOTE: Under certain circumstances the borrower and seller may be permitted to waive the 12-day period which must normally occur between advance disclosure and settlement. In the event such a waiver is made, copies of the statements of waiver, executed as provided in the regulations of the Department of Housing and Urban Development, shall be attached to and made a part of this form when the form is used as a settlement statement.

HUD-1B (5-75)   AS & AS (1323)

RESPA. This form, coupled with the information booklet received by the borrower when the loan application is made, which defines and illustrates costs on a line-by-line basis, should enable the borrower to make a better judgment concerning the reasonableness of closing costs to be paid.

Advance Inspection of Uniform Settlement Statement. Not only must a uniform settlement statement, which details all closing costs, be used at the closing, but the borrower has the right to inspect this statement *one day prior to closing.* At that time, information on the additional closing costs not required to be disclosed when the loan application is made must be disclosed to the borrower. These costs include those in the second category mentioned earlier, such as loan origination fees, loan discount, fees for mortgage insurance application, any assumption or refinancing fees, any prepaid mortgage or hazard insurance premiums, escrow deposits, and prepaid interest.

All of these costs must be disclosed to the extent that they are known to the lender on the day prior to closing. Also, the good faith estimates of other closing costs made when the loan application was completed by the borrower must be revised, if necessary, to reflect actual costs at that time. Both groups of costs must be entered on the uniform disclosure statement for inspection by the borrower, unless the borrower waives right of inspection. This can be done by the borrower signing a statement waiving this right. If the borrower inspects the closing statement and agrees to all of the closing charges, the next step is to close the loan the following day.

The intent of RESPA can be summarized at this point by observing that with the information booklet, with advance disclosure of some closing costs, and with the right of a borrower to inspect the uniform settlement statement *prior* to closing, the borrower is able to shop around for the most competitive loan terms *and* closing costs. Any costs that are not understood by the borrower can be better explained and the borrower is in a better position to judge whether closing costs are excessive and can be obtained from another lender on better terms.

Closing Statement—Example To illustrate the development of the uniform settlement statement required under RESPA, we consider the example that follows. The property, located at 200 Heavenly Drive, has been contracted for purchase at a price of $50,000 and scheduled for closing on January 31. Data pertinent to the transaction are detailed below. The buyer has asked for and received an advance disclosure of settlement costs on a form exactly like the one shown in Exhibit 10–7. Since the disclosure was made by the lender one day prior to closing, accurate information was available on all costs and fees associated with the closing. Therefore, it is assumed in this example that the advance disclosure estimate and final disclosure of settlement cost statements are the same. Recall that they do not necessarily have to be identical since estimates are made on the advance disclosure. Recall also that some items; e.g., attorney's fees, pest inspection, etc., may be paid outside of the closing. In addition, the lender is not requiring private mortgage insurance on the conventional loan, nor is a hazard insurance escrow account to be established as the borrower has presented an insurance binder evidencing a prepaid, one-year hazard insurance policy. The

---

Buyer: George and Alice Smith
          100 Dirt Road
          Anytown, USA

Seller: Ralph and Pearl Brown
          200 Heavenly Drive
          Anytown, USA

Lender: ABC Savings and Loan Association
          Anytown, USA

Settlement agent: Land Title Co.
          Anytown, USA
Loan commitment date: January 10
Advance disclosure date: January 30
Actual settlement date (closing date):   January 31

I.   Buyer and seller information:
 a.   Purchase price $50,000.00
 b.   Deposit 500.00
 c.   Real estate tax proration (taxes due Jan. 1 and July 1,
      $960 per year, $480 per half. Taxes unpaid by seller:
      Jan. 1–30, 30 days or 30/365 × $960 = $78.90 ....   78.90

II. Buyer/borrower and lender information:
 a.   Amount of loan (9% interest, 25 years, conventional loan).......... 40,000.00
 b.   Prepaid interest Jan. 31–Feb. 1 (1 day) or
      1/365 × 0.09 × ($40,000) = $9.86 ....   9.86
 c.   Property tax escrow (1 month accrued since Jan 1,
      plus 3 mos. additional escrow @ $80 mo.) 320.00
 d.   Loan origination fee (2%) 800.00

III. Transactions between buyer/borrower and others:
 a.   Title insurance fees (Land Title Co.) $335, survey
      endorsement $10, notary charge $5.00 ....   350.00
 b.   Recording fees (deed $10, mortgage $15) 25.00
 c.   Real estate transfer tax (½ of 1%) 250.00
 d.   Larry Lawyer–attorney fee..   100.00

IV. Transactions between seller and others:
 a.   Land Title Company–closing fee 10.00
 b.   Release statement–seller's mortgage 5.00
 c.   Payoff–seller's mortgage (Anytown State Bank) 21,284.15
 d.   Real estate brokerage fee (6%) (Anytown Realty Co.) 3,000.00
 e.   Connie Counsel–attorney fee 100.00
 f.   Pest inspection (Anytime Pest Co.) 20.00

borrower has elected not to purchase mortgage cancellation life insurance; however, the borrower has agreed to establish a property tax escrow account with the lender for payment of property taxes due on July 1 and has agreed to pay a monthly installment equal to one twelfth of estimated annual taxes.

Based on the preceding information, which shows how the seller and buyer have agreed to split costs and fees and financing costs, the statement detailing actual settlement costs is shown in Exhibit 10–7. Note that, on the basis of the summary of all costs and expenses, the buyer will have to provide $11,275.96 at the time of closing. This represents the selling price of $50,000 less the $40,000 amount borrowed, less the $500 deposit paid to the seller, plus $1,854.86 which represents financing charges, settlement costs and escrow requirements detailed on the second page of Exhibit 10–7. The seller will receive a check from the lender for $25,501.95 which represents the $50,000 sale price less the $21,284.15 mortgage balance owned, less $3,135.00 which represents primarily the $3,000 real estate commission and the seller's share of settlement costs, detailed on the second page of Exhibit 10–7.

Federal Truth-in-Lending Requirements   In addition to disclosure requirements affecting settlement costs under RESPA, disclosure requirements under the federal Truth-in-Lending Act,[23] dealing with finance charges, has been a requirement affecting lenders since 1968. The truth-in-lending provision, like the RESPA legislation, is intended to provide the buyer/borrower with disclosure of financing costs and is not intended to regulate financing costs or interest rates. In addition to the disclosure of costs, the Truth-in-Lending Act requires the computation of the effective loan yield (cost) on a given loan according to an actuarial method as prescribed by the act. This effective loan yield (cost) is called the annual percentage rate (APR) and its computation was demonstrated in the preceding chapter in connection with mortgage yields when origination fees were considered.

Coverage and Requirements of Truth in Lending   Transactions that fall under RESPA requirements will generally be covered by the Truth-in-Lending Act. Under provisions of the act, the lender must disclose to the buyer/borrower information in six vital areas associated with the loan closing and this information must be included in a uniform Truth-in-Lending statement (see Exhibit 10–8).

Finance Charges and Prepaid Finance Charges.   Finance charges are generally interpreted to mean interest; however, certain other categories of charges must be included as finance charges and must be disclosed to the borrower. These items include:

---

[23] Public Law 90–321 (1968) as amended. Development of specific regulations and supplementation under the act were charged to the Federal Reserve Board, which issued Regulation Z in 1968.

EXHIBIT 10–8

Federal Truth-in-Lending Statement

I. A. Cash price (contract sales price)............................ $50,000.00

    1. Less any cash down payment $10,000.00

    2. Less any trade-in ....$ —

    3.   Total down payment $10,000.00

  B. Equals unpaid balance of cash price $40,000.00

  C. Plus any other amounts financed:

    1. Property insurance premiums ....$ —

    2. _____ ....$ —

    3.   Total other amounts financed .... $ —

  D. Equals unpaid balance $40,000.00

  E. Less any prepaid finance charges:

    1. Origination fee or points paid by borrower ....$ 800.00

    2. Loan discount or points paid by seller ....$ —

    3. Interest from (1–31–77) to (2–1–77) ....$ 9.86

    4. Mortgage guaranty insurance ....$ —

    5. _____ ....$ —

    6.   Total prepaid finance charge .... $ 809.86

  F. Equals amount financed $39,190.14

II. The FINANCE CHARGE consists of

  A. Interest (simple annual rate of 9%) $60,680.00

  B. Total prepaid finance charge (I. E. 6.) ....$ 809.86

  C. _____ $ —

  D.   Total FINANCE CHARGE $61,489.86

III. A. The ANNUAL PERCENTAGE RATE on the

    amount financed is 9.25%

  B. If the contract includes a provision for variation in the interest rate, describe: none

IV. The repayment terms are: 300 monthly installments of $335.60 beginning on the 1st day of March, 1977 and due on the 1st day of each month thereafter.

V. The finance charge begins to accrue on: February 1, 1977

VI. In the event of late payments, charges may be assessed as follows: After 30 days, interest will be assessed at 9% on all amounts past due.

VII. (Use either A or B as appropriate)

  A. Conditions and penalties for prepaying this obligation are: none

  B. Identification of method of rebate of unearned finance charge is:

VIII. Insurance taken in connection with this obligation: none

IX. The security for this obligation is: 1st mortgage on property located at 200 Heavenly Drive, Anytown, USA (Zip)

a. FHA or private mortgage insurance *required* by the lender.
b. Mortgage cancellation insurance when *required* by the lender, unless the borrower is informed of the nature and cost of the insurance and the lender obtains, in writing, from the borrower a statement that he desires the coverage.
c. Property insurance when *required* by the lender, unless the borrower acknowledges in writing that he is aware of the cost of such insurance and that he can obtain such insurance from any supplier he desires.

Prepaid finance charges must be treated as a cost of borrowing and include:

a. Loan application fees or fees charged by the lender to evaluate and compile data on a loan applicant.
b. Loan commitment fees or a fee charged by lenders for issuing a loan commitment whether the loan is accepted or refused by the borrower.
c. Loan origination fees including discount points charged by lenders to increase loan yields, usually paid by borrowers in conventional loan transactions.
d. Discount points, or fees charged by lenders to raise the yield on FHA/VA loans, paid by the seller.
e. Escrow charges (not to be confused with the escrow reserve for future payments), or a charge made by the lender for establishing an escrow account.
f. Prepaid interest, or interest due the lender from date of closing until the beginning of the period covered by the first mortgage payment.
g. Any prepaid FHA or private mortgage insurance premiums.
h. Assumption fees, or charges levied against the borrower by the lender when an existing mortgage is assumed rather than making a new loan when a property is purchased.
i. Preparation of an amortization schedule by the lender and charged to the borrower.

Both categories—finance charges and prepaid finance charges—are treated as part of loan costs and must be included in determining the effective cost of the loan, or *APR,* by deducting such charges as they are paid over the life of the loan. For example, interest charges and mortgage insurance fees occur over the life of the loan and will be included as they are paid. However, prepaid finance charges generally occur at the time of closing and will be deducted from the amount actually borrowed by the buyer. (This process will be illustrated in the section that follows on the annual percentage rate.)

Other Closing Costs and Statutory Fees. These items are specifically *excluded* from the determination of finance charges as they are legal fees and are customarily present in any real estate transfer. They generally provide no income or return to the lender. Costs in these categories include:

a. Title search, opinion or title insurance costs.

b. Preparation of deeds, settlement statements, and loan documents.

c. Escrow accounts and funds accumulated for future payment of taxes, insurance, water, sewer, etc.

d. Appraisal fees, credit reports, notary fees.

e. Transfer taxes, deed recording, etc.

Charges Financed by Lender. Any fees, insurance, or payments made to third parties connected with the loan closing, which the lender agrees to finance, must be included in determining financing costs. To illustrate; if the first year's hazard insurance premium is borrowed by the buyer, interest charges on this loan are also included with mortgage interest in computing the effective cost of the loan.

The Annual Percentage Rate. This requirement simply specifies that the lender will disclose to the borrower the amount actually financed by the lender, the dollar amount of finance charges made by the lender, and the resultant actual percentage interest rate charged, termed the annual percentage rate (*APR*).

To show how the disclosure is made on the uniform federal Truth-in-Lending statement, the preceding loan closing is again used as an example in Exhibit 10–8. Referring back to Exhibit 10–7, which illustrated the uniform loan closing disclosure statement under RESPA, the necessary information can be gathered for completion of the truth-in-lending portion of RESPA requirements. Looking down Exhibit 10–8, it can be seen that the unpaid loan balance (Items I–D) is straightforward in our example, since there were no trade-ins or items in addition to the purchase of the property financed by the lender. Hence the unpaid balance is $40,000 and represents the contractual amount to be repaid by the borrower.

In determining how much the borrower will have for actual use, or the amount actually financed, various deductions must be made from the unpaid loan balance when necessary. In our example there was a loan origination fee of $800 charged by the lender and prepaid interest in the amount of $9.86, leaving the amount financed at $39,190.14. In other words, the lender is actually financing $39,190.14; however, the borrower has contracted to repay $40,000 plus 9 percent interest over a time of 25 years. Other prepaid items such as loan application fees, assumption fees, commitment fees, discount points, and other items discussed in connection with prepaid finance charges will also be deducted, when appropriate, in the determination of the amount actually financed.

Another required disclosure to the borrower under the Truth-in-Lending statement is the actual dollar amount of finance charges (Section II, Exhibit 10–8). This is simply determined as total interest to be paid over the mortgage term plus prepaid finance charges. Total interest payments are easily determined in our example by first computing the monthly mortgage payment for the $40,000 loan amount, at 9 percent for 25 years, or $40,000 × 0.00839 = $335.60; then by multiplying the monthly payment of $335.60 × 300, or the number of monthly payments to be made over the life of the loan (12 × 25 years). This product shows that total dollars to be paid by the borrower over the life of the loan are $100,680. The contract loan amount is $40,000. Therefore, the amount of interest collected by the lender over 25 years is $100,680 − $40,000, or $60,680. When the $809.86 in prepaid finance charges is added to the interest to be collected by the lender over the term of the loan, the total dollar finance charge of $61,489.86 is determined. Item C under Section II in Exhibit 10–8 also provides for additional charges for FHA insurance, and private mortgage insurance premiums, when appropriate, which represent additional finance charges paid over the life of the mortgage loan.

Section III in Exhibit 10–8 deals with the determination of the annual percentage rate (*APR*) which is the true rate being charged on the loan by the lender. This computation has been demonstrated in the preceding chapter. It is carried out as follows:

$$\$335.60 \ (IF, PV \text{ of } \$1 \text{ per mo., } ?\%, 25 \text{ yrs.}) = \$39,190.14$$
$$(IF, PV \text{ of } \$1 \text{ per mo., } ?\%, 25 \text{ yrs.}) = \quad 116.77$$

Looking to the interest tables provided in the Appendix, and considering interest factors in column 4 for 25 years for various interest rates, we see that in the 9.25 percent tables, the *IF* is equal to 116.77; hence the true interest cost for the loan in our example, or the *APR*, is 9.25 percent.[24] This interest rate is obviously higher than the 9 percent contract interest rate that appears on the note accompanying the mortgage.[25]

Method of Repayment, Late Payments and Prepayment Penalites. Disclosure requirements under truth-in-lending also provide that in the time intervals allowed for loan repayment, interest penalties for late payments, and prepayment penalties must be fully disclosed. In our example, such disclosures are illustrated in Sections IV through VII of

---

[24] It should be recalled that the 9.25 rate is the true rate assuming the mortgage loan is repaid after 25 years. If repaid earlier, the true yield on the loan will be *greater* than 9.25 percent. In addition, prepayment penalties are not included in the computation of the *APR*, hence if the loan is prepaid during the penalty period this will also serve to increase the cost of the loan.

[25] Tables have been compiled by and are available from the Federal Reserve System to provide the *APR* for various loans, given the contract interest rate and prepaid finance charges.

Exhibit 10–8. However, if a loan is not fully amortized, but involves unequal payments as might be the case with a construction loan, a demand loan, or a partially amortized loan, either a loan repayment schedule disclosing what portion of each payment is interest and principal or a full explanation of how interest is to be computed and any terms and conditions for refinancing must be included.

Security Interests. The fact that a lien will be placed on real property must be clearly disclosed. The property that is being made subject to the lien must be described, usually by attaching a copy of the mortgage or note to the Truth-in-Lending statement.

Special Types of Residential Financing

Condominiums Many buyers of residential properties have come to know the concept of condominium propery ownership. The term "condominium" means individual ownership of one-family units within a multifamily structure (such as a high rise) or complex (such as a planned unit development). This ownership is coupled with an individual ownership interest in the land and common areas (halls, recreation facilities, etc.) which are a part of the condominium development. In other words, the owner of a condominium unit owns the unit and has an ownership interest in all common areas. The ownership interest in the common areas is usually determined by either: (1) the ratio of the value of an owner's unit to the total project value; or (2) the ratio of square footage contained in an owner's unit to the total square footage in a project. This ownership interest also determines the extent to which each owner must contribute to operating the owners' association which is the legal entity created to operate and manage the common areas within the development.

For a condominium to be created, most states have provided that certain statutory requirements be fulfilled. In Ohio, for instance, the condominium statute provides for a declaration containing:

1. A legal description of the land.
2. The name of the condominium property, including the word "condominium."
3. Purposes and restrictions in the use of the property.
4. A plot or floor plan of the building, including principal materials and the number of stories, basements, and units therein.
5. Unit designation, together with access areas.
6. A description of the common areas and facilities, and the percentage of the total interest appertaining to each unit.
7. A statement that each owner shall be a member of a unit owners'

association which shall be established for the administration of
condominium property.

8. Designation of the person to receive service of process for the unit
owners' association.

9. A method for amending the declaration, requiring approval of not
less than 75 percent of the voting power.

The declaration must be filed with the county recorder and the county
auditor.

The unit owners' association is operated by a board of managers
duly elected by the membership. This board normally provides for the
prompt repair of common areas, assessment of common expenses, and
the distribution of common profits. A lien upon an individual unit is
provided for failure of a member to pay his properly allocated share of
common expenses. Common profits, like losses, are assigned to the
unit owners according to their percentages of interest in the common
areas and facilities as set forth in the declaration. These percentages also
determine members' voting strength in the unit owners' association.

There are features associated with condominium ownership that many
buyers find attractive. The primary advantages include: maintenance
and repair being performed by professional management, retention of
the tax deductibility of interest enjoyed by single-family owners, possible
lower costs of construction when compared to single-family units of the
same size, location in highly desirable areas that would not be afford-
able if a single-family detached unit were considered, to name a few.

With respect to financing, there is not much difference between financing a single-family unit and a condominium unit. Both require
a mortgage loan commitment and a down payment and are closed in
a similar fashion. The uniform statement of settlement and truth-in-
lending requirements detailed in this chapter contain many of the
same closing costs. The primary differences between financing condominium units and single-family units lie in the underwriting process
that is performed prior to the loan commitment and the annual or
monthly fee charged for management and maintenance of the condominium, in addition to the monthly mortgage payment.

One area in underwriting loans on condominiums that sometimes
causes difficulty for lenders and borrowers lies in the appraisal of the
interest in common areas owned with the purchase of a single unit.
This problem is not too difficult to resolve if the unit is purchased
when the development is new, because cost data for the entire development can be relied on to some extent in establishing the value of a
buyer's interest in common elements. However, when the development
is not a new one and a unit is being resold, the lender may be very

cautious in accepting an appraisal containing a value for the interest in common elements. This is because the entire development may have to be appraised in order to establish the value of an owner's interest in them. This is very difficult to do and lenders will consider such appraisals carefully.

The lending institution making individual mortgage loans to prospective buyers of condominium units will be very cautious in examining the declaration on file with the county recorder and the by-laws governing the operation of the condominium owners' association. For example, of importance to the lender are the conditions in the owner association bylaws that restrict sales to tenants. An agreement may specify that buyers of condominiums must be retired, or over a certain age. This restriction in the lender's view may decrease the future marketability of the unit and, therefore, increase the lending risk.

Other areas of vital concern to the lender, particularly when the condominium project is a new one, are:

1. Provision for maintenance costs. A statement of the amount of the monthly operating fee and what services are covered must be presented to the lender. Most lenders know what "normal" fees should be from loans previously made and by continuous updating of information from condominium management companies. Any attempt by a developer of a condominium project to sell units while quoting buyers abnormally low operating costs will be frowned on by the lender. This practice will ultimately lead to the dissatisfaction of the buyer and poor future marketability of units.

2. Voting control of the owners' association during development or until all units are sold. During the period when initial sales of condominium units are made, the developer retains voting control because most of the units are yet to be sold. Consequently, if sales slow down or the developer becomes financially troubled, expenditures on maintenance may be deferred in an attempt to save operating cash and to keep the monthly maintenance fee low to attract other buyers. This can be a source of irritation to previous buyers and, should the development become known to have poor management, make for even poorer marketability. Hence many lenders require that voting control of the owners' association be relinquished by the developer after a reasonable time period, so that present individual owners may safeguard their investment.

3. Added expansion. When a loan on a condominium unit is being considered, the lender will want to see the *entire* development plan of the project, or additional phases of expansion expected to be completed by the developer. This is important because rapid expansion may result in over-use of existing recreational facilities and other common areas and make for poor future marketability. The lender wants to be sure that common facilities are adequate to service the entire number of occupants, both present and future.

4. *Ownership of recreation and vital common areas.* Some developers of condominiums have been known to *retain* ownership of a few vital facilities such as a swimming pool or sewerage plant within a development. These facilities are then leased to the owners' association *after* all units are sold. Sometimes the lease payments are extremely high and raise the monthly fee paid by individual owners. Most lenders will refuse to lend in such a case and will require that these facilities be a part of each buyer's ownership interest in all common areas. In this way, a developer cannot take advantage of owners after units are completed and sold.

5. *Escrow provisions for down payments.* Since many buyers of condominiums make purchase commitments before units are actually constructed, they should require that down payments made on units when the loan is closed be placed in an escrow account until the units are completed. If funds are not placed in escrow and if a developer uses these funds to complete the project and then defaults, buyers will have a difficult time recovering down payments. The developer should have adequate funds from construction and development loan commitments obtained before construction and should not have to resort to using down payments to complete construction.

Cooperatives To combat high rents following World War I and at intermittent intervals since that time, cooperative apartments have been promoted in some American cities, notably Chicago, Los Angeles, New York, and Philadelphia. The pattern of their financing is as follows: First, there is organized a corporation whose assets consist of the land and building that constitute the apartment. Then as large a mortgage as possible is obtained, with the land and building as security. Each apartment is assigned a price dependent upon the arrangement, the relative location, the number and size of rooms, and so on. The purchaser of each apartment secures the right to use it so long as he meets his obligations to the corporation, together with a percentage of stock that represents the purchase price. The total amount of stock issued is expected to be sold for an amount sufficient to make up the difference between the net proceeds of the mortgage and the total cost of the project. The cost here includes cost for land, construction, selling, and profit to the promoters.

If the building to be used for the cooperative venture is already in existence, the financing follows the pattern just outlined. If the building is not yet built, the promoter may prefer to play safe by "selling the blueprints" instead of the building. In other words, he has plans drawn for the proposed building and selects a site for its location. Then sales-men sell apartments from the plans, making sure to get substantial down payments, 25 percent or more, but giving a contract for purchase which enables the promoter to return the deposit should he decide not to go through with the deal. It is found that the venture is not likely to attract enough buyers, he can abandon or postpone the construction. If, on the other hand, buyers are sufficiently numerous to justify com-pletion of the program, construction will proceed. The remainder of the buyer's commitment, above the down payment, will be due at some future date, perhaps at the time of possession.

The "blueprint" plan assumes complete ownership by all who occupy apartments in the project. It is sometimes designated as the 100 per-cent plan. In addition, a modification of this plan, variously designated as semi-cooperative, group ownership, joint ownership, 40 percent plan, and so on, is sometimes financed by only a portion of the tenants with the remaining units rented to non-owners. Under either the 100 percent plan or any variation of it, the ground floor may be used for stores. These stores may be included in the cooperative scheme or may be rented separately at whatever they will bring in the market.

Types of Ownership of Cooperative Apartments   The three common types of ownership of cooperative apartments are: trust, corporate, and individual. In the trust type, legal ownership is in the name of a bank or trust company. Purchasers of units are given certificates of benefi-cial interest or participation certificates. The ownership of such a certifi-cate carries the right to lease a unit in the building. The lease defines the rights and obligations of its owner, including any restrictions upon sale and transfer, subletting rights, and so forth. Management of a trust type of apartment ownership may be vested in the trustee or other-wise, as defined in the agreement.

In the corporate type of ownership, title rests with the corporation of which the purchasers are shareholders. Management is determined by the board of directors. Here also restrictions may be placed upon the sale of stock and the transfer of leases by those originally entitled to them. The stock is frequently pledged with the directors of the cor-poration as additional assurance that its owners will meet their obliga-tions to the corporation. This practice parallels the pledging of certifi-cates with the trustee—in the previous type described above—for the same purpose.

In the third type of cooperative ownership, individuals have title to the units assigned for their use. Ownership may take one or two forms: tenancy in common or condominium. Under the tenancy in common type of ownership, the purchaser receives by deed an undivided interest in the whole with the right to occupy a particular unit. Under the condominium concept, the purchaser acquires by deed a fee simple title to a specific unit and common ownership of the public areas and the underlying ground. Tenancy in common has many of the disadvantages of the traditional cooperatives. Condominiums have recently received numerous statutory assists and are becoming increasingly popular. Prior to 1963 only six states had condominium laws on their books. Now this form of ownership is generally accepted.

QUESTIONS

1. What does underwriting mean in real estate lending?
2. What are some standard guidelines used in underwriting residential mortgage loans?
3. What are the differences between the cost and market comparison approaches to appraising property?
4. Why are lenders concerned with the value of a property over time in addition to its present appraised value?
5. Define financial leverage.
6. What does the incremental, or marginal, cost of borrowing mean?
7. Should borrowers always choose to maximize the use of financial leverage by borrowing as much as possible?
8. What are loan origination fees? List various types.
9. What is an escrow account? What does proration of property taxes mean?
10. What is private mortgage insurance coverage? Why is it used? How does it differ from mortgage cancellation insurance and hazzard insurance?
11. What is the Real Estate Settlement and Procedures Act? What is its intent?
12. What are requirements under RESPA? Discuss the process of disclosure of settlement costs from loan application to loan closing. What types of fees and conditions are prohibited under RESPA?
13. What is the Truth-in-Lending Act? How does it affect real estate lending? What must be disclosed under the uniform Truth-in-Lending Statement?
14. When a person buys a condominium, what is being purchased? What is the condominium declaration?
15. What are lenders especially cautious about when underwriting mortgage loans in condominiums?

CASE PROBLEMS

1. Ms. Sally Strutter is considering the following loan alternatives to finance the $60,000 house she would like to purchase. Loan A can be made for 80% of value, $48,000, at 8¾% for 25 years. Loan B can be made for 90% of value, or $54,000, at 9% for 25 years.

    a. What should be the monthly mortgage payments under Alternatives A and B?

    b. What is the marginal or incremental cost of borrowing the additional $6,000 under Alternative B?

c. If the property were held only 10 years, would this change the answer in *b?*

d. Assuming the price of the property is expected to appreciate to $62,000 after one year, what would be the rate of equity appreciation under both alternatives? Based on the results obtained, should financing Alternative B be chosen?

2. Referring back to problem 1, assume a new loan, Alternative C, can be obtained for $54,000 at 9% for 30 years. Comparing Alternatives A and C:

a. What would be monthly mortgage payments under Alternatives A and C?

b. Assuming the property is expected to be held only 10 years, what would be the marginal cost of borrowing the additional $6,000 under Alternative C?

c. If the property were held for 15 years, would the answer in *b* be different? Explain; do not work out a solution.

d. Assuming the property is expected to increase in value to $62,000 after one year, what would be the rate of equity appreciation on Alternative C as compared to Alternative A?

3. Mr. Robert Bedford, who is in the 40% tax bracket, makes the following loan: $50,000 for 25 years at 8½ percent. What is his interest deduction for tax purposes after the first year (assume the property is purchased on January 1) of ownership? What average monthly reduction in mortgage payment does this tax deduction represent?

4. Ms. Marion Marty bought a property for $30,000 five years ago. She presently could sell it for $38,000. Assuming Ms. Marty is over 65 years old, on what amount must capital gains tax be paid?

5. On August 20, Mr. and Mrs. Newton decided to buy a property from Mr. and Mrs. Oldton for $40,000. On August 30, Mr. and Mrs. Newton obtained a loan commitment from ABC Savings and Loan for a $30,000 conventional loan at 9% for 25 years. The lender informed Mr. and Mrs. Newton that an $800 loan origination fee will be required to obtain the loan. The loan closing is to take place September 15. In addition, escrow accounts will be required for both property taxes and hazard insurance; however, no mortgage insurance is necessary. A breakdown of expected settlement costs has been provided by ABC Savings and Loan when Mr. and Mrs. Newton inspect the Uniform Settlement Statement required under RESPA on September 14 as follows:

I. Buyer and seller information:
   a. Purchase price $40,000.00
   b. Deposit paid by Newtons to Oldtons (paid in escrow to
   ABC Savings and Loan) 500.00
   c. Real estate tax preparation (taxes due to county
   January 1 and July 1, $800 per year, $400 per half)
   (July 1–September 15 unpaid by seller) 77 days or
   (77/365 × $800) 168.77

II. Buyer/borrower and lender information:
   a. Amount of loan $30,000.00
   b. Prepaid interest—(regular monthly payments to begin on
   November 1—from closing through September = 16 days
   [16/365 × (0.09 × $30,000)] 118.36
   c. Property tax escrow—2 months required 133.33
   d. Hazard insurance escrow—2 months or $20 required 20.00
   e. Loan origination fee 800.00

III. Transactions between buyer/borrower and third parties:
    a. Title insurance fee (Landco Title Co.) ....$ 300.00
    b. Recording fees—mortgage and deed 25.00
    c. Real estate transfer tax (½ of 1% of purchase price) 200.00
    d. Barry Barrister—attorney 100.00
IV. Transactions between seller and third parties:
    a. Landco Title Co.—closing fee ....$ 60.00
    b. Release statement—seller's mortgage 5.00
    c. Payoff—seller's mortgage (XYZ State Bank) 15,215.00
    d. Real estate brokerage fee (6% Plain Deal Realty) 2,400.00
    e. Linda Lawyer—attorney 100.00
    f. Pest inspection 20.00

On September 15, Mr. and Mrs. Newton again inspect the uniform Settlement Statement as required under RESPA and none of the estimates has changed. Complete the closing statement using an approach similar to that used under RESPA.

   a. What are the amounts due from the borrower and due to the seller?
   b. What would the disclosed annual percentage rate be as required under the Truth-in-Lending Act?

APPENDIX: SPECIAL CONSIDERATIONS—RESIDENTIAL FINANCING

Sometimes, years after a real estate transaction has been closed, individuals are faced with decisions involving various aspects of their mortgage loan, For example, many individuals may be thinking of paying a part of their loan off early, of refinancing their loan, or possibly of selling their house on the basis of a mortgage assumption. This section deals with some of the decisions borrowers may face during the time over which they are paying off an existing loan and includes a framework through which various alternatives which confront them may be analyzed.

Loan Refinancing On occasion, an opportunity may arise for an individual to refinance a mortgage loan at a reduced rate of interest. Indeed, during the period of rapidly rising interest rates encountered in late 1973 and early 1974 and the reverse pattern of late 1975 and early 1976, some opportunities for refinancing existed, and many borrowers took advantage of it.

To illustrate the fundamental relationships in any refinancing decision, at least three ingredients must be known: (1) terms on the present outstanding loan, (2) new loan terms being considered, and (3) any charges associated with paying off the existing loan or acquiring the new loan (such as prepayment penalties on the existing loan or origination and closing fees on the new loan). To illustrate, assume a borrower makes a mortgage loan for $40,000 at 9 percent interest for 30 years. After five years, interest rates fall and a new mortgage loan is available at 8¾ percent for 25 years. The loan balance on the existing loan is $38,352 and a prepayment penalty of 1 percent must be paid on the existing loan. The lender who is making the new loan available also requires an origination fee of $200 plus $16 for incidental legal fees for recording, etc., if the new loan is made. Should the borrower refinance?

In answering this question, we must analyze the costs associated with refinancing and the benefits or savings which will accrue due to the reduction in interest charges, should the borrower choose to refinance. The costs associated with refinancing are detailed below.

Cost to refinance:
Prepayment penalty: 1% × $38,352 = $384
Origination fee, new loan   =   200
Recording, etc., new loan   =   16
       Total Costs $600

Benefits from refinancing are obviously the interest savings that result from a lower interest rate. Hence if refinancing occurs, the monthly mortgage payment under the new loan terms will be lower than payments under the existing mortgage. Monthly benefits would be $6.75 as shown:

Monthly savings due to refinancing:
Monthly payments, existing loan, $40,000, 9%, 30 years $322.00
Monthly payments, new loan $38,352, 8¾%, 25 years 315.25

Difference in monthly payments ....$ 6.75

The issue faced by the borrower now becomes whether or not it is worth investing, or paying out, $600 (charges for refinancing) to save $6.75 per month over the term of the loan. Perhaps the $600 could be reinvested in a more profitable alternative? To analyze this question, we should determine what rate of return is earned on the investment of $600 for 25 years, given that $6.75 per month represents the return. This is easily done as follows:

$6.75 × (*IF, PV* of $1 per month, ?%, 25 years) = $600
(*IF, PV* of $1 per month, ?%, 25 years) = $600/$6.75
(*IF, PV* of $1 per month, ?%, 25 years) =   88.88

Referring to the Appendix, we want to find the *IF* in column 4 for 25 years for some interest rate which is equal to 88.88. A search reveals that the 13 percent table shows an *IF* in column 4 equal to 88.67 for 25 years. Therefore, we know that the yield on our $600 dollar investment, with returns (savings) of $6.75 per month over 25 years, would be equivalent to earning slightly over 13 percent per year. If another alternative equal in risk cannot be found which provides a 13 percent annual return, the refinancing should be undertaken.

Early Repayment—Loan Refinancing One additional point must be made concerning refinancing, however, if the property is not held for the full 25 years. In that event, monthly savings of $6.75 do not occur for the entire 25-year term and therefore the refinancing is not as attractive. To demonstrate, if we assume the borrower plans to hold the property for only 10 more years after refinancing, is it still worthwhile? To analyze this alternative, note that the $600 cost will not change should the refinancing be undertaken; however, the benefits (savings) will change. The $6.75 monthly benefits will be realized for only 10 years. In addition, since the refinanced loan is expected to be repaid after 10 years, there will be a difference between loan balances on the existing loan and the new loan, due to different amortization rates.

Loan balance, 15th year–existing loan° $31,732
Loan balance, 10th year–new loan† 31,548

Difference ....$ 184

   ° Based on: $40,000, 9%, 30 years, prepaid after 15 years (col. 7, 9% table).
     † Based on: $38,352, 8¾%, 25 years, prepaid after 10 years (col. 6, 8¾% table).

The calculation comparing loan balances under the existing loan and under the new loan terms shows that if refinancing occurs, the amount saved because of a lower loan balance is $184, should the new loan be made. Hence, total savings in the event of refinancing would be $6.75 per month for 10 years, plus $184 at the end of 10 years. Do these savings justify an outlay of $600 in refinancing costs? To answer this question, we compute the return on the $600 outlay as follows:

$ 6.75 (*IF, PV* of $1 per month, ?%, 10 years)
+ 184.00 (*IF, PV* of $1, ?%, 10 years) = $600

Computing a simple yield on monthly returns, or ($6.75 × 12) ÷ $600, yields 13.5 percent; however, we note that $184 is far less than $600; hence we know that 13.5 percent greatly overstates the actual return. After trial and error with different interest rates, we will finally choose 9½ percent and discount as follows:

$ 6.75 (77.28121) = $522
$184.00 (0.38819) =   71

Present value: $593

    We see that when discounting at 9½ percent, the solution $593 is very close to the desired present value, or investment, of $600. Now we know the yield earned due to refinancing in this case will be slightly lower than 9½ percent per year for the ten-year period.

    Obviously, this return is much lower than the 13 percent return computed assuming the loan was repaid after 25 years. This is true because the refinancing cost of $600 remained the same, while the savings stream of $6.75 was shortened from 25 years to 10 years. Although an additional $184 was saved because of differences in loan balances, it did not offset the reduction in monthly savings that will have occurred from the 10th through the 25th year.

In analyzing refinancing decisions, then, not only must costs and benefits (savings) be compared but the time period one expects to hold a property must also enter into the decision. In our example, it is obvious that if the time period over which the mortgage is to be repaid is shortened, the rate earned on interest savings will be lower and consequently less attractive. In our last example, if an investor desired a return greater than the 9½ percent that the $600 outlay for refinancing would bring over the ten-year period, it would not be worthwhile to refinance. On the other hand, if the borrower was content with a rate of return lower than 9½ percent, the ten-year repayment period would still make it worthwhile to undertake the refinancing. Hence the refinancing decision should be based on what $600 investment alternatives are available at the time refinancing is being considered, and whether such alternatives will provide a return greater than 9½ percent over 10 years.[1]

Mortgage Loan Assumptions—Financial Implications   The final topic to be covered in this chapter deals with the possible advantage of purchasing a property by assuming the seller's mortgage loan. Mortgage loan assumptions are possible in some cases, depending on original borrowing terms.[2] The real advantage to selling under an assumption is for the buyer to retain the seller's mortgage terms, particularly if interest rates have risen significantly since the seller's mortgage was made.[3] For example, if an individual bought a $40,000 property and made a mortgage loan 5 years ago for $30,000 at 7 percent interest for a term of 25 years, the possibility of assuming such a loan might appear attractive if interest rates have risen. However, due to price appreciation and the fact that the loan has been amortized for 5 years, the amount of cash necessary for the buyer to assume the mortgage may be prohibitive for a buyer. For example, if the property has risen in value over the past 5 years to

---

[1] Another point to be considered here is the probability the loan will be held for less than 10 years. Obviously, if one expects to sell a property and to pay off the mortgage within 10 years, the interest savings on the $600 will be even less. Hence, if a borrower expects to sell a property within a short time after refinancing, it will be difficult to justify refinancing to begin with.

[2] In many areas of the United States, properties are sold on assumption. However, in many other areas, the right to sell on assumption is precluded explicitly in the mortgage or by the lender not approving the new buyer. Lending practices vary widely depending on tradition and economic conditions in a given area.

[3] It should also be pointed out that when selling under an assumption, in the event a buyer defaults on an assumed loan, the seller becomes liable for payment. However, a release from liability may be obtained by the seller from the lender, making the new buyer the only party liable in the event of default.

$50,000, the amount of cash equity required by the buyer to assume the seller's loan in our example would be $22,652, determined as follows:

Purchase price: $50,000
Seller's mortgage balance
   ($30,000, 7%, 25 years, after 5 years) 27,348
Cash equity required to assume: $22,652

If the buyer does not have $22,652 in cash, even though he desires an assumption, he may be unable to conclude the transaction.

Loan Assumptions and Second Mortgages   One alternative open to the buyer who could not make the large cash outlay in the above example may be to obtain a second mortgage. However, using a second mortgage will be justified in this case only if the terms of the second mortgage, when combined with terms on the assumed mortgage, will make the borrower as well or better off than if the entire purchase had been financed with a new mortgage. If the entire purchase can be financed with a new 80 percent mortgage loan for $40,000 at 9 percent for 20 years, we need to know how we may combine a second mortgage with the assumed mortgage to make the assumption as attractive as the new mortgage loan. If a second mortgage cannot be made on the required terms, a new mortgage loan will be made on current market terms. To analyze this problem we first compare monthly payments and amounts borrowed under a new loan, with monthly payments and amounts borrowed if an assumption is made:

	Amount Borrowed	Monthly Payments
New loan 9%, 20 years $40,000		$360.00
Assumed loan 7%, 25 years .... 27,348°		212.10†
Difference: $12,652		$147.90

° Outstanding balance based on $30,000, 7%, 25 years, after 5 years.
† Payments based on $30,000, 7%, 25 year term.

From the above calculation if an assumption is made, the borrower will have to provide $12,652 more than will be borrowed if a new loan is made for $40,000.[4] By assuming the mortgage, $147.90 per month will be saved when compared to making a new loan. However, if the borrower does not have the extra $12,652 to assume the loan, but can find a second mortgage for that amount, up to what rate can he pay on the second mortgage and still remain as well off as if he financed with the $40,000 loan at 9 percent for 20 years?

---

[4] It should be pointed out that under the assumption and the second mortgage, the buyer would pay the seller $10,000 down, assume the $27,348 mortgage balance, and find a second mortgage for $12,652, making the total purchase price of $50,000.

The answer to this question is easily determined. If the second mortgage is to be fully amortized over a 20 year period, the solution can be obtained by finding the rate of interest that monthly payments of $147.90 would yield on a loan of $12,652. This is accomplished as:

$147.90 (*IF, PV* of $1 per month, ?%, 20 years) = $12,652
  (*IF, PV* of $1 per month, ?%, 20 years) = $12,652/$147.90
  (*IF, PV* of $1 per month, ?%, 20 years) = 85.54

By consulting the tables in the Appendix for an *IF* in column 4 for 20 years, a search shows that the 13 percent table provides us with 85.36, or a solution very near 85.54. In other words, if a second mortgage bearing an interest rate of 13 percent for 20 years can be obtained, the combination of the assumed mortgage terms plus the second mortgage terms will be equivalent to financing the purchase with a new mortgage of $40,000 at 9 percent for 20 years.

The relationship can be seen more clearly by computing the combined mortgage payments on the assumed loan and a second mortgage loan made for 20 years at 13 percent.

Monthly payment assumed loan* $212.10
Monthly payment second mortgage loan†........... 148.28
                                                    $360.38 or
                                                    $360.00 (rounded)
* Based on original $30,000 loan, at 7%, for 25 years.
† Based on second mortgage loan of $12,652 at 13%, for 20 years.

We can now see that the combined monthly payments equal $360, an a $40,000 loan at 9 percent interest for 20 years. *Obviously if a second mortgage can be found bearing an effective interest rate less than 13 percent for 20 years, the buyer will be much better off by assuming the existing loan, as the combined monthly payments will be lower than making a new loan at 9%.*[5]

Second Mortgages and Shorter Maturities. In many cases second mortgages may not be available for a 20-year period. If a ten-year term were available on a second mortage loan at 12 percent interest, would the borrower be better off by assuming the existing mortgage and making a second mortgage, or should the entire $40,000 loan be refinanced at 9 percent? To answer this question we must determine the combined interest

---

[5] It should be apparent that such a high interest rate can be paid on the second mortgage because $27,348, or the amount assumed, carries a 7 percent rate and represents about two thirds of the $40,000 to be financed, while the second mortgage of $12,652 represents only one third. When weighted together by the respective interest rates, the total rate paid on the combined amounts is influenced more by the amount assumed at 7 percent.

cost on the assumed mortgage which carries a rate of 7 percent for 20 remaining years and the second mortgage which would carry a rate of 12 percent for 10 years. This combined rate can then be compared to the current 9 percent rate for 20 years presently available, should the property be financed with an entirely new mortgage loan.

To combine terms on the assumable mortgage and second mortgage we add monthly payments together as shown below.

	Monthly Payments
Assumed loan°	$212.10
Second mortgage†	181.56
Total	$393.66

° Based on original terms: $30,000, 7%, 20 years.
† Based on $12,652, 12%, 10 years (loan constant 0.01435).

The sum of the two monthly payments is equal to $393.66, which is far greater than the $360 payment required if a new loan for $40,000 is made at 9 percent interest for 20 years. However, the combined $393.66 monthly payments are made for only 10 years. After 10 years the second mortgage is completely repaid and only the $212.10 payments on the assumed loan will be made through the twentieth year. This pattern compares to $360 under an entirely new loan made for 20 years at 9 percent interest.

Whether or not the combined mortgages should be used by the borrower can now be determined by solving for the combined cost of borrowing. This cost is based on the monthly payments under both the assumed loan and second mortgage, for the respective number of months payments must be made, in relation to the $40,000 amount being financed. This can be seen easily to be the monthly payments of $181.56 on the second mortage for *10 years* and the $212.10 payments on the assumed mortgage for *20 years*, both discounted by an interest rate that results in the present value of $40,000.

$$\$181.56 \ (IF, PV \text{ of } \$1 \text{ per month, } ?\%, 10 \text{ years})$$
$$+ \ 212.10 \ (IF, PV \text{ of } \$1 \text{ per month, } ?\%, 20 \text{ years}) = \$40,000$$

By trial and error we search for the interest rate that gives the combinations of *IF*'s that make the present value of the combined monthly mortgage payments equal to $40,000.

Discounting at 8 percent:

$181.56 (82.42148	= $14,965
$212.10 (119.55429)	= 25,357
Present value	= $40,322

Discounting at 8.25 percent:

$181.56 (81.53107)	= $14,803
$212.10 (117.36184)	= 24,892
Present value	= $39,695

Interpolating:

Present value at 8%	= $40,322
— Desired present value	= 40,000
Difference	= $ 322
Present value at 8%	= $40,322
— Present value at 8.25%	= 39,695
Difference 0.25	= $ 627

$$\$322/\$627 \times 0.25\% = 0.128\%$$
Combined cost: 8% + 0.128% = 8.128%

By discounting at 8 percent and 8.25 percent and interpolating, the combined interest cost on both the existing mortgage if assumed for 20 years and the second mortgage made for 10 years is 8.128 percent. This combined package of financing still compares vary favorably to the 9 percent interest rate currently available on a $40,000 mortgage for 20 years.[6]

Loan Assumptions and Open-End Mortgages   The importance of an assumable open-end mortgage also becomes apparent when interest rates have risen since the seller of a property made his mortgage. Suppose the seller of the property is willing to increase the amount of the loan under an open-end mortgage provision that allows additional amounts, up to 80 percent of value, to be borrowed *at any time* on current lending terms. Returning to our example above, instead of the borrower having to find a second mortgage, the seller might merely exercise the open-end provision by borrowing an additional $12,652 which, when coupled with the outstanding balance of $27,348, would provide the necessary $40,000 which would be assumed by the borrower.[7] The $27,348 loan balance would still bear an interest charge of 7 percent. But the incremental amount borrowed, or $12,652, would cost 9 percent for the remaining

---

[6] It should be noted, however, that the combined monthly payments of $393.65, should the assumption and second mortgage combination be made, is much higher than the $360 payments available under a new mortgage for the first ten years. Although this is offset by the much lower $212.10 payments after ten years, the borrower must decide which pattern of monthly loan payments best fits his income pattern, in addition to simply choosing the loan alternative with the lower interest cost.

[7] The seller would still realize the sales price $50,000, less the outstanding loan balance of $27,348, or $22,652. This is true because the buyer must pay $10,000 down to the seller and the seller keeps the additional $12,652 borrowed under the open-end borrowing. The buyer assumes the full debt owed by the seller of $40,000, or $27,348 plus $12,652.

		Monthly Payment
Existing loan $27,348		$212.10°
Additional borrowing 12,652		113.87†
Total $40,000		$325.97

° Based on original loan $30,000, 7%, 25 years.
† Based on $12,652, 9%, 20 years.

The main advantage in assuming the existing loan can be seen in the 20 years because it must be borrowed at current market interest rates. Combining the terms on the $27,348 balance with the $12,652 additional amount borrowed results in a total monthly payment of $325.97.
difference between monthly payments on a new loan for $40,000 at 9 percent for 20 years which would be $360.00, and the combined payments if the loan is assumed *and* the seller exercises the open-end provision, which would be $325.97. By assuming the existing loan, the borrower will save $34.03 per month ($360 − $325.97).[8] Further, the combined effective interest cost on the assumed loan would be determined by finding the interest rate which would make the $325.97 combined payment on assumption equal to the $40,000 amount borrowed. This is done as follows:

$325.97 (*IF*, PV of $1 per mo., ?%, 20 yrs.) = $40,000
(*IF*, PV of $1 per mo., ?%, 20 yrs.) = $40,000/$325.97
(*IF*, PV of $1 per mo., ?%, 20 yrs.) = 122.71

Looking to the interest tables in the Appendix, we see that in column 4 in that 7.75 percent tables the *IF* corresponding to 20 years is 121.81, which is extremely close to 122.71. Consequently, the combined payments of $325.97 on the mortgage assumption of $40,000, represent an effective cost of approximately 7.75 percent.[9] *Clearly the 7.75 percent effective interest cost on the mortgage assumption is far better than the 9 percent rate that would have to be paid if the new loan were made.*

APPENDIX—CASE PROBLEMS

1. Barry Borrower made a 30 year, 9½% loan for $35,000 five years ago. Since then interest rates have fallen to 8¾ percent. He has contacted a lender who is willing to refinance the loan balance of $33,684 at 8¾% for 25 years.

---

[8] It should be pointed out that the seller will also recognize this saving and will probably raise his selling price to partially offset this advantage. It is clear that the $34.03 monthly saving is worth a considerable amount. If one looked at the $34.03 as an investment return, and if 9 percent represented a reasonable return on investment, the present value of those savings over 20 years would be $34.03 × (*PV* of $1 per month, 9%, 20 years) or $34.03 × (111.14) = $3,782. How much of this amount the buyer would be willing to pay over the $50,000 price would depend on competitive conditions and how much the buyer valued the interest savings.

[9] Interpolation results in a more precise yield of 7.76%.

However, there will be $1,365 in loan origination and legal fees if the new loan is made.

    a.   Assuming the new loan is held to maturity, how should Mr. Borrower decide whether or not to refinance?

    b.   If Mr. Borrower's property is expected to be sold ten years from now, how should Mr. Borrower decide whether or not to refinance?

    2.   Ms. Mary Maeker has an opportunity to buy a property with a loan assumption. The price of the property is $50,000 and it has an outstanding loan balance of $30,000 for 25 years remaining at 7% interest. Monthly mortgage payments are $212.10.

    a.   How much equity would Ms Maeker have to pay the seller to assume the loan if the property was purchased?

    b.   Assume Ms. Maeker could not provide the necessary equity in (*a*), but could finance an additional $10,000 with a second mortgage at 10% interest for 10 years, or finance the entire purchase with a $40,000 loan at 9% interest for 25 years. Which alternative would be the least costly?

    3.   Mr. Ralph Brown has an opportunity to purchase a property with a loan assumption. The selling price is $40,000 and the owner has an open-end mortgage. The present mortgage balance is $25,000, carries a 7½% interest rate, and has a remaining 20 years to maturity. Present monthly payments are $201.50. The owner of the property has agreed to exercise the open-end provision of the mortgage and to increase the loan amount to $35,000. However, this additional $10,000 amount would be financed at 9% interest over the remaining 20 years. Mr. Brown also has the option of financing the entire purchase with a $35,000 mortgage for 20 years at 9%.

    a.   Is the combined cost of financing more desirable than making a new $35,000 loan for 20 years at 9%?

    b.   What is the effective interest rate on the combined loans if the property is bought with the loan assumption?

11

Financing Income-Producing Properties

Introduction

This chapter deals with the *permanent* financing of income-producing properties such as apartment complexes, office buildings, and shopping centers. Financing these types of real estate differs considerably from residential financing. Risks associated with the economic condition of the national economy, local economy, competitive pressures from other businesses, and locational considerations all come to bear on the profitability of a given income-producing property. Consequently, the ability of an investor to repay a mortgage loan is affected by all of these forces in combination.

With the many types of risks to consider, the lender and borrower are faced with complex decisions when evaluating income-producing properties and the amount of financing that may be provided for a given venture. Modern techniques used in financial analysis are available which help in the assessment of risk and profitability of a particular investment. These techniques form the basis of this chapter. Knowledge of these techniques and their application will create a better understanding of the economic requirements of a project that must be met to obtain financing.

Two types of income-producing properties are illustrated and analyzed in this chapter: residential income-producing properties, such as apartment complexes; and commercial properties, including shopping centers and office buildings. Financial considerations from the lender's viewpoint, as well as financial and investment considerations from the investor's viewpoint, are carefully considered.

Residential Income Properties

Borrowers on residential income-producing properties such as apartment complexes must provide appropriate documentation with a loan application when seeking funds from a financial institution. Generally, the documentation required for review by the loan officer at a lending institution will include at least an income or operating statement and an appraisal report. In the case of a new apartment complex, the income statement will be an estimated statement based on a market survey, or feasibility study. This study is conducted separately or as part of the appraisal process to ascertain whether such a venture is economically feasible. When a loan analysis is made on an existing property, the lender will usually rely on an operating statement that is available from the present owner of the property.

With regard to the appraisal, if the project is a new one, the appraisal is made from plans and the market study. If it is an existing property, the appraisal will be based on a combination of past operating statements and market data.

Market Studies—*Economic Feasibility*   In beginning the appraisal process, a *market study* dealing with supply and demand factors, property characteristics, and other relevant information must be conducted to ascertain the *economic feasibility* of the proposed project. In the case of income-producing apartment complexes, trends and forecasts in the following areas are vital in establishing whether the local market can absorb the proposed number of units being planned at the desired rent levels.

Demand factors:
1. Population forecasts—by size of household, by age of head of household.
2. Income forecasts—by size of household, by age of head of household.
3. Employment levels.
4. Rate of industrial and business expansion.
5. Diversity of business activity in economic base.

Supply factors:
1. Vacancy levels—in the entire housing market and in rental range of proposed project.
2. New construction—in the entire housing market and in rental range of proposed project.
3. Trends in construction costs.
4. Geographical analysis of vacancy levels and new construction.

Neighborhood analysis:
1. Age of adjacent structures, condition, quality.
2. Conformity with surrounding structures and land uses.

3. Property taxes.
4. Public expenditures on community services.
5. Expenditures on education.
6. Accessibility to major work centers.
7. Proximity of convenience shopping, recreation.
8. Topographical and geographical considerations.
9. Zoning, land use plans in future development.

This checklist is illustrative, not exhaustive, of data necessary for a market study that would accompany an appraisal report. From this market study, support for projected operating statements is provided based on a careful evaluation of vacancy rates and new construction occurring in the rental range of the proposed apartment complex, coupled with the strength in local market demand. This study in turn provides the information that is essential to the development of an operating statement.

Operating Statements—Lender Considerations   The primary function of the operating statement from the lender's point of view is to determine the ability of a borrower to repay a loan, should one be granted. In order to make such a determination, the lender will perform a *financial ratio analysis* of the operating statement. The results of this analysis will then be compared with financial data from comparable properties to judge the accuracy of the operating statement. Results from the analysis will also aid the lender in determining the income potential of the property and its ability to cover loan payments.

To illustrate the use of financial ratio analysis, Exhibit 11–1 provides a breakdown of the income and expenses for Sandalwood Apartments, a proposed new 120-unit, low-rise apartment complex for which the borrower is seeking a permanent mortgage loan commitment. The 120-unit complex will have 60 two-bedroom apartments, 30 one-bedroom apartments, and 30 three-bedroom apartments. Laundry facilities will be provided and will generate other income for the project. The borrower has developed the projected statement in Exhibit 11–1, based on a market study. This statement is part of the documentation accompanying the loan application and is to be analyzed by the lender.

Initially, the borrower is seeking a permanent 25-year loan for 75 percent of value, or $1,687,500. The borrower has had a market study conducted and an appraisal made by an independent appraiser. The project's appraised value is $2.25 million ($500,000 land and $1.75 million building). How would the lender make a financial analysis of the project?

Debt Service Coverage   One of the primary considerations of the lender is the project's ability to generate sufficient income to cover mortgage payments. To help make this determination, the debt service coverage ratio is widely used by lenders. Using data from the operating state-

EXHIBIT 11–1
Projected Operating Statement, Sandalwood
Apartment Complex*

Rental income	$342,000
Other income	3,600
Gross potential income	345,600
Less vacancy and collection loss	17,280
Effective gross income	328,320
Less operating expeneses:	
Personnel–wages expense	25,920
Utilities–common areas	12,095
Management expense	17,280
Painting and decorating	6,912
Maintenance–repairs	12,095
Miscellaneous	5,185
Insurance	5,185
Real estate taxes	40,098
Total operating expenses	124,770
Net operating income	$203,550

* Rental schedule: $180 per month, 1 bedroom; $235 per month, 2 bedrooms; and $300 per month, 3-bedroom apartments. No utilities included in rent.

ment, this ratio is simply defined as net operating income (NOI), divided by the mortgage payments made during the year for a given loan amount and terms.

Assuming that current lending terms available at the time the borrower is seeking financing are 8.5 percent interest for 25 years, the debt service coverage ratio is calculated as:

Mortgage payment: $1,687,500 × 0.00805* = $13,584.38
Total mortgage payment per year: $13,584.38 × 12 = $163,013 (rounded)

* Loan constant, 8.5%, 25 years.

$$\text{Debt service coverage} = \frac{NOI}{\text{Total mortgage payment}} = \frac{\$203,550}{\$163,013} = 1.25$$

Based on the computation of debt service coverage, it can be seen that income after operating expenses, or NOI, covers the annual mortgage payments 1.25 times. In other words, if the 75 percent loan is granted, there is a cushion or margin of safety for the lender of ($203,550 − $163,013) $40,537. This means that net operating income can fall by $40,537 before the lender will be in any danger of not receiving mortgage payments.

Generally, the coverage ratio acceptable to the lender is determined by policy established by the particular lending institution based on *past loan experience* on comparable properties. In cases where loans have gone into default, coverage ratios used when these loans were originated may tend to represent a minimum acceptable or cut-off point for a given lender. A standard cut-off rate commonly used in the real estate industry for debt coverage ratios on residential income property is 1.25. In other words, most lenders set a 1.25 coverage ratio as the *minimum* amount of coverage they require for any prospective loan in that category. If that industry yardstick is applied in the preceding example, the 75 percent loan, if granted, should result in a debt service coverage ratio that will just meet the acceptable minimum.

Operating Expense Ratio It must be stressed that no one ratio computation made by the lender is sufficient to indicate whether a loan should be made or how much should be loaned. The lender must rely on a series of ratios and review all of them together as part of an overall financial analysis. Another equally important ratio, which is computed by most lenders, is the operating expense ratio. This is simply the ratio of total expenses to effective gross income. In our illustration it is computed as:

$$\text{Operating expense ratio} = \frac{\text{Operating expenses}}{\text{Effective gross income}} = \frac{\$124,770}{\$328,320} = 38.0\%$$

This ratio can then be compared to operating ratios compiled from comparable properties or from published industry data.[1] If there is a significant deviation from operating expense ratios reported from comparable properties, the lender will then make an item-by-item percentage comparison from data in the operating statement. In this way it can be determined what expense category caused the difference. An industry standard used by lenders for the operating expense ratio on residential income properties ranges from 35 percent to 40 percent of gross potential income. This means that the ratio computed in our example, or 38.0 percent, generally falls within the range of operating expenses reported on a national basis by apartment managers.

It is clear that a higher operating ratio, say significantly above 40 percent, will leave very little net operating income to cover debt service and will probably make lenders reluctant to finance a project. Does it also follow that a significantly lower operating expense ratio, say less than 35 percent, will make a lender more eager to finance a project? Not necessarily, as many developer/borrowers have been known to "dress up" operating statements by reducing expenses in order to show a higher net operating income. They then argue that with the higher net operating income, more can be borrowed since the debt service coverage will be acceptable, even with greater amounts borrowed. Lenders are usually aware of such possibilities and will closely question any operating expense

---

[1] A commonly used source of industry data for apartment complexes is: National Association of Realtors, Institute of Real Estate Management, *Apartment Building Expense Analysis* (Chicago: National Association of Realtors), annual issues.

ratio that is considerably lower than the industry average. The borrower then has to prove how the project might be managed more efficiently and at a lower cost than comparable properties.

Vacancy and Collection Loss Ratio   Another part of the operating statement that will be given careful attention by the lender is the adequacy of the vacancy and collection loss estimate. Obviously, this ratio must bear a close relationship with vacancy rates reported by managers of other apartment complexes in locations similar to the subject property. This ratio is highly sensitive to local economic conditions and signals when housing or other investment property has reached a saturation point, or a point of oversupply which may be critical to the market absorption of any new units. Lenders are aware of vacancy rates in their lending areas and constantly monitor and update this information.

While no hard and fast industry ratios exist for vacancy rates, it is generally believed that when residential income properties consistently run vacancies in excess of 5 to 7 percent of potential revenue, they may be risky ventures and have difficulty in meeting debt service.[2] Similarly, any attempt on an investor's part to use a ratio below 5 percent will also be questioned closely by a lender. As was the case with the operating expense ratio, this may simply be an attempt by the investor to "dress up" the operating statement and the lender will challenge any attempt to do so. Therefore, the ratio used in this case should be a reflection of the current rate experienced in the local apartment market, unless the borrower has a compelling reason to do otherwise.[3]

Break-Even Ratio   Another commonly used ratio indicates the amount of occupancy required before a project can meet all cash outlays associated with operation and debt service. This ratio is called the break-even ratio and is computed as:

$$\text{Break-even ratio} = \frac{\text{Operating expenses} + \text{Debt service}}{\text{Gross potential income}}$$

In our example, based on the 75 percent loan being considered by the lender, the break-even ratio is:

$$\frac{\$124{,}770 + \$163{,}013}{\$345{,}600} = 83.3\%$$

This ratio indicates that should the 75 percent loan be granted, the complex must be rented up to 83.3 percent of its potential revenue before all cash outlays for operations and debt service can be met. At that point the owner is earning a zero operating profit, or is "breaking even."

---

[2] For commercial properties such as shopping centers and office buildings, less than a 5 percent vacancy factor would be normal because of the long-term leases usually applicable in those situations.

[3] Such a reason may be that the subject property has a distinct locational or design advantage over other complexes, or perhaps has a better amenity package than its competition. However, a lender would still have to be convinced of such an advantage.

Another way of looking at the same ratio is to consider the maximum vacancy rate tolerable, if the loan is granted, that will still enable the owner to break even. This vacancy rate in our example is simply 100 percent, representing gross potential income, less the break-even ratio, or 83.3 percent, leaving 16.7 percent as the maximum amount of revenue that can be lost because of vacancies, before the owner incurs losses.[4]

Standard break-even occupancy ratios used in underwriting income producing residential property range from 80 to 85 percent of gross potential income. In fact, in many cases when properties are to be developed, some permanent lenders *require a minimum occupancy ratio* before the lending commitment becomes effective.[5] Obviously, a lower break-even occupancy ratio is desirable for both lender and borrower, given an accurate operating statement, as both are better off after the break-even point is reached. In our example, the break-even point of 83.3 percent estimated for the property in question, falls within the 80–85 percent suggested as an industry underwriting standard.

Gross Return on Asset Investment Another ratio used widely by lenders in underwriting decisions involving income-producing properties is gross return on asset investment. This ratio indicates how much income before debt service is being earned on total invested capital and is also a measure of profitability to the investor. In our example, this ratio is computed as:

$$\text{Gross return on asset investment} = \frac{NOI}{\text{Total assets}} = \frac{\$203,550}{\$2,250,000} = 9.0\%$$

The importance of this ratio lies in the fact that lenders desire some indication of a property's gross return. Unless an owner is earning a reasonable profit, property management and maintenance may suffer. One researcher in the field of real estate investment has indicated that a yield of about 10 percent has historically prevailed in the larger scale real estate developments such as apartment complexes and shopping centers.[6] Consequently the property being analyzed in our example is expected to return a gross yield that is roughly competitive with yields historically earned by other investors in similar properties. However, this yield will fluctuate over time depending on the supply and demand of

---

[4] When these ratios are used, it is assumed that all operating expenses tend to be fixed, that is, not dependent on occupancy. To the extent some of the expenses are variable, they may be lower as occupancy declines and should be reflected in the computation. Another assumption made here is that actual occupancy is proportional to gross potential income.

[5] In these cases a permanent commitment is made that involves the sale of a construction loan to the permanent lender. When an occupancy standard is used as a contingency in the permanent commitment, the lender is not required to purchase the construction loan until that standard is reached.

[6] See Paul F. Wendt and Alan R. Cerf, *Real Estate Investment Analysis and Taxation* (New York: McGraw-Hill Publishing Co., 1969).

comparable units, inflationary pressures, and the rate of return on capital available in other industries. During periods of heavy inflationary pressures, for example, the yield on real estate will be expected to increase to cover upward movements in mortgage interest rates and to keep pace with returns earned in other industries. Therefore, this ratio must be interpreted strictly in accordance with what comparable properties are yielding at a given point in time, as a historical yield may be somewhat misleading.

The Property Appraisal—Lender Considerations The role of property appraisals cannot be overemphasized in lending decisions because, as discussed in Chapter 10, appraised values are also used as a basis for lending. Methods and procedures used in establishing values are thoroughly reviewed and evaluated by the lender to prevent over-borrowing on a particular property.[7] The lender wants to be assured that both the initial property value and the pattern of property value over time exceed the outstanding loan balance for any given property over the term of the loan.

In making income property appraisals, usually one or a combination of three techniques is used. These techniques are the cost approach, the market approach, and the income capitalization approach. The basic essentials of each of these approaches are reviewed here to provide insight into the process followed by appraisers in establishing the values considered as a basis for financing by lenders.

Cost Approach The cost approach ordinarily involves determining the construction cost of building a given improvement, usually on a square footage basis, adding any amenities and extraordinary equipment requirements. In the case of existing buildings, the reproduction cost is normally reduced by estimating any physical, functional, or economic depreciation in arriving at final estimated value. This approach is procedurally identical to the cost approach detailed in Chapter 10 (see Exhibit 10–1). However, in the case of income-producing property, the variations in structural design, equipment, and locational influences make the cost estimation process much more complex. Consequently, the cost approach may be at times difficult to apply, particularly if the property is not a new one.

Market Approach The market approach as used in appraising income-producing properties relies on market comparables for judgments concerning value. As pointed out in Chapter 10, recently sold market comparables are chosen that are locationally adjacent to the subject property; and adjustments are made for size, physical characteristics, quality, and locational differences. However, two additional variations of the market

---

[7] Generally both the borrower and permanent lender will have appraisals made to ascertain what the basis for financing should be.

approach can be used when appraising income properties. These variations involve the gross income multiplier and the net income multiplier.

Gross Income Multiplier. If a truly comparable property has recently sold and can be accurately compared to the property being appraised, there may be operating statements available on the comparable property that can be used in appraising the subject property. Therefore, in addition to arriving at value using only sales prices on comparables, adjusted for various property differences, the relationship between gross income and sale price may also be significant in establishing value. For example, assume that a property very comparable to the Sandalwood apartment complex recently sold for $3 million. If operating statements are available and show that gross income for that property was $450,000, this would indicate that the property sold for approximately 6.67 times gross income. In other words, a gross income multiplier is simply the sale price of a particular property divided by gross income, or:

$$\text{Gross income multiplier } (GIM) = \frac{\text{Sale price}}{\text{Gross income}} = \frac{\$3,000,000}{\$450,000} = 6.67 \times$$

If a group of properties very comparable to the subject property have recently sold, a range of *GIM*s can be developed to support the multiplier used in the subject appraisal. For instance, if two other properties comparable to the Sandalwood property have recently sold and operating statements are available, additional *GIM*s can be developed as shown in Exhibit 11–2.

EXHIBIT 11–2
Development of Gross Income Multipliers for Comparable Properties

	Comparable Property		
	I	*II*	*III*
Date of sale	1/30/77	11/25/76	10/1/76
Sale price	$3,000,000	$2,500,000	$2,100,000
Gross income	$ 450,000	$ 385,000	$ 320,000
Gross income multiplier (*GIM*)	6.67 ×	6.49 ×	6.56 ×

After considerable analysis of each of these comparable properties, taking into account all differences among them, the appraiser may conclude that the appropriate multiplier to use on Sandalwood is 6.5 ×. Since the estimated gross income for Sandalwood is $345,600 (per the operating statement in Exhibit 11–1), use of this multiplier would result in an appraised value of $345,600 × 6.5, or $2,246,400.

Net Income Multiplier. In addition to gross income multipliers, some appraisers, when possible, develop net income multipliers as an additional basis for comparison. The net income multiplier is defined as the ratio of sale price to net operating income. For the three properties being used as a basis for comparing Sandalwood, net income multipliers are developed as shown in Exhibit 11–3.

The primary reason for considering net income multipliers is that operating expenses may vary somewhat among properties. If operating expenses vary significantly, this difference will show up in gross income, as higher operating costs must be recovered through higher rents.

EXHIBIT 11–3
Development of Net Income Multipliers for Comparable Properties

	Comparable Property		
	I	*II*	*III*
Sale Price	$3,000,000	$2,500,000	$2,100,000
Net operating income	$ 272,700	$ 223,215	$ 189,190
Net income multipliers (NIM)	11.0	11.2	11.1

Significant differences in operating expenses also indicate a lack of comparability, to a degree, which will have to be justified in the appraisal report. Therefore, the net income multiplier serves as a check on the gross income multiplier and, to some extent, indicates the relative comparability of properties used in the appraisal. In the case at hand, after an appraiser has considered the net income multipliers developed in Exhibit 11–3, he will arrive at an appropriate net income multiplier for the subject property. This multiplier will be based on a judgment of property characteristics both similar and dissimilar to comparable properties. Assuming a net income multiplier of 11.1 is deemed appropriate for Sandalwood, the value derived would be $203,550 × 11.1 = $2,259,405.

A Concluding Note on Market Multipliers. Although multipliers based on market income and sale prices can be important in deriving appraised values, a few words of caution are in order. These multipliers are meaningful only if the properties chosen for market comparables *are truly comparable*. Significant differences in building age, location, and quality make judgment in determining the appropriate multiplier a larger part of the decision process and so more room for error exists. In addition, use of these multipliers is helpful only for sales that have occurred a short time prior to the appraisal. This is true because expectations with regard to inflationary pressures and supply-demand conditions in the local market change from time to time and these expectations are reflected in market prices.

Income Capitalization Approach   The final approach to appraising income producing properties, and perhaps the most important of the three discussed here, is the income capitalization approach. This approach relies completely on the operating statement (provided in Exhibit 11–1) and views income from a particular project (before financing, depreciation, and taxes) as return on capital invested. In other words, net operating income of $203,550 in Exhibit 11–1 is viewed as a return on invested capital at some market rate of return. The key determinants to appraised value under the income capitalization approach are (1) accuracy of estimated net operating income and (2) selection of a market capitalization rate, or rate of return on invested capital. — **straight Cap**

Income Capitalization—Direct Capitalization. What follows is one of many approaches that may be used in estimating value by income capitalization.[8] This method is known as *direct capitalization* and is a very simple approach to income property valuation. It involves allocating a portion of net operating income as return on land value, then assigning the remainder of the income stream as a return on building value. The portion of the net operating income stream assigned to the land is based on the known present land value, or $500,000 in our case, capitalized by some market capitalization rate, adjusted for any anticipated increases in income earned on the land value due to inflation or real economic growth.

In choosing a capitalization rate, the appraiser usually looks to a number of external market yields, such as returns on bonds and other securities and comparable capitalization rates that have recently been used on similar properties. In the Sandalwood appraisal it is assumed that the appraiser selected a basic capitalization rate of 10 percent and that this rate will be adjusted for long-term inflation and economic growth at an assumed rate of 3 percent per year. Consequently, the portion of net operating income that represents return on land value is determined by the following valuation formula:

$$\frac{LI}{k\text{-}g} = \text{Land value}$$

In this formulation LI is the portion of net income attributable to land, k is the basic capitalization rate of 10 percent, and g is the expected 3 percent growth rate in the income stream accruing to the land.[9] Substituting these values for the appropriate terms yields the following:

---

[8] For a more complete description of various income capitalization approaches to value see William N. Kinnard, Jr., *Income Property Valuation* (Lexington, Mass.: D. C. Heath and Company, 1971) and L. W. Ellwood, *Ellwood Tables for Real Estate Appraisal and Financing* (Chicago: The American Institute of Real Estate Appraisers, 1967).

[9] Many appraisers do not show both k and g separately when using this method. They simply combine k-g, in this case $0.10 - 0.03 = 0.07$, and use the 0.07 as an overall capitalization rate. We show both k and g separately in order to make it clear that the income stream is expected to rise at the rate of three percent and the return on the land is actually 10 percent.

$$\frac{LI}{0.10-0.03} = \$500,000$$
$$LI = \$500,000 \times .07$$
$$LI = \$35,000$$

The portion of current net operating income attributable to land is $35,000, and this amount is expected to grow at the rate of 3 percent per year due to inflation and increased demand. Since net operating income from Exhibit 11–1 is $203,550 and $35,000 is attributable to land, the *residual* amount of net operating income allocated to the building is $203,550 − $35,000, or $168,550.

Assuming that the building has an economic life of 40 years, the building investment must be recovered during that time period, or at a rate of 2.5 percent per year (2.5 percent × 40 = 100 percent). Therefore adding a new term *d*, representing recapture of capital, to the land value formulation gives the following formulation for building value.[10]

$$\frac{BI}{k - g + d} = \text{Building value}$$

Making the appropriate substitutions gives the following result:

$$\frac{\$168,550}{0.10 - 0.03 + 0.025} = \text{Building value}$$
$$\$1,774,210 = \text{Building value}$$

Adding the land value of $500,000 to the building value of $1,774,210 results in a total estimated property value of $2,274,210 under the direct income capitalization method.

The uses of capitalization rates, growth rates, capital recovery rates, land value, and economic life are all specifically set out under this methodology, and the appraiser must be prepared to defend all of them as inputs to the appraisal. Justification must be provided for all inputs from comparable properties recently appraised and financed, or from market data that have been gathered. The lender will then seriously consider the estimated value under this approach as a basis for a permanent loan commitment.

Final Correlation   Based on individual estimates made under all three valuation approaches, that is, cost, market, and income capitalization, the appraiser will make a final judgment by choosing a value believed to be most indicative of market value. It may be equal to the value obtained under any of the three approaches, or it may be somewhere between the three estimated values. Exhibit 11–4 summarizes values derived under the approaches used for Sandalwood.

---

[10] Recapture rates do not apply to land value because it is assumed to have an unlimited economic life.

EXHIBIT 11–4
Summary of Appraised Values under Various
Appraisal Methods

Method	Dollar Value
Cost	$2,250,000
Market Comparison (*GIM*)	2,246,400
Market Comparison (*NIM*)	2,259,405
Income Capitalization	2,274,210

The appraiser makes the final judgment, giving weight to the method for which the best qualitative information was available and based on experience in appraising similar properties. In our illustration we assume the final appraised value chosen was $2.25 million.

Appraised Values and Financing—Summary   From the foregoing analysis, it is clear that the appraisal of income-producing properties is a fairly complex undertaking. Since the lender is vitally concerned about the collateral value of the property being mortgaged, the three approaches used in the appraisal report will be scrutinized for accuracy of data, comparability, and validity of the assumptions.

A valuable aspect of the appraisal report is that it lays out all of the market data that went into the estimation of value and provides an opportunity for the lender to satisfy himself as to whether or not the amount of funds being applied for is reasonable. By careful examination of the market research report and market data, and by making other assumptions deemed necessary, the lender can also derive a subjective estimate of value from the information provided in the appraisal report.

Financing Income Property—Borrower Considerations   Thus far, much of the analysis presented here has centered on the lender's analysis of documentation accompanying the loan application. We now turn to factors and influences that motivate the *borrower* to seek financing. Proper analysis of borrower considerations requires that new material involving financial leverage, depreciation, tax provisions, and cash flow be explored. This material forms the basis for *investment analysis,* which is used in analyzing the profitability of a project by a borrower/owner. However, investment decisions necessarily involve borrowing and financing decisions; hence, a complete treatment of the fundamentals of real estate investment analysis is essential for a better understanding of real estate finance.

Determination of Cash Flow   The purpose of investment analysis by a borrower/owner is to develop data that will answer three fundamental questions: What cash returns will the project provide before and after tax? What will be the overall yield on investment from operating returns and capital gains? How will return on investment be affected by the amount borrowed?

First, consideration is given to before-tax cash flow from operating the property. From the operating statement in Exhibit 11–1, we summarize the following information in Exhibit 11–5.

EXHIBIT 11–5
Condensed Operating Statement, Sandalwood Apartment Complex

Gross possible income	$345,600
Vacancy and collection loss	17,280
Operating expenses	124,770
Net operating income	$203,550
Less:	
Debt service	$163,013
Cash flow before tax	$ 40,537

Cash flow before tax is defined as cash revenues minus cash outlays for expenses and debt service. The project being considered has an appraised value of $2,250,000 and the amount of loan being discussed is $1,687,500, or 75 percent of value, leaving $562,500 as equity invested in the project. The annual debt service of $163,013, when subtracted from net operating income, results in cash flow before tax of $40,537 in the first year of the project's operation, as shown in Exhibit 11–5. The $40,537 represents a *before-tax cash return on equity* of 7.2 percent during the first year the project is operating ($40,537 ÷ $562,500). This relationship is sometimes referred to as a "cash on cash" return, as it represents the actual cash return from operating the project on equity invested.

After-Tax Cash Flow   Although before-tax cash flow and its relationship to equity invested is important to the borrower, it reveals only ~~on an~~ one half the picture of total return in a project. After-tax cash flow and ~~individual~~ its relationship to equity invested is perhaps the most important concept ~~basis~~ in investment analysis. The development of after-tax cash flow requires ~~only~~ the computation of taxable income, which involves depreciation and interest expense, both of which are deductible from net operating income in establishing taxable income.

In our illustration, the estimated economic life of the improvement is 40 years. The $2.25 million appraised value of the project is comprised of $500,000 in land and $1.75 million for the building. Assuming $100,000 salvage value for the building after 40 years, the annual depreciation charge on a straight-line basis will be the building value less salvage value, divided by 40 years, or ($1,750,000 − $100,000) ÷ 40 = $41,250;

and a straight-line rate of $41,250 ÷ $1,650,000 = 2.5$ percent. Since this is a new residential property, the internal revenue code will allow double declining balance depreciation, or two times the straight-line rate, as the depreciation charge in the first year. Therefore, $1,750,000 × 0.05$, or $87,500, is the depreciation charge allowable during the first year.[11]

Interest expense, also allowed as a deduction from net operating income, is computed by subtracting from total debt service of $163,013, the amount of principal reduction or amortization that occurred during the first year. Principal reduction is determined for the mortgage in our illustration by referring to the 8.5 percent interest tables and selecting the mortgage balance factor for a 25-year loan after *one year*. This factor is 0.9879 which, when multiplied by the original loan balance of $1,687,500, indicates that the mortgage balance after one year is $1,667,081. Hence principal reduction during the first year was $1,687,500 − $1,667,081, or $20,419. Of the total debt service of $163,013, therefore, $20,419 was amortization, leaving $142,594 as interest expense for the year.

With depreciation and interest expense determined, we can proceed with the computation of taxable income. Exhibit 11–6 contains a summary of relationships necessary in determining taxable income or loss.

EXHIBIT 11–6
Computation of Taxable Income, Sandalwood
Apartment Complex

Net operating income	$203,550
Less:	
Interest expense	142,594
Depreciation expense	87,500
Net income (loss)	($26,544)

From Exhibit 11–6, it is apparent that the owner of the Sandalwood project will report a *taxable loss* for the year. This loss is reportable even though $40,537 was realized in before-tax cash flow from the operation of the property (Exhibit 11–5). How is it possible to receive $40,537 in cash during the year and report a taxable loss of $26,544? The answer lies primarily in the $87,500 accelerated depreciation charge, which is a non-cash expense, yet allowed as a deductible expense for tax purposes. The accelerated depreciation charge is allowable because of a desire on

---

[11] Note that salvage value is ignored when computing depreciation under this method. For a discussion of current depreciation methods and other tax relationships important in real estate investment, see the tax environment appendix to this chapter. Readers who are not familiar with these tax relationships should read the appendix before continuing.

the part of government to stimulate investment in residential real estate. The net effect of this government policy is to allow the owner of this project to receive $40,537 in tax-free cash and also to deduct the $26,544 loss against income earned elsewhere in the determination of personal tax liability on all income for the year.[12] Consequently, an investor in a 50 percent tax bracket would have two sources of return in this case (1) before-tax or tax-free cash flow, and (2) a tax shelter resulting from the tax loss which may be netted against taxable income earned from other sources. Total after-tax cash flow for the first year is computed as follows:

Cash flow before tax $40,537
Plus: Tax saving: $26,544 × 0.50 13,272
After-tax cash flow $53,809

The *after-tax return on equity* in this case is computed by taking after-tax cash flow of $53,809 during the first year of operation and by dividing by the $562,500 equity invested by the owner. Therefore, the *after-tax return on equity* is 9.6 percent for the first year ($53,809 ÷ $562,500).

    After-Tax Cash Flow over the Investment Period. The *after-tax return on equity* computed in the preceding section is an indicator of the current return on investment for the initial year of operation. However, most investors are concerned with a measurement of return for the *entire investment period* during which they own the property. This return would include operating returns as well as any capital gain realized in the year in which a property is sold. Indeed, the capital gain may be the largest component of total return to be realized on an investment and certainly is not overlooked in a sound investment analysis.

    To determine the rate of return over the entire investment period, we assume Sandalwood will be held for five years.[13] As the direct income capitalization appraisal indicated previously, net operating income during this period is expected to increase at an average rate of 3 percent per year because of changes in demand and inflationary pressures. The property value is also expected to grow in value and at the end of five years is estimated to bring $2,613,600 when sold. Under these assumptions, what would be the after-tax rate of return on the entire investment?

    [12] The deduction of the $26,544 loss against other income is allowable only if the form of business used to own and operate the apartment project is a sole proprietorship or partnership. Corporations may *not* "pass through" tax losses to stockholders.

    [13] This assumption is only a convenience. One challenging exercise in investment analysis is to determine when an investment should be sold to maximize investment return. This requires a computer program such as ones used in Wendt and Cerf, *Real Estate Investment Analysis and Taxation.*

Exhibit 11–7 summarizes the determination of annual after-tax cash flows for the five years the project is to be held. It should be noticed in the exhibit that in addition to net operating income growing at 3 percent, two key relationships emerge that considerably influence after-tax cash flow from year to year. These two variables are depreciation and interest expense.

EXHIBIT 11–7
After-Tax Cash Flow, Five-Year Investment Period, 75% Loan, Sandalwood Apartment Complex

Year	(1)	(2)	(3)	(4)	(5)
a. Net operating income	$203,550	$209,657	$215,946	$222,424	$229,097
b. Less debt service	163,013	163,013	163,013	163,013	163,013
c. Cash flow before tax	40,537	46,644	52,933	59,411	66,084
Percent return on equity	7.2%	8.3%	9.4%	10.6%	11.7%
d. Net operating income	$203,550	$209,657	$215,946	$222,424	$229,097
e. — interest expense	142,594	140,738	138,882	136,688	134,494
f. — depreciation expense	87,500	83,125	78,969	75,020	71,269
g. Taxable income (loss)	(26,544)	(14,206)	(1,905)	10,716	23,334
× tax rate	0.50	0.50	0.50	0.50	0.50
h. Taxes or (tax savings) ....(	13,272)	(7,103)	(953)	5,358	11,667
Cash flow before tax (c)	40,537	46,644	52,933	59,411	66,084
+ tax savings (or — taxes) (h) ....+	13,272	+7,103	+ 953	— 5,358	— 11,667
i. Cash flow after tax	$ 53,809	$ 53,747	$ 53,886	$ 54,053	$ 54,417
Percent return on equity	9.6%	9.6%	9.6%	9.6%	9.7%

Depreciation decreases in accordance with the double declining balance method, which is explained in the tax environment appendix to this chapter. Interest expense also declines because over time principal reduction is occurring and interest comprises a smaller proportion of fixed debt service.[14]

According to the projections and assumptions made with regard to the project, before-tax cash flow is computed (line c, Exhibit 11–7) and

[14] It should be noted that interest expense for each year can be computed by determining the loan balance at the end of each year and by subtracting it from the loan balance for the preceding year to arrive at the amount of amortization applicable to a one year period. The amount of amortization applicable for that year, when subtracted from the fixed debt service, leaves interest expense for that year. For example, interest expense in year 3 can be determined by finding the loan balance at the end of year 2, or $1,687,500 × 0.9747 = $1,644,806, and the loan balance at the end of year 3, or $1,687,500 × 0.9604 = $1,620,675, and subtracting ($1,644,806 — $1,620,675), leaving $24,131 as the amount of amortization during the third year. When subtracted from the $163,013 debt service, this leaves $138,882 as interest during the third year.

is coupled with the tax savings or taxes payable (line *h*) resulting from reportable tax losses. It should be noted, however, that beginning with the fourth year of operation, taxable income occurs and must be *subtracted* from before-tax cash flow. With respect to profitability, the annual *before-tax return on equity* ranges from 7.2 percent to 11.7 percent, while the annual *percentage return after-tax* stays relatively stable at 9.6 percent per year.[15]

Cash Flow—Sale Year. To complete the rate of return computation in the investment analysis shown here, the *after-tax cash proceeds must be included when the property is sold* at the end of the fifth year of operation. Two basic calculations are necessary to determine after-tax cash flow from sale: (1) cash flow after repayment of the mortgage and (2) taxes due in the sale year.

Cash flow after repayment of the mortgage is easily computed as:

Sale price	$2,613,600
Less: Mortgage Balance:	
($1,687,500 × .9279°)	1,565,831
Cash flow after mortgage repayment	$1,047,769

    ° Balance on 25 year loan at 8.5%, after 5 years.

The second calculation determining taxes to be paid in the sale year requires a slightly more complicated procedure. To begin, book value for the property must be established. Book value is defined as the asset cost less all depreciation expense charged over the five-year investment period.

Cost basis	$2,250,000
Accumulated depreciation (Exhibit 11–7)	395,883
Book value	$1,854,117

Once book value is determined, total gain on the sale of the asset is arrived at by subtracting book value from the sale price of the asset at the end of the fifth year.

---

[15] Some syndicators and promoters also add annual loan amortization (repayment of loan principal) to the cash flow figures in measuring before-tax and after-tax return on equity. They refer to this as "equity buildup," or a return to the investor stemming from increased equity arising from a decline in the loan balance. This practice is inappropriate, as no cash will actually be received from this source until the property is sold and the outstanding loan balance is repaid. This cash return should then be combined with the cash flow realized in each year in the determination of the overall, or internal, rate of return on invested equity.

Sale price $2,613,600
Book value 1,854,117
Taxable gain ....$ 759,483

Since the property in our illustration was held for 5 years, a portion of the taxable gain is subject to capital gains tax with the remainder subject to ordinary tax rates. To determine what portion of the gain is subject to ordinary tax rates requires that the recapture of depreciation rule be considered.[16] This rule requires that all depreciation taken by accelerated methods in excess of straight line depreciation during the investment period must be taxed at ordinary rates to the extent of total taxable gain. The remainder of any gain, after deduction of ordinary income, is subject to capital gains tax rates. To illustrate:

Accumulated depreciation $395,883
Straight-line depreciation 206,250
Ordinary income 189,633

Total taxable gain 759,483
Ordinary income 189,633
Capital gain 569,850

Total taxes:
Ordinary income $189,633 × .50 = ... 94,817
Capital gain $569,850 × .25° = ... 142,463
    Total taxes at sale $237,280

° Based on one half the ordinary tax rate.

Note that in computing ordinary income, an annual straight-line depreciation charge is computed and subtracted from accumulated depreciation actually taken. The rationale for this procedure is that if a property does not depreciate in value (and may in fact appreciate in value) only a normal allowance for depreciation can be taken. Therefore, the excess of accelerated depreciation over what would have been taken had straight-line depreciation been used must be taxed at ordinary rates.

Now that taxes payable on the sale year have been determined, cash flow after-tax in the sale year can be summarized as shown in Exhibit 11–8.

From Exhibit 11–7 the annual cash flow after-tax from operations may now be combined with cash flow after-tax at sale in Exhibit 11–8. This provides total returns over the five-year holding period for the investment. The after-tax rate of return on these cash flows, when discounted

---

[16] For a more detailed explanation of recapture of depreciation see the tax environment appendix to this chapter.

EXHIBIT 11–8
After-Tax Cash Flow at Sale, Five-Year Investment
Period, Sandalwood Apartment Complex

Cash flow after mortgage repayment:
Sale price $2,613,600
Less: Mortgage balance° 1,565,831

Cash flow before tax $1,047,769
Less taxes at sale:
Taxes on ordinary income 94,817
Taxes on capital gain 142,463

Cash flow after tax at sale ....$ 810,489

° $1,687,500 mortgage at 8.5%, for 25 years, after 5 years.

to equal the $562,500 in equity invested in the project, can be determined as follows:

Year	Cash Flow after Tax	Discounted at 15 Percent: IF°	PV
1	.............................$ 53,809	0.86151	$ 46,357
2	 53,747	0.74220	39,891
3	 53,886	0.63941	34,455
4	 54,053	0.55086	29,776
5	 54,417	0.47457	25,824
5	 810,489	0.47457	384,634
Present value			$560,937

° PV of $1, 15%.

Since the desired present value of $562,500 is very close to the solution obtained when the after-tax cash flow is discounted at 15 percent, for all practical purposes the after-tax rate of return on the Sandalwood project is 15 percent per year.[17] This *internal rate of return* is obviously higher than the simple annual percentage returns computed on a before- and after-tax basis in Exhibit 11–7. The computational procedure followed in deriving the 15 percent return is the recommended approach in determining the true return. *This is the return that should be used in decision-making by the investor.*

Leverage and Borrower Considerations An analysis of Sandalwood apartments under the assumption of 75 percent financing indicates that an internal rate of return of about 15 percent per year will be earned on the $562,500 investment made by the owner over a five-year period.

[17] Interpolating provides a slightly more exact solution of 14.9%.

What follows is a brief investment analysis under the assumption of *80 percent financing* on the same loan terms. In other words, the loan is $1.8 million at 8.5 percent interest for 25 years; the equity is only $450,000. The intent of this section is to demonstrate the effect of increased *financial leverage* on the investment rate of return for Sandalwood, while keeping all other assumptions made in the preceding analysis the same. The result of this analysis will show why borrowers desire the use of financial leverage in order to maximize after-tax return on equity investment.

Exhibit 11–9 contains the after-tax cash flow computed for Sandalwood

EXHIBIT 11–9

After-Tax Cash Flow, Five-Year Investment Period, 80% Leverage, Sandalwood Apartment Complex

Year	(1)	(2)	(3)	(4)	(5)
a. Net operating income ....$	203,550	$209,657	$215,946	$222,424	$229,097
b. Debt service	173,880	173,880	173,880	173,880	173,880
c. Cash flow before tax	29,670	35,777	42,066	48,544	55,217
Percent return on equity	6.6%	8.0%	9.3%	10.8%	12.3%
d. Net operating income ....$	203,550	$209,657	$215,946	$222,424	$229,097
e. −Interest expense	152,100	150,120	148,140	145,800	143,460
f. −Depreciation expense	87,500	83,125	78,969	75,020	71,269
g. Taxable income (loss) ....(	36,050)	(23,588)	(11,163)	1,604	14,368
× tax rate	0.50	0.50	0.50	0.50	0.50
h. Taxes or (tax savings) ......(	18,025)	(11,794)	(5,582)	802	7,184
Cash flow before tax (c)	29,670	35,777	42,066	48,544	55,217
+ tax savings or (−taxes) ..+	18,025	+11,794	+ 5,582	− 802	− 7,184
i. Cash flow after tax ....$	47,695	$ 47,571	$ 47,648	$ 47,742	$ 48,033
Percent return on equity	10.6%	10.6%	10.6%	10.6%	10.7%

under the assumption of 80 percent financing. Comparing Exhibit 11–9 with 11–7, note that net operating income and depreciation income expense are unchanged. The only variables changed in the analysis are interest expense and debt service, which are based on the assumption of the new 80 percent loan. Interest expense in each year is computed in the manner explained in conjunction with Exhibit 11–7. Note that when compared with Exhibit 11–7, before-tax cash flow in Exhibit 11–9 is lower due to the higher debt service associated with the larger amount borrowed; but since equity requirements are only $450,000 in this case, the percentage return on equity before-tax becomes larger under this alternative during the third year. In addition, since interest expense is tax-deductible, the reportable tax loss under the 80 percent loan is much greater than the corresponding tax loss reportable under the 75 percent loan. When before-tax cash flow is coupled with the tax savings under the 80 percent loan assumption, the resulting cash flow after-tax figure is lower than that reported on the 75 percent loan example in Exhibit 11–7. The amount of equity required, however, under the 80 percent loan is far less than the equity required under the 75 percent loan. This becomes apparent when the annual after-tax return on equity is compared in Exhibits 11–7 and 11–9. Note that the return under the 80 percent loan alternative is approximately 10.6 percent per year as compared to 9.6 percent under the 75 percent alternative.

Looking to Exhibit 11–10, cash flow after tax in the sale year is com-

EXHIBIT 11–10
After-Tax Cash Flow at Sale, 80% Leverage, Sandalwood Apartment Complex

Sale price	$ 2,613,600
Mortgage balance ($1,800,000 × .9279*)	−1,670,220
Cash flow after mortgage repayment	$ 943,380
Taxes in sale year:	
Taxes on ordinary income†	− 94,817
Taxes on capital gain†	− 142,463
Cash flow after tax at sale	$ 706,100

* Based on 25 year loan, 8.5%, after 5 years.
† Taxes are unchanged from preceding example with 75% mortgage loan.

puted by the methodology used in the 75 percent loan illustration in Exhibit 11–8. Note that the only variable that changes, when compared to the 75 percent loan results, is the cash flow after mortgage repayment. This is true because when compared to the 75 percent mortgage, the 80 percent mortgage has a greater loan balance outstanding after five years. Since taxes payable at sale are unaffected by simply changing financing arrangements, the taxes computed in the 75 percent loan illustration are deducted from cash flow after mortgage repayment. This results in cash flow after-tax at sale of $706,100. This figure is also less than the cash flow after-tax at sale computed in the 75 percent illustration.

The question now to be considered is: How does financial leverage affect the after-tax internal rate of return on investment in this case? It is clear that both cash flow after-tax in each operating period and cash flow after-tax at sale are lower if 80 percent financing is obtained. The equity required, however, under the 80 percent loan is only $450,000 versus $562,500, or $112,500 less than with the 75 percent loan. To compare returns under both alternatives, we compute the after-tax internal rate of return on cash flows from the 80 percent loan as follows:

Year	Cash Flow after Tax	Discounting at 17 Percent: IF°	PV	Discounting at 18 Percent: IF†	PV
1 ....$	47,695	.84467	$ 40,287	.83639	$ 39,892
2	47,571	.71347	33,940	.69954	33,278
3	47,648	.60265	28,715	.58509	27,878
4	47,742	.50904	24,303	.48936	23,363
5	48,033	.42997	20,652	.40930	19,660
5	706,100	.42997	303,602	.40930	289,007
Present value			$451,499		$433,078

° PV of $1, 17%.
† PV of $1, 18%

The foregoing computation shows that the after-tax internal rate of return on equity with an 80 percent loan is very close to 17 percent. Compared to the 15 percent return on equity if the 75 percent loan alternative is taken, the borrower would probably prefer the 80 percent loan in this case in order to earn the increased yield.[18]

Rating Loan Terms The financial analysis performed by the lender and the investment analysis performed by the borrower set the stage for bargaining over the amount to be borrowed and the terms desired by each party. The financial ratio analysis that would be performed by the lender was illustrated at the beginning of the chapter, based on a 75 percent loan to value ratio and an appraised value of $2.25 million. That analysis resulted in the financial ratios summarized in the first column of Exhibit 11–11. In the second column these ratios have been *recomputed* assuming the 80 percent loan is made. In Exhibit 11–12, the annual percentage returns and internal rates of return, earned by the borrower under each loan alternative, are also summarized. From Exhibit 11–11, it is clear that if the 80 percent loan is obtained, the lender will clearly be taking more risk. Note that the debt service coverage ratio and the break-even occupancy ratio both fall below the industry standard. On the other hand, the borrower is better off if the 80 percent loan is granted, as the summary of profitability ratios in Exhibit 11–12 indicates. Clearly, the borrower will prefer to bargain for the 80 percent loan unless he is risk averse.

[18] After interpolation the yield on the 80 percent alternative is about 17.1 percent. Whether this alternative is selected over the 75 percent alternative depends on whether the difference in equity requirements under the two alternatives, $562,500 − $450,000, or $112,500, can be reinvested at a rate greater than the marginal cost of borrowing, per our discussion in Chapter 10. The marginal cost of borrowing in this case is 8.5 percent since it was assumed that the 80 percent loan would be obtainable on the same terms as the 75 percent loan.

EXHIBIT 11–11

Comparison of Key Financial Ratios under Two Loan Alternatives, Sandalwood Apartment Complex

Financial Ratios	*75 Percent Loan*	*80 Percent Loan*	*Industry Standard*
Debt service coverage	1.25 X	1.17 X	1.25 X
Operating expense ratio	38.0%	38.0%	35%–40%
Vacancy and collection loss	5.0%	5.0%	5%– 7%
Break-even ratio	83.3%	86.4%	80%–85%
Gross return on assets	9.0%	9.0%	10%

EXHIBIT 11–12

Comparison of Investment Returns under Two Loan Alternatives, Sandalwood Apartment Complex

Return Measure	*Year*				
	1	*2*	*3*	*4*	*5*
Cash flow before tax on equity					
75% loan	7.2%	8.3	9.4	10.6	11.7
80% loan	6.6%	8.0	9.3	10.8	12.3
Cash flow after tax on equity					
75% loan	9.6%	9.6	9.6	9.6	9.7
80% loan	10.6%	10.6	10.6	10.6	10.7
Overall rate of return					
75% loan					15%
80% loan					17%

Which loan alternative would be granted? To the extent the lender views the increased risk undertaken if the 80 percent loan is granted as being the dominant consideration, he would be unlikely to budge from a 75 percent loan offer. Perhaps the borrower can demonstrate convincingly through the market study that rents and net operating are expected to increase consistently in the immediate future (note that *NOI* in Exhibit 11–9 increases at 3 percent per year while the debt service remains the same) and that the initial debt service coverage of 1.17 $\times$ will improve to 1.21 $\times$ in the second year ($209,657 ÷ $173,880), and 1.24 $\times$ by the third year. Possibly on these grounds the lender may be persuaded to increase the loan commitment.[19]

Final terms are negotiated between lender and borrower with regard

---

[19] It should also be pointed out that the loan-to-value ratio is also declining over time as the mortgage balance is paid down. In addition, if the property value is expected to increase, the loan-to-value ratio will decline even faster.

to competitive conditions in the loan market. If credit is relatively tight, the lender will be less likely to grant the 80 percent loan as other borrowers may be perfectly satisfied with a 75 percent loan. On the other hand, if the supply of mortgage credit is plentiful and loan demand is slack, a lender may be willing to take a second look at the 80 percent loan possibility.

Financing Commercial Properties

Shopping Centers Another important area of real estate lending involving income-producing properties is the financing of shopping centers. Shopping centers have developed widely since World War II with the advent of modern highways, automobile transportation, and the consequent suburban relocation of households. Generally, three categories can be used to classify shopping centers. The *neighborhood center* is primarily comprised of businesses providing essential goods and services as well as some convenience goods. This category will average approximately 50,000 square feet of leasable area. The *community center* contains businesses which, in addition to essentials and convenience goods, provide some consumer durables such as furniture and appliances as well as clothing apparel. These centers average about 175,000 square feet of leasable floor area. The third category is the *regional center* which is fully diversified, including a larger number of the business activities contained in neighborhood and community centers, and also recreation, eating establishments, and banking. These centers contain about 500,000 square feet, or more, of leasable floor space.

Approaches to Development and Financing Generally there are three approaches to developing and financing shopping centers and other commercial properties. Each approach affects the risk of financing as viewed by a lender. One approach is referred to as the *primary tenant-owner* approach. This approach is used when a large, well established retail department store, for example, takes it upon itself to develop and finance a shopping center, making itself the primary tenant. The idea behind this approach is that since its retail business will be the primary economic attraction for most consumers in the trading area, by developing the center itself, the store can exert control over its competition as well as complementary business lines. In addition, the store can earn investment returns from leasing space to other firms. Ordinarily, if the firm is a financially sound enterprise and if the locational and market analyses are favorable, most lenders find financing of this kind of center very desirable. This approach is not frequently used, however, as many large retailers do not have the expertise or desire to become involved in real estate development and management.

The second approach to financing and developing shopping centers is the *preleased* approach. This approach usually involves the developer contacting prospective tenants during the design and planning stages. Lease commitments are obtained from them in advance of actual development. Often a developer can prelease space to prospective tenants if a major retailer has signed a long-term lease. Indeed, a developer may offer a major tenant a below-market rental inducement to obtain a lease. If the market analysis is sound, a major tenant will help draw customers for other business establishments, thereby making additional preleasing much easier. With preleasing, terms established at the time the lease agreement is made are binding commitments. Consequently, the revenue to be generated from the center after completion is viewed with more certainty by lenders. This in turn implies that debt service will be covered with more certainty, making the loan more attractive to lenders. The preleased approach to shopping center development is the method most widely used by developers.

The last approach is referred to as *speculative* development. Under this approach a developer has a market study and site analysis made. If development proceeds immediately, before competitors see the opportunity, space can be leased easily and quickly. In other words, little preleasing takes place under this method; financing occurs on the strength of the location, market study, and background of the developer. The developer must be established and financially sound to obtain mortgage financing for such an endeavor. The risks are greater under this approach, compared to the other two approaches. Lenders are extremely reluctant to finance such projects unless convinced otherwise. This technique is used least in the development of shopping centers because of the great risk involved.

Market and Location Analysis   A market study and location analysis are vital in obtaining financing for shopping centers. These studies must be as technically correct as possible when used as a basis for financing. Items which must be considered in the market analysis, and which will be analyzed closely by lenders, include the following:

a. Establishment of a trading area for the center.
b. Projection of population, income within the trade area.
c. Breakdowns of retail expenditure patterns of households in the trade area.
d. Attitude surveys of nearby residents who may use the shopping facilities.
e. Traffic count of vehicles on main traffic arteries adjacent to the center.
f. Competition from other shopping centers.
g. The supply of available space in other shopping centers.
h. Rent levels on available space in other centers.
i. Appropriateness of the business mix planned in the center.
j. Adequacy of parking space.

Financial Analysis—Shopping Centers When a developer leases space to a prospective tenant, there are three basic methods used in determining the lease payments. These lease payment patterns are referred to as *straight, net,* and *percentage.* Any one of these lease patterns may be used in a given situation but in many cases facets of all three patterns are combined when a lease agreement is written.

Straight Lease. Under a straight lease agreement, rent is generally negotiated at a fixed price based on the square footage in the area to be leased. The price per square foot generally will vary somewhat with the location within the center and with the total quantity of space leased by a particular tenant. The lease will be made for a specific time period and will usually contain provisions for escalation in the event insurance costs, taxes, or other specific costs increase during the term of the lease.

Smaller businesses in shopping centers generally contract under a straight lease agreement. This is because their sales volume is not enough to induce them to enter into a percentage lease agreement. Sometimes a major tenant also may be able to negotiate a fixed straight lease agreement on favorable terms, especially if the lease is somewhat vital to preleasing and development of the entire project.

Net lease. The net lease usually contains the same provisions as the fixed or straight lease with additional provisions that all operating expenses, maintenance, utilities, insurance, and taxes are to be paid by the tenant. The rent negotiated in this case represents a net return to the owner of the shopping center. With proceeds under the net lease, the owner pays only debt service and perhaps costs associated with maintaining common areas in the shopping center.

The net lease relieves the owner of the shopping center from managerial burdens which are shifted to the tenant. In many cases, this form of lease comes into being when tenants have personnel requirements that are essential to the business, such as food stores that are maintained continuously or department stores with changing display areas and redecorating done by store personnel.

Percentage Lease. The percentage lease gets its name from the fact that rents are partially determined by the sales volume of the business that is leasing space. Generally rents in this situation are determined in two parts. A fixed, or flat, charge per square foot is made, which is the minimum rental requirement regardless of the sales volume. Then a percentage is negotiated which is applied to all sales volume above a specific sales level. For example, a store may pay $1.75 a square foot annually, payable in monthly installments, plus 2 percent on annual sales volume over $1 million. In this event, the $1.75 per square foot represents the minimum rental that a tenant can expect to pay. The additional 2 percent over the $1 million sales volume is applicable only if sales exceed $1 million. The amount of rent received over and above the minimum price per square foot is called *overage.*

Under a percentage lease, the minimum price per square foot available to a tenant is lower than the rent under a straight lease. This is because the owner of the shopping center is actually assuming somewhat of an equity position in each of the businesses in the shopping center, as part of the lease payments may come from overage. Since a potentially higher rental income can be earned with higher levels of sales, the owner must also share in the risk of decline in sales. This will be reflected in a lower minimum price per square foot, compared to what would be paid under a straight lease.

In some cases percentage leases are also net leases in the sense that all taxes, insurance, maintenance, etc., are paid for by the tenant. The cost of this service, when paid for by the tenant, is reflected in the rental determination as negotiated between the owner and tenant.

Lenders analyze provisions in all leases executed between developers and tenants very carefully. The credit standing of the businesses and their ability to make the lease payment are scrutinized closely by lenders. This is necessary because lease payments from tenants ultimately provide the income that the owner of the shopping center will use for debt service. Special consideration is given to situations in which many of the leases executed in a given shopping center are of the percentage-lease type. This is true because, contrary to the fixed or straight lease, the rental income to the developer will change with sales from establishments in the center. Consequently, the ability of the borrower to repay debt will also change, depending on business activity.

Additional items that the lender will closely evaluate when approached by a developer for financing include:

a.   The length or time of executed leases—if obtained from high quality tenants, longer leases reduce risk to the borrower and lender.
b.   Lease restrictions regarding changes in tenants. To what extent are existing tenants protected from competing businesses?
c.   Are tenants required to join a merchant's association for promoting business of the entire shopping center?
d.   How are common areas to be maintained? If the management of the shopping center is expected to maintain these areas, is there sufficient income from leases to cover it?
e.   What conditions exist in leases for increases in taxes, insurance, etc., which may face the owner of the center?
f.   What is the minimum income from leases? How much overage is expected? What have been trends in the sales of tenants in comparable locations?

Operating Statement   As was the case with residential income-producing property, the operating statement forms the basis for financial ratio analysis by the lender and borrower. What follows is a hypothetical example of River Oaks, a proposed shopping center development. A break-down of estimated construction cost is provided in Exhibit 11–13 and an operating statement is provided in Exhibit 11–14.

EXHIBIT 11–13
River Oaks Shopping Center, Cost and Revenue Data

Gross leasable square feet: 500,000
Parking area: 1,500,000 sq.ft.
Other sidewalks, malls, paved areas: 60,000 sq.ft.
Total acreage: 48

Tenant Classification	Total Sq. Footage	Base Rent (per square foot)°	Total Rent
(1) Supermarket	43,000	$2.00	$ 86,000
(2) Department stores	218,000	2.00	436,000
(10) Boutique-specialty	200,000	3.75	750,000
(1) Drug store	10,000	3.70	37,000
(2) Variety stores	20,000	3.20	64,000
(1) Bank	9,000	3.00	27,000
Totals	500,000	$2.80 (avg.)	$1,400,000

Building and Development Costs:
Land	$1,070,000
Building (basic structure $14.00 sq.ft.)	7,000,000
Architect–engineering	65,000
Offsite improvements	100,000
Onsite improvements	360,000
Construction finance charges	205,000
Fixtures	110,000
Miscellaneous	90,000
Total cost	$9,000,000

° Does not include overages.

The total development cost of the proposed River Oaks shopping center is $9,000,000 based on data in Exhibit 11–13. The estimated lease revenue from operation of the center is $1,400,000 annually, excluding overages. When overages are included, total annual rents are estimated at $1,500,000. Approximately 70 percent of the space has been preleased, primarily on a net lease basis, for terms ranging from three to seven years. The operating statement provided in Exhibit 11–14, details the estimated expenses and revenues for the center.

Financial Ratio Analysis. River Oaks is applying for 80 percent financing for 25 years. The current market interest rate for loans on this type of commercial property is 9.75 percent. If these terms are granted to River Oaks, the loan will be made for $7.2 million and annual debt

EXHIBIT 11–14
Operating Statement, River Oaks Shopping Center

Gross potential income without overages		$1,400,000
Estimated overages		100,000
Gross potential income with overages		1,500,000
Vacancy and collection loss		70,000
Effective gross income		$1,430,000
Expenses:		
Property taxes	$101,250	
Less: Tenants' share of taxes	30,000	$ 71,250
Insurance		30,000
Management		105,000
Merchant's association–advertising		15,000
Common area maintenance, repairs		70,000
Common area–utilities		60,000
Security–parking and common areas		30,000
Miscellaneous		10,000
Total operating expenses		391,250
Net operating income		$1,038,750

service will be $769,824.[20] What follows is a summary of the financial ratio analysis that will usually be applied to such a statement. Details concerning computations of the ratio have already been provided in the preceding section on residential income properties.

When a financial analysis of shopping centers is undertaken, usually two sets of ratios are considered, one set including estimated overages and one set excluding overages. Based on Exhibit 11–14, then, the gross potential income for computing the two sets of ratios will be either $1,500,000 (with overages) or $1,400,000 (without overages); consequently, net operating income will be either $1,038,750 (with overages) or $938,750 (without overages). The computation of ratios using definitions for cash ratios explained in the preceding section is summarized in Exhibit 11–15.

The rationale for computing ratios including and excluding overages stems from the lender's concern with the amount of debt service a shopping center is capable of carrying under favorable and unfavorable economic conditions. The most favorable condition for granting the loan will occur if the overages are actually realized. The ratios compiled excluding overages, however, are based on the *minimum* lease payments expected from tenants in the shopping center. They tend to be the set of ratios conservative lenders weigh most heavily when analyzing an operating statement.

[20] Based on $7,200,000 × 0.00891 (loan constant for 9.75%, 25 years) = $64,152 per month.

EXHIBIT 11-15
Summary–Key Financial Ratios, River Oaks Shopping Center

Financial Ratios	Overage Included	Overage Excluded	Industry Standard
Debt service coverage ....1.35 ×	1.22 ×	1.25 ×
Operating expense ratio 27.4%	29.4%	33%
Vacancy and collection loss 4.7%	5.0%	5%
Break-even ratio 77.4%	82.9%	80%
Gross return on assets 11.5%	10.4%	10%
Leasable area/total area 24.3%	24.3%	25%

One additional ratio that is particularly important for shopping centers and is included in Exhibit 11–15, is the ratio of leasable area to total square footage to be used in the center. This ratio is defined as:

$$\frac{\text{Leasable area}}{\text{Leasable area + parking area + common area}}$$

From the data provided for River Oaks in Exhibit 11–13, the ratio is determined as:

$$\frac{500,000}{500,000 + 1,500,000 + 60,000} = 24.3\%$$

Essentially this ratio represents the proportion of land on which lease income will be earned relative to the total land requirements necessary for the project. It is a very important ratio, because if too much land is used for nonleasable area such as parking, etc., lease income may never be high enough relative to total project investment to provide an adequate return. On the other hand, if too little space is provided for parking and adequate common areas of movement into and around the shopping center, the resulting inconvenience may hinder the sales volume of individual business establishments.

Looking at Exhibit 11–15, the ratios computed for River Oaks with and without overages are compared to industry standards[21] for regional shopping centers actually in operation. The analysis shows that with overages excluded, the debt coverage and break-even ratios are noticeably weak in relation to ratios experienced by other regional centers presently operating. When overages are included in the computations all ratios computed for River Oaks appear relatively sound. The operating expense

---

[21] These standards are based on data gathered by the authors from lenders in the Ohio and Midwest area and may vary somewhat geographically. The 10 percent standard used for gross return on assets will vary with economic conditions, as discussed earlier in the chapter.

ratios are noticeably below industry standards. This results in a significantly higher gross return on assets. Data used in estimating expenses in this case would probably be analyzed in more detail by the lender.

The question to be pondered here is will the borrower get the 80 percent loan as requested? Based on the ratios compiled in Exhibit 11–15, the accuracy of predicted overages and the percentage of available space preleased are among the most critical variables to the lender. If the overages estimated in Exhibit 11–14 are accurate from the lender's analysis of the market study, since a high percentage of space has been preleased, the loan will probably be granted.[22] If the overages are too optimistic in outlook, and only a small amount of preleasing has occurred, the lender may counter-offer with a smaller loan. This smaller loan would reduce the required debt service and would bring the ratios computed excluding overages more into line with industry standards.

Investment Analysis—Shopping Centers Assuming that an 80 precent loan of $7,200,000 is obtained by the borrower at 9.75 percent interest for 25 years, that would be the rate of return to the owner of the River Oaks development? To analyze the project from the investor's point of view, Exhibit 11–16 contains a schedule of before- and after-tax cash

EXHIBIT 11–16
After-Tax Cash Flow, Five Year Investment Period, River Oaks Shopping Center

	Year	(1)	(2)	(3)	(4)	(5)
a.	Net operating income	$1,038,750	$1,059,525	$1,080,716	$1,102,330	$1,124,376
b.	Less debt service	769,824	769,824	769,824	769,824	769,824
c.	Cash flow before tax	$ 268,926	$ 289,701	$ 310,892	$ 332,506	$ 354,552
	Percent return on equity	14.9%	16.1%	17.3%	18.5%	19.7%
d.	Net operating income........	$1,038,750	$1,059,525	$1,080,716	$1,102,330	$1,124,376
e.	Less interest expense	698,544	692,064	683,424	674,784	664,704
f.	Less depreciation expense	297,375	286,223	275,490	265,159	255,216
g.	Taxable income	$ 42,831	$ 81,238	$ 121,802	$ 162,387	$ 204,456
	Times tax rate	× 0.50	× 0.50	× 0.50	× 0.50	× 0.50
h.	Taxes	$ 21,416	$ 40,619	$ 60,901	$ 81,194	$ 102,228
	Cash flow before tax c	$ 268,926	$ 289,701	$ 310,892	$ 332,506	$ 354,552
	Less taxes h	21,416	40,619	60,901	81,194	102,228
i.	Cash flow after tax	$ 247,510	$ 249,082	$ 249,991	$ 251,312	$ 252,324
	Percent return on equity ..	13.8%	13.8%	13.9%	14.0%	14.0%

[22] This assumes that the market study and appraisal reports are considered accurate by the lender. The three methods used in appraising income-producing properties have been discussed in the preceding section. These same three techniques are used in appraising commercial properties such as shopping centers and office buildings.

flow. Important assumptions made in the schedule are that net operating income and the total project value will increase at the rate of 2 percent annually. Beginning net operating income is taken from Exhibit 11–14 and therefore includes overages. Further, since this project qualifies as new commercial property, a declining balance method of depreciation is used. Depreciation is charged at 150 percent of the straight line rate over an estimated economic life of 40 years. Of the $9 million cost of the project, the depreciable basis of improvements is $7,930,000, or all development costs excluding land acquisition cost.

It should be noted in Exhibit 11–16 that the after-tax cash flow is less than the before-tax cash flow because in this case no operating loss is reported for tax purposes. In each year of operation the project reports taxable income (line g). This result is different from the outcome when the residential income property was analyzed at the beginning of the chapter. The reason lies in the smaller depreciation charge allowed on commercial property. Recall that in the Sandalwood analysis, the double declining balance method, resulting in two times the straight line depreciation rate, was allowed. In the present case, only 150 percent of the straight line depreciation rate may be used. Consequently, after-tax cash flow and after-tax return on equity are both less than before-tax cash flow and before-tax return on equity.

After-tax cash flow at sale is determined in Exhibit 11–17 to be $2,469,226.

EXHIBIT 11–17
After-Tax Cash Flow at Sale, River Oaks Shopping Center

Sale price		$9,936,727
Mortgage balance ($7,200,000 × .9395*)		6,764,400
Before-tax cash flow at sale		3,172,327
Taxes:		
Sale price	$9,936,727	
Book value	7,620,537	
Taxable gain	2,316,190	
Recapture of depreciation:		
Accumulated depreciation	1,379,463	
Straight-line depreciation	991,250	
Ordinary income	388,213	
Tax rate	× .50	
		194,107
Taxable gain	2,316,190	
Ordinary income	388,213	
Capital gain	1,927,977	
Tax rate	× .25	
		481,994
After-tax cash flow		$2,496,226

* Loan balance factor for 9¾%, 25 year loan after 5 years.

This result is based on an increase in the value of the project of about 2 percent per year over the five-year investment period. Therefore, the property value is assumed to have risen from $9 million to $9,936,727 after five years. The determination of after-tax cash flow at sale follows the procedure used in the Sandalwood apartment analysis.

To compute the after-tax rate of return on the entire project, the after-tax cash flows in the five operating years combined with the after-tax cash flow at sale represent the cash returns in equity of $1,800,000. To determine the after-tax internal rate of return on the investment, we search for an interest rate which, when used to discount the cash returns, results in a present value equal to the equity invested.[23] This is done as follows:

| Year | After-Tax Cash Flow | Discounting at 17 Percent: | | Discounting at 18 Percent: | |
		IF*	PV	IF†	PV
1	.............$ 247,510	.84467	$ 209,064	.83639	$ 207,015
2	 249,082	.71347	177,713	.69954	174,243
3	 249,991	.60265	150,657	.58509	146,267
4	 251,312	.50904	127,928	.48936	122,982
5	 252,324	.42997	108.492	.40930	103,276
5	 2,496,226	.42997	1,073,302	.40930	1,021,705
Total present value	....$1,847,156				$1,775,488

* IF, PV of $1, 17%.
† IF, PV of $1, 18%.

Since the equity invested is $1.8 million, the result obtained here indicates that the internal rate of return lies between 17 and 18 percent. Interpolating from the above present values results in a more precise yield of 17.7 percent.

While the estimated rate of return on River Oaks is about 17.7 percent annually, there are other considerations which should be made by an investor in such a project. Since a component of the rental income for River Oaks comes from overages based on the sales volume of tenants in the center, the investor will be somewhat protected from general inflationary price increases in the future. This aspect of the investment makes it more attractive than if straight leasing had been used. Straight leasing would

---

[23] The average return on equity is about 14% per year, and the net cash flow in the sale year of $2,469,226 is higher than $1.8 million originally invested. The internal rate of return on the entire investment will therefore be greater than 14%. The trial and error process should start at a rate greater than 14%.

have resulted more or less in a fixed rental income pattern over the duration of the leases executed with tenants.

Another favorable aspect of this investment from the investor's standpoint is that it appears that the use of 80 percent leverage is possible. Based on financial ratio analysis performed on the operating statement from River Oaks, it appears that because of a high percentage of preleased space, the income generated from the operation will probably be sufficient to cover debt service if an 80 percent loan is granted. This relatively high amount of leverage, which does not expose either the investor or lender to excessive financial risk, provides a considerably higher return on equity than if a smaller loan were made.

Many other types of financing can be applied to shopping center financing and development. Sale and leaseback and equity participations are also extensively used in financing this type of development. These topics are discussed separately in different chapters of the text.

Office Buildings   Financing office buildings, another form of commercial property, is similar to financing shopping centers. Generally, development and financing consists of the primary owner-tenant, preleased, and speculative approaches—the same basic concepts discussed in connection with shopping centers. As to the types of lease executed between owner and tenant, the straight lease or net lease is used most often. Both usually include an escalator provision for possible increases in insurance and taxes. In the case of special purpose, preleased office space (such as in medical buildings), the unit is generally unfinished with the tenant taking responsibility for equipment installations. Long-term leases are normally executed in these cases with escalator provisions for general price increases between lease renewal periods.

Market Study   A major area of departure between shopping center and office building development lies in the market study. The general office building market has traditionally been in central-city areas. Suburban locations have developed more slowly because of the necessity of a central work place in urban areas which is generally accessible to the urban labor market. For firms utilizing relatively large quantities of labor, the central city areas have been the most feasible location for most types of office buildings.

The first category of office complex to move into suburban areas has been the special purpose type. The reason for this arises because of the services provided and the need for proximity to the households served. The advent of interstate highways with inner-belt and outer-belt connections has modified the traditional journey to work pattern in central cities. Locations on outer-belt perimeters are now as accessible as downtown locations for much of the labor force. As a result, many general office building complexes that would formerly have located in central city areas are locating in suburban areas. Increased accessibility, coupled with rising center city property taxes and income taxes on employees, also has made suburban locations more attractive to both businesses and employees. This changing pattern of development has made the market study for office buildings increasingly more complicated because of the even greater importance attributable to location.

In market studies for office buildings, many factors are closely evaluated by lenders:

a. Population growth in the market study area.
b. The historical ratio of office space to population.
c. A market survey of all available market space in the market area.
d. A breakdown of vacancies at the time of the market study by:
    1. Location.
    2. Size of building.
    3. Age and condition of structure.
    4. Rent range per square foot.
e. An historical analysis of the *absorption rate* of office building space, or how rapidly new office space developed in recent years has been absorbed by market demand.
f. An accounting of all proposed office building construction slated to occur in the market area, by location and rent range.

Essentially what the market study must provide is enough data to support the fact that population increases warrant the development of additional office space. Coupled with a current inventory of available space by location and rent range, the lender wants assurance that a loan is not being made on an office complex in a market that is already, or will soon be, overbuilt. Particular attention, therefore, is given to the historical ratio of population to office space and present *absorption rates* on new, recently developed office space.

To the extent that the proposed complex is preleased or is to be an owner-occupied situation, the lender will be more disposed to make a loan commitment. In this event, the lender is able to perform a financial analysis on the prospective tenants and to determine their ability to make the expected lease payments. This does not relieve the investor of performing an adequate market study, because leases are not permanent. A poor location or an inadequate analysis of the structure of market demand may result in future problems for the investor when leases are to be renewed.

Operating Statement   What follows is a brief illustration of a proposed office building development. The development, called Professional Plaza, is a suburban two-story (walk-up) complex with 80,000 square feet of leasable space. Approximately 50 percent of the space has been preleased for terms ranging from three to five years. Straight lease terms have been negotiated and include escalators for any property tax or insurance increases with all such increases to be prorated among tenants on the basis of square footage leased. A brief summary of estimated cost data and an operating statement for Professional Plaze is contained in Exhibit 11–18.

EXHIBIT 11–18
Projected Statements, Professional Plaza Office Building

Cost data:

Land	$ 533,800	
Building and improvements	1,601,200	
Total cost	$2,135,000	

Operating data:

Gross potential income ($5.50 per sq.ft.)	$ 440,000	100.0%
Vacancy and collection allowance	22,000	5.0
Effective gross income	418,000	95.0%
Less expenses:		
Personnel–wages	39,600	9.0
Utilities–common areas	15,400	3.5
Management	22,000	5.0
Painting–decorating	13,200	3.0
Maintenance–repairs	22,000	5.0
Insurance	8,800	2.0
Real Estate taxes $104,000		
Less: Tenants' share .... – 60,000	44,000	10.0
Total operating expenses	$ 165,000	37.5
Net operating income	$ 253,000	57.5

The operating data show that based on operating revenues and expense projections, Professional Plaza should provide approximately 58 cents on every dollar on rental revenue generated for coverage of debt service and taxes. The investors in Professional Plaza are negotiating for an 80 percent loan, or $1,708,000 for 25 years. Interest rates presently available on similar developments are 9.5 percent. Monthly debt service on such a loan would be $14,928, or a total of $179,136 annually.

Financial Ratio Analysis The financial ratio analysis computations are carried out in the same manner as defined at the beginning of the chapter. These ratios are summarized in Exhibit 11–19. Industry standards used here are based on data gathered from appraisers and lenders in Ohio and the Midwest. Industry ratios will vary depending on the type of building, height, and size, as well as location. Sources for financial ratios for specific buildings in specific locations are published annually and are available to the public.[24]

---

[24] National Association of Building Owners and Managers, *Annual Office Building Experience Exchange Report* (Chicago: National Association of Building Owners and Managers, various years).

EXHIBIT 11–19
Summary–Key Financial Ratios, Professional Plaza Office Building

Financial Ratio	Professional Plaza	Industry Standard
Debt service coverage	1.41 ×	1.25 ×
Operating expense ratio 39.5%		35–40%
Vacancy and collection loss	5.0%	5.0%
Break-even ratio 78.2%		80–85%
Gross return on assets 11.9%		10%

In addition to financial ratio analysis, the lender will also closely evaluate the operating statement, market study, and appraisal report accompanying the loan application. The financial ratios computed here show that the loan, if granted, will place Professional Plaze well within acceptable risk limits (again, assuming the market study and appraisal report are also acceptable to the lender). The lender, however, will also examine the lease agreements and will determine the financial condition of all tenants and their ability to meet lease obligations.

Investment Analysis—Borrower Considerations   The investment analysis that should be undertaken by the borrower parallels the analysis illustrated in conjunction with shopping centers. Consequently it is not repeated here. As with shopping centers, depreciation methods allowable for commercial property are applicable. With the operating statement, mortgage terms, and depreciation method shown, a statement of after-tax cash flow for each operating period should be formulated. Cash flow, less taxes payable when the property is sold, is then combined with operating returns to determine the over-all return on equity invested.

QUESTIONS

1. When determining the economic feasibility of an income-producing property, what particular factors is a lender most likely to be concerned with?
2. What is financial ratio analysis and how does it aid the lender in underwriting loans for income-producing property?
3. Besides physically comparing properties recently sold, what are the two additional methods used under the market approach to appraising?
4. Briefly explain the income capitalization approach to value.
5. How are investment analysis, used by borrowers, and real estate financing related? Why must an investment analysis perspective be taken by borrowers in evaluating financing alternatives?
6. What is referred to as a "cash-on-cash return?"
7. What is recapture of depreciation?
8. What are the three basic approaches to shopping center development?

9. What are the three basic methods for determining rentals in shopping center leases? Briefly explain the differences among them.

10. Distinguish between depreciation methods that are permissible for residential properties and for commercial properties.

CASE PROBLEMS

1. Briarwood Apartments is a new concept in apartment design promoted by L. Z. Wells, who can attractively locate the complex in a natural setting that is close to shopping and work-center areas. He has approached Acme Life Insurance Company for a loan commitment on the project. Based on a market study done by his appraiser the following operating statement is estimated:

BRIARWOOD APARTMENTS
Projected Operating Statement

Rental income	$470,000
Other income	5,000
Gross potential income	475,000
Less:	
Vacancy and collection loss	19,000
Effective gross income	456,000
Personnel–wages	35,625
Utilities–common areas	16,625
Management expense	23,750
Painting and decorating	9,500
Maintenance–repairs	14,250
Miscellaneous	7,125
Insurance	7,125
Real estate taxes	42,750
Total operating expenses	156,750
Net operating income	$299,250

Mr. Wells has had the property appraised for $2.3 million and is seeking 75% permanent loan financing. At present, terms available on such a loan would be 9.5 percent interest for 25 years. What financial analysis would the lender perform? What are the financial strengths and weaknesses of this operating statement when compared to industry standards?

2. Ms. Martha Jones has an excellent opportunity to make an investment in a small residential income property. She has had the project appraised for $360,000 and can obtain a loan from Mutual of Bigville Life Insurance Company for 70% of value, at 9 percent interest for 25 years.

She can obtain the land for $72,000 and a building contractor can deliver the improvement at a cost of $288,000. The economic life of the improvements will be 40 years for tax purposes. The following condensed operating statement is provided below:

PHASE 3 APARTMENT COMPLEX
Operating Statement

Rents	$60,000
Vacancy and collection	3,000
Total operating expenses	22,000
Net operating income	$35,000

Assuming that she is in the 50% tax bracket, she elects to use the 200% declining balance method of depreciation, net operating income will increase at 2% per year, and the entire property can be sold for $390,000 after four years:

    a.   Construct a statement of after-tax cash flow for Ms. Jones.

    b.   What after-tax internal rate of return would Ms. Jones earn?

    c.   Assuming a loan for 80% of value can be obtained on the same loan terms, what would the return now be?

APPENDIX: THE TAX ENVIRONMENT

Depreciation

Depreciation expense is one of the most important charges affecting taxes paid by real estate investors. Generally, all assets decrease in value due to physical wasting or wear and tear and are subject to depreciation. This definition usually includes buildings and other improvements such as sidewalks, parking areas, and other land betterments. However, land itself is not depreciable.

Establishment of Value and Economic Life Generally, the purchase price paid for a property plus its acquisition expenses serves as the *basis* for depreciation calculations. Acquisition expenses typically include title fees, broker's commissions, attorney's fees, appraisal costs, and surveys.

The economic life of an improvement is an estimate based on a term over which the asset in question will be useful to the particular taxpayer. This estimate is extremely important as it serves as a major component in all depreciation methods allowable under tax regulations. Usually, the shorter the estimated economic life for a given improvement, the greater the depreciation charge (under all methods of computation) and the lower the tax liability during the economic life. Normally, a taxpayer is expected to use past experience when possible in establishing an asset's economic life. Economic lives established by independent appraisals made on a property are also permissible for tax purposes. The Internal Revenue Service has also established guidelines suggesting economic lives under some 75 categories of assets. Taxpayers are not required to use these guidelines, however, if they can provide justification for using a different economic life.

Component versus Composite Depreciation   The same economic life does not have to be used for the entire improvement. It is possible to establish *different* economic lives for different components within the same project or development. For example, one economic life can be chosen for the building shell, another for the roof, and still another for sidewalks. This approach is referred to as *component* depreciation. It may be valuable for a particular investor if the depreciation charge derived by assigning different economic lives to components exceeds the charge computed under an overall *composite* depreciation rate selected for the entire improvement.

Generally, the component method is justifiable when a property is new and evidence can be presented to the effect that some parts of an improvement will wear faster than others. However, when an existing property is purchased, it is more difficult to justify assigning different economic lives to different components. This is particularly true if the property in question has been in existence for some time.

Allowable Methods of Computation   Whether the component or composite approach is chosen, there are generally three basic methods used to compute depreciation on real property. The first approach is referred to as the *straight-line method*. Under this approach the basis of the property less any salvage value is divided by the economic life of the asset, resulting in an annual depreciation charge.

Example: A new property is purchased for $100,000. The land is valued at $20,000 with improvements valued at $80,000. The improvement is estimated to have an economic life of 40 years at the end of which time the building shell is estimated to have $10,000 salvage value. The annual depreciation charge would be:

$$\frac{\text{Improvement value} - \text{Salvage value}}{\text{Economic life}} = \text{Straight-line depreciation charge}$$

$$\frac{\$80,000 - \$10,000}{40} = \$1,750$$

Accelerated Depreciation Methods.   These methods of depreciation are allowable for certain categories of property to be discussed below. The first methods demonstrated here are called the *declining balance methods* of depreciation. The technique for computing the depreciation charges under all declining balance methods is based on the *depreciation rate* obtained under the straight-line method. For example, in the example above, $1,750 is the amount chargeable under the straight-line method. The straight-line depreciation *rate* is computed as:

$$\frac{\textit{Annual straight-line charge}}{\textit{Cost—salvage value}} = \frac{\$1,750}{\$80,000 - \$10,000} = 2.5\%$$

a. Double Declining Balance Method. Under this method, up to twice the straight-line depreciation rate may be taken on an improvement over its economic life. The depreciation charge is computed by doubling the straight-line rate ($2 \times 2.5\% = 5\%$) and applying the rate obtained to the basis of the improvement (ignoring salvage value). In each succeeding year, the depreciable basis of the asset is reduced by the amount of depreciation taken in the preceding year, hence the term declining balance.

To illustrate this method using the same example above, a partial depreciation schedule is shown in Exhibit 11A–1.

EXHIBIT 11A–1
Depreciation Schedule–Double Declining Balance Method

Year	Depreciable Basis	Rate	Depreciation Charge
1	..........................$80,000	× 5% =	$4,000
2	 76,000	× 5% =	3,800
3	 72,200	× 5% =	3,610
4	 68,590	× 5% =	3,430
5	 65,160	× 5% =	3,258

Note in the exhibit that under this method, the depreciation rate remains the same and the depreciable basis of the asset declines with each year. The schedule seen above can be carried out for 40 years or the economic life of the asset.

b. 150% Declining Balance Method. This technique is allowable on certain categories of real estate. The computation process is the same as under the double declining balance method, except that the depreciation rate differs. The rate is computed simply as $1.50 \times 02.5\% = 3.75\%$ or one and one-half times the straight line rate. The 3.75% rate obtained would be substituted in the depreciation schedule in Exhibit 11A–1, in the rate column and the annual depreciation charge determined accordingly.

c. 125% Declining Balance Method. Under this technique the depreciation rate would be $1.25 \times 2.5\% = 3.125\%$. This rate would be used in place of the 5% rate in Exhibit 11A–1 in completing the depreciation schedule, should this method be used.

The second major method allowable under accelerated depreciation methods is referred to as the *sum of the years' digits* method. Under this technique, the depreciation rate used on each year changes while the depreciable basis remains the same. Its computation is carried out by first cumulatively summing over the number of years contained in the assets economic life. In our example, this would be done as follows:

$1 + 2 + 3 \ldots + 40 = 820$. However, a short cut solution is also obtained through the following formula:

$$N\left(\frac{N + 1}{2}\right) = \text{sum-of-the-years' digits}$$

where N equals the economic life of the improvement, in our example:

$$40\left(\frac{40 + 1}{2}\right) = 820$$

The depreciation charge under this method is then determined by taking the last year in the sequence of digits (40 in our example) and dividing it by the sum-of-the-years' digits (820) to obtain the depreciation rate in the first year. In each succeeding year, the numerator changes by the next year in the reverse sequence. To demonstrate this technique a partial depreciation schedule is completed in Exhibit 11A–2. Note in the exhibit that the depreciable basis of the asset remains the same while the rate changes in each year. The initial depreciable basis under this method is cost *minus salvage value*, when salvage value is estimated. This differs from the declining balance techniques which *ignore* salvage value altogether in determining the depreciable charge.

EXHIBIT 11A–2
Depreciation Schedule–Sum-of-the-Years' Digits Method

Year	Depreciable Basis		Rate		Depreciation Charge
1	.....................$70,000	×	40/820	=	$3,415
2	 70,000	×	39/820	=	3,329
3	 70,000	×	38/820	=	3,244
4	 70,000	×	37/820	=	3,159
5	 70,000	×	36/820	=	3,073

Changing Depreciation Methods. Once a depreciation method has been chosen by the taxpayer, it can only be changed once during an asset's economic life. The taxpayer may elect to change from any method to straight-line depreciation only. This may be worthwhile for an investor to do when the depreciation charge under an accelerated method falls below the straight-line charge which would be effective at that point in the asset's life. By comparing the straight-line charge computed in any given year (based on the *undepreciated basis* less salvage value divided by the *remaining* economic life at that point) it may be that the straight-line charge will exceed the charge under an accelerated method. However, once the election to switch to straight line is made, the taxpayer may not change depreciation methods for that asset again.

Comparing Depreciation Charges. Exhibit 11A–3 contains a summary of charges under the various depreciation methods computed in our basic example. Note that in the exhibit, the depreciation charges vary considerably depending on the method selected. Generally, the taxpayer

EXHIBIT 11A–3
Summary of Depreciation Charges under Various Methods

Year	Straight Line	Double Declining Balance	Declining Balance		Sum-of-the Years' Digits
			150 Percent	*125 Percent*	
1	$1,750	$4,000	$3,000	$2,500	$3,415
2	1,750	3,800	2,888	2,422	3,329
3	1,750	3,610	2,779	2,346	3,244
4	1,750	3,430	2,675	2,273	3,159
5	1,750	3,258	2,575	2,202	3,073

will select, from the methods allowable to him, the method which results in the greatest depreciation charges early in the life of the asset. By doing so, taxes are reduced in the early years of the investment. This means that most investors choose one of the accelerated methods (when allowed) over straight-line depreciation. Although all depreciation methods ultimately result in the same total depreciation being charged over the entire life of the investment, by choosing those methods with the greatest depreciation charges early in an asset's life, taxpayers can use (reinvest) tax savings in some other endeavor during the periods in which the lower tax liability occurs.

It should be pointed out that the choice of depreciation methods will not be consistently the same. It will depend on the cost, estimated salvage value, economic life, and holding period of a particular investment. Consequently, the taxpayer should always compute depreciation charges on all options available and observe the pattern of charges over the number of years the investment is to be held. Only then can the proper choice of depreciation methods be made.

Choice of Depreciation Methods—Specific Types of Real Estate The choice of depreciation methods allowed under tax regulations is very rigid and depends on specific categories of real estate being depreciated. The four major criteria for classification of real estate on *property acquired after July 25, 1969* can be best seen in Exhibit 11A–4. The major criteria used to categorize property are whether a property is *residential* or *other* and whether a property is *new* or *existing*.

EXHIBIT 11A–4
Depreciation Methods Allowed on Specific Types of Real Estate

	Residential	All Other
New	Sum-of-the-years' digits Double declining balance 150% Declining balance 125% Declining balance Straight line	· 150% Declining balance Straight line
Existing	125% Declining balance Straight line	Straight line

Residential real estate generally refers to income-producing (rental) residential property. At least 80 percent of rental revenue must be derived from residential use for a property to be categorized as residential real estate. This rule is sometimes important for mixed properties or properties which have a commercial and residential mix within the same improvement. All *other* real estate generally refers to commercial properties such as shopping centers, office buildings, and industrial properties.

Gain on Sale of Real Estate Investments

As pointed out in Chapter 11, special care must be given in the determination of taxes when a property is sold. For properties acquired after July 25, 1969, when a gain is realized on the sale of an asset, the *recapture of depreciation* provision must be applied. This regulation requires that if a property is sold for more than its taxable basis, all depreciation charged over what would have been charged had the straight line method of depreciation been used is treated as ordinary income and must be taxed at ordinary tax rates. The total gain on sale is then reduced by the amount of depreciation recaptured and the remainder is subject to capital gains tax.[1]

To illustrate, we return to our example of the new $100,000 property ($80,000 building and $20,000 land) with an economic life of 40 years and $10,000 salvage value. We assume that it was acquired after July 25, 1969, held for five years, and sold for $120,000. It was depreciated using the double declining balance method depreciation. Assuming the investor is in the 50 percent tax bracket what would be the taxes at sale?

---

[1] It should also be pointed out that during 1976 any asset must be held for more than six months to qualify for long-term capital gains treatment. Beginning in 1977, capital assets will have to be held over nine months to qualify, and beginning in 1978 capital assets will have to be held more than one year to qualify for capital gains treatment.

Step 1. Computing Gain

Sale price		..$120,000
Book value, 5th year		
Cost $100,000		
Less: Accumulated depreciation 18,098		81,902
Total Gain		..$ 38,098

Step 2. Recapture of Depreciation

Accumulated depreciation, DDB ....$ 18,098		
Less: Straight line ($1,750 × 5) 8,750		
Ordinary income		9,348
Capital gain		..$ 28,750

Step 3. Computation of Taxes—Assume taxpayer in 50% tax bracket

Ordinary income ....$ 9,348		
Ordinary tax rate .... .50		
Ordinary tax		..$ 4,674
Capital gain ....$ 28,750		
Capital gain tax rate° .... .25		
Capital gain tax		..$ 7,188
Total tax		..$ 11,862

° It is assumed that the capital gains tax rate is one half the ordinary tax rate in this illustration. Actually, the capital gain shown here would have to be combined with other capital gains and losses, if any, reported by the taxpayer and the combined gains and losses would be taxed. Also, the reader should be aware that after 1972, taxpayers are subject to a minimum tax on tax preference items which include long-term capital gains and interest.

Based on the three step procedure just illustrated, the taxpayer would have to pay a total of $11,862 if the property was sold after five years. It should be noted that the recapture provision must be taken into account anytime (1) a gain is realized on a property and (2) an accelerated depreciation method is used.

A Final Note. The brief summary of tax factors affecting real estate presented here is intended to demonstrated the more basic or fundamental influences on investment analysis. Tax laws change from time to time, and therefore the instructor must keep up to date on changes in tax legislation. The examples should be modified to recognize significant changes as appropriate.

12

Construction and Land Development Loans

Introduction

Perhaps two of the most complex areas of lending in real estate finance, both from the standpoint of lenders and investors, are construction loans and land development loans. This chapter contains a description of the basic characteristics of each type of financing, as well as illustrations designed to provide the reader with some insight as to how these loans are negotiated by lenders and borrowers, and how terms for disbursement and repayment are determined. In addition to financial characteristics, considerable emphasis is also given to procedural matters ranging from obtaining loan commitments to the closing of each type of loan and control over the disbursement and repayment of funds. This emphasis is necessary in understanding these particular methods of financing, because of the technical characteristics of the construction and development process.

Construction Lending and Permanent Financing Commitments

Before construction loans on income-producing properties are negotiated between developers and lenders, the developer first makes contact with a lender who might be willing to make the long-term or *permanent loan* on a proposed project. This procedure is followed because most construction lenders are short-term lenders who do not want to make long-term loans. Rather, they specialize in construction lending which is usually short-term in nature. Because the construction lender is only interested in the short-term financing of a project, assurance must usually be provided by the developer that a long-term lender has been found who is willing to finance the project when it is completed. In this way, since another lender will provide funds when the project is completed, the construction lender's involvement in financing usually ceases with completion of the project.

In order to gain insight into how most construction loans are made, it is necessary to understand how long-term loan commitments are negotiated between developers and permanent lenders. This section of the chapter provides a brief overview of how *permanent financing* is arranged in *advance* of construction loans.

Take-Out Commitment   It should be stressed that any long-term or permanent lender will first evaluate a proposed project, whether it is an apartment complex, shopping center, or office building, by using the financial analysis provided in the preceding chapter. The market study, building plans and costs, as well as the operating statement are analyzed carefully by the lender, who determines whether a loan should be made and, if so, on what terms. Should the loan be approved and the borrower and lender agree on the terms, the lender issues what is known as a take-out commitment. This represents a commitment to *become* the permanent lender. In other words, since the project has not yet been developed, the borrower must find a construction lender to finance development. However, construction lenders are usually unwilling to make loans unless they are certain that a developer has found a permanent mortgage lender who will provide funds that will be used to pay off the construction loan when the project is complete. If a lender is making both the construction loan and the permanent mortgage loan, such an arrangement is unnecessary. However, in practice it is more common to find different lenders making the construction loan and the permanent loan.[1] Consequently the take-out commitment for the permanent mortgage usually must be found by the developer *before* the construction loan will be granted by a local lender.[2]

Take-out commitments issued by most long-term lenders contain *contingencies* that must be met by the borrower before the lender's commitment becomes legally binding. If these contingencies are not met,

---

[1] Usually, construction loans are made by short-term lenders with an excellent knowledge of the local real estate market, such as commercial banks and some savings and loan associations. The permanent lenders on income-producing properties tend to be large life insurance companies, who rely on the local lender to make construction loans and to control the disbursement of funds. For a good review of construction lending practices, see Peter A. Schulkin, *Commercial Bank Construction Lending* (Research Report No. 47, Federal Reserve Bank of Boston, 1970).

[2] Some lenders may be willing to lend without a take-out commitment, speculating that the permanent loan will be found before completion of the project. However, in light of the disastrous results experienced by real estate lenders in the mid 1970s, this practice has practically ceased.

the lender does not have to release funds on the completion date. A list of common contingencies contained in take-out commitments might include the following:

a. The proposed development must be completed by a specific date called the completion date.
b. Title must be clear of liens at the date of completion.
c. Certification is required that a minimum percentage of units have been leased as of the delivery date of the permanent mortgage funds by the lender. This date usually coincides with the completion date.
d. The permanent lender must approve all change orders affecting building plans and specifications previously approved by the permanent lender.
e. The permanent lender must approve all long-term leases.
f. Evidence must be given to the permanent lender, by the borrower, that a construction loan has been obtained from another lender within a specific time period.
g. Final certification of the development by an architect must be received to insure adherence to plans previously approved.

These contingencies are very important from the standpoint of both borrower and lender. Although many of them are obvious, some elaboration is required. Item *c* is generally included to assure a certain level of occupancy in a project by the completion date. For example, if an apartment complex, office building, or shopping center is being financed, usually a provision is included in the commitment that 70 or 80 percent of leasable area must be under contract by the completion date. The purpose of this provision is to shift some of the risk to the construction lender who is to be repaid from funds disbursed by the permanent lender. If the construction lender, who should be well informed on local real estate conditions, is willing to make a loan with such a provision in the take-out agreement, then the permanent lender is somewhat protected also, since the construction lender will bear the risk of the development until the required occupancy is achieved.[3] Should construction lenders in a given market be unwilling to make a loan with such a contingency in the take-out commitment, this may be a sign of a very risky development. Therefore, the permanent lender may not be willing to extend the deadline for obtaining a construction loan.

Item *d* is a very controversial contingency that may affect both building cost and design and must be approved by the lender. Usually,

---

[3] When construction lenders make loans, a completion date is usually specified. If it is anticipated that the required occupancy level will not be met by the completion date, the construction lender may require a provision for "gap financing." This is discussed later in the chapter.

only major changes must be reported to the lender. However, differences in opinion frequently occur as to what constitutes a major change. This difference is sometimes difficult to resolve and may cause problems when the permanent lender is scheduled to commit the permanent funds. These problems may also occur if, after completion of the project, the permanent lender has had "second thoughts" about why the take-out commitment was extended to begin with.

Some additional provisions which protect the borrower are usually included in the commitment. Provisions concerning construction delays due to forces beyond the control of the lender will usually be included and will automatically extend the completion date. Should the development be completed early, the delivery date for funds provided by the permanent lender is usually automatically advanced.

Commitment Fees—Take-Out Commitments. The lender normally charges a nonrefundable fee for making a take-out loan commitment. This fee must be paid by the borrower at the time of commitment. The fee is usually comprised of two parts: (1) the out-of-pocket costs and overhead incurred by the lender when the financial and credit analyses of the loan application and loan applicant are performed, and (2) an indirect charge for the loss of investment opportunities associated with funds that have been committed to the borrower for delivery at a future date and that cannot be invested at maximum advantage during the interim period.[4] Should the developer not meet the completion date or fail to fulfill contingency provisions in the take-out commitment, the commitment fee is forfeited.

Take-Out Commitments—Buy and Sell Agreements. In past years many borrowers may have obtained a take-out commitment from a lender and intentionally forfeited the commitment fee by not closing the permanent loan. This may have been profitable if mortgage interest rates fell significantly during the time development was being completed or if the borrower found another permanent lender willing to offer better loan terms. In more recent years, permanent lenders have required what is called a *buy and sell agreement.* This agreement is signed by the borrower, the permanent lender, and the construction lender and essentially provides that the construction loan mortgage will be delivered to the permanent lender on the completion date. In essence, the permanent lender *buys* the construction loan mortgage from the construction lender. In this way, the constructon loan is repaid and the permanent loan is closed simultaneously. Under this approach, the permanent lender receives more assurance that the permanent loan will be made and that both the borrower and construction lender will

---

[4] Some short-term investments may be available, but returns on these would more than likely be less than returns on loans normally made by the lender.

endeavor to complete the project on time and to fulfill all contingency requirements.

Gap Financing. An additional commitment that may be made by the permanent lender, the construction lender, or perhaps even a third lender is called gap financing. This may be a separate loan commitment or a contingency in the take-out commitment negotiated with the permanent lender. The purpose of gap *financing* is to finance a particular property in the event that a contingency in the take-out commitment, usually an occupancy requirement, is not met.

To illustrate the use of gap financing, assume that a take-out commitment is issued for $1.8 million as of a scheduled completion date. The commitment is contingent on the condition that 75 percent of the space in the property is leased. If the contingency is not met, the gap financing commitment might provide that only $1.5 million will be advanced under the terms of the take-out commitment. The remaining $300,000 is disbursed subject to another set of terms usually including a *higher* interest rate for a specified term generally ranging from 6 to 12 months. After the term of the gap financing commitment, if the occupancy standard is met, the $300,000 is refinanced on the same terms as the $1.5 million advanced on the completion date.

With regard to the desirability of gap financing, it is obvious that neither the borrower nor the lender hope that it will have to be used. This is true because if the occupancy standard cannot be met on the completion date the project will have a very low cash flow. Adding an additional interest requirement at that time may jeopardize the solvency of the project and force early default.

Standby Commitments Standby commitments also arise in cases where the borrower is seeking a permanent commitment in order to obtain a construction loan from another lender. Standby commitments differ from take-outs in that neither the borrower or the lender expects the standby commitment to become binding. The borrower generally expects to find more favorable terms on the permanent loan elsewhere. However, the borrower wants to begin development and needs a commitment to obtain the construction loan, but he believes that better terms will be found during the development period. The borrower will continue to search for more favorable terms until the completion date becomes effective under the standby commitment. If more favorable terms are found elsewhere, the borrower will complete the requirements for the permanent mortgage with another lender. If more favorable terms are not found by the completion date, then the standby commitment will be used and the permanent loan will be closed with the lender who issued the standby commitment.

Even though permanent lenders who offer standby commitments charge a commitment fee and are legally bound to deliver mortgage funds on the completion date (if the borrower decides to use the commitment), many construction lenders are unwilling to make construction loans when a borrower has only a standby commitment. Neither the borrower nor the permanent lender really expects to complete the transaction. Should the borrower decide to use the commitment, the permanent lender may balk at his responsibility. For example, if a period of tight credit occurs in the economy after the commitment is made, the permanent lender may not have the full amount of funds necessary to make good on the commitment. In situations such as these, lenders who have issued standbys may look for "technical violations" of contingencies in the commitment (for example, minor changes in construction plans not approved by the permanent lender, and so on). For this reason, very few construction lenders are willing to make loans when the borrower has only a standby commitment. A recent study of commercial bank lending practices showed that 45 percent of banks surveyed would under no circumstances make a construction loan when the borrower had only a standby commitment. In *only special instances* would the remaining 55 percent of banks surveyed make a construction loan when the borrower had only a standby commitment, or no take-out commitment at all.[5]

The Construction Loan

Generally a construction loan is secured by a mortgage for future advances, or an open-end mortgage. Under this type of mortgage, the lender has first lien on the land and all subsequent improvements as funds are disbursed for labor and materials used in the development of the improvements. With the exception of loans made for single-family properties, most construction loans are made by commercial banks. This is because these banks are local in orientation and are very familiar with local lending conditions. They are also usually in a good position to control disbursement of funds and to monitor construction progress.[6] As indicated previously, most construction lenders generally require evidence from the borrower that a permanent take-out commitment has been obtained from a long-term lender as a precondition of obtaining a construction loan. This is not always true for developers of single-family properties who, based on their own financial strength as well as the local demand for housing, may be able to obtain construction loans for a number of houses to be built on speculation. However, when a loan for a home to be custom-built is negotiated, usually the buyer has already obtained a permanent mortgage commit-

---

[5] See Schulkin, *Commercial Bank Construction Lending*, pp. 32–53.

[6] A sizable number of construction loans on residential income properties are also made by savings and loan associations.

ment, which may be used as the basis for a builder to obtain a construction loan.

Special Risks in Construction Lending Even though most construction loans are made with relative assurance of permanent financing, special risks must be recognized in conjunction with this type of lending. Many sources of risk in construction lending can result in project failure or other difficulties for both the construction lender and borrower. First, there are the possibilities of strikes, inclement weather, or unforeseen problems with building design or geologic structure, which may slow down construction and consequently increase costs. If a slowdown occurs, interest charges, overhead, inflation in material costs, and real estate taxes accumulate. This may eventually require that the borrower invest additional equity funds or that the bank increase the loan over the initial amount of the construction loan commitment. A second area of risk that may cause problems in construction lending lies in the possibility of poor management in the development firm or a firm's inexperience in a particular field of construction. These conditions can lead to cost overruns and delays that can threaten the solvency of the developer and the economic feasibility of a project.

Finally, although most construction loans are made to borrowers with take-out commitments, contingencies in the take-out commitment, if not met, can cause the permanent lender to retract the commitment. It may be recalled that most take-out commitments require a completion date for construction, the right of the permanent lender to approve all construction change orders, a specific lease rental achievement, and other possible conditions before the commitment becomes binding. Unforeseen problems with construction can delay the project beyond the completion date, result in structural design changes unsuitable to the permanent lender, or cause the devolper not to meet the necessary rental achievement. If any or all of these events should occur, the permanent lender can retract the commitment and the construction lender may have to carry the completed project until a new permanent lender can be found.

Construction Loan Analysis Even though a take-out commitment may be obtained by a given borrower, construction lenders must perform their own underwriting function. Based on the special categories of risk just discussed, it is apparent that the construction lender faces the possibility of loss even when a take-out commitment exists.

First to be considered in the construction lending underwriting process is the financial adequacy and past construction experience of the developer. In making construction lending decisions, the lender must be assured that the builder has had successful building experience in the type of project for which financing is being sought. Lenders are reluctant to extend credit to inexperienced developers or to developers who have not demonstrated ability within specialized areas of construction. A developer's financial adequacy is equally important. In the event that slowdowns in construction are encountered, the developer must have adequate working capital to see a project through to completion without reliance on additional borrowing from the bank. Consequently, the bank normally will require as part of the loan application documentation, a complete set of financial statements from the developer along with a record of past construction experience, which may be thoroughly investigated by the lender. Assuming that the lender finds the data obtained on the developer satisfactory, personal guarantees may be required of the developer as a condition for obtaining the loan. These guarantees generally allow the lender to look to the developer's personal financial assets for satisfaction in the event a project goes into default.

Project Review   If a developer has a take-out commitment for a project from a permanent lender, this usually means that a market study and an appraisal report have been compiled and extensively studied by the long-term lender. The construction lender generally reviews the market study and appraisal to determine how much should be loaned based on economic value. Should the market study or appraisal not be adequate in the eyes of the construction lender, new studies may be conducted by the construction lender, ordinarily by staff appraisers. In any event, the construction lender seldom, if ever, agrees to lend an amount greater than the amount of the take-out commitment, regardless of the appraised value. Further, some construction lenders will not lend any more than the cost of the improvement being constructed, exclusive of the land value.

Risk Analysis   In addition to reviewing the appraisal and market reports, the construction lender normally performs a detailed ratio analysis of projected operating statements submitted by the developer. These statements accompany loan documentation given to the permanent lender and already have been analyzed in the manner shown in the preceding chapter. Nevertheless, the construction lender, who is very familiar with local market conditions in real estate, reviews these statements to see if assumptions made in the estimates are realistic. Then, after computing key financial ratios and comparing them to industry standards and present local market conditions, the construction lender makes a judgment as to whether the project should be underwritten. In addition to the appraisal review, other requirements are imposed on the developer by the construction lender. These items are outlined below.

Detailed Cost Breakdown.   The developer usually must submit detailed cost estimates and plans for constructing the improvement. The cost breakdown generally must be certified by an architect chosen by the lender, usually at the expense of the developer, for accuracy in accordance with building plans and specifications. Then the lender usually requires the developer to contract with the architect, again at the developer's expense, to verify on a monthly basis all costs as construction work progresses and as the lender disburses funds.

Building Contracts and Subcontracts. Normally, lenders require developers to obtain fixed-price contracts for specified amounts of construction from subcontractors. The lender may require these contracts as a means of protecting against cost overruns that may occur if material or labor prices rise during construction.

Labor and Material Payment Bonds/Completion Bonds. Many lenders require that developers purchase labor and material payment bonds and completion bonds. The first type of bond assures the lender that any unpaid bills for labor and material will be paid by the bonding company should a developer default. The completion bond assures the lender that the construction will be completed by the bonding company in the event that the developer defaults during construction.

Title Insurance. As a condition for obtaining a construction loan, title insurance generally must be purchased by the developer. This is to assure the lender that no liens superior to its lien exist on the property when construction commences. In addition, as funds are disbursed and construction progresses, the lender usually requires that the title company continually update the title abstract in order to verify that no liens have been filed before each disbursement is made by the lender. In fact, many lenders disburse construction funds directly to a title company which makes payment to the developer, or directly to subcontractors, *after* verifying the absence of any liens. This practice is used to assure the lender that no mechanics' liens have been filed during construction. Should a lien exist, and if the title company makes disbursement, the title company becomes liable for any loss to the owner, and ultimately to the lender.

Assignment of Lease Rents. In cases where long-term leases have been obtained by the developer, the lender may require assignment of these leases until the construction loan is liquidated. This assures the lender of receiving all rental payments should the project be completed and occupied with the developer in default.

Assignment of Commitment Letter. The construction lender usually requires the borrower to assign the take-out commitment letter obtained from a permanent lender to the construction lender. In this way, if the project is finished by the completion date and all contingencies are met, the permanent mortgage funds can be collected directly from the permanent lender by the construction lender, bypassing the developer.

Tri-Party Buy-Sell Agreement. In lieu of assignment of the commitment letter, the borrower, developer, and long-term lender may enter into an agreement whereby the permanent lender agrees to buy the construction mortgage loan directly from the construction lender on the completion date, assuming all contingencies are met. As previously indicated, this agreement gives the construction lender greater assurance that funds will be delivered when the construction project is completed and all contingencies honored.

Other Requirements Prior to Closing. In addition to the foregoing, other requirements must be fulfilled by the developer prior to closing. These include boundary surveys, soil samples and tests, verification of payment of all outstanding property taxes, checking zoning status and building permits, determination of the availability of necessary public utilities, a binder evidencing the purchase of hazard insurance coverage during the construction period, and establishment of the date on which construction is to commence and to end.

Rating Loan Terms and Fees For large scale construction projects, construction lenders may also charge nonrefundable loan commitment fees. These fees are forfeited in the event that a loan commitment is not accepted by the borrower within a specified time period. As with fees charged for take-out commitments, these fees range upward from amounts necessary to cover out-of-pocket underwriting costs, depending on market conditions. In addition, loan origination fees, intended to increase the loan yield to the lender, are charged at closing. Origination fees usually range from 1 to 3 percent of the loan commitment.

Interest rates on construction loans generally reflect short-term borrowing rates. Since the term of a construction loan is almost always less than three years, the rates charged on new loans vary considerably from period to period in response to current lending conditions. Many lenders, particularly commercial banks, have begun to rely on a system of *floating interest rates* on construction loans. A system of floating rates is based on the bank's *prime lending rate,* or short-term interest rate charged on commercial loans to the bank's most creditworthy customers. A construction loan normally is evaluated as to risk during the underwriting process and the interest rate quoted on the loan is made in conjunction with the prime rate. For example, an interest rate on a construction loan may be quoted as "two points over prime." This means that if the prime lending rate is 7 percent at closing, the interest rate charged on the construction loan is 9 percent. More importantly, however, if the prime lending rate increases during the construction period, the interest rate on the construction loan also increases, maintaining the 2 percent difference over the prime lending rate. In addition, some lenders have used a *floor,* or lower limit, on declines in interest rates permissible on construction loans with floating rates. Usually this floor is equivalent to the initial rate at which the construction loan was originated. Hence, in our example, the rate on the construction loan would be two points over prime with a floor of 9 percent.

Disbursement of Funds   As indicated in an earlier chapter, a cardinal rule followed by real estate lenders is never to loan more than the economic value of the property that serves as security for the loan. This rule applies equally well in construction lending. Generally, as construction progresses, disbursements are made by the lender in one of three ways. In the *stage method*, funds are disbursed as stages of construction are completed. For example, when a building is under roof and work has been verified by the lender, the first disbursement is made. As construction progresses and the building is plastered, the second disbursement is released. Completion of the project qualifies the builder for the final disbursement. This technique, used primarily in single-family construction, assures that the economic value being created in construction is in place and subject to a lien by the lender as disbursements are made. Consequently, the security for the loan is being improved continuously with the disbursement of funds.

The second way to disburse funds is the *monthly draw method*. This method is used extensively in the construction of larger scale projects requiring sizeable loans. The developer requests a draw each month based on the work completed in the preceding month. If an architect verifies that such work is in place, the lender disburses the funds. Again, the collateral value for the loan increases simultaneously with the disbursement of funds.

The final method of disbursement is a *voucher system.* The developer submits invoices from subcontractors for actual work completed to date. These invoices are submitted to the lender or to a title insurance company, depending on whether the lender is using the services of a title company for updating the title abstract, and then they are paid. With all these methods of disbursement, as payments are made, contractors and subcontractors sign an agreement that they have been paid for work done to date. This precludes their filing mechanics' liens.

Holdbacks.   In many cases, construction lenders "hold back" a portion of each disbursement payable to a developer. This occurs when a developer is using a number of subcontractors and is holding back a portion of the funds due under subcontracts. The developer holds back to be sure that subcontractors perform all work completely prior to receiving final payment. Consequently, the construction lender holds back from the developer so that no excess funds are made available to the developer during the period the developer is holding back from subcontractors.

Construction Lending Illustrated   Global Development Company has approached State City Bank for a construction loan for an apartment complex. Global has already obtained a take-out commitment from

Acme Life Insurance Company for up to $1.1 million on a total appraisal value of $1.5 million. Major contingencies in the take-out commitment specify that the project must be completed within 12 months and that 70 percent of all units must be leased before the commitment is binding.

State City Bank has reviewed the appraisal report and analyzed the cost estimates based on the market study. It believes the project to be economically feasible. If State City makes the loan, financing is available at a floating rate of 9 percent interest, or 2 percent over prime, with a 3 percent loan origination fee. The bank will not make a construction loan commitment for more than the take-out commitment. The appraised value of the project is $1.5 million. Of that amount, land value constitutes $400,000. Global owns the land free and clear and is willing to give State City first lien on the land as a condition of obtaining the construction loan.

A summary of detailed cost estimates submitted by Global is shown in Exhibit 12–1. The total estimated cost of building the improvement,

EXHIBIT 12–1
Summary of Cost Estimates, Global Development Company

Hard Costs:		
On Site		
Building ($17.00 sq.ft.)	$810,000	
Fixtures	60,000	
Landscaping	5,000	
Parking area	42,000	$917,000
Off Site		
Water and sewer extension	50,000	50,000
Soft Costs:		
Closing fees and taxes	10,000	
Loan origination fees	33,000	
Construction interest	61,000	
Architect–Engineering	8,000	
Architect inspections	5,000	117,000
Total Costs		$1,084,000

excluding land, is $1,084,000, which is slightly less than the take-out commitment of $1.1 million. This cost must be certified by an architect who judges conformance with building plans and specifications before the construction lender will make a loan commitment. It should also be noted that as part of the "soft costs" anticipated by the developer an estimate for construction interest cost has been included. This is customary in many construction lending situations, as no cash flow will begin from the project until it is completed. Consequently, unless the developer chooses to pay interest from internal sources, it is effectively carried forward in the construction loan balance, which is then purchased by the permanent lender. This point will be developed more fully as the illustration is completed.

Assuming State City Bank agrees to make the loan, all bonding requirements, surveys, title and hazard insurance policies, the tri-party or buy-sell agreement, payment of property taxes, and other requirements of the construction lender must be completed by the developer prior to closing. At closing, soft costs, including closing costs and taxes, origination fees, and layout costs will be advanced.[7] A summary of closing costs and soft costs approved for disbursement is provided in Exhibit 12–2.

EXHIBIT 12–2
Summary of Closing Costs and Soft Costs, Construction Loan—Global Development Company

Legal, layout costs	$ 5,000
Engineering fees–survey	8,000
Title abstract	500
Title insurance	2,000
Taxes and recording fees	2,500
Origination fee–State City Bank (3%)	33,000
Amount authorized for disbursement	$51,000

Based on the rate at which construction progresses, Global will be requesting draws against the construction loan commitment extended by State City Bank. Exhibit 12–3 shows a hypothetical schedule of monthly draws that might occur as Global completes the project and as construction is verified by an independent architect. Looking closely at the exhibit, it should be noted that as actual monthly draws are taken down by Global, *interest* is included as part of the draw on each month. This means that the developer is borrowing, as part of the draw, current interest charges each month. Since a construction loan is an "interest-only" loan, only interest is paid by the developer each month and no reduction in loan principal occurs.[8] Therefore, the balance due to the bank will increase each month by the full amount of *construction cost plus interest* that is borrowed by the developer. The *net cash* amounts taken down by the developer are shown in the last column of Exhibit 12–3. They reflect the proceeds the developer has for use each month

---

[7] In some cases, lenders may be willing to make an additional advance for materials at closing. This depends on the financial condition of the developer and whether bonding is in effect. Conservative lenders prefer the developer to use internal funds for initially acquiring materials. Reimbursement is then made after the materials are in place.

[8] This is true unless the developer chooses to make payments in excess of interest due for the month from internal funds. This amounts to the developer paying down the loan balance or loan principal.

EXHIBIT 12–3

Draw Schedule-Loan Statement, Construction Loan—Global Development Company

| | Actual Draws | | | | | |
Month	Construction Costs	Interest[°]	Total Monthly Draw[†]	Cumulative Loan Balance	Interest Payments	Net Cash to Developer
Close	$ 51,000	$ —	$ 51,000	$ 51,000	$ —	$ 18,000
1	—	383	383	51,383	383	—
2	175,000	385	175,385	226,768	385	175,000
3	175,000	1,701	176,701	403,469	1,701	175,000
4	150,000	3,026	153,026	556,495	3,026	150,000
5	125,000	4,174	129,174	685,669	4,174	125,000
6	100,000	5,143	105,143	790,812	5,143	100,000
7	90,000	6,564	96,564	887,376	6,564	90,000
8	50,000	7,365	57,365	944,741	7,365	50,000
9	30,000	7,841	37,841	982,582	7,841	30,000
10	20,000	8,155	28,155	1,010,737	8,155	20,000
11	20,000	8,389	28,389	1,039,126	8,389	20,000
12	10,000	8,625	18,625	1,057,751	8,625	10,000

[°] Computed on previous month's ending balance at .75% for months 1–6, and .83% for months 7–12.

[†] End of month.

after the draw is made and interest charges are paid.[9] Also at closing, the amount drawn is $51,000; however, the loan origination fee of $33,000 charged by State City Bank actually leaves $18,000 in cash for the developer to pay closing and soft costs.

Recalling that this loan was made with a floating interest rate initially at 9 percent, we assume that the prime lending rate increases 1 percent at the beginning of the seventh month, making the interest rate on this loan 10 percent. Based on the draw schedule in Exhibit 12–3 and taking into account the interest rate change, the total amount owed State City Bank at the end of 12 months is $1,057,751. This is slightly less than the construction loan commitment of $1.1 million and the take-out commitment which was also $1.1 million.

The draw schedule and corresponding interest and loan balance computations serve as the construction lender's *financial control* on the project. Should the loan balance as a percentage of the total commitment become higher than the percentage of construction completed, this would signal a possible cost overrun due perhaps to rising material or labor prices. Similarly, if the developer and the architect, who is verifying the construction in place, differ on the amount of draw necessary

[9] We assume that the developer makes the draw and immediately pays interest from the draw each month.

to pay for materials and labor used in the preceding month, this may signal a potential problem both for the developer and the lender.

Project Completion and Sale of the Construction Mortgage   Assuming that the project is ready to begin leasing space by the end of 10 months[10] and that the 70 percent occupancy contingency and all other contingencies in the take-out commitment are met at the end of 12 months, the construction mortgage is ready for sale to the permanent lender. Since the $1,057,751 mortgage amount shown in Exhibit 12–3 is slightly below the $1.1 million commitment made by the permanent lender, that lender will issue payment for $1,057,751 to the construction lender in exchange for the construction mortgage and note.[11]

Effective Interest Cost and Construction Loans   An interesting question for the developer now arises concerning the actual cost of this construction loan. What would State City Bank's yield, or internal rate of return, be on this loan? Since the original interest rate on the loan was 9 percent and since the prime rate went up by 1 percent at the beginning of the seventh month, making the monthly interest charge 10 percent, and a loan origination fee of $33,000 was charged by State City Bank, it is not clear precisely what the effective cost (yield) to the developer (lender) is in this case. The solution to this problem can be determined by again reviewing the data in Exhibit 12–3. The last column in the exhibit shows the actual net cash outflow from State City Bank to Global. This outflow represents State City's net *investment* in the construction loan made to Global. Since the construction loan is sold to Acme Life Insurance Company for $1,057,751, this represents the *net cash return* to State City Bank. Hence, the yield on this construction loan can be determined by *finding the interest rate that makes the present value of the return equal to the present value of the investment outlays.* This unknown interest rate is the internal rate of return or true yield on the construction loan.

The procedure used to find the interest rate that will make the present value of inflows and outflows equal is detailed in Exhibit 12–4. The series of cash flows is unusual in this case because the net cash outflows from the bank go out over different time intervals and the single cash return comes in at the end of the loan period. By discounting *all cash*

---

[10] Rentals usually begin before the last draws are made by the developer. By obtaining leases as soon as possible, the 70 percent rental achievement, which is a contingency in the take-out commitment, has a better chance of being met.

[11] If the construction mortgage balance should exceed $1.1 million, the permanent lender would be committed to only $1.1 million if the project were finished on the completion date and all other contingencies were satisfied. The construction lender would then be forced to hold a second mortgage for the difference between the construction loan balance and $1.1 million, since the construction lender approved the additional draws.

EXHIBIT 12–4
Determining the Effective Interest Cost of Construction Loans

Month	Net Cash Outflows	IF, PV of $1 (16 percent)	PV	IF, PV of $1 (15 percent)	PV
Outflows:					
Close ....$ 18,000		—	$ 18,000	—	$ 18,000
1	—	—	—	—	—
2	175,000	.97386	170,426	.97546	170,706
3	175,000	.96104	168,182	.96342	168,599
4	150,000	.94840	142,260	.95152	142,728
5	125,000	.93592	116,990	.93978	117,473
6	100,000	.92360	92,360	.92817	92,817
7	90,000	.91145	82,031	.91672	82,505
8	50,000	.89946	44,973	.90540	45,270
9	30,000	.88762	26,629	.89442	26,827
10	20,000	.87594	17,519	.88318	17,664
11	20,000	.86442	17,288	.87228	17,446
12	10,000	.85305	8,531	.86151	8,615
Present value total outflows $905,189					$908,650

Month	Net Cash Inflow	IF, PV of $1 (16 percent)	PV	IF, PV of $1 (15 percent)	PV
Inflows:					
12 ....$1,057,751		.85305	$902,314	.86151	$911,263

inflows and outflows during the period in which the flows occur, we take into account the important fact that interest is earned *on loan amounts only as those amounts are actually disbursed.*

In computing the present values, we do not know what interest rate to use. (This is what we are searching for.) We must use a trial and error approach.[12] Note in Exhibit 12–4 that the first interest rate used for discounting, 16 percent, results in a present value of outflows equal to $905,189 and a present value of inflows of $902,314. If 16 percent were the correct internal rate of return, the present value of inflows and outflows would be equal. Since they are not equal, we know that 16 percent is not the correct rate. However, we do know that the present value of inflows is less than the present value of outflows when 16

---

[12] The rate is found as a part of the trial and error process. However, we do know from Exhibit 12–3 that total net cash flow to the developer is $963,000 and the loan balance totaled $1,057,751 after 12 months. The difference, or $94,751, is the net cash return received by the bank over the undiscounted outlays ($963,000). If we assume for the moment that the $1,057,751 loan balance occurred evenly over 12 months, the *average* loan balance would be one half, or $528,876. The cash return of $94,751 divided by $528,826 is about 18%. This rough average percentage gives us a starting point.

percent is used; hence, we know that 16 percent is too large. By trying 15 percent, we see that the present value of inflows, $911,263, is now greater than the present value of outflows, $908,650.[13] We know now that the true yield on this loan falls between 15 and 16 percent.[14] This yield is obviously much higher than either the original interest rate on the loan of 9 percent or the increase to 10 percent that occurred after six months. This higher yield is primarily caused by the $33,000 origination fee charged at closing, which the borrower has paid back with loan funds obtained from the take-out commitment.

Interpolation—Construction Loans. Should the solution of between 15 and 16 percent not be precise enough for the lender or borrower, interpolation will result in a closer approximation to the actual yield. Interpolation is slightly more complicated in this situation than in examples shown in earlier chapters because we do not have a desired present value. However, we can proceed according to the following formula:

$$PV \text{ of Inflows} - PV \text{ of Outflows} = \text{Difference}$$

Discounting at 16 percent:	$902,314	− $905,189	= − $2,875
Discounting at 15 percent:	$911,263	− $908,650	= $2,613

We would like to know the interest rate which when used for discounting will make the difference in present values of all inflows and outflows equal to zero. By looking at the relative size of differences in present values obtained after discounting, we can see that the difference obtained when 15 percent is used, or $2,613, is closer to zero. This indicates that the solution is closer to 15 percent. To estimate the actual yield, we first determine the total difference from zero that results when both 15 and 16 percent are used for discounting. This total difference is $2,613 + $2,875 or $5,488. Note that when finding this total difference we ignore the fact that $2,875 is negative. This is because when interpolating we are interested only in how far each difference is from zero without regard to whether the difference is positive or negative. To solve for the yield we proceed as follows:

Difference in interest rate (16% − 15%)	= 1%
Sum of differences in present values	= $5,488
Difference in present value for *lowest* interest rate (15%)	= $2,613
Ratio of ($2,613 ÷ $5,488) × 1%	= 0.48%
Adding 15% + 0.48%	= 15.48%

---

[13] Note that both the present values of inflows *and* outflows change when the discount rate is changed.

[14] The internal rate of return procedure shown here can be used in any case when a loan is taken down in draws and repayment of the loan balance occurs in one or more payments. Computer programs exist which facilitate solutions to these types of problems.

This interpolation procedure shows that a better estimate of the true yield (cost) on this loan to the lender (developer) is 15.48 percent.

Land Development Loans

To raise the capital necessary to acquire undeveloped land, make onsite and offsite improvements, and then subdivide and sell parcels for homesites, developers rely on land development loans. As with construction loan, funds are borrowed or "taken down" in stages, usually monthly, based on the percentage of development work completed and verified. An open-end mortgage is used as security for the loan. It usually gives the lender first lien on the land being developed and first lien on all improvements when completed and as funds are disbursed. As in the case of a construction loan, the lender normally requires bonding and personal guarantees by the developer as a condition for obtaining the loan.

Unlike the construction loan, however, repayment of the land development loan is dependent on the sale of building sites to individuals and other developers. In other words, in the case of a construction loan, a take-out commitment generally is obtained by a builder, assuring the construction lender that the loan will be purchased by a long-term lender. This is usually *not* the case in land development situations, as loan repayments are made when parcels are sold to *individual buyers*. As a result, land development loans are usually *more risky* than most construction loans. The lender must accurately assess the risk of the project and the rate at which parcels will be sold in order to determine whether the loan can be repaid.

Much of the analysis and many requirements used in construction lending are also utilized in land development lending. Financial statements, appraisal reports, and market studies are analyzed closely by the lender. In addition, detailed plans and costs are reviewed by an architect or engineer. As development progresses, monthly inspections must be made to verify all work done before a draw can be made against the loan commitment. All pre-closing requirements relating to bonding, subcontracts, title insurance, hazard insurance, zoning verification, building permits, etc., discussed in connection with construction loans, also commonly apply to land development loans. However, since usually no take-out commitment exists in land development situations, the lender making the development loan assumes the full financial risk associated with the success or failure of the project.

Funds for repaying the loan come from the sale of individual parcels by the developer; therefore, a portion of the proceeds from each parcel sale must be paid to the lender. This amount, negotiated by the lender and developer, is referred to as the *release price*. When a parcel is sold and the developer pays the release price to the lender, the lender in turn signs a release statement waiving all liens against the parcel sold. Clear title may then pass to the buyer of the parcel. The lender uses this release clause in the mortgage as a control on the development loan, to assure repayment as parcels are sold.

Land Development Loans Illustrated   Landco Development Company has approached Mid City Mortgage Company concerning a 50 acre tract of land, which it would like to improve and subdivide into 120 building sites. The land is available at $8,000 per acre, or $400,000 and has been zoned R-1 for residential development. Each parcel should sell in a price range of $8,000 to $12,000 depending on location within the subdivision. An appraisal has been made on the project based on comparable building sites available in the market. At an average value of $10,000 per parcel, it is estimated that the project will have an appraised value of $1.2 million when completed. Landco figures that direct costs on the project will total $733,000 as shown in detail in Exhibit 12–5.

EXHIBIT 12–5
Landco Development Company, Project Cost Estimates

Land	$300,000
Closing costs	20,000
Other direct costs:	
$30 per lineal foot	300,000
1. Grading	
2. Streets	
3. Subsurface improvements	
Taxes	3,000
Engineering and other field work	20,000
General and administrative expenses directly	
associated with development	80,000
Miscellaneous	10,000
Total	$733,000

Landco wants to borrow this amount from Mid City. Landco has made a $100,000 down payment on the land.

Mid City will make a careful analysis of Landco's appraisal report, cost estimates, and market study. Then it will conduct its own appraisal, based on comparable land sales, to confirm whether the $1.2 million value estimated for the completed project is reasonable. If granted, the loan will represent approximately 61 percent of value ($733,000 ÷ $1,200,000). This loan-to-value ratio falls within the range acceptable by most lenders.[15] Based on current financial market conditions, if Mid City agrees to make the loan, it will be made at 12 percent interest and, in addition, a loan origination fee of $15,000 will be charged.

A breakdown of the amount of funds to be disbursed at the loan closing between Mid City and Landco is shown in Exhibit 12–6. A monthly schedule of the draws estimated by Landco as necessary to complete the project on time is detailed in Exhibit 12–7.

Landco believes that sales of parcels should start seven months after development begins and that sales will progress according to the following schedule:

EXHIBIT 12–6
Landco Development Company, Estimates of Loan Fees and Disbursement at Closing

Cost Items

Land costs	$300,000
Accounting, legal, layout costs	9,440
Appraisal fees	1,000
Engineering fees–survey	2,000
Title abstract and insurance premium	5,200
Review by counsel	500
Liability premium	310
Recording fees	100
Real estate taxes due	1,450
Total costs authorized to be disbursed at closing	$320,000
Add: Loan origination fee	15,000
Initial loan balance at closing	$335,000

EXHIBIT 12–7
Schedule of Estimated Monthly Cash Draws, Landco Development Company

Month	Amount	Month	Amount
Closing	$320,000	7	$ 33,333
1	50,000	8	33,333
2	50,000	9	33,333
3	50,000	10	18,833
4	35,500	11	18,833
5	35,500	12	18,333
6	35,500	Total	$733,000

---

[15] Most lenders will not allow the loan-to-value ratio on land development loans to exceed a range of 60 to 70 percent of value, or the actual cost of improvements.

Months	Sales per Month	Cumulative Sales
7–12 4		24
13–24 5		60
25–36 3		36
		120

Based on this estimate, all the parcels should be sold three years from the beginning of the development.

Repayment Pattern—Land Development Loans   The first item to be negotiated between the developer and lender is the *release price* for each parcel, that is, the amount that must be repaid by the developer to the lender from the proceeds of each parcel sale. To accomplish this, the lender will first estimate the *average loan and interest per parcel* available for sale. This is computed by taking from Exhibit 12–7 (1) the monthly estimates of draws necessary for Landco to complete the project and (2) the estimated rate at which parcels will be sold, and then combining these estimates in a schedule such as the one in Exhibit 12–8. Recalling that the first draw of $320,000 will be taken down at closing, and that a $15,000 loan origination fee will be charged, the loan balance payable as of the closing date is $335,000. Exhibit 12–8 summarizes the way in which the cash inflows and outflows must occur from the closing date for Landco to repay the initial $335,000 loan balance and all subsequent draws at the end of three years.

Looking at Exhibit 12–8 more closely, column (*a*) represents the

EXHIBIT 12–8
Schedule of Monthly Draws and Loan Repayments, Landco Development Project

(*a*) Month	(*b*) Repayment	(*c*) Draws	(*d*) IF, PV of $1 per Mo. 12%	(*e*) Present Value (*b*) × (*d*) Repayment	(*c*) × (*d*) Draws
Close	0	$335,000	—	0	$335,000
1–3	0	50,000	2.941	0	147,050
4–6	0	35,500	5.795– 2.941	0	101,317
7–9	4(*x*)	33,333	8.566– 5.795	11.084(*x*)	92,366
10–12	4(*x*)	18,833	11.255– 8.566	10.576(*x*)	50,642
13–24	5(*x*)	0	21.243–11.255	49.940(*x*)	0
25–36	3(*x*)	0	30.108–21.243	26.595(*x*)	0
				98.195(*x*)	$726,375

months during which future inflows and outflows are expected to occur. Column (b) represents the loan and interest per lot that must be paid to the lender by the developer to assure that the loan is repaid during the 36 month period in which sales are to occur. Since we do not know yet how much must be paid to the lender from parcel sales, we designate those dollar payments as x, or the unknown we are trying to determine. We do know, however, that these unknown amounts x will be repaid at the rate of four payments per month during months 7–12. Five payments per month during months 13–24, and three payments per month during months 25–36. Column (c) represents loan draws that are expected during the period of development and parcel sales.

Column (d) in Exhibit 12–8 contains interest factors for the PV of $1 per month at 12 percent. As was done in the previous section on construction lending, these factors are applied against the amounts in both columns (b) and (c). This assures that when x is determined, it will be great enough to earn the lender 12 percent on all net loan amounts outstanding over the 36 month period. Discounting all outflows by 12 percent assures that interest will be earned on loan amounts only when they are drawn down. By discounting the inflows at 12 percent, account is taken of the fact that the repayments do not occur all at once, but rather, over time. Hence, the return being earned by the lender is occurring over time.[16] It should be noted that the IFs used in column (d) must also be netted out, so that only the *portion* of the IF applicable to a given time period is used. For example, in months 7–9, the IF for nine months, 8.566, must be reduced by the IF for six months, 5.795, so that the difference, 2.771, representing the specific 7–9 month interval, is used in the computation. This netting of IFs must be done each time the cash inflow or outflow changes during a specified time interval, such as three months, a year, etc.[17] Column (e) represents the present value of all inflows and outflows occurring over the 36 month period. Since the original loan balance of $335,000 must be repaid from the net repayments, it should now be clear that x, the unknown amount of loan repayment, must be large enough to repay the initial $335,000 loan balance and all subsequent draws, plus 12 percent interest.

With all of the information assembled in Exhibit 12–8, the estimated

---

[16] This procedure is exactly the same as that used earlier in determining the internal rate of return on the constructon loan. Only now we knew the rate of return on which repayments are to be based is 12% and we are trying to determine the loan repayments. This situation also differs from construction lending in that like the draws, the returns also occur over time. In the construction lending case, only one return was realized by the lender when the loan was sold to the permanent lender.

[17] It should be recalled from the problems at the end of Chapter 8 that what is being done here is netting out IFs to correspond to annuities received during specified time intervals.

loan and interest per parcel can be determined. Since the present value of all loan draws, $726,375, must equal the present value of x payments, x can be solved as follows:

$$\$726,375 = 98.195(x)$$
$$\$726,375 \div 98.195 = (x)$$
$$\$7,397 = (x)$$

From this analysis it can be seen that from the average parcel sale price of $10,000, if the lender wanted the loan fully repaid after 36 months when all parcels are sold, the amount of loan repayment would be $7,397 per parcel, or effectively 74 percent of the average parcel price.[18]

Determination of the Release Price   Based on the estimated loan and interest per parcel of $7,397, if sales of building sites proceed as scheduled, the borrower will have the development loan repaid when all 120 parcels are sold, or after 36 months. When most land development loans are made, however, the lender will demand a release price *greater* than the estimated loan and interest per parcel. This is true because the lender usually does not want to take the risk associated with a possible slowdown in sales in the later stages of the project. In many land developments, choice parcels are sold early and less desirable ones remain unsold over time. Since some parcels are difficult to sell, the lender wants assurance that the developer takes this added risk. Consequently, the lender will bargain for a high release price, hoping that the loan will be repaid before all 120 parcels are sold.

Another reason for negotiating a higher release price is that since Mid City puts most of the "front-end" money into the development during the first 12 months (see the draws in column c of Exhibit 12–8), it wants assurance that the loan repayment is given preference as sales proceeds are realized. In addition, since the average sales price is estimated to be $10,000, if the loan repayment is set at $7,397, the developer will share in proceeds in the amount of $10,000 − $7,397, or $2,603 for each parcel sold. Since the lender wants the loan repaid more rapidly, there is still room to negotiate for a higher release price, such that the developer retains a smaller portion of the $2,603 available from each sale.

In most land development loans, the release price per parcel ranges from 110 to 120 percent of the estimated loan and interest per parcel. The exact price is negotiated based on how soon the lender wants the loan repaid, how much cash the developer must retain from each parcel

---

[18] At this point, the reader can return to Exhibit 12–8 and substitute $7,397, for all of the ($x$'s) in column ($b$). When discounted by 12 percent [column (d)], carried over to column (e), and totaled, it can be seen that the present value of repayments would equal $726,375, or the present value of all draws. This proves that the loan is fully repaid and that the lender has earned 12 percent on the monthly outstanding loan balance.

sale to cover other expenses and profit, and conditions in the loan market. For example, if a 110 percent release price is chosen, the developer retains about $1,863 per sale ($10,000 less $7,397 × 1.10); and if 120 percent is used, the developer will retain only $1,124. Most lenders prefer to have the loan fully repaid when approximately 80 percent of all parcels are sold. They try to negotiate a release price to accomplish this end. In our illustration, this would mean that after 96 parcels are sold the lender would like to have the loan repaid.

Obviously the release price chosen will affect the cash flow of both the lender and developer and will be determined by competition among lenders desiring to make the loan. The developer usually prefers the loan offer with the *lowest* release price to increase cash flow in the early stages of development. In practice, the effects of any particular release price must be projected to determine: (1) when the loan can be repaid and (2) whether the cash position of the developer is strong enough to maintain cash solvency over the development and marketing period.

Loan Repayment Schedule—Land Development Loans   To estimate when the land development loan will be repaid by Landco under a negotiated release price, we assume that the release price is set at 120 percent of the $7,397 loan and interest per parcel. This results in a $8,875 (rounded) release price per parcel. Based on an average appraised value of $10,000 per parcel, the release price represents 88.75 percent of the value of individual parcels.[19] With the schedule of draws, the forecasted sales schedule, and the release price known, a repayment schedule like the one shown in Exhibit 12–9 can be developed to ascertain when, and after how many parcels are sold, the loan will be repaid.

Looking at Exhibit 12–9, the first column contains the beginning loan balance in each month the loan is outstanding. The second column shows the monthly draws required by the developer to complete construction (Exhibit 12–7). Interest is computed at an annual rate of 12 percent compounded monthly, or at a monthly rate of 1 percent (12% ÷ 12 months). No payments are made for 6 months until parcel sales begin. Interest is accrued during that time period and carried in the loan balance. The loan payments, based on the $8,875 release price times the number of monthly parcel sales, are shown in the third column. If development proceeds as scheduled, draws are taken down as estimated, and parcel sales are made as projected, the developer will repay the loan during the 29th month. In terms of parcel sales, as of the 28th

---

[19] In practice, the developer will provide the lender with a schedule of lot prices for each parcel within the development. The lender will in turn apply approximately 88.75 percent to each parcel price to obtain the schedule of release prices for all parcels in the project. When each parcel is sold and the scheduled release price is paid, the lender then signs the release form giving clear title to the buyer.

EXHIBIT 12–9
Loan Repayment Schedule, Landco Development Company

Month	(1) Beginning Balance	(2) Draws°	(3) Payments°	(4) Interest†	(5) Ending Balance
Close		$335,000		—	$335,000
1	$335,000	50,000		$ 3,350	388,350
2	388,350	50,000		3,884	442,234
3	442,234	50,000		4,422	496,656
4	496,656	35,500		4,967	537,123
5	537,123	35,500		5,371	577,994
6	577,994	35,500		5,780	619,274
7	619,274	33,333	$ 35,500	6,193	623,300
8	623,300	33,333	35,500	6,233	627,366
9	627,366	33,333	35,500	6,274	631,473
10	631,473	18,833	35,500	6,315	621,121
11	621,121	18,833	35,500	6,211	610,665
12	610,665	18,833	35,500	6,107	600,105
13	600,105		44,375	6,001	561,731
14	561,731		44,375	5,617	522,973
15	522,973		44,375	5,230	483,828
16	483,828		44,375	4,838	444,291
17	444,291		44,375.	4,443	404,359
18	404,359		44,375	4,044	364,028
19	364,028		44,375	3,640	323,293
20	323,293		44,375	3,233	282,151
21	282,151		44,375	2,822	240,598
22	240,598		44,375	2,406	198,629
23	198,629		44,375	1,986	156,240
24	156,240		44,375	1,562	113,427
25	113,427		26,625	1,134	87,936
26	87,936		26,625	879	62,190
27	62,190		26,625	622	36,187
28	36,187		26,625	362	9,924
29	9,924		10,023	99	—
		$748,000	$862,025	$114,025	0

° Draws and payments occur at the end of the month; columns do not total because of rounding.
† Computed at 1% per month on the beginning monthly loan balance.

month, 96 parcels would be sold. Since a $9,924 loan balance remains going into the 29th month and the release price is $8,875, this means that the loan will be repaid with the sale of two additional parcels in the 29th month, or after a total of 98 parcels are sold. With the sale of 98 parcels required to repay the loan, this represents about 82 percent of the 120 parcels available. This percentage is close to the 80 percent requirement specified by most lenders on land development projects.

   Developer—Cash Flow, Profitability From the loan repayment schedule just detailed, with a negotiated $8,875 release price based on an average sale price of $10,000, the developer will retain an average of $1,125 ($10,000 − $8,875) from each parcel sale until the 29th month, or until the 98th parcel is sold. After that point is reached, the developer will retain the full $10,000 average sale price through the sale of the 120th parcel. Clearly, this is when the greatest profit will be earned by the developer. However, during the development period and until the sale of the 98th parcel, a question arises concerning the developer's ability to meet operating expenses and other requirements. The amount loaned to the developer is to cover only the *direct costs* associated with development. Other obligations, such as sales commissions, property taxes, and general and administrative expenses after actual development is complete, must be covered from the cash retained by the developer from each parcel sale or from internal working capital.

To investigate the developer's ability to carry this project until the loan is repaid, a schedule of cash flows for the developer must be constructed that contains not only the direct cost elements, but also additional day-to-day operating expenses. In this way, the developer's cash position can be projected and the risk of loan default better analyzed. Exhibit 12–10 contains a quarterly summary of all cash inflows and outflows for Landco over the entire life of the project. The outflows for direct costs in the cash flow schedule are taken from the schedule of monthly draws (Exhibit 12–7). Loan repayments are taken from the schedule of loan repayments (Exhibit 12–9). Other operating expenses, including general and administrative expenses, sales commissions, and property taxes, have been estimated on a quarterly basis and included in the exhibit.

An analysis of Exhibit 12–10 provides insight into Landco's ability to carry the cash needs of the entire project. It should be noted that in the first two quarters there is no net cash flow available to Landco, and from the third through ninth quarters, cash flow is positive but a very small amount. It is during such periods that estimates concerning costs, sales rates, and repayment conditions become crucial to both Landco and Mid City. If the time needed for development exceeds initial estimates, if development costs exceed estimates, or if sales do not materialize as projected, it is clear that Landco's cash flow position will change dramatically. Similarly, if Mid City requires a release price that is too high, this may also serve to reduce the cash flow to Landco, which may jeopardize Landco's ability to carry out the project and to repay the loan. For this reason, Landco's own financial resources must be considered by Mid City in the event that any of these adverse factors materializes. Clearly, if Landco's cash position in this project becomes questionable, Mid City will be reluctant to advance funds for operating expenses in addition to direct costs. In this event, Landco will be expected to share in some of the risk by contributing working capital

EXHIBIT 12–10

Schedule of Cash Flow, Landco Development Company

Quarter	Close	(1)	(2)	(3)	(4)	(5)	(6)	(7)	(8)	(9)	(10)	(11)	(12)
Inflow:													
Sales				$120,000	$120,000	$150,000	$150,000	$150,000	$150,000	$90,000	$90,000	$90,000	$90,000
Loan draws	$335,000	$150,000	$106,500	100,000	56,500								
Total inflow	$335,000	$150,000	$106,500	$220,000	$176,500	$150,000	$150,000	$150,000	$150,000	$90,000	$90,000	$90,000	$90,000
Outflow:													
Land purchase .	300,000												
Closing fees	35,000												
Loan repayment		150,000	106,500	106,500	106,500	133,125	133,125	133,125	133,125	79,875	36,648		
Direct costs				100,000	56,500								
Other expenses:													
General and administrative					3,000	3,000	3,000	3,000	3,000	3,000	2,000	2,000	2,000
Property tax					3,000		2,500		2,500		2,000		1,500
Sales expense				6,000	6,000	7,500	7,500	7,500	7,500	4,500	4,500	4,500	4,500
Total outflow	$335,000	$150,000	$106,500	$212,500	$175,000	$143,625	$146,125	$143,625	$146,125	$87,375	$45,148	$6,500	$8,000
Net cash in (out)	0	0	0	$ 7,500	$ 1,500	$ 6,375	$ 3,875	$ 6,375	$ 3,875	$ 2,625	$44,852	$83,500	$82,000

from its own resources to complete sale of the project successfully. To analyze Landco"s ability to advance working capital, should it be necessary, Mid City will thoroughly review the company's income statement and balance sheet as well as possibly requiring additional loan security or guarantees from Landco beyond this particular project.

Finally it should be noted that based on Exhibit 12–10, Landco's profitability does not materialize significantly until the last three quarters of the project. This is in keeping with the way in which risk is taken during the project. Because the lender puts in "front-end" capital, it wants assurance of a high priority in the sales proceeds as the development matures. Consequently, Landco must wait until the lender's prior claim is satisfied before it realizes a return. However, from Landco's viewpoint, since its equity in the project increases with the market value of the project as actual development occurs, and since its front-end investment is virtually zero, all returns are appropriately deferred to the later stages of the project.

Extension Agreements   In the land development case just illustrated, the date that Mid City anticipates that the loan will be repaid is during the 29th month. Since it is possible that the loan will not be paid at that time due to development problems or the slow sale of parcels, the lender will usually require an extension clause in the initial loan contract. This clause specifies that an additional charge will be made for any extra time needed to repay the loan. This amounts to gap financing, or additional interim financing, and the lender will usually charge an extension fee in addition to interest on the outstanding loan balance, if an extension is needed.

QUESTIONS

1.   For undeveloped properties on which borrowers seek permanent financing, what are the two major types of loan commitments? Which category do construction lenders prefer and why?

2.   What contingencies are commonly contained in take-out commitments at the insistance of the permanent lender?

3.   What is a buy and sell agreement? Why have these agreements been used with increasing frequency?

4.   What is gap financing? Why is it necessary? Is its use desirable by both borrowers and lenders?

5.   "The fact that take-out commitments are commonly required as a condition for obtaining a construction loan takes a lot of the risk out of the situation for the construction lender." Evaluate this statement.

6.   What are some of the requirements that lenders impose on developers when making construction loans?

7.   What does bonding mean? When is it used?

8.   What does a floating interest rate loan mean? How does it work?

9. What controls are usually employed by the construction lender when disbursement of loan funds is made? How does the lender attempt to control risks of cost overruns?

10. When a construction loan is made, interest charges are often built into cost estimates by the developer. Why is this done? How does this affect the monthly cash position of both the lender and borrower? Since the interest is effectively borrowed, how and when does the bank earn its return?

11. What is usually the maximum loan amount that a construction lender will make a commitment for?

12. If a construction loan totals more than the take-out commitment due to a cost overrun or other cause, what are the obligations of the construction lender and the permanent lender who made the take-out commitment?

13. How do land development loans and construction loans differ with respect to lending risks?

14. What is a release price? How is it determined? Why is it used?

15. How does use of a release price in a land development loan tend to even out the risks to the borrower and developer in land development situations? Why do lenders usually insist that land development loans be repaid when approximately 80 percent of parcels are sold?

16. How can the lender and developer be assured that the release price in a land development loan is reasonable and that the developer will be able to carry the projects until all parcels are sold?

CASE PROBLEMS

1. ABC Development Company has approached National County Bank concerning a construction loan for a shopping center on land owned by ABC. ABC has a take-out commitment for up to $1,000,000 from Rock of Gibraltar Insurance Company. National County Bank has reviewed the project costs, ABC's financial statements, the appraisal, and the take-out commitment and has decided to make the construction loan. The loan commitment will be for up to the same amount as the take-out commitment and will carry a 9 percent interest rate plus a 2 percent loan origination fee ($20,000).

ABC has provided the estimates of monthly construction costs which National City agrees are realistic. Closing costs are included in this schedule and the $20,000 loan origination fee is included in closing costs.

Monthly Construction Cost Estimate
ABC Development Company

Month			
Close	$ 40,000	7	50,000
1	–	8	50,000
2	200,000	9	40,000
3	200,000	10	40,000
4	100,000	11	30,000
5	75,000	12	10,000
6	75,000		

Based on the estimated completion schedule, the permanent lender is scheduled to buy the construction loan from National County Bank 12 months after closing the construction loan.

   a. Complete a draw schedule and loan statement like the one in Exhibit 12–3 (assume the estimated monthly construction costs are accurate).

   b. Assuming the permanent lender buys the construction loan for the balance outstanding after 12 months, what is the yield (cost) to the lender (developer)?

   2. Community Development Corporation (CDC) is seeking financing for acquisition and development of 90 home sites. The land acquisition will cost $350,000 and direct development costs are estimated to be an additional $350,000. City Federal Bank has indicated that it is interested in making the loan at 12 percent interest with additional closing costs of $10,000 and a loan origination fee of $20,000. The appraised value of the project, based on an average parcel price of $10,500, is $945,000. After making a down payment of $100,000, CDC believes that it will have to take down $250,000 of the land cost, the closing fee of $10,000, and the $20,000 origination fee when the loan is actually closed. The remaining direct cost of $350,000 will be taken down in 10 equal installments of $35,000 beginning the first month after closing. Parcel sales are expected to begin during the seventh month after closing at the rate of 5 parcels per month. The company and the bank have also agreed to a release price of 120 percent of the estimated loan and interest per parcel.

   a. Based on the above information, compute an estimate of the loan and interest per parcel for sale by CDC.

   b. From your answer in (*a*), what will be the release price?

   c. Based on (*b*) and the pattern of loan draws, when will CDC have the loan fully repaid?

   d. Besides the computations above, what other factors will the lender consider in evaluating CDC's loan proposal?

13

Special Techniques Used in Financing Real Estate

Techniques Considered

In recent years several adaptations of principles well known to those acquainted with real estate finance have received considerable acclaim as new approaches to financing real estate. The important techniques to be considered in this chapter are:

1. Sale and leaseback.
2. Equity participations of institutional lenders.
3. Wraparound mortgages.

PART 1: SALE AND LEASEBACK

Meaning

Although referred to in connection with long-term leases in chapter 6, the technique of sale and leaseback was not discussed in depth. Its popularity justifies a fuller consideration herein. This financing arrangement contains two steps which are taken simultaneously, although they appear to be separate and distinct. First, an institution with funds to invest, such as a life insurance company, a college or university, a religious body, or a charitable institution, purchases the real estate owned and used by a well-established business corporation—usually a retailer or a manufacturer. Second, the property is leased back to the seller by the purchaser. From these two steps we obtain the name— "sale and leaseback." Other names used to designate this practice are "purchase and leaseback" and "liquidating lease."

The property need not be in existence at the time such an arrangement is made. Some contractors agree to purchase a site to be selected by the lessee, construct a building according to his plans and specifications, turn the complete product over to him for his use, and finance it according to the sale and leaseback principle, all without any capital outlay by the lessee.

Lease Terms

The test of investment quality in such an arrangement depends primarily upon the financial stability of the lessee. The customary term of such a lease ranges from 20 to 40 years. Leases on retail property are customarily for longer terms than on industrial real estate. The lease may provide for a renewal or even for a repurchase at or before the expiration date. The rental is net to the lessor. The lessee pays all taxes and assessments, insurance, maintenance and repair costs, utility charges, and so on. The net rent is fixed at such a level that it is expected that, within the original term of the lease, the lessor will have recovered at least the purchase price of the building; and in the meantime he will have enjoyed a final net return at least comparable to currently available returns on government or Aaa corporate bonds. In some such leases the rate of return is not flat for the entire life of the lease but may be graded, with highest rates in the early years, followed by declining rates for successive periods. This practice permits the lessor to write down his investment more rapidly.

In the event of the failure of the lessee to meet any of the charges assumed by him, the lessor is empowered to make the payments required and collect from the lessee. This follows the usual pattern of long-term leases. Defaults—whether due to nonpayment of rent, assignment for the benefit of creditors, or any other action of the lessee that may jeopardize the position of the lessor—usually give the latter the right to terminate the lease. Condemnation clauses are usually well defined. Total destruction of structures is dealt with both in leases and in state laws governing them.

Reasons for Recent Use

As pointed out above, the principles involved in sale and leaseback arrangements are not new. Indeed, at least one instance of the specific practice has been cited as early as 1882. The widespread use of this device has been confined to recent years. The reasons are as follows: (1) Equity capital from outside capital markets has been scarce. The alternative was to resort to borrowed capital, which traditionally was limited to 50 to 60 percent of the appraised value of the real estate offered as security for the loan. Where more capital was needed, the opportunity to secure 100 percent of value was eagerly accepted. Even where the borrower could get along with a 50 percent loan, he might prefer to sell his real estate and lease it back for reasons that will be developed later. (2) Financial institutions have at times been hard put to find outlets for their tremendous resources. The amount of the resources of life insurance companies pressing for investment will be discussed in Chapter 17. Other reasons for the use of sale and leaseback arrangements will be discussed later in this chapter.

Types of Real Estate Used

As already indicated, the most common use of the device of purchase and leaseback is in the mercantile field of business. It is not strange that this is so. Traditionally many large distributors, including some very strong institutions and some chains, have not looked with favor upon real estate ownership. Leases of property owned by others have been common. In explaining the reasons for the sale of its properties to the Union College, the president of Allied Stores wrote his stockholders as follows: "This Company has long recognized a preference for renting land and buildings, where leases were obtainable on favorable terms, rather than investing its own funds in real estate." Also, merchandise corporations are thought to be more stable than some other users of real estate. Sears, Roebuck and Company; Federated Department Stores, Inc.; Spiegel, Inc.; J. C. Penney Co.; Allied Stores Corporation; and numerous other department stores have used the sale and leaseback device extensively. Chain stores in fields covering shoes, variety merchandise, wearing apparel, drugs and cigars, and foods; restaurants; and candy and even smaller individual stores have been similarly financed in substantial numbers.

Next in order of use are industrial corporations. Not all that have become interested in this type of financing have been permitted to use it because of the highly specialized character of their operations. The real estate used by a department store would at least be available for use by another department store. But that used by some manufacturers might be worth very much less for any other alternative purpose. Many well-known industrial corporations have made some use of this device. It is not necessary that a company achieve the strength of an industrial giant, however, to utilize the sale and leaseback method of financing. Many lesser industrial corporations of sound credit have taken the same route.

Office buildings in the large cities, and even in many smaller ones have been sold and leased back to their former owners. To some extent, banks have also used financing of this type. Construction companies engaged in building more office space regularly use the commitment to sell and lease back as a means of financing major construction. They have worked extensively with life insurance companies in this manner.

Sources of Funds

Life insurance companies constitute a major source of funds for sale and leaseback financing. Other sources of funds include college and university endownment funds and charitable and religious investment funds. Like life insurance companies, educational institutions have been hard pressed to earn the best possible returns on their investment funds. Pension funds have engaged in sale and leaseback financing to a limited extent. Since liberalization of the income tax laws permitting accelerated depreciation deductions, affluent individuals in high tax brackets have found these investments attractive when they can largely offset rental income against depreciation and interest deductions.

Legal Character of Lease Contract

The sale and leaseback contract contemplates an actual sale of the property with delivery of both legal and equitable title to the purchaser. Upon attaining the status of ownership, the purchaser then executes a valid lease upon terms agreed upon at the time the two-step agreement was made. Since the sale follows traditional real estate transfers, there is nothing peculiar about it. It is the lease that must be scrutinized most carefully, because each lease is drawn to meet a specific situation. Here there is ample opportunity for mistakes that amateurs would not recognize until it is too late. One very important question is: Is the lease so drawn that it tends to substitute a mortgage for the sale?

For example, as has been pointed out elsewhere in this text, a deed given to secure a debt becomes an equitable mortgage. If the lease contains a purchase option, does this amount to a relationship between the lessor and lessee that a court may construe to be that of mortgagor and mortgagee instead? In fear of this possibility, some lessors refuse to grant repurchase rights. The lessee, on the other hand, would prefer an option to repurchase the property if he thinks it may appreciate in value during the term of the lease. Presumably the court will weigh all the evidence in each case before reaching a decision about the existence of an equitable mortgage when a repurchase option is included in the lease. Doubtful cases may lean in the direction of a mortgage interpretation.

As at least a partial offset to the uncertain attitude of courts concerning the legal character of the lease contract where repurchase options are included, some leases provide such options only in conjunction with cancellation privileges. For example, the lessee might be permitted to request cancellation of the lease at stated intervals during its life, in consideration for his willingness to repurchase the property upon such cancellation. The amount of the purchase price is usually the amortized value of the lessor's purchase price, plus a premium of 1 to 4 percent, depending upon the remaining life of the lease. If the lessor elects not to sell, then the lease is expected to be terminated as of the cancellation date.

In other words, this is not an absolute right to repurchase, since the request may be refused by the lessor. If the specialized character of the building results in pressure upon the lessor to grant the request, the effect is the same as if the lessee had a right to repurchase the property. This situation may be weighed by a court asked to determine whether or not an equitable mortgage exists in a sale and leaseback arrangement. This possibility has deterred the inclusion of any reference to a repurchase clause in some leases recently executed. On the other hand, the lessee may not dare to request a cancellation of the lease for fear of refusal by the lessor, followed by termination of the lease and dispossession of the lessee. The result is the same as if the lease were noncancelable.

Renewal Options Options to renew a lease, at its expiration, for another term, perhaps for the same length of time as the original lease, are sometimes used as a substitute for a repurchase option. Renewals are usually provided for at much lower cost than the rent originally charged. The reduction may be 1 or 2 percent or as much as 5 percent or more of the original cost of the property. Where such renewals are permitted, two questions arise, the answers to which may affect the amount of tax deductions: (1) Shall the cost of improvement paid for by the lessee be spread over the remaining life of the original lease only, or shall it be spread over this period plus the period of lease renewal? (2) Shall rentals paid during each period be deducted as they accrue, or shall they be averaged over the life of the lease plus the life of the extension? For example, if the rental during the first 20 years is $25,000 annually, and the rental is only $10,000 per year for the next 20 years, shall these amounts determine annual deductions for tax purposes or will the average of $17,500 be so used? The answer seems to rest upon the probability of renewal of the lease. This, in turn, frequently hinges upon the favorableness of renewal terms.

Sales to Establish Losses Occasionally, sale and leaseback plans involve unusual features. If they are set up for the purpose of obtaining an additional tax advantage, they are usually scrutinized very carefully by the Internal Revenue Service. For example, a foundry located in St. Louis, Missouri, and carried on the tax records at $531,700, was sold to a small college for $150,000 and leased back in the conventional manner to the original owner. The difference, $381,700, was taken as a business loss. The Commissioner disallowed the deduction. The government contended that the transaction represented a gift for the most part and not a sale of the property at its fair value. For a gift to an educational institution, the donor was entitled to deduct not more than the usual allowance from its total net income for this purpose and not the difference noted above. Even after taking legal deductions into account, the result might still be a gain to the vendor instead of a loss.

Advantages Claimed for Lessee

The advantages usually claimed for business corporations which sell their real estate and lease it back include the following: (1) This plan will provide more funds for expansion of business and for working capital at lower cost and for a longer period of time than will be available from any source. (2) The funds so released from the sale of real estate can be invested to better advantage and at a higher rate of return when used to expand business operations. (3) This device simplifies the financial plan of the business corporation, makes possible a smaller debt structure, and avoids the hazards of refunding bonds or other forms of debt. (4) It enables a business corporation, admittedly not skilled in the solution of real estate problems, to pass them along to the purchaser of the property. (5) It is a flexible form of financing the business, resulting in a minimum of investment in fixed assets. (6) Where cancellation clauses are included, they enable the lessee to select a new location for his business, should he see fit to do so. (7) The tax advantage will be discussed in the next section.

In considering the above-named advantages, we must not overlook the fact that, as in the financing of all long-term leases, the financial capacity and stability of the lessee is of prime importance. Sale and leaseback arrangements are most often available to well-established business enterprises with a long record of successful operation under an outstanding management. Presumably such a management weighs the advantages and disadvantages of alternative financing plans before selling its real estate and leasing it back.

Admittedly not all of the above-claimed advantages are of equal weight. For example, does the sale and leaseback plan relieve the lessee of concern about real estate problems and permit him to pass them along to the lessor for solution? Under the terms of the lease, the lessor receives a net return. All problems involving taxes, maintenance, repairs, insurance, and so on, remain with the lessee. In other words, the lease does not relieve him of the disadvantages of real estate management and operation. Unless it contains a repurchase option, it may relieve him of any advantage that might accrue from appreciation in the value of the real estate, however. To this extent the lease may be a disadvantage to the lessee instead of an advantage.

This may be a very significant factor to take into account. In the past, at least, 100 percent locations have continued to show appreciation in site values for long periods of time. Whether or not there is any appreciation in value, any remaining value at the expiration of the lease would accrue to the advantage of the lessor, even though his investment had been amortized in the meantime. Should any loss suffered in this manner by the lessee be substantial, it would necessarily need to be taken into account as an additional cost of rentals paid for the use of property owned by the lessor. As an offset, the amount of differential gain between the rentals paid and the return on the funds released by the sale and leaseback plan would need to be taken into account.

Tax Advantages to Lessee: The Lease or Own Decision   The considerations involved in the determination of the tax impact of leasing as compared with owning real estate are perhaps best illustrated by an assumed example.

Evergood Corporation owns land and a building housing its home office. The building has a remaining life of 20 years and a book value of $1.8 million. Straight-line depreciation is used. The land has a book value of $500,000. The company is projecting that at the end of 20 years the bare land can be sold for $1 million. Site clearing costs are estimated at $100,000. The company figures its internal return on investments at 9 percent, compounded monthly, after tax.

Reliable Insurance Company has offered to pay Evergood Corporation $2.3 million for the land and building and to lease the property back to Evergood for a 20-year period at a net rental of $285,000 per year, the last year's rental to be paid at the closing, with other rental payments monthly.

For simplicity in evaluating the proposal, assume that Evergood is taxed at a 50 percent rate on its ordinary income and at a 30 percent rate on its capital gains.

The present value of owning the building may be compared with the present value of sale and leaseback. The suggested solution follows:

A. Present value of retaining property ownership
    1. Annual depreciation deduction .... $ 90,000
    2. Annual tax savings at 50% tax rate   45,000
    3. Tax savings per month   3,750
    4. PV of $1 per month for 240 months at 9%° 111.1450
    3. Times *4*. Present value of tax savings from depreciation .... $ 416.794

    5. Net proceeds from sale of land in 20 years
       ($1,000,000 — $100,000 clearing costs) .... $ 900,000
    6. Tax basis of land–nondepreciable   500,000

5. Less 6. Capital gain .... $ 400,000
7. Federal tax on capital gain at 30% 120,000

8. Capital gain after tax .... $ 280,000
9. Add back tax basis of land (item 6 above) 500,000

10. After-tax proceeds of sale of property in year 20 .... $ 780,000
11. PV of $1 discounted 240 months at 9%° 0.1664

10. Times 11. Present value of after-tax property sale proceeds ...... $ 129,792
12. Add present value of tax savings from depreciation 416,794

13. Present value of retaining property ownership .... $ 546,586

B. Present value of sale and leaseback
  1. Gross cash receipts from sale to insurance company $2,300,000
  2. One year lease rental paid in advance 285,000

  3. Net proceeds of sale to Reliable Insurance Company .... + $2,015,000
  4. Lease rental payable for 228 months (19 years) $23,750
  5. After-tax rental costs at 50% rate 11,875
  6. PV of $1 per month for 228 months at 9% 109.0635
  5. Times 6. Present value of after-tax cost of 228 rental payments.... − $1,295,129
  7. Add back present value of tax shield in 20th year
     provided by advance rental payment of $285,000:
     $142,500 × interest factor for discount of
     240 months at 9% (0.1664) .... + 23,712

  8. Present value of sale and leaseback .... $ 743,583

C. The difference between the present value of retaining the
  building and the present value of sale and leaseback is
  $196,997 in favor of the decision to lease.

° Refer to tables in the Appendix under the 9% rate.

The foregoing problem and suggested solution points out a way to structure a consideration of the interrelationship between income tax effects of the alternative methods of holding the property and the potential earning power of the funds that can be released in case of sale. Note that implicit in this solution is a 9 percent return on available funds, and this may not eventuate. If the company is thrown into a loss position, the calculation will be greatly changed. Furthermore, residual values may be widely different in actuality, and lease renewal options were not taken into account.

Advantages to Lessor

The advantages of the sale and leaseback device to the purchaser who becomes the lessor center around the following: (1) The term of the investment is relatively long, and there is no need to bother about early prepayments. (2) The amounts invested are relatively large. (3) Only well-seasoned, well-managed corporations are accepted as lessees. (4) The rate of return after amortization of the principal of the investment is relatively high. (5) The lessor has more control over real estate which it owns than over that on which it merely holds a mortgage. (6) There may be a substantial remainder of value after the lease expires which will serve as a hidden reserve for the lessor. (7) There may be possible income tax advantages in this method of financing real estate.

Whether the long term of the investment is an advantage or may prove ultimately to be a disadvantage depends upon the future level of prices. During the period when many of the leasebacks now in effect were executed, real estate has been priced at high levels. In making their arrangements, the lessors have had the advantage of the services of the best appraisers to help them fix prices they were willing to pay for the properties purchased. They have not blindly purchased real estate merely because the sellers were willing to lease it back for a long period of time. Mortgages likewise have been written for as long a period as the leases discussed in this chapter. Presumably, where mortgages were used the mortgagor has had a cushion of value, over and above the mortgage, which served as protection to the mortgage.

The amounts invested have been relatively large in comparison with many other individual investments made by insurance companies and other institutional investors that have engaged in leaseback financing. As a consequence, the cost of servicing these large investments may be less than for smaller commitments. Only well-seasoned, well-managed corporations have been accepted as lessees. Indeed, some insurance companies have dealt only with large corporations with assets of at least $100 million. Few of the leases have involved corporations with assets of less than $10 million. With only a limited amount permitted to be used for the purchase of investment real estate, the purchaser has been able to select his purchases with great care.

The relatively high rate of return has been due to several factors. Since the lessee saw a distinct advantage in the leaseback plan and since he found a limited market for his real estate because of the necessity for tax-exempt protection to the lessor, the latter has been able to charge what the traffic will bear. Then, too, the sale and leaseback plan provides a form of investment that is less liquid than listed bonds, for example. While a purchaser could sell its real estate subject to the lease, it must find a purchaser that enjoys the same tax-exempt status as itself.

Finally, there is greater risk in taking title to the real estate at a price which represents 100 percent of its value than in granting a 60 percent loan with the same real estate as security. In general, the rate of return has been sufficient to permit the amortization of the investment in the building at least, and in some cases in the land and building, within the term of the original lease, and still leave a rate of return upon the reducing balance of the investment somewhat higher than the best return obtainable upon government or Aaa corporate bonds.

The alleged advantage of greater control over the real estate that is owned and leased back to the seller, in comparison with a mortgage on the same real estate, is of doubtful validity. In practice, quite the contrary may prove to be the case. Real estate mortgages commonly contain restrictive clauses giving the mortgagee considerable control over subsequent financial operations of the mortgagor. In general, leases seldom give the lessor such control. Restrictive clauses have not been much used in the leases discussed in this chapter.

In the absence of repurchase and renewal options, the potential remainder value to the purchaser-lessor may be real for several reasons. While the structure value is amortized over the period of the lease, its effective life may be much longer. If the structure will render effective service for 50 years and is completely amortized in 25, its value at the end of the lease would probably not be 50 percent of its original value—changes in price levels being disregarded—but it could be a substantial percentage of the original value. Any residual value in the structure would add to the rate of return received by the lessor. If the site is so located that it continues to increase in value, the remainder could very substantially add to the hidden reserves of the lessor. In this case also, any remainder value increases the rate of return enjoyed by the lessor.

The tax advantage of leasebacks is limited generally to the federal corporate income tax. Insurance company lessors could not avoid state and local real estate taxes even if they wished to do so. While educational and religious bodies might possibly avoid real estate taxes and assessments, they commonly require the lessee to pay them as a precaution against too great opposition from the public. The federal corporate income tax exemption has been freely used up to this time. As previously mentioned, abuse of this exemption has been controlled in considerable measure by recent changes in the tax law. Tax-exempt institutions are now required to pay income taxes on unrelated business income, including substantial amounts of rents received under sale and leaseback arrangements. Changes in regulations governing corporate income taxes on life insurance companies have reduced, but have not eliminated, their preferred status in the field of real estate financing by the use of the sale and leaseback device.

Tax Exemption of Lessor   Prior to 1950, certain classes of investors enjoyed a sweeping federal income tax immunity which provided a direct stimulus to purchase and leaseback programs. Had it not been that nonprofit enterprises were totally exempt from corporate income taxes, it is not likely that this plan would have developed to its present proportions. By specific provision of the Internal Revenue Code, educational, charitable, and religious institutions were exempt from the payment of income taxes. In practice, life insurance companies were also given virtual exemption because of the formula permitted by the Treasury Department for the computation of their taxable income. Hence, institutions in these classes that became lessors under the sale and leaseback program had little concern about the tax consequences of their receipt of one type of income as compared with receipt of another type.

Nonexempt investors cannot be as free in their choices of investment outlets. If a financial institution lends money on an amortized real estate mortgage as security, it need report for income tax purposes only that part of the payments which represents interest on its investment. Amortization of principal is not considered to be taxable income. But if it purchases the real estate and leases it back, it must report as taxable income all rents received, minus only such amounts as are properly deductible for allowed depreciation.

For example, on an amortized loan for $500,000 for 20 years at 8 percent interest, payable annually, the first year's receipt would be $50,926, of which $40,000 would be interest and $10,926 a principal installment. Only $40,000 would be taxable. Assuming interest computed on the reducing balance of the loan, the taxable income would decline year by year. If the nontax-exempt institution purchased a property for $500,000 and leased it back at a net return of 10 percent, the annual income would be $50,000 for each and every year. Assuming that the land is valued at $200,000 and the building at $300,000 for tax purposes, the latter amount only would be depreciable. At a rate of 2½ percent, the allowable depreciation for tax purposes on a straight-line basis would be $7,500, leaving a taxable income of $42,500 for each year. Over a 20-year period the lessor would pay much more in corporate income taxes from its net return of 10 percent on a purchase and leaseback arrangement than from its 8 percent interest on a real estate mortgage.

An amendment to the Internal Revenue Code in 1950 made tax-exempt organizations subject to income tax on their "unrelated business net income." Included in unrelated business income are rentals received from property leased to others for a period exceeding five years, where the lessor with the tax exemption borrowed funds to effect the purchase or acquisition of the property and such indebtedness is still outstanding. The purchase and leaseback situation commonly fits this pattern.

The taxable business lease income of exempt organizations is determined by application of the following formula:

$$\frac{\text{Business lease indebtedness at end of tax year}}{\substack{\text{Adjusted basis of premises} \\ \text{covered by business lease at} \\ \text{end of tax year}}} \times \substack{\text{Annual business lease} \\ \text{rental (less allocable} \\ \text{expenses)}} = \substack{\text{Unrelated business} \\ \text{taxable income}}$$

The following example is adapted from the *Income Tax Regulations*.[1] Assume that an exempt educational institution purchased a building 12 years ago for $600,000. It used borrowed funds and leased the building for a period of 20 years. At the present time, the end of the 12th year of ownership, the building has an adjusted tax basis of $500,000, and the unpaid balance of the indebtedness to acquire the property is $200,000. The annual rental from the lease is $55,000. Taxes, interest, and depreciation total $20,000 for the year. Unrelated business taxable income from the business lease is computed as follows:

$$\frac{\$200,000}{\$500,000} \times \$35,000 = \$14,000$$

A study of this example shows that the current tax law has moved in the direction of limiting the flexibility of a tax-exempt lessor in dealing with a taxable lessee. Note, however, that the annual business lease income equal to the proportion of the actual capital investment of the tax-exempt investor is still excluded from taxable income. Thus, the leasehold rental income of a tax-exempt investor who does not borrow to finance his acquisition of property is still tax-exempt.

There has also been a reduction in the tax advantages afforded life insurance companies. Whereas their taxes through the mid-1950s were negligible, these companies now find an increasing percentage of their income subject to federal tax. The amended tax formula results in a substantial increase in the proportion of life insurance company investment income subject to tax. The new formula, however, still leaves these companies with a decisive advantage over the ordinary corporate investor, whose income from interest on mortgage loans or from leasehold rentals is fully taxable.

Future of Sale and Leaseback

The future of sale and leaseback arrangements depends upon a number of variable factors. The amount of real estate involved in such financing is already substantial. Institutions that have been organized over the years to foster self-help through mutual insurance, education, religion, charity, and thrift have been encouraged by legislation granting them tax exemption, in comparison with ordinary business enterprises. Except for these tax exemptions, it does not appear that sale and leaseback arrangements would be so popular. In effect, the purchasing institutions have used a legal device to pass along to sellers the use of their tax-exemption privilege. We have seen that Congress has taken away several of the advantages of the leasing arrangement through

[1] Reg. § 1.514 (a)-1.

changes in classification of income of tax-exempt or tax-sheltered institutions and through extension of use of accelerated depreciation methods. Court decisions may invite either extensions or contractions of the use of this program by the manner in which they interpret leases that are brought before them for adjudication. State legislatures may either liberalize the percentage of life insurance company assets that may be invested in this manner, or they may decide that the sale and leaseback principle is not in the public interest and may legislate against its extension.

Under the present structure of the income tax law the purchase and leaseback is particularly advantageous for investments by pension funds paying no taxes and by individuals in high tax brackets. They can offset rental income by accelerated depreciation charges and mortgage interest costs of the financed portion. These sources are becoming relatively more important, as life insurance companies have recently signified general preference for mortgage-lending programs on income properties at high loan-to-value ratios where the net rent will support the loan. Recently, the New York Insurance Department issued a regulation making 100 percent loans permissible when supported by leases from tenants of unquestioned financial responsibility. This leaves the sale and leaseback market even more generally today the province of tax-exempt institutions and highly taxable individuals for whom real estate ownership can provide a depreciation writeoff and an inflation hedge.

PART 2: EQUITY PARTICIPATIONS OF INSTITUTIONAL LENDERS

Origins

In recent years, institutional lenders have become increasingly interested in equity participations in projects in which they have a lending interest. There are several forces at work in the economy that have induced this trend. Savings deposit institutions have had to respond to increased interest payment demands of depositors and higher costs of administration. Statutory restraints have been liberalized. Certainly equally important has been the willingness of hopeful borrowers to grant some degree of equity participation to tilt the scales in their favor in a tight market for mortgage money. Philosophically, mortgage loan officers feel entitled to equity participation when they provide up to 100 percent of the financing and in many cases assume equity-type risks.

Usually associated with equity participations is a less secure legal and financial position. This may take the form of a second mortgage, a wraparound loan, a mortgage or purchase and leaseback of a subordinated fee, or a subordinated convertible debenture. Often, lenders will accept higher loan-to-value ratios, lower interest rates, and slower repayment terms as well. Occasionally, they may provide the "front money" to prime the pump for the flow of construction money at an early stage of development. To be of interest to institutional lenders, the projects usually involve investments in excess of $1 million. Thus, the borrowers are highly experienced and reliable developers and they are working with prime real estate.

The more commonly used participation formats include the following:

1. Percentage of gross or net income.
2. Participation in income over a break-even point.
3. Land sale and leasehold mortgage.
4. Sale and buy-back agreement.
5. Joint venture with "front money" partner.
6. Convertible mortgage.

Percentage of Gross or Net Income   Perhaps the most usual form of participation, which may be incorporated in the conventional financing forms such as mortgages and leases, is a stipulated percentage of gross or net income above some agreed base figure. The more commonly accepted measure is gross income because of its ease of determination. This kind of provision is common in financing motels and nursing homes.

Participation in gross income normally ranges from 2 to 5 percent. Thus, on a $3,000,000 loan on a property grossing $600,000, a participation of 3 percent would add $18,000, or 0.6 percent, to the lender's yield. Even better, the yield would improve with an increasing gross income.

Participation in Income over a "Break-Even" Point   A typical arrangement may provide a "kicker" to the lender of, say, 20 percent of all income over a "break-even" point, defined as a definite expense figure either at a certain dollar amount or as computed by a prescribed formula, plus debt service as required by the mortgage constant. For example, on a $3,000,000 loan at 9 percent interest with a 10 percent constant, the results might be as follows:

Effective gross income	$600,000
Expenses per agreement (40% of effective gross income)	240,000
Debt service ($3,000,000 × 0.10)	300,000
Excess over break-even point	$ 60,000
$60,000 × 0.20 =	$ 12,000
$3,000,000 × 0.9 =	270,000
Interest plus participation due lender	$282,000

$$\frac{282,000}{3,000,000} = 0.094, \text{ or 9.4 percent yield to lender}$$

Land Sale and Leasehold Mortgage Combination of a land sale and a leasehold mortgage may be used by a developer either (1) where the land investor is a different party from the one funding the development improvements or (2) where the same investor buys the land on a purchase-leaseback and makes the mortgage loan on the leasehold estate. The use of the subordinated ground lease in the case where a new land investor is brought in under arrangements to support the construction financing was discussed at length in Chapter 6. An example showing how such financing may improve the developer's leverage and tax position follows.

Use of a Sale and a Subordinated Ground Lease. Assume a shopping center development with the following summary data:

1. Equity contribution ....$ 2,000,000
   First mortgage 8,000,000

   Total cost of project $10,000,000

2. Cash flow projection
   Rental and other income ....$ 1,500,000
   Cash expenses 400,000

                                          $ 1,100,000
   Debt service (9% interest, 10% constant) 800,000

   Excess cash flow over financing requirements ....$ 300,000

Assume further that the developer is able to sell the land for $1.5 million and he can lease it back for a 50-year primary period with two ten-year renewal options at $175,000 annually. This would give the investor an 11.67 percent return, which could be improved upon by providing for a 20 percent participation in all gross rentals over, say, $1.7 million in any one year.

For the developer the comparison of owning land versus leasing would reflect as follows:

	Owning	*Leasing*
Excess cash flow to developer ....$	300,000	$ 125,000
Investment by developer ....:..............$2,000,000		500,000
Percent return—Excess cash to investment	15	25

Extending the comparison to after-tax consequences demonstrates that the yield differences after tax are even more pronounced:

	Owning	Leasing
Rental and other income	$1,500,000	$1,500,000
Cash expenses	$ 400,000	$ 400,000
Depreciation (assumed figure)	400,000	400,000
Interest	720,000	720,000
Land rental cost		175,000
Total tax deductible expenses	$1,520,000	$1,695,000
Net tax loss	$ 20,000	$ 195,000
Savings on income tax at 50% rate	$ 10,000	$ 97,500

Effective benefits to the developer in each case are the sum of his favorable cash flow from the project and his tax savings because of the tax loss generated by the project. Thus:

	Owning	Leasing
Excess cash flow to the developer	$ 300,000	$125,000
Savings from tax loss	10,000	97,500
Total after-tax benefits to developer	$ 310,000	$222,500
Percentage of after-tax benefits to developer's investment	$\frac{310,000}{2,000,000} = 15.5$	$\frac{222,500}{500,000} = 44.5$

In comparing the after-tax yields, the substantially higher gain in effective return on the developer's investment under the leasing alternative is readily apparent. In all cases in the foregoing example, on the basis of income and expense projections alone, the use of a ground lease indicates a considerably greater earning potential.

Of course, if he continues to own the land, the developer will be recovering his investment out of cash flow and possible site value of the land at the end of the economic life of the shopping center. On the other hand, if he sells the land to an investor and leases it back, the developer must look only to the cash flow, as the residual value of the land belongs to the investor. In the latter case, however, the developer's investment has been greatly reduced by the proceeds from the sale of the land and, abetted by increased tax shelter, his payback period is substantially shortened.

Use of Land Sale and Leasehold Mortgage with the Same Investor One investor, for appropriate participation, may fund both the fee and the leasehold estate. In this instance, the investor buys the land at its fair value and leases it back to the developer. The investor then makes a mortgage loan on the leasehold estate. The lease normally provides for a base rate plus overages based on sales volume of occupant tenants of the developed property. In this case, the investor has a fixed return, plus possible overages, and he retains the residual property values through fee ownership. The developer, on the other hand, has the advantage of a high loan-to-value ratio, a 100 percent depreciable asset, and lower payout requirements, since he does not need to amortize the investment in land.

Since this method is unusually complicated, an example may be helpful. Assume a development with a building costing $3,220,000 on land valued at $580,000. The investor, often an insurance company or its subsidiary in this case, buys the land for $580,000 and leases it to the developer at 9 percent constant, or $52,200 per year. The investor then makes a 75 percent loan on leasehold improvements, which totals $2,415,000, to bear 9 percent interest and be amortized over 30 years (9.66 percent constant). The investor then contracts to receive a participation (say 30 percent) of "net defined income," which is determined by deducting from effective gross income all debt service payments, ground rents, and cash expenses, to arrive at cash flow. On a defined net income of $100,000, the investor's participation would be $30,000. His total return and yield would be computed as follows:

Ground rent ....$	52,200
Contract interest rate	217,350
Participation in defined net income	30,000
Total ....$	299,550
Total investment ($580,000 + $2,415,000)	$2,995,000

Yield to investors is thus about 10 percent plus reversion of land.

The developer's return, of course, is determined by relating his residual cash flows to his equity investment, initially $70,000 of cash flow as a return on ($3,220,000 − $2,415,000) $805,000, but subject to adjustment as effective gross income changes.

Sale and Buy-Back Agreement   A related type of financing is the "sale and buy-back," or installment sales contract. Under this arrangement, the investor buys the property from the developer and simultaneously sells it back to him under a long-term installment agreement whereby the investor retains legal title. The developer-buyer obtains an equitable interest in the title and may claim depreciation. His payments are set approximately equal to the current mortgage constant for the purchase price, plus a contingent payment related to property performance. The buyer normally has prepayment privileges in the form of contract termination options which when exercised will also result in a profit windfall to the investor.

To visualize the fact pattern for "sale and buy-back" financing, assume that Brown has just completed for $2.5 million a 170-unit garden apartment complex on land that he has owned for several years. The current land value is $400,000. The economic value of the land and buildings is $3.5 million, based on the following projection of income and expenses (10 percent capitalization rate):

Effective gross income $500,000
Fixed and operating expenses 150,000
Net income $350,000

Brown now sells this project to a real estate investment trust for $2.9 million, his total investment value, and at the same time agrees to buy back the property over a 30-year period. At $300,000 paid annually, the installment payments will amortize the total cost over approximately a 27-year term at 9½ percent interest annually. Under this arrangement, the trust will receive its special participation by virtue of the last three annual payments as a bonus.

Joint Venture with "Front Money" Partner   Recently, there has been a decided emergence of "front money" transactions. Quite commonly, experienced developers team up with partners who have no development experience but who can provide cash outlays necessary to carry a development through its initial stages. The split on net income and relative positions in regard to control of the venture are negotiated. Terms of a joint venture of this kind might follow the general outlines of this example: Brown, a developer, enters into a joint venture agreement with Green, the "money partner," to acquire and develop land and build a condominium on it. With the land to cost $500,000 and the improvements to cost an additional $4,000,000, the project might be projected to gross $5,500,000 on sale of the units. Green lends $500,000 to the venture to buy the land. A construction loan is arranged for $3,700,000. To make up the deficiency between building costs and the construction loan and to provide working capital, each partner contributes $300,000. As sales of the condominium units are made, the proceeds are distributed according to the agreement as follows:

1.   The construction loan is repaid.
2.   Green receives back the $500,000 advanced for land purchase.
3.   Interest is paid on Green's loan at the rate of 10 percent per annum.
4.   Any proceeds left over are distributed equally to Brown and Green to return their capital contributions and pay out the profits.

Convertible Mortgage[2]   The diluting effect of inflation on fixed earnings rates and unadjusted return of principal dollars at maturity has caused the development of yet another financing device called the "con-

---

[2] For an excellent treatment of this subject, refer to Lois A. Vitt and Joel H. Bernstein, "Convertible Mortgages: New Financing Tool," *Real Estate Review*, vol. 6, no. 1 (Spring 1976), pp. 33–37; also Lois A. Vitt, "Convertible Mortgage Seen as New Approach to Realty Financing," *Mortgage Banker*, August 1975, pp. 5–11.

vertible mortgage." This form can offer significant advantages to both the developer and the institutional lender. From the standpoint of the developer, all financing is derived from one reliable source. The institutional lender benefits by becoming a progressively greater participant in the equity ownership by taking loan amortization through increased equity while at the same time receiving the contract rate of interest on its total investment.

The essentials of the arrangement provide that the institutional investor will make both mortgage and equity investments to finance a new income-producing project. The amount of the mortgage will be an acceptable percentage of the appraised economic value of the property and the remainder of the funds will be provided as equity, presumably mostly from the institutional investor, since the developer's costs are normally substantially below the economic value of the project. The investor's equity participation will be based upon the relationship between the total equity funds advanced and the total value of the project. In many cases, the developer will be able to "finance out" the total costs, thus earning his total equity position in the completed project as his profit without net cash outlay. An example will demonstrate the technique more clearly.

A shopping center is expected to generate $396,000 annual net income before financing costs. Capitalized at 11 percent, it has an economic value of $3.6 million. On the basis of the appraisal value, the investor is willing to lend $2.4 million (75 percent of an estimated loan value of $3.2 million) at 10 percent interest and will invest an additional $800,000 for a 25 percent equity position. If the developer is able to complete the project for not more than 3.2 million, he has a 75 percent initial equity with no cash outlay and a substantial income expectancy over a great many years. According to the convertible mortgage plan, the investor will receive 10 percent on his total investment annually, but his mortgage balance is to be amortized annually by conversion to increased equity participation at any agreed rate, say 2 percent. The following table reflects the first three years of activity under such an arrangement:

(1)	(2)	(3)	(4)	(5)	(6)	(7)	(8)
			Financing	Net	Investor's	Yield to	Cash
	Mortgage	Investor's	Payments	Cash	Share of	Investor	to
Year	Balance[a]	Equity	at 10%	Flow[b]	Column (5)[c]	(%)[d]	Developer[e]
1 ..	$2,400,000	$800,000	$320,000	$76,000	$19,000 (25%)	·10.59	$57,000
2 ..	2,352,000	848,000	320,000	76,000	20,520 (27%)	10.64	55,480
3 ..	2,304,000	896,000	320,000	76,000	22,040 (29%)	10.69	53,960

[a] Reduces 2% of original balance annually; transferred to equity (column 3).
[b] $396,00 — $320,000 = $76,000 cash flow after financing costs.
[c] Investor's portion starts at 25% and increases 2% annually.
[d] The sum of columns 4 and 6 divided by the sum of columns 2 and 3.
[e] Column 5 — column 6 = residential cash flow to developer.

It should be noted that both participants develop substantial tax shelter from depreciation attributable to the equity positions. Furthermore, an interesting analysis can be developed to determine reasonable expectations of benefits to be derived from the impact of earnings increases that may follow the effects of inflation over a number of years. Of course, if the developer totally finances out, his yield is infinite.

Other Forms of Participation   A less-used form of equity participation more commonly associated with stable income streams, has the investor or lender taking an actual conveyance of title to all or part of the property at the expiration of the tenant's lease or at the end of the mortgage payback period. This arrangement, of course, has the disadvantage of many years of deferral in the opportunity to participate.

In large projects, the institutional investor's position is usually secured throughout the construction period by fee ownership or a first mortgage lien on the property. Arrangements may provide that as buildings are constructed and sold the investor will release the property and participate in the profit or, if buildings are leased, that it will share in certain leasing overage benefits with the developer.

Many institutions are developing a specialty of standby commitments for 100 percent of the cost of a building project. By this arrangement, the developer is assured an unconditional takeout when the project is completed. This gives him the financial strength to arrange for a construction loan and time to arrange cheaper, more conventional permanent financing. In the event that the standby commitment is used, in normal course the institution becomes a partner with the developer under terms providing for substantial participation in profits in addition to loan repayment requirements, including interest.

PART 3: WRAPAROUND MORTGAGES

The recent period of historically high-interest rates has brought the wraparound mortgage into considerable acceptance. Often, when an owner requires additional financing, he arranges for the placement of a new first mortgage in a larger amount than is presently owing on an existing property. A part of the proceeds of the new loan is used to satisfy the old mortgage. Sometimes it is not possible or even good judgment to pay off this prior mortgage. Prepayment penalties may be high or interest rates may be attractively low on the existing mortgage. In this case, a wraparound mortgage may be arranged whereby the owner obtains the benefits of additional financing without the prior mortgage being extinguished. The second lender takes over servicing the prior mortgage out of payments he receives from the owner as debt service. For example, assume that Jones owes $400,000 on an apartment building secured by a first mortgage requiring debt service of $40,000 annually with interest first deducted at 6 percent. In order to expand the building at a cost of $300,000, the owner arranges with an insurance company for a wraparound mortgage of $700,000 bearing interest at 8 percent and requiring debt service of $64,750 (9.25 percent constant) annually. At the closing, the owner executes mortgage documents supporting his $700,000 obligation and receives $300,000 cash. The insurance company relieves him of his $400,000 savings and loan obligation and will proceed to pay it off at the rate of $40,000 per year out of the $64,750 it receives. By servicing the prior debt at a lower interest rate, the insurance company leverages its own return to well above the 8 percent nominal return on its mortgage note.

It should be noted that there are serious limitations to the use of the wraparound mortgage. These limitations have related to "due on sale" clauses in the original mortgage notes and important problems in regard to laws defining the legality of the wraparound mortgage lien as an institutional investment and the danger of usury.

A "due on sale" clause permits a mortgagee to accelerate the first mortgage note in event of any assignment of title. Most institutional lenders are including this provision in loan arrangements today. The price of waiver of this right to accelerate the original note in favor of a wraparound lender will likely be the payment of points or a higher rate of interest on the existing loan. Such demands will probably defeat the purpose of the wraparound loan.

The wraparound mortgage form is that of a second mortgage, or inferior, lien and, therefore, an apparently ineligible investment for most financial institutions. Some state regulatory authorities, however, have looked at the overall substance of the transaction and have accorded the wraparound instrument first lien status. In numerous states, regulated institutions have made wraparound loans under their leeway provisions, whereby they are permitted to make a limited proportion of investments on the basis of prudent business judgment, without regard to lien priority.

The effective return to the wraparound lender is normally substantially above the nominal rate stated in the wraparound mortgage note. Whether the transaction is usurious should be resolved by recourse to local counsel in the state having jurisdiction.

QUESTIONS

1. What are the chief reasons for the sale and leaseback of real estate?
2. What kinds of real estate can be used most successfully in a sale and leaseback arrangement?
3. What are the general qualifications required of a vendor-lessee for acceptance as a party to a sale and leaseback transaction?

4. What are the principal sources of funds for sale and leaseback financing, and why are these sources most interested in this arrangement?

5. To what degree are life insurance companies eligible to participate in sale and leaseback financing?

6. Under what conditions is a sale leaseback contract likely to be treated by the courts as an equitable mortgage?

7. How would tax treatment of a sale and leaseback contract as an equitable mortgage differ from its treatment as a true sale and leaseback transaction?

8. What advantages are claimed for the lessor under the sale and leaseback arrangement? What advantages are claimed for the lessee?

9. Give examples of current techniques being used to provide equity participation for institutional investors.

10. What are the advantages and limitations of wraparound mortgages?

CASE PROBLEMS

1. Utopia Corporation sold the land and building housing its manufacturing operation to the We-Do-All Leasing Company for $2 million and immediately leased it back for 25 years at an annual rental. In the lease, Utopia Corporation set up an option to repurchase the total property at the end of the 25-year period for $100. Is this a proper sale transaction?

2. Star Transportation Company owns a trucking terminal. It estimates the remaining life of the buildings at 25 years and carries them at a book value of $2.4 million. It uses straight line depreciation. The land has a book value of $700,000, but is estimated to be worth $1.5 million as land alone in 25 years. Clearing costs would probably run $150,000. The company estimates its opportunity cost of funds at 11 percent, compounded monthly, after tax. Assume that the company has a 50 percent tax rate on ordinary income and a 30 percent capital gain rate.

As an alternative, the company can sell the terminal to the Universal Leasing Company for $3.1 million and lease it back for a 25-year period at a net rental of $330,000 per year, the last year rental to be paid at closing, with other rentals payable monthly.

Compare the net present values of the terminal under the owning and leasing alternatives. What other factors should be considered?

3. The Westwind Apartments partnership owns a development that is financed as follows:

Partners' capital contribution	$1,000,000
First mortgage of Reliance Insurance Company	5,000,000
Total land and building cost	$6,000,000
Cash flow projection:	
Rental and other income	$ 850,000
Cash expenses	190,000
Cash flow before financing service	$ 660,000
Debt service (9.5% interest, 10.2% constant)	510,000
Estimated cash flow after financing service	$ 150,000

The partnership is presently entertaining an offer from First Real Estate Trust to buy the underlying apartment building site at its appraisal value of $600,000 and to lease it back under a subordinated ground lease to Westwind Apartments for 30 years, with two favorable renewal options. The rent for the primary period would be $70,000 annually with a 15 percent participation in all rentals and other income over $900,000 per year. Assuming the building is depreciable at 4 percent annually and the overall income tax rate of the partners is 50 percent, compare the returns to the partners on the basis of land ownership versus leasing the land.

4.   Green built a large warehouse on land that he inherited. His warehouse cost him $2 million. His land is currently appraised at $300,000. He owes $2 million on his construction loan from the local bank. Based on projected net cash inflows from the warehouse operation ($300,000), Green's appraisal of the total property is $2.8 million. To pay off the construction loan and to provide some working capital, Green seeks to sell his total project for $2.3 million and to buy it back over 35 years. He is willing to pay 10 percent interest and to amortize the full cost over 30 years in monthly payments. The last 5 years would be treated as bonus payments to the investor for his participation.

a.   Under Green's sale and buy-back plan, what would his payments be annually? What would be the rate of return on his residual investment?

b.   If you were the potential investor in Green's venture, what factors would you consider to evaluate the attractiveness of this offer?

5.   The owner of an office building has had a 7 percent mortgage on it with an unpaid balance of $500,000. Annual debt service is $48,000. He wants to add an additional floor at a cost of $200,000. The owner arranges with a wraparound lender for a total mortgage of $700,000 at 9 percent and total debt service of $68,000 annually. The new lender disburses $200,000 and takes back mortgage documents evidencing a $700,000 obligation. Henceforth, the owner must pay the wraparound lender $68,000 annually as his full requirement. The wraparound lender, in turn, will make the required $48,000 payment to the original mortgagee. What return will the wraparound mortgagee earn on its investment during the first year of its loan?

part three
Sources of Real Estate Credit

14

Introduction to the Mortgage Market

This chapter serves as an introduction to the mortgage market. It includes a discussion of the sources of funds available for mortgage lending and the major institutional participants in the market for mortgage loans. These institutions are identified as to specialization by type of mortgage lending. In addition, the major causes of instability in the availability of mortgage credit from period to period are investigated. The intent herein is not to furnish an exhaustive analysis of the mortgage market. The objective is to provide a basic understanding of funds flows, as subsequent chapters deal with each institutional source in fuller detail.

Flow of Funds and the Financial System

To understand the nature of the mortgage market, it is helpful to place it in context with other financial markets in our economy. Generally, when referring to financial markets, a distinction is made between money markets and capital markets. Money markets are usually defined as markets for financial claims with maturities of less than one year. Examples of claims with maturities of less than one year include: U.S. government Treasury bills, some securities of U.S. government agencies, and commercial paper issued by corporations, to mention a few. Capital markets generally refer to markets in which obligations with maturities greater than one year are bought and sold. Examples of these obligations include corporate bonds and stocks, mortgages, long-term bonds issued by the federal government, and long-term bonds issued by state and local governments. Hence, the stock market, bond market, and mortgage market can be thought of as component parts of capital markets.

While it is sometimes useful to analyze money and capital markets separately, a greater understanding of our financial system can be obtained through flow of funds analysis. Flow of funds analysis integrates money and capital markets into a framework that enables one to trace the primary flows between economic sectors in the economy. Exhibit 14–1 contains a simplified flow of funds diagram that enables tracing of money and capital flows from sources that supply funds to economic units that use or demand funds in our economy.

Sources and Uses of Funds   Beginning with sources of funds, over any given time period sources of funds available for investment include primarily savings of households and earnings from business.[1] Determinants of savings, in the case of households, include the amount of income earned over the period and the amount of current consumption of that income. The amount consumed partially depends on interest rates that can be earned for not consuming, or saving, and expected price levels. Determinants of business earnings are generally governed by competitive forces in the economy governing sales, cost of output, and expected capital investment less necessary dividend payments to investors. What remains after dividend payments is the amount business has for future investment.

Primary uses of funds are shown in the upper right corner of Exhibit 14–1. Generally, part of the demand for funds comes from households desiring to acquire consumer durable goods, such as automobiles and appliances, and to construct new residences. In addition, businesses requiring expansion in production facilities, including new plants and machinery, as well as increases in inventory levels, provide additional demand for funds. Therefore, a considerable amount of funds generated by businesses and households as sources, is invested directly in *real assets*[2] as shown at the top of the figure.

Channels of Funds Flows   One of the main purposes of the diagram in Exhibit 14–1 is to show how funds provided by individual households and businesses are channeled to other individual households and businesses, and perhaps government, which demand funds in excess of their current levels of savings and earnings. Many individual households and businesses that provide funds may not invest exactly the amount of funds at their disposal in real assets. Those individual households and businesses will have an excess or surplus of funds during any one period of time. However, other individual households and businesses will have a need for funds in excess of amounts which they can derive from their own sources. Consequently, over any given period of time, some individual households and businesses will be seeking funds to use for investment in real assets, while others will have excess funds the use

---

[1] More specifically, this includes retained earnings plus capital consumption allowances.

[2] Real assets are meant here to include stocks of physical goods which are expected to yield productive service over time.

EXHIBIT 14–1
Simplified Flow of Funds Diagram

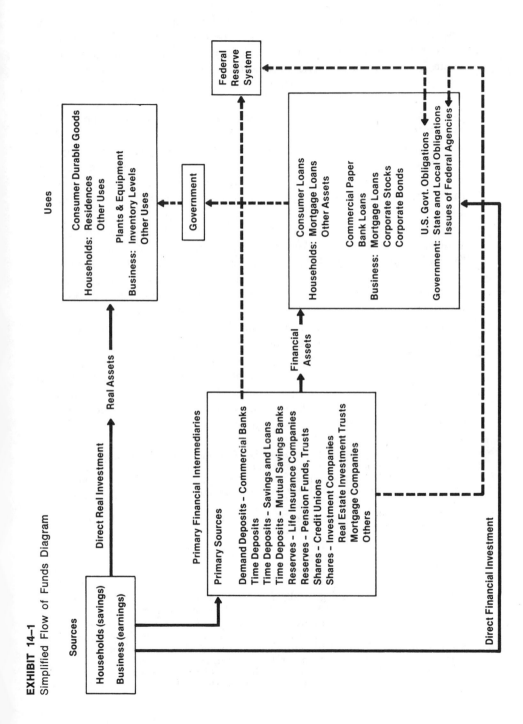

of which they are willing to sell. Government at the federal, state, and local levels may also enter the market for funds depending on their respective budgetary-expenditure patterns over a given period in time.[3]

To raise the necessary funds, households, business, and government create financial claims and obligations. For households these claims usually take the form of consumer and mortgage loans. Businesses generally make business and mortgage loans and issue stock, commercial paper, and bonds; while government agencies usually issue bonds, bills, and notes.[4] These financial claims become *financial assets* for lenders, who will supply funds for some specified period and earn either interest or dividends in return for the use of funds.[5] A summary listing of financial assets used by households, business, and government to raise funds in money and capital markets is shown in the lower right corner of Exhibit 14–1.

Financial assets can be sold to suppliers of funds directly through the various bond or stock markets (see direct financial investment arrow at the bottom of Exhibit 14–1).[6] However, most funds available for investment in financial assets are channeled through financial intermediaries.

Financial Intermediaries and Funds Flow   Because direct financial investment of savings by households (shown at the bottom of Exhibit 14–1) requires: (1) a certain amount of knowledge concerning financial assets (how to buy securities and other financial assets), (2) a willingness to take certain risks (price fluctuation on securities or bankruptcy by the issuer), (3) some minimum amount of funds to buy certain financial assets (mortgages, for example), and (4) the necessary underwriting knowledge to make large business loans, mortgage loans, etc., it is usually not practical for most households to invest in financial assets directly.[7]

---

[3] Whether government enters the market for funds depends in large part on tax revenues and expenditures. If a governmental unit runs a budgetary deficit over a given period, it must raise funds. On the other hand, if a unit runs a budgetary surplus, it will enter the market to retire outstanding obligations from preceding periods.

[4] Depending on the maturity of these financial claims, they may be classified as money market instruments or capital market instruments.

[5] We refer here to new issues or additional amounts of financial assets only. It should be recalled that existing issues of stocks, bonds, etc. that are traded among individuals provide no net increase in funds to households and businesses seeking to expand or invest in real assets.

[6] A direct purchase will generally require the services of a broker or investment banking firm. Nonetheless, it still constitutes a direct purchase in our discussion.

[7] Businesses with surplus funds also face some of these problems. However, these surpluses tend to be very short-term in nature. Because of the dynamic nature of the economy, individual firms with surpluses in one period may be large borrowers in the next. Hence, most firms keep surplus funds in short-term investments. Since our focus here is on the mortgage market, which is a long-term capital market, we are more interested in long-term sources of savings. Hence, our discussion centers more on households.

Most individuals do not meet one or more of the four criteria listed above because of the specialization required to underwrite or purchase assets, or because they have small savings balances which they do not want to risk the possibility of losing. Consequently financial intermediaries have developed that specialize in: (1) consolidating many small amounts of savings from individuals and making large loans (mortgages, business loans, etc.); (2) diversifying funds over many different types of financial assets so as not to risk all funds in one investment; and (3) underwriting and studying characteristics associated with investments, which requires managerial expertise. Clearly these functions could not be performed by individual households.

In the middle of Exhibit 14–1 an abbreviated list of major financial intermediaries and their primary methods of attracting savings from households is provided. Basically each institution, either by design or by government regulation, offers a certain inducement such as interest, dividends, or a service in return for savings flows. These flows are then aggregated and invested in diversified portfolio of financial assets (loans, mortgages, bonds, etc.) on which a return is earned by the intermediary.[8] The intermediary in turn pays individual households in the form of interest, service, etc., for the use of savings flows and earns a profit for performing this intermediation function. As will be seen later in this chapter, the degree to which households choose to use financial intermediaries or purchase financial assets directly can drastically affect funds available for mortgage lending.

Government Debt and Financial Markets   Government influence is felt in financial markets when that sector (particularly the federal government) increases a budgetary deficit or surplus. Deficits occur when tax receipts fall short of expenditures (see the Government sector in Exhibit 14–1). To finance a deficit, government, like households and business, must borrow by creating financial claims, as it is a net user of funds. When such deficits occur at the federal level, debt obligations are issued consisting of short-term U.S. Treasury bills, notes, and bonds which are bought by individuals and intermediaries. When budgetary receipts exceed expenditures, a surplus occurs. In this event, government usually repurchases obligations issued in previous periods or adds to the flow of funds.[9]

The impact of government deficits on financial markets partially depends on the magnitude of the deficit and on the timing. If a large gov-

---

[8] It must be pointed out here that most intermediaries are highly regulated by either state or federal government as to the types of financial assets they may invest in. Hence, this discussion must be interpreted by the reader in general terms at this point.

[9] Since World War II, government, particularly at the federal level, has been in the position of financing deficits.

ernmental deficit occurs simultaneously with rapid business expansion, for example, there is a tendency for interest rates on financial assets to increase in the short run as households and business compete with government for funds. On the other hand, in periods of declining economic activity, such deficits are used to stimulate investment in the business sector through increased government spending. In the latter case, the impact on interest rates tends to be slight due to low levels of demand for funds.

The Federal Reserve System and Financial Markets   Another significant way in which government can influence financial markets is through actions taken by the Federal Reserve System (see Federal Reserve System at the extreme right of Exhibit 14–1). This public agency is charged with management of the nation's monetary system while promoting the attainment of maximum economic income, minimum unemployment, and stable prices. The supply of money is defined as currency in circulation and demand deposits at commercial banks. Only about one half of the commercial banks belong to the Federal Reserve System; however, they account for about 80 percent of deposits in all banks in the United States. These banks are required to keep a specific percentage of demand and time deposits on reserve in district Federal Reserve banks. This is referred to as the reserve requirement for member banks. The Federal Reserve System, in turn, provides them with check clearing services, transfer of funds services, and currency. It will also lend money to member banks and will supervise and audit their performance.

Reserve Requirements.   One way in which the Federal Reserve influences financial markets and the supply of money is through changes in the reserve requirements. By requiring more reserves, the Federal Reserve System reduces the amount of funds available for investment. This occurs because commercial banks have to increase their reserves at district banks. These funds are withheld by district banks from financial markets, thereby reducing funds available for investment (see relationship between commercial banks and the Federal Reserve System in Exhibit 14–1).

Changes in reserve requirements may be used when the economy is expanding too rapidly and inflationary pressure develops. To reduce the rate of expansion, the Federal Reserve may choose to increase reserve requirements and to reduce the supply of money and hence funds available for investment. Interest rates are driven up as business, households, and perhaps government agencies compete for a smaller supply of funds. Eventually, as interest rates rise high enough, some investment outlays are postponed or eliminated and the economy begins to return to stability. During this period, however, mortgage interest rates as well as rates on all financial assets rise rapidly and credit is extremely difficult to obtain. While changing reserve requirements is certainly an effective way to reduce the availability of funds, it is considered a somewhat drastic step to be taken and is not used frequently by the Federal Reserve.[10]

Open Market Operations Another, more commonly used method of monetary management by the Federal Reserve is open market operations. With this technique, the Federal Open Market Committee of the Federal Reserve System decides whether to buy or sell U.S. Treasury obligations in an attempt to increase or decrease the supply of money. The Federal Reserve System maintains a portfolio of U.S. Treasury securities which it adds to by buying additional securities or which it reduces by selling securities. Sales of securities tend to *reduce* the money supply and funds available for investment, while purchases of securities tend to *increase* the money supply. Sales of securities by the Federal Reserve reduce the money supply because as they are sold, checks are drawn against demand deposits (checking accounts) at commercial banks by individuals and businesses making purchases. Hence, demand deposits are reduced, and the amount of loanable funds is reduced because the Federal Reserve does not allow these funds to reenter the banking system (see relationship between government securities and the Federal Reserve System in Exhibit 14–1).[11]

Open market sales of securities by the Federal Reserve System causes a contraction in the supply of money and hence in loanable funds. It serves to drive interest rates upward as competition by households and business for a smaller quantity of funds increases. Open market operations, like reserve requirements, can be used in an attempt to reduce the rate of expansion and inflationary pressure in the economy, or to stimulate activity in the economy. However, these operations are used much more frequently than changes in reserve requirements. This is the case because changing reserve requirements can have a more sudden and drastic effect on the money supply and hence the flow of funds. Open market operations, however, are used as part of a continuous system of monitoring and management of the money supply by the Federal Reserve. Through gradual increases and decreases in holdings of securities, the desired effects on financial markets can be achieved with an element of timing that may be more desirable by monetary authorities.

Changing the Discount Rate and Credit Restrictions. The final tool at the disposal of the Federal Reserve System for altering the money supply, and hence the funds flow in the economy, is changing the discount

---

[10] The reverse process can also occur during a period of economic recession. By reducing reserve requirements, more funds become available for investment at lower interest rates. With lower interest costs, the Federal Reserve hopes to stimulate investment.

[11] Purchases of treasury securities by the Federal Reserve has the opposite effect. In this case sellers of securities receive checks from the Federal Reserve which are deposited at banks. This would increase demand deposits and loanable funds.

rate. The discount rate measures charges made to member banks for borrowing from the Federal Reserve System. Changing the discount rate affects the flow of funds because if commercial banks desire to borrow from their district Federal Reserve Bank to make additional loans to business and individuals, the price or interest rate charged on loans made by the Federal Reserve System will partially determine whether the commercial bank borrows and how much. Obviously if the Federal Reserve chooses to raise the rate on loans made to commercial banks, fewer loans will be made, and vice versa.

Experience has shown that changing the discount rate has a much less important direct effect on the supply of money than either open market operations or changing reserve requirements. In practice, changing the discount rate has generally served as a signal given by the Federal Reserve System as to the policy it plans to implement concerning the money supply in the near future. Raising the discount rate is usually a signal that a reduction in the money supply, or a period of "tighter money," is desired by the Federal Reserve and generally open market operations will reflect that policy objective. Lowering the discount rate usually signals that an increase in the money supply, or a period of "easy money," may be in the offing. The Federal Reserve is also empowered to impose credit restrictions on various kinds of loans made to businesses and households should the economic situation warrant it. This power, however, is seldom used, as emergency conditions would have to exist in the economy before the Federal Reserve would enact credit restrictions on any broad scale.

Flow of Funds—Illustrated   To familiarize the reader with the flow of funds concept, a summarized segment of a flow of funds statement for the period 1965–1975 is presented in Exhibit 14–2. The segment presented deals with: (1) the portion of the flow of funds diagram relating to the flow between financial intermediaries and users of capital (middle of Exhibit 14–1) and (2) the portion of the diagram dealing with direct financial investment by households (bottom of Exhibit 14–1). In other words, we are focusing on how individual firms, households and government obtained funds in financial markets either: (1) from financial intermediaries or (2) directly from households and businesses buying financial assets.

The top half of Exhibit 14–2 concentrates on the types of financial claims created by households, business, and government to raise funds These claims, also listed in Exhibit 14–1, include mortgages used by households and business for real estate improvements and bonds and stocks issued by corporations for plant expansions and equipment outlays, as well as securities and obligations used by government at all levels to raise capital. Note the increases and decreases in funds invested in mortgages during each of the years from 1965–1975. This fluctuation

Funds Raised and Advanced in Credit Markets, 1965–1975 (in billions of dollars)

	1965	1966	1967	1968	1969	1970	1971	1972	1973	1974	1975
Funds Raised by Type:											
Mortgages	$25.6	21.3	23.0	27.4	27.8	26.4	48.9	68.8	71.9	54.5	57.3
Corporate Bonds	8.6	11.8	17.2	15.0	14.5	23.8	24.8	20.2	12.5	23.3	36.7
Corporate Stock	3.5	4.8	5.5	6.4	10.0	10.5	14.9	13.1	8.0	5.6	11.7
U.S. government securities	1.6	4.0	13.1	13.2	-3.3	12.9	26.6	17.4	9.8	11.4	84.4
Sponsored credit agencies	2.1	4.8	-.6	3.5	8.8	8.2	3.8	6.2	19.6	22.1	11.0
State and local obligations	7.3	5.6	7.8	9.5	9.9	11.2	17.6	14.4	13.7	17.4	15.4
Consumer credit loans	9.6	6.4	4.5	10.0	10.4	6.0	11.2	19.2	22.9	9.6	5.3
Bank loans and commercial paper	18.3	14.1	11.5	20.9	31.7	4.6	13.3	31.8	63.7	53.1	-11.7
Other loans	6.5	6.9	2.5	8.3	15.8	7.3	3.9	7.4	17.2	21.1	6.4
Total*	$83.2	79.6	84.4	114.3	125.5	110.9	164.0	198.5	239.3	218.1	216.6
Funds Advanced by:											
Financial Institutions	$68.7	49.5	75.3	88.5	68.9	97.2	157.2	180.2	175.6	149.6	140.8
Commercial banks	28.8	17.5	35.9	38.8	18.3	35.2	50.6	70.7	86.7	64.6	27.3
Savings and loan associations	9.6	4.2	9.2	10.2	9.9	11.6	29.2	36.4	27.1	21.0	40.5
Life insurance companies	8.2	8.0	8.4	9.0	8.4	9.0	11.8	13.8	15.6	16.1	19.2
Mutual savings banks	3.9	2.7	5.2	4.3	3.2	4.1	10.0	10.4	5.4	3.3	10.5
Pension or retirement funds	8.5	6.1	9.3	10.5	11.6	13.0	13.6	14.3	16.4	20.4	25.7
Real estate investment trusts	—	—	—	.2	.9	2.1	2.5	4.9	4.5	.9	-2.5
Other—rest of world	9.7	11.0	7.3	15.5	16.6	22.2	39.5	29.7	19.9	23.3	20.1
Government and related institutions	$11.6	15.3	9.0	14.1	22.4	18.1	13.3	13.5	32.9	38.0	40.9
Sponsored credit agencies	2.2	5.7	-.1	3.2	8.9	10.0	3.2	7.0	20.3	24.1	12.6
Federal Reserve System	3.8	3.5	4.8	3.7	4.2	5.0	8.9	.3	9.2	6.2	8.5
U.S. government and state–local governments	5.6	6.7	4.3	7.2	9.3	3.1	1.2	6.2	3.4	7.7	19.8
Direct Advances	$ 2.9	14.9	.2	11.6	34.3	-4.4	-6.5	5.0	30.8	30.5	35.0
Households	2.3	16.4	-1.6	5.2	31.2	-2.7	-14.2	1.3	21.6	22.1	15.4
Business	.6	-1.5	1.8	6.4	3.1	-1.7	7.7	3.7	9.2	8.4	19.6
Total	$83.2	79.6	84.4	114.3	125.5	110.9	164.0	198.5	239.3	218.1	216.6

* Totals are rounded.
Source: Adapted from Board of Governors, Federal Reserve System (Washington), *Flow of Funds Accounts*, May 1976.

is very important as it shows that funds flowing into the mortgage market were more available in some periods than others. The availability of mortgage funds has a direct bearing on housing construction and other real estate development, a point to be explored further later in this chapter. It should also be pointed out that funds flowing into each of the sectors detailed in the top half of the table are also a reflection of the competition for funds. Each claim created by business, households, and government has either an interest or dividend rate, which reflects the price each borrower is willing to pay to raise funds. Hence, the relative share of total funds available for borrowing from each sector will be determined by competition.

The bottom half of Exhibit 14–2 lists financial intermediaries that advanced funds by buying financial assets or claims created by households, business, and government with funds flowing through such intermediaries. It also provides categories for federally related institutions and government as well as for households and businesses that invested or advanced funds into the financial system by buying financial assets directly. Special note should be taken of funds advanced by financial institutions that fluctuated significantly from 1965 to 1975. As will be developed later, funds advanced by intermediaries are especially critical to the mortgage market since deposit-type intermediaries are the most significant mortgage lenders in our economy. When funds advanced by these intermediaries decline in a particular year, it is likely to be a result of a slowdown in savings deposits from households which choose to make more direct investments in financial assets such as stocks and bonds. Direct advances made by households and business are shown at the bottom of Exhibit 14–2 and are a good indication as to whether funds are flowing away from financial intermediaries in a particular year. This flow, in turn, affects the mortgage market. This concept will also be explored in more detail later in this chapter.

The Mortgage Market

From the discussion to this point, we have seen that the flow of funds from sectors of the economy with a surplus of funds to sectors with a net demand for funds depends, in part, on a complex system of financial intermediaries. In addition, the flow of funds can be altered by actions taken by government financing debt and policies of the Federal Reserve System. Since the mortgage market is only one component of the financial system just described, it is definitely affected by changes that occur in the overall flow of funds. Although we discuss the mortgage market in isolation here, it must be kept in mind that it is a part of the overall financial system and is responsive to changes affecting that system.

In this section, we separate the mortgage market from the rest of the

financial system and provide more detail on mortgage market participants. A simplified diagram of the mortgage market is presented in Exhibit 14–3. The intent of the diagram is to identify the major participants
in the mortgage markets and to depict how the interaction of the supply
and demand for mortgage funds sets the terms for mortgage lending and
borrowing.

The Demand for Mortgage Funds   The demand for mortgage funds
emanates from business and households desiring to make investments
in real assets, such as single-family residential housing, multifamily
housing, apartment complexes, and commercial developments (shopping
centers, hotels, and office buildings), which require financing. This group
is depicted in the left portion of Exhibit 14–3. There are many determinants of demand for housing and other real assets requiring mortgage

EXHIBIT 14–3
The Mortgage Market

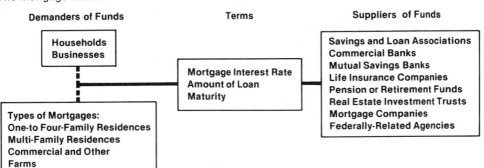

financing. Many of these factors were discussed in Chapter 10 when we
dealt with economic factors affecting the value of residential property
and in Chapter 11 when market studies for income-producing properties
was discussed. A general list of these demand factors is provided below.
While many of these demand characteristics are more relevant in determining the demand for housing and residential mortgage loans, most
of these characteristics are also important in the demand for commercial
structures and commercial mortgage financing.

1. Changes in Population
    a. Changes in the number of household formations.
    b. Changes in the structure of households.
        1. Age of head of household.
        2. Size of household.
        3. Age distribution of members of household.

    c. Changes in geographical distribution of households.
       1. Rural-urban shifts.
       2. Urban-suburban shifts.
2. Changes in Income and Employment
    a. Current levels of income.
    b. Changes in the distribution of income.
       1. By size and age distribution of households.
    c. Changes in industrial and business location.
       1. Skilled and unskilled employment demand.
       2. Wage structure.
3. Changes in Construction Costs
    a. Price of construction materials, land, and labor.
    b. Price of financing and credit costs.
    c. Changes in consumer tastes, style preferences.
    d. Changes in environmental conditions.
       1. Changes in relative price of fuel used for power and heat.
       2. Environmental restrictions of air and water pollution.
4. Changes in Housing-Related Services
    a. Property tax structure.
    b. Quantity and quality of public services provided.
    c. Federal tax structure.
       1. Treatment of homeowners–renters.
    d. Changes in maintenance costs.
    e. Changes in utility costs.
5. Stock of Existing Supply of Structures
    a. Vacancies.
    b. Distribution of rents and prices by type of structure.
    c. Distribution of stock by type of structure and location.
    d. Demolitions, conversions.

Based on the flow diagram in Exhibit 14–3, it can be seen that the interaction of the demand for mortgage funds with the supply of available funds determines the mortgage interest rate and market terms on which funds are available. However, it should also be kept in mind that there are risk differentials among individual loan transactions, based on the relative financial strength of borrowers, geographical differences in project location, and other factors. These differences result in a distribution of mortgage interest rates and terms. Hence, when reference is made to the interest rate on mortgages, these differentials must be kept in mind. In addition, although the mortgage market diagram in Exhibit 14–3 excludes other sectors of the financial system, it must be kept in mind that the mortgage market is a part of the larger system. Further, the demand for mortgage funds is a part of the demand for all funds in the economy, and competition among all sectors influences mortgage interest rates.

The Supply of Mortgage Funds Referring again to Exhibit 14–3, suppliers of mortgage funds are listed on the right side of the diagram. The institutions listed are different from those listed in Exhibit 14–1 because these financial intermediaries are the most important participants in the mortgage market. While other institutions in Exhibit 14–1 may make some mortgage loans, they are not significant in dollar amount. Hence our discussion will focus on only the most important intermediaries in the mortgage market, though it must be kept in mind that there are other intermediaries competing for savings flows.

The institutions listed in Exhibit 14–3 may be classified into one of three categories. Depository-type institutions include savings and loan associations, commercial banks, and mutual savings banks, as these intermediaries offer a variety of deposit accounts to savers. Contractual-type institutions include life insurance companies and pension and retirement funds as these intermediaries usually provide a service to individuals that involves a contractual commitment of savings over a long period of time. The third category, including mortgage companies, real estate investment trusts, and federally related agencies, might be called specialized mortgage market intermediaries. These intermediaries restrict their investment activity to the mortgage market primarily, and most of the funds that they use for making investments in mortgages do not come directly from savers. The following section briefly describes some of the overall functions of each institution.[12]

Mortgage Lenders in the Mortgage Market Insight into the operation of the mortgage market can be gained by becoming familiar with the major financial institutions involved in mortgage lending and the type of lending in which each tends to specialize. There are four major private institutions that are significantly involved in the mortgage market: savings and loan associations, mutual savings banks, commercial banks, and life insurance companies. Exhibit 14–4 provides a breakdown of total real estate mortgage loans held by each of the major private lenders, plus a breakdown of loans held by federally related agencies and other lenders, by category of loan.

Looking to the last column in Exhibit 14–4 it is clear that savings and loan associations are the largest real estate lenders in the United States. Of the four largest private real estate lenders, savings and loan associations held approximately 34.8 percent of total mortgage loans outstanding at the end of 1975. They were followed by commercial banks (17.0 percent), life insurance companies (11.2 percent), and mutual savings banks (9.6 percent). These institutions accounted for about 72.6 percent of total mortgage loans outstanding at the end of 1975 and are by far the most important institutions in the mortgage market. Federally re-

---

[12] A more complete discussion of each institution is contained in subsequent chapters.

EXHIBIT 14-4
Total Mortgage Debt* by Type of Loan and Lender, 1975 (in billions of dollars)

Institution	One- to Four- Family (percent)	Multi- family (percent)	Com- mercial and Other (percent)	Farm (percent)	Total (percent)
Major Lenders:					
Savings and Loans	$224.7	$25.4	$28.6	—	$278.7
	(45.6)	(25.6)	(18.1)	—	(34.8)
Commercial Banks	77.0	5.9	46.9	6.4	136.2
	(15.6)	(5.9)	(29.8)	(12.5)	(17.0)
Life Insurance Companies	17.6	19.7	45.3	6.8	89.4
	(3.6)	(19.8)	(28.7)	(13.3)	(11.2)
Mutual Savings Banks	50.0	13.8	13.4	—	77.2
	(10.1)	(13.9)	(8.5)	—	(9.6)
Federally Related Agencies†	66.4	13.6	2.1	19.4	101.5
	(13.5)	(13.7)	(1.3)	(37.9)	(12.7)
Other Lenders:					
Real Estate Investment Trusts	1.4	4.2	5.9	—	11.5
	(.3)	(4.2)	(3.7)	—	(1.4)
Mortgage Companies	5.8	1.6	1.9	—	9.3
	(1.2)	(1.6)	(1.2)	—	(1.2)
State and Local Agencies	4.2	6.4	1.3	.5	12.4
	(.8)	(6.4)	(.8)	(1.0)	(1.5)
Pension Funds	3.6	2.9	3.5	—	10.0
	(.9)	(2.9)	(2.2)	—	(1.2)
Others	41.5	5.8	8.8	18.2	74.2
	(8.4)	(5.8)	(5.6)	(35.5)	(9.3)
Total	$492.2	$99.4	$157.6	$51.2	$800.4
	(100.0)	(100.0)	(100.0)	(100.0)	(100.0)

* Includes construction, land development and permanent mortgage loans.
† Includes GNMA-backed mortgage pools, mortgage holdings of FNMA, FHLMC, GNMA, Farmers Home Administration, Federal Land Banks, and other federal agencies.
Source: Board of Governors of the Federal Reserve System—preliminary.

lated agencies including the Federal National Mortgage Association (FNMA), the Federal Home Loan Mortgage Corporation (FHLMC), the Farmers Home Administration and the Federal Land Bank System, have increased their holdings dramatically in the post war period. By the end of 1975, they held almost 13 percent of all real estate mortgages. Other categories of lenders detailed in Exhibit 14-4, including pension funds, mortgage companies, real estate investment trusts, and state and local credit agencies together accounted for about 5.3 percent of total mortgage debt.

Specialization in Real Estate Lending: An Overview In addition to total mortgage lending activity, data in Exhibit 14-4 show areas of lending specialization by category of loan and lender. For example, data in column one show that savings and loan associations are by far the largest holder of one- to four-family mortgage loans. Of the $492.2 billion in single-family loans (one- to four-family category) outstanding in 1975, savings and loans held over 45 percent of the total. They were followed by commercial banks (15.6 percent), federally related agencies (13.5 percent), mutual savings banks (10.1 percent), and life insurance companies (3.6 percent). In the multifamily loan category, detailed in column two, savings and loan associations accounted for about 25.6 percent of the $99.4 billion in loans outstanding, followed by life insurance companies (19.8 percent), mutual savings banks (13.9 percent), federally related agencies (13.7 percent), and commercial banks (5.9 percent). The pattern of commercial mortgages held by major financial institutions is completely different from both the one- to four-family and multifamily categories, with commercial banks accounting for the largest percentage (29.8 percent) of the $157.6 billion in total loans outstanding in that category, followed by life insurance companies (28.7 percent), savings and loans (18.1 percent), and mutual savings banks (8.5 percent). These patterns of mortgage investment indicate clearly that lenders specialize in certain areas of real estate lending. Exhibit 14–5 contains a summary of selected characteristics of the major participants in the mortgage market. The intent of this summary is to provide an overview of the role that each intermediary plays in the mortgage market as well as being useful as a convenient reference for the discussion in in this and subsequent chapters.

Savings and Loan Associations. As the summary in Exhibit 14–5 shows, these institutions are specialists in underwriting residential mortgage loans, both in the one- to four-family and multifamily categories. This specialized lending pattern follows from the fact that government regulations have historically allowed savings and loan associations to offer higher interest rates on savings deposits than commercial banks. These regulations have generally provided savings and loans with a relatively stable source of funds for lending purposes; consequently, they are in a good position to make long-term loans. Government regulations have also restricted the investment policy of savings and loans by requiring the origination of primarily residential loans in their local lending area. Consequently, these institutions have developed underwriting expertise in underwriting both construction loans and permanent loans on single-family and multifamily residential real estate and have evolved into the most important lending institution in those categories.

During the period 1965–75, of all loans made by savings and loan associations, 80 to 85 percent were made on single-family (one- to four-family category) properties. Although loans on single-family properties have been the mainstay of savings and loans, the share of loans made on multifamily and commercial mortgage loans has been increasing in recent years with the two categories accounting for about 20 percent

EXHIBIT 14–5

Participants in the Mortgage Market—Selected Characteristics

Characteristics	Source of Funds	Stability of Funds Flow	Percent of Funds Invested in Mortgages*	Preferred Mortgage Loans and Recent Lending Trends	
				Long-Term Mortgage Loans*	Short-Term Loans
Savings and loan associations	Time deposits	Moderate	97–100% of deposits	Largest of all lenders on single-family properties (80–85% of loans made). Most single-family loans conventional. FHA/VA loans account for only 12–15% of single-family loans made. Multifamily and commercial mortgages growing relative to single-family mortgages in recent years.	Largest single-family construction lenders. Also make considerable amounts of construction and land development loans for multifamily residences.
Commercial banks	Time and demand deposits	Low	15–20% of deposits	Make primarily single-family loans (55–65% of all loans made). FHA and VA mortgages range 11–30% of single-family loans. Largest of all lenders on commercial properties (28–35% of all loans made). Share of multifamily and commercial mortgages growing in recent years.	Largest construction lenders in multifamily and commercial categories. Extend large short-term loans to mortgage companies and REITs.
Mutual savings banks	Time deposits	Moderate	73–85% of deposits	Make primarily single-family loans (50–65% of all loans made). Second largest holder of FHA/VA mortgages (50–70% of single-family loans made). Make significant numbers of multifamily loans. Mortgage loans as a percent of deposits declining in recent years.	Very little construction lending due to geographic separation from developers. Make long-term commitments to mortgage companies and REITs that make construction loans.

	Source of funds	Liquidity	Mortgages as % of assets	Mortgage lending	Construction lending
Life insurance Companies	Reserves	High	30–38% of assets	Make primarily commercial and multi-family mortgage loans. Commercial and multifamily loans increasing in recent years. Loans on single-family properties declining in recent years. Total mortgage loans as a percentage of assets declining in recent years.	Very little construction lending due to geographic separation from developers. Make long-term commitments to mortgage companies and REITs.
Mortgage companies	Equity and short-term loans	Low	nearly 100% of assets	Long-term mortgages not a preferred investment. Although a high percentage of assets held in mortgages, this represents principally year-end balances of unsold mortgages. Largest originator of FHA/VA mortgage loans. Primary function—loan origination and servicing.	Significant number of loans for construction and land development.
REITs	Equity and short-term loans	Low	nearly 100% of assets	Long-term multifamily and commercial mortgages preferred by some trusts.	Significant number of loans for construction and land development for specialized projects—primary function of many trusts.
Pension funds	Payroll deductions/ contributions	High	10% of assets	Increased activity in multifamily and commercial mortgages. Rely on other institutions for originations.	Very little activity due to inexperience in underwriting mortgage loans.
Federally related agencies	Notes and bonds	Moderate	90–100% of assets	Largest holder of FHA/VA mortgage loans. Significant holder of multifamily mortgage loans. Purchase mortgage loans from lenders in secondary market. Share of mortgage holdings growing significantly.	Very little activity in direct lending for construction and land development.

* All statistics in table are high and low percentages applicable to the period 1965–75.
Source: Board of Governors, Federal Reserve System.

of total loans by the end of 1975. Most residential loans made are conventional; i.e., loans underwritten by individual institutions with no FHA insurance or VA guarantee, although private mortgage insurance is required on many loans.

Because of their relatively stable source of funds, savings and loan associations have kept about 100 percent of time deposits invested in real estate loans, with cash and other liquid investments accounting for only a relatively small percentage of total assets.[13] Since savings and loan associations are the second largest group of financial institutions in the United States, their role in the mortgage market is clearly a dominant one. Consequently, changes in economic conditions and government policies affecting these intermediaries clearly have a tremendous effect on the mortgage market.

Commercial Banks. In contrast to savings and loan associations, commercial banks, the largest group of financial institutions in the United States, have relatively low stability in their sources of funds. Since about 45 to 50 percent of their funds come primarily in the form of demand deposits, the availability of funds for mortgage lending on a long-term basis is considerably lessened because of the short-term and fluctuating nature of demand deposit balances. Hence, as Exhibit 14–5 indicates, commercial banks invest only 15 to 20 percent of total demand and time deposits in mortgage loans. In keeping with the relatively unstable nature of deposit flows, commercial banks have developed expertise in short-term lending in primarily business and consumer loans, while keeping reserves in highly marketable government obligations.

In addition to being the second largest holder of single-family mortgage loans among private lenders, commercial banks tend to specialize in commercial mortgage loans and in all phases of construction lending. Specialization in commercial mortgages follows from their relationship with business customers who make short-term business loans and rely on these banks for mortgage loans when new plants and office buildings are needed. Since banks are familiar with business organizations from continuing short-term lending relationships, development of commercial mortgage lending is a natural outgrowth of that activity.

Many of the mortgages made by banks are construction and land development loans which will ultimately be held by another lender, such as a life insurance company, upon completion of construction. Banks also make short-term loans to mortgage companies and real estate investment trusts (REITs), which are not reported as mortgage loans in Exhibit 14–4, but are nonetheless related to the real estate industry.

Life Insurance Companies. These contractual-type intermediaries

---

[13] Cash and liquid assets have been roughly equivalent to equity and reserves for most associations in recent years.

enjoy a relatively high degree of stability in the availability of funds for investment when compared with both commercial banks and savings and loan associations. This stability follows from the contractual nature of premiums on insurance policies and the amount of benefit payouts required at any point in time. As a consequence, investments in long-term assets are more desirable for these intermediaries.

As shown in Exhibit 14–4, life insurance companies, like commercial banks, make substantial investments in commercial mortgage loans and loans on multifamily properties. Their commercial lending activity lies more in large shopping center developments, motels, and larger-scale office buildings throughout the entire United States, as contrasted with more local, smaller-scale loans made by commercial banks. Life insurance companies tend not to be interested in underwriting smaller-scale projects but prefer larger-scale projects that involve large outlays of funds. They rely on mortgage bankers and commercial banks to make construction loans and to monitor construction at the local level. Local lenders, because of their geographic proximity to the construction and development, are more efficient in performing that function. As a result, life insurance companies are more interested in only the permanent financing on large projects.

Mutual Savings Banks. Like savings and loan associations, mutual savings have a relatively stable source of funds in the form of time deposits and therefore they also tend to specialize in single-family lending. However, as shown in Exhibit 14–4, a larger portion of lending by mutual savings banks occurs in multifamily and commercial lending when compared to savings and loan associations. This is the case because mutual savings banks are located primarily in the northeastern section of the United States and must seek out loans in other areas of the country when savings inflows exceed the level of loan demand in their respective local lending markets. When this occurs, like life insurance companies, they prefer larger-scale projects on which they issue commitments for permanent financing, with commercial banks, mortgage companies, or perhaps savings and loan associations making the construction loan and overseeing the project at the local level.

Also because of their geographical location, mutual savings banks purchase FHA-insured and VA-guaranteed mortgages from other parts of the United States. The FHA insurance and VA guarantee make mortgages on one- to four-family properties (usually originated by mortgage bankers in other areas) marketable investments for mutual savings banks. Hence, next to federally related agencies, they are the largest holders of FHA and VA mortgages in the United States.

Federally-Related Agencies. These agencies have become a very important force in the markets for single-family loans, multifamily loans, and farm lending. The development of the Federal National Mortgage

Association, Federal Home Loan Mortgage Corporation, and various other agencies[14] has occurred primarily in response to recurrent problems[15] faced by private lenders during periods of rapidly rising interest rates. Essentially, these institutions provide a secondary market for existing single-family and multifamily loans for lenders who seek an outlet for mortgages made during periods of rising interest rates, when funds for originating new loans become scarce. By raising capital with various types of obligations and notes, these federally related institutions then purchase loans from private lenders during periods of capital shortages, thereby providing funds with which lenders may originate new loans. Because of recurrent problems in financial markets, these institutions have continuously increased their holdings of mortgage loans in recent years.

Mortgage Companies. These lenders held $9.3 billion in mortgage debt at the end of 1975. However, most of this debt was held in the form of construction loans and loans on newly completed properties, many of which were originated as construction loans by mortgage companies. This characterizes much of the mortgage banker's role in the mortgage market, that is, an originator and seller of mortgages to other financial institutions.

Mortgage companies are usually privately owned concerns with limited funds for outright mortgage lending. They usually operate on the basis of commitments which they obtain from other financial institutions to buy loans to be closed by mortgage companies at a future date. With this commitment, mortgage companies can usually obtain short-term loans from commercial banks to originate loans that are to be delivered to other lenders in the future, at which time they repay short-term loans. They may repeat this activity many times during one year and, as a result, the year-end figures shown in Exhibit 14–4 do not reflect total originations made during the year.

Mortgage companies tend to be very active in the one- to four-family market, obtaining commitments from primarily federal agencies and then originating FHA-insured and VA-guaranteed loans. In the market for multifamily and commercial mortgages, mortgage companies also act as middlemen by seeking permanent loan commitments for developers and investors and then making the construction loan themselves, or arranging construction financing with another lender. In most cases, after construction is completed, mortgage companies retain the loan servicing function for the permanent lender.

Real Estate Investment Trusts. Although they accounted for $11.5 billion in loans outstanding at the end of 1975, real estate investment

---

[14] Farm credit programs are discussed in Chapter 22.

[15] These problems are discussed later in the chapter.

trusts have been the most rapidly growing participant in the mortgage market over the past ten years. These trusts are usually categorized as mortgage trusts or equity trusts, depending on whether they specialize in making mortgage loans or in purchasing property. Mortgage trusts, however, dominate as the major type of real estate investment trust.

Mortgage trusts generally raise capital from equity investors and make short-term loans from commercial banks. These funds are used primarily to originate construction loans and land development loans in the multifamily and commercial loan category. Some of these loans are held as investments by the trusts; however, many are sold to other financial institutions. Consequently, like mortgage companies, total loan originations made during a year may far exceed mortgage loans held by these institutions at year-end. Although real estate investment trusts have been rapidly expanding over the past ten years, the industry faced a severe downturn in lending activity in 1974–75. Problems faced by these trusts are taken up in Chapter 18.

Pension–Retirement Funds. Another group of institutions that are increasing in importance in the mortgage market are insured and non-insured pension and retirement funds. As shown in Exhibit 14–4, mortgage holdings by these institutions totaled approximately $10 billion at the end of 1975. Stringently regulated by state law, these institutions have traditionally made investments in high quality stocks and bonds. However, with a growing realization of the relatively high yields available on high quality mortgage loans and the acquisition of underwriting expertise by administrators of these funds, they have slowly increased their commitments to purchase mortgages made in the multifamily and commercial loan categories.

Growth and Instability in the Mortgage Market

Growth in Mortgage Lending Mortgage loans constitute the largest type of credit outstanding in the United States. Further, residential mortgage loans constitute the largest category of loans among the various types of mortgages made in the United States. To show the importance of mortgage credit relative to all other forms of credit, Exhibit 14–6 provides a summary of growth in selected types of credit in the United States from 1950 to 1975.

From Exhibit 14–6, it can be seen that at the end of 1975 total mortgage credit outstanding totaled $800.4 billion. Compared to the other major categories of credit use, mortgage credit is by far the single largest use of credit in our economy. At the end of 1975, mortgage credit accounted for 33.4 percent of total credit outstanding in the United States. This far exceeds credit usage by corporations, state and local government, consumers, and even the federal government.

EXHIBIT 14–6

Growth in Selected Types of Credit (in billions of dollars)

Type of Credit	1950		1975		Increase	
Total credit outstanding	$418.6	100.0%	$2,399.7	100.0%	$1,981.1	100.0%
Real estate mortgage loans:						
One- to four-family homes	45.2	10.8	492.2	20.5	447.0	22.6
Multifamily units	10.1	2.4	99.4	4.1	89.3	4.5
Commercial properties	11.5	2.7	157.6	6.6	146.1	7.4
Farm properties	6.1	1.5	51.2	2.1	45.1	2.3
Total	$ 72.9	17.4	$ 800.4	33.4	$ 727.5	36.7
Corporate bonds	35.6	8.5	254.2	10.6	218.5	11.0
State and local government						
obligations	24.4	5.8	222.8	9.3	198.4	10.0
Consumer credit	21.5	5.1	195.4	8.1	173.9	8.8
Federal debt	216.5	51.7	451.1	18.8	234.6	11.8

Source: Adapted from data obtained from the U.S. League of Savings Associations and the Board of Governors of the Federal Reserve System.

Not only is mortgage debt the single most important use of credit in the United States, but its role has increased in importance in the post-World War II period. As shown in Exhibit 14–6, of the $1,981.1 billion increase in credit outstanding from 1950 to 1975, mortgage credit accounted for 36.7 percent of the increase, or over $1 for every $3 in total credit raised during that time period. Indeed, total credit outstanding increased over five and one half times from 1950 to 1975, while total mortgage credit increased well over ten times during the same period. These facts give some indication of the relative importance of mortgage credit as well as its growth as the major use of credit in the economy.

Changes in the Availability of Mortgage Credit

While the growth in mortgage credit during 1950–75 might be characterized as phenomenal by some, it must be stressed that during this same time period, the availability of mortgage credit in *individual years* changed dramatically. Exhibit 14–7 provides some basic information concerning mortgage interest rates and housing starts during the ten-year period 1965–75. Data in the table reveal that sharp declines in housing starts occurred during the years 1966, 1969, and 1973–74. During the same three periods, mortgage interest rates increased sharply. These years, particularly 1966 and 1973–74, have been characterized as the most severe downturns in housing starts and real estate development in the post-World War II period. In other years, notably 1967, 1971, and 1972, data in Exhibit 14–7 show sharp reversals in the mortgage interest

EXHIBIT 14–7

Mortgage Interest Rates and Housing Starts

Year	Total Private Housing Starts (in millions)	Percent Change from Preceding Year	Mortgage Interest Rate° (percent)	Percent Change from Preceding Year
1965 1,473		—	5.47	—
1966 1,165		−20.9	6.38	+16.6
1967 1,292		+10.9	6.55	+ 2.7
1968 1,508		+16.7	7.21	+10.1
1969 1,467		− 2.7	8.62	+19.6
1970 1,434		− 2.0	9.03	+ 4.8
1971 2,052		+43.1	7.70	−14.7
1972 2,357		+14.9	7.53	− 2.2
1973 2,045		−13.2	8.19	+ 8.8
1974 1,336		−34.7	9.55	+16.6
1975 1,164		−12.9	9.32	− 2.4

° Yield on FHA mortgages purchased in secondary mortgage market.
Source: Federal Reserve Bulletin.

rate and substantial increases in housing starts. In the following section we investigate instability in the mortgage market and discuss its causes.

The Degree of Financial Intermediation   As discussed previously in relation to the flow of funds diagram in Exhibit 14–1 and the data pertaining to flow of funds in Exhibit 14–2, it was emphasized that funds may be channeled into investment in one of two ways. Funds may be channeled through financial intermediaries or invested directly into financial assets. When the economy is growing at a moderate pace and incomes are rising, prices and interest rates tend to be relatively stable. During these periods, a substantial amount of funds available for investment tend to be channeled through financial intermediaries, particularly depositary-type intermediaries, as opposed to being invested directly. As also previously discussed, it is generally more efficient for individuals to use intermediaries than to invest directly in securities and other financial assets.

If for some reason, however, yields and interest rates rise on securities, such as corporate bonds or U.S. Treasury obligations of state and local governments, relative to interest rates available on deposits offered by financial intermediaries, an increasing number of individuals will find it more attractive to invest *directly* in securities and to shift funds away from financial intermediaries.[16] These financial intermediaries

---

[16] Furthermore, if price levels are rising, households will also tend to save less and to consume more out of fear of paying higher prices later, and hence funds available for investment may be reduced in total. This would happen in addition to individuals seeking higher returns on savings they produce over a given period.

cannot easily respond to changes in yields offered in other markets because of government regulations on deposit interest rates. Therefore, since depository-type institutions are the primary participants in the mortgage market, when individuals choose to shift savings flows away from financial intermediaries, the degree of financial intermediation is reduced and funds that flow to the major lenders in the mortgage market are also reduced. Since no accessible market for mortgages exists so that individuals can easily acquire them, even though mortgage interest rates may increase along with other interest rates, funds will not readily flow into mortgage loans.

Financial Disintermediation   When substantial shifts in funds flows occur from financial intermediaries and flow directly into the market for securities and other financial assets, this process is usually called *financial disintermediation.* This process occurred to a significant degree during the years 1966, 1969, and 1973–74 when, as has been seen in Exhibit 14–7, mortgage interest rates increased sharply and housing starts decreased sharply. To focus on this process and its causes, Exhibit 14–8 presents a listing of yields that were available on deposits made at selected depository-type institutions and on investments in selected corporate and U.S. government bonds and state and local obligations. While the data show that all yields have generally risen from 1950

EXHIBIT 14–8

Average Annual Yield on Selected Types of Investments (in percent)

Year	Savings Deposits in Savings Associ- ations	Savings Deposits in Mutual Savings Banks	Time and Savings Deposits in Commercial Banks	U.S. Government Bonds	State and Local Bonds	Corporate (Aaa) Bonds
1950	2.52	1.84	0.94	2.32	1.90	2.62
1955	2.94	2.64	1.38	2.84	2.57	3.06
1960	3.86	3.47	2.56	4.01	3.69	4.41
1965	4.23	4.11	3.69	4.21	3.34	4.49
1966	4.45	4.45	4.04	4.66	3.90	5.13
1967	4.67	4.74	4.24	4.85	3.99	5.51
1968	4.68	4.76	4.48	5.25	4.48	6.18
1969	4.80	4.89	4.87	6.10	5.73	7.03
1970	5.06	5.01	4.95	6.59	6.42	8.04
1971	5.33	5.14	4.78	5.74	5.62	7.39
1972	5.39	5.23	4.66	5.63	5.30	7.21
1973	5.55	5.45	5.71	6.30	5.22	7.44
1974	5.98	5.76	5.93	6.99	6.19	8.57
1975°	6.22	5.89	5.90	6.98	7.05	8.83

° Preliminary.

Source: Federal Deposit Insurance Corporation; Federal Home Loan Bank Board; Federal Reserve Board; Moody's Investors Service; National Association of Mutual Savings Banks; United States League of Savings Associations. Courtesy of U.S. League of Savings Associations.

to 1975, special attention should be paid to the spread or difference between yields available on deposits and yields available on the securities listed in the table. In 1965, for example, deposit yields offered at savings and loan associations averaged 4.23 percent while the yield on U.S. government bonds averaged 4.21; or savings and loan associations offered 0.02 percent more for deposits. This same spread computed in 1966 showed government bond yields exceeded interest rates offered by savings and loan associations by 0.21 percent, by 1.30 percent in 1969, by 0.75 percent in 1973, and by 1.01 percent in 1974. The same general pattern is found if comparisons are made among the various yields shown in the table during the same periods. The spread between yields on securities and deposit interest rates widened greatly during 1966, 1969, and 1973–74 when compared to spreads in preceding periods.

Deposit Flows. The general widening in yields for the years discussed above, resulted in more and more households and businesses shifting funds from financial intermediaries by making direct investments in various types of government bonds, corporate bonds, and stocks. To provide some idea of the magnitude of the shift, Exhibit 14–9

EXHIBIT 14–9

Changes in Deposits and Reserves at Selected Financial Institutions, 1965–1975 (in billions of dollars)

	Commercial Banks		Other Savings Institutions	Insurance and Pension Fund Reserves	Total
	Demand	*Time*			
1965	$ 7.3	$20.1	$13.1	$17.0	$57.5
1966	3.9	13.3	6.9	19.4	43.5
1967	15.0	23.9	17.0	19.6	75.5
1968	14.8	20.7	12.7	20.1	68.3
1969	8.2	−9.5	7.9	21.3	27.9
1970	14.3	38.0	17.0	24.3	93.6
1971	17.4	41.4	40.6	27.7	127.1
1972	19.6	42.3	46.1	30.3	138.3
1973	16.0	50.9	28.1	31.6	126.6
1974	11.1	57.0	22.1	38.9	129.1
1975	16.2	30.1	59.8	41.3	147.4

Source: Board of Governors, Federal Reserve System, *Flow of Funds Accounts,* May 1976.

provides a summary of changes in demand and time deposits at commercial banks and time deposits at other depositary institutions, including primarily savings and loan associations and mutual savings banks,[17] and changes in reserves at life insurance companies and pension and

---

[17] Credit unions are also included in this category.

retirement funds. As shown in Exhibit 14–4, and described in more detail in Exhibit 14–5, these institutions are by far the most important lenders in the mortgage market.

Based on the data shown in Exhibit 14–9, changes in deposits declined significantly in each of the years 1966, 1969, 1973, and 1974 relative to periods immediately preceding these years. As changes in deposits decreased, loanable funds for mortgages of all types declined considerably, causing credit shortages and high mortgage interest rates. These high interest rates and shortages caused the demand for mortgage loans to decrease and, hence, activity in the real estate industry to drop off sharply. However, it must be pointed out that lending in many sectors of the economy also dropped off because of credit shortages and high interest rates. An interesting question concerning relative declines in economic sectors now arises. Was the mortgage market affected more than other financial markets? While this question is difficult to answer, some tentative observations can be made.

The Mortgage Market and Other Markets for Credit. Exhibit 14–10

EXHIBIT 14–10

Mortgage Funds Raised Relative to All Funds Raised in Financial Markets, 1965–1975 (in billions of dollars)

	Total Funds	Mortgage Funds	Ratio of Mortgage Funds to Total Funds
1965	$ 83.2	$25.6	30.8%
1966	79.6	21.3	26.8
1967	84.4	23.0	27.3
1968	114.3	27.4	24.0
1969	125.5	27.8	22.2
1970	110.9	26.4	23.8
1971	164.0	48.9	29.8
1972	198.5	68.8	34.7
1973	239.3	71.9	30.0
1974	218.1	54.5	25.0
1975	216.6	57.3	26.5

Source: Board of Governors, Federal Reserve System, *Flow of Funds Accounts,* May 1976.

provides data on the purchase of funds raised for mortgage lending in real estate relative to total funds available for all forms of lending during the period 1965–75. As can be seen from the data presented, mortgage lending declined during 1966, 1969, and 1973–74, relative to total funds available for lending. This implies that funds flowing into mortgage lending declined not only in amount but also *relative* to funds raised in others sectors of the economy. These sectors, most notably corporations and government, increased their share of total funds during these periods as their percentages of capital raised increased relative to funds loaned in the mortgage market. The share of other borrowers in credit markets can be estimated by subtracting the percentages shown in Exhibit 14–10 from 100 percent.

This pattern illustrated in Exhibit 14–10 has led many individuals to argue that the real estate industry is more adversely affected during periods of rising interest rates than are other sectors of the economy. These critics maintain that because corporations and government can issue securities with a broad market appeal, they can compete more effectively for funds directly than can financial intermediaries with interest rates on deposits stringently regulated by the government. Further, while the flow of funds to the mortgage market increases significantly when interest rates stabilize, the "boom or bust" pattern of credit shortages and increases causes significant displacement in the real estate industry and, it is argued, an inefficient use of resources.

Fundamental Causes—Financial Disintermediation While the process just described illustrates the market forces that cause financial disintermediation, more basic questions arise concerning what causes: (1) total funds available for lending to decline in some periods and to increase in others and (2) yield spreads to widen on bonds and other securities relative to deposit interest rates offered by financial institutions, which are so important to the mortgage market.

In answering these questions, it is generally acknowledged that the periods of significant financial disintermediation are usually accompanied by rapidly rising price levels or inflationary pressures. While the causes of inflation are many, most economists would attribute it to a combination of rapid expansion in the business sector, large deficit spending by government, and perhaps periods of easy monetary policy by the Federal Reserve.[18]

If households expect prices to continue to rise, they tend to consume more from income and to reduce their rate of savings. Consequently, in the short-run there will be a reduction in total funds flow through the financial system for investment. Expansionary plans by business and the necessity of government to finance deficits cause keen competition for a generally smaller supply of funds. This, in turn, causes sharp increases in interest rates on financial claims created to raise funds. More households become aware of these rising interest rates on bonds and other securities and begin to invest directly in them, bypassing financial intermediaries. Financial intermediaries cannot raise interest rates on deposits because of government regulations; hence, disintermediation results.

---

[18] This discussion oversimplifies the complex forces at work that cause economic instability. However, the discussion does highlight many of the probable causes and their effects in the mortgage market.

To dampen investment plans of business, the Federal Reserve generally slows the growth in the money supply through one or a combination of open market operations, changing reserve requirements or raising the discount rate. This action tends to increase interest rates even further as the money supply and funds available for investment are reduced. Eventually, investment subsides and, as the price level stabilizes, savings flows increase and the economy returns to relative stability. However, in the interim period the flow of funds into the mortgage market is drastically reduced and activity in the real estate sector of the economy is slowed considerably.

Instability in the Mortgage Market and Proposed Remedies Based on material presented to this point, it is apparent that the relative instability in availability of mortgage funds has brought many problems to the real estate industry. One remedy that has been suggested by students of the problem has to do with lifting government-regulated ceilings on interest rates paid on deposits made at financial institutions. As has been pointed out, because of the regulatory lag in adjusting interest rates payable on deposits, the spread between yields on direct investments and deposits increases and provides incentives for financial disintermediation. After deregulation of ceiling rates, institutions could compete for savings by offering higher interest rates on deposits, and the flow of funds to the mortgage market might be maintained.

At least one argument has been advanced for not deregulating deposit interest rate ceilings. It has to do with the fact that the yield fluctuations and disintermediation are short-term in nature and any attempt to prevent yields from spreading might be counter-productive to Federal Reserve policy at certain times. In other words, if the Federal Reserve Board wants to slow down the general rate of investment because of inflationary pressure in the economy, it may choose to initiate a rise in interest rates. Generally, increases in interest rates will be initiated by the Federal Reserve Board by sales of government bonds in the open market.[19] The effect of these sales is to drive up yields on government securities. This result, in turn, causes yields on other investments such as corporate bonds, business loans, etc., to rise. The intent, of course, is to make borrowing more expensive and to slow down the rate of investment. Consequently, some argue that if ceiling rates were deregulated, although the housing industry might benefit, deregulation would also result in general increases in investment that would be contrary to Federal Reserve policy.

---

[19] It might also choose to increase reserve requirements for member commercial banks and/or raise the discount rate on funds borrowed by member banks from federal reserve banks. Both of these policies, like the open market operation, would restrict the amount of funds available for lending at commercial banks and tend to drive up interest rates.

Another, more realistic, argument concerning ceiling deposit rates asserts that deregulation would be largely ineffective anyway. This is true because during periods of rising interest rates large mortgage lenders, such as savings and loan associations, can pay only small increases in deposit rates, even though mortgage loans are being made at higher interest rates. This limitation occurs because only *new mortgage loans* being made will earn the current or high interest rates. Older mortgage loans carried as assets by these lenders will continue to earn rates in effect when they were made. Consequently, the average interest rate earned on all mortgages held by mortgage lenders will increase only slightly. On the other hand, when ceiling rates on deposits are changed, all savings irrespective of when they were first deposited will earn the new interest rate. As a result, interest costs associated with increasing deposit rates will rise faster than the average yield on all mortgage loans held by major mortgage lenders. Hence, the increases in deposit rates that may occur under deregulation of ceiling rates will very likely be small as long as the average yield on all mortgages remains low.

The Variable Interest Rate Mortgage.   One suggested solution to deregulation of deposit ceiling rates is to institute a system of mortgages with variable interest rates. These mortgages, previously discussed in Chapter 9, have a provision allowing the interest rate originally negotiated on the loan to change with a market index. This would allow the mortgage interest rate to change on *all mortgages* made with such a provision, as interest rates are changing. Consequently, with income rising from changes in the interest rate on all mortgage loans, savings institutions could raise interest rates on deposits to compete for additional savings. It is argued that this in turn would result in a more stable flow of funds to the mortgage market and would eliminate much of the boom-bust cycle in real estate lending.

At the present time, use of variable rate mortgages is not allowed at federally chartered savings and loan associations. Only state chartered associations, primarily in California, are using them with any success. However, if the cycles in real estate lending experienced in recent years continue, there is good reason to expect an increase in the use of variable rate mortgages.

Other Alternatives.   To help cushion the blow on real estate lending and housing starts, the federal government has chosen to create a system of federally-related, private institutions in the secondary mortgage market. These institutions, including primarily the FNMA, GNMA, and FHLMC, have been created to act as a buffer during periods of rising interest rates. By issuing government-backed securities during periods of high interest rates, these institutions raise capital to buy mortgages from mortgage lenders and thus provide funds to the lenders for additional loans. This technique, along with various subsidy schemes which are used in conjunction with these federally-related institutions, provides some funds for mortgage lending even during periods of financial disintermediation. These institutions, their functions, and the operation of private mortgage lenders are taken up in detail in the chapters that follow.

QUESTIONS

1. From data provided in this chapter, describe the areas of mortgage lending in which the four major private financial institutions specialize.

2. Rank the four major financial institutions in the mortgage market in terms of total mortgage investment.

3. Based on the discussion in this chapter, what are the fundamental determinants of savings by households?What determines how savings are allocated among depositary institutions and investments in our economy?

4. What is financial disintermediation? How does this process come about? What is its effect on the housing and mortgage markets?

5. What remedies have been proposed as a solution to the problem of financial disintermediation as it affects the housing and mortgage markets?

15

Financing of Real Estate by Savings and Loan Associations

Early Associations

The foundation stones of modern savings and loan associations are two in number: thrift and homeownership. Neither is currently placed ahead of the other in importance. In the day-to-day operation of an institution of this character, if the savings and investment funds pile up because of lack of mortgage demand, the progressive manager tries to stimulate loan applications. If the latter exceed the capacity of the institution to supply funds, efforts are made to increase savings. Within reasonable limits, liquidity requirements taken into consideration, an attempt is made to maintain a balance between receipts and disbursements. As a matter of fact, until quite recently the statement that interested savings and loan managers most was neither the balance sheet nor the income statement based upon accruals, but the statement showing cash receipts and disbursements.

In the early days there was a definite difference in emphasis. Homeownership by its members was the goal of the early "building societies" organized by our forefathers of English origin and of the "Bauvereine" organized by their German neighbors. The end was homeownership; the means was a kind of forced savings which were no longer considered essential once the home was paid for. The emphasis upon homeownership was so great that our usual concept of saving for a purpose was definitely reversed. Today we are accustomed to think that those who save accumulate funds against their use for a specific purpose which involves their expenditure at a later date. In other words, saving precedes spending. The basic idea in building associations was to encourage the borrower to borrow, with his home as security, funds which he would then repay from future savings. In this case, spending precedes saving.

The ambition for homeownership was not an indigenous American plan. Neither was the plan for cooperative financing of homes. Both were imported from Europe. Except among the German settlers, early American building societies followed the Anglo-Saxon model. Without benefit of parliamentary sanction, the English had made considerable progress with voluntary associations before the first American counterpart was started in Frankford, Pennsylvania, in 1831. The avowed purpose of this first American cooperative home-financing institution, known as the Oxford Provident Building Association, was to "enable the contributors thereof to build or purchase dwelling houses."

This first association could not even qualify as a mortgage finance institution as we know this term today. It gave no heed to the financial needs of those who owned homes already; its purpose was to help its nonhomeowning members to acquire homes for themselves by purchase or construction. Neither was it concerned with thrift as a desirable objective by itself, since it had nothing to offer to the person who wished to save for some purpose other than homeownership.

Share-Accumulation Sinking-Fund Loan Plan   The early American associations used a loan plan that few members of the associations ever understood; and not even the elected nonsalaried managers could forecast its full meaning. It operated in this manner: Suppose that A subscribes for five shares of stock and later borrows $1,000 from the association. He gives a mortgage on his home for this amount. In effect this is an unamortized term loan without any definite term stated. Each month he pays the interest, which is credited to the income of the association. In addition, he continues to make his regular payments on his shares.

More often than not, the interest rate was 6 percent. The borrower would pay each month to the association $5 for interest and an additional $5 dues to be credited on his share account. This was the beginning of requiring the borrower to pay 1 percent of his original loan principal per month, regardless of the percentage of loan to property value, and so forth. While most modern lending practices have adjusted monthly payments to a variety of factors, savings and loan associations have remained with a monthly reduction formula.

High percentage loans were common in the early building associations. While the borrower was expected to have some capital to put into his home, the amount required was likely to be a token amount only as a gesture of good faith on the part of the borrower. Even this rule was relaxed, when the board of directors felt that the property was being acquired at a bargain, if the borrower enjoyed a reputation for honesty, sobriety, and industry. In any event both the real estate acquired and the member's stock were put up as collateral to protect the loan.

Since funds were limited to the amount paid in on stock subscriptions and earnings on loans, the money available had to be allocated. Often the loan was made to the member willing to pay the highest premium, commonly determined by auction. Some associations had a fixed premium rate; others gave the loans to borrowing members in the order of filing applications or by lot.

At the end of the year the earnings of the association, minus any expenses, which were small, and any losses, which had to be calculated annually, were credited to the share accounts on a pro rata basis. The credits to the share account thus cumulated from dues and from credited income. Charged against this account were unpaid fees, fines, and forfeitures of stock or dividend credits for failure to make required payments or premature withdrawals. Whenever these net credits were equal to the amount of the original mortgage, the shares were declared to be matured and were used to offset and cancel the loan. In the beginning, this terminated the member's need for the association. He had reached the goal for which he had set out. Other members would continue paying their dues and borrowing funds needed to finance the purchase or construction of their homes. The "last man" would in effect borrow his own savings and hence have no obligation to pay interest. As his obligations were met, the association terminated.

Serial Associations In order not to put a premium upon late joiners in a terminating association, anyone joining after the date of organization was forced to make an initial contributon equal to the existing credits per share. Lack of accumulated capital foreclosed this possibility after the credits were of substantial size. This denied participation to many who would have liked to join the association. With the machinery all set up and in operation, an American idea was added that had not been commonly used in England. Why not start a new series with new members? Thus was the serial association born. In effect it amounted to a succession of terminating associations. Whenever it appeared that there was sufficient demand, a new series was started. This meant increasing the number of meetings, perhaps to one a week instead of one each month.

Managerial duties increased, and the secretary and attorney began to receive compensation in the form of fees. Directors, who supplanted the trustees of early voluntary associations when the corporate form of organization was introduced, still served without compensation. The mere introduction of the use of serial associations did not change the methods of operating these associations. The same methods of lending their money on mortgages were continued.

Savings Members Gradually the need for more attention to the desires of savings members began to be felt in the operation of building associations. In some cases the member who started with full expectations of acquiring a home by this means changed his plans or had them changed for him. Perhaps the lady of his choice said "No" instead of "Yes." There were other members who were not ready to buy or build a home even when the credits to their shares accumulated to a point where they reached their face value. Other thrifty people wanted an opportunity to accumulate savings but had no interest in homeownership. Even the member who had secured a debt-free home through the aid of his building association wished to continue as a member of the association, because he had acquired thrifty habits and liked them.

While homeownership was the major objective of these building associations, there was nothing to prevent a member from taking out cash by the maturity of his shares instead of through the process of giving back a mortgage as evidence of a loan. Hence, the practice of maturing shares in cash gradually developed. Even in such event some members, well satisfied with the returns they had received from their investment, were loath to withdraw the cash due them. They preferred to leave their investment intact or even to add to it as before.

Modern Associations

With the emergence of the savings member who did not borrow from the association, the whole character of the association underwent a radical change. From a purely local community association of friends, anxious to help one another acquire homes, it was on the verge of becoming a financial institution equipped to serve two distinct groups of people, many of whom had no direct interest in the others. On the one hand, there were the thrifty people who needed the assistance of a financial institution equipped to care for their savings against the time when they would be needed for any purpose. On the other hand, another group of people needed financial assistance in financing the homes of their choice. Some might save systematically until they accumulated enough to make the down payment on a home. Thereafter they preferred to make payments on a mortgage debt instead of on share accounts to be later offset against the mortgage. Others might continue to build savings accounts after the mortgage was paid off. Still others preferred to borrow the amount needed over and above the funds accumulated by other means to buy a home.

This change in character broadened the scope of operations and brought other changes in thrift and home-financing institution operations. Among these was a gradual change in name to recognize the new position of savings members. The word "savings" began to be used in some combination with "building" and "loan." Gradually the modern standard pattern of the savings and loan association began to take shape. This is the one most commonly used today, except in Louisiana where those operating under a state charter are still called "homestead associations," and in Massachusetts where the corresponding name is "cooperative bank." This latter name has become so well established that even federal savings and loan associations are commonly spoken of in that state as banks.

With the change in the character of these associations, the older emphasis upon forced savings gradually disappeared. With its disappearance went most of the use of fees, fines, and forfeitures. Investing members were encouraged to bring in their savings in either regular or irregular amounts and at regular or irregular intervals, and to withdraw them as they needed them. Penalties took the form of loss or reduction of income. Borrowers were put on their own responsibility without reference to the performance of other borrowers. Delinquencies were dealt with in terms of those responsible, but losses were not charged against those who met their obligations promptly.

Types of Accounts   With the new emphasis upon savings accounts came a classification of shares into groups that undertook to represent the needs of various types of investors. For the investor whose shares had matured but who nevertheless wished to retain his investment, "full-paid shares" (sometimes called "income shares") were provided. These came to have a face value of $100. Dividends were paid in cash. "Prepaid shares" set a pattern that has since been followed by E bonds issued by the government. Purchased at $75, they matured at $100 through the credit of dividends over a series of years. There is no magic in these amounts: $700 could be left to grow into $1,000; or $360 to grow into $500; and so on. The prepaid share is simply the plan arranged for the lump-sum investor who does not need his dividends in the form of cash as they accrue. Many of these then became full-paid shares. "Installment thrift shares" encouraged the small investor dependent upon earnings to set aside a definite amount each month to add to his account in his savings and loan association. This type of share emphasizes the advantages of regular savings habits. To clinch the argument in their favor, some associations either penalized failure to make all payments on time by the assessment of fines for late payments or rewarded the shareholder who met all payments as scheduled by giving him an extra bonus in the form of an increased dividend payment.

In contrast to the emphasis upon regularity of payments under installment thrift shares, the Dayton plan (originated in Dayton, Ohio) encouraged thrifty people to make additions to their investments when and as their resources permitted. Each account holder established his own pattern of savings, and his contributions were rewarded in proportion to his individual accomplishments. In keeping with the removal of pressure to save, these shares were given the name "optional savings shares." While some associations still favor the practice of encouraging regular savings, most savings and loan associations have long since adopted the practice of accepting savings at the option of their owners.

Savings and loan associations started out as mutual institutions with no distinction among the claims of those who contributed capital. Later, some were organized with a permanent capital in the form of nonwithdrawable "guarantee stock," so-called because it was supposed to serve as a cushion to absorb possible losses which might otherwise have been assessed against ordinary shares. Where guarantee stock was used, its ownership was concentrated in the management. Other investors received as evidence of their commitments a variety of certificates—full-paid, prepaid, installment, accumulative, and so forth. These corresponded to the types of shares already discussed. The accumulative certificate was similar to the Dayton plan share.

Deposits, used by some Ohio associations, were sometimes protected by nonwithdrawable stock. In other cases no cushion of investment was provided, since shares as well as deposits were freely withdrawable. In fact, in many instances shares and deposits were so similar in character that great confusion resulted. Some investors never were sure whether they owned shares or deposits.

In recent years there has been a distinct movement in the direction of simplifying the capital structure of savings and loan associations. The pattern followed by mutual associations—the predominant type—calls for only two types of accounts: savings accounts and investment accounts. The former are optional as to amounts and times of deposit, although systematic saving is still encouraged in some quarters. Earnings are credited to these accounts. Investment accounts serve the needs of lump-sum investors who prefer to receive their earnings distributions in cash.

With the passage of the Housing and Urban Development Act of 1968, savings and loan associations were permitted to use the terms "deposit" and "interest" in place of "share accounts" and "dividends." They were also allowed to issue notes, bonds, debentures, and long-term certificates of deposit for the first time.

Need for a Central System

Out of the Great Depression of the 1930s several weaknesses of home mortgage financing became starkly apparent. Under the heading of causes of financial distress, the following stood out:

1. The instability of real estate values in this country—due to a combination of factors which we need not stop to discuss here—resulted

in low-percentage loans in relation to values. Even normally low percentages were further reduced in periods of economic distress, so that
refinancing became very much restricted when most needed.

2.   Low-percentage first mortgages required supplementary financing
for many real estate owners. This took the form of short-term second
and third mortgages. Refunding of these short-term obligations was
costly under the best of circumstances because of the prevalence of
heavy discounts. Under circumstances which represented less than the
best, mortgagees, fearing the future, pressed for liquidation of their
claims, precipitating numerous foreclosure actions.

3.   The prevalence of short-term primary financing in some sections
of the country resulted in increases in demands for repayment when
the mortgagor had least opportunity for refinancing with other lenders
on mortgage security. Because these short-term mortgages made no provision for amortization, the mortgagees lacked this source of liquidity
with which mortgagors could have been assisted. Unsatisfied demands
for repayment of matured mortgages invited increased foreclosures.

4.   Short-term funds invested in long-term mortgages became frozen
at a time when the demand for the withdrawal of these funds was
greatest. In general, whether a real estate mortgage is written for a
long or a short term, it is to be considered a frozen asset unless the
debt secured by it is actually amortized. If you list the cities where
commercial banks were in greatest difficulties during the early 1930s
and then make another list of localities where banks were heavy lenders
on real estate mortgages, you will find a striking coincidence.

5.   Inefficient and unsystematic appraisal practices resulted in the
virtual purchases of many real estate parcels at the time mortgages
were placed against them. Many lenders had only vague ideas on the
subject of appraisal techniques. They let some of their borrowers make
their appraisals for them by shopping around for loans until they found
the highest bidder for their business. If what is said in this paragraph
seems to be in conflict with what is said under "1," keep this in mind.
Some loans were actually 40 or 50 percent loans. Others, labeled 40
or 50 percent loans, were actually 110 percent loans because of excessive
appraisals. Frequently the amount of the loan was agreed upon, and
the appraisal was adjusted to make the loan fit the announced lending
policy of the mortgagee.

6.   The dependence of real estate lenders upon purely local sources
of loanable funds created an uneven flow of mortgage money in different
parts of the country at the same time. Under normal economic conditions, one city might have a plethora of funds and a dearth of loan
demand; another city might have a great backlog of loan demand and
insufficient funds with which to meet it. In the absence of any kind
of mechanism to shift funds from one section of the country to another

for this purpose, real estate lenders were shut off from access to national capital markets.

7. There was a lack of standards for quality of construction. Lenders did not ordinarily undertake to tell contractors and owners what type of structures to build. Indeed, some of them had no yardstick by which to measure construction quality. They merely responded favorably or unfavorably to applications for loans. Since the nature of the response to such applications was conditioned, in part at least, by their anxiety to put to work the surpluses of cash that they might have on hand, in times of surplus jerry-builders undoubtedly received more encouragement and support than in times of shortages.

8. Too many real estate parcels were held by weak holders who lacked the capacity to meet their obligations when their economic circumstances were disturbed ever so little. Like some of their more fortunate friends and acquaintances, they, too, made an emotional response to the sentimental appeal for homeownership. But lacking the financial resources with which to back up their emotions, they fell easy prey to foreclosure action as soon as the economic road became rough. These foreclosures flooded a market already glutted with unwanted properties, caused wider fluctuations in all real estate values, and raised doubts in the minds of even strong holders about the desirability of investment in real estate.

The Federal Home Loan Bank System

To deal with these and other shortcomings of the thrift and home financing institutions, largely the savings and loan associations, the Federal Home Loan Bank System was created by authority of the Federal Home Loan Bank Act which was approved on July 22, 1932. Operating in twelve districts, encompassing the United States, Puerto Rico, the Virgin Islands, and Guam, the Federal Home Loan Banks function as a central credit facility for all federally chartered savings and loan associations, and on a voluntary basis to qualified state-chartered savings and loan associations, mutual savings banks, and life insurance companies.

Objectives of the Home Loan Bank System   By its design, the Home Loan Bank System, except through the Federal Home Loan Mortgage Corporation as discussed in Chapter 21, does not and cannot inject liquidity into individual mortgages. What it does is to provide liquidity for the institution that holds the mortgage. As a credit reserve system, it is not necessary for it to undertake the difficult task of making mortgages marketable. It merely accepts them as security for advances to members of the Home Loan Bank System. In some cases, unsecured advances are also made.

In providing this service it gives its members an alternative source of funds. Before the Home Loan Bank System was organized, savings and loan associations were accustomed to obtain cash on occasion from the commercial banks of their locality. Usually such loans were collateralized with mortgages held by the borrower. In this manner local banks aided the plans of mortgage lenders materially. One difficulty with such a plan was the limitation of availability of funds at a time when such funds were most urgently needed.

Of necessity, commercial bank loans were made for short periods of time only. They were extended with care in such manner as to protect the lending institution. When the borrower most needed new advances, the lender was least likely to look with favor upon granting them. In addition, such advances as had already been made were likely to be called at most embarrassing times for the borrower.

The Home Loan Bank System was not intended to take business away from local commercial banks. Instead, it was developed for the purpose of providing more dependable liquidity for its members, for a longer period of time, if necessary, than that for which commercial banks could commit their funds. Some members of the Home Loan Bank System still depend upon their local commercial banks for at least a part of their short-term needs for cash. The reasons for this practice are several. In some cases the close relationship between the savings and loan association manager and his banker is so cordial that friendship dictates the use of local bank credit. On other occasions, the local bank may be so anxious to get loans that it will lend money at lower rates of interest than those currently charged by the Home Loan Bank of the district. Even when local banks are used as sources of cash, the member-borrower enjoys the feeling of security that membership in the Home Loan Bank System affords it.

As a precaution against excessive demands by members upon the regional banks, the System regulates interest rate ceilings and liquidity. The interest rate ceilings do much to stabilize the competitive climate for savers' funds, both among associations and with respect to other types of thrift institutions or investment vehicles. Sufficient liquidity reserves of short-term or highly marketable securities held by member institutions cushion the demands upon the regional banks in times of unusual withdrawal demand.

Sources of Home Loan Bank Funds   Since July 2, 1951, all of the stock of Home Loan Banks has been owned by the membership. Subscription requirements are based on the amount of home mortgage loans held by the institution.

In addition to the capital of the Home Loan Banks, other sources of funds consist of:

1.   Consolidated bonds and notes which are sold in the open market by the Home Loan Bank Board as they are needed, with the proceeds

distributed among the various regional banks on the basis of their probable loan demands. These bonds and notes carry such maturity as best seems to meet the needs of the system. Interest rates reflect the cost of money for that type of paper at the time the bonds and notes are issued. By the sale of these bonds and notes, the member institutions have access to the capital markets of the country.

2.   Deposits of members who have excess funds. Demand deposits pay no return to their owners. Interest rates on time deposits vary with the length of time and with the needs of the banks. Recently a new pattern using a definite maturity certificate of deposit has been introduced into the system. Under the theory of system operations, it is expected that excess deposits in one bank can be borrowed by another bank in the system.

Provision for Federal Savings and Loans   Federal chartering of savings and loan associations was originally authorized in the Home Owners Loan Act of 1933. In brief, the act set up a plan for chartering and supervising federal savings and loan associations under the Home Loan Bank Board, which is the senior governing body of the Federal Home Loan Bank System. In addition to newly chartered federal associations, the Board was authorized to set up rules and regulations for converting state-chartered associations into federal associations. At the present time, about 98 percent of the assets of all savings and loan associations are held by members of the Federal Home Loan Bank System. The fact of this broad-encompassing acceptance testifies to the need for this leadership and stabilizing influence.

Nature of Federal Associations   Whereas each state savings and loan association operates under its own local laws, the federal associations are governed by a uniform law. State-chartered associations that have sought membership in the Federal Home Loan Bank System qualify for that membership by meeting standards comparable to those set for the federal associations.

This type of association is intended to be primarily a local thrift and home-financing institution, mutually owned by its investors. Borrowers are given the right to attend shareholders' meetings and to cast one vote each. No deposits may be accepted upon which a definite rate of return is promised. Every federal association is required to be a member of the Home Loan Bank System and is expected to make use of its facilities if and when it can use them to advantage. Borrowing from other sources is much more definitely restricted. In addition, the federal association must have its accounts insured by the Federal Savings and Loan Insurance Corporation.

Loan plans are simplified. In general, federal associations are confined to restricting their loans to residential real estate as security, with enough leeway to take care of community needs for other types of real estate. Not more than $55,000 may be loaned on the security of any one single-family home; limits on multiple-dwelling units are subject to regulation of the Home Loan Bank Board. Also, not over 20 percent of assets may be loaned on other improved real estate without regard to limitations on loan amount and without regard to territorial limits; and, furthermore, additional sums not exceeding 20 percent of the assets of the associations may be used without regard to area restrictions to make or purchase participating interests in loans that are otherwise eligible holdings for federal associations. All such loans must be secured by first liens. In addition, federal associations may invest in bonds and notes of the United States and state and municipal governments, obligations of the Federal National Mortgage Association, stock or debentures of the Home Loan Banks, and National Housing Partnerships, discussed later.

Lending Operations   The specific lending programs of federal savings and loan associations are as follows: (1) Installment loans may be made on homes or on combinations of home and business property up to 75 percent of the appraised value. (A home is defined is a residential property which provides not more than four-family units.) These loans must be repaid in monthly installments within a period of 30 years. With the consent of the members of the association, the ratio of loan to appraised value may be increased to 90 percent. Such loans may also be made up to 95 percent of value, provided the excess over 90 percent is covered with private insurance or the association creates a loss reserve. If the loan is insured or guaranteed by an agency of the United States, it may follow the pattern of insured or guaranteed loans. (2) Term or straight loans may be made for periods not to exceed five years, provided that they do not exceed 50 percent of the appraised value of the property. With the approval of the members, term loans may be made up to three years for an amount not in excess of 60 percent of the appraisal. (3) Loans may be made on other improved real estate for an amount not in excess of 50 percent of the appraised value, to be repaid in monthly installments over a period of not more than 20 years. With the approval of the members, the percentage may be increased for apartment loans to 80 percent of appraised value, provided the loan is amortized in 30 years; it may also be increased to the maximum allowable for insured or guaranteed loans. Associations may make construction loans on the security of apartments or commercial property for periods up to three years. The maximum loan-to-value ratio for loans on commercial property is 75 percent, to be amortized over a period not to exceed 25 years.

Federal associations may invest in leaseholds with a primary or renewal period extending at least 10 years beyond the loan maturity date. They may invest up to 5 percent of total assets directly in real estate located in urban renewal areas and in loans secured by first liens on such property. Direct investments, however, may not exceed 2 percent of total assets. These associations may also make 90 percent loans on first mortgages amortized over 30 years to provide single- and multiple-housing accommodations, including rest and nursing homes, suitable for and limited principally to occupancy by persons over 55 years of age. If their general reserves, surplus, and undivided profits are over 5 percent of withdrawable accounts, federal associations may also lend for land acquisition, site improvement, and developmental housing construction. They may make loans of this type up to 5 percent of their withdrawable accounts. The specific terms and limitations under which the loans are made are subject to regulation by the Home Loan Bank Board. In 1964, the Board regulations provided that development loans could be made up to 70 percent of the appraised value of undeveloped land and improved building site and up to 80 percent of the appraised value of the total property as houses were completed on the sites. The developer was required to begin improvements within nine months of land acquisition and the development loan had to be retired completely by the end of six years. Federal associations may purchase any loans that they are eligible to make. However, loans purchased from affiliated institutions or from an officer or employee must be approved by the Home Loan Bank Board.

In early 1972, the Home Loan Bank Board made a move designed to stimulate lending in poor neighborhoods. It modified its regulations to permit federal associations to make partially amortized loans on residential and commercial buildings. These loans can have maturities of as few as 10 years with monthly installments based on terms as long as 30 years. Since payments under these conditions are smaller than for a straight 10-year mortgage, there is a "balloon" payment required at maturity. Meanwhile, the lender can study the loan and the borrower's performance. If refinancing is justified, the lender may elect to make a new loan at maturity under appropriate terms.

In its 1972 action, the Board also authorized federal associations to make mortgages with diminishing monthly payments. These loans are intended to assist persons nearing retirement. Under this plan, a borrower can make large payments in the 10 years or so before he retires, with smaller payments after his retirement, when his income is lower, until the mortgage is extinguished.

The Consumer Home Mortgage Assistance Act of 1974 increased the lending authority of federal savings and loan associations. For the first time, savings and loan associations were authorized to make line of credit construction loans on residential real estate relying on the borrower's general credit rating or other security. Such loans, however, are not permitted to exceed the greater of (*a*) the sum of surplus, undivided profits, and reserves, or (b) 3 percent of assets. The associations were further authorized to invest, subject to Federal Home Loan Bank Board conditions, in loans, advances of credit, and interests therein for primarily residential purposes, without regard to limitations in existing law. Such investments may not exceed 5 percent of assets. The 1974 act further authorized savings and loans to borrow funds from state mortgage finance agencies and to reloan such borrowings at interest rates not to exceed 1.75 percent of the rate paid the state finance agency.

At the present time, it appears that the whole scope of activities of savings and loan associations is about to undergo sweeping changes. These changes point toward the associations becoming much more like commercial banks with greatly expanded authority. They will be affected by a financial institutions act presently under consideration by the Congress. The details of the changes as now contemplated are outlined in the appendix to Chapter 16.

Lending Policies

As specialists in the field of real estate finance, savings and loan associations are the primary sources of financial assistance for a great many mortgagors. For that reason their lending policies become a matter of great importance to anyone interested in financing real estate. Although each association is managed by its officers and its board of directors, we must first take a look outside of the management if we would understand its lending policies. These are determined in part by general economic conditions, in part by governmental actions, and in part by competitors.

General economic conditions play a major part in setting the lending pattern of any association at a particular time. If the general level of interest rates is low, savings and loan associations must take this into account or go out of business. If new money is coming in slowly, loan applications will be more carefully screened than if idle funds are piling up. If collections of outstanding loans become more difficult because of reduced incomes of borrowers, refinancing of loans for new borrowers will not be as easy. If real estate activity begins to slow down in the face of the maintenance of a high level of cash receipts, the association may be forced to liberalize policy to keep its funds employed.

Governmental actions affect the lending policies of savings and loan associations both positively and negatively. On the negative side, regulatory bodies set boundaries beyond which associations may not go. It is not uncommon to prohibit loans on property located more than 100 miles from the home office of the association. Experience has taught that adequate servicing of loans requires a concentration of security within a readily accessible area. Likewise, similar restrictions prohibit:

the taking of a junior lien as the primary security for a loan; loans on unimproved property; the making of loans without the signed reports of appraisers; loans to officers and directors except on their own homes; loans in excess of statutory or regulatory percentages of loan to appraised value; and so forth.

On the positive side, the actions of government agencies frequently determine the lending policies of savings and loan associations, whether the latter like such actions or not. In recent years, the lending patterns approved by such agencies as the FHA and the Veterans Administration in setting up regulations for GI home loans have set in motion irresistible forces affecting all lenders. Even though the assistance offered by these agencies is not used, lending policies are nevertheless colored by their programs. Relatively lower interest rates, high-percentage loans, prepayment privileges, common use of the monthly payment direct reduction loan plan, and so on, have all been forced upon lenders of all types by governmental agencies.

Competitors, with or without the assistance of governmental agencies, frequently serve notice upon savings and loan managements that they must change their lending policies, "or else." An aggressive management that adopts a liberal lending policy and convinces the potential borrowers in its market that it has a more advantageous lending plan can soon develop imitators among its competitors. Indeed, the competitors who fail to conform to changes which appear to be permanent in character will probably cease to be competitors.

With this background of lending policies to which the management of each association must conform, we now turn to certain elements of a lending program which are subject to the discretion of individual association management.

Loan Rating Systems Savings and loan associations and other lenders on residential housing have consistently sought to improve their loan underwriting practices. A number of institutions now use loan rating systems. Such systems are usually implemented by filling out a loan rating form on each loan applicant. In completion of this form, points are awarded to the potential borrower in accordance with how he scores on a list of weighted criteria that the lending institution has established as crucial to its decision. The borrower's score is then compared with standards set by the lender. In some instances, a lender may approve all applicants above a certain score, reject all below an established lower score, and hold for further consideration all those scoring in between.

The Federal Home Loan Mortgage Corporation has a single-family loan underwriting matrix with primary test criteria relating to documentation of the loan and secondary criteria dealing with credit and appraisal items. The stated goal of this matrix system is to standardize underwriting procedures and to speed loan handling.

Great Western Savings of California has developed a more complex statistical analytical system. On the basis of loans already in the association's portfolio, factors pointing to desirable and undesirable loans were determined. A formula was then developed using 20 weighted single-family mortgage loan characteristics to compute the degree of risk involved in making a particular loan.

Arguments for development and adoption of a good rating system are strong. Such a system should assist in:

1. Identifying and not mistakenly rejecting sound loans.
2. Evaluating risk of default.
3. Ranking for quality when lendable funds are rationed.
4. Uniformity in application of lending standards.
5. Reduction of underwriting costs by quick elimination of patently undesirable loans.
6. Documentation of reasons for approval or rejection.

Mortgage loan ratings forms are most useful for screening loan applicants where initial interviewing is done at branch offices by under-qualified personnel. Any type of rating form, because it is based on historical data, will tend to ignore many potentials, good or bad, for the borrower. These can only be taken into account by the interveiwer's additional comments. The rating form will not reflect health factors or domestic relations problems unless these subjects are an item of special inquiry. No scoring model can be developed to deal with all types of customers for various loan purposes. Some borrowers may be too old for the type of loan requested; or the predictability of their income may not be high enough. Some institutions do not use a rating form because they want their loan officers to develop expertise by making their own personal borrower evaluations.

The act of filling out a loan rating form will point out the typical items considered and the weights assigned to each item. Students desiring to study the application of such a form are invited to complete the case problem at the end of this chapter. The form shown there was developed by the U.S. League of Savings Associations. A number of institutions have picked a score of about half the points possible as the minimum acceptable for loan approval. On that basis, for the form shown at the end of the case, a score of 28 to 30 would be marginal. The precise loan cut-off point to be used by an institution is a management decision, which is affected by how the form is used.

Interest Rates For many years the percentage of loan to appraised value was commonly used to measure and to offset the risk element of what were then considered to be unusually risky loans. As already indicated in an earlier part of this chapter, fairly low ceilings of loan percentages were established both by managements and by regulatory bodies. Higher risk loans might be financed below these ceilings. Interest rates were fixed with less regard to risks assumed. They were likely to be standardized for all loans granted within any economic period. Even today, some associations charge the same rate of interest on all conventional loans. Their managements seem to feel that they cannot justify variations in rates or that they should just as well charge rates that are commonly accepted in their markets. Because such rates are likely to be higher than those charged on FHA and GI loans, some associations refuse to make insured or guaranteed loans.

Other associations use the interest rate as a means of compensating for risks assumed in making real estate loans. On this basis, loans that entail greater risks and costs are required to pay higher interest rates. Small loans, even though lacking the element of great risk, may still be charged the higher rate because of the higher costs per dollar of bookkeeping, servicing, and so on. Associations which use various interest rates on mortgage loans frequently start with a base rate on a loan equal to perhaps 40 percent of the appraised value, using as security property in good neighborhoods built less than 12 years before and with low moral hazard. Additions to this base rate to compensate for added risks are sometimes established more or less on a rule-of-thumb basis. In other cases, an elaborate schedule is used which takes into account such items as: tenant- or owner-occupancy; specific age of property; design and construction of main buildings; maturity of loan; location of security; loan percentage; life insurance protection with mortgagee as beneficiary as his interest may appear; amount and apparent stability of income of borrower; other obligations of borrower; special hazards; and so forth.

Those who have used discriminatory interest rates on mortgage loans have found little difficulty in explaining to their borrowers the reasons for this practice. These interest rates are like the prices of shoes. Shoes can be purchased at from $5 to $50 or more a pair, depending upon the quality. Discriminatory interest rates measure qualitative differences in service rendered to borrowers. To the occasional borrower who might question whether discrimination is being practiced against him, the association should be able to state the conditions under which his loan too will merit the lower rate of interest. In some cases interest rates are reduced, with or without the request of the borrower, when risks are reduced through amortization of the loan balance.

One factor that influences the level of interest charges on real estate loans is the amount and aggressiveness of competition. If competition is weak or absent, higher rates may be charged. If the race for available mortgage loans is close, rates may be cut by the successful bidder. When mortgagors recognize this possibility, they may shop around for low rates as they sometimes do for liberal loans.

Savings and Loan Service Corporations

Savings and loan associations in recent years have been permitted to spin off service corporations. Such corporations may engage in many areas of business activity denied the parent corporation. A mere listing of allowable areas suggests the great potential in this direction. Of particular interest in real estate finance are:

1. Originating and servicing real estate loans, even under less restrictive conditions than those imposed upon the association.
2. Purchasing, servicing, and brokering mobile home loans.
3. Making combined loans on property improvement and household furnishings.
4. Investing in National Housing Corporation loans.[1]
5. Providing consulting and allied professional services, including appraisal, maintenance and management, construction loan inspection, bulk purchasing, and advertising.
6. Acting as agent or broker in areas of hazard and title insurance.

Although the service corporations are fairly new to the savings and loan industry, they have shown a significant degree of success in generating new loans and participations which are, in turn, often passed on to their parent corporations. It should also be noted that with the passing of the financial institutions act, now in an advanced stage of congressional review, savings and loan associations themselves will have broader powers. This eventuality will probably thrust the financial service corporations into the more specialized areas.

Private Mortgage Insurance Companies

Of increasing importance to savings and loan associations has been a capability to make higher percentage loans with safety. A welcome response to this need has been the emergence of private mortgage insurance. Where buyers have been reluctant to seek FHA/VA government assistance, if in fact they were eligible, and both borrowers and lenders have sought to avoid delays and paperwork, private mortgage insurors have offered attractive alternatives. So rapid has been the growth that, since 1971, private mortgage insurance has been covering more new 1–4 family mortgage loans each year than the FHA/VA programs.

---

[1] See discussion of the National Corporation for Housing Partnerships in Chapter 20.

History   Prior to the provision of mortgage insurance by the federal government during the 1930s, the field was exclusively occupied by private companies. These companies sold insurance coverage principally on mortgage loans on large commercial and high-rise apartment buildings with little or no emphasis on insurance on loans for single-family dwellings. Further, their operations were for the most part on a regional basis with inadequate regulation, and the insured loans were not regularly amortized. Under the impact of the Great Depression, these firms either failed or ceased operations as a matter of good judgment.

From the depression period until 1957, the mortgage insurance and guarantee field was left to the federal government with its Federal Housing Administration and Veterans Administration programs. In 1957, however, the Mortgage Guaranty Insurance Corporation was organized and licensed by the Wisconsin Insurance Commissioner. It is now authorized to do business nationwide. From the time of its organization to December 31, 1974, its insurance in force has increased sharply, amounting to $20.7 billion at the 1974 year-end. The business is generated about equally from new housing and from sale of existing homes. The bulk of the company's business has been with savings and loan associations. Recently, however, a growing number of banks, credit unions, and insurance companies have been using this protection. There are several private insurance companies from which private and federal institutions accept insurance in their conventional loan programs. The Mortgage Guaranty Insurance Corporation is the most important, however, by a wide margin. It accounts for over 60 percent of the loans insured by private companies.

Method of Operation   These companies offer insurance to approved mortgage lenders against financial loss on first mortgage loans where mortgagors fail to make required payments. This insurance is ordinarily not utilized unless the loan exceeds 80 percent of appraised value. Mortgage Guaranty Insurance Corporation coverage, for instance, insures the top 20 percent of the mortgage loan regardless of balance, to a maximum limit of 95 percent of appraisal value. Such protection makes it possible for lenders to increase the volume of conventional loans by lending at loan-to-value ratios that would be excluded under their normal lending policies.

An institution becomes an approved lender by applying to an insurer and having a master policy issued in its favor. Factors considered by the insurance company as part of its approval process include: size, supervisory history with regulatory agencies, appraisal experience and qualifications, operating policy, and membership in the Federal Savings and Loan Insurance Corporation or (for commercial banks) the Federal Deposit Insurance Corporation. Most applicants have been savings and loan associations, although commercial banks, mutual savings banks, and mortgage bankers are also extensive users of the service.

By the terms of the master policy, a "default" is declared when payments have not been made for four months. The insured institution must give notice to the insurer within ten days after the insured loan has become in default. The insurer may then direct the insured institution to initiate appropriate legal proceedings. In any event, the proceedings must be instituted within nine months of the time the loan first went into arrears. Within 60 days after completion of the legal proceedings, the insured institution files notice of loss and conveys its title to the insured. The amount of loss payable to the insured institution includes the principal balance due under the mortgage, back interest, real estate taxes, hazard insurance premiums, all expenses incurred in preservation of the property, and all legal expenses, including court costs and reasonable attorney's fees. In the determination of the loss payable, the insurer may exercise an option not to acquire the property, but to leave it with the insured institution, and thereby limit liability to 20 percent of the allowable claim. The effect of this option is to shift the risk of 80 percent of the allowable claim to the institutional lender, which for satisfaction of its claim must look to the value of the property it has as security.

These insurance companies approve only loans that meet their underwriting standards. When approved, one of two types of loan policies will normally be issued. The policy most frequently used provides for a year term with annual renewals, called the "annual plan." The premium for the first year is 1 percent of the amount of the loan; and for succeeding years it is ¼ of 1 percent of the declining balance of the loan. Under the second plan, a single premium is paid in the amount of 2½ percent of the initial amount of the loan to cover a ten-year term. The premium under all plans is paid by the borrower. The policies are subject to cancellation by the insured institution, and it may then receive a partial refund of premium. The insurance companies also require that the borrower pay an appraisal fee of $20 to accompany each application for insurance where the loan exceeds 80 percent of appraised value. This fee provides a fund to finance additional appraisals by agents of the insurer to verify the quality of the lender's appraisals.

Extension of Coverage   Private insurance companies now cover over 14 percent of the total home mortgage debt outstanding. It is also interesting to note that they are now extending this type of insurance to multifamily, commercial, and industrial properties. Commercial Loan Insurance Corporation, a subsidiary of MGIC Investment Corporation, for example, extends loans to every type of commercial and industrial real estate, including shopping centers, factories, nursing homes, retail stores, and warehouses. As in insurance of home mortgages, the protection extends to the top 20 percent of the outstanding loan balance. A five-year noncancellable policy may be purchased for a single premium of 2.9 percent of the loan, or for an annual premium of 1.2 percent of the loan for the first year and ½ of 1 percent of the outstanding principal balance at the beginning of each year thereafter. The renewal premium is ½ of 1 percent of the outstanding principal balance at the beginning of each renewal term.

Lease guarantee insurance has been assuming importance in recent years. It has been typical in the financing of shopping centers and other commercial or industrial developments that the bulk of the mortgage payments be covered by prime tenants. These tenants, occupying a major part of the space, therefore command lower rental rates because of the developer's reliance upon their credit. Since many mortgage lenders will accept minor lessees whose leases are insured in lieu of a prime tenant, there is often an advantage in increasing the occupancy percentage for insured minor tenants and cutting back the space alloted to major tenants. The insurance premium is usually only a fraction of the differential gain from the higher rents obtained through the shift in space allocation.

The possible advantage of lease guarantee insurance may be illustrated by assuming alternative uses of a 100,000 square foot warehouse costing $1 million. This space may be rented to:

1. An AAA-1 tenant for $95,000 annually, or 9.5 percent; or
2. Two minor tenants at a combined rental of $120,000, or 12 percent. To qualify with the lender on the warehouse mortgage, however, these tenants must be covered by lease guarantee insurance.

Over a 15-year span, at $25,000 per year higher rentals, the lesser tenants would pay the developer/owner $375,000 more in rentals than would be received from the AAA-1 tenant. The cost of the insurance for the two minor tenants might run $50,000. Deducting this amount from the rental advantage of $375,000 still leaves a net cumulative overage of $325,000 in favor of the second alternative.

Risk   The character of the risk inherent in private mortgage insurance is well-stated in a prospectus filed in 1961 with the United States Securities and Exchange Commission by Mortgage Guaranty Insurance Corporation:

In common with insurers of other types of risk, the mortgage loan insurer proceeds on the assumption that past experience, adjusted for applicable changes in conditions, will prevail on average in the future.

Application of this basic assumption to the field of mortgage loan insurance is believed to involve substantially greater dependence on broad estimates, and consequently less likelihood of accuracy, than most other forms of insurance. Losses on first mortgage loans do not necessarily follow a generally steady and reasonably predictable pattern from year to year. Under favorable economic conditions, losses are likely to be small. The great risk in the residential mortgage loan insurance field would appear to be a period of adverse general economic conditions of substantial duration. However, a localized depression affecting an area in which a significant amount of loans has been insured might also affect its operations materially. . . . Whether and when a period of adverse economic conditions will occur and the extent of the losses which may be suffered by first mortgage residential lenders and insurers are all unpredictable.[2]

How the inherent risk is being dealt with in Wisconsin is described in a 1963 prospectus of the Mortgage Guaranty Insurance Corporation:

Regulations of the Wisconsin Insurance Department require MGIC to maintain two separate reserves for losses, a case basis reserve and a contingency reserve. . . . The contingency reserve is designed to protect against the effect of adverse economic cycles. MGIC is required to credit to this reserve (by charges of surplus and not to income) an amount equal to 50% of all premiums earned. Subject to the approval of the Wisconsin Commissioner of Insurance, this reserve is available for payment of losses to the extent losses in a given year exceed 30% of the premiums earned in that year. Funds credited to the contingency reserve, to the extent not used in payment of losses, must remain in the reserve for fifteen years.[3]

A recent study was made under the direction of Dr. Chester Rapkin, former chairman of the Urban Studies Group of the Institute of Environmental Studies and professor of finance at the Wharton School of Finance and Commerce at the University of Pennsylvania, to determine the soundness of the MGIC insurance protection. By computer analysis, MGIC was subjected in "model" form to 30 different combinations of foreclosure experience and economic decline. The study concluded that the company ". . . appears to have the size and balance to withstand immediate catastrophic losses, and only with assumptions of acute and unprecedented mortgage foreclosures exceeding even the worst period of the 1930s does the simulation analysis place the model company in jeopardy."

In April 1975 Professor Rapkin's conclusions were confirmed in a report by Arthur D. Little, Inc., the well-known business consultants. This report emerged from a 14-month study of the private mortgage insurance business for the U.S. Department of Housing and Urban Development, the Federal National Mortgage Association, and the Federal Home Loan Mortgage Corporation. Testing economic models from "optimistic" to "doomsday," the researchers concluded that the twelve private mortgage insurors used in the study—including MGIC—could

---

[2] "Prospectus," Mortgage Guaranty Insurance Corporation, October 17, 1961, p. 5.

[3] "Prospectus," Mortgage Guaranty Insurance Corporation, May 14, 1963, pp. 17–18.

survive severe economic reversals. The report stated, in part, "... it appears probable that the typical MIC (mortgage insurance company) could survive economic conditions like those which led to the Great Depression if they were to present themselves in the future."[4]

The question will always remain whether the reserves are sufficient to meet the requirements of a future occasion. Should the reserves run short, there is not the availability of Congress to appropriate for inadequacies in protection that are considered a likelihood in the case of the federal underwriting programs.

QUESTIONS

1. What were the origins of the savings and loan association?
2. What were terminating associations and how did they differ from serial associations?
3. Describe the share-accumulation sinking-fund loan plan.
4. Under the practices of early associations, what penalties were assessed against a member who withdrew from the organization before completion of the project for which the association was organized?
5. What were Dayton plan associations, and how did they expand the scope of savings and loan activities?
6. What weaknesses existed in the home mortgage financing structure in the early 1930s?
7. What are the objectives of the Federal Home Loan Bank System and how does it accomplish these objectives?
8. In addition to equity capital, what other sources of funds do the Federal Home Loan Banks have?
9. What are the chief factors affecting lending policies of savings and loan associations?
10. Why do savings and loan associations prefer to make loans on single-family dwellings over other forms of residential or commercial real estate?
11. Why do these institutions make loans on nonresidential properties, and under what restrictions do they operate?
12. What has been the trend of the percentage of loan to appraised value in recent years, and what conditions have influenced this trend?
13. What justification can you give for granting savings and loan associations broader lending powers? What recent changes in this direction have been made? See appendix to Chapter 16.

CASE PROBLEMS

1. A developer is planning a 400,000 square foot shopping center. He is considering two plans of tenant recruitment:

Plan 1:   Lease 70% of the space to major tenants at $3.50 per square foot and the remaining 30% to local tenants at $6.00 per square foot.
Plan 2:   Lease 60% of the space to major tenants at $3.50 per square foot

---

[4] *MGIC Fact Book, 1975,* Mortgage Guaranty Insurance Corporation, MGIC Plaza, Milwaukee, Wisconsin, p. 22.

and the remaining 40% to local tenants at $6.00 per square foot. To obtain the credit equivalent of Plan 1 from the mortgage lender, lease guarantee insurance would have to be taken out costing $100,000.

Evaluate the alternative plans for tenant allocation.

2.   Mr. and Mrs. Arthur Green are applying to Home Savings and Loan Association to refinance a loan of $25,000 at 9% for about 25 years with monthly payments of $210. The property is located on a regular-sized lot in an exclusively residential neighborhood developed over the past 5 years and still under development. The savings and loan appraiser has valued the property at $32,000, which is slightly under average for the community. Real estate taxes and hazard insurance are, respectively, $750 and $300 annually.

Mr. and Mrs. Green are both in their early 30s with 3 children of elementary school age. Mr. Green has been employed by the Sun City Fire Department for 3 years. His current salary is $15,000 per year. Mr. Green has also operated his own life insurance agency for 3 years, netting about $5,000 per year before income tax. His overall income tax rate is 25%. Mrs. Green does not work outside the home.

Mr. and Mrs. Green currently owe about $8,000 in installment debt. They are making monthly payments on this debt totaling $450.

The Green personal balance sheet indicates assets and liabilities and proprietorship as follows:

Assets		Liabilities and Proprietorship	
Cash and savings	$ 2,000	Credit card debt	$ 500
Note receivable	3,000	Installment debt	8,000
Common stocks	1,000	Home mortgage debt	25,000
Life insurance—cash			
surrender value	1,000	Green—proprietorship	18,500
Investment—life insurance			
agency	5,000		
Automobiles	4,000		
Family residence	32,000		
Household goods	4,000		
Total	$52,000		$52,000

Mr. Green carries $75,000 of life insurance—$50,000 in a whole life policy and $25,000 in term insurance. The Greens have maintained savings accounts at the Home Savings and Loan Association averaging $1,500 since 1970. The present balance is $1,200. Bank and mortgage company references show payments have been made as agreed. The Greens have lived at their present address for the past four years.

Required: 1.   Evaluate the foregoing loan application using the following mortgage loan rating form.
            2.   Consider the advantages and limitations of the rating form. What does it fail to take into account in this case?

LOAN RATING FORM °

BORROWER'S NAME_____

CO-BORROWER'S NAME_____

ANNUAL INCOME (First Borrower)

Income from Primary Employment $ _____

Income from Secondary Employment   _____

Overtime Bonuses, etc.   _____

Other Income from Investments, etc.   _____

GROSS ANNUAL INCOME $ _____

ANNUAL INCOME (Second Borrower)

Income from Primary Employment $ _____

Income from Secondary Employment   _____

Overtime Bonuses, etc.   _____

Other Income from Investments, etc.   _____

GROSS ANNUAL INCOME $ _____

TOTAL GROSS ANNUAL INCOME OF
BOTH CO-BORROWERS $ _____

Less Total Annual Debt
(excluding mortgage payment)   _____

TOTAL NET ANNUAL INCOME $ _____

CARRY–CHARGE RATIO
Total net annual income from above divided
by the monthly mortgage payment, includ-
ing tax and insurance reserve .... $ _____

1. CARRY–CHARGE RATIO

Under 40 = 0
41–50   = 1
51–55   = 2
55–60   = 3
61–69   = 4
70–75   = 5
76–80   = 6
Over 80   = 7

SCORE: _____

° Reprint is permitted by courtesy of the U.S. League of Savings Associations.

2. DOLLAR AMOUNT PRESENTLY OWED ON
    SHORT-TERM DEBT WITH CO-BORROWERS
    (REVOLVING CHARGE ACCOUNTS, CREDIT
    CARDS, ETC.) THIS DOES *NOT* INCLUDE
    OBLIGATIONS SHOWN IN TOTAL ANNUAL
    DEBT FIGURE INDICATED ABOVE
    TOTAL AMOUNT OF SHORT-TERM DEBT

    More than 25% of net monthly salary = 0
    10–24% of net monthly salary   = 1
    0–9% of net monthly salary   = 2

    SCORE _____

3. AGE OF BORROWERS

    Under 23 = 0
    24–26   = 1
    27–29   = 2
    30–33   = 3
    34–38   = 4
    39–49   = 5
    50–54   = 3
    55–65   = 2
    Over 65 = 0

    SCORE _____

4. NUMBER OF DEPENDENTS OTHER THAN SPOUSE

    0 dependents   = 1
    1 or 2 dependents = 4
    3–5 dependents   = 2
    5 or more   = 0

    SCORE _____

5. OCCUPATION

    Unskilled workers
      and commissioned salesman   = 0
    Salaried salesmen   = 1
    Self–employed (nonprofessional) = 1
    White-collar workers   = 2
    Skilled labor   = 2
    City government employees   = 3
    Federal government employees   = 3
    Professionals   = 5

    SCORE _____

6. EMPLOYMENT RECORD

    Less than 2 years on job = 0
    2–5 years   = 1
    5–10 years   = 2
    10 or more years   = 3

    SCORE _____

7. CREDIT REFERENCES
        Small loan companies &
          auto finance companies   = 0
        Credit card companies   = 1
        Retail trade & merchants   = 2
        Bank & mortgage companies = 3

                                       SCORE _____

8. ATTITUDE TOWARD OBLIGATIONS
        Credit report shows many slow
        pays—judgments, bankruptcy   = 0
        1 or 2 slow pays   = 2
        No slow pays—as agreed   = 4
        Better than agreed   = 6
        Cash buyer   = 7

                                         SCORE _____

9. TERM OF LOAN
        26 years and over = 0
        15–25 years   = 1
        Under 15 years   = 2

                                         SCORE _____

10. LOAN PURPOSE
        Refinance   = 0
        Purchase or construction = 2

                                         SCORE _____

11. MARKETABILITY OF PROPERTY
        Poor   = 0
        Average = 1
        Good   = 2

                                         SCORE _____

12. WILL THE LOAN BE COVERED BY PRIVATE MORTGAGE INSURANCE? (THIS QUESTION TO BE USED ONLY ON LOANS IN EXCESS OF 80% OF VALUE.)
        Yes = 3
        No = 0

                                         SCORE _____

13. AGE OF PROPERTY
        Over 50 years,
          no remodernization = 0
        21–50 years,
           no remodernization = 1
        10–20 years   = 2
        New to 10 years   = 3

                                         SCORE _____

14. EQUITY IN PROPERTY
                  5% or less = 0
                  6–10%   = 1
                  11–15%   = 2
                  16–20%   = 3
                  21–25%   = 4
                  26–30%   = 5
                  31–50%   = 6
                  Over 50%   = 7
                                                  SCORE _____
15. PROPERTY TO BE OCCUPIED BY
                  Owner = 2
                  Other = 0
                                                  SCORE _____

                                          TOTAL SCORE _____

16

Financing of Real Estate by Banks

Current Real Estate Lending by Banks

In this chapter are discussed real estate lending practices of three kinds of banks: mutual savings banks, state-chartered commercial banks, and national banks. Since the policies of all commercial banks have much in common, they will be discussed as one class, except for the differences noted below. Real estate mortgages are expected to involve long-term commitment of funds, regardless of the specific terms for which mortgages are written. Therefore, it is to be expected that both experience and regulations should dictate that only capital, surplus, and time deposits be used by commercial banks for making real estate loans. Since mutual savings banks are not looked upon in the same light as commercial banks, most deposits in the former are considered to be time deposits.

As of December 31, 1975, the total savings and time deposits of all banks in this country were $555 billion. Of this total, commercial banks held $445 billion and mutual savings banks $110 billion. The relatively small number of saving banks, scattered throughout the country, that are owned by stockholders are classed as commercial banks for our purposes, since their operations more nearly parallel those of state-chartered commercial banks than of mutual savings banks.

The real estate mortgage holdings of all banks as of December 31,

1975, are set forth in Exhibit 16–1. It is interesting to note the concentration of real estate mortgages on residential property as security, with commercial loans in second position and farm real estate in third.

EXHIBIT 16–1
Mortgage Holdings of All Banks as of December 31, 1975 (in $ billion)

	Nonfarm Residential	*Farm*	*Commercial*	*Total*
Commercial Banks	$ 83.2	$6.4	$45.5	$135.1
Mutual Savings Banks	63.7	.1	13.3	77.1
Total	$146.9	$7.5	$58.8	$212.2

Source: *Federal Reserve Bulletin,* March 1976, p. A42.

MUTUAL SAVINGS BANKS

Origin of Mutual Savings Banks[1]

The origin of mutual savings banks in this country has much in common with the origin of savings and loan associations. Both had their impetus outside of the group to be served. Like their predecessors in England and on the continent of Europe, the clergy, philanthropically minded people, and others interested wished to encourage thrifty habits and frugality among the growing numbers of working people. The sponsors of these "frugality banks" recognized the need for institutions which could care for the savings of those dependent upon wages for a living against the time when incomes might be reduced for one reason or another. Even the names of some of the early savings banks attempt to describe their purposes. The first to start business in this country was the Philadelphia Savings Fund Society, which opened for business in the fall of 1816. It is fitting that the first institution of this kind should have been started in the city made famous by the thrift teachings of Poor Richard. This was soon followed by the Provident Institute for Savings, started in Boston in the spring of 1817. The idea of such banks soon spread to other cities. All contemporary accounts of their operation lay emphasis upon the services rendered to humble people of small means who would probably squander their earnings except for the exhortations of savings banks to save something against the time of need.

[1] See also the monograph prepared for the Commission of Money and Credit titled *Mutual Savings Banking* (Englewood Cliffs, N.J.: Prentice-Hall, Inc., 1962).

Concentration of Mutual Savings Banks[2]

Today mutual savings banks are found in only 17 states and Puerto Rico. Most of them are concentrated in three states—Massachusetts, New York, and Connecticut. In these three states, savings banks have attracted much more savings funds than have all other types of banks and savings and loan associations combined. Outside New England New York, New Jersey, Delaware, Pennsylvania, and Maryland, there are only a few mutual savings banks—8 in the Middle West and 11 in the far West, including Alaska. The three states first mentioned above account for nearly three fourths in number and more than that in proportion of assets of all mutual savings banks in the country. On December 31, 1975, Massachusetts had 166 savings banks; New York, 118; Connecticut, 67; other New England states, collectively, 72; New Jersey, 20; Pennsylvania, 8; Delaware, 2; and Maryland, 3. Outside of this area, the other locations are: Indiana, 4; Wisconsin, 3; Minnesota, 1; Washington, 8; Oregon, 1; Alaska, 2; and Puerto Rico, 1.

Management of Mutual Savings Banks

Savings banks have no stockholders. By a broad use of language, their owners are called "depositors." The return they receive upon their investments is called "interest" in spite of the fact that no one makes a commitment to pay them a fixed return. There is no backstop of stock to protect deposits against the shocks of losses. As a mutual institution only, the deposits, plus whatever reserves have been retained in the business to absorb losses, may be looked to for the purpose of meeting the effects of unusual losses.

Since the depositors are not considered to be stockholders, they have no voice in the management of their own funds. This task is entrusted to a self-perpetuating board of trustees. The original board was selected by the organizers of the bank. Vacancies resulting from resignations, deaths, or other causes are filled by the remaining board members. This system has worked quite satisfactorily over the years. In actual practice it differs only in form from the manner of selecting the boards of directors of many American corporations whose stockholders enjoy voting rights that are seldom or never exercised. In such corporations, boards of directors are virtually self-perpetuating bodies.

Growth of Savings Banks

There can be no question about the need for savings banks, the

---

[2] Important data for this discussion were derived from the 1976 *National Fact Book of Mutual Savings Banking,* National Association of Mutual Savings Banks, 200 Park Avenue, New York, N.Y. 10017. Updating may be accomplished by reference to later annual publications of this fact book.

quality of the services rendered, or the nature of the responses by the people who took advantage of these services. The number of such banks increased steadily for a time, both in total assets and in number of depositors. The number of banks grew steadily until it reached a maximum about 100 years ago. Since then the number of banks has shown a considerable decline which is especially marked in recent years.

In 1820 there were ten mutual savings banks in the United States with total assets of $1 million. The number increased to a peak of 674 in 1875, when total assets amounted to $850 million. Since that date the number has declined to a low of 476 in 1975. By the end of 1975, total assets amounted to about $121 billion.

Undoubtedly the growth of savings and loan associations and savings departments of commercial banks played their part in other sections of the country, leaving the bulk of savings business in the above-described "savings bank" area to the mutual savings banks. The recent rapid growth of federal savings and loan associations in New York and New England suggests that there may be other reasons for the failure of savings banks to expand into new areas in recent years.

Savings Banks and Their Investors

Since the owners of deposits in mutual savings banks expect to withdraw their savings on demand, the banks must operate in such a manner as to meet these requirements. The laws under which they operate permit them to "go on notice" for 30 to 90 days before paying withdrawal demands. Except in times of emergency, they make no use of this protection. To make common use of it would discourage patronage. While some banks have suffered more than others, in general, withdrawal demands have not frequently been unduly burdensome to most savings banks. Since withdrawals are closely associated with confidence of the investors, the strong reputation of savings banks has helped to keep down "fear" withdrawals.

For the protection of safety of deposits, the states in which savings banks operate have enacted laws restricting the investments of such institutions to "legals" which are supposed to be of high quality. Within statutory limits that set forth the categories of investment opportunities available to savings banks, the management has wide latitude of choice in selecting what seems to it to serve best its requirements for safety, liquidity, and return.

Restrictions upon Real Estate Lending

All mutual savings banks receive their charters from states. The laws regulating their operation represent quite a wide range of patterns in their mortgage-lending programs. The ratio of maximum loan to value varies from 50 to 90 percent (except for FHA and GI loans).

Savings banks are also subject to restrictions on the percentage of assets or deposits that may be placed in mortgages. In New York, the maximum amount of conventional mortgage loans that may be held by a savings bank is 65 percent of the assets of the bank. There is no ceiling, however, on the proportion of assets that may be invested in FHA or VA loans. In Massachusetts, generally, 70 percent of deposits may be invested in mortgages, plus an additional 15 percent of deposits in federally underwritten mortgages. Similarly, in Connecticut 85 percent of assets may be invested in mortgage loans, but all loans in excess of 70 percent of assets must be FHA or VA.

State laws regulate maximum terms for loans, as well as other characteristics. New York provides the terms on its "90 percent" loans shall not exceed three fourths of the useful life of the property or 30 years, whichever is less. Massachusetts and Connecticut have a 25-year maximum term for their "80 percent" loans.

Because trustees of mutual savings banks are traditionally conservative, self-imposed restrictions may be even more rigid than those imposed by law. In general they prefer loans on single-family dwellings. Only the largest institutions, whose investment funds present constant pressure for investment, get into the fields of investment in apartment-house, commercial, and industrial mortgages.

Lending territories are usually determined by their short distance from the home office, so that the problems of servicing will not be so difficult as they are when property securing mortgage loans is located at great distances. In recent years the pressure of investment funds has recommended removal of distance restrictions when mortgage loans are insured by the FHA or are guaranteed by the VA. In New York state, where more than half of all assets of mutual savings banks are located, recent changes in legislation governing lending territory have been expanded to permit such banks to make even conventional loans in the neighboring states of Connecticut, Massachusetts, New Jersey, Pennsylvania, Rhode Island, and Vermont. Similarly, Massachusetts and Connecticut may make loans in their own and adjoining states. In the case of the latter states, however, the loans must be located in a city or town situated within a specified distance of the bank. By way of contrast, there are no state territorial limitations for savings banks located in some other states such as Delaware, Maryland, Pennsylvania, Rhode Island, Vermont, and Washington. In all cases, geographic limitations do not apply to FHA and VA loans.

Mortgage Experience of Savings Banks

Before the depression of the 1930s, savings banks had long been the major source of mortgage money in the areas in which they operated. From the time that savings banks became significant caretakers of savings funds until the 1930 depression, real estate mortgages had been looked upon with favor as satisfactory investment outlets for funds deposited with them. During the last quarter of the last century and the first three decades of this one, mortgages always absorbed at least a third and frequently as much as half of the total resources of savings banks. After 1932 the mortgages held by all savings banks in the United States decreased year by year. While there was some recovery in the decade of the 1940s, by the middle of that decade the total amount of mortgages in their portfolios was still less than in the previous decade. Meantime, corresponding figures for savings and loan associations on a national basis showed an increase of approximately two thirds. The percentage increase in residential mortgages held by insurance companies from the middle 1930s to the middle 1940s was even greater.

Changes in Policy The factors that accounted for this change in policy concerning real estate mortgages as investments are not too clearly defined in the record. Patriotic desire to help finance the needs of the government during World War II undoubtedly played some part. The decline in the demand for real estate financial assistance was also a factor. The supply of real estate buyers had undoubtedly declined for a part of this period, while the supply of government bonds for most of it was ample to meet all requirements. During this period, interest rates on mortgage loans declined somewhat, but government bond interest rates declined relatively more.

The above evidence leads to the conclusion that, for reasons best known to their managements, the savings banks definitely decided to restrict their holdings of real estate mortgages. This of course was their right. The only purpose of emphasizing it here is to show that borrowers had that much of their opportunities contracted. They were required to look elsewhere for real estate financial assistance.

Reasons for Decline The search for the reasons for the decline in the volume of real estate mortgages held by savings banks suggests two outstanding conclusions. In the first place, their managements resisted strongly the acceptance of "newfangled" lending plans. Long accustomed to the use of one-year or demand mortgages, the savings banks with some reluctance made a concession to the popularity of competitors' loan plans when they secured legislative permission to write loans for three years instead of one. At the end of three years such mortgages were frequently kept alive as demand instruments. The monthly payment direct reduction loan plan did not immediately appeal to savings bank managers even after further changes in legislation permitted them to use it. Likewise, the high percentage loans made by federal savings and loan associations and other competitors did not cast a shadow which was heeded by savings banks. Even their legislative authority to make

FHA loans—which were high-percentage, monthly payment, direct reduction loans for the most part—was not freely used.

In the second place, it does not appear that this loss of mortgage business was accompanied by any great measure of regret. Perhaps it would be more accurate to state that savings banks were willing to lose mortgage business rather than to compete for it, under the terms desired by borrowers and aggressively offered by competitors. During the depression they had suffered losses from this type of investment even though they had limited their loans to low percentages of appraised value and even though they had the legal right to demand repayment of the debt at their convenience. The loss suffered on mortgage loans was relatively greater than on all other types of investments. In the face of this experience, they hesitated to grant high percentage loans whose repayment could not so easily be demanded because the new and more popular loan contract did not fix a maturity date for the entire amount advanced.

Since about 1947, savings banks have generally experienced another change in attitude toward mortgage investments, particularly those insured by the FHA or guaranteed by the VA. This change was due in part to a desire to decrease their holdings of U.S. government bonds. When they liquidated sizable quantities of governments, they again turned to corporate bonds and to real estate mortgages as outlets for their funds.

Meanwhile, their continued growth posed investment problems, which were solved in part by a return to favoritism of mortgages. Less than one fourth of their assets were in mortgages at the end of World War II. By 1954, about one half of their assets were in mortgages. In 1960, the ratio of mortgage loans to total assets ranged from about one half in Pennsylvania, Maryland, and Maine, to nearly three fourths in New York and Vermont. During the period from 1965 to 1975, of total net uses of funds received by mutual savings banks amounting to $49.8 billion the amount channeled into residential mortgages totaled $34.2 billion, or 69 percent.

Several factors have combined to make mortgages especially attractive to savings banks. Regular amortization, improved marketability, better yields than were otherwise available, and federal underwriting have provided liquidity and earning power in the same investment, together with security of principal. Their investment program was given nationwide significance by legislative changes in most savings bank states permitting out-of-state lending both conventionally and through the purchase of FHA and VA mortgages derived in other sections of the country.

Volume of Mortgage Holdings   At the end of 1975, the mutual savings banks of the United States held a total of $77,249 million in real estate mortgages. The distribution of these mortgages was approximately two thirds within and one third outside the state. The percentage distribution of the types of loans of these banks at the end of 1975 was:

	Percent
Conventional	65.3
FHA	18.7
VA	16.0
Total	100.0

Breakdown by type of property was:

	Percent
Residential	82.6
1-to-4 family	59.6
Multifamily	23.0
Nonresidential	17.3
Farm	0.1
Total	100.0

Proposed Legislation Affecting Mutual Savings Banks

In a proposed congressional financial institutions act, the powers and activities of mutual savings banks would be greatly expanded. The nature of the contemplated changes, affecting commercial banks and savings and loan associations as well, is presented in summarized form in the appendix of this chapter.

COMMERCIAL BANKS

Nature of Commercial Banks

As the name implies, commercial banks—whether national or state chartered—are the reservoirs of credit for the commerce of the country. Unlike savings and loan associations and savings banks, they are not mutual in character. Their financial plan is based upon stockownership, frequently quite closely held; the investors look upon their commitment as a source of profit through the dividends they receive. The people who supply most of the funds of commercial banks, the depositors, have no voice in management and do not share in the dividends distributed to the shareholders.

Bank depositors are divided into two groups. Demand depositors consist of individuals, corporations, and other groups of people, who place their working capital in their local banks for safekeeping, to be drawn out as needed by the owner. Such funds are not looked upon as investment money. They are simply placed where they are more secure than if they were left in the home or the office. Because they are withdrawable on demand, the bank's use of them is necessarily greatly restricted. In contrast, those who place time deposits in commercial banks look upon such an operation as an investment on which they expect an interest return. Because such funds are expected to remain in the bank longer than are demand deposits, they can be invested in long-term commitments, including real estate mortgages. While commercial banks reserve the right to require 30 days' notice before time deposits can be withdrawn, this right is seldom exercised.

Savings Growth in Commercial Banks

Up to the turn of the century, savings accounts in commercial banks were incidental to the major operations of these banks in other financial fields. The law which created national banks made no mention of savings accounts. In 1903, a significant ruling of the Comptroller of the Currency gave the green light to the opening of savings accounts by national banks. The effect of this ruling was that, since the legislation establishing these banks failed either to authorize or to prohibit savings accounts, each bank was free to make its own choice on this question. Nearly half of the national banks chose to open savings departments within the next decade. Then the Federal Reserve Act of 1913 specifically sanctioned such departments by encouraging their operation.

The development of savings departments in state-chartered commercial banks more or less paralleled that of savings departments in national banks. In general, state banks gave favorable consideration to savings accounts somewhat ahead of national banks. Even then it was not until 1917 that the savings deposits of all commercial banks in the country equaled the deposits of all mutual savings banks. Thereafter the commercial banks forged ahead rapidly until the depression years of the 1930s. In 1932, the commercial banks fell behind for the first time in a decade and a half. Taking the lead again in 1935, the commercial banks never lost it. At the present time, their savings and time deposits are about four times those of savings banks.

There are, however, many who question the propriety of commercial banks taking advantage of the total increased mortgage lending potential created by their present time deposits, because of the increased need for liquidity in connection with their commercial banking function. They point out that a great part of the increase in savings and time deposits is represented by certificates of deposit (CDs), which the banks first began issuing in 1961. Two types of certificates are issued. One type is the large-unit (probably $100,000 or more), negotiable certificate issued to the larger business firms; the other is the small-unit, non-negotiable certificate issued to smaller businesses and individuals. A corporation, which was previously carrying funds in a commercial account at no interest, can now place the same money at interest with the bank and receive a certificate therefor which is as negotiable as a stock or bond. If it needs the funds again, all it has to do is sell the certificate in the market. Savings and loan associations as well as other corporations have extensive holdings of CDs for funds deposited in commercial banks. Business firms are now also permitted to have regular passbook savings accounts up to a maximum of $150,000.

In light of this reliance on the liquidity of these instruments, the attendant hazards should be noted. Since these certificates are for a term at a higher money cost, the funds they represent must be put to work at a relatively high interest rate to yield a profit. On the other hand, since CDs have early maturities, all banks could be stripped of CD money quickly if short-term rates rose above the highest rate for CDs. Banks making mortgage loans with reliance upon the permanency of CD money would then be pressed. This, of course, points up the need for a reliable secondary market for conventional, as well as federally underwritten mortgages. The problem of secondary markets is discussed in Chapter 21.

Trusteed Funds   In addition to the resources in savings accounts that may be used for mortgage lending, commercial banks may have trusteed funds in their trust departments which must be invested. In general, such funds have been left with the bank by individuals who may have very definite ideas about their investment. As a consequence, one trust may be so set up as to prevent the investment of its funds in real estate mortgages. Another may set limits upon the amounts that may be so invested. It might even specify the types of real estate security acceptable for real estate loans. Still another may leave wider discretion to the trustee. Since trusts are enjoying substantial growth, it is likely that an increasing amount of money for real estate lending will be available from this source.

History of Real Estate Lending by Commercial Banks

As originally passed in 1863, the national bank law permitted national banks to make loans on both real and personal property as security. A year later the law was amended in such manner that the term "real property" was taken out. Thereafter and until the second decade of this century, national banks were not permitted to make loans on real estate directly. However, they were permitted to accept real estate mortgages as secondary collateral to prevent losses on loans previously made in good faith on legal types of collateral.

Until state banks and trust companies used their authority to grant real estate loans in a manner to place competing national banks at a distinct disadvantage, the latter kept out of the field of real estate mortgage lending. But when the competitive advantage possessed by state banks began to embarrass the operating plans of national banks, supervision of the latter was relaxed in a manner to give more leeway in making mortgage loans, even though the laws under which they operated failed to sanction such practices.

It is fortunate that commercial banks—both state and national—did find it advantageous to grant real estate loans. In many sections of the country there have been neither savings banks nor savings and loan associations to assist in the financing of real estate purchases. Even today there are areas where mortgage money is restricted to that made available by commercial banks. While this is less true than formerly, it still describes some real estate markets.

Lending Authority

As originally enacted in 1913, the Federal Reserve Act opened the door to real estate loans by national banks by providing that they could make loans on improved and unencumbered farms for periods up to five years and for amounts not in excess of 50 percent of their value. No national bank could invest for this purpose more than one fourth of its capital and surplus or one third of its time deposits.

In 1916, this law was amended to permit national banks to make loans on improved and unencumbered real estate other than farms. The same limitations were imposed as stated above for farm loans, with the further restriction that, on real estate other than farms, the maturity of the loans was limited to one year instead of five. It is significant to note that one-year loans on urban real estate was the common pattern at that time for many of the competitors of national banks in some areas. Consequently the one-year limitation placed national banks in a competitive framework in such markets. Not all of the state banks limited real estate loans to one year as a matter of practice. Because of this, a demand arose almost immediately for further liberalization of the lending powers of national banks in the real estate field. This demand presently received the active support of the Comptroller of the Currency. No changes were made, however, until the passage of the McFadden Act of 1927. This law permitted five-year, 50 percent loans on urban real estate. For unamortized loans, this law has remained intact to date.

Beginning in 1935, the Federal Reserve Act was further amended to permit national banks to make loans at progressively higher loan-to-value ratios where the loan was amortized. In 1970, the authority was increased to permit home loans up to 90 percent of appraised value with an amortization not to exceed 30 years. The Federal Reserve Act was further amended in 1974.

Current provisions of the law governing real estate loans by national banks include the following:

1. National banks may not make real estate loans in excess of the greater of unimpaired capital and surplus or time and savings deposits, except that real estate loans secured by other than first liens, when added to unpaid prior liens, are to be limited to 30 percent of unimpaired capital and unimpaired surplus combined. Furthermore, they are authorized to make real estate loans in excess of 70 percent of time and savings deposits only if the total unpaid amount loaned does not exceed 10 percent of the maximum amount that may be invested in real estate loans.

2. Under present law, national banks are authorized to make various loan-to-value ratio loans secured by other than first liens where the lien, when added to prior liens, does not exceed the applicable loan-to-value ratio for the particular type of loan.

3. National banks are not required to classify as real estate loans various loans insured, guaranteed, or backed by the full faith and credit of the federal government or a state.

4. Loans with maturities of less than 60 months are classified as commercial loans when made for construction of buildings and secured by a commitment to advance the full amount of the loan upon completion.

5. Loans made for the construction of residential or farm buildings with maturities of not more than 9 months are eligible for discount as commercial paper if accompanied by an agreement for firm takeout upon completion of the building.

6. National banks are permitted to make loans on leaseholds that have at least 10 years to run beyond the terminal date of the loan.

7. Loans made to manufacturing or industrial businesses are exempt from real estate loan limitations even though the bank takes a mortgage on real estate as security where the bank relies primarily on the general credit standing and earning power of the business as the source of repayment.

Volume of Mortgage Loans Held by Banks

For all commercial banks of the country, real estate mortgage loans constitute about one seventh of total assets and about one third of the amount of time deposits. Loans on residential properties, including apartments, account for approximately two thirds of the dollar volume of all mortgages, with all other types of real estate security making up the other one third. In number of mortgages held, residential loans represent an even higher percentage than is true for dollar volume. Approximately nine tenths of the total number of loans on real estate as security are residential loans.

The distribution of mortgage holdings among different sizes of commercial banks varies somewhat, although the differences are not too significant. In general, the largest banks have a smaller percentage of assets invested in real estate mortgages. The greatest concentration is recorded for banks in the smaller asset categories, though not in the very smallest groups.

Grouped as a single type of financial institution, commercial banks at the end of 1975 held about 18 percent of the dollar volume of all real estate mortgages in the United States. Commercial bank nonfarm loans are overall about two thirds for residential and one third for commercial purposes.

Fluctuations in Mortgage Holdings

Unlike savings and loan associations whose major outlet for funds is real estate mortgages, commercial banks vary greatly in the dollar volume of mortgages held. Two conditions account for these fluctuations. In the first place, many commercial banks—particularly the larger ones—would prefer to invest their funds elsewhere. Consequently, whenever the demand for money for commercial loans is great, they show less interest in real estate mortgage commitments. In the absence of a commercial loan demand of sufficient magnitude to absorb their available funds, some of them become more interested in loans against real estate as security.

In the second place, commercial banks have in the past approached the business of making loans on real estate with considerable caution. In general, they have followed smaller loan-to-value ratios than have savings and loan associations. Also, in periods of smaller demand for real estate mortgage credit, commercial banks are generally content to let their competitors make most of the available loans. In the middle 1930s commercial banks were not active bidders for mortgage loans. Their proportion of total mortgage debt dropped considerably from its level at the beginning of the depression. By contrast, in the post-World War II period the proportion of total real estate mortgage debt held by commercial banks rose to a point approximately double the ratio of the middle 1930s. It must be remembered that insurance of loans by the FHA and the guarantee of loans by the VA entered into the picture in the postwar period. Commercial banks made more generous use of both insurance and guarantee of mortgages than did some of their competitors. The use of insurance and guarantee is reflected also in loans made by the larger banks. In general, the larger the commercial bank which holds mortgages, the more generous the use of insurance and guarantee of mortgage loans.

During the late 1960s and early 1970s, many commercial banks sponsored real estate mortgage investment trusts. As described in Chapter 18, their adverse experience in this type of venture has added a new tinge of conservatism to their real estate lending practices.

Methods of Acquiring Mortgages

Commercial banks follow either of two practices in acquiring mortgages on real estate. Some have mortgage loan departments that are so well organized that they are active competitors within their markets for real estate loans. Indeed, their advertising for mortgages may be pitched on a very aggressive plane. If their time deposits are large and dependable over a period of years, they are likely to be more active bidders for real estate mortgages. As pointed out in Chapter 18, they may even have become sponsors of mortgage investment trusts. They not only originate the loans which they carry in their portfolios, but they service them as well. In some communities that lack specialized real estate financial institutions, commercial banks may be the most reliable agencies for making loans on real estate.

Other commercial banks, which place less emphasis upon real estate mortgages as sources of income, may not even have a mortgage department worthy of the name. Such mortgages as they may acquire from time to time are purchased from mortgage bankers or dealers. As pointed out in Chapter 19, commercial banks that purchase their real estate mortgages are likely to be "in-and-outers" so far as their mortgage acquisitions are concerned. Some of them may even let their mortgages be serviced by their loan correspondents, particularly if the security is located in a city other than the one in which the bank is located. Finally, some commercial banks prefer not to engage in mortgage lending under any circumstances.

Interim Financing

Even banks without particular expertise in real estate lending may engage in mortgage loan "warehousing" with mortgage bankers as the principal originators. In this type of lending, commercial bankers' loans are secured by institutional takeout commitments held by mortgage bankers who seek interim development and construction loans from the commercial banks until final placement with the permanent lenders at completion of the project.

Institutional Commitments in Mortgage Lending   In many respects the mortgage banker stands in about the same relationship to the institutions and other investors to whom he sells his mortgages as the investment banker stands to the investing public which buys his corporate securities. He must originate a satisfactory obligation and he must finance it until such time as it is sold to the ultimate investor. Prior to the time that a real estate mortgage is ready for sale, however, there has often been a long gestation period, and many arrangements for interim credits have had to be made—often more complicated and of longer duration than the investment banker must undertake. These interim financing problems arise because of the basic conditions out of which a new mortgage is derived. Often a new property or a new development is being constructed. The builder is ill equipped to provide his own financing, and the mortgage banker with a thin capital equity is not able to give him much help from his own funds. To accomplish their objectives, both need a construction loan. To support the construction loan credit, a commercial bank or other lender which might make such a loan often requires a firm commitment from an institutional investor to take over the mortgage on the property once the building has been completed. In fact, such commitments have proved to be increasingly important to the mortgage-lending operation in recent years. The commitments have been principally of two types: (1) "advance" or "forward" commitments and (2) "standby" commitments.

The first type of commitment, called an "advance" commitment by the Federal Housing Administration and termed a "forward" commitment by the Life Insurance Association of America, is virtually a purchase order for a mortgage on property to be constructed. A firm obligation is undertaken for the period of the commitment to purchase the federally underwritten mortgage on property to be constructed in accordance with acceptable plans and specifications. On the strength of the knowledge that the mortgage has a market once the property is completed, other institutions are willing to provide the necessary interim financing to bring the property to such a state of completion that the mortgage is eligible for sale under the commitment.

The "standby" commitment is an arrangement, usually worked out with a commercial bank, whereby the latter will buy mortgages, generally from a mortgage banker, at a substantial discount in event they cannot be sold more favorably to an institutional or other investor by the end of the commitment period.

The advance, or forward, commitment has been used in greatest volume at those times when credit conditions have eased, and the institutions with large volumes of funds to place have taken this means of providing for ready investment of their cash inflow. As money rates tighten, the institutional lenders find alternative uses for their funds equally attractive, and they are less inclined to enter into such commitments, as they feel overcommitted at lower rates on the obligations that they have already undertaken. Furthermore, rising interest rates with declining bond prices tend to make the sale of bonds for the purpose of obtaining funds for an alternative use an unattractive prospect.

A correlative of a restriction in advance commitments is an increased need for the standby commitment. In the absence of a certain market for the mortgage once construction is complete, the mortgage banker or the builder will accept an alternative avenue for disposition at a substantial discount, on the chance that a more desirable buyer can be found after origination of the permanent mortgage and before expiration of the commitment period. The use of this device tends to exert a stabilizing influence upon the availability of funds at times when a tight money market tends to dry up the supply. The effect is limited, however, by the fact that as the volume of standby commitments increases, the bank issuing the commitments will lower its forfeiture price until the potential financing costs become prohibitive and the plans for more construction are dropped.

Mortgage Inventory Loans, or "Mortgage Warehousing"   Interim loans by commercial banks to nonbank lenders are often specifically designated as "mortgage inventory" loans. Bankers commonly identify as inventory loans those made on securities being underwritten by an investment banker while the issues are being prepared for sale and distribution to individuals and financial institutions who buy them for their investment portfolios. Mortgage inventory loans serve exactly the same purpose for the mortgage banker, as he requires financing to expedite the origination, sale, and distribution of his mortgages to permanent investors. The practice of granting such loans has been called "mortgage warehousing." The notion of warehousing arises from the temporary nature of the advance as the mortgage passes from its originator to the ultimate lender.

There are three general types of warehouse loans. Two of these commonly involve mortgage bankers directly. The most common is the "committed-technical" warehousing loan, which has been made for many years. Under this arrangement, the commercial bank simply lends to the mortgage banker to provide financing between the time of payment for construction and the time when he can deliver perfected mortgages to the permanent investor. This loan is supported by a prior commitment of the investor to purchase the mortgages when completed. Numerous details must be handled before the mortgage is ready for purchase. The loan must be closed; the credit of the owner of the property must be checked; the FHA insurance or the VA guarantee must be obtained; title insurance or a counsel's opinion must afford adequate title protection; other appropriate insurance must be bound; and delivery and recordation of necessary documents must be effected. All of these processes, together with assembling mortgages in the proper amounts, usually take five to six months. The amount of the warehousing loan is usually based upon the commitment of the permanent investor. The lending bank will be limited to the amount of the commitment or to a figure slightly less than that amount.

A second type of warehousing loan is called the "uncommitted-technical" loan. It differs from the first only in that there is no prior commitment of a permanent investor to take up the loan from the mortgage banker. When a commercial bank lends under this arrangement, it may lend either with or without recourse. If the loan is with recourse and a permanent investor has not been found by the end of the interim lending period, the mortgage banker must take up the loan from the commercial bank. He must then either carry the financing himself or arrange it elsewhere until he manages to sell the mortgage. If the warehousing loan from the bank is without recourse, there is a different result. In case the mortgage banker has not placed the mortgage with a permanent investor before the maturity date of the interim loan, the commercial bank retires the loan by purchasing the mortgage given as security at its prearranged forfeiture price, which is normally at a discount. The obligation of the commercial bank in this situation is the previously mentioned standby commitment for which it is paid a fee irrespective of whether a forfeiture is declared.

Still a third type of warehousing loan has come into prominence since the mid-1950s. It has been designated as "committed-institutional" warehousing. This type of loan is made directly to large institutional investors rather than to mortgage bankers, and the credit is designed to give investors more flexibility in arranging for mortgage investments by providing for their unusual requirements for investable funds which will later be met permanently out of the receipts of funds in the ordinary course of business. These loans by the commercial bank are usually of longer duration, ranging from a year to 18 months, with the borrower having a prepayment option. The use of this financing method is largely the result of the decline in the bond markets in recent years, rendering these securities relatively unavailable for sale by institutional investors to provide funds to meet advance commitments to mortgage bankers. As bond prices rise again, so that capital gains instead of capital losses may result from bond sales, it may be presumed that committed-institutional warehousing tends to become less important for this purpose. The method is available, however, to deal with any situation in which the cash inflow of an institution does not meet its expectations.

Social and Economic Impact of Mortgage Warehousing It becomes apparent from studying the operating methods of mortgage bankers today that mortgage warehousing is essential to the smooth and orderly performance of their present functions. They do not need and are not organized to provide directly the funds necessary to carry the large volume of mortgages which they may originate for institutional investors. Commercial banks can meet this requirement for them on a flexible and economic basis, with credits expanding or contracting consistently with their commitments. In uncommitted warehousing, commercial banks can again be of real assistance in appraisal of the investment demand, the mortgage market, and other significant factors in the process of granting the credit line. Through the establishment of this line and a forfeiture price, mortgage bankers are afforded a platform from which they can work with some assurance while they proceed during the period of the interim loan to seek out new markets on a national basis. They are thus enabled to originate mortgages beyond the time that they could remain in the market if they were limited to reliance upon prior commitments. Similarly, committed institutional warehousing permits large mortgage investors to anticipate their cash inflows for as long as two years, or more, in advance and to issue forward commitments to their correspondent mortgage originators. Such commitments enable the correspondents to maintain an uninterrupted lending program, without breakdown or cutoffs, and thus support the building industry in a continuous construction program.

Although it may generally be presumed that mortgage warehousing has a stabilizing effect, it has been pointed out that such great dependence upon the commercial banks renders the supply of current funds available for real estate lending directly subject to commercial bank policies. Bankers point out that they may cease lending on this type of credit when they feel they have reached proper and judicious limits. A decision by bankers en masse not to make further warehousing loans, whether for reasons of money market conditions or better alternative uses of funds, can bring about a disturbing result in an otherwise stable market. Of course, if the bankers decide that a reversal in real estate market conditions has made further such loans unwise, the impact is inevitable.

Economists point out that under certain conditions the provision of warehousing credit may be inflationary. Under conditions of full employment, with productive resources in short supply, any additional credit expansion has this effect. Thus, any new demand for productive resources injected into the housing industry would be competing for resources already in demand and prices would be driven upward. Should this situation develop in critical proportions, a problem in credit control will arise. It has been suggested that for such a special form of credit, with regard to which quantitative and qualitative controls as generally conceived would be too broad and the need for prompt action would be paramount, a program of "moral suasion" would probably be most effective.

Bank Holding Companies in Real Estate Finance

Under the Bank Holding Company Act of 1956 as amended in 1970, bank holding companies are required to register with the Federal Reserve System. These companies are permitted to engage in nonbank activities determined by the Federal Reserve Board to be closely related to banking. Included in the permissible activities that may affect real estate in particular are mortgage banking, leasing of real and personal property, trust services, insurance, data processing, management consulting, and debt or equity investment for community development. Until now, many banks have found entry into broader areas of real estate finance a mixed blessing. Too little experience and expertise set the conditions for many questionable real estate loans now being digested by the commercial banking system. These mortgages were largely generated through bank management services acting for real estate investment trusts sponsored by bank holding companies. It is to be expected, of course, that once the shake-out has taken place, the survivors will expand to enjoy the opportunities offered by the bank holding company form and that communities will benefit from the fuller service.

QUESTIONS

1. How do mutual savings banks and commercial banks differ in their general purposes?

2. How have the differences in the purposes of mutual savings banks and commercial banks affected their lending policies with respect to mortgage loans on real estate?

3. Where are most of the mutual savings banks located? Why are they not found in other parts of the country?

4. How has recent legislation liberalized the lending practices of mutual savings banks?

5. Why have commercial banks been so slow in entering the real estate lending field?

6. How important statistically are commercial banks and mutual savings

banks as sources of mortgage money to finance real estate purchases?

7. How do commercial banks and mutual savings banks acquire their mortgages?

8. Do you expect the commercial banks to be relatively more important or less important as a source of real estate financing in the future? What considerations have influenced your opinion?

9. Distinguish between "advance" or "forward" commitments and "stand-by" commitments and define each.

10. What is mortgage warehousing?

11. What are the three general types of mortgage warehouse loans? Describe each.

12. Is the practice of mortgage warehousing a favorable influence on economic conditions? Why or why not?

CASE PROBLEM

Study the impact of the Financial Institutions Act on one or more real estate financing institutions in your community.

APPENDIX

In 1971, a Presidential commission, commonly called the Hunt Commission, after extensive study issued a report setting forth 89 recommendations designed to improve the health and stability of the nation's financial institutions, housing industry, and general economy.[1] In essence, the report contained a series of recommendations that would change savings and loan associations, mutual savings banks, and even credit unions into near-commercial banks; and commercial banks would be induced to expand the proportion of their activities in areas of real estate finance. All of the institutions would handle their assets and liabilities in similar fashion and be uniformly regulated and taxed. Further, permission of all institutions to convert their charters to commercial banks was recommended.

In 1973, the Hunt Commission conclusions led to the introduction of the Financial Institutions Act. It has gone through several changes until it now appears near passage. How the Congress has reacted to date to the Hunt Commission recommendations can be discerned in a general way from a summary of a recent form of the bill, printed from a publication titled *The Financial Institutions Act of 1975*, U.S. Department of the Treasury, March 19, 1975. This summary is as follows:

[1] *The Report of the President's Commission on Financial Structure and Regulation* (Washington, D.C.: U.S. Government Printing Office, 1971).

BEFORE AND AFTER STATUS OF FINANCIAL INSTITUTIONS

Commercial Banks

Before	*After*

Deposit Powers

payment of interest: ceilings on deposit rates set by Federal Reserve Board.

payment of interest: ceilings eliminated after five and one-half years. Secretary of the Treasury to report findings and recommendations to Congress five years after enactment of the FIA.

demand accounts: full powers; individual and corporate.

demand accounts: full powers; individual and corporate (no change).

Negotiable Order of Withdrawal (interest-bearing checking accounts) (NOW) accounts: not permitted.

NOW accounts: full powers; individual and corporate.

savings accounts: individuals only.

savings accounts: individual and corporate.

Lending and Investment Powers

real estate loans: severe restrictions re collateral, loan size, maturity and method of repayment.

real estate loans: modest restrictions re collateral, loan size, maturity and method of payment; plus community rehabilitation loans under a 3 percent leeway authority.

equities: holdings severely restricted.

equities: holdings severely restricted (no change).

Taxes

tax credits: none.

tax credits: special mortgage interest tax credit for investing in residential mortgages: significant incentive to invest at least 10 percent of assets in residential mortgages.

Chartering Alternatives

federal: yes
state: yes

federal: yes $\Big\}$ no change.
state: yes

Commercial Banks (*continued*)

| | *Before* | *After* |

Branching

national banks: \
state banks: 〉 state law governs location of branches.

national banks: \
state banks: 〉 state law governs location of branches (no change).

Summary

Consumer interests penalized. Prohibitions restrict direct participation in housing and real estate finance. Absence of mortgage investment incentives given S&L's.

Consumer interests given high priority. Restriction against housing and real estate finance modified, and positive incentives for such investment, identical to those given S&L's.

Savings and Loan Associations and Mutual Savings Banks

Deposit Powers

payment of interest: ceilings on deposit rates set by FHLBB or FDIC.

payment of interest: ceilings eliminated after five and one-half years. Secretary of the Treasury to report findings and recommendations to Congress on competitive strength of all financial institutions five years after enactment of the FIA.

savings accounts: full powers; individual and corporate.

savings accounts: full powers; individual and corporate (no change).

demand accounts: not permitted.

demand accounts: full powers; individual and corporate.

NOW accounts: not permitted.

NOW accounts: full powers; individual and corporate.

Lending and Investment Powers

loans for housing and closely related areas.

loans for housing and closely related areas; real estate loans under same conditions as commercial banks; plus (on a limited basis) consumer loans (up to 10 percent of assets); construction loans not tied to permanent financing; community rehabilitation loans under a 3 percent leeway authority.

equities: no acquisition of private sector issues.

equities: no acquisition of private sector issues (no change).

Savings and Loan Associations and Mutual Savings Banks (*continued*)

Before	*After*
securities: no acquisition of private debt securities.	securities: limited acquisition of commercial paper, bankers' acceptances, and high grade corporate debt (up to 10 percent of assets).

Taxes

loan loss deductions: preferential treatment compared to banks.	loan loss deductions: will move to same treatment as banks by 1979, or earlier, at their option.
tax credits: none.	tax credits: special tax credits for investment in residential mortgages; significant incentive to retain high percentage of portfolio in residential mortgages.

Chartering Alternatives

federal: mutual associations only.	federal: mutual and stock associations.
state: mutual and stock associations.	state: mutual and stock associations (no change).

Branching

federally chartered: governed by FHLBB.	federally chartered: governed by FHLBB (no change).
state-chartered: governed by state law.	state chartered: governed by state law (no change).
	provides freedom of conversion from state to federal, federal to state, mutual to stock and stock to mutual.

Summary

Consumer interests penalized owing to prohibitions against service competition and forced specialization among financial institutions.	Consumer interests strengthened by availability of new sources of supply of both deposit services and lending services and the promise of direct price competition between thrift institutions and banks.
Opportunities to compete for funds limited and little ability to withstand tight-money pressures without substantial government support.	Virtually unlimited opportunities to compete for funds. Ability to withstand tight-money pressures strengthened, minimizing need for government rescue operations.

Credit Unions

Deposit Powers

Only share accounts permitted.

Share accounts plus variable share certificates similar to certificates of deposit.

Lending and Investment Powers

Severely restricted consumer lending. Statutory 12 percent ceiling on loans.

Maximum term of unsecured loans extended from five to seven years. Maximum term of secured loans extended from ten to twelve years. Loan limits increased and made more flexible. Ceiling on lending rate to be raised at the discretion of the NCUA administrator.

no authority to offer mortgage loans.

allowed to offer 30 year mortgage loans to members.

no lines of credit permitted.

authority to offer lines of credit varying with the credit-worthiness of the member.

Chartering Alternatives

conversion to mutual thrift institutions not permitted.

conversion to mutual thrift institutions permitted.

Sources of Liquidity

private sector institutions only.

private sector institutions, *plus* NCUA-administered Central Discount Fund for emergency, temporary liquidity purposes only.

Taxes

tax-exempt.

tax-exempt (no change).

Summary

Prohibitions against other than basic consumer lending.

Expanded depositor and borrower services including mortgage lending. Emphasis on greater flow of services to consumer-saver.

17

Financing of Real Estate by Life Insurance Companies

Life Insurance Companies as Lenders on Real Estate Security

Like some other types of financial institutions, life insurance companies have followed a pattern in lending on real estate as security that has adjusted itself to changing economic conditions. At one time farm loans were popular outlets for investable resources of insurance companies. Later, enthusiasm for this type of investment cooled materially. From time to time mortgages on urban real estate have been favored. Since life insurance companies, unlike savings and loan associations, for example, were not organized primarily for the purpose of financing homes, it is to be expected that they will seek the outlets for their investment funds which will best meet the requirements of the investor at the time the investment is made.

One of the reasons real estate mortgages are in current favor with life insurance companies is the pressure for investment of enormous resources at a time when interest rates on other types of investment are relatively lower.

Life Insurance Assets According to the *Life Insurance Fact Book,*[1] total assets of life insurance companies in 1890 were $771 million. They doubled in each decade until, in 1960, they totaled about $120 billion. As of December 1975, they were estimated at $289 billion, indicating continued rapid growth. In recent years insurance companies have experienced quite a change in their investments in real estate mortgages.

---

[1] A considerable part of the statistical material contained in this chapter has been adapted from the *Life Insurance Fact Book.* Updating may be accomplished by reference to the most current issue.

In 1930 slightly more than 40 percent of all assets were so invested. This percentage declined to a low point of just under 15 percent in 1946. Since that year there has been a consistent increase in the proportion of assets invested in mortgages. At the end of 1975, the percentage was approximately 30.8. Meantime, because of the very rapid growth of total assets, the dollar volume of mortgages held in 1975 was over twice as great as the 1961 volume.

The magnitude of the investment problems of life insurance companies is indicated from the fact that in 1950 new investments amounted to $12.3 billion; in 1959, to $19.8 billion; and in 1975, to $132.4 billion. New investments represent not only new assets but refundings and pay-offs of old investments. For example, purchases of short-term securities, usually involving reinvestment of the funds several times during the year, amounted to $90 billion in 1975. Of the remainder, approximately $16 billion were derived from matured or redeemed bonds, mortgage amortizations or prepayments, and sales of holdings.

Earnings on Investment   The net average return on life insurance investments in 1923 was 5.18 percent. In the following year this average rate of return started on a long, steady period of decline which reached a low of 2.88 percent in 1947. Since 1948 there have been annual increases to about 6.36 percent in 1975. The continued decline in the earnings rate for insurance companies through the mid-1940s helped to account for a return of interest in real estate mortgages, because they have consistently paid higher rates than government bonds or even Aaa corporate bonds. The yield differential has generally remained even as bond yields have risen.

Restrictions upon Real Estate Loans by Insurance Companies

Most of the states have passed laws governing the operations of insurance companies. These fall into two classes: laws governing the operations of companies domiciled within the state; and those controlling activities of companies domiciled elsewhere, but doing business within the state that passed the law. Since the major purpose of both types of laws is the protection of the policyholders, the features of the legislation dealing with investments are more or less incidental to this major purpose. For this reason, a brief discussion of legislation of the latter type must be presented.

While most laws dealing with insurance companies domiciled within the state permit investments in real estate mortgages, such permission is usually hedged about with various types of restrictions. Only the most common restrictions will be discussed here. Those interested in the less common types are referred to the laws of the various states for such information. In general, the permission to make loans on real estate is limited, for example, to "improved land," including farms. While such improved land is supposed to be unencumbered, such encumbrances as taxes, assessments, easements, and building restrictions are excepted.

One common type of restriction that impinges heavily upon real estate finance, and that will probably be subject to review from time to time, is the upper limit of individual loans and the limit of assets which may be devoted to this type of investment. For example, in New York an insurance company may not invest more than $30,000 or 2 percent of its total assets (whichever is greater) in a mortgage on a single property. If the company's assets are less than $1 million, it is effectively restricted to loans on residential or small business properties, including farms. If its assets exceed $100 million, this 2 percent limitation loses much of its meaning. In New York, also, not more than 50 percent of the total assets of a life insurance company may be invested in all real estate mortgages held by it at one time. Again the size of the company has an important bearing upon its competitive position in the field of real estate finance.

Where legislation governing the operation of life insurance companies makes specific mention of such subjects as leaseholds and land contracts, they too are subject to the restrictions defined in the law. For example, no loan may be made by an insurance company domiciled in the state of New York on a leasehold whose unexpired term is not at least equal to the lesser of 40 years or a sufficient term that normal amortization will have been completed within four-fifths of the remaining leasehold period. In Minnesota the corresponding term is 40 years; in Ohio 99 years, renewable forever; and in Texas for a period at least 10 years beyond the term of the loan.

Where restrictions of the kind mentioned above are included in the law which governs the operation of insurance companies domiciled in another state but doing business in the state that passes the law, the purpose is to protect the domestic companies against unfair competition as well as to protect the policyholders.

Restrictions setting the upper limits of loans in relation to the value of the security therefor are considered to be quite conservative in today's markets. Such loan-to-value ratios usually range between 66⅔ and 75 percent for conventional mortgages. FHA and VA loans are usually exempted from these as well as from most of the other restrictions discussed herein. In general, while a few laws make gestures in the direction of a recognition of the importance of appraisals in the administration of such loan-to-value restrictions, they cannot be said to give the full protection intended. In the absence of appraisal standards which are not yet available, such limitations are more theological than practical. In making this statement there is no intent to imply that loan-to-value restrictions operate any differently for insurance company lenders than for any other kinds of real estate financial institutions.

In respect to one type of restriction, not mentioned above, insurance companies usually enjoy greater freedom than their competitors. They are not usually required to amortize their real estate loans nor to limit them to any maximum maturity. Recent changes in policy on such questions have been dictated more by competition than by law. For example, insurance companies are making freer use of amortized loans on residential properties than was their practice a quarter of a century ago. Recently, several states have passed laws permitting higher loan-to-value ratios, usually 75 percent, if the loan is fully amortized within a prescribed term of years.

Geographical Limitations Here is an area in which laws governing insurance companies operate quite differently from those governing the operations of other types of lending institutions. For example, in Chapter 16 it was pointed out that savings and loan associations are usually discouraged from making loans outside of a restricted lending area defined in the regulatory laws. Until recently savings banks have been subjected to geographical limitations somewhat more liberal than those for savings and loan associations, but nevertheless restrictive.

Geographical limitations for insurance companies are much more liberal. For the most part the lending area for them is considered to be the United States. In some state laws even Canada is added. One potent reason for this difference is that insurance companies are commonly national in their markets for writing insurance policies. It has been thought fair to allow them to invest their funds in areas from which they have been obtained in the usual course of conducting their insurance business. Indeed, some states have been so insistent that this be done that their legislation is slanted in this direction. For example, Texas laws require that a foreign insurance company, as a consideration for the right to do business in that state, must invest at least three fourths of the reserves required to protect Texas policyholders in Texas real estate finance and in Texas securities.

Geographical Distribution of Mortgage Holdings At the end of 1975, the states which supplied the largest holdings of farm mortgages in the portfolios of life insurance companies were, in the order named: California, Texas, Iowa, and Illinois. The largest holdings of FHA nonfarm mortgages were in the following states, in the order named: California, Texas, Florida, and Washington. Corresponding figures for VA nonfarm loans place the following states at the top of the list: California, Texas, Virginia, Ohio, and Illinois. Other nonfarm mortgages showed greatest totals in the following states: California, Texas, New York, Florida, and Illinois. The "other nonfarm" classification includes mortgages on commercial and industrial properties. Total real estate mortgages held by insurance companies at the end of 1975 were greatest in the following states: California ($11.5 billion), Texas ($8.8 billion), Florida ($4.5 billion), New York ($4.4 billion), Illinois ($4.2 billion), and finally, Ohio ($3.0 billion).

Self-Imposed Restrictions While it can be said that savings and loan associations, for example, are all interested in making loans on real estate as security, the same generalization cannot be applied to all life insurance companies. Great differences appear in the mortgage-lending operations of the latter. These differences are accounted for by variations in size, investment experience, and mental attitudes of those who manage the companies. As may be expected, smaller companies are less well equipped to handle mortgage lending than are their larger competitors. Some companies limit their mortgage holdings to residential properties as security, while others lend on commercial, financial, and even industrial property as well.

In spite of the pressure of funds for investment and for reinvestment, life insurance companies occasionally experience something akin to the "in-and-out" policies of commercial banks in their mortgage investment programs. This is particularly true of advance commitments. At times they will gladly indicate to their correspondents their willingness to purchase agreed-upon quantities of mortgages for future delivery. On other occasions they become more cautious and prefer to consider purchases only as mortgages are offered to them. In unusual situations—where money rates appear quite uncertain—they may even withdraw from the market temporarily.

Mortgage Experience

On the whole, the distribution of real estate loans in recent years has shown a distinct trend toward apartment complexes and commercial and industrial properties. Mortgage holdings of one- to four-family residential properties represented over half of all mortgage holdings from 1950 through 1964, reaching a high of 61 percent in 1956. Since 1964, this proportion has steadily declined. At the 1975 year-end, it was about 20 percent. At that time, over 73 percent of total mortgage holdings were on apartment developments and commercial properties, with the balance on farms.

The predominance of FHA loans in the period from 1940 to 1946 was particularly marked, being 57 percent in number and 31 percent in dollar volume of all home loans closed or purchased. The VA loans had not yet had a chance to come into favor during this period. Two thirds in number and 43 percent in dollar volume were written for 20 years or more. Increases in the maturity of loans and in the loan-to-value ratios of real estate loans made by life insurance companies during the past quarter century have been especially marked.

The types of mortgages held by life insurance companies at the end of 1947, 1959, and 1975 are shown in Exhibit 17–1. The relative shift from

EXHIBIT 17–1
Types of Mortgages Held by Life Insurance Companies (000,000 omitted)

	1947		1959		1975	
	Total	*Percent*	*Total*	*Percent*	*Total*	*Percent*
Nonfarm loans						
FHA	$1,398	16.3	$ 8,523	21.7	$ 8,502	9.5
VA	844	9.8	7,086	18.1	3,903	4.4
Conventional	5,538	63.6	20,744	53.0	70,009	78.4
Farm loans	975	10.3	2,844	7.2	6,753	7.7
Total	$8,755	100.0	$39,197	100.0	$89,167	100.0

conventional to FHA and VA loans between 1947 and 1959 is quite noticeable from the exhibit. The dollar volume of conventional nonfarm loans increased over 12 times from 1947 to 1976. The outstanding FHA and VA loans increased markedly in significance and then went into a decline relatively, although maintaining fairly constant dollar amounts in recent years. The increasing relative importance of conventional nonfarm loans in a large measure is attributable to recent demands by business for external financing which have diverted funds that might otherwise have flowed into home mortgages under FHA and VA programs.

Preference for Larger Loans Although life insurance companies make loans on single-family residences, many of them prefer the larger loans in this category. Seldom will they compete actively for smaller residential loans except when they are buying them in bulk. To an even more marked degree, they prefer loans on multifamily dwellings and on commercial properties such as hotels and office and loft buildings. Even in the field of industrial real estate, they are an important financial influence.

Another development in the mortgage market affecting life companies is the rapidly growing importance of local lenders, especially savings and loan associations and commercial banks. Insurance companies are experiencing increasing difficulty in competing for conventional residential loans. For this reason, also, these companies are seeking loans on income property occupied by tenants with superior credit ratings. The advantages of purchase-and-leaseback arrangements have been sharply curtailed during the past few years by changes in the federal income tax law. Out of the leaseback experience, however, life companies have learned that they can accomplish an approximate equivalent by 100 percent loans. Since the definite approval of such loans in New York state, insurance companies have been looking with increasing favor on 100 percent loans on income property when the tenants are of unquestioned financial responsibility and the net rent will support the loan. Relative freedom from maximum loan limitations and territorial restrictions gives the life companies an advantage over their competitors in regard to this type of property.

Proportion of Assets in Mortgages   In 1890, 40 percent of insurance company assets was invested in real estate mortgages. For the next 40 years this ratio varied from year to year until in 1930 it was again 40 percent. From 1930 the ratio declined steadily until in 1945 it was just under 15 percent. Increases since 1945 brought the ratio of mortgages to total assets up to about 32 percent in 1976. During this latter period most of the shift in investments was from government bonds to mortgages. The present ratio is somewhat lower than during the immediately past years because of the extremely attractive yields in the bond markets in the recent past. At the end of 1975 life insurance companies held about one ninth of all real estate mortgages in the country.

Mortgage Loan Department

Because of the geographical extent of mortgage loan operations, the problem of organization of the mortgage loan department of a life insurance company is quite unlike that faced by its competitors in this field of operations. Investment in mortgages can be national in scope for any particular company. Their origination and servicing must be conducted at the local level to be most successful. Because of differences in practices among insurance companies, several plans of operating mortgage loan departments are in common use. The more extensive the mortgage-lending operations, the larger the number of loans outstanding and the more far-flung their geographical distribution; the more varied the kinds of property which secures them, the more complicated the mortgage loan department becomes.

The institution which has outstanding a large number of insured or guaranteed loans on residential property, widely scattered geographically without any great amount of concentration in any contiguous area, may well find one type of mortgage loan department most satisfactory. One which has a similar amount of money invested in a small number of large commercial and multiple-family residence loans, concentrated in a few metropolitan areas, might find a different form of organization best adapted to its needs.

There are two major types of organization to be considered. In addition, variations and combinations of these two types are in use. These two major types are branch offices and outside correspondents. They have been known to succeed each other, following a pattern of alternation that is dictated by experience which ends in disappointment. If one system is tried continuously to the satisfaction of the management, it is not likely to be disturbed. But if its results are unsatisfactory, regardless of the reasons, it is not uncommon that a major operation is performed in order that a change of pattern may be substituted.

Where the branch office type of organization is used, it is manned by salaried employees of the insurance company. Here the control is direct. Both lending and servicing facilities can be set up by the home office, and supervisory personnel can see to it that company policies are carried out to the letter. Under this plan of organization, the lending institution can literally build a loan portfolio according to its own pattern, instead of picking and choosing among the types of loans offered for its purchase.

Branch offices may be located in the same physical quarters as the respective local offices of the insurance division of the insurance corporation, or they may occupy separate space. In either event, the employees of the mortgage loan department are under the supervision of the home-office staff engaged in mortgage loan operations. In addition they may be subject to some measure of direction by the roving field representatives who visit them from time to time. Arm's-length supervision of small staffs needed to man branch offices may be one of the reasons that this plan of organization is less commonly used than the correspondent system next described.

Loan Correspondents

As an alternative to branch offices for the purpose of making and servicing loans, some insurance companies prefer to appoint outside companies or individuals to handle this part of their mortgage business. From the standpoint of loan origination only, the service performed by such a correspondent is that of a finder, for whose service a finder's fee is paid. Here both the mortgage banker and the mortgage broker are used. Some insurance companies use either in ways that best suit their purposes. In some instances, the finder's job is completed when he points out an opportunity for making a real estate loan. Or he may take the next step and assemble information about it, leaving decisions to be made by salaried representatives of the insurance company.

Perhaps, instead, the finder assembles the information, prepares the necessary papers, and in fact does all but the closing of the loan, leaving only the latter function to be performed by the more direct representatives of the lender, if they find it desirable to complete the transaction.

Finally, in the case of mortgage bankers (or mortgage companies, as they are sometimes called) the finder may use its own funds to close the loan, which is then offered for sale to the insurance company. Some of the sellers of such mortgages are properly classed as correspondents of the insurance company purchaser, because of their contractual and continuing relationships. Others are not properly called correspondents, since the relationship between buyer and seller is casual and discontinuous.

Where the finder is compensated for the service of finding mortgage opportunities only, other arrangements must be made for servicing the loans which he originates. Where the correspondent is a mortgage banker, he may also service loans made by him for the insurance company or sold by him, receiving therefor a separate service fee. A variety of plans are used to provide compensation for loan correspondents. Among them are monthly payments, a percentage of collections made, and a percentage of original loans. As pointed out elsewhere in this text, a high finder's fee may be accompanied by a low servicing fee and vice versa.

Even those insurance companies that have had extensive experience with both branch offices and loan correspondents seem to encounter difficulty in deciding which plan is better. One reason for this apparent indecision is the problem of changing conditions. At one period of the business cycle, one plan appears to meet requirements best; at another period, another plan may be preferred. Some companies combine the two, using branches to establish patterns and loan correspondents to operate within patterns so established. Some companies alternate plans. Some use both at the same time. Historically speaking, correspondents appeared first. They still predominate.

Undoubtedly, branch operation provides a better opportunity for close control than does the loan correspondent plan. For that reason, times of stress are likely to emphasize the contributions of branches in contrast with those of the more independent correspondents. On the other hand, aggressive correspondents who produce results satisfactory to their principals are likely to find continued demand for their services.

Originating and Service Fees   Originating fees paid loan correspondents by life insurance companies vary from 0.25 to more than 2 percent. Probably the greatest number of cases fall within a range close to 1 percent. The maximum for FHA/VA originations is 1 percent.

Originating or finders' fees are of particular significance where mortgage loans are repaid within a relatively short period of time. If a finder's fee is paid in placing a loan on the books, this reduces the effective interest rate on the loan correspondingly. For example, if the finder's fee is 1.5 percent and the loan is repaid within five years, the 1.5 percent commission must be amortized within the five-year period, unless a corresponding penalty is charged against the borrower for the privilege of prepaying his loan. That is one reason why insurance companies frequently make no provision for mortgage loan prepayments or for such prepayments only when penalties are assessed. One common provision is to permit not more than 20 percent of the loan principal to be repaid within any consecutive period of 12 months. In the recent period of extremely high interest rates, it is not uncommon to have total "lock-in" of the loan for a minimum period, often five to seven years. Currently, finders' fees are commonly paid by the borrower.

Servicing fees commonly range from ⅛ to ¾ of 1 percent. The rate is often related to the size of the loan to be serviced. The Federal National Mortgage Association and the Federal Home Loan Mortgage Corporation commonly allow a ⅜ of one percent servicing fee, while the Government National Mortgage Association commonly pays 0.44 percent. These practices tend to influence the standards for mortgage banking services to life insurance companies.

Home-Office Operations

In addition to the supervision exercised by home-office mortgage loan departments of life insurance companies, some such departments are largely depended upon to originate and service loans. This is particularly true of some small companies, of those which have only an unusually small proportion of their assets invested in mortgage loans, and of those which concentrate their mortgage loans in one or a few areas with close geographical contact with the home office. Some home offices make no use of either branch offices or loan correspondents either for loan originations or for loan servicing. Some rely in part upon loan finders of one kind or another and do all the servicing from the home office. Some find their mortgage loan operations so widely distributed that they farm out both loan origination and servicing.

In general, the functions of the home-office mortgage loan department may be classified under the following heads: (1) the determination of mortgage loan policies, including the kinds of property on which loans will be made or purchased, the geographical areas in which they are to be favored, and the loan plans to be used; (2) the consideration of loan applications and of mortgage-purchase opportunities and the recommendations to be made thereon to the investment committee; (3) the establishment and operation of a plan of supervising home-office staff, field representatives, branch-office personnel, etc.; (4) the study of performance records of loans on the books; and (5) periodic checks to determine the status of mortgage loan investments. From time to time property management arrangements may be required to handle the management, operation, and disposal of properties acquired through foreclosures of delinquent mortgages.

Except in those intermittent periods when unusually large amounts of foreclosed real estate are acquired, the management of property presents no particularly difficult problem. Under so-called normal circumstances, which produce only occasional property acquisitions, the probability is that a local representative or agent will be assigned the task of property disposal. If a mistake was made in making the loan, the insurance company will absorb its loss, if any, as one of the calculated risks of the mortgage loan business. If foreclosure results from causes that could not have been foreseen when the loan was acquired, the same procedure is followed. Only when there is no reasonable market for foreclosed properties will the problem of property management become acute. Then heroic steps may be needed to minimize losses. The home office will then assume greater responsibility for more direct control of owned real estate.

Ownership versus Lending

Financial institutions that have learned from experience that mortgages sometimes turn out to be deferred certificates of real estate ownership have pondered this question: Which is safer, to start with ownership or to end with it? In other words, as an alternative to making a very high percentage loan against a property owned by the borrower, some lenders are experimenting with direct ownership of income property. When a financial institution takes a mortgage on an existing property, it can only take or leave this kind of investment. If it builds the building instead, it can exercise such choices as location, arrangement, and standards of construction. If it makes a loan, it has no direct control over the property as long as the obligations of the mortgagor are met. When it invests its funds directly in the real estate, management rests with the owner. There is no mortgagor. Equities in owned real estate are out in the open. Equities in mortgaged real estate may be just as definitely established in the mortgagee, even though they may be concealed for a time until legal title passes when a default results finally in foreclosure or in an adequate substitute in the form of a voluntary conveyance.

Other factors are also present in the determination to own the real estate from the beginning in contrast with lending against it as security. These include legal complications surrounding foreclosure proceedings. Tax problems play their part also. With the prospect of high taxes for the indefinite future, financial institutions still arrive at investment policies in the boardroom, but only after the tax angles have been fully explored.

In some instances the probabilities lean in the direction of recommending outright ownership of some investment property instead of depending upon interest from mortgages only.

Life insurance companies are among those experimenting with real estate ownership for investment purposes. Such properties are either owned directly by the insurance companies or by wholly owned subsidiaries. The total directly owned real estate in 1947 was $860 million. Of this, $582 million was utilized for company operational requirements. At the end of 1975, the total had grown to $9.6 billion. The life companies' own home and branch offices required about $2 billion of that amount. The other $6.6 billion represented direct ownership of commercial and residential properties. Although this is a favorable trend toward making possible more business facilities and housing, it should be pointed out that $9.6 billion is only slightly more than 3 percent of the total life insurance company assets at that time. Many of these properties are held under leaseback arrangements, discussed elsewhere in this text. A number of recent acquisitions have resulted from forfeitures under distressed mortgages held by the insurance companies.

Commercial Real Estate as an Investment Because of its increasing importance to the life insurance company investment program, commercial real estate should be analyzed in regard to the primary objectives of safety of principal, liquidity, and yield. Its attractiveness depends upon its ability to meet these objectives.

The safety of principal in a direct investment in real estate must be determined by whether the investor can recapture his capital (1) by sale of the property for an amount equal to his unamortized investment or (2) by a full return of his capital in the amortization process, together with a rent equivalent for interest. The measure of marketability of the property, of course, depends upon such factors as its diversity of uses, site, and architectural appeal. Increasing rates of general price inflation and a rising level of real estate prices have also had important impacts in increasing salability of such properties. Critics of commitments to effect a hedge against inflation urge that such uses of funds are of a speculative, rather than investment, nature and consequently improper.

Where reliance for recapture of capital is on the full amortization process, the financial strength of the lessee is paramount. This financial condition is required to meet the objections of those who claim that 100 percent financed rental properties are less secure than mortgages granted for lower percentages of the property value. It is suggested by those favoring direct investment that if the financial strength of the lessee is unquestionable in the early years of the lease, by the time financial conditions of the company will have had time to change, the unamortized cost will be adequately secured by excess property values.

Even in event of financial reverses, they point out, most corporations reorganize and continue operations, with the result that reorganization trustees affirm real estate leases and preserve the owners' claims to continued rental income.

In regard to the liquidity factor in direct real estate investment, it must be accepted that large individual parcels are not readily salable. This is particularly true in periods of economic adversity. Life companies must therefore evaluate this characteristic in light of their overall portfolio requirements. They must accept the limitations of the degree of liquidity provided by the normal amortization of principal implicit in rent income under a long-term lease.

The most attractive feature of this form of investment has been its yield. Directly owned commercial real estate has been consistently acquired to yield effective interest rates ½ percent or more above those on mortgages on comparable property. In addition, recently, bonus interest based on rental overages and equity participations have been written into the loan agreements. In addition, a most important inducement has been the opportunity for capital appreciation either in the residual value after the property has been fully amortized or as result of rising price levels.

There have also been administrative advantages claimed for direct investment. Proponents believe that the supply of commercial real estate at attractive yields is great. It is true that investments in the commercial sector over the last decade or longer have been in tremendous volume. It is not so certain, however, that placement of funds in this area is any less competitive than in other types of investment.

An additional advantage claimed for real estate investment has been the unlikelihood of refinancing or early prepayment so often characteristic of mortgage loans. Although the point seems to be well taken, the advantage seems to be purely one of degree. Both direct ownership and mortgage lending also carry the obligation of periodic reinvestment of funds released by amortization.

Still another advantage claimed for direct investment in real estate is that it permits management, by specially tailored terms of purchase and leaseback, to control net income to some degree. For some purposes, many of them tax-related, this possibility is desirable.

On the other side of the coin, in addition to the questions raised in the foregoing discussion, the problems of staffing skilled persons to administer such real estate investment programs are great, often prohibitive for small insurance companies. Many fear the possibility of having to manage the property in event of reversals. There is also still a strong prejudice among older, senior executives against direct ownership of real estate. Recent experiences have confirmed their wisdom.

Private Placements

One method of financing that is essentially a part of real estate finance was developed during the 1930s and has since grown to enormous proportions. This is variously known as private placement, direct sale, private sale, and so forth. In effect, the business enterprise that needs money obtains it directly from the financial institution that is expected to be the ultimate investor in the securities purchased. There is no middleman such as an investment banker, a security underwriter, or a security salesman.

While not all of the securities that have been purchased by financial institutions in the form of private placements can be classified as real estate bonds, enough of them fit into this category to warrant a brief discussion of private placements in a text on real estate finance. As a matter of fact, the successful experience of financial institutions with large real estate mortgages laid the foundations for their participation in the broader field of private placements.

Origin of Private Placements   The depression of the 1930s focused attention upon the need for security in an uncertain world. In a very real sense, life insurance companies were the beneficiaries of the misfortunes of investors and speculators who lost money from the decline in the prices of stocks and bonds. Disillusioned and discouraged security purchasers in great numbers turned to life insurance as a more certain means of protecting their dependents. This also had the effect of placing upon the insurance companies the burden of investing funds supplied by their policyholders.

For more than two decades we have witnessed a marked trend in the direction of institutionalizing the savings of the American people. Many who lack confidence in their capacity to manage their own affairs have shifted the burden to financial institutions such as life insurance companies. As a result, life insurance companies have become the largest single class of institutions entrusted with the care of the savings of thrifty people. Following the many bank failures in the early 1930s, life insurance companies for a time were about the only source of funds available to industrial enterprises in need of financial assistance. Demand matched supply when those in need of loans went to those who had money to lend.

Influence of Security Regulation   Another factor that has influenced the wide use of private placements was the enactment of the Securities Act of 1933, which gave an agency of the federal government police power over the sale of securities offered in the open market. The element of cost in preparing applications for approval by the Securities and Exchange Commission, while an item of some importance, is probably not the major factor considered by those who sought to bypass such need for seeking approval of the issuance of securities to be offered for sale. The time element was undoubtedly much more significant in the early stages of the use of private placements of securities.

For example, if corporation X should decide at a regular meeting of its board of directors that it should raise money by the sale of a mortgage bond issue at a time when the market for such bonds was reasonably favorable, it would have to prepare its registration statement and supporting documents for submission to the SEC in support of its application for the approval of the sale of its securities in the open market. Thereafter the SEC must be given sufficient time to examine the evidence before reaching a decision. Consequently, from the date of a determination to borrow money to the sale of the bonds in the open market, a few months' time could easily be consumed. Meantime, the market for this class of security might easily turn against it in a fast-moving world. Instead of disposing of the bonds in a favorable market, as had been hoped, the issuing corporation might find itself in a position where it could not dispose of its bonds under reasonably favorable conditions.

By contrast with the above method of an open-market offer of its bonds to all and sundry investors, the corporation could negotiate with a single financial institution such as a life insurance company—or a few such institutions—for the sale of the entire bond issue. Since in such case there would be no public offering of the securities, the SEC would have no jurisdiction over the sale of the bonds. The time, trouble, and expense of preparing registration statements and supporting documents could be saved. Within a few hours instead of a few weeks or months, the borrowing corporation could negotiate a deal with the institutional purchaser or purchasers of its bonds and know just what to expect. Details of preparing the bond issue could follow.

Presumably, also, in the absence of middlemen, the borrowing corporation could realize a bit more from the sale of its bond issue. The amount so saved, if any, depends upon several considerations, including the relative bargaining ability of the seller and the buyer of the bonds.

Continued Use of Private Placements   Even after the conditions that gave rise to private placements in the early 1930s had been succeeded by easier money markets, the use of private placements continued. In some years the tempo of their use has been faster than in the early 1930s. In recent years, sizable proportions of the proceeds of all new security issues have come from private placements. Meantime the investable resources of life insurance companies have mounted year by year. The pressure of putting to work these increased resources have caused an extension of the use of private placements for corporate securities.

QUESTIONS

1. Review briefly the general history of life insurance companies as lenders on real estate security.

2. Are life insurance companies more likely than savings and loan associations to invoke penalties for prepayment of mortgage loans? Why or why not?

3. How do geographical limitations on mortgage lending by insurance companies differ from those governing the operations of other types of lending institutions?

4. By what methods do insurance companies place their investable funds in real estate mortgages? What are the advantages and disadvantages of each method?

5. What reasons can you suggest for the trend toward a decreased proportion of government-underwritten mortgages in insurance company loan portfolios in recent years?

6. Evaluate life insurance companies as investors in mortgages on commercial and industrial real estate.

7. What is the usual range of originating fees paid by life insurance companies to loan correspondents? What is the range of servicing fees?

8. In what types of real estate have life insurance companies invested most extensively as equity owners? Why?

9. How important is private placement to life insurance companies as a means of acquiring corporate securities? Why?

10. What are the most important factors considered in a decision by an insurance company whether to invest in real estate mortgages or corporate bonds?

CASE PROBLEMS

The property, with income and expenses as set forth below, has been used in three examples typical of life insurance company loan arrangements.

Type of property: Apartment—144 units

Value:	Land	$ 300,000
	Building improvements	1,700,000
	Total	$2,000,000
Operations:	Gross income	$ 340,000
	Less 5% vacancy allowance	17,000
	Effective gross income	$ 323,000
	Less cash operating expenses:	
	40% of effective gross income	129,200
	Net income before debt service	$ 193,800

1. In this case the insurance company arranged for participation to the extent of 3% of effective gross income in addition to 9% interest with amortization

of the mortgage loan over 25 years (10.07% constant). Initial mortgage: $1.5 million.

a. Compute the first-year percentage return on investment to the lender.

b. Compute the first-year percentage return on investment to the owner based on cash flow.

c. Assuming an annual rate of increase in income and expenses of 4% compounded monthly in accordance with the tables incorporated in the Appendix to this text, compute the estimated yield to the insurance company in the fifth and tenth years of this loan.

2. In this case the insurance company provided for a 20 percent participation in all income over the "break-even point," defined as 40% of effective gross income plus debt service. This is in addition to 9% interest (10.07% constant) with 25-year amortization. Initial mortgage: $1.5 million.

a. Compute the first-year percentage return on investment to the lender.

b. Compute the first-year percentage return on investment to the owner based on cash flow.

c. Assuming an annual rate of increase in income and expenses of 4% compounded monthly in accordance with the tables incorporated in the Appendix to this text, compute the estimated yield to the insurance company in the fifth and tenth years of this loan.

3. In this case the insurance company invested in accordance with what has sometimes been called the "John Hancock plan." This has often been used in development situations.

Step 1: The investor bought the land for $300,000 cash and leased it back to the developer at a 9% rate.

Step 2: The investor made a 75% loan on leasehold improvements ($1,700,000 × .75) for $1,275,000 at 9% for 30 years (9.66% constant).

Step 3: The investor contracted also to receive 30% of "defined net income." This is equal to the difference between effective gross income and the total of 40% of effective gross income taken as operating expenses, debt service, and the ground rent.

a. Compute the first-year percentage of return on investment to the investor.

b. Compute the first-year percentage of return on investment to the developer based on cash flow.

18

Real Estate Investment Trusts and Syndication

PART 1: REAL ESTATE INVESTMENT TRUSTS

Background of the Real Estate Investment Trusts

The concept of the real estate investment trust goes back to the 1880s. In the early years, trusts were not taxed if the income therefrom was distributed to beneficiaries. A Supreme Court decision in the 1930s, however, resulted in classifying all passive investment vehicles that were centrally organized and managed like corporations as "associations" taxable as corporations. This covered real estate investment trusts.

The stock and bond investment companies, also affected by the Supreme Court decision, promptly secured legislation (in 1936) which exempted regulated investment companies from federal taxation. At this time the real estate trusts were not organized to press for equal consideration and the trust did not develop into importance as a legal form for investing in real estate.

After World War II, however, the need for large sums of real estate equity and mortgage funds renewed interest in more extensive use of the real estate investment trust (which also became known as the "REIT," pronounced "reet"), and a campaign was begun to achieve for the REIT special tax considerations comparable to those accorded mutual funds. In 1960 such legislation cleared the Congress.

Legal Requirements Effective January 1, 1961, special income tax benefits were accorded a new type of investment institution by an amendment to the Internal Revenue Code (Section 856–858). Under this amendment, a real estate investment trust meeting prescribed require-

461

ments during the taxable year may be treated simply as a conduit with respect to the income distributed to beneficiaries of the trust. Thus the unincorporated trust or association, ordinarily taxed as a corporation, is not taxed on distributed taxable income when it qualifies for the special tax benefits. Only the beneficiaries pay the tax on such distributed income. To qualify as a "real estate investment trust" for tax purposes, the following requirements must be met:

1. Ownership must be in an unincorporated trust or association managed by at least one trustee, with transferable certificates of beneficial interest or shares, and ordinarily taxable as a domestic corporation.
2. There must be at least 100 beneficial owners.
3. The trust must not be a personal holding company even though all of its gross income constitutes personal holding company income.
4. The trust may not hold any property primarily for sale to customers in the ordinary course of business, that is, dealer property.
5. It must elect to be treated as a real estate investment trust.

At least 90 percent of the income of a real estate investment trust must come from real property rentals, dividends, interest, or gains from the sale of securities or real estate. Seventy-five percent or more of the trust income must be directly attributable to real property, and another 15 percent must be derived from real estate or any other source from which a regulated investment company would derive most of its income, such as interest and dividends. There is also a 30 percent test, which requires that not more than 30 percent of the gross income of the trust come from short-term gains on security sales and gains on the sale of real estate held for less than four years.

The trust must distribute at least 90 percent of its ordinary income to its shareholders. Any amount that the trust retains is subject to the regular corporate income tax.

When the new law initially went into effect, it appeared that if the real estate required active management and if the trustees participated in such management, the trust would not be accorded exempt status. The final Treasury regulations have defined the duties and powers of the trustees, shareholders or beneficiaries, and independent contracting managers, however, with some liberality. The property manager may perform and bill the trust for operating costs; he may hire and fire employees; he may collect rents and remit differences with proper accounting for collections and expenses. The trustee is permitted to make some important decisions, such as whether to make major repairs.

When the law was passed, real-estate investment trusts where the trustee was required to be "passive" were prohibited in many states. As a result, enabling legislation was required before such trusts could be formed. At the present time, the states generally have laws on the books permitting the establishment of real estate investment trusts that may qualify for special federal income tax benefits.

Types of Trusts   The two principal types of real estate investment trusts are equity trusts and mortgage trusts. In the early years of this REIT form, the equity trust was generally used, but later the mortgage trust became the more important.

The difference between the assets held by the equity trust and those held by the mortgage trust is fairly obvious. The equity trust acquires proprietary interests, while the mortgage trust purchases mortgage obligations and thus becomes a creditor with mortgage liens given priority to equity holders. Of course, as time has progressed, more heterogeneous investment policies have been developed, combining the advantages of both types of trusts to suit specific investment objectives. Such combinations are called "hybrid" trusts.

For purposes of description, equity trusts have been categorized into five groups.[1] These groups, their advantages, and their disadvantages are as follows:

1. *Blank Check Trusts.* A blank check trust is one that is organized to buy properties judged by the trustees to meet the investment goals of the trust. Participating interests in the trust are sold on the strength of the reputations of the promoters, trustees, and independent contractors with management responsibility. The advantage of this type of trust is its flexibility; but a major disadvantage results from the lapse of time between the date the investors' shares are offered to the public and the time when the funds can be profitably invested. During this period, the investors' shares tend to suffer depressed conditions in the securities market.

2. *Exchange Trusts.* Exchange trusts involve the exchange of property for shares in the trust immediately after its organization. Such a transfer qualifies as a tax-free exchange for income tax purposes, and the trust acquires the shareholder's cost basis with respect to the property for depreciation purposes. The disadvantage of failing to acquire a stepped-up basis for higher depreciation deductions is offset by the tax-free diversification that the investor achieves. The trust also benefits in that it obtains a seasoned property with a known income potential.

3. *Purchasing Trusts.* A purchasing trust is one that has been organized to purchase property described in a prospectus. The advantage of this form is that the potential investor is fully informed about the property to be acquired. Possible disadvantages to the purchasing trust may lie in the lack of diversification and, from an administrative point

---

[1] John C. Williamson, "The Real Estate Investment Trust Act—The Catalyst Which Is Making Real Estate 'Go Public'," *Journal of Property Management,* vol. 27, no. 2 (Winter 1961), pp. 68–79.

of view, in the difficulty of gathering sufficient historical data to meet state or federal securities registration requirements.

4. *Mixed Trusts.* Mixed trusts are organized to invest part of the funds raised in a specific property and the balance on a "blank check" basis. Being a hybrid, this trust will have the advantage of providing almost immediate income; but since a part of the funds will be invested over a period of time, the overall return will be relatively low until, at least, the total investment has been made.

5. *Existing Trusts.* Existing trusts are those which were in effect at the time the federal income tax law was revised to permit special treatment and which have since reorganized to qualify under the pertinent Revenue Code Sections. These trusts have the advantage of seasoned management and virtually no new organization costs. They also have an investment history to show prospective investors. Many of their properties will have been written down to the point that depreciation charges are not as great as they would like, but the trusts can cope with this problem by advantageous upgrading.

The equity trusts are distinguishable from the mortgage trusts in many respects regarding investment objectives served. Equity trusts receive rent as a primary source of income, while mortgage trust income is largely in the form of interest income and discounts earned through mortgage amortization. Capital gains in the equity trust come largely through the sale of the real estate. The mortgage trust derives its capital gains from selling mortgages at prices above cost, as a result of a change in money rates or because the mortgages have become more secure instruments. As owner of the physical property, the equity trust may obtain a depreciation deduction as a tax benefit not available to the mortgage trust, but by the same token it must assume the owner's management responsibilities. The mortgage trust income from interest and discounts is fixed in nature, whereas the rental income of the equity trust may be fixed, as in a "net lease," or volatile, where the rents are determined as a percentage of sales. Expenses of operation may also be involved in determining the return to the equity trust. Because they are constantly amortizing, the assets of the mortgage trust have been considered more liquid than the real estate owned by the equity trust. The experience of recent years, however, has demonstrated that where there are widespread delinquencies on mortgage loans, the highly leveraged mortgage trust is likely to be less viable than the equity trust.

A review of these characteristics suggests at least two distinct markets of real estate investors that the trusts serve. The equity trust has been used by the relatively small investor desiring to participate in the ownership and operation of large improved real properties—such as commercial, industrial, or apartment buildings. The mortgage trust, on the other hand, has developed as a vehicle of institutions with increasing surpluses of uninvested savings needing a fixed return or with underutilized mortgage underwriting talent that can be applied to a profitable new venture.

The Appeal of Equity Trusts as an Investment

From a negligible figure in the early 1960s, equity trust ownership of real estate grew to $4.3 billion, or 22 percent of all REIT assets (the other being principally mortgages), at the 1974 year-end. This growth was largely occasioned by investors seeking an opportunity to place funds in real estate under professional guidance as to investment selection with management provided and with somewhat greater liquidity than investment in a real estate parcel provides.

The real estate investment trust is well adapted to fulfilling these requirements. By affording the individual investor an opportunity to pool his resources with those of persons of like interests, funds are assembled to permit purchase of buildings, shopping centers, land and developments—or whatever seems to offer the most attractive returns. Investment must be approved by a board of trustees who are ordinarily well qualified to make such decisions. The trust certificate holder buys an interest in diversified holdings, and his shares are usually readily salable in the over-the-counter market. The tax exemption places the small shareholder in a position for tax payments similar to what he might have if he had made the same investment as an individual real estate operator.

The advantages of the trust to the small private investor depend, in the final analysis, on the fundamental soundness of real estate as an investment. The attractiveness of real estate as an investment closely follows its economic value. These values are largely determined by growth in population and its purchasing power in relation to a uniquely immobile and indestructible site with improvements thereon. According to many real estate analysts, the probable physical and economic life of residential buildings is from 80 to 90 years. The indestructible nature of land and the physical durability of buildings makes it possible for the same parcel to experience diverse successive uses over a period of years or centuries. It follows that improvements with the least special-ized purposes have the greatest flexibility of use and probable longest economic life.

It is a mistake to assume that land values always rise. Even in a prosperous, expanding economy certain segments of the real estate market, whether classified geographically or functionally, may experience distress. It is for this reason that, if one is to take advantage of the possible physical and economic durability of real estate, investment deci-sions should be made by competent, foresighted appraisers with a full appreciation of local and general economic conditions. As the management counsel of mutual funds provide this judgment for investors in such funds, so also the trustees of real estate investment trusts provide this service to their investors.

Leverage Much has been written about the advantages of real estate investment as an opportunity for leverage on equity capital. Leverage, also called "trading on the equity," is the use of borrowed capital to increase the profitability of the equity, or shareholder's interest. The use of borrowed capital is profitable as long as the assets financed by borrowed funds earn more than the borrower's overall cost of capital. Of course, if the earnings on the borrowed funds do not equal the borrower's money costs, the leverage works in reverse. For this reason, only stable operations such as public utilities and real estate, with high predictability and stability of earnings, can use leverage to a great extent. An example of the effects of leverage is given in Exhibit 18–1.

EXHIBIT 18–1
Effects of Leverage

	Venture A[*] All Equity Capital $250,000			Venture B[*] Equity Capital, $250,000 Borrowed Capital, $125,000		
Item	*Average Year*	*Better Year*	*Poor Year*	*Average Year*	*Better Year*	*Poor Year*
Gross income	$50,000	$65,000	$35,000	$75,000	$97,500	$52,500
Operating expenses	30,000	33,600	26,400	45,000	50,400	39,600
Net operating income	$20,000	$31,400	$ 8,600	$30,000	$47,100	$12,900
Fixed charges (interest on borrowed capital)	–0–	–0–	–0–	7,500	7,500	7,500
Return on equity capital	$20,000	$31,400	$ 8,600	$22,500	$39,600	$ 5,400
Rate of return on equity capital (before taxes)	8.0%	12.6%	3.4%	9.0%	15.8%	2.2%

[*] This example assumes an operation in both instances providing gross revenue equal to 20% of its capital with operating expenses equal to 60% of gross revenue in average year.

This example suggests three conclusions:

1. Leverage properly used can be an extremely profitable technique.

2. Higher leverage can increase the required rate of return because of the greater riskiness of the venture.
3. Leverage improperly used reduces an investment to a speculation and is extremely dangerous.

For these reasons, trading on the equity should be done cautiously and only by knowledgeable technicians. It has been found to be more

useful in real estate, because of stability of income, than in any other area of business activity. The real estate investment trust makes extensive use of the leverage opportunity.

Real Estate as a Hedge against Rising Price Levels   Anyone who bought real estate during or shortly after World War II realizes how rising price levels or production costs of new structures—residential, commerical, or industrial, where production is to a demand—can cause the property values to rise. A study of price levels in America from the Revolutionary War days to the present, where periods of as long as 20 years are considered as a span, has shown a steady rise.

The value of real estate that maintains its economic utility tends to move with the cost of reproduction of a new facility to render a comparable service. Particularly where leverage is used to finance ownership of a larger property subject to possibly higher reproduction cost, a properly selected, functional real estate property can serve as a hedge against higher price levels.

Tax Shelters in Real Estate Investments   Much has been written pointing out the tax advantages that may be derived from liberal depreciation allowances deductible from taxable income. The advantage lies in the fact that the functional or economic life of a property often extends far beyond the depreciable life used for income tax purposes. In many instances, the decline in value as a result of depreciation or obsolescence has been substantially or totally offset by rising replacement costs of similar properties when demand for such properties is high in relation to supply. Thus, older properties may sell today at prices above original cost of construction, and yet they may have been substantially depreciated for income tax purposes.

This possibility has been greatly enhanced by the use of accelerated depreciation methods. Such methods permit heavier depreciation charges in the earlier years of the life of the building, and they thus effect a deferral of income tax.

It should be pointed out, however, that to the extent a depreciation charge is taken, the investor has recognized a retrieval of his capital, and not income on his investment. A statement of income and expenses may demonstrate why this is true:

Total revenues received	$100,000
Total cash expenses	60,000
Net cash earnings	$ 40,000
Depreciation charge allowable	
(Write-off to reduce property carrying value)	30,000
Net taxable income	$ 10,000

If this property is managed by a tax-exempt real estate investment trust and the $40,000 of net cash earnings are distributed to trust certificate holders, only one fourth of the earnings (in the ratio of $10,000 to $40,000) will be taxable to the individual recipients. The other three fourths will constitute a nontaxable return of capital. For tax accounting purposes, the individual investor cannot measure his precise return on his investment by his cash receipts. Distributions paid out of depreciation (as the $30,000 above) instead of net income ($10,000 above) are considered a return of capital until the investor receives the full cost of his shares or sells them. After full recovery of costs he realizes taxable gains.

From a practical investor's standpoint, however, where the trust shares have a ready marketability, a current yield may be effectively determined by comparing the cash dividend received (trust payout) with the current market price. A history of gain or loss in capital may be derived from comparing issue price and market price. Because a large portion of real estate investment trust distributions is usually nontaxable, the after-tax value of such dividends is often substantially greater to the individual taxpaying investor than a like amount of fully taxable dividends of an ordinary corporation.

The 1974–75 Reversal. The business recession and tight money rates of the 1974–75 period brought major difficulties to the equity real estate investment trusts. Although they did not suffer the severe losses of the mortgage trusts, as will be discussed later, the value of their shares in the public markets declined substantially.

Large-scale unemployment created rental vacancies as families merged into fewer housing units. Rental overages on leases disappeared or businesses defaulted or discontinued operations. Meanwhile, maintenance costs rose under the inflationary pressures. It was generally not possible to acquire new properties under conditions of favorable leverage because of relatively higher long-term mortgage interest rates. Consequently, net income was reduced or losses were incurred and dividends were reduced or suspended.

Although banking relationships deteriorated in these years, a return to a more orderly mortgage market can do much to make refinancing and resale of properties a possibility and thus to restore liquidity to the equity trusts. Emergence from the recession will bring about a restoration of income to the trust properties. This income, in turn, will be flowed through to the equity trust shareholders.

It is a few years away, but ultimately, after the banks have dealt with the surfeit of mortgages that they have had to take over, mostly from the mortgage trusts, the equity trusts may again be considered eligible borrowers, albeit under cautionary terms. As these trends develop, the equity trusts may again be in a position to offer the attractions that brought such a generous flow of funds into the real estate market during the 1960s and early 1970s.

The Development of Mortgage Trusts[2]   The mortgage lending segment of the REIT industry by the 1974 year-end encompassed $15.29 billion, or about 72 percent, of the total industry assets of $21.18 billion. This development took place largely from 1969 through 1974. At the latter year-end, trust sponsor-advisors included 39 commercial banks, 42 mortgage bankers or real estate companies, and 10 insurance companies, accounting for nearly 60 percent of the total assets of the industry.

Accounting for such institutional growth, fostered by so many institutions so quickly, was the expectation of material advantages to the sponsors of the trusts. The main advantages sought were:

1. An additional source of funds to lend on mortgages that could be serviced by the sponsor or its affiliate.
2. Advisory fees.
3. An opportunity to support projects by loans beyond the legal or policy limits of the sponsoring institution.

The Appeal of Mortgage Trusts as an Investment.   The mortgage trust is unlike the equity trust in that it does not own the real property. Rather, it owns mortgage paper secured by the underlying real property. Income generated by the mortgage paper is affected by the nominal interest rate on the mortgage note, the discount (or premium) at which the obligation is acquired, and the amount of funds outstanding on loan. The trust expenses applicable against this income are, generally, interest paid for the funds derived to put out on loan, management company costs, and other lesser expenses incident to the operations of this kind of investment company.

During the late 1960s and early 1970s, prior to the débacle of mortgage defaults in 1974 and 1975, this trust form held forth great promise as a source of loans, particularly for construction and development, that were beyond the legal or policy limits of the highly regulated banks, savings and loans, insurance companies, or other real estate-oriented

---

[2] Financial data presented in this section were derived from *REIT Fact Book—1975*, National Association of Real Estate Investment Trusts, Inc., 1101 Seventeenth St., N.W., Washington, D.C. 20036. The current *Fact Book* is recommended supplementary reading for this chapter.

financing institutions. Because their lending policies were relatively unregulated and because they had access to public securities markets, mortgage trusts were in a position to fill a great void in the real estate financing market.

Equity funds were raised through sale of shares to the public and these funds were usually placed in a portfolio of FHA and VA government-backed mortgages. This investment immediately provided an effective yield on assets of 7 to 8 percent. In addition, the FHA-VA mortgages provided an equity-derived asset base that would support bank lines of credit of up to four times the amount of the equity. Thus, $1 million of shareholders' equity would support up to $4 million of bank credit lines, or similar access to the commercial paper market. Even though the cost of the short-term borrowed funds might be relatively high, there was always the reasonable expectation that the trust could put the funds out on a construction or development loan at a 3½ to 4 percent higher rate. The spread between borrowing costs and loan income thus held promise of increasing earnings on the shareholders' equity as the loan portfolio grew. Such growth in earnings would support further sales of shares in the trust at higher prices, and so on. Following this pattern, the expansion of mortgage trusts during the early 1970s was spectacular.

The 1974–75 Recession. During 1974 a general economic recession set in and the prime bank lending rate rose to an unprecedented high of 12 percent. Because of the unanticipated rise in money costs, many mortgage trusts were forced into an operating loss position because they were not able to pass on a sufficient amount of these higher costs to their borrowing customers. Their advance mortgage commitments had been made at lower rates with inadequate flexibility for upward rate adjustments. Beyond this, many developers were unable to sell their completed units or could not complete their projects because of rapidly inflating construction costs and, consequently, were thrown into default on their construction loans. The equity share values of mortgage trusts plummeted, thus foreclosing further stock sales as a source of funds.

Because of the loan default expectations, the commercial paper market dried up for the trusts and forced them to rely almost exclusively on bank credit lines. As the defaults continued to increase during 1975, many large commercial banks were placed in the position of having to extend the maturities on notes taken pursuant to these credit lines which had usually been extended by banks as a group under a revolving credit agreement. The extensions were granted to avoid the cumulative impact on the total financial system if the trusts were forced to undertake mass foreclosures in a time of serious business recession. A number of bank sponsors took large blocks of mortgages out of the trust portfolios and into their own loan and liquidation accounts to reduce trust debts where stringencies became so severe that commercial bank lines could not otherwise be reasonably renewed. Such actions had an impact on overall commercial bank liquidity and removed the mortgage trusts generally from the construction and development loan markets as a supplier of funds for the foreseeable future. There still remains, however, a real need for a significant amount of construction and development financing under proper restraints. It is possible that after the shakeout a few stronger trusts will survive and will return to this market to become viable lenders in this important field of real estate finance.

The lessons learned from this experience were costly and many. They included numerous excesses: excessive expectations of trust profitability; excessive loan-to-value ratios; excessive use of credit lines; and excessive reliance on too little expertise of too few trust executives in times of rampant inflation and confiscatory money costs.

Types of REIT Mortgage Loans   Since it is reasonable to expect an eventual return of stabilized mortgage trusts to the lending markets, it is important to note the kinds of mortgage lending to which they have made a significant contribution. In order of importance, mortgage trust loans include:

1. Construction loans.
2. Development loans.
3. Long-term conventional loans on apartment and commercial properties.
4. Short- and intermediate-term loans on completed properties.
5. Junior lien loans.

Construction Loans.   Nearly half of REIT mortgage loans are construction loans. This has historically been an area of great need for funds because this type of lending has been subordinated to many others by savings and loan associations, commercial banks, insurance companies, and other institutional lenders. Because the bulk of mortgage trust funds were usually raised on a short-term basis, the construction loan with high interest rates and attractive commitment fees with maturities normally falling within one to two years seemed an appropriate investment. At the 1974 year-end, about two thirds of the construction loans outstanding were for residential housing. Office buildings and shopping centers accounted for a substantial amount of the other loans for construction.

Development Loans.   About 15 percent of the mortgage trust loans have gone for land development. Such loans are granted a developer to make site improvements necessary with building construction. The major items of cost in development are clearing and grading the land and putting in roads and utility lines. Usually a development loan is accompanied by a construction loan on the same property.

Long-Term Mortgage Loans. Some mortgage trusts have taken the more conservative route of investing in long-term (10 to 20 years) mortgage loans. After 1971, however, REIT long-term mortgage lending fell off markedly because the costs of long-term funds, rising along with short-term rates, rendered such commitments unprofitable.

Short- and Intermediate-Term Loans. Loans for the short or intermediate term (up to 10 years) are typically not substantially amortized. They are made on completed properties to carry the developer through an interim period during which he hopes to build a favorable operating experience, to improve significantly his bargaining position for favorable terms on his long-term mortgage loans. Particularly in recent years, loans of this type have been made when the developer found his construction loan maturing with no long-term take-out commitment to pay it off. Many such interim loans have been thrown into default because of recent deterioration in the real estate market and inability of the developer to obtain long-term financing.

Junior Lien Loans. With rising interest rates, wraparound mortgages have been used significantly in connection with financing improvements to existing properties or to refinance for purposes of raising additional funds for expansion at another site. Junior liens also arise as auxiliary forms in connection with other transactions. Liens of this type represent only about 9 percent of all trust mortgage loans.

Balance Sheet of the REIT Industry The National Association of Real Estate Investment Trusts, Inc. published the following balance sheet of the REIT industry as of the 1974 year-end (in $ billions):

Assets		*Liabilities and Shareholders' Equity*	
First mortgages:		Commercial paper	$ 0.71
Land loans	$ 0.90	Bank term loans and	
Development	2.34	revolving credit in use	5.78
Construction	7.75	Bank lines in use	5.29
Completed properties:		Senior nonconvertible debt	0.38
0–10 years	1.51	Subordinated nonconvertible	
10+ years	1.95	debt	1.01
Junior mortgages		Convertible debt	0.68
Land, dev., & construction	0.39	Mortgages on property	
Completed properties	1.05	owned	1.65
Loan loss reserves	(0.61)	Other liabilities	0.47
Land leasebacks	0.54		$15.97
Property owned	3.72	Shareholders' equity	5.20
Cash and other assets	1.63		
Total	$21.18°	Total	$12.18°

° Does not total due to rounding.
Source: *REIT Fact Book—1975*, p. 37. This balance sheet was derived by the NAREIT from data provided by the 208 trusts of which it has records excluding those trusts not filing as REITS for tax purposes.

PART 2: REAL ESTATE SYNDICATION

Meaning

The concept of real estate syndication extends generally to any group of investors who have contributed funds for the common purpose of carrying out a real estate project requiring a concentration of capital. It may take the business form of:

1. Corporation.
2. Joint ownership.
3. Joint venture.
4. Partnership.

The Corporate Form Incorporation of the business generally provides such advantages as continuity of life, marketability of ownership shares, and ease of estate planning, since security values are more ascertainable. It also limits the liability of the shareholders to the amount of the cost of their shares. A major disadvantage of this form, however, is the exposure of the investor to double taxation. The corporation pays income tax on the project earnings and the investor-shareholder pays income tax on the residual earnings at his rate as they are paid to him as dividends by the corporation. For this reason, the corporate form has been less attractive than others providing less vulnerability to taxation.

Joint Ownership There are also difficulties attendant upon the use of joint ownership, usually tenancy-in-common. Death of a syndicate investor brings problems of estate administration into the project. The refusal of one member to cooperate may under some conditions create a general stalemate.

Joint Venture This form has been used extensively for private real estate syndicates. Groups may acquire a succession of properties calling for differing arrangements with investors and for financing with each separate property. The precise tailoring required for each venture limits the usefulness of this form for public syndication.

Partnership The partnership, usually modified to a limited partnership, has become the most popular syndicate form. The partnership is not treated as a separate entity for tax purposes, and, therefore, the profits are flowed directly to each member of the firm in proportion to his participation. When the limited partnership form is used, the investor may become a limited partner and thereby limit his liability to loss to his capital contribution. Only the general partner carries unlimited liability for creditor obligations of the firm. Properly established, the limited partnership provides most of the advantages, without the tax disadvantages, of the corporate form. This explains its attraction for public syndication.

Types of Syndicates

There are two important types of syndicates: private and public. A private syndication is so limited in the number of participants in the offering as to render compliance with securities laws a minimal task. A public offering, on the other hand, is characterized by rigorous compliance requirements of the federal and state securities divisions governing the sale of securities to the public. Numerous reports, brochures, prospectuses, and the like are required to qualify an issue for sale to the public.

Private Real Estate Syndicates Private real estate syndicates are usually made up of a few local friends and business associates who think they see a speculative opportunity in real estate operations. They operate informally, sometimes to their disadvantage, and the public seldom knows of their existence. They pool their resources to establish a fund, either for the purpose of purchasing an equity in a property already encumbered by a mortgage or upon which a mortgage is placed as a part of the deal, or for the purpose of paying for a property so that they may own it free from encumbrances. Different circumstances may dictate one or the other of these methods of financing the property.

Each separate transaction is set up as a joint venture, even though the same individuals may participate in successive deals of this kind. Title to the property purchased may be taken in the name of one member of the syndicate who serves as its manager or in the name of some corporate trustee. In either event, the terms of the syndicate agreement should be set forth with greater particularity than is usually followed. Misunderstandings and miscalculations may be better avoided by more explicit written agreements. Even though an elaborate agreement is drawn up, it is usually known only to participants in the syndicate. No representation is made to outsiders that would lead them to consider this type of syndicate as a general partnership.

As in any other business venture, numerous questions may arise in the future that should be anticipated at the time the deal is made. Among them are the following: (1) responsibility, compensation, and authority of manager and trustee, if one is used; (2) method of voting upon issues to be settled by members—one vote per man or votes distributed according to amount of financial contribution to the resources of the syndicate; (3) improvement policies—modernization of old building or even replacement as the best means of realizing greatest profits from the venture; (4) assessments of members and methods of collecting them; (5) metohds of dealing with members who refuse or are unable to meet assessments; (6) methods of disposal of syndicate interests of members wishing or forced to dispose of them; and (7) names of syndicate members, the amounts of their individual contributions and the manner of sharing profits or losses.

This type of syndicate is normally used to finance a real estate speculative venture. It can, however, be used for investment purposes as well. The kinds of properties dealt in include: vacant land thought to be about ready for subdividing; apartment or office buildings, or even factories; or any kind of property the present owners of which may be in need of immediate financial rescue. In other words, real estate syndicates may be associated with financial distress.

The qualifications of members of real estate syndicates of this type should include the following: (1) They should have available resources that could be devoted to such a venture for whatever period of time is necessary without embarrassment. (2) They should have the courage required to embark upon a type of business operation that may involve considerable risk. (3) They should have the patience needed to stay with the program which they undertake until they test their best opportunities for profit from it. In some cases this may take several years with annual expenses and taxes to pay but no income to offset them. (4) They should be well enough acquainted with each other to be able to act in harmony, come what may. Ventures of this kind require a high degree of mutual confidence, both among the members and in the syndicate manager.

Various practices are followed with respect to the determination of issues to be settled involving the interests of syndicate members. Under one method of operation, the chief contribution made by the members is financial. They pay their money over to the manager and let him make all decisions concerning its use. This has the advantage of avoiding conflicts of opinions, but places a considerable burden of choice upon one man. Under other methods, all major decisions are made by syndicate members. This is the more democratic approach, but may result in differences that are not easily resolved. If a trustee holds title to the property in trust for the members, it is not expected that he will be required or permitted to make major decisions affecting their interests. The agreement should make this clear, to avoid future complications.

Public Real Estate Syndicates   Particularly since the mid-1950s, a number of large syndicators have spearheaded a new trend involving the public in real estate syndication. Certificates of participation have been sold in units as low as $500, $1,000, or $5,000—amounts which were previously considered too small. The result has been that, instead of a few participants of substantial means and risk-taking ability, the syndicate membership may be composed of thousands of small investors who have been intrigued by promises of a tax-sheltered high return per year. An early example of the operation finds the syndicator and his chosen associates advancing $100,000 for the general partnership interest. Limited partnership interests are then offered to the public in $1,000 or $5,000 units for a total of $4.4 million. With the $4.5 million of equity funds, the syndicate can buy a real estate complex costing up to $10 million, mortgaging the property for the difference. The promised high return to limited partners must to a great extent be conditional on the income potential of the property. Furthermore, at least a portion of the return is considered for tax purposes to be a recovery of capital for depreciation of the property. Many investors assume a permanently rising price level which will offset actual dollar depreciation in real estate. If this condition does not hold, however, the investor finds that his depreciation deduction is a true cost as well as a tax item, and that his return is lower by that amount.

In an operation of this kind the syndicate general partners share few of the risks. They may have originally bought the property through another business entity and sold it to the syndicate at a profit. Through another company which they own they may receive substantial remuneration for management services. Above all, as the general partners, all earnings and capital gains not contracted away to the limited partners accrue to their benefit. They stand to gain all residual benefits. For a $10 million real estate holding, for example, $1 million net income should not be excessive for a one-year operation. Distributions on the capitalization might be as follows:

```
Net rent income (before interest) ................................$1,000,000
Less:
    Mortgage ($5,500,000 @ 7½%) ...............$385,000
    Limited partners ($4,400,000 @ 12%) ...... 528,000
                                                          913,000
        Residual to general partners (syndicators) .........$   87,000
```

On the $100,000 invested by the syndicators the return for the year would be 87 percent. Upon later sale of the property at a capital gain, the syndicators' participation usually would take a major portion of the gains above a refund to limited partners of their original investment.

It is readily apparent from the thin band of coverage of the limited partners' return of 12 percent that their risk is relatively high. This has been a matter of increasingly grave concern to state and federal securities sales regulators.

Limited Partnership Syndicates for Publicly Assisted Housing The limited partnership business form has recently emerged as a favored vehicle for the ownership of residential rental real estate for low and moderate income groups where constructed under the aegis of the National Housing Act or similarly directed state statutes. The limited partnership form is attractive because it offers to all limited partners the major advantage of a corporation—liability for firm business obligations limited to a specific capital contribution—and does not incur the disadvantage of the corporate form of not being able to pass business operating losses through to the firm owners. The limited partnership is not treated as a separate taxable entity like the corporation. The partnership losses, therefore, are distributable directly to the partners in accordance with their loss-sharing ratio, whereas in a corporation such losses can only be offset against corporate income of other periods.

In establishing the limited partnership, great care must be taken that the contractual terms identify it in effect as a partnership and not as an "association" as understood by the Internal Revenue Service. An association is taxed like a corporation. The six criteria for treatment like a corporation are the presence of:

1. Business associates.
2. An objective to carry on the business and divide the gains therefrom.
3. Continuity of life.
4. Centralization of management.
5. Limited liability.
6. Free transferability of interest.

A corporation must have more corporate than noncorporate characteristics to be classified as a corporation for tax purposes. Criteria 1 and 2 above are common to both corporations and partnerships. It is, therefore, commonly understood that a business firm will receive treatment as a partnership if two of the criteria 3 through 6 are absent.

Most limited partnerships have a centralization of management similar to corporations, so differentiation normally will take place in 3, 5, and 6. Under the Uniform Partnership Act, after which most state statutes are patterned, the general partner has the power to dissolve the partnership at any time, thus denying it continuity of life. Otherwise, a terminal date may be provided for in the partnership articles. The criterion of limited liability is negated by the very fact that one partner is a general partner with unlimited liability. Finally, free transferability of interests can be limited by requiring permission of the general or other limited partners to effectuate a change of ownership. This restriction has been deemed by the Treasury regulations such an impingement as to constitute a legal curtailment of transferability of interests. By proper combination of these provisions, tax treatment as a partnership can be achieved.

The sole general partner of a limited partnership is often a corporation. The advantage of this arrangement lies in the limited personal liability the builder-sponsor of a project can achieve by holding his interest in the limited partnership in his corporation. An incorporated general partner can also provide better continuity of management. To avoid "dummy" characteristics in the sole corporate general partner, the Internal Revenue Service follows internal guidelines (called "safe harbor rules") imposing certain ownership and minimum capital requirements. In regard to ownership, limited partners may not own, individually or in the aggregate, more than 20 percent of the corporate stock. The tax rules of attribution of ownership relating to members of the partners' families also apply. The net worth requirement of the corporate general partner depends upon the total contributed capital of the partnership: If the contributed capital is less than $2.5 million, the corporate general partner must have a net worth at least equal to 15 percent of the total partnership capital, but not to exceed $250,000. Where the contributed partnership capital is $2.5 million or more, the corporate general partner must maintain at all times a net worth of at least 10 percent of the partnership capital.

It is a uniform rule that property can be depreciated only to the extent of its tax basis, usually cost. In a general partnership, where all partners have unlimited liability, the tax basis, or cost, includes both equity contributions and debts for which all partners are responsible. Thus, the full cost, whether financed by equity or debt, can be claimed as a depreciation deduction over time for income tax purposes. A consistent application of this rule to limited partners would seem to limit their depreciation deduction to their equity interest, since they assume no liability beyond that amount. In this instance, however, there is an exception where none of the partners has any liability in connection with the property acquisition.[2] This is true in regard to a mortgage on real estate acquired by a partnership on a "subject to" basis without assumption by the partnership or any of the partners of any liability on the mortgage. Under such conditions, the full cost of the property, whether acquired by funds provided by equity or debt, may be taken as a depreciation deduction by the partners, whether general or limited. Thus, where a depreciable property was financed by $9 of debt for each $1 of equity, the partner has leveraged his depreciation deduction to 10 to 1. Over time, the taxpayer partner may claim $10 of depreciation deductions against taxable income for each $1 of equity invested. In a 50 percent tax bracket, his cumulative tax savings could amount to $5, or five times his equity investment.

Although the Tax Reform Act of 1969 extended the recapture provisions of the income tax law whereby excess depreciation taken by accelerated methods is treated as ordinary income rather than capital gain upon sale of the property, more liberal treatment was accorded government-assisted projects and rehabilitation expenditures for low-income rental housing. Furthermore, a new 60-month straight-line write-off was provided for rehabilitation expenditures for low-income rental housing

---

[2] Treas. Regs. § 1.752–1 (e); see also Sheldon Schwartz, "How to Find Tax Shelter as a Limited Partner," *Real Estate Review*, vol. 1, no. 2 (Summer 1971), pp. 54–59.

where the dwelling units are held for occupancy by persons of low or moderate income consistent with the policies of the Housing and Urban Development Act of 1968. Publicly assisted housing has thus become particularly attractive for syndication to the taxpayer in the high bracket who is seeking deductible losses to pose against income he is receiving from other sources.

In summary, the appeals of the limited partnership syndicate for publicly assisted housing lie in combining maximum depreciation deductions, relatively favorable capital gain treatment under the recapture rules, and government-assisted financing with delegated management responsibility and limited liability. Such a marriage of investment advantages has made it possible for many builder-sponsors to complete qualified construction projects without any equity investment of their own.

Regulation of Public Real Estate Syndicates

From substantial beginnings during the 1950s and early 1960s, there was a veritable stampede into real estate investment through syndicates during the late 1960s and early 1970s. Investors were aggressively seeking a hedge against high rates of inflation, highly predictable returns, and tax shelters. The most respected Wall Street underwriters began to bring out SEC-registered limited partnerships to invest in properties, and less distinguished promoters were active across the country.

The great flexibility of the limited partnership led to abuses, particularly in investment policies, promoters' and managers' compensation, and investor suitability standards. It is in these areas that federal and state regulatory authorities have expressed the greatest concern.

Investment Policies   In the early experience with limited partnerships and until the late 1960s, capital was normally raised to finance identifiable parcels, which were described in the prospectus or offering circular in detail. Such specific definition of the investment assets set the standards of securities commissioners in a fairly rigid pattern.

In 1969, however, Goodbody & Co. underwrote Burnham Properties, a $20 million public limited partnership with an undefined portfolio. Approval of the sale was obtained in California on the principle that there should be no greater objection to public investing in an undescribed portfolio for real estate than to mutual funds investing in stocks and bonds on a discretionary basis. In a short time, several similar issues were permitted in other states. Although such offerings are not looked upon with favor, state securities commissioners have generally come to accept them. They are known as "blind pool" syndications and should be recognized as pure venture capital funds, since there can be no property descriptions or relevant economic or financial data available for the investors' guidance. After a review of abuses invited by blind pool offerings, a real estate advisory committee established by the SEC recommended that if such offerings are to be permitted at all, specific investment criteria should be disclosed in the prospectus, as well as the sponsor's background, experience, and previous results.[3] In addition, the committee recommended that the issuer be required to file annual reports on its operations with the SEC and to send them as well to its investors. These reports should show investment results in detail and demonstrate how the use of the funds conformed with the standards enunciated in the prospectus.

Promoters' and Managers' Compensation   A second major area creating problems for syndicate investors arises in connection with promotional and management fees. Keeping these fees to reasonable levels becomes especially difficult in the field of real estate because of the many ways in which compensation can be paid. It may be in the form of a brokerage fee, portfolio management fee, a promotional interest as a general partner, or an insurance commission, to name a few.

Management fees have been based on gross assets, net assets, gross rentals, net income, and cash flow. Each method will yield its own unique results dependent upon the fortunes of the syndicate operation. Unfortunately, projections of results are often based on hypotheticals without valid underlying assumptions. Bad projections will distort judgments regarding what is appropriate compensation, or, for that matter, what is a proper method for determining it. In all instances, full disclosure of conflicts of interest of principals, as well as all direct and indirect compensation payable by the partners to promoters, general partners, underwriters, and affiliates, should be made. This disclosure should describe the compensation as to time of payment and amount and it should detail the service rendered to earn it.

Investor Suitability Standards   An outstanding weakness of a limited partnership interest as an investment is its lack of liquidity or marketability. By virtue of the restrictions on the assignability of the capital interest, a new partner must have the consent of the existing partners to acquire and enjoy the full interest of a selling partner. Furthermore, state-imposed requirements of financial responsibility of potential investors have complicated the problem of developing a secondary market for such interests. Even an issue of certificates of beneficial interest in a limited partnership interest is complicated by the fact that the limited partner becomes a securities issuer and subject to separate registration requirements.

Another weakness of the syndicate lies in the fact that it often has limited appeal to any but the investor in the high tax brackets. Yields on other than a tax shelter basis may be negligible. The low-income

---

[3] These results were published by the Real Estate Advisory Committee, established May 3, 1973, by the SEC. See also the article titled "What Lies Ahead for Real Estate Regulation?" by the Committee chairman Raymond R. Dickey, in *Real Estate Review*, vol. 3, no. 1, Spring 1973, pp. 13–19.

investor may acquire a syndicate interest with too little appreciation of the weak economic viability of the venture. The nature of the investor's expected return in the traditional sense, as well as the hypothetical tax savings, should be clearly delineated in all cases.

Federal and State Securities Authorities   The federal and state securities laws and regulations are relevant to any real estate syndication. Disclosure requirements under the Securities Act of 1933 and the Securities Exchange Act of 1934 set the federal basis for civil liability to investors and criminal fraud liability of principals and their professional counsel for failure to disclose full information about a public issue. State blue sky laws require securities salesmen to be registered in the local jurisdiction. These laws often go beyond the federal requirements in permitting the state commissioner to disqualify a security on its merits, in addition to determining the required degree of disclosure of specific facts about the issue. Neglect of the issuer to qualify the issue may permit the investor to rescind the whole transaction and demand his money back. Beyond these laws are the state antifraud statutes to deal with fraudulent practices in connection with security registration. Although the degree of applicability of federal or state laws and regulations differs with the characteristics of each issue, full and active compliance will yield the best results for both the syndicator and his investors.

QUESTIONS

1.   How does a real estate investment trust qualify for favored tax treatment under the Internal Revenue Code? What is that treatment?

2.   Distinguish among the principal types of real estate investment trusts and show how each may be useful.

3.   What are the chief differences in the tax advantages generated by the equity trust and the mortgage trust?

4.   What are the major appeals of the equity trust to the public investor? What are the shortcomings of this trust as evidenced in the recent period of recession and high interest rates?

5.   Answer question 4 for mortgage trusts.

6.   What problems do you see to the return of equity trusts as an important institutional source of funds for financing real estate?

7.   Answer question 6 for mortgage trusts.

8.   Why is the limited partnership such a popular form for real estate syndication?

9.   How are limited partnerships used in public assisted housing?

10.   What are the principal governmental regulatory problems in connection with public real estate syndications?

CASE PROBLEMS

1.   Public Equity Real Estate Trust has assets of $2 million. Its annual

revenues last year totaled $240,000. Cash expenses, exclusive of financing, were $60,000. The trust has mortgage debt of $1.2 million, with an effective interest rate of 9% and a loan constant of 10%. Annual depreciation is $50,000.

Required: 1.   Compute the annual cash flow of the trust. Assuming the full amount of the cash flow was paid to the shareholders, what percentage return would they receive?

2.   Determine the minimum dividend that the trustees must pay if the trust is to qualify for exemption from federal income taxes on net income paid to shareholders.

2.   Mortgage Trust of America (MTA) had strong institutional sponsorship. It had bank lines permitting it to borrow up to $4 million for each $1 million of unimpaired equity invested in government-backed mortgages. MTA sold 1 million shares to the public at $20. These funds were invested in FHA-VA mortgages to yield effectively 8%. Trust bank credit lines permitted borrowing at an effective rate of two points above the bank prime lending rate. The trust felt confident that it could generally lend the short-term funds for construction or development with a 4% spread. If demand contracted, it could pay off its bank borrowings. Operating expenses were estimated at 20% of total yield.

Show how the trust might expect to increase earnings and to support further equity financing as the credit lines were used. Test debt/equity ratios of 1/1, 2/1, and 3/1.

3.   Real Estate Packaging Company, Inc. established a limited partnership with its subsidiary, Expertise, Inc., as the general partner and investors Gray and Black as limited partners. A $2 million property was assigned to the partnership subject to a $1.6 million 10% mortgage from the Security Insurance Company. With estimated land value at $100,000, the annual depreciation on the building and fixtures at 4% was $76,000. Financing for the total property was as follows:

Institutional mortgage	$1,600,000
Limited partner Gray–40% of capital	160,000
Limited partner Black–40% of capital	160,000
General partner Expertise, Inc.–20% of capital	80,000
Total cost of property	$2,0000,000

Projected effective cash income:

Rentals		$ 250,000
Cash expenses, excluding interest	$ 70,000	
Interest, assuming no amortization of mortgage principal	160,000	
Total cash expenses		230,000
Projected cash flow to partners		$ 20,000

Assuming that partner Gray participates in proportion to his capital contribution and is in an overall 50% tax range on his income, how long will it take for him to achieve a payback of his investment in total cash flow and tax savings? What do you estimate to be the amount of the tax shield from his share of depreciation over the life of the property?

19

Mortgage Banking

Meaning

Mortgage bankers are sometimes known as mortgage companies or mortgage dealers. Those included under this appellation as defined in the Constitution of the Mortgage Bankers Association of America are as follows:

Any person, firm or corporation . . . engaged in the business of lending money on the security of improved real estate in the United States, and who publicly offers such securities, or certificates, bonds or debentures based thereon, for sale as a dealer therein, or who is an investor in real estate securities, or is the recognized agent of an insurance company or other direct purchaser of first mortgage real estate securities for investment only.

The principal activity of the modern mortgage banker is originating and servicing income property and residential mortgage loans for institutional investors. Some mortgage bankers are essentially one-man concerns, with all of the small capital owned by the manager. In other cases, the corporate form of organization is used, with more than one class of security sometimes sold to obtain capital. In some cases, operations are extensive enough to warrant the maintenance of offices in several cities by one corporation. Since mortgage bankers are essentially merchandisers of mortgages, they expect to turn their capital rapidly. Their relatively small equity capital is sometimes supplemented by the use of bank credit. Even when bonds or debentures are sold, the resulting capital of mortgage bankers is not large in comparison with the annual volume of business done.

Mortgage Loan Broker Distinguished

Closely related to the mortgage banker, yet distinct from him, is the mortgage loan broker. The relationship is so close that there is frequent confusion among those who fail to see any major difference. In other cases the mortgage loan broker is considered, often without justification, to be the black sheep of the mortgage-financing family. On another branch of the family tree, the mortgage loan broker is closely related to the better understood real estate broker whose activity is centered around the sale of real estate. Indeed, the same individual acts frequently in a dual capacity of real estate broker and mortgage loan broker.

Unlike the mortgage banker, the mortgage loan broker never invests his own capital in a mortgage. He is strictly an agent and not a merchandiser. To be sure, he may act from time to time as an agent without a principal, since he frequently is put in the position of peddling a loan application until he finds an investor interested in it. When this is accomplished, the broker then becomes the agent of the investor for the purpose of closing the deal for a loan.

Mortgage loan brokers may operate "under their hats," from a small office devoted to this business only, or in conjunction with insurance brokerage and other related businesses. They may even use their real estate brokerage offices as their places of business. They may be individuals, partnerships, or corporations. They seldom advertise their business in any formal way, but depend upon personal contacts to secure their loan applications. Their chief function is to originate real estate loans for insurance companies, banks, and others.

Mortgage Bank Departments

In the smaller offices, manned by the owner and a couple of clerks, the owner-mannager is a jack-of-all-trades. He takes care of all parts of the business. In the large mortgage banks, departmentalization may be carried out in some detail, with each major department operated more or less as a unit. Among the most common of such departments are: (1) the promotional department, which develops new business, processes applications for loans, obtains purchase commitments, and so on; (2) the title department, which drafts papers, records them, takes care of title problems, and delivers the mortgages; (3) the servicing department, which makes collections, and so forth; (4) the accounting department, which keeps all records; and (5) the insurance department, which handles all insurance problems. Sometimes separate departments handle taxes, FHA/VA transactions, and so forth.

Need for Soliciting Business

Some mortgage bankers look with disfavor upon dependence on customers calling at their places of business to apply for real estate loans.

Unless he has a previous association with the mortgage banker, the walk-in customer tends to be someone shopping a poor loan around, or trying to find which lender will make the highest appraisal, or seeking a rate at less than the prevailing one. Reliance on this kind of customer is not conducive to building the strongest mortgage loan portfolio.

Since the lender has no means of knowing in advance the people who are likely to become applicants for real estate loans, many mortgage bankers find their best source of business to be real estate brokers. Since most transfers of real estate title which give rise to the need for loans occur as the result of sales efforts of brokers, the latter are in the best position to know what loans will be needed. Field agents contact brokers regularly and undertake to render service of a kind that will win their goodwill.

Next in order of solicitation are builders. Some field agents make a practice of calling upon builders on their construction jobs, since it is frequently difficult to find them at their offices. When construction loans are granted, the fieldmen who contact the builders to solicit their business sometimes serve as inspectors as well. Where permitted to do so, field agents attend meetings of both real estate brokers and builders, thereby keeping abreast with their thinking on matters affecting the financial problems which they face.

Payments to Outsiders

One problem faced by all institutions engaged in making loans on real estate as security is the question of making payments to those not actively engaged in the business. Such payments usually assume two forms: First, a finder's fee is sometimes paid to the real estate broker or the builder who is responsible for bringing the loan application to the attention of the mortgage banker. This is a sort of bribe to induce the broker or builder to give preference to the banker who pays it. But if all lenders in a given market pay the same finder's fee, it ceases to be effective as a business-producing device. Also, where it is used it becomes habitual whether the broker really "finds" the loan application or not. For example, if A buys a property through broker B and insists upon securing his mortgage loan from banker X, B still expects his finder's fee even though he had no choice of lender. In some markets, finder's fees are the rule. In others they are not used at all. In still others, some lenders use them while others do not. Prompt service may produce loan applications in spite of the absence of a finder's fee.

The other type of outside payment is indirect. The absorption of all or a part of loan fees is a form of payment to outsiders for the loan. This, too, is subject to wide variations, dependent upon the practices of competitors and upon the amount of money pressing for investment in real estate mortgages. Like the payment of finder's fees, the absorption of loan costs tends to lose its effectiveness if all lenders in a given market follow the practice. Sometimes the loan applicant demands that he be paid the finder's fee, if he knows that it is customary in his market to pay one.

Sideline Business

Some mortgage bankers are not greatly disturbed if they fail to make a profit from mortgage loan acquisitions. By making the loan they acquire various types of sideline business. Among these are the writing of fire insurance premiums, sales commissions, property management fees, real estate brokerage, sale of leases, appraisal fees, and loan-servicing fees. The latter are normally most important. Depending upon the combination of circumstances, loan-acquisition profits and servicing profits may be alternatives. For example, one banker may be willing to accept a servicing contract at no profit if the commission from disposing of the mortgage is great enough. Another may be willing to forgo such profit if the servicing fee is large enough to show a profit.

One of the arguments used by mortgage bankers with insurance companies interested in establishing branch offices for the purpose of soliciting and servicing real estate loans is that the mortgage banker can render the service at less cost because of its sideline business operations. The branch office of the insurance company would be concerned with loans only. With approximately the same overheard costs, the mortgage banker can conduct several types of business, as listed earlier. In addition, mortgage bankers sometimes render services to real estate brokers and builders, in order to build or keep their goodwill—services which insurance companies are not permitted to render.

The recent emergence of real estate investment trusts provided an attractive new market for mortgage bankers. Subsequent difficulties experienced by the trusts have placed heavy demands upon these same bankers. The well-qualified and diversified mortgage banker has been viewed as a natural manager to handle the originating, servicing, and advisory functions for a mortgage trust. Some mortgage bankers saw fit to sponsor mortgage trusts themselves so that publicly derived trust funds and credit generated therefrom could be made available to them for placement. Until the recent traumatic disruption in the mortgage markets, this was considered a boon to the construction loan markets. Now it is apparent there will be a several year interval before the mortgage trusts can again become an important factor in the lending business. Meanwhile, the mortgage bankers will be called upon to exercise their highest form of expertise in liquidating the outstanding loans currently unsupported by earning assets.

Procedure in Making Loans

Flash appraisals and informal commitments are sometimes made in advance of the receipt of loan applications. The more formal procedure is to get the loan application, have the property appraised, secure photographs of it, and get a credit report on the borrower. The latter may be obtained by telephone for the purpose of arriving at a conclusion, with a written report to follow before the loan is closed. If the commitment for the purchase of the mortgage is required before the loan is closed, further time is consumed. In general, the mortgage banker will know what types of loans to submit to each of his principal purchasers to make sure of their acceptance. Where the mortgage banker uses his own funds to close the loan, he can save time at the expense of making a loan that he may not dispose of readily.

Some parts of loan processing may be started in anticipation of the acceptance of the loan by the insurance company. For example, the check on the title is often time consuming. If it can be started before a commitment is received, closing time can be expedited.

Where the mortgage banker sells loans to several insurance companies or commercial banks, he usually wishes to make sure that all receive fair treatment, in order to retain their business. He may distribute the loans made in an equitable fashion. To do so he may prefer to use his own capital in making the loans instead of receiving an advance commitment for purchase. On the other hand, he must cater to the wishes of those to whom he sells mortgages. This means that he must offer only such loans as he knows will meet the approval of the purchaser.

Where a long-standing relationship between mortgage banker and insurance company investor has taught each to know what to expect of the other, authority may be granted by the latter to commit it up to certain amounts in making loans. In other words, the mortgage banker is permitted to close the loan promptly, knowing that the insurance company will not refuse to buy the mortgage. By speeding up the decision to make the loan, both borrower and lender are given more prompt service. Frequently, promptness in making decisions is what gets the mortgage.

Methods of Financing Mortgages

In general, mortgage banks finance real estate loans according to one of the following patterns:

1. The loan is made only after the banker has received the prior approval of the insurance company for which it is a loan correspondent. The insurance company which agrees to take the loan

may even advance to the mortgage banker the amount of money needed by the mortgagor. Otherwise the mortgage banker uses its own funds, knowing that within a short time it will recoup the amounts so invested from the institution which has contracted to take the loan. In such a transaction, the banker is, in effect, the agent for the insurance company.

2. The mortgage banker may act as a real merchandiser, investing its own funds in the mortgage and then offering it for sale to some investor seeking this type of outlet for its funds. In this case it may keep its own funds invested at all times, selling only such mortgages as it needs to free its funds for the purchase of a new supply. Since its capital is small in comparison with its volume of business, this is not its major objective. Whenever it makes a loan without the prior approval of some purchaser, it runs the risk of acquiring stale merchandise that no purchaser will take off its hands at an advantageous price. Then it may unwillingly find its capital tied up in nonmerchantable mortgages.

Growing Significance of Mortgage Companies

There are over 1,400 institutions listed as mortgage companies in the membership of the Mortgage Bankers Association of America. A number of these, however, undoubtedly perform mortgage banking as an incidental rather than as a principal function. It appears that there are many fewer mortgage companies than commercial banks and savings and loan associations in the country. In fact the number of mortgage companies is nearer that of life insurance companies, their best customers.

From small beginnings before World War II, the growth since that time has been spectacular. During 1975, mortgage bankers closed $20.6 billion in mortgage loans. Over half were FHA/VA one- to four-family loans. The distribution of loan originations was as follows (in $ billions):[1]

```
1- to 4-family
   FHA/VA ...........................................................11.9
   Conventional ..................................................... 3.1
5+ family ............................................................ 1.2
Nonfarm residential ............................................. 4.4
                                                                    ____
   Total ..............................................................20.6
                                                                    ____
```

Taken with the estimated total loan originations during 1975 by life insurance companies, mutual savings banks, savings and loan associations, and commercial banks, mortgage bankers accounted for about one fifth of the total activity.

The substantial postwar growth of mortgage bankers, as well as their

---

[1] *Mortgage Banker,* March 1976, p. 30.

present structure and operational methods, can be attributed largely to the federal mortgage assistance program. The Federal Housing Administration insurance and the Veterans administration guarantee programs have offered what was needed to create a national mortgage market. These agencies provided minimum property requirements, subdivision standards, and credit review which gave insured or guaranteed mortgages a quality upon which distant lending institutions could rely with little individual review or investigation. The federal underwriting itself permitted institutional investors to make loans of higher risk than would otherwise be prudent or legally possible from the standpoint either of loan-to-value ratio or of distance from lender to liened property.

The FHA or VA mortgage has emerged as a standard article, subject to ready trade in the national marketplace. It has an additional unique feature. It is eligible, under certain limitations, for purchase by federally-oriented secondary market facilities. Of particular significance to mortgage bankers in this respect is the Federal National Mortgage Association (FNMA). The availability of this resource as a buyer in the market at times of temporary credit stringency has provided a stability in the supply of mortgage funds that did not previously exist.

The mortgage banker, operating in a localized area, has been the natural beneficiary of the increased need by nonresident investors for a local agency to originate and service mortgages. Accordingly, the market increase in federally underwritten mortgages has given impetus to mortgage banking.

Mortgage bankers are also deeply concerned with the support they may be able to rely upon from the Federal National Mortgage Association in a tight market. To them, this agency stands in much the same relationship as the Federal Reserve System to commercial banks or the Federal Home Loan Bank System to savings and loan associations. Yet its objectives have not been set forth with sufficient definiteness in this regard to induce reasonable reliance at all times.

Although the Federal Home Loan Mortgage Corporation (discussed in Chapter 21) has been developed in recent years as an additional secondary market facility, it has never recognized mortgage bankers as acceptable sellers to it. The justification offered for this denial has been the relatively unregulated status of mortgage bankers as compared with members of the Federal Home Loan Bank System. Mortgage bankers have benefited somewhat from this new development, however, through their acceptance as appropriate agents of eligible sellers under properly circumscribed conditions.

Purchasers of Mortgages

The great majority of real estate mortgages acquired by mortgage bankers find their way into the portfolios of *life insurance companies.*

The second most important customer in recent years has been the *mutual savings banks*. Through new legislation, savings banks in some states are permitted to own mortgages on properties located at a distance from their home offices and they have been utilizing mortgage bankers to an increasing degree. Other investors through mortgage companies include chiefly commercial banks, savings and loan associations, and the Federal National Mortgage Association.

The demand of *commercial banks* for the services of a mortgage banker largely emanates from the rural areas where cash is more plentiful than local investment outlets. City banks that are interested in real estate mortgages as investments frequently originate their own mortgages. Country banks depend upon mortgage bankers instead. Frequently, if their cash resources are large, they may pay higher premiums for loans than insurance companies. Some smaller mortgage bankers cater to this trade because of the high premiums paid for loans. Larger companies usually find it more advantageous to deal instead with the few insurance companies for which each is a correspondent. Then, too, the demand for loans by country banks is likely to be intermittent, depending upon the state of their cash and upon their outlook concerning future business conditions. They are in-and-out buyers.

One further difference between commercial banks and insurance companies as purchasers of real estate mortgages is that the former are subject to fewer rules than the latter. Because the insurance companies are mass purchasers, they find it necessary to standardize the rules under which they operate. For example, a specific company may set a minimum of 720 square feet of floor space for a single residence that it will finance. In such case it is useless to offer it a loan on a smaller house, regardless of its quality. Or the insurance company may not be interested in VA loans. Commercial banks normally do not have enough mortgage experience at any one time to make them unwilling to consider the purchase of any loan which the mortgage banker may offer to them.

However, because of the restrictions under which commercial banks are forced to operate in the purchase of mortgages, the mortgage banker may make sure that he can dispose of a "bank" loan before he makes it. Some use a submission sheet in offering mortgages to commercial banks. It contains a description of the property; the terms of the loan and the price asked for it; the necessary information about the borrower—such as his occupation, annual income, and credit rating; the amount of the appraisal, FHA or otherwise; and any other pertinent information about the application. Sometimes submission sheets are sent out on the same day to several commercial bankers. The first one to accept by telephone, telegraph, or letter gets the loan, and it is closed on that basis.

Savings and loan associations do not ordinarily purchase mortgages from mortgage bankers. They do not like to pay any premiums for the purchase of mortgages. Occasionally an individual may liquidate his mortgage holdings by selling them to a savings and loan association through a mortgage banker. Or on occasion the association may purchase an individual loan which it would have liked to make originally but which for some reason it did not have the opportunity to make. One exception to the rule about savings and loan associations' purchases of mortgages from mortgage bankers occurs when the association, like the country bank, operates in a community where savings funds greatly exceed investment opportunities. In such cases a mortgage banker, or a mortgage broker in a neighboring city which can use excess funds, serves as the investment agent for the savings and loan association.

The Federal National Mortgage Association is an agency created by Congress to provide a secondary market for federally underwritten mortgages. In view of the importance of mortgage bankers in the origination of these mortgages, it is to be expected that FNMA should become their customer. Activity of the FNMA in the insured mortgage market has provided an important new business channel for mortgage bankers. The history and current status of the FNMA is discussed in Chapter 21.

Mortgage loans are sometimes sold to *individuals, estates, or trustees*. Here there is even less rigidity in purchaser requirements than in the case of commercial banks. Loans purchased by such buyers may be safe but off-color loans. Perhaps they should be called off-standard. For example, insurance companies will not ordinarily consider a loan against a motel or a motor freight terminal. It may carry a high rate of return and may represent a low percentage loan. Because of the difficulty in placing such loans, the borrower usually pays all costs, including the fees to the mortgage banker.

On the other hand, some mortgage bankers prefer not to deal with individual investors except when off-standard property is involved. Volume of sales to one individual is not likely to be large. Each may have his own ideas about appraisals, location, and so on, so that the time spent in trying to sell an individual mortgage may be out of proportion to the amount of business generated. In general, the individual purchaser of mortgages expects a higher yield on his investment than does an insurance company, for example. One reason for this demand is the high-income taxes paid by the individual. To net a yield comparable to that enjoyed by an insurance company, the individual must obtain a higher interest rate.

Mortgage Assembly Occasionally a mortgage banker has found that he can get a better price for a large inventory of mortgages than for a single mortgage or a small number. Hence by the use of his own capital, supplemented by bank loans, he accumulates whatever inventory he can carry before offering it to institutional buyers. In doing so he is taking the risk that interest rates will change before he is able to liquidate his holdings. For example, if the larger purchaser will pay a 2 percent premium on $500,000 or $1 million of 9 percent loans, the mortgage banker will work toward that amount as his goal. Meantime, if investment committees of large buyers decide suddenly that they no longer want to buy 9 percent mortgages, the mortgage banker may find sticky merchandise on his shelves. Since his bank loans are for short periods of time, he must adjust his price to the new bid price of the buyers and, if necessary, take his loss.

This type of business has become of increasing importance with the recent development and public marketing of government-backed mortgage pools through participation certificates. Mortgage bankers, both by virtue of experience and facilities, are ideally suited in many instances to move ahead in this field as mortgage assemblers. They are further abetted by the action of the Chicago Board of Trade in establishing a mortgage interest-rate futures options market. By the purchase or sale of these options, originating mortgage bankers are able to shift their interest-rate risk to speculators by hedging. These developments are discussed in detail in Chapter 21.

Pension Funds   Although as yet they have been an elusive market, pension funds offer appealing possibilities as customers of mortgage bankers. As an industry, mortgage bankers are becoming increasingly cognizant of the magnitude of the pension fund market, and they are more aware of their own excellent position to compete for fund investments.

In essence, pension funds are simply accumulations of money over the working life of an individual to provide income to him during his retirement. Before World War II, these funds were largely established by corporations or by govermental units on a voluntary basis and on a relatively small scale. In the postwar labor climate, desirable pension plans became an important method of attracting scarce workers into employment with a particular firm. Favorable tax treatment was accorded acceptable pension plans. Pensions became an important issue at the labor-management bargaining table. Under this impetus, the amount of investable funds held to underwrite retirement and related benefits grew spectacularly.

The asset volume held for investment by private pension funds alone is of the order of that of the life insurance industry. It is growing at the rate of from $9 to $10 billion annually.

The shifting of the flow of these funds from bank accounts and corporate bonds and stocks into mortgages has been a slow process. The present percentage of pension trust funds invested in mortgages is insignificant compared with the potential. The reason for the small proportion of funds invested in mortgages seems to be that investment committees and counselors, and even bank trust departments, are unfamiliar with the safety and ease with which these investments can be handled through mortgage bankers. Many trustees have been concerned that there is no market quotation on mortgages. As the secondary market for mortgages improves and their security becomes better defined, this objection can be overcome. The trustees have also had an abiding fear of additional, unanticipated costs of handling mortgage investments. In this respect the mortgage banker is admirably equipped to relieve their burden. Over a period of time, as the mortgage banker reaches the decision-making groups and dispels their fear of the unknown, he will find a lucrative market. He can demonstrate, for example, that in its important aspects a federally underwritten mortgage can be handled as safely and simply as bonds and stocks through the proper employment of mortgage banking services.

Considerable thought is constantly being directed toward the development of securities based on packages of mortgages that are serviced on a "carefree" basis by others than fund administrators. These securities are being made available in conveniently large denominations. The composite yield of the mortgage package is normally sufficient to provide a satisfactory income to the mortgage servicer as well as an attractive return to the pension fund or other institution seeking exoneration from management responsibilities and possible embarrassment with delinquencies.

Programs launched by the federal government to provide mortgage-backed securities guaranteed by the Government National Mortgage Association (GNMA) were partly inspired to lure more pension fund money into real estate financing. Details of these programs, and the allied activities of the Federal National Mortgage Association and the Federal Home Loan Mortgage Corporation, are discussed in Chapter 21.

Types of Loans

Mortgage bankers typically provide their major services in arranging permanent financing for new rather than existing properties. They frequently assist builders by establishing short-term credit for new construction. This credit may be arranged for the builder directly from a commercial bank, or the mortgage banker may advance the construction costs and borrow from the commercial bank in its own name. In either event, the funds for construction are ultimately provided by the commercial bank. Mortgage bankers usually gain an additional fee when they finance the builder themselves, but the typical 1 or 2 percent additional compensation involved often does not justify the higher risks and larger staff required in observation and supervision of the construction process.

As previously indicated, a survey of representative mortgage bankers shows a high degree of concentration of real estate loans on one- to four-family properties. By statutory limitations and practice, most FHA and VA loans are on one- to four-family dwellings; and, with few exceptions, the conventional mortgage loans derived by mortgage bankers are on similar properties.

The small proportion of conventional loans on income properties handled through mortgage bankers can be explained in the decision of most institutional investors to originate such loans directly. Lending on larger building units requires specialized knowledge of appraisal techniques and legal problems, and the loans are usually large enough and in sufficient volume to justify the institutional lender in maintaining its own staff for direct negotiations with such borrowers. This practice is particularly common among insurance companies and savings banks in the highly industrialized areas of the country, especially in the East.

Exclusive Outlets

The goal of every mortgage banker is to establish relationships with investment institutions which are so satisfactory to both the buyer and the seller of mortgages that the seller will always know where he can dispose of his inventory and the buyer will know where he can secure supplies of new mortgages. Some of these relationships crystallize into exclusive contracts. The mortgage banker agrees to sell only to one or to a very few investors; and each of these in turn agrees to buy in that market only from the mortgage banker whose name is signed to the exclusive contract. The signatures to the contract are not as important in the long run as the manner in which both parties deal with each other. If each is satisfied with the service it receives from the other, no formal contract is needed. If either is dissatisfied, a formal contract will probably be terminated at the earliest opportunity.

Most investment institutions do not object to the mortgage banker having more than one purchaser of its mortgages. In fact, they prefer such an arrangement, since it removes pressure from the investor to absorb all offerings of the seller at all times. In taking on its list of investors, however, the mortgage banker should exercise care in avoiding too much competition among them. For example, one investor may prefer FHA or VA loans; another, conventional loans; a third, apartment or commercial loans; and so on.

Indemnity Policies

In spite of the general practice of securing prior approval of the purchaser of the mortgage before it is granted, the mortgage banker still has a responsibility for making sure that the loans he processes do not result in a loss to the purchaser. For example, if such a loan is paid off within the first year, it is frequently replaced with another of similar amount, premium free, or the mortgage banker may return whatever premium was collected in disposing of the mortgage. At other times only the loss that is due to a negative yield will be made up. In some cases these obligations of the mortgage banker are a part of the contract between the insurance company and its correspondents. In other cases, unwritten understandings are sufficient to fix responsibility. In general, the mortgage banker is more likely to be dependent upon the continued business of the purchasing insurance company than the reverse.

The prepayment privilege in mortgages is particularly troublesome in mortgage banking because of the premiums and other fees paid by the investor in acquiring the mortgage. Because of the common practice of competitors who originate loans to include this privilege, its exclusion might result in a loss of business. From the standpoint of the investor, if he permits prepayment freely, he may lose money if the privilege is exercised early in the life of the loan. One common answer to the problem is to permit limited prepayment privilege—to become operative only after from two to five years, for example. Another is to permit prepayment on any interest date but with a penalty of a few months' interest or of a flat percentage of the amount of the mortgage. In still other cases, the amount of prepayment without penalty is limited to 20 percent per year.

Servicing Department

The mortgage banker owes two obligations to the investor whose funds he handles: (1) to invest his money safely and (2) to get it back according to the loan contract. Lending money is fairly simple. Getting it back may be more difficult. Servicing involves more than serving as a clearinghouse for checks transmitted by the borrower. Adequate servicing involves at least four major operations:

1. Current payments made by the borrower must be processed and the net proceeds, after retaining tax, mortgage, and hazard insurance quotas and service fees, must be transmitted to the investor that holds the mortgage. In rare cases the investor insists that all escrow deposits for taxes, mortgage insurance, and hazard insurance be transmitted to it to be held in trust for the borrower.

2. The security must be inspected periodically to make sure that it is not being subjected to waste or unusual depreciation.

3. When the property changes hands and the new owner assumes the mortgage debt, a whole series of records in the office of the mortgage banker must be changed. The collection department must get the proper name and address of the new owner and set up new records to check

against delinquency by him. Insurance papers must reflect the change of ownership. The tax department must change its records in order to make sure about new tax bills. The accounting department must set up new records in line with the new obligor on the loan. If the mortgage is insured by the FHA or guaranteed by the VA, the proper governmental agency must be notified. Even where the present mortgage is completely paid off rather than assumed by the new owner, the mortgage banker must protect the interests of the holder of the mortgage by making sure that the proper amount is paid in the proper manner.

4. Finally, in serious cases of delinquency, steps must be taken to protect the holder of the mortgage, by foreclosure if necessary.

Among these four steps in servicing, too many lending agencies think primarily of the first. They may neglect the second. The third is thrust upon them perhaps more than once during the life of the mortgage. At such a time, outside forces call the tune and the mortgage banker must dance to it. The fourth step is the one that nobody likes to contemplate and that no one has ever quite made adequate provisions to meet. Plans of borrowers sometimes go awry, perhaps through no fault of their own. Delinquencies follow. They are costly to the investor and to the mortgage banker. They are frequently disastrous to the borrower, who may lose his equity if he cannot maintain his payments on his loan.

It is not uncommon for the delinquent borrower to be delinquent in payments on his other financial obligations at the same time. Cumulative pressure from all creditors may make it impossible for him to meet any one creditor's claims fully. It is not easy for a mortgage banker to reach a conclusion about forebearance that is always wise, even though the holder of the mortgage counsels patience so long as there appears ample protection of his interests. We are primarily concerned here with servicing costs. This much appears certain. No fee has probably ever been adopted that is based upon a pattern of chronic delinquency with its letters, its telephone calls, its personal contacts, all pointed toward the collection of nonexistent funds. Temporary delinquencies may be cured. They may be prevented from becoming chronic. But the servicing of even temporary delinquencies probably results in an outlay that is in excess of current receipts for servicing purposes. When times are prosperous, a skeleton crew is sufficient to man the collection department. When unemployment and decreased incomes become the order of the day for our general economy, the number of employees in the collection department of a mortgage bank may be stepped up appreciably.

Fees

As discussed in Chapter 17 in connection with life insurance company loan administration, mortgage bankers earn two types of fees: (1) for loan origination and (2) for servicing the loan during its existence.

Origination Fees Origination fees are most often assessed against the borrower. They fall into two major classes: (1) All expenses of making the loan are expected to be covered. Such fees for FHA and VA loans are standard. There is no such standardization for conventional loans. Sometimes they cover out-of-pocket costs. At other times they cover what the traffic will bear. Costs cover appraisal fees, title insurance, if any, title check fees, and office expense. As pointed out elsewhere, competitive practices help to determine the amount of costs charged to the borrower. Sometimes appraisal fees are charged only if the loan is made; sometimes whether or not the loan is approved; and sometimes they are absorbed by the lender. (2) Off-standard loans—those made against properties that holders of mortgage paper do not like as security—frequently cost the borrower a fee in addition to those mentioned above. Instead of a sellers' market for such mortgages, it is generally a buyers' market. Because the mortgage banker may have unusual difficulty in disposing of them, he expects the mortgagor to pay his fees.

Servicing Fees Compensation for servicing the loan from the time it is made until it is paid off is collected by the mortgage banker out of the borrower's periodic payments. If the servicing fee is ⅜ percent, for example, and the contract interest rate on the mortgage note is 9½ percent, when the borrower's payment is received by the mortgage banker, only 9⅛ percent is forwarded to the lender as interest, the other ⅜ percent being retained as compensation for the collection service. Of course, all amortization of principal amounts is forwarded to the lender. The servicing fee is based on the unpaid loan balance and becomes less as the loan is amortized. Many loans on the books with unpaid balances too low to earn fees enough to cover the costs of carrying them can create problems for the mortgage banker.

Loan Insurance and Guarantee

Loans insured by the FHA or guaranteed by the VA are not necessarily free from servicing problems. On the contrary, it is probable that many such loans were made by their lenders with less than normal attention to the problems of future loan servicing. If guaranteed or insured loans are made because of the guarantee or insurance, and particularly if they would not have been granted otherwise, trouble may develop. While neither the FHA nor the VA would intentionally sanction a loan which it considered too heavy for the borrower to carry, there is a tendency on the part of some lending institutions to assume that they have shifted their loan-servicing problems to a governmental agency when they make insured and guaranteed loans. This is not the case.

The major purpose of these governmental agencies is to be of service to the borrower. If the borrower could have obtained liberal loans without insurance or guarantee of his mortgage, there would probably never have been either an FHA or a VA lending program. Because sufficiently liberal loans were not available, these agencies were developed. Since their interest is primarily centered in assistance to the borrower, neither the VA nor the FHA will permit the borrower to lose his property by foreclosure of the mortgage until every reasonable effort to solve his financial difficulties has been made. This means loan servicing by the mortgagee.

Furthermore, much of the cost of loan servicing, even where loans are insured or guaranteed, is not recoverable from the borrower or from a governmental agency. While the principal of the loan and the delinquent interest are intended to be recoverable, the costs of working out programs of forbearance and adjustment are not.

In general, the safety but not the soundness of such loans is insured or guaranteed. This is accepted as part of the program. For example, when a mortgagee makes a guaranteed loan to a veteran, it must satisfy itself that the borrower's income, present and prospective, is sufficient to meet the carrying charges of the loan. In other words, the burden of the soundness of the loan is not shifted to the VA. In time of crisis, the VA does not undertake to make loan payments continuously, thus keeping the loan account alive on the books of the lender. While this may be done on a temporary basis, sooner or later the degree of safety of the loan will be demonstrated when foreclosure proceedings are directed, to be followed by indemnification of the lender on account of lost principal and delinquent interest.

A Forward Look at Mortgage Banking

The exceedingly rapid rise of the mortgage banking industry over the past quarter century by its very nature engendered conditions that invited correction in event of economic recession. The industry flourished in the development of a national market for federally-underwritten mortgages at favorable yields to investors in new construction. Conditions were so favorable for growth in the field of mortgage origination and servicing that competition during the 1960s and early 1970s became more intense both outside the industry and from within.

Commercial banks became increasingly interested in programs of originating and servicing mortgages for investors other than themselves. In fact, commercial banks are in a particularly favorable position to move into mortgage banking because they have immediately available any funds necessary to provide interim financing or to maintain a mortgage inventory for sale. The American Bankers Association was active in pointing out the advantages of a broad mortgage program to its membership, and the commercial banks became more conscious of the advantages to be gained by offering mortgage origination and service facilities for bank-administered pension and welfare funds. These funds have been important investors through mortgage bankers in recent years.

To maximize their current opportunities, some banks acquired mortgage banking expertise by buying out mortgage banking firms. Some firms so acquired were simply absorbed into the bank assets and operations; others, secured by the one-bank holding company route, maintained their separate integrity as mortgage bankers.

Many banks even sponsored real estate mortgage investment trusts to become additional lending elements in the development and construction areas. As set forth in Chapter 18, the recession of 1974, and thereafter, placed heavy strains on most banks with this involvement, together with their mortgage servicing arms, because of massive defaults not only in their own mortgage loan portfolios but also in those of the mortgage trusts to which they had legal or moral obligations.

Savings and loan associations have also taken new cognizance of potentials in the national secondary markets. Whereas they were limited to competition in local markets in earlier days, they now find it possible to participate in loans made anywhere in the country. Through new techniques of participation and mortgage pooling, small savings and loans are enabled to originate or invest in much larger construction programs than would otherwise be possible. It is a short step from active participation in loan origination in the national market to adoption of a policy of sales of loans to other investors. Although insured savings and loans are now limited in the sale of such loans to 20 percent of their portfolio, such a limitation allows a substantial participation, and the limitation can always be changed.

The recent blight in real estate development and construction has cast a long shadow across the mortgage banking industry. Delinquency rates have risen to the highest levels since the Great Depression of the 1930s. With inflation at full gallop in 1974 and continuing high, both origination and servicing costs have risen sharply. A study by the Mortgage Bankers Association revealed as early as 1972 that the cost of originating a single-family mortgage loan was $488 for reporting members.[2] This was approximately 2.33 percent of the average loan made, far in excess of the 1 percent maximum allowed for FHA/VA originations. Costs of servicing home mortgages in 1972 were estimated at $35.80 per loan. This amount, added to servicing purchased from others in the amount of $4.30, brought the gross servicing costs to $40.10 per loan. The average servicing fee for the portfolios was 0.405 percent. It can be determined from these figures that the minimum average-sized loan to break even was about ($40.10 ÷ 0.00405) $9,900.

---

[2] John M. Wetmore, "Inflation Hits Mortgage Banking—Origination and Servicing Costs Jump," *Mortgage Banker*, February 1974, pp. 85–87.

The obvious conclusions to be drawn from these data are that mortgage bankers will be resorting wherever possible to higher discount points or stipulated loan origination fees. In many cases larger loans only will be sought to upgrade the overall portfolio average loan balance. Where possible, a step-up percentage for loan service fees might be arranged to take effect whenever the unpaid balance is brought down to the break-even point.

Many companies are also considering expansion into real estate operations and insurance as logical auxiliary fields which may take on primary importance when income from servicing mortgages begins to fall short. This diversification will relieve the company from such a high degree of dependence on the federal housing programs and will give it greater stability.

QUESTIONS

1. What is a mortgage banker?
2. Why are mortgage bankers important to both borrowers and lenders?
3. How does a mortgage banker originate new business?
4. What is a finder's fee? Do you approve of payment of finders' fees? Why or why not?
5. How does a mortgage banker finance the mortgages which it originates?
6. How do you account for the spectacular growth of mortgage companies since the end of World War II?
7. Who are the principal purchasers of mortgages generated through mortgage companies?
8. What types of loans are most attractive to mortgage bankers? Why?
9. How is the mortgage banker compensated for his services?
10. What is a takeout letter and how is it used to aid in construction financing?
11. What are the four stages of mortgage loan servicing?
12. "Loan servicing" is fairly synonymous with "loan collection." What are the indicia of a good loan collection policy?
13. Has the expansion of the federal loan insurance and guarantee program simplified or complicated mortgage-servicing problems? In what respects?
14. What are the obligations of a mortgage banker to the investor in the real estate mortgages which the mortgage banker originates and services?
15. If you were a mortgage banker today, what areas would you be exploring for possible expansion of your services?

CASE PROBLEMS

1. As an executive of the Universal Mortgage Company, you are servicing a mortgage loan for the Tinsel Makers' Pension Fund. The mortgagor is the Bi-Lo Department Store. The department store premises burn completely to the ground and the insurance proceeds have been received. The mortgagor

desires to rebuild. What problems do you foresee and how would you act to resolve them?

2. You are asked to develop criteria for servicing an income property loan and point out how they might be different from those for servicing a loan on an owner-occupied residential unit. Be explicit in your response.

3. The Universal Mortgage Company services mortgages for a fee of 0.5% of unpaid mortgage balances annually. It collects this fee out of loan payments received from borrowers. It then remits the remaining proceeds to the Reliable Insurance Company for whom the loans are being serviced. For the past year, total servicing costs were $200,000. It has 4,000 loans to service.

    a. What is the average servicing cost per loan?

    b. What is the minimum average unpaid balance of the loans in the portfolio that the company can tolerate to break even?

    c. How can it improve its net servicing income?

4. The convertible mortgage, discussed in Chapter 13 as a new financing technique with good potential, can have particular appeal to a mortgage banker. Since the mortgage company manages collections on the total investment, both mortgage loan and equity buildup, the servicing fee for asset management does not decline over the life of the loan. Consider the returns to the institutional investor, the developer, and the mortgage banker in the following example.

A warehouse facility is expected to earn $220,000 annual net income before financing costs. The appropriate capitalization rate is 10.5%. The investor is willing to fund $2,000,000, of which $1,500,000 will be by mortgage loan and $500,000 as equity with a 10% rate of return to be paid on the total funding, net to investor after payment of 0.2% servicing fees to a mortgage banker to administer the investment. The initial equity participation to the investor is 25%, and the mortgage is to be amortized solely by a transfer to investor's equity of 2½% of the initial balance annually. By virtue of this transfer, the developer's initial 75% claim will decrease by 2½% annually.

    a. Prepare a schedule showing the investor's and developer's investment income and yield positions during the 1st, 2nd, 5th, and 21st years of the plan. Assume a constant earning stream. The format for this schedule follows the explanation in Chapter 13.

    b. Do the same exercise as in *a* above assuming an increasing earnings stream at the rate of 3% annually using the compounding tables in the Appendix to estimate earnings growth.

    c. Calculate the equity positions of the investor and the developer at the beginning of the 1st, 2nd, 5th, and 21st years assuming that depreciation is more than offset by inflation with the result that the property increases in value at the rate of 3% annually (compounded monthly as per tables). Assume also that the loan agreement gives the investor his equity participation in the gross amount of the property value upon reappraisal. Thus, compute gross value less investor's equity to derive the developer's claim to assets. Then deduct the mortgage balance due investor to determine developer's residual equity value.

    d. What will the mortgage banker earn in asset management fees under requirements *a* and *b* above?

part four
Government and Real Estate Finance

20

Federal Assistance in Housing

Order of Discussion

Because of the complex nature of federal activities, their discussion is separated into several segments. In order, in the present chapter, there follow a general description of the governmental administrative organization handling various programs, a summary of the Federal Housing Administration and public housing programs, and a similar consideration of the support function of the Veterans Administration in loans to veterans.

In Chapter 21, the development of secondary markets for mortgages and federal support activities in these markets are discussed in detail. Finally, the whole question of rural real estate credit and the function of the Farmers Home Administration in aid of rural housing are dealt with in Chapter 22.

Administrative Agencies

The agency principally responsible for the housing and urban development activities of the federal government is the Department of Housing and Urban Development (HUD). Its head is designated as "Secretary," who serves as a member of the President's Cabinet. The Department was created in 1965 to extend and intensify the activities and programs of the Housing and Home Finance agency.

The creation of HUD in 1965 marked the combination of several well-known governmental agencies. The Federal Housing Administration (FHA) had been in operation since 1934, when it was created to handle the underwriting of federally-backed mortgage insurance as a much-needed aid to real estate credit at the time. The Public Housing Administration (PHA) was established in 1937 to administer federal aid to public housing. The Urban Renewal Administration (URA) was formed in 1949 to develop and promote urban renewal programs. The Housing and Home Finance Agency was established in 1947, and it became the umbrella under which FHA, PHA, and URA functioned in loose collaboration until they were taken into HUD. The FHA is now officially designated "HUD-FHA," but it is still simply referred to without the prefix. The PHA is now the Housing Assistance Administration, and the URA is now the Renewal Assistance Administration.

Certain federal housing and home finance activities have been delegated to other departments. The Department of Agriculture operates a farm housing program authorized under Title V of the Housing Act of 1949. The administrative agency handling this program is the Farmers Home Administration. The Department of Defense is responsible for certifying the need for military housing financed by mortgages insured under the federal program or for the provision of family housing where necessary in the interests of national defense. The Small Business Administration makes loans to victims of disasters so that they may restore their damaged homes or buy or build new ones. It also assists small businesses in becoming reestablished where they have suffered substantial economic injury as result of displacement by an urban renewal program or similar government project. The Departments of Commerce and Labor are of particular assistance to the national housing program in providing housing and construction statistics and in setting standards for construction materials and labor.

Functional Divisions of HUD   The major areas of HUD activities are headed by assistant secretaries. Important secretarial designations and program areas include:

1.   The assistant secretary for housing production and mortgage credit, also called the federal housing commissioner, who handles the private housing market and mortgage credit (including the FHA).

2.   The assistant secretary for renewal and housing assistance, who deals with problems of the inner city, in particular through the Housing Assistance Administration and the Renewal Assistance Administration.

3.   The assistant secretaries for community development and for community planning and management, who are charged with the problems of growth in metropolitan areas and with the administration of the Community Development Act of 1974 to assist communities in their physical development and improvement, including the removal and prevention of slums and blight.

Functions of the FHA

Since its organization in 1934, a variety of functions have been added to the FHA program. As expressed by statutory authority, these functions involve the operation of housing loan insurance programs designed to encourage improvement in housing standards and conditions, to facilitate sound home financing on reasonable terms, and to exert a stabilizing influence in the mortgage market. The FHA is not a direct lender, nor does it plan or build houses. It does markedly affect lending terms and building plans and specifications, as well as selection of housing sites, by the conditions under which it permits insurance to be granted. The various types of loans on which insurance is issued by the FHA are defined by several titles of the National Housing Act of 1934, as amended.

Title I insures lending institutions against loss on loans which finance the alteration, repair, improvement, or conversion of existing structures and the construction of new, small, nonresidential structures. The FHA liability is limited to 90 percent of loss on individual loans and to 10 percent of all such loans made by any institution.

Title II covers all residential mortgage insurance programs. The major programs are listed and capsulized in later paragraphs by statutory sections.

Operation of Title II Title II of the Federal Housing Administration law set up a system of mutual mortgage insurance which at the outset was intended to encourage the construction of new homes, thus providing a market for building materials and employment for building laborers. Later it was extended to cover rental housing projects as well. In return for insurance of mortgages made by private lenders, an insurance premium was charged which was expected eventually to build reserves sufficiently large to put this title on a self-sustaining basis. The amount of insurance coverage was limited to 80 percent of the appraisal of the property insured, as set by the FHA. This insurance percentage has since been liberalized and applied to different sections of this title according to varying formulas, which usually result in insurance from 85 to 100 percent of the appraisal value. The interest rate was fixed at 5 percent, to which could be added originally 0.5 percent for service charge and 0.5 percent of the original amount of the loan for insurance premium. The net result was a charge of 6.42 percent to the borrower, computed over the life of a 20-year loan. Later the service charge was eliminated, the interest rate was reduced to 4.5 percent, and the insurance premium was reduced to 0.5 percent on the unpaid principal of the loan, producing a charge to the borrower of 5 percent. The interest rate has been administered following the cost of mortgage money in the free markets, but subject to statutory limits, from the beginning. This practice, at times, has caused a wide divergence between FHA and conventional lending rates, and has given rise to the requirement that the seller of a property being financed through the FHA pay discount points to induce a lender to make a loan at the FHA rate. Special concession rates of interest have been authorized for certain programs.

The lender must use a monthly payment direct reduction first mortgage, the maturity of which was originally limited to 20 years. This was later increased to 25 years, and then to 30 years or three fourths of the remaining economic life of the property, whichever might be less. Certain loans under sections relating to cooperative housing, slum clearance, or housing for the elderly may have repayment periods extending for as long as 40 years. In case of uncured default, the lender is entitled to receive, from the FHA, debentures equivalent to the amount of the debt then unpaid. These debentures are issued in the name of the mortgage insurance fund but are fully guaranteed as to principal and interest by the government. The interest rate varies in relation to the government's ongoing cost of money, and the maturity is three years after the maturity of the defaulted mortgage.

Approved Participants The FHA is charged with administering the housing law in conformity with both its letter and its spirit. Both lenders and borrowers, as well as the property involved, must therefore be qualified by the FHA.

Automatic approval to become a lender is extended to members of the Federal Reserve System, the Federal Deposit Insurance Corporation, the Federal Savings and Loan Insurance Corporation, and certain other agencies. Lenders not qualified by this kind of membership must earn the specific approval of the federal housing commissioner by giving evidence of appropriate experience in making and servicing mortgage loans, sufficient capital, and capacity to continue a satisfactory business, preferably through a charter.

Once the property meets eligibility standards by type, location, and appraisal, the borrower must also be qualified for the loan. When the lender makes application for mortgage insurance, it submits information about the personal history and the financial responsibility of the mortgagor. If the FHA is not satisfied with this, it may make its own credit investigation of the borrower. Its effort is directed to a determination of the debt-paying capacity of the borrower and the degree of risk that the financial capacity of the borrower introduces into the mortgage transaction.

In attempting to measure the borrower's financial capacity to meet his obligations, the FHA is interested in the current income of the borrower and its probable continuity. It is interested also in such charges against this income as mortgage payments, insurance taxes, maintenance, and household operating expenses, as well as income taxes, life insurance premiums, payments on installment accounts, and similar payments. In the light of all these factors the borrower is given a rating that may range from "excellent" to "reject."

Major Sections of Title II in FHA Program   The most important sections of Title II that are administered by the FHA are listed in succeeding paragraphs.

Section 203 of this title provides for insuring mortgages on one- to four-family dwellings. This section has accounted for about 70 percent of all mortgage insurance written by FHA.

Section 207 authorizes the insurance of mortgages, including construction advances, on rental housing projects of eight or more family units. It also covers projects undertaken by nonprofit corporations for occupation by the elderly. Its authority further extends to insurance of loans on mobile home courts.

Section 213 authorizes the insurance of mortgages on cooperative housing projects of eight or more family units. The section provides for two types of FHA-insured cooperative housing projects—the management type and the sales type. Under the management type, the mortgagor must be a nonprofit ownership housing corporation or trust, with permanent occupancy of the housing facility restricted to members. In a sales-type project each individual member is a stockholder of the cooperative corporation, or a beneficiary of the trust, undertaking the construction of the housing project. Upon completion of the sales-type project, provision is made for the acquisition of title to an individual housing unit by each member and the insurance of an individual mortgage thereon.

Section 220 permits insurance in connection with financing the rehabilitation of existing salable housing and the replacement of slums with new housing.

Section 221 authorizes mortgage insurance on low-cost housing for relocation of families in connection with urban renewal and slum clearance programs. Its benefits are also extended to any family of low or moderate income, or individuals who are handicapped or aged 62 or over.

Section 221 (d) (2), as amended in 1968, provides for insurance of mortgages for single homes, permits a mortgagor to contribute the value of his labor to the acquisition of his dwelling, and authorizes the Secretary of HUD to reimburse the mortgagee for its expenses in handling the mortgage. The ratio of the loan to property value can be 100 percent for an owner-occupant, except when the home was not constructed under FHA or VA inspection or over a year has passed since its completion. In the latter case, the maximum ratio is 90 percent. The minimum cash investment is $200 for a displaced family and 3 percent of acquisition cost for other families. Normal FHA ceiling interest rates apply, and a ½ percent mortgage insurance premium is charged. In the case of displaced families the term of the mortgage can be up to 40 years. For other families, it is generally 30 years.

Section 221 (d) (3) provides special terms for construction or rehabilitation of housing located in approved urban renewal areas for mortgagors approved by the Federal Housing Commissioner. Where the mortgagor accepts regulation in regard to rents, charges, and methods of operation in a manner designed to effectuate the purposes of the program, a below-market interest rate will be allowed. Under such conditions, construction financing is charged at the FHA market rate, but at time of completion of construction and final endorsement of the mortgage for insurance, the rate can be reduced to 3 percent. On mortgages carrying this rate, FHA waives its mortgage insurance premium and the mortgages will be purchased by the Federal National Mortgage Association.

The rent supplement program was also established by Section 221 (d) (3) in 1965. By this authority, low-income individuals of families who are either elderly, handicapped, displaced by government action, occupants of substandard housing, or occupants or former occupants of homes damaged by acts of God are eligible for admission as tenants to new or rehabilitated housing owned by a nonprofit organization participating in the below market interest rate (BMIR) program. The housing owner contracts with the Secretary of HUD for federal rent supplement payments. The contracts run for terms up to 40 years. The rent supplement payments are limited to the excess of the fair rental value of the unit over one fourth of the tenant's income. When the tenant can afford to pay the whole rent by this standard he may continue to live in the unit without a rent supplement payment.

The Housing and Urban Development Act of 1968 extended the rent supplement program to owners of housing projects financed under a state or local program which provided assistance through loans, loan insurance, or tax abatements, provided the project meets the approval of the Secretary of HUD for rent supplement benefits before completion of construction or rehabilitation. Rent supplement benefits may also be extended to housing financed by direct loans under Section 202 of the Housing Act of 1959.

Section 221 (h) of the Federal Housing Act was added in 1966 to establish a program to promote homeownership for low-income families with the assistance of FHA mortgage insurance. Under this authority, the FHA insures mortgages of nonprofit organizations to finance the purchase and rehabilitation of deteriorating and substandard housing. Mortgages may also be insured to finance the resale of housing to low-income families or individuals who are eligible for rent supplements under the rent supplement program.

The mortgage to the nonprofit organization may be insured for an amount equal to the appraised value of the property plus estimated rehabilitation costs. Its maturity is set by the FHA. Under the 1966 legislation, the regular FHA ceiling interest rate was prescribed until final endorsement of the mortgage for insurance, then 3 percent. Under the 1968 amendment, the interest rate may be as low as 1 percent for purchasers whose income is low enough to warrant the lower rate. As a result, individual mortgages insured under this section may bear interest between 1 and 3 percent, depending on the individual incomes and needs of the homeowners. The mortgage of the homeowner in any individual case can be an amount equal to the unpaid balance of the mortgage of the nonprofit corporation selling the property that is allocable to the dwelling being sold. The minimum down payment required is $200, but this may be applied to closing costs. The maximum mortgage term is 25 years. The mortgage must contain a provision that the interest rate will increase to the highest rate permitted by FHA if the mortgagor does not continue to occupy the property; however, this provision is not applicable to a case of resale back to the nonprofit organization from whom the property was originally purchased, or a sale to a local housing authority or another low-income purchaser approved by the FHA.

Section 222 authorizes FHA insurance for mortgages on dwellings owned by members of the Armed Forces or the Coast Guard upon proper certification by the Department of Defense, or the Treasury Department as to Coast Guard personnel. The underlying objectives of such a program in the interests of national security, particularly at the more remote outposts, are apparent.

Section 231 provides insurance for the construction or rehabilitation of rental housing for the elderly or handicapped. The facility constructed must contain at least eight units.

Section 232 authorizes FHA insurance of mortgages on urgently needed nursing homes. The insurance is applicable to convalescents who do not require hospitalization but who do need nursing care. To qualify a home for such insurance, the appropriate state agency charged with licensing and regulating such establishments must certify that the home is needed and that minimum operating standards will be enforced in the home. The property may be new or rehabilitated, but it must have at least 20 beds.

Section 233 gives the FHA authority to insure mortgages on experimental housing. This insurance is available for mortgages or home-improvement loans meeting the requirements of any of FHA's Title II programs. The program extends to all types of operations. The experimentation may involve the utilization or testing of new design, materials, construction methods, or experimental property standards for neighborhood design. Major effort is directed toward improving low-income housing construction.

Section 234 authorizes FHA to insure a mortgage covering a family unit in a multifamily building of five or more units and an undivided interest in common areas and facilities serving the structure. This kind of ownership is known as "condominium." Under the 1961 Housing Act, the insurance was limited to a mortgage on a structure carrying mortgage insurance under one of the FHA multifamily insurance programs other than Section 213. By the Housing Act of 1964, insurance was authorized for blanket mortgages to finance the construction or rehabilitation of multifamily projects to be sold as condominiums, provided the mortgagor certifies that it intends to sell the project as a condominium and will make all reasonable efforts to sell the family units to FHA-approved purchasers.

Section 235 (added in 1968) was designed to establish a homeownership assistance program for the purchase of new, single-family homes by low and moderate income families, handicapped persons, or single persons 62 years of age or older. The assistance takes the form of periodic payments to the mortgagee by the Secretary of HUD to make up the difference between 20 percent of the family's monthly income and the required monthly payment under the mortgage for principal, interest, taxes, insurance, and mortgage insurance premium. The amount of the subsidy varies according to the income of the homeowner.

Because of shoddy construction by developers under this program, further funding was halted in January 1973. The program was restarted in 1976. Changes were made to prevent some of the earlier abuses. The average incomes of participants in the program were raised somewhat by the new formula adopted for establishing eligibility. Further, to preclude the possibility of more subsidized slums, regulations were revised to require that HUD insure no more than 30 percent of the homes built in a subdivision. Higher down payments were required. They must now at least equal 3 percent of the first $25,000 of acquisition cost, plus 10 percent of all cost over $25,000.

Example of Subsidy. As an illustration of how a subsidy works, the revised Section 235 is described herein in greater detail and by example. This section provides assistance in the form of a monthly payment to the mortgagee from HUD, reducing the interest cost to as low as 5 percent of the loan balance but not less than 20 percent of the homeowner's adjusted monthly family income. To be eligible for assistance, the family must have an adjusted income not exceeding 80 percent of the median income for the area, with appropriate adjustments for family size. A deduction of $300 is made for each family member under 21 years of age and the earnings of such minors are not included.

An assistance payment computation is made to determine the lesser of:

a. The difference between the total monthly payment under the mortgage for principal, interest at the market rate, mortgage insurance

(0.7 percent), taxes and hazard insurance and 20 percent of the mortgagor's adjusted monthly income; or

.... *b.* The difference between the monthly payment of principal, interest at the market rate, and mortgage insurance premium (MIP) under the mortgage and the monthly payment that would be required at a 5 percent interest rate excluding the monthly insurance premium (MIP).

For example, assume a family has an adjusted annual income of $8,088, or a monthly income of $674. Other transaction items are as follows:

Sale price: $25,600	Computation of monthly mortgage payment:
Down payment: $1,400	Principal and interest (see tables) $190.40
Mortgage amount: $24,200	MIP (0.007 × $24,200) ÷ 12 .... 14.12
Term in months: 360	Taxes and hazard insurance 31.00
Interest rate: 8¾%	Total $235.52

Assistance calculation:

1. Monthly mortgage payment as above $235.52
2. 20% of adjusted monthly income 134.80

1.–2. Monthly subsidy per formula (a) above $100.72

3. Monthly payment (principal + market interest + MIP excluding taxes and hazard insurance) $204.52
4. Monthly payment (principal + interest at 5%) 129.95

3.–4. Monthly subsidy under formula (b) above ....$ 74.57

Since formula (b) provides the lesser subsidy, the amount computed by that method is the authorized assistance payment. The mortgagor's monthly payment, therefore, is $235.52–$74.57 = $160.95.

Section 236 (added in 1968) was established to provide the counterpart of Section 235 for rental and cooperative housing for low and moderate income families. This section emerged from the below-market interest rate program authorized under Section 221 (d) (3) which has been successful in providing needed rental and cooperative housing for families whose incomes are too high for public housing and too low for standard housing available in the competitive market.

Section 221 (d) (3) has suffered from the limitation of depending on direct federal lending from the special assistance funds of FNMA to support its 3 percent mortgages. The limited availability of these funds greatly restricted the activity. The new subsidy program made it possible to obtain funds from the private mortgage market.

Under the Section 236 program the mortgagor-owner of the housing must make a monthly payment for principal and interest under the mortgage as though it bore a 1 percent interest rate. The difference between this amount and the monthly payment due under the mortgage, which bears the market rate of interest, for principal, interest, and mortgage insurance premium is paid to the mortgagee on behalf of the mortgagor by the federal government.

From the standpoint of the tenant, a basic rental charge is established on the basis of a 1 percent mortgage interest rate. The tenant is then required to pay either the basic rental charge or 25 percent of his income, whichever is greater.

Funding for construction under Section 236 was frozen in January 1973 for the same reasons as for the suspension of Section 235—the creation of "instant slums" by loose practices. Future operations under Section 236 are contingent upon the government making more funds available for use in this manner.

Section 237 was added in 1968 to extend FHA mortgage insurance to families of low or moderate income with impaired credit histories or irregular income patterns. Such families may become eligible if the Secretary of HUD finds them to be reasonably satisfactory credit risks and capable of homeownership with proper financial counseling. Mortgages insured under this program must generally meet the requirements of the specific FHA program for financing under which the applicant seeks assistance. The credit and income requirements do not apply, however. Insurance will not be authorized under Section 237 unless the monthly mortgage payments for principal and interest, plus real estate taxes, can be paid with 25 percent or less of the mortgagor's monthly income, based on the last year or the past three-year average, whichever is greater.

In addition to the relaxation of credit restrictions, the 1968 legislation gave the FHA more flexible authority to accept insurance on properties in declining urban areas. Insurance may now be accepted in areas that do not meet normal eligibility requirements. Acceptance of these mortgages is permitted when the FHA is able to establish that the area is "reasonably viable," giving consideration to the need to provide adequate housing for families of low or moderate income in the area, and that the property is a reasonably acceptable risk in view of such consideration. This authority enlarges upon the 1966 amendment to Section 203 of the National Housing Act whereby the secretary of HUD was authorized to insure one- to four-family dwellings in areas fraught with riots or other disorders, without regard to economic soundness, in view of the urgent need for adequate housing for low and moderate income families in the area.

Section 238 established a "Special Risk Insurance Fund" to receive premiums from and pay claims under programs that are not intended to be actuarially sound. These include mortgages insured under the new Sections 235, 236, and 237, as it relates to properties in declining areas that do not pass minimum standard tests for economic soundness, as discussed in the preceding paragraph. Also included in this fund are mortgages issued under Section 233, primarily oriented to the development of new technologies for lower income housing.

New "Section 8" Housing Assistance Program. In the Housing and

Community Development Act of 1974 a new low income housing subsidy program was authorized by Section 8 of the Housing Act of 1937 as amended. Under this new program, designed to replace the faltering Section 236 program previously described, HUD is authorized to render aid through "assistance payments contracts." These contracts are made on behalf of eligible families occupying new, substantially rehabilitated, or existing rental units. The HUD Secretary is authorized to contract directly with private owners or public housing agencies agreeing to construct or rehabilitate housing.

Assistance payments contracts may run as long as 15 years for an existing unit and up to 20 years for a new or rehabilitated one (or up to 40 years where the project is owned by, or financed by a loan or guarantee from, a state or local agency). The contracts must specify the maximum monthly rent which is to be charged for each assisted unit. The maximum monthly rent can not exceed by more than 10 percent the fair market rental established for comparable rental units in the area suitable for occupancy by the assisted person. However, the maximum rent can be up to 20 percent higher than fair market rental where the Secretary determines that special circumstances warrant the higher rent.

The amount of assistance provided with respect to a unit is an amount equal to the difference between the established maximum rent for the unit and the occupant family's required contribution to rent. Aided families are required to contribute between 15 and 20 percent of their total income to rent as prescribed by the Secretary. A 15 percent maximum is established for certain large families.

In general, eligible families are those who, at the time of initial renting of the units, have total incomes not in excess of 80 percent of area median income. At least 30 percent of the families assisted under all of the annual contract authority allocations must be families with gross incomes not in excess of 50 percent of area median income. These rules are subject to substantial adjustment by the Secretary to take into account construction cost variables, unusually high or low family incomes, and other factors.

Through the spring of 1976, at least, the Section 8 program had not been productive of much new housing. HUD had expected that state housing agencies would provide financing for these projects. There were 31 qualified state agencies across the country that had their own borrowing power and capability of participating in a Section 8 program. Their potential, however, became clouded with the deep recession and the problems of New York City and the collapse of the New York Development Corporation.

Private lenders, too, held back, since these subsidies are in lieu of mortgage loan insurance or guaranties. As previously stated, assistance payments contracts run for 15- to 20-year terms, but mortgages continue for 30 to 40 years. Such a condition leaves the second half of the mortgage repayment period unsupported. No one is certain of the future economic viability of such projects.

Other Titles in the FHA Program Among other titles of the National Housing Act that should be mentioned are Title VII, Title X, and Title XI. Title VII—Section 701 provides for insurance of the yield from investment in rental housing projects for moderate income families. This insurance extends to commercial space and community facilities. Title X relates to land development and new communities, allowing insurance to back the financing to purchase land and develop building sites, including streets, water and sewer systems, and similar costs. Title XI authorizes mortgage insurance for financing construction and equipment of local group practice facilities for doctors, dentists, and optometrists. In certain localities, one practitioner will be sufficient to qualify.

National Corporation for Housing Partnerships This corporation was formed pursuant to 1968 legislation authorizing the President of the United States to create one or more private corporations to engage in activities directed at providing more and better housing for low and moderate income families. The corporation was authorized to enter into and participate in all forms of partnerships and associations, to conduct research and study projects, to provide technical assistance, and to provide financing assistance to other organizations in connection with its activities. The corporation was specifically authorized to form a limited partnership in which the corporation is the general partner and each stockholder is a limited partner. The scope of activities of the limited partnership is the same as those of the corporation.

The limited partnership formed under this authority was titled the National Housing Partnership (NHP). Its initial capital was $42 million invested by 270 leading industrial corporations, utilities, financial organizations, and labor unions. Additional funds may be raised by the sale of portions of NHP's interests in projects on a continuing basis. NHP offers assistance in various ways:

1. Co-sponsorship with local sponsors in joint housing ventures.
2. Purchase of as much as 99 percent of the equity in a multifamily housing development.
3. Seed money loans.
4. Sponsorship with nonprofit and community organizations.
5. Staff services.

NHP now has projects in about two-thirds of the states in a variety of locations.

Public Housing

Under the U.S. Housing Act of 1937, the federal government assumed responsibility for the administration of a public housing program. Under this program, the federal government has provided financial aid for housing owned and operated by local housing authorities for the benefit of low-income families who otherwise would be unable to afford decent housing in the locality. Single elderly persons of 62 years of age or older, or persons who, regardless of age, are under disabilities which entitle them to retirement benefits under the Social Security Act, are eligible for admission as "families of low income," except when restrictive state housing laws prevail.

This segment of the federal public housing program has always been in a great measure the responsibility of the local community concerned. The actual construction and operation of housing projects is the responsibility of local housing authorities. These are nonprofit public agencies which own and operate the project. Construction is performed by private contractors under contract to the housing authority. Costs of this construction are met through the public sale of bonds by the local housing authority. Such obligations are exempt from federal income tax. To encourage further the private purchase of local housing authority obligations, the federal government guarantees the repayment of both principal and interest. All such private financing is under the control of the HUD administrator, who determines maximum maturities, interest rates, and so on. The interest rates are fixed in conformity with a formula outlined in the law which relates them to the rates on applicable government bonds.

Federal aid takes the form of (1) loans to help finance the preliminary development and (2) annual contributions to permit operation of the housing development at rents within the means of low-income families. Actually, the local housing authority pays all operating costs from rental income, and the federal contribution goes only toward bond retirement.

As a part of its complementary service, HUD also sets standards and offers technical assistance to the local housing authorities. In the consummation of new construction programs, the local authorities often undertake a simultaneous elimination of a number of substandard dwellings, either by demolition or by rehabilitation, equal to the number of units constructed for public housing.

No annual contribution will be made by the federal government unless the housing project to which it applies is exempt from all real and personal property taxes imposed by state, city, county, or other political subdivision. In lieu of such taxes, the local housing authority may contract to make payments to taxing districts not to exceed 10 percent of the annual shelter rent charged in the housing project.

Prior to 1965, public housing was geared to new construction, specifically built for the purpose. In 1965, Congress authorized local housing agencies to acquire existing housing or privately built new housing for low-rent tenants. Such programs are now known as "instant housing" or "turnkey" acquisitions. They are backed by an annual contribution contract under which HUD provides financial assistance to the local housing authority for acquisition and operation of the projects.

Also in 1965, for the first time Congress authorized the use of federal assistance to permit local housing authorities to lease private dwellings to low-income tenants. This program is initiated by the governing body of the community approving by resolution the application of this plan to the community. Upon HUD approval, listings of available homes and apartments are obtained from private owners and real estate companies. The public housing authority and the property owner usually sign a lease which provides for subleasing to eligible tenants. Other leasing arrangements are possible. The local housing authority pays the federal contribution either to the owner directly or to the tenants. If the latter, the tenant places the contribution with the balance of the rent and makes the total payment to the owner.

Local housing authorities have recently become more interested in housing specially designed to meet the need of the aging and physically handicapped. More liberal cost allowances have been allowed. In addition, in view of the low incomes of a large number of the elderly and handicapped, additional operating subsidies have been authorized for each dwelling where it is necessary to maintain project solvency.

Community Development[1]

The Housing and Community Development Act of 1974 fundamentally revamped the federal government's financial assistance program for communities for physical development and improvement, including the removal and prevention of slums and blight. The change substitutes a single program of 100 percent grants (with certain related guarantees of loans) to communities on basically a formula plan for several ongoing categorical programs. Within a few restrictive limits, communities now have authority to formulate their own development plans and programs, to be assisted instead of conforming to federal programs and decisions. This approach obviously gives the communities greater authority and flexibility in determining the assisted operations to be undertaken.

Several categorical programs of several years history were terminated (as to commitment on January 1, 1975). These included:

---

[1] The material on community development was derived from *Evolution of Role of the Federal Government in Housing and Community Development*, Subcommittee on Housing and Community Development of the Committee on Banking, Currency and Housing, House of Representatives, 94th Congress, First Session, October, 1975, U.S. Government Printing Office, Washington, D.C., pp. 201–3. This pamphlet is an excellent chronology of legislation and selected legislative actions, 1892–1974.

Open space—urban beautification—historic preservation grants.
Public facility loans.
Water and sewer and neighborhood facilities grants.
Urban renewal and neighborhood development program grants.
Model cities supplemental grants.
Authority to make rehabilitation loans.

Eligible Recipients   States, cities, counties, and other units of local government (including certain designated types of public agencies) are the eligible recipients of community development block grants (and guarantee of loans). The legislation also extends this eligibility to certain private "new community" developers and citizens associations.

Eligible Activities   In general, eligible activities include the broad range of development activities typical in a community. They encompass those dealt with under the earlier programs now terminated. The activities include:

Acquisition, disposition or retention of real property that is blighted, deteriorated, or inappropriately developed; appropriation for rehabilitation or conservation activities; or appropriation for conservation of open space or historical sites and public purposes

Acquisition, construction, or installation of most types of public works, utilities, facilities, and site and other improvements

Code enforcement in deteriorating areas

Clearance, demolition, removal, and rehabilitation of buildings and improvement, including interim assistance and financing of rehabilitation of privately-owned property incident to other activities

Other related activities such as public services not otherwise available, relocation payments for those displaced, and administration of the program

Payment of the nonfederal share of other federal programs related to development

Development of a comprehensive plan and the policy-planning-management capacity of the community

Requirements in Application for Community Development Grants   To obtain HUD approval of an assisted activity, a properly prepared application must contain:

1.   A summary of a three-year plan that identifies community development needs and objectives developed in accordance with area-wide development planning and national urban growth policies and which demonstrates a comprehensive strategy for meeting these needs.

2.   Formulation of a program which includes activities to meet

community development needs and objectives, indicates resources other than federal assistance expected to be available to meet such needs and objectives, and takes account of environment factors.

3. A description of a program to eliminate or prevent slums, blight, and deterioration where such conditions or needs exist, and provide improved community facilities and public improvements, including supporting health and social services where necessary and appropriate.

4. A housing assistance plan which:

accurately surveys the condition of the community's housing stock and assesses the housing assistance needs of lower income persons residing or expected to reside in the community;

specifies a realistic annual goal for the number of units, or persons to be assisted, including the mix of new, existing, and rehabilitated units, and the size and types of projects and assistance best suited to the needs of the lower income persons in the area; and

indicates the general locations of proposed lower income housing with a view to further revitalization, promoting greater housing choice, avoiding undue concentration of low income persons, and assuring availability of adequate public facilities and services for such housing.

Financing Homes for Veterans[2]

When World War II ended, the deluge of returning veterans and new family formations created an acute housing shortage. A high level of economic activity provided the veteran with income sufficient to amortize a mortgage in lieu of rent, but he usually did not have the cash down payment required to permit him to buy a home under conventional lending methods. It had been the practice for many years, in compliance with investment restriction laws of the states, for institutional lenders to limit their loans to from 60 to 75 percent of the appraised value of the property. Experience had taught them to require a cushion against depreciation in value that takes place in a forced sale on foreclosure.

Legislative History It was therefore a revolutionary step when a grateful Congress enacted legislation providing World War II veterans a guarantee by the United States of mortgage debt incurred to acquire a home. This guarantee was intended to be sufficient to substitute, in substantial measure at least, for lack of a cash down payment. The first law, passed in 1944, provided for a 50 percent guarantee up to $2,000 with the interest rate on the loan not to exceed 4 percent.

The original construction of the guarantee law was strict. Lenders

---

[2] The authors are indebted to R. C. Coon, Director, Loan Guaranty Service, Department of Veterans Benefits, Veterans Administration, Washington, D.C., for assistance in providing information for the current revision in regard to VA assistance to veterans in financing real estate. The authors, of course, are solely responsible for the accuracy and interpretation of the material contained in this chapter.

were skeptical and few were willing to make loans except on an experimental basis. The $2,000 maximum was only sufficient to provide a substitute for the 40 percent cash down payment required by many investing institutions on a $5,000 home, and any veteran wanting to buy a home for $6,000, $8,000, or $10,000 would be faced with an increasingly prohibitive problem with the cash down payment required.

In 1945, the law was amended to raise the guarantee limit to $4,000 (the limit on nonrealty loans remaining at $2,000). The new provision permitted a $4,000 substitute for the cash down payment up to 50 percent on a $8,000 home, and a more expensive home could be obtained by an added cash down payment by the veteran; or the lender might satisfy itself with less than a 50 percent guarantee. Now, the program began to function. Furthermore, by regulation of the Veterans Administration, lenders were permitted to recoup advances made for delinquent taxes and insurance and the costs of foreclosure plus attorney fees. Lenders learned by experience that their guarantee claims were quickly honored and that the program was managed by the VA so as to honor just claims and to avoid technicalities, thereby encouraging more lenders to enter the program.

By 1950, several things had come to pass which had encouraged Congress to liberalize the VA loan law. First, inflation caused the price of housing to increase, and this in turn made the $4,000 guarantee inadequate. Second, experience proved that the veterans were unexpectedly good credit risks and that the cost to the government was far less than had been anticipated—so much so that the loss due to defaulted loans was substantially less than the historical average loss in ordinary commercial lending made by ordinary financing sources to good credit risks. This disposed Congress to increase the maximum guarantee to 60 percent of the loan, not to exceed $7,500. The increase allowed "no down payment loans" in the $12,000 to $13,000 area with larger purchase prices by using a percentage of guarantee of less than 60 percent or by making additional cash down payment, or both. While the inflation of values was going on, there was also a development of a shortage of mortgage loan money at the statutory rate limit for federal guarantee, resulting in 1959 in an advance of the maximum interest rate to 5¼ percent. Incidentally, the VA secured amendments to state and federal laws, permitting VA-guaranteed loans as an exception to other laws imposing restrictions on loan-to-value ratios for institutional investors.

Qualified Veterans   Guaranteed or insured loans may be made to veterans of World War II or the Korean conflict who served on active duty for 90 days or more. Other veterans in active service over 180 days may also qualify. Special eligibility is granted to veterans in the above classes with less than the required service but who were separated with service-connected disabilities or to unmarried widows of veterans who died in service or as a result of service-connected disabilities. Wives of members of the armed forces who have been listed as missing in action or prisoners of war for 90 days may also qualify. In all cases, eligibility is conditioned on a separation from the service that is other than dishonorable.

All termination dates for eligibility to apply for VA-guaranteed housing were removed by the Veterans Administration Act of 1970. This act also provided that mobile homes are acceptable security for loan guarantees by the Veterans Administration.

Nature of GI Obligation   The legal nature of the VA guarantee is that of an absolute guarantee in which the Administrator becomes liable for the entire amount of the existing guarantee immediately on default. The guarantee has always been a percentage guarantee with a maximum amount fixed by law. Thus, an original loan of $10,000 made today will be guaranteed for 60 percent (or $6,000) and this percentage will adhere to the loan as the debt is decreased by payments or increased by unpaid interest. The practical aspects of the GI loan obligation are set forth by the VA in the foreword to the 1969 edition of the *Lender's Handbook* in the following terms:

The execution of a guaranteed or insured loan involves the assumption of a substantial responsibility by all parties concerned. Upon the veteran rests the obligation to repay in full the amount borrowed; the lender assumes the responsibility of servicing the loan adequately and effectually, exerting every reasonable means in default cases to assist the veteran borrower against loss of his home, farm, or business; and the Veterans Administration, on behalf of the Government, must require that both parties fully discharge their responsibilities.

The elements of the above quotation to be emphasized are: the debt obligation of the borrower; the necessity for tempered leniency on the part of the lender; and the determination of the VA to administer the law in a manner to protect the veteran, the lender, and the government. This definition should also be taken seriously by lending institutions. Few veterans have any conception of the responsibilities that go with homeownership. Most of them have had little or no experience as rent-paying tenants—much less as homeowners. Most of them need the financial assistance which the GI law gives them. They need also a great deal of homely advice about homeownership and its responsibilities. In many cases they need to be advised against the purchase of a certain property, even though it will appraise for enough to qualify for a guaranteed loan.

Eligible Lenders   Any person, firm, association, corporation, or state or federal agency can be an eligible lender under the GI law. It is expected, however, that most loans will be made by commercial banks—national, state, or private; savings and loan associations; savings banks; insurance companies; credit unions; and other mortgage institutions which are subject to supervision by a governmental agency. Lenders operating under federal laws, including national banks, federal savings and loan association, and all banks, savings and loan associations, and insurance companies authorized to do business in the District of Columbia, are permitted to grant GI loans without reference to the limitations or restrictions of any other statute. These restrictions are waived in respect to: ratio of loan to property value; maturity of loan; security requirements; dignity of lien; and percentage of assets which may be invested in loans against real estate as security.

Eligible lenders whose operations are supervised by a governmental agency—state or national—may make loans that are automatically guaranteed so long as they keep within the requirements of the VA. Nonsupervised lenders who meet VA regulatory standards may also arrange to have their loans approved on an automatic basis. By automatic guarantee is meant that the lender need not secure the prior approval of the VA before making the loan. Approximately 18.6 percent of all GI loans have been automatically guaranteed during the past 15 years, but only 7 percent in the 1975 fiscal year. In short, processing on an automatic basis has become a less important part of the program except in certain areas such as Boston where most business is conducted this way. Most lenders prefer to secure prior approval on all loans granted by them. This is their privilege. By this means they minimize the risk of having the guarantee questioned on technical grounds at a later time.

Insured Loans   Any loan eligible for a guarantee under this law may be eligible for insurance as well, if made or purchased by a supervised lender. The lender which elects to use the insurance program must notify the VA of its intent at the time the loan is reported. Otherwise it is guaranteed instead of insured. When insurance is elected, the lender's insurance account is credited with 15 percent of each loan insured, provided that it keeps within the maximum amount of the guarantee. In case of default on an insured loan, the lender is entitled to obtain from the VA the full amount of its net loss, regardless of the percentage of loss to value of the property. For example, suppose that the lender has made or purchased $1 million of GI loans. Its insurance credit would be $150,000, which is 15 percent coverage. If the loans are paid down to $600,000, the coverage becomes 25 percent; to $300,000, 50 percent; and so forth. Meantime, any losses suffered by the lender would be charged against its insurance credit. If an $8,000 loan against a property resulted in an $8,000 loss, full recovery could be obtained if the balance to the insurance credit of the lender amounted to that much. Insured home loans are negligible in number and amount.

Purposes of Home Loan   A guaranteed home loan may be used to purchase a residential property to be occupied by the veteran as his home; for financing the construction of his home; or for paying for alterations, repairs, or improvement to the home he already owns. Loans for the purchase of real estate primarily for investment purposes are not eligible for guarantees. Residential properties may consist of not more than four-family units, provided that one is to be occupied by the veteran as his home. Where the property is to be purchased or constructed through joint ownership of two or more veterans, one additional unit may be added for each added veteran. This is being interpreted to mean that two veterans may purchase a six-family unit. In states where home appliances are included as fixtures, they can be included in the guaranteed loan. Where there is doubt, they may not be included, since Title 38 U.S. Code, Chapter 37, which establishes the guaranty, applies only to real estate loans.

GI Home Purchase as Hedge   The purchase of homes by veterans using the liberal financing terms of the GI law has been looked upon by some of them as a kind of double hedge. In the first place, it has provided a hedge against decisions by landlords. By owning a home being financed by a GI loan, the veteran is assured a place to live at no increase in housing cost so long as he keeps up his payments. He cannot be dispossessed, and his rent cannot be increased. Only taxes, utilities, and repair costs may go higher. Financing costs are fixed for the life of the loan. These are usually no higher than rental payments for comparable accommodations.

In the second place, the ownership of his home affords the veteran a hedge against further inflation in real estate prices. If real estate prices go up substantially, the cost of housing accommodations to tenants sooner or later reflects the increase. Of course, if costs should drop, then the prices of existing properties will follow after a time. Even in such event the homeowner is in a more advantageous position than the real estate speculator or investor. The investor who retains his property after prices decline will probably suffer loss of income. The speculator who buys when prices are high and sells at a lower price will lose a part of his principal. But the owner-occupant of a home still has the use of his property.

Lending Plans   Early VA guarantees amounted to 50 percent of the amount of the loan, or $4,000, whichever was less. Under the 1950 amendment to the law this maximum guarantee was raised to 60 percent, with a ceiling of $7,500. In 1968 the mortgage guarantee ceiling was raised to $12,500, and in 1974 to $17,500, to help finance more expensive homes. The Administrator of Veterans Affairs is authorized to establish maximum interest rates in accord with loan market demands, not to exceed limitations by Section 203 (b) (5) of the National Housing Act. The maximum term is now 30 years and 32 days; it was formerly 25 years. In 1970 the guarantee authority was broadened to include loans to refinance mortgages and other liens of record on homes owned and occupied by eligible veterans. There is no maximum loan except that the loan cannot exceed the reasonable value of the property established by the VA.

Although Congress had in mind 100 percent loans to veterans, if necessary, including all costs of making the loan, the amount of any loan is subject to negotiation with the lender selected for financing assistance. In addition, the provision of the law relating to refinancing allows the VA to guarantee a loan not to exceed the reasonable value and also the veteran is allowed to pay the discount in these cases. Furthermore, the veteran may receive cash from the transaction resulting from the difference between the loan amount (which can not exceed the reasonable value) and the mortgages or other liens or debts which are to be paid in full from the loan proceeds. Some of this cash may be used by the veteran to pay the closing costs and prepaid items which are allowable; however, these are not technically part of the loan amount. They are disclosed to the VA because only certain charges are authorized as allowable to be paid by a veteran. This disclosure is not necessary because the VA considers them to be a part of the loan. It should be emphasized that only loans provided for in 38 U.S. Code, Sec. 1803 (c), which includes refinances, carry permission to the veterans to pay discounts.

Maturity of Loans   Term loans for five years or less are eligible for guarantee under the GI home-financing plan. Experience has shown, however, that most home loans are monthly payment direct reduction loans. Amortization may follow the standard plan, which provides for a level monthly payment throughout the life of the loan. Under this plan, the same monthly payment will result in a declining interest charge and an increasing proportion of the monthly payments being used to reduce the principal balance. The Springfield plan is also acceptable to the VA. Under it, the same amount must be paid each month to reduce the principal balance, but the interest charge will constantly decline. As a consequence, the total monthly payment will decline month by month. Most of the loans granted follow the standard plan. The maximum maturity allowed is 30 years and 32 days.

The law provides that payments must be approximately equal; but it also provides that amortization of the indebtedness may follow established procedure in the community where the property is situated. In accordance with this provision, loan plans have been approved which call either for somewhat larger payments in the beginning with reductions later, or for small payments at the start when the borrower's expenses are great, with increases later when income applicable to the loan payments promises to be greater. Extreme variations in payments are not sanctioned by the VA.

Many lenders do not look with favor upon the maximum maturities provided under the GI law. In spite of the loan guarantee, the following reasons are set forth in support of shorter maturities for GI borrowers: (1) The shorter the maturity, the smaller is the amount of interest paid by the borrower. (2) Shorter maturities result in building equities faster at a time when family obligations are not as great as they will be later. (3) The larger the equity, the greater is the probability of forebearance if the borrower needs it.

Down Payment   Under the GI law, home loans are guaranteed with or without down payment. The amount of the down payment is subject to negotiation between the borrower and the lender. Some lenders have been willing to make 100 percent loans if other factors have been favorable. Others have insisted upon at least a small down payment in order to make sure that the borrower feels a sense of ownership in the property. Even where the owner's equity is small, he may feel that this can be amortized over a period of a few years as a part of the cost of having an assurance of a place to live. As a general rule, small equities do not give the same sense of ownership that is present when the equity is larger. By the same token, an equity created by a gift is less significant in the mind of the recipient than one created from his own savings.

For the above reasons, some lenders to whom the GI loans are otherwise acceptable have insisted upon substantial down payments of 20 percent or more. Others have considered "sweat" equities as at least a partial substitute for a down payment. If some of the work needed to make the home livable is performed by the veteran, the increase in value—which also means an increase in his equity—is called a "sweat" equity. In some areas where loans are made with uncompleted houses as security, with the assumption that the borrower will complete the structure with his own labor and that of his friends, the name given to such a mortgage is "shell loan." The VA requires a minimum of property improvements to qualify for guaranty, and proper escrow procedures must be followed with regard to work to be completed.

Prepayments   All GI loans on homes must grant the privilege of prepayment of any part or all of the indebtedness at any time. The lender is not required to accept as a prepayment less than one installment or $100, whichever, is smaller. Prepayments may be used to cure defaults, unless they have been once used for this purpose. For example, if prepayments have been applied to reduce the principal balance of the loan and later the borrower defaults, the amounts prepaid may be applied, through a recalculation of the payments, to cure or to prevent a default. The veteran can thus obtain the double advantage of interest reductions and of building a cushion against possible future defaults. In addition, if prepayments are substantial, the veteran may request that the loan be reamortized, reducing future payments; assuming that the reamortization schedule will provide that the entire loan be repaid within the original loan period.

Taxes and Insurance By mutual agreement between the veteran borrower and the lender, the latter may collect with each loan payment a proportion of taxes, assessments, and insurance premiums applicable to the property. The method of collecting and disbursing such payments should be clearly set forth in the mortgage contract. If such added payments are provided for and if the contract so stipulates, failure to meet any such payments may constitute a default just as if the borrower had failed to pay interest or principal installment when due. Custom, rather than the regulations of the VA, generally governs the collection of these added amounts. If the lender is accustomed to collect them on conventional or FHA loans, it will probably collect them on GI loans also. Some lenders have not become acquainted with the advantages of collecting taxes and insurance from their borrowers.

In 1971, VA and HUD conducted a survey of both lenders and borrowers regarding the practice of escrowing taxes and insurance as a part of the loan payment. They found this to be the common procedure. Lenders favored this policy particularly to make sure that the taxes and insurance premiums were paid in a manner not to jeopardize guaranties.

Appraisals Appraisal procedure under the GI law has suffered many pains. As originally written, the law prohibited the application of loan guaranties if the price paid for the property exceeded the "reasonable normal value" of the property, as determined by the appraisers responsible to the VA. Nobody ever knew how to measure "normal" value. Presumably it was intended to provide only for long-term value, from which must be eliminated elements of inflation resulting from temporary scarcity. But the veterans who needed the assistance of the guarantee most urgently were those who were homeless in a period of extreme housing shortages. To bar them from the purchase of homes, even at admittedly inflated prices, meant the practical nullification of the purposes of the GI law.

Subsequently the word "normal" was stricken from the law. Had it been omitted originally, the administrators of this law might have had equally great difficulty in defining "reasonable value." But when "normal" was dropped, its omission was interpreted to mean that reasonable value must take into account current market conditions. This change made it possible for veterans to benefit from the law. By that time, the VA defined reasonable value in its regulations as "that figure which represents the amount a designated appraiser, unaffected by personal interest or prejudice, would recommend as a proper price or cost to a prospective purchaser, whom the appraiser represents in a relationship of trust, as being a fair price or cost in the light of prevailing conditions." This concept abandons the idea of long-term value and places greatest emphasis upon prevailing conditions.

Interests Covered   The GI law on home financing applies to: (1) a fee simple estate, whether legal or equitable; (2) a leasehold estate, running originally for a period not less than 14 years beyond the maturity of the loan, or which is renewable for such a period; and (3) a life estate, if the remainder and reversionary interests are made subject to the lien.

Forbearance   The Congress, in passing the GI home loan provisions, sought a means of providing homes for veterans of World War II by the use of a financing program which shifts much of the risk from the shoulders of the lender to the government. It is recognized that some who take advantage of this plan will have at least temporary difficulty in living up to the obligations they assume. Lenders are expected to exercise forbearance whenever borrowers have difficulty in meeting their obligations under their mortgages. This can be accomplished by recasting the loan in such a manner as to extend the term of repayment of the principal balance. This is encouraged by the VA. Filing of notice of default with the VA still leaves the lender free to exercise patience and leniency with his delinquent borrower. He is not forced to bring foreclosure suit in order to protect his guarantee.

Hopeless cases are dealt with as such when it is determined that there is no probability that the loan will be reinstated and the default cured. When it appears that the borrower can no longer carry the property, all parties concerned are urged to find a buyer for the property. If a new buyer can take over the mortgage and pay the mortgagor something for his equity, if any, well and good. If the real estate market is not favorable; if the condition of the property is such that it does not attract buyers; and if forbearance has been carried to such a point that the sale price of the property is less than. the guarantee: then the VA will consider a proposal for the sale of the property at a price that will require it to make up to the lender the difference between the mortgage indebtedness and the amount assumed by the purchaser, but not in excess of the loan guarantee.

As an alternative, the mortgagee may accept a voluntary conveyance in lieu of foreclosure, with the prior consent of the VA. The policy of the VA is to encourage the acceptance of voluntary conveyances because of the saving of time and money.

Open Mortgages   The VA regulations authorize the use of open mortgages in those states that have legislation authorizing their use. Lenders are encouraged to inspect the properties securing VA loans at least once a year for the purpose of determining their physical condition. Such an inspection may disclose evidence of intentional or unintentional waste as well as any unusual conditions that cause the property to depreciate in value more rapidly than usual. Even ordinary wear and tear needs to be offset by maintenance and repair. Mortgages protecting GI loans are permitted to contain clauses allowing the lender to make advances to cover the cost of expenditures for these purposes. As noted above, the lender is still obligated to observe due caution to make sure that, in his locality, such advances may not jeopardize the dignity of his lien. The VA discourages the use of open-end mortgages and although the VA mortgage form affords a lien to the holder for advances made for taxes and insurance, none of its printed forms contains a general provision for any state. But, the view of the VA is that it cannot prevent their use, which might nevertheless be followed by a reduction of a claim on a guarantee.

Filing of Claims   Should a borrower become delinquent, the lender may file a claim with the VA. The VA may elect to make good the amount of the delinquency, bringing the loan current again. Any payments made by the VA to the lender in this fashion do not reduce the amount of the debtor's obligation. The VA becomes subrogated to the amount of claim against him that is paid to the lender. Subsequently the VA may assert this claim in any manner it sees fit. It may determine that conditions are such as to require the VA to pay off the claim of the lender and take over the mortgage. Meantime it may help the veteran and the lender to dispose of the property, in case it appears clear that the mortgagor can no longer carry it. Generally, a claim for guaranty will be submitted after liquidation of the security.

In isolated cases where for any reason a foreclosure sale is conducted, the VA does not encourage the lender to take a deficiency judgment unless it appears clear that it can probably be collected. In no event is the lender obligated to undertake to collect, by resort to legal proceedings, any debts owed by the veteran borrower to the government on account of a GI home loan.

Custody of Property   As soon as the holder of a VA-guaranteed mortgage elects to convey property to the VA after acquiring it through foreclosure or voluntary deed, it must so notify the VA. Thereupon the VA expects to assume custody of the property. By this means the former lender is relieved of any responsibility for loss to the property or damage for personal injuries in connection therewith. Since the VA is a self-insurer, it has no need for any kind of commercial insurance coverage. If the holder of the title sees fit to renew any insurance policy or to place insurance against the property following its acquisition, it does so at its own risk.

In turning over property to the VA, the holder of the title has no responsibility for securing the eviction of any occupant who is a trespasser on the property. But the VA will require a showing that any occupant is not claiming to own the property, because every purchaser of property is charged with notice of all rights of all parties in possession. In case title is obtained by foreclosure action, the occupants should be joined in the suit in order to cut off whatever rights they may attempt to assert.

Title Evidence   In cases of conveyance of a property to the VA, it is the holder's responsibility (supervised or otherwise) to deliver clear title and appropriate evidence thereof to the VA. In all cases, the VA reviews the title evidence to assure itself that the title is clear. Although the VA does not directly pay for the procurement of such title evidence, the holder can be reimbursed by including those costs in the computation of the claim.

Sale of Property   A veteran who purchases a home with financial assistance afforded by a GI loan may sell his home without restrictions so far as the VA is concerned. Because of the favorable interest rate and small monthly payments, the purchaser will usually want to assume the mortgage rather than to refinance and discharge the mortgagee. But there is a pitfall in so doing, for the veteran will remain liable on the debt to the holder of the loan; and if the purchaser defaults, and the VA pays on the guarantee, the veteran will be indebted to the VA for the amount paid on the guarantee. This debt is actively enforced by both the VA and the Department of Justice. On the other hand, if the purchaser not only assumes the mortgage debt, but also the obligation of the veteran to reimburse the VA in case it has to pay on its guarantee, and if the purchaser meets the VA requirements as a good credit risk, the veteran and the purchaser may apply to the VA to have the veteran released from all obligation on the debt, including reimbursement to the VA. When the VA accepts the purchaser fully in lieu of the veteran, the latter will be completely released, even though the originally guaranteed debt remains in force and effect against the purchaser. Some veterans have taken advantage of these circumstances and have sold their homes at a profit. In some cases real estate salesmen have sought out veterans interested in disposing of their homes, because of the appeal of the GI financing plan. In summary, a VA mortgage is attractive as an assumption because of the ease of transfer, the absence of a prepayment penalty, and in respect to older homes, a lower interest rate. During the past ten years, in times of tight money, an assumption for many sellers was often the only means of selling a home.

Since 1950, a veteran has been able to obtain another loan even after using full entitlement provided the requirements for restoration can be met. Currently the requirements are quite simple: The veteran must have disposed of the security for the property and the loan must have been paid in full. In some cases of assumption, if a veteran-buyer has sufficient entitlement and is willing to substitute his or her entitlement for that of the veteran-seller, restoration can be accomplished in this manner. This is known as substitution of entitlement and became effective April 1, 1975.

Direct Lending   At the time the GI bill was first discussed in Congress, there was considerable pressure to provide direct loans by the government to the veterans of World War II. Private lending guaranteed by the VA was finally substituted for direct lending. From time to time since the law was originally enacted, there has been pressure to add direct lending features. Finally, in 1950, the law was amended to provide that:

Upon application by a veteran eligible for the benefit of a home loan guarantee who has not previously availed himself of this privilege, if the VA finds that private capital is not available for the purchase or construction of a home, the VA may make a loan directly under the following conditions:

A.   That he is a satisfactory credit risk,

B.   that the monthly payments to be required under the proposed loan bear a proper relation to the veteran's present and anticipated income and expenses,

C.   that he is unable to obtain from private lending sources in such area at an interest rate not in excess of 4 percentum per annum a loan for such purpose for which he is qualified under Section 501—of this title.

Loans made under this amendment were to bear interest at the rate of 4 percent (increased in subsequent years consistently with the guarantee and insurance programs) and were subject to the following limitations:

1.   The original amount of such loan shall not exceed $10,000 (since increased in steps to as much as $25,000); and

2.   The guaranty entitlement of the veteran shall be charged with the same amount that would be deducted if the loan had been guaranteed to the maxima permitted under Section 500 (a) of this title.

The VA is authorized to sell mortgages to any private lending institution evidencing ability to service loans with the proviso that it may guarantee any loan thus sold subject to the same conditions, terms, and limitations which would be applicable to privately originated loans with an automatic guarantee.

The direct lending program has had considerable activity in capital-short areas. It has enjoyed a favorable collection experience.

Default Experience and Losses   At the end of December 1975, only 48,000 (1.2 percent) of the nearly 4 million GI home loans outstanding were in default. Historically, efforts to restore defaulted loans to good standing have been successful in 84 percent of the cases. Only 322,668 GI home loans, or 3.6 percent of the 9 million loans closed, have resulted in a claim.

A summary of the operations and financial position of the program through June 30, 1975 follows:

Expenses and Losses:
Losses from claims ....$ 308.8
Operating expenses and losses 919.6
Total expenses and losses $1,228.4

Income:
Interest collection on veterans indebtedness 4.1
Operating income 1,049.8
Total income $1,053.9

Net loss ....$ 174.5

Loan Guaranty Program Balance Sheet

Assets:
Cash ....$ 334.2
Accounts receivable, net 6.7
Loans receivable, net 1,086.9
Claims receivable, net 28.6
Net equity in real property 164.9
Total assets $1,621.3

Liabilities:
Accounts payable ....$ 47.2
Securities outstanding 561.0
Borrowing from Treasury 505.7
Total liabilities $1,113.9
Net government equity 507.4

Total liabilities and government equity $1,621.3

All amounts in millions of dollars.

The loss of $174.5 million represents less than 0.15 of 1 percent of the total $119.4 billion of loans guaranteed or insured by the program.

Participation in FHA and VA Programs A sense of the relative importance of the lending sources to the federal underwriting programs can be gathered from a review of Exhibit 20–1.

EXHIBIT 20–1
Holdings of Federally Underwritten Mortgage Debt by Main Types of Financial Institutions for Selected Years, 1955 through 1975 (in $ billion)

		FHA				VA			
Year	Total FHA & VA Debt.*	Mutual Savings Banks	Commercial Banks	Life Ins. Cos.	Savings & Loan Ass'ns	Mutual Savings Banks	Commercial Banks	Life Ins. Cos.	Savings & Loan Ass'ns
1955.....	42.9	4.1	4.6	6.4	1.4	5.8	3.7	6.1	5.9
1965.....	81.2	13.8	7.7	12.1	5.1	11.4	2.7	6.3	6.4
1975.....	144.9	14.5	6.4	8.1	n.a.**	12.5	3.3	4.0	n.a.**

* Institutional holdings listed above do not add up to total FHA and VA debt shown in first column because of other holdings, such as those by government agencies and pension funds.
** Data are as of September 30, 1975. Total combined federally-underwritten holdings of savings and loan associations were $30.4 billion, breakdown not available.
Source: *National Fact Book of Mutual Savings Banking, July 1975,* National Association of Mutual Savings Banks, 200 Park Ave., New York, N.Y., p. 54. Additional source: *Federal Reserve Bulletin,* March 1976, p. A44.

It will be noted that mutual savings banks have consistently been major FHA and VA lenders. Savings and loan associations, after a slow start in terms of their potential, have become progressively more important. Life insurance companies have been somewhat down the line, and commercial banks have been even less important as credit suppliers under these programs.

The FHA activities in recent years have become overburdened in many areas by excessive loan defaults under subsidy programs. Private mortgage insurors of conventional loans have also taken over a substantial portion of the market. On the positive side, however, the FHA has made homeownership possible for many Americans. The default experience has not been unmanageable under the unsubsidized programs.

Similarly, the VA program has shown a favorable default experience. It, too, has played an important part in converting this nation from one of predominantly renters to homeowners.

The Road Ahead

What has been said in this chapter emphasizes growing recognition of the existence of a serious problem—the inadequate housing of many American families. Nothing in this chapter has been posed as the final answer to this problem. With each passing year the magnitude of the problem has grown in size and complexity. The country is forced to face, rather than look beyond, the needs and entitlements of minority groups, particularly at the core of the inner city. The proportions of the national malaise are amorphous and multidimensional. Financial factors are affected by noneconomic illnesses in the ghetto culture—crime in the streets, dope traffic, weak school systems, and undeveloped work habits, to name a few.

There is no mistaking that the American system is sending more and more dollars in the direction of achieving "a decent home and a suitable environment for every American family." Through current legislation, federal subsidy is becoming a greater support to the private housing system. Many now see an approach to our national housing problem like that of the Marshall Plan for European economic recovery after World War II as not only appropriate but necessary to achievement of a satisfactory standard of housing for all—to restore personal esteem, pride in family, appreciation of economic opportunity, and respect for the rights of others.

This was much of what was in the minds of Congress as expressed in Title XVI of the Housing and Urban Development Act of 1968 establishing the machinery for the ten-year plan to meet all of the nation's housing needs and eliminate all of its substandard housing by 1978. The ten-year plan set a goal for housing production at 26 million units, of which 20 million would be private financed and 6 million government subsidized. Although total production through most of the ten years has lagged far below the 2.6 million units required annual average, it does not seem too far-fetched to start from now and hope for achievement of this goal over the next decade.

The high priority for this type of federal assistance is now more formalized than previously. It will work, however, only through combined efforts of private and governmental interests. In this way, job creation, for example, may be coordinated with improvement in education and living facilities. Private and state and local financial resources will become exhausted and it will be to the federal government that the community will look for residual loans and grants in aid.

By simple mathematics, it is apparent that at $15,000 per unit the ten-year cost of 26 million new housing units would require $390 billion of financing. The magnitude of this need is of the order of the cost of waging a war. Such figures, of course, are hypothetical and meaningless unless they are derived with respect to direct applications to real situations. Much of any investment could be recovered through employment of the previously unemployable, increase in the property tax rolls, and decrease in the welfare rolls.

The challenge of housing the population of America lies not only in seeking the best solution to some part of the problem, but more often in learning what the facets of the problem are and how they interrelate.

QUESTIONS

1. How is the federal housing program administered?
2. What are the functions of Titles I and II of the National Housing Act?
3. What are the general terms and characteristics of a Title II loan?
4. Who may participate as lenders in the FHA program? Who may participate as borrowers?
5. How do the problems involved in urban redevelopment differ from those of original city planning?
6. What are the shortcomings of complete reliance upon private capital for the elimination of substandard housing and slum areas?
7. What are the arguments for and against public housing?
8. What action has HUD taken to meet the need of housing for families with lower incomes? Distinguish the programs. How appropriate are they?
9. What is the role of the Veterans Administration in assisting GI housing?
10. It has been stated that a GI loan may provide the buyer with a "double hedge." Explain.
11. Review the relative importance of FHA-insured and VA-guaranteed mortgages to various types of financial institutions. Determine where insurance is relatively important and suggest reasons why.

12. How should we determine what are appropriate housing goals for the next decade?

CASE PROBLEMS

1. The Alexanders have an existing mortgage balance of $28,000 on a property with an FHA appraisal value of $40,000. Their present mortgage is conventional, at a 7.5% interest rate, with monthly payments for interest and amortization of $300. The mortgage provides for a prepayment penalty of interest for 90 days on the unpaid balance at date of prepayment. They are considering the possibility of refinancing with a Section 203 FHA-insured mortgage. The current FHA interest rate is 8.75%. Assume that there are 3 discount points required for closing costs and to adjust to the current market interest rate.

    a. The 1974 housing act established maximum loan-to-value ratios on unsubsidized home mortgages as follows:

        97% of the first $25,000 of value;

        90% of value between $25,000 and $35,000; and

        80% percent of value over $35,000.

    What is the maximum loan the Alexanders may obtain?

    b. Compute the following:

      1. Prepayment penalty.

      2. How much cash the Alexanders would receive if they should take out a maximum mortgage loan.

      3. Their new monthly payment on a 30-year mortgage at 8.75% interest plus 0.5% mortgage insurance premium. Do not include taxes or hazard insurance costs.

2. John Brown is applying for a homeowner's loan subsidized under Section 235 of the National Housing Act. His adjusted annual income as determined by the FHA is $8,400. He is below the area income limit of $8,500 that would exclude him. Other transaction data:

Sale price: $24,000   Term: 360 months

Down payment: $ 1,000   Interest rate: 8.75%

Mortgage amount: $23,000   Taxes and hazard insurance: $28 monthly

On the basis of the model included in the chapter, compute the authorized subsidy for this case and the mortgagor's required monthly payment.

3. Harry Gray, a veteran, has bought his home and financed the purchase by a GI loan. He desires to sell his home. He seeks your advice. If he sells to a nonveteran, what advantages may he achieve and what are the disadvantages? How may the results be different if he sells to another veteran?

21

Secondary Mortgage Markets

Growth of Mortgage Loans

Since World War II, total mortgage debt has expanded in massive terms. During the decade of the 1950s the debt doubled, expanding about $128 billion. By January 1, 1970, outstanding mortgage loans had more than doubled again, reaching over $425 billion. At the 1975 year-end, six years later, the outstanding mortgage debt had risen to $800 billion. This remarkable growth took place in spite of periods of extreme credit stringency during recent years.

The great increase in the demand for mortgage money can be accounted for principally as the result of three major demand factors. First, and perhaps most obvious, is the rapidly increasing national population. This factor, however, has not been as important as two others: (1) the rising unit cost of homes and (2) the higher loan-to-value ratios. For federally underwritten mortgages on single-family homes, the increased average loan between 1950 and 1975 reflected a rise in purchase price of from 4 to 10 percent per year. For the same period the loan-to-value ratio rose from 76 percent to over 90 percent. A similar trend has been confirmed for conventional loans closed by insured savings and loan associations, where the average amount of the loan more than doubled and average loan-to-value ratios rose from 58 percent to over 70 percent during the period. Another factor, longer maturity dates for loans, has also had an impact on the increased amount of borrowing.

The very policy of increased liberalization of financing terms for homeownership as supported by the federal program has had a contradictory effect. Through stimulated demand for housing and concomitant higher prices, home market values are highly dependent upon a continuation of such liberal policies. With low down payments, conservative interest rates, and long maturities, such loans may quickly become submarginal from the point of view of the private lender. It is at this point that another need arises. That is the need for a reliable secondary market for real estate mortgages to which institutions may resort to release funds for a continuation of a lending program under continually favorable conditions in an expanding real estate construction program.

Changing Character of Real Estate Mortgages   Until recent years investment in real estate mortgages was a highly specialized type of money commitment. Few investors were willing to undertake the risks associated with such a commitment except where they had personal knowledge of the security, based upon inspection and appraisal, and where they could keep in touch with the debt-paying habits of the borrower by performing their own servicing operations. While this is still true of conventional loans, even here the urgency of the need for personal knowledge of the security and of direct servicing is not as great as it once was.

The coming of government guarantee and insurance of mortgages, accompanied by the increasing use of title insurance, has changed the above pattern materially. No longer does the ultimate holder of a real estate mortgage think of his commitment as the financing of a real estate project. Instead he gives prime attention to the insured or guaranteed paper which he holds as a receipt for his investment. Knowledge of the security for the mortgage is subordinated to faith in the guarantee or insurance of the mortgage, supported by title insurance. This change in the concept of real estate mortgages adds greatly to their liquidity and thereby points up the need for secondary markets for mortgages.

Supply of versus Demand for Mortgage Funds   If the supply of funds available for mortgages were just equal to the demand for such funds in each market area, there would be little need for a secondary market for mortgages. Mortgages could be retained by the individuals and the institutions that originated them until they were amortized in an orderly fashion. There would be no occasion either to buy or sell such mortgages.

While this kind of situation obtains in some sections of the country, in large and growing areas our economy is not simply organized. In some sections we face what amounts to mortgage money surpluses. Here the supply of funds available for investment in real estate mortgages exceeds the demand for mortgage money. In other areas, where the population is growing at rates faster than the average for the entire country, the reverse is true. The demand for mortgage funds far exceeds the local supply. Means must be found to permit money-surplus areas to supplement mortgage funds in money-scarce areas; and conversely to permit money-scarce areas to provide investment outlets for a part of the funds available in money-surplus areas. Secondary markets provide one answer to this problem.

Development of a Secondary Mortgage Market The development of a secondary mortgage market system for all types of sound real estate mortgages has been a slow process and it is still in an intermediate stage. Since 1913 commercial banks have been able to maintain liquidity through privileges of rediscounting certain paper with the Federal Reserve System or of receiving temporary advances from the Federal Reserve Bank in return for the pledge of acceptable collateral. Although the credit reserve principle prevailed over the mortgage discounting system in the establishment of the Federal Home Loan Bank System in 1932, there was a clearly defined purpose that the Home Loan Banks should provide liquidity to their member institutions. A serious limitation of the Home Loan Banks from a practical aspect, however, lies in the relative concentration of its membership in savings and loan associations. Although eligible, few mutual savings banks and insurance companies have joined the system, largely it may be presumed because of reluctance to become a part of a minority group in the membership. Furthermore, the use of the credit reserve principle of providing liquidity through advances rather than by purchase of mortgages has greatly limited the volume of funds that can be provided by the Home Loan Banks. The concept that the credit is temporary or that any loan with a maturity beyond one year must be amortized over the period of the advance seriously limits the use of the advanced funds in the hands of the borrowing institution.

Institutions without recourse to the Federal Reserve or Home Loan Bank systems have no direct and assured means of achieving liquidity for funds committed to real estate mortgages. Mortgage bankers, in particular, who are not eligible to Home Loan Bank membership and who are typically thinly margined on capital, feel a special need for a strongly supporting secondary mortgage market system. The federal government made gestures toward the setting up of a secondary market for mortgages with the establishment of the federal assistance program for real estate during the 1930s. Only fairly recently, however, has there been a secondary market worthy of the term. The secondary real estate mortgage market has been defined as the aggregate of all purchase and sale transactions in such mortgages. For such a market to be effective and worthy of acceptance, private or governmental funds must be available at all times to permit the purchase of mortgage loans meeting prescribed standards. The investor in mortgages can deal with greater confidence if he can be assured of the existence of a secondary market where he can liquidate his holdings on a reasonable basis under the conditions then current. Often the ability to sell existing mortgages in the secondary market is the only means by which the holder of such mortgages can regain the liquidity necessary to finance new housing or to recover funds for an alternative use.

A purchasing institution may acquire mortgages in the secondary market either for resale or for retention as investments. Thus, to a certain extent, private institutional investors provide a secondary mortgage market to mortgagees, investors, and other holders of mortgage loans. By far the most important factors, however, in the secondary market for mortgage loans are the Federal National Mortgage Association, the Government National Mortgage Association, and the Federal Home Loan Mortgage Corporation. These agencies will each be discussed in succeeding sections of this chapter.

Federal National Mortgage Association

Failing in its efforts to induce private capital to form national mortgage associations for the purpose of providing a secondary market for insured mortgages, Congress in 1938 authorized the Reconstruction Finance Corporation (RFC) to form a subsidiary to be known as the Federal National Mortgage Association. This institution is familiarly known as "Fannie Mae," and commonly designated by its initials, FNMA. Its original capital was $10 million, with a paid-in surplus of $1 million, all provided by the RFC Its original purposes were to purchase insured mortgages and to assist in the financing of large-scale rental projects. In purchasing mortgages from approved mortgagees, it permitted them to continue to service the loans, retaining a fee of 0.25 to 1 percent for this purpose, according to the requirements as viewed by the RFC. FNMA was authorized to issue notes when it needed resources greater than its original capital and surplus.

Although established to provide a secondary market for insured mortgages, FNMA was not freely used at the time it was chartered. The restrictions it placed upon purchases tended to discourage mortgagees from selling their mortgages in this market. This was particularly true because a more satisfactory market was provided by banks, insurance companies, and so forth, which made their purchases on terms more liberal to the sellers. As a consequence, FNMA was not a major factor in the insured mortgage market until it was revived in the postwar years.

FNMA after World War II   The principal initial objectives of FNMA were:

1.   To establish a market for the purchase and sale of first mortgages insured by FHA covering properties upon which were located newly constructed houses or housing projects.

2. To facilitate the construction and financing of economically sound rental housing projects or groups of houses for rent or sale through direct lending on FHA-insured first mortgages.

3. To make FNMA bonds or debentures available to institutional and individual investors.

Since July 1, 1948, FNMA has also been permitted to purchase certain VA mortgages guaranteed under the provisions of the Servicemen's Readjustment Act of 1944, as amended. At the same time, the Association's authority to make direct FHA-insured multifamily housing loans was discontinued.

FNMA was a subsidiary of the RFC until 1950 when it was transferred to the Housing and Home Finance Agency which had been created in 1942. By becoming a part of the federal agency primarily concerned with housing and home finance, FNMA's activities in the secondary market for home mortgages could thereafter be more closely coordinated with the Home Loan Bank Board and its affiliated agencies as well as with those of the FHA.

The demand for assistance from FNMA developed after World War II because of the differential between interest rates on FHA-insured and VA-guaranteed loans and yields on government bonds. Originally VA loans were made at 4 percent and, at the same time, FHA loans were made at 4¼ percent. For some time, government bonds were selling to yield less than 2½ percent. This differential created a favorable climate for investing in federally underwritten mortgages rather than government bonds, even considering additional risk factors and servicing costs involved with investments in mortgages. As general interest rates began to rise in the late 1940s, lenders became reluctant to make commitments to large builders because of the danger that by the time of completion of projects the current interest rates might be still higher and their mortgages worth less than face value. At this point FNMA rendered an invaluable service to both lenders and builders by entering the secondary market on a commitment basis. By its commitment, FNMA agreed to purchase at an established rate the lender's mortgage paper during the commitment period. This assured a continuing flow of funds from lenders to the mortgage market.

An additional complication has always existed with reference to both FHA and VA mortgage loans. This complication is that they have a ceiling interest rate. As the market rate of interest on government bonds, for example, rose above 3 percent, while FHA and VA loans were at 4¼ percent and 4 percent, respectively, most investors considered bonds more desirable than the federally underwritten mortgages, all costs and risks considered. At this time, FHA and VA mortgages had few takers except to the extent that FNMA made advance commitment to lenders to take such loans off their hands. Under such circumstances, FNMA placed itself virtually in the position of a primary supplier of real estate mortgage funds.

Secondary Market Operations since 1954   In 1954, the Congress rechartered FNMA. The new Charter Act assigned to FNMA three separate and distinct activities: (1) secondary market operations in federally insured and guaranteed mortgages, (2) management and liquidating functions, and (3) special assistance functions. Each function was carried out as though it represented the operation of a separate corporation. Each had its own assets, liabilities, and separate borrowing authority.

By a wide margin, the secondary market operations became FNMA's most important direction of activity. Furthermore, it became apparent that the operation, properly managed, could support itself.

Secondary Market Operations and Their Financing   For several years, organizations such as the National Association of Home Builders, the Mortgage Bankers Association of America, the National Association of Real Estate Boards, and the United States Savings and Loan League had advocated the formation of a new secondary market facility to be expanded from a nucleus of the FNMA mortgage portfolio. Dominant among the recommendations was the position that governmental participation in the operation of the principal secondary market facility should gradually be replaced by private enterprise. A major objective of the FNMA Charter Act was to set up a procedure whereby FNMA would over a period of time be transformed into a privately owned and managed organization. By converting FNMA to a private operation rather than setting up a new one, it was contemplated to take advantage of FNMA's years of experience in the secondary market during the transition period and eventually to concentrate the whole operation in private hands.

The Charter Act authorized issuance of nonvoting $100 par preferred and common stock for the financing of secondary market operations. The preferred stock was issued to the Secretary of the Treasury and the common was issued only to sellers of mortgages or borrowers as they participated in FNMA's secondary market operations.

Parties utilizing the services of FNMA have been required to buy certain amounts of its capital shares in accordance with established criteria. If the purchasers of the shares have not wanted to continue to hold them, they have had a ready resale market on the New York Stock Exchange, where the shares are listed.

The Housing and Urban Development Act of 1968   Under the Housing and Urban Development Act of 1968, the assets and liabilities in connection with, and control and management of, the secondary market operations were transferred to a private corporation. This became the new Federal National Mortgage Association. Prior to this time, FNMA had been jointly financed by government and private investors. The 1968 law made it a government-sponsored corporation owned solely by private investors. All Treasury-held preferred shares were retired.

The special assistance and management and liquidating functions, largely dealing with subsidized mortgage purchases for special federal housing programs, remain in the Department of Housing and Urban Development. To perform these functions the law created another corporation titled the Government National Mortgage Association (GNMA), now familiarly known as "Ginnie Mae."

The 1968 legislation expanded the purchasing power of FNMA to include certain mortgage-backed securities guaranteed by GNMA, so that, when desirable, FNMA can support the secondary market for such securities. The authority for this mutual support has provided the basis for attracting funds into the mortgage market to a far greater degree.

Besides FNMA debentures and short-term notes, two new forms of borrowing were provided for by the 1968 legislation. First, FNMA was permitted to issue subordinated notes, in a manner similar to the "capital notes" permitted banking institutions. These obligations are usually issued for long terms and may include provisions for convertibility to common shares.

The second new borrowing form authorized issuance and marketing of securities backed by earmarked pools of portfolio mortgages. GNMA is authorized to guarantee the payment of principal and interest on any such securities issued by FNMA. Incidentally, GNMA is authorized in a similar manner to guarantee securities issued by other agencies or private parties approved for this purpose, when the securities are backed by federally underwritten mortgages and subjected to a trust similar to that established by FNMA. The gain sought here is to create a soundly backed security that will attract new money into the mortgage market, particularly from pension and retirement funds.

The Secretary of HUD continues to have general regulatory powers to assure that the purposes of the Charter Act are served. This office must authorize all issues of corporate securities and obligations. It participates in the decision-making process regarding the levels of mortgage purchases under varying economic conditions. It may also require that a reasonable portion of FNMA mortgage purchases be related to low and moderate income housing, but only under conditions of a reasonable economic return.

Later Legislation   Authority of FNMA to buy, sell, and otherwise deal in mortgages not federally insured or guaranteed (so-called conventional mortgages) was conferred by the Emergency Home Finance Act of 1970. A conventional single-family mortgage purchase program began in February 1972. FNMA continues to recognize that its primary responsibility is to the market for federally underwritten mortgages and expects for the foreseeable future that conventional mortgages will represent a small proportion of its total mortgage portfolio. Strict qualifications will be enforced to assure proper limitations on the additional risk inherent in operating in the conventional mortgage market.

Recent legislation has also extended the powers of FNMA to permit it to deal in loans made for the construction and modernization of hospital facilities. Authority to receive federal subsidies has been further extended to allow FNMA to absorb losses from ownership and disposition of federally insured low- and middle-income mortgages acquired at prices above those warranted by the going rates in the mortgage market.

FNMA Purchasing Procedure[1]   The prices paid for mortgages are competitively determined by a procedure called the "Free Market System Auction." FNMA offers 4-month and 12-month forward commitments that guarantee the availability of funds to purchase mortgages at a fixed rate. Separate auctions are held for conventional and federally-underwritten mortgages. The mortgages may cover either new or existing homes or condominiums. Auctions are usually held on Mondays on a biweekly basis. Sellers are lending institutions such as banks, savings and loan associations, insurance companies, and mortgage bankers. Bids on the four-month commitment are called in by telephone on a yield basis. FNMA reviews the bids and decides how much it will commit that day.

Alternatively, a seller may submit a "noncompetitive" bid. By this bid a request is made for a commitment at the average yield accepted by FNMA on that auction day. The highest acceptable commitment amount for this type of bid is $200,000, whereas competitive bids may be accepted up to $3 million. However, the lender submitting the noncompetitive bid is assured that he will get a commitment and not lose out in the bidding.

The results of the bidding are usually announced in financial publications, such as *The Wall Street Journal,* on the Tuesday following the auction. The range of yields accepted and the average yield applicable to noncompetitive bids are stated. These yields are net to FNMA after deduction of servicing fees.

In order to convert these yields to mortgage prices, FNMA uses the *FNMA Yield Book,* which it makes available to sellers upon request. Tables contained in this book are based on the assumption of a 30-year amortization schedule with a prepayment in 12 years. Any yield premium required above the nominal mortgage rate and after the ⅜ percent servicing fee is made up by discount points passed on to the builder or home owner. By rule-of-thumb, to effect about ¼ percent higher yield, the

---

[1] For an excellent discussion of purchasing procedures of all governmental secondary market agencies, see Charles E. Wiggin, "Doing Business in the Secondary Mortgage Market," *Real Estate Review,* vol. 5, no. 2 (Summer 1975), pp. 84–95.

mortgage loan disbursement at original issue must be at approximately 1¾ percent discount, or 98.25 percent of the stated obligation of the note.

Under FNMA's 12-month commitment procedure, the yield at which a commitment will be made is adjusted periodically and is usually published along with the free market auction results. The 12-month yields do not necessarily follow the free market pricing.

For these commitments, FNMA charges a fee of ½ percent which is due when it issues its acceptance statement, with an additional 1/100 percent (one basis point) for a competitive bid, whether or not it is accepted. There is an additional ⅛ percent fee on condominium loans when they are delivered.

Prior to sale of condominium loans conventionally financed, the lender must secure approval from FNMA. Such approval requires a formal application and review of all pertinent data regarding the project, such as plans and specifications, engineering and appraisal reports, and the builder's insurance and bonding protection. Condominiums financed under a FHA program do not require the same approval.

Purchasers of commitments may choose among three alternatives during the commitment period. They may (1) exercise their right to sell to FNMA, (2) decide to retain the mortgages for their own portfolio, or (3) sell the mortgages to another buyer. If option (2) or (3) is elected, FNMA simply receives the commitment fee for its agreement to stand ready to purchase.

Servicing of Mortgages   For every mortgage offered to FNMA for purchase, the seller must provide a satisfactory service agreement. If the seller is itself qualified as an eligible servicer by FNMA standards, it will oridinarily be permitted to service the mortgage upon signing a servicing agreement with FNMA. In either event, the servicer must have an office with servicing facilities satisfactory to the Association within 100 miles of the mortgaged propety. FNMA provides direct servicing of mortgages on multifamily dwellings. The duties of the servicer include collecting the mortgage installments and tax and insurance deposits, paying taxes and insurance premiums when due, and handling assessments and other charges against the property in such a manner as to keep the mortgage security good. The servicer is also required to make inspections of the property, personally service accounts that have become delinquent, maintain appropriate records, make a proper accounting for the funds it receives, and report what action it has taken on delinquent accounts. After it becomes apparent that a delinquent account cannot be salvaged short of foreclosure, the account may be turned over to the Association for further action.

FNMA Sales Procedure   Although the major emphasis in the FNMA programs has been in the areas of mortgage purchases, at times an equally important function may be mortgage sales. Inherent in the performance of secondary market functions is that under certain conditions it is in the best interests of an orderly market that FNMA be a seller as well as a buyer. Sales from the portfolio of the secondary market operations are made at prices based on prevailing prices for similar classes of mortgages in the general secondary market, with due regard for the impact that the contemplated sales will have on future prices. Sales of home mortgages from the special assistance portfolio are not made at less than cost, while multifamily mortgages are sold on a negotiated basis.

Lists of mortgages for sale are available to prospective purchasers in the various Association agency offices. With respect to multifamily dwellings, FNMA will issue sales options under proper circumstances. As to other mortgages, those selected by a potential buyer will be reserved for his consideration and will not be available to any other investor for a period of 15 days. This period is allowed to give the prospective purchaser an opportunity to inspect the mortgage premises and examine the notes, mortgages, and other documents related to the security at the Association agency office. A sales price is quoted in the reservation letter sent by the Association to the prospective purchaser. This price, however, is subject to change without notice during the reservation period. The actual price paid is that in effect at the time of the signing of the FNMA mortgage sales agreement when the investor consummates his purchase. Upon receipt of the sales price, the investor is assigned the mortgage without recourse, subject to the servicing agreement between the Association and the servicer, which may be canceled on 30 days' notice.

Administration of FNMA   The board of directors of FNMA consists of 15 members, one third of whom are appointed by the President of the United States and the remainder of whom are elected by the stockholders. All terms are for one year. The presidential appointments are required to include one person each from the homebuilding, real estate, and mortgage lending industries. All directors are removable by the President but only for good cause shown.

The chief executive officer of FNMA is its president. Other officers include a vice president, general counsel, secretary, treasurer, and controller. Because of the technical nature of the functions performed, employees are usually specialists who must meet high professional standards. The Association by its very nature, in its secondary market and other operations, must be exclusively sensitive to the national need and impervious to the exhortations of special interests if it is to fulfill its highest objectives as a supplement to the existing privately financed institutions. To assist the board of directors in its establishment of sound financial policies, in 1959 the Association established a FNMA General Advisory Committee consisting of eight representatives of the housing and home financing industries. The broad purpose of the committee is to provide advice and counsel directed toward increasing the effectiveness of FNMA in the various phases of its operations. The work is conducted out of five agency offices strategically located across the country.

The Government National Mortgage Association

The Government National Mortgage Corporation, as previously mentioned, performs three principal functions. Briefly, these are: (1) management and liquidating of previously acquired mortgages, (2) special assistance government lending in support of federal programs, and (3) guarantee of eligible mortgages to support a public market for mortgage pools and to assist FNMA. Its operations are financed through funds from the U.S. Treasury and from public borrowing.

Management and Liquidating Functions   The Charter Act of 1954 authorized FNMA to manage and to liquidate the existing mortgage portfolio at the close of its former operation as of October 31, 1954. In September 1959, Congress expanded the management and liquidating functions to authorize FNMA to purchase or make commitments to purchase, service, and sell any mortgages offered it by the Housing and Home Finance Agency (now the Department of Housing and Urban Development) where the Administrator deemed their acquisition by FNMA to be in the best interest of efficient management and liquidation. This authorization has been actively used. The management and liquidating functions are directed by statute to be carried out in an orderly manner with a minimum of adverse effect upon the residential mortgage market and a minimum loss to the federal government. This responsibility is now the obligation of GNMA.

Special Assistance Functions   In its assumption of responsibility for government special assistance functions, GNMA has acceded to the responsibility placed upon FNMA in the Charter Act of 1954. This act charged the Association with the obligation to provide special assistance in connection with certain residential mortgages when, and to the extent that, the President of the United States determines such assistance to be in the public interest. Under this function the Association also supports special housing programs as designated by the Congress. The special assistance program is specifically intended to meet two general needs. The first need relates to housing in underdeveloped areas. GNMA is charged with the responsibility, when the President so directs, of making financing available for selected types of residential mortgages (pending establishment of their marketability) which are originated under special housing programs designed to provide housing in areas where it cannot be provided under established home financing programs.

The second great need arises when a decline in mortgage lending and home building threatens the stability of a high-level national economy.

To carry out the purposes of the special assistance functions, GNMA is authorized to purchase or enter into commitments to purchase mortgages or participations therein as directed by the president or as prescribed by law. So far as practicable, mortgages purchased under these functions must meet the purchase standards imposed by private institutional investors. The crucial factor justifying the purchase by GNMA is that, because of other circumstances surrounding the location of the property, the borrower, or economic conditions, the mortgages are not likely to be readily acceptable to private lenders.

As with the other operations, the special assistance functions are contemplated to be fully self-supporting. Both commitment fees and purchase and marketing fees are charged. The principal source of income, of course, is interest from mortgages held. Income earned is retained as a reserve for losses and contingencies.

The Mortgage-Backed Security Program   GNMA is authorized by Section 06(g) of Title III of the National Housing Act to guarantee the timely payment of the principal and interest on securities that are based on or backed by a pool of mortgages insured by the FHA or Farmers Home Administration or guaranteed by the VA. The Department of Justice has rendered an opinion that the GNMA guarantee constitutes a full faith and credit obligation of the United States, and the Secretary of the Treasury has ruled that GNMA may properly borrow from the Treasury to meet its obligations under the guarantee.

The process of pool organization is initiated by a mortgage originator who becomes the issuer of the certificates. An issuer must be an FHA-approved mortgagee and GNMA seller-servicer in good standing; it must further meet a specific net worth test. FNMA and the Federal Home Loan Mortgage Corporation are also active as issuers. The issuer applies to GNMA for permission to issue certificates against the mortgage pool that the issuer has assembled or expects to assemble. The aggregate value of the pool must usually be at least $2 million. The mortgages must meet standards of homogeneity as to type, interest rates, and maturity. For example, single-family mortgages cannot be mixed with multifamily mortgages. Furthermore, the mortgages are required to be insured or guaranteed no more than one year prior to the date on which GNMA issues its commitment to guarantee the certificates.

Upon favorable response to the issuer's application, GNMA issues a commitment to guarantee the issuer's certificates at such time as the issuer can verify that it has good title to an acceptable pool of mortgages. Documents showing proper formation of the pool are then submitted to the bank or fiduciary that is to act as custodian. Upon appropriate acknowledgment of receipt of documents by the custodian, GNMA prepares the certificates for issue.

After the certificates are issued, the issuer assumes responsibility for servicing the loans and passing through to certificate holders their proportional share of monthly interest and amortization payments. The issues must also provide accounting statements reflecting the results of the certificate holders' participation in the pool.

In addition to the GNMA guarantee, several other features commend these securities to the whole investment spectrum, including savings and loan associations, savings banks, credit union, pension funds, commercial banks, insurance companies, corporations, and partnerships, as well as individuals. Although the security has many of the characteristics normally associated with direct investment in a first mortgage loan portfolio, it has the advantage of avoiding the management problems of loan origination and servicing. The improved marketability of the GNMA certificate over individual mortgages is a decided plus factor, particularly as the secondary market is expanding through active participation of major financial institutions. The price varies, of course, with current interest rates. Hence, if prevailing interest rates for comparable securities are lower than the face rate on the certificate, the security will sell at a premium; if higher, it will sell at a discount. The Internal Revenue Service has ruled that these certificates are "loans secured by an interest in real property." This ruling is of particular interest to savings and loan associations and savings banks, since it means that such securities do not jeopardize their eligibility for special bad debt reserve deductions permitted under the Internal Revenue Code. For income tax purposes, real estate investment trusts are to treat these securities as direct mortgage investments. The Internal Revenue Service has further held that the exempt status of employees' pension and profit-sharing funds is not adversely affected by ownership of these securities.

Many developments of the mortgage-backed security program are taking place. For example, "serial maturities" and pools of FHA-insured mobile home loans are logical extensions. A mortgage-backed security guaranteeing the interim payments on a construction loan can assist substantially in the financing of multifamily projects.

There are two basic groups of mortgage-backed securities: (1) pass-through securities and (2) mortgage-backed bonds. Each group has unique appeals and some different risk characteristics.

Pass-Through Securities. Pass-through securities are of two types: (1) standard and (2) modified.

Under the *standard* plan the total interest payment and principal amortization are passed through to the certificate holders on a monthly basis. As any mortgages become delinquent, they are immediately replaced from a reserve pool. In the alternative, a reserve fund may be established to offset principal losses from foreclosure. This plan terminates when all mortgages in the pool are paid off.

With *modified* pass-through securities, the investor has the interest and principal passed through less frequently than monthly, perhaps quarterly, semiannually, or annually. The payment is typically made to the investor at due date whether or not the funds are actually received from the mortgagor. Excess mortgage reserve pools or guarantee reserve funds are required of issuers under the modified plan as with the standard plan. This prevents loss of principal or interest by the security holders. There is some exposure to risk, however, in the modified plan where funds need to be reinvested pending disbursement to investors. In both standard and modified plans, prepayments are passed through to investors.

Mortgage-Backed Bonds. There are two classifications of mortgage-backed bonds: (1) sinking fund and (2) staggered maturity.

The *sinking fund* mortgage-backed bond is similar to the modified pass-through security in that principal repaid from the underlying pool of mortgages is accumulated in a fund from which payments are later made to bondholders. The basic distinction from the pass-through obligation is that principal is paid in predetermined specific amounts, whether or not they are accumulated from the underlying mortgages. Similarly, interest obligations on the bonds must be met without regard to interest collections on the underlying mortgages. The bond principal maturity schedule can run ahead of mortgage amortization. The possibility of interest and principal payment demands exceeding collections places a contingent demand on the reserve financial strength of the issuer.

Staggered maturity bonds come due in a pattern designed to coincide with the expected accumulation of principal from the underlying pool of mortgages. Interest and principal payments are made on the bonds as they come due without regard to the amount collected on the mortgages. If mortgagors prepay or principal funds accumulate prior to bond maturity, there is a substantial reinvestment risk. Interest rates may have fallen, and the issuer may be hard-pressed to reinvest at a rate sufficient to keep up bond coupon payments at the higher rate. Issuers of such bonds must have a large enough net worth to absorb potential losses created by changes in the money market. The minimum net worth requirement has been $50 million. The minimum amount permitted in a single issue is $100 million. FNMA and the Federal Home Loan Mortgage Corporation have both issued bonds backed by federally-underwritten mortgages. It is interesting to note, incidentally, that the Mortgage Guaranty Insurance Corporation (MGIC) has issued mortgage-backed bonds supported by privately-insured conventional mortgages.

Optional-Delivery Commitment for Purchase of GNMA Securities Because of the lapse of time necessary to assemble eligible mortgages in required quantities, potential issuers have prevailed upon GNMA to develop a standby commitment procedure to protect them from market risk during assembly. This is called an "Optional-Delivery Commitment for Purchase of GNMA Securities." The commitment is issued for a nonrefundable fee of 1 to 1½ percent, according to its duration. The interest rate of the commitment is determined by the "asked" side of the mortgage market. In this way, if rates move higher, the issuer is protected by this upper limit standby; while, if the rates decline, he simply disregards this protection and takes his securities directly to the market as originally planned.

The Tandem Plan Besides supporting a public market for mortgage pools, GNMA also has the function of purchase and sale of FHA/VA mortgages pursuant to a cooperative system with FNMA known as the "tandem plan." The program combines the GNMA guarantee with the FNMA secondary market operation to maximize the utilization of special assistance funds voted by Congress.

By this plan, financing is afforded eligible project sponsors in two steps. In the first step, GNMA issues a commitment to buy at par a mortgage upon completion of the qualified project. By prior arrangement, FNMA has agreed to purchase a certain amount of these mortgages at market prices. As the second step, the long-term mortgage may be sold to FNMA at the market price, with GNMA making up the difference of the discount between par and the market price.

The great advantage of this arrangement is its leverage to provide government assistance. Authorities state that the tandem plan can provide as much as 30 times the financing possible if GNMA were to buy and hold the mortgages outright. This is true because the privately derived funds of FNMA actually carry the mortgage with GNMA merely absorbing the discount.

Shortly after the tandem plan developed, GNMA discovered that it could mitigate its losses by selling the mortgages directly in the open market rather than to FNMA. First, GNMA determined that all such mortgages were eligible for inclusion in GNMA pass-though pools. Second, it recognized that mortgage bankers and other institutions seeking to build loan servicing volume would be willing to pay favorable prices, accepting some front-end losses, which could be more than offset against future GNMA loan-servicing business. The GNMA loan servicing fee of 0.44 percent is particularly attractive as compared with the ⅜ percent more commonly paid. By taking advantage of this program, therefore, mortgage bankers and others may develop mortgage-backed securities pools and generate loan servicing business as phases of one overall operation.

Federal Home Loan Mortgage Corporation

Title III of the Emergency Home Finance Act of 1970 provided for the establishment of the Federal Home Loan Mortgage Corporation

(FHLMC), often called "Freddie Mac." Its designated purpose is to serve as a secondary market facility for real estate mortgages under the sponsorship of the Federal Home Loan Bank System.

The Corporation is financed by $100 million of capital shares issued to the 12 district Federal Home Loan Banks. The stock may be retired by FHLMC if such retirement will not reduce surplus and reserves below $100 million. The FHLMC board of directors is composed of the three members of the Federal Home Loan Bank Board, whose chairman is also the chairman of the FHLMC board.

FHLMC has authority to buy and sell FHA and VA loans, conventional loans, and mortgage participations. It was particularly created to improve secondary market facilities for residential conventional mortgages, which have not had the benefit of federal insurance or guarantees. In order to increase availability of mortgage credit in this direction, FHLMC has authority to purchase conventional, as well as FHA or VA, mortgages from any Federal Home Loan Bank, the Federal Savings and Loan Insurance Corporation, any member of a Federal Home Loan Bank, or any financial institution whose deposits or accounts are insured by an agency of the United States. Mortgage bankers cannot sell loans to FHLMC. Under certain prescribed conditions, however, a legal seller to FHLMC may contract with FHA-approved mortgagees—including mortgage bankers—to perform servicing as authorized agents.

FHLMC makes no direct loans to home buyers. It merely provides funds by an intermediary process following this pattern:

1. A home buyer seeks a mortgage loan from an institution eligible to sell to FHLMC.

2. As the institution becomes short of mortgage money to lend out, it may sell some of its existing mortgages to FHLMC.

3. FHLMC may then either sell these mortgages directly or market securities backed by the mortgages in the open capital market.

Mortgage Production[2]   FHLMC has five ongoing "over-the-counter" programs whereby it contracts to buy mortgages on a continuing basis. Delivery by the seller is mandatory. Failure to deliver may disqualify a seller for up to two years. Loans delivered must meet certain quality standards as well as specific legal requirements clearly defined by the enabling statute and the corporation. For example, loan amounts, loan-to-value ratios, private mortgage insurance coverage required, term, age, and necessary documentation are all delineated. Effective January 1, 1976, FHLMC/FNMA Uniform Mortgage Documents were instituted as a general requirement. The contract amount may range between $100,000 and $5 million. There is no contract fee for a Federal Home

---

[2] The authors gratefully acknowledge assistance from materials developed by Ronald D. Struck, Assistant Vice President, in regard to FHLMC operations.

Loan Bank System member. For nonmembers, a fee of ⅜ percent of the contract amount is assessed.

Over-the-Counter Programs   The purchase programs are as follows:

1. *Whole Loan—Single-Family.* FHLMC will purchase entire interests in eligible single-family conventional residential mortgages. The deal creating the mortgage may be closed after the date of contract, but the mortgage must be delivered within 60 days of that date. The maximum purchase price can never exceed par and will be adjusted to the nominal mortgage rate and contract yield requirements to FHLMC. The servicing fee to the seller is ⅜ percent.

2. *Whole Loan—Multifamily.* FHLMC will purchase entire interests in eligible multifamily conventional residential mortgages. Rules for the closure, delivery, and maximum purchase price are similar to the single-family loans discussed above. The servicing fee runs to ¼ percent of the first $250,000 of unpaid principal balance and ⅛ percent of the amount in excess.

3. *Participation—Class A Offering.* FHLMC will purchase from 50 to 85 percent interests in eligible multifamily conventional mortgages. Mortgages must be closed prior to date of contract and delivery must be within 30 days. In this case, mortgages are purchased at a required. net yield to FHLMC, so no servicing fee is paid as such. The seller retains any interest income over FMLMC's yield requirement as servicing income.

4. *Participation—Class B Offering.* Under this program single-family conventional mortgages are included along with the multifamily mortgages listed in the Class A offering. The contracts will be to purchase 50 to 85 percent participations, but the multifamily mortgages may not exceed 50 percent of the total acquired under one contract. Closing and servicing fee provisions are the same as for the Class A offering.

5. *FHA/VA Loans.* FHLMC will purchase entire interests in FHA- or VA-underwritten residential mortgages. Rules for closure, delivery, maximum purchase price, and servicing fees are similar to those applied to single family conventional loans discussed above.

Loan Commitments   Over and above its over-the-counter purchase programs, FHLMC has offered forward commitments to purchase mortgages with delivery of the mortgage at the seller's option. These commitments have been for periods ranging from 6 to 24 months. They have been for virtually all types of eligible conventional and FHA/VA mortgages acceptable under the purchase programs. The interest rates for all FHLMC contract and commitment programs are established on a nationwide basis in the light of current conditions in the capital markets. Commitments are issued in dollar amounts only and never for specific projects. The seller or another party must originate the loan and deal with the mortgagor/builder. In this way FHLMC avoids direct competition with any primary mortgage lender.

Mortgage Marketing   To finance its operations, FHLMC relies upon four principal methods. In order of importance, these are:

1. Borrowing from the Federal Home Loan Banks.
2. Issuance of GNMA-guaranteed mortgage backed bonds.
3. Issuance of participation sale certificates.
4. Direct sale of mortgages held.

FHLMC does not view its operation as simply mortgage warehousing. Its borrowing from the Federal Home Loan Banks is rather to facilitate a flow of mortgages from sellers to buyers in the secondary market. GNMA mortgage-backed bonds have been previously discussed in this chapter as important vehicles to achieve the standardization, quality, and ease of administration so important to an efficient secondary market. Mortgages directly sold suffer in several respects by comparison and are acceptable in a much more limited market. Participation sale certificates, on the other hand, offer in a different way the aforementioned advantages of GNMA mortgage-backed securities. Their security is broadened to encompass the area of conventional mortgages. Typical certificates represent undivided interests in specified conventional mortgage participations owned by FHLMC. The total obligation is guaranteed by FHLMC.

Automated Mortgage Market Information Network   As another assist to the secondary market for mortgages, FHLMC has played a key role in establishing a new corporation called AMMINET (an acronym for Automated Mortgage Market Information Network). Its purpose is to establish a direct electronic communication network among subscribers to the system. Subscribers may use the service to list specific terms of offers to buy or sell mortgages. Deals may be concluded over the telephone without reliance on an intermediary.

The Mortgage Interest-Rate Futures Market

The advance commitment from investors has long been a major tool of mortgage bankers to support interim financing to allow completion of construction and loan closing. The necessity for advance commitments has not changed, although the nature of the transaction is different, in the creation and marketing of mortgage pools to public investors. In the last few years, wide fluctuations in interest rates have accentuated the risks assumed by mortgage bankers, savings and loan institutions, commercial bankers, and other financial institutions assembling underlying mortgages over time for sale at a future date. A modest interest rate change during the period of packaging can easily wipe out the narrow profit spread that the issuer seeks. If he makes a commitment in June, for example, to deliver mortgages in September at a fixed rate and the market rate decreases, he cannot acquire the mortgages at yields high enough to match his commitment and he must lose his expected profits or incur a net loss. A facility for shifting the interest rate risk to those willing to assume it has been sorely needed.

On October 20, 1975, the Chicago Board of Trade instituted trading in mortgage interest-rate futures options. These options were developed primarily to provide a capability for institutional hedging against mortgate interest-rate risk. This market operates on the same pattern as futures options for wheat, soybeans, cotton, shell eggs, pork bellies, and many other commodities. Hedgers are those who must accept ownership risks in these commodities and who seek to avert the risk of price fluctuation by taking an opposite position in the futures market, selling against their inventories to speculators. These sales are customarily made to option buyers who are not interested in the commodities as such, merely in their price fluctuations.

The commodity-like trading unit established for trading mortgage interest-rate options is a GNMA-backed modified pass-though certificate in the amount of $100,000 at 8 percent per annum. Prices are quoted as a percentage of par. The minimum fluctuation is $\frac{1}{32}$ percent of par, or $31.25 per contract. The daily limit of price movement is $750 per contract. Contract delivery months are March, June, September, and December.

To make the conversion from yield to price of the security, or vice versa, tables have been developed.[3] The yields are computed under the assumption of simple, uncompounded monthly payments of principal and interest at 8 percent on a 30-year mortgage, with prepayment in the 12th year. A partial listing of the price-yield relationship is presented in the following tabulation:

Yield (percent)	Price*
7.00	107–12
7.50	103–12
8.00	99–22
8.50	96–03
9.00	92–22
9.50	89–15
10.00	86–12
10.50	83–14
11.00	80–20

* Numbers to the right of the dash are 32nds. Thus, 107-12 means 107 12/32 percent of par. Prices are quoted as points and 32nds.

[3] *GNMA Yield and Price Equivalent Tables* may be acquired through Financial Publishing Company, 82 Brookline Avenue, Boston, Mass., 02215.

Quotations in terms of the prices shown above may be found daily in *The Wall Street Journal* and other publications carrying Chicago Board of Trade reports.

An example will illustrate how the hedging process may be useful to a mortgage assembler. The transaction may be summarized as follows:

Cash Market	*Futures Market*
June 1	*June 1*
He sells $1 million 8% GNMA-backed mortgages to a bank at a price of 92–22 to yield about 9% for delivery on December 1.	He buys $1 million (10) December futures contracts at 92–22.

If the assembler continues to originate 8 percent mortgages and the market acquisition rate drops to 8½ percent for the period, assuming the options market follows the same pattern, the following theoretical result may be achieved:

Cash Market	*Futures Market*
December 1	*December 1*
He delivers the $1 million mortgages costing 96–03 to the bank at 92–22. A *loss* of 3–13 (3¹³⁄₃₂) points is realized. This amounts to $34,062.	He sells back his $1 million December futures contracts costing 92–22 for 96–03. He thus *gains* 3–13 points, or $34,062.

If, instead, the market acquisition rate rises to 9½ percent, with a similar move in the options market, the December results would be:

Cash Market	*Futures Market*
December 1	*December 1*
He delivers the $1 million mortgages costing 89–15 to the bank at 92–22. A *gain* of 3–7 (3⁷⁄₃₂) points is realized. This amounts to $32,188.	He sells back his $1 million futures contracts costing 92–22 for 89–15. He therefore *loses* 3–7 points, or $32,188.

In this case, it will be seen that the mortgage assembler has successfully shifted his interest rate risk from himself to the options market. Of course, entailed in this shift is the sacrifice of any profits that might accrue from a favorable rate change during the risk period. Furthermore, it must be recognized that the futures market does not follow the cash markets precisely, and there are transactions costs. The trends and degrees of change, however, are close enough to make the exercise desirable under many conditions.

The foregoing example is known as a "long," or "buy," hedge, where the hedger seeks initially to lock in his delivery price. A different type of protection is afforded by the "short," or "sell," hedge. The latter pattern is typically used by a mortgage banker who is planning to market his pool at a future date to investors who will be willing to pay the current market rate at the time of marketing the pool certificates. He sells futures options as he acquires mortgages, thus locking in protection at his acquisition rate for each mortgage parcel of his pool.

The mortgage interest-rate futures market also holds attraction to mortgage bankers assembling conventional mortgages for thrift institutions or FNMA. When these institutions curtail their purchases and the mortgage bankers find they must warehouse their "homeless" mortgages for a while, hedging can protect them from major losses from interest rate fluctuations. The availability of the futures market further enhances the potential of the FHLMC commitment program for its approved sellers/services. For this reason, FHLMC has been a strong advocate of the development of the options market. To students of interest rates, there are numerous market strategies to which a use of the options market may be adapted.

QUESTIONS

1. What is a secondary mortgage market and why is it necessary?
2. What were the three principal activities of FNMA under its 1954 charter? How are they now administered? What is GNMA?
3. How are the secondary market operations of FNMA financed?
4. Describe the purchasing procedures whereby FNMA acquires mortgages in connection with its secondary market operations.
5. How are mortgages acquired by FNMA serviced?
6. What are the principal activities of GNMA?
7. Describe the federally insured mortgage-backed securities program as administered through GNMA. What is the "tandem plan"?
8. What is the Federal Home Loan Mortgage Corporation (FHLMC)? Why was it created?
9. What are the principal sources of funds from which FHLMC finances its operations?
10. What are the major FHLMC secondary market programs?
11. What are the functions of the mortgage interest-rate futures market?

CASE PROBLEMS

1. You are an institutional mortgage lender. Your local market is too restricted to generate enough loans to utilize your facilities fully. You seek out a mortgage banker with an active market in a neighboring locality. He agrees to close $500,000 of mortgage loans meeting FHLMC specifications in your name at 9% plus 2 points. To accomplish this for you, it is agreed that

he is to receive 1 point and out-of-pocket costs in connection with loan origination.

How may the secondary market provided by FHLMC be used to your advantage?

2.   Trace through the consequences and compute the yield to the mortgage assembler from the following transaction:

Assume you have $1,176,470 in mortgages yielding an aggregate of 8%—about 50% single-family and 50% multifamily and eligible for FHLMC Class B participation—available for sale. FHLMC purchased 85% of the total ($1,000,000) under its participation plan to yield 7.75% to FHLMC.

3.   a.   On August 1, a mortgage assembler sells $1 billion 8% GNMA-backed mortgages to a bank to yield 8½%. Delivery was contracted for December 1. How may he establish a hedge to protect himself against the possibility of a drop in interest rates during his acquisition period?

b.   Assuming that the market acquisition rate did in fact drop to 8% for the period, and that the cash and options markets moved together, what will be the results of a hedge transaction entered into on the August 1st date?

4.   a.   On March 1, a mortgage banker makes a commitment to acquire a $1 million mortgage pool, based on current GNMA-backed 8% certificates, at 99–22 (approximately 8% yield). How may he hedge to protect himself if he will not be marketing the mortgages until September 15?

b.   Assuming the yield on this class of mortgages rises to 8½% by September 15, what will be the results as the mortgage pool certificates are sold in the market and the hedge is closed?

5.   Several brokerage houses and banks have worked as dealers in GNMA-backed securities. Obtain a prospectus of a GNMA-backed security issue marketed through one of your local houses, and study it in depth. You may particularly want to study the functions of origination, trading, and management of the security position (long or short), sales activities to thrift institutions and others, and cashier obligations, as well as the terms of the issue itself.

22

Rural Real Estate Credit and the Farmers Home Administration

Meaning of Farms

The American farm combines, in its real estate relationship, both residential and business uses. It affords a place for the owner-operator and his family to live while it provides them with their means of livelihood. In times past, the farmer has been looked upon as a grower of crops and farm animals. To an increasing extent he has become a businessman. Like any other type of business, farming requires capital. Requirements for this purpose cover real estate capital, machinery, working capital, and contributions to cooperative ventures.

Real estate capital, with which we are primarily concerned in this study, covers the cost of land and its more or less permanent improvements. The latter include the home, various types of farm buildings, fences, drainage, and, in some cases, irrigation and terracing. These costs add up to the greatest proportion of the capital investment of the farmer.

Determinants of Amount of Investment

The amount invested by an individual farmer in his real estate is governed by several unrelated factors. The type of farming, of course, helps to set the pattern of investment. The size of the farm in turn helps to determine the use made of it. The period of the business cycle is a major factor in the pricing of farms. The price paid measures the kind and amount of financing needed. One interesting feature of farm financing that has assumed greater importance in recent years is the competition of city folk in the purchase of farms. There has always been a feeling on the part of many city dwellers that ownership of a farm is quite desirable. More recently, several new factors have accentuated this feeling. In groping for security in an uncertain world, people seem to feel that farming offers a better than usual sense of protection to farm owners. Many people feel that nothing can happen to interfere materially with farm ownership. Some city people have purchased farms as a hedge against inflation. Others have purchased run-down farms as a means of equalizing income tax burdens. Whatever the incentive that impels city people to purchase farms, the effects of their competition complicate the financial problems of farmers who hope to make a business of farming.

Sources of Farm Capital

Traditionally, the typical cycle that eventually leads to farm ownership, by those who make farming a business as owner-operators, begins with the small savings of a boy on the farm. These are added to as the young man works as a hired hand until the equity capital necessary for a venture on his own takes form. Seldom can a young man hope to own a farm unless he inherits it. Ownership comes in the middle life of the farmer who buys a farm. Until the person ambitious to become a farm owner acquires some capital through savings, he will probably maintain his status as a laborer working for someone else.

With some capital accumulated through savings, the farmer may become his own manager through one of the following processes: (1) He may enter into partnership with someone else. (2) He may become a tenant instead of a laborer for hire. (3) He may use some kind of credit arrangement to add to his equity capital the amount needed for acquiring a farm.

Partnership Partnerships are commonly used in farm operation. One partner, frequently the inactive one, owns the farm and takes into partnership a younger man with experience and usually some capital. Sometimes even the capital is absent. The owner of the farm matches his capital against the skill of the younger man. Father and son and father and son-in-law partnerships are very common. Two brothers may become partners. Or partnerships are arranged in which no blood or marital relationship exists between the participants.

Farm partnerships have the advantage of encouraging long-range planning which may end in a transfer of title to the land at the death of the older member of the firm. They are frequently entered into without written or formal agreement. The imposition of personal income taxes probably did more to require an accounting of income between partners than had ever been done before. As a general rule, farmers have not been accustomed to distinguishing sharply between income and capital investment. This has been true of partnerships as well as of other types of business organization on the farm.

Because of the prevalence of the father-son origin of farm partnerships, the problem of lines of authority takes on interesting patterns. The older man tends to make the decisions at the outset, but, if all goes well, more and more he defers to the wishes of the younger partner, until finally the original position is reversed. Eventually the son may, to all intents and purposes, become the owner, with the father being supported by the son as his share in the fruits of the partnership.

Leasing   In the absence of a father-son partnership, and particularly if the farm owned by the father is not large enough to support two families, the younger man may lease a farm instead. Although he is expected to have some capital, he can enter the farming business by using the real estate capital of someone else. In return for the use of this capital, he pays a share of the crops, or a cash rental, or a combination of the two. Some farmers prefer a lease to farm ownership, especially in times when the price of land is very high. By renting land owned by someone else, they can continue to add to their savings, pending a decline in prices.

Some farmers own the place that provides them with a home and lease additional land for productive purposes. Sometimes the partnership arrangement discussed above is made possible by leasing adjoining or nearby land. By this means not only is additional land acquired, but a home needed for the younger member of the partnership is made available also. Some city people who own farms but are unacquainted with their operation are very glad to shift the burdens of management to a tenant skilled in farm operation.

The lease arrangement avoids some of the difficulties occasionally encountered in partnerships. Under a proper form of lease, the landlord is concerned only with end results. Meantime, management is centered in the tenant. At the same time, tenancy lacks the stability of a partnership arrangement. Leases are likely to run one year at a time or on a year-to-year basis. Some of the work on a farm and some of the investment by the tenant must necessarily look beyond this short period for results.

A modification of farm leasing takes the form of a manager-operator agreement. The owner of the farm hires a manager who operates the farm, with all capital being supplied by the owner. By a kind of profit sharing plan, the hired manager is permitted to share in the results of his labors over and above a stipulated salary for his services.

Like partnerships, leases are frequently informal and oral rather than written. As in other business matters, a more formal written lease is recommended. Like other leases, farm leases should include all practicable provisions to make sure of complete meeting of minds between the tenant and the landlord. In general, a lease that leans too far in the direction of protecting either party to the disadvantage of the other is not likely to endure for long or to produce satisfactory results.

Use of Credit   As a business loan, the financing of farm real estate is expected to be repaid from the income from farm operations. While the lender will look to the appraisal of the security for the loan as a basis for his decisions, neither he nor the borrower expects to have the loan repaid from the proceeds of the sale of the property. Here, as elsewhere in real estate finance, a distinction must be made between a safe loan and a sound one. A lender may feel safe in making a loan if the liquidating value of the security will be at least equal to the amount of the loan. But a borrower who would expect to use this means of meeting his obligations would not be making a sound business commitment.

Because most farms are family operated, the personal equation in farm loans is particularly significant. The lender gives great weight to the moral hazard. An ambitious, experienced farmer can obtain real estate financing of greater advantage to him than he could if his reputation for integrity and skill were less favorable. The lender knows that he is taking the risk of managerial ability and acts accordingly. In analyzing the moral hazard, the family is included in the lender's calculations. As a family-operated business, farming reflects the type of family as well as the type of head of the household. The attitude of the wife toward farming and farm life may be nearly as important as that of the borrower. Farm productivity, in terms of dollar income, is frequently definitely related to the interest taken by the wife in farm operations.

Increasing Demand for Credit   In looking into the future, it seems probable that farmers will depend more upon credit facilities in financing their operations than has been true in the past. The reasons for this change are: (1) The average size of farms is increasing. Increased mechanization makes possible the handling of more acres with the same man power. (2) This increased mechanization calls for larger capital investment. (3) Soil exhaustion requires greater attention to and investment in rehabilitation and conservation programs. (4) Many farmers are reaching an age when they are no longer able to continue to handle their acreage. With higher prices of farms, the transfer of these holdings to younger men will call for more credit than was needed when the present farmers acquired their holdings.

Factors Considered by Lender   In addition to the moral hazard, the lender on farm real estate takes into account various factors that may not be present in considering urban real estate as security for loans. Loans are made not on acres alone but upon the productivity of those acres. Erosion and wastage as well as fertility must be studied, since the loan will be repaid over a long period of time. The lender must look to the productivity of the farm over a series of years as the source of repayment of his loan. Hence he tries to measure it as best he can.

The size of the farm is important. Since it must first afford a living to its owners, the lender wants to make sure that there will be enough left to pay taxes and operating expenses—including reasonable allowances to maintain the productivity of the land—and still leave a balance of income from which the mortgage can be amortized. Even a well-operated small farm might be a poor lending risk because of the absence of a debt-paying balance of income.

As a businessman seeking a business loan, the farmer must be able to demonstrate his efficiency as a manager. Operating costs should be consistent with a productive unit of the kind that a borrower should offer as security for a loan. Evidence of lack of balance in the investment of capital or in the use of labor will not produce a high credit rating for lending purposes. For example, some farms are inefficiently operated because their owners or operators economize too much in the use of laborsaving machinery; others lean in the opposite direction and are burdened with more mechanization than the particular farm can support.

To an increasing extent farmers are required, for one reason or another, to keep accounting records of their operations. When the owner of a farm makes an application for a real estate loan, he must be in a position to tell what he owns and what he owes. His net worth will go a long way toward determining his borrowing capacity. Not only will the lender be interested in the use of a microscope, but he will want to use his telescope also. He will want to know in detail the current condition of the business and also the progress of the operations as compared with those in preceding periods. An increase in assets or a decrease in debts indicates an increase in net worth. The opposite tendency in either would speak against an extension of too much credit to the applicant for a real estate loan. Changes in price levels are taken into account in measuring changes in net worth.

In some respects an income statement is even more useful in measuring debt-paying capacities than is a balance sheet. The latter is somewhat of a liquidation measure; the former tests the farm operation as a going concern. As might be expected, adequate and accurate income statements for farm operations are more rare than balance sheets. They are becoming more common. County extension agents are rendering worthwhile service in encouraging accounting records. The farmer who keeps them is a better credit risk than one who does not.

Types of Farm Mortgages   As stated above, farm mortgages should be paid out of income. The type of mortgage most likely to meet the needs of most farmers runs for a long period of time—10, 20, 30 or, in some cases, as long as 40 years; is payable in annual or semiannual installments; and carries a low rate of interest, since the average return on farm capital is low. Some years may show higher than average returns, but others will show lower rates of return, depending upon prices of farm products, crop yields, and other factors.

Term loans fail to meet the needs of most farmers. If a lump-sum mortgage falls due at an inopportune time, when renewals are not favored and refinancing is unavailable, trouble for the borrower may result. Foreclosure marks the end of the trail for many such mortgages.

Sinking Fund for Future Payments   Because of the irregularity of farm income, some farm mortgages provide that the borrower may build up in high-income years what amounts to a sinking fund to take care of installments in lean years. If such funds are credited with the same rate of interest as is charged on the mortgage, the effect is about the same as if prepayments had been allowed. The difference lies in the fact that prepayments might not be considered by the lender as an offset to no payments when farm income is low. Both the Federal Land Bank System and some private lenders on farm security encourage the practice of developing a fund to take care of some future payments.

Timing of Payments   Unlike mortgage payments on residential properties in urban areas, where the monthly payment direct reduction loan plan has become the common pattern, farmers make their payments less frequently. Payments are most commonly made on an annual, semiannual, or quarterly basis. Which of these plans is followed is determined by the nature of the farming operations. In areas where cash crops are harvested once a year, annual payments best meet the requirements of the borrower. Where tradition dictates a semiannual contract, borrowers frequently become six months in arrears unless their cash income permits payments more often than once a year. In the infrequent cases where income is collected more frequently, the payments may even be met quarterly without inconvenience to the borrower. For example, dairy farmers might readily meet quarterly payments on their mortgages.

Rehabilitation Financing   Where farmers undertake a program of soil rehabilitation or a conservation program, the amounts so invested cover a series of years. Some mortgages are so written as to provide for advances as needed for this purpose. The repayment of these advances is arranged in such a manner as to permit the anticipated increase in yield to pay the cost of the program. In order to play safe, only a portion of the anticipated increased yield—perhaps 75 percent—is required to repay the loan. In some cases only a small part of the advances is required to be repaid annually until the entire program is completed. Then the repayments are increased to amortize the advances over a period comparable to those of ordinary farm mortgage loans.

In financing any such operations, the lender must make sure that the borrower proceeds under the guidance of experts, so that the funds advanced will be spent in such a manner that their recovery within a reasonable time may be expected. The usual period for repayment of such loans runs from 5 to 15 years. This is an area of financing in which neither the lender nor the borrower is presumed to be expert. Both need the advice and guidance of specialists capable of fitting a conservation program to the needs of a specific farm.

Appraisals for Farm Loans The average appraiser who appraises property for the purpose of making loans on urban real estate would be of little use to lenders on farm property. Since farm loans are made on the business of farming, the appraiser must be able to set loan values on more than land and permanent improvements. He must be able to measure the selling price of the land and also its earning capacity. The latter is conditioned by the character of the management of the farm, so that this must be reviewed also.

Unlike loans against urban real estate, farm mortgages do not really constitute the first private claim against the property offered as security. Since the farmer-borrower and his family make their living from the operation of the farm, their living expenses constitute the first deduction from farm income. To be sure, their standard of living will probably be lowered in times of reduced income, but they nevertheless depend upon farm income to pay their family expenses. Then, unless the lender is willing to foreclose his mortgage at the first sign of default, he must allow the borrower enough to continue to pay operating expenses, including ordinary repairs and maintenance costs. All of these considerations must be taken into account in appraising farms for lending purposes.

Because the lender must always take into account the possibility of foreclosure as a last resort, he must consider the problem of future salability of the farm. Here even apparently extraneous factors must be studied. Among them are such subjects as the condition of roads, the proximity of schools, and the availability of markets.

Sources of Funds for Farm Mortgages

The sources of funds for loans on farm mortgages as security are, in order of volume: individuals and others; Federal Land Banks; insurance companies; and commercial banks. The miscellaneous group of individuals and others account for approximately 40 percent of farm mortgage loans. Individual lenders are present when the seller of a farm takes back a purchase-money mortgage as part payment for his property; when a father or other relative sets up a young man in the farming business; or when the funds needed by the borrower are obtained for a person of means who is willing to invest funds in farm mortgages.

In spite of the prevalence of farm mortgages held by individuals, this class of loans is ordinarily made with less attention to safeguarding the interests of both mortgagor and mortgagee than is true of institutional lenders. In many cases no expert appraiser is asked to give an opinion of value. The borrower and the lender agree upon the value of the property for lending purposes. Particularly if a purchase-money mortgage is involved, the needs of the borrower rather than the value of the property may determine the amount of the loan. This may later cause trouble for both borrower and lender.

As a general rule, the term of mortgages made by individuals is shorter than is that of mortgages held by financial institutions. Interest rates are relatively high where no family relationships are involved, with wide variations in specific cases. Short terms and high interest rates result in higher than average installment payments. Unless the payments are carefully geared to the income-producing capacity of the farm, trouble may result.

Included in the miscellaneous category of farm mortgage lenders are the usual sources of real estate finance with urban land as security. They cover savings and loan associations, mortgage loan companies which represent life insurance companies and other institutional investors, and so forth. In some localities, school funds are invested in farm mortgages. Endowment funds of educational and charitable institutions provide sources of farm mortgage finance. As with individuals who invest in farm mortgages, there is no common pattern of mortgage lending by miscellaneous sources. Expert appraisals may be lacking, and attention to details of sound mortgage lending may be overlooked.

In general, individual and miscellaneous lenders do not hold enough mortgages to give them a wide distribution of risks. With limited resources they may not be able to pursue policies more flexible than those set forth in the mortgage instrument. Under the best of circumstances, they may not be able to help the borrower meet unusually difficult financial problems. Since the lender usually dictates the terms of an unstandardized loan pattern, he is likely to make sure that his interests rather than those of the borrower are taken care of.

Life Insurance Companies   Life insurance companies have experienced a long and varied history as holders of farm mortgages. They tend to concentrate their farm loans in the best-developed areas and upon relatively large individual loans. In some cases they make loans directly through their branch offices, and in other cases they purchase farm mortgages from mortgage bankers and others. Even commercial banks sometimes have purchase agreements with life insurance companies by which the bank may hold a mortgage for a short period of time—as much as two years—and then dispose of it to an insurance company.

Some insurance companies offer long-term farm financing at low rates of interest. Some of these loans may run as long as 40 years. Several amortization plans are used, most of which provide for some kind of prepayment privileges, provided that these advance payments arise from farm income. While farm mortgages held by life insurance companies currently amount to $6.3 billion, less than 3 percent of their assets are invested in this class of paper. This is a much lower percentage than was formerly so invested.

Commercial Banks   In their real estate lending operations, commercial banks are subject to various kinds of limitations. The laws and regulations under which they operate set standards that must be observed. In addition to legal restrictions, policies established by boards of directors of commercial banks limit their real estate lending operations. Some will make no farm loans under any circumstances; others favor this type of lending. Still others prefer a balanced program in which farm loans play some part.

In rural areas, commercial banks constitute the largest segment of institutional lenders who hold farm mortgages. Here again, governmental restrictions determine the kinds of loans made. National banks may make unamortized five-year loans up to 50 percent of appraised value. They may also make amortized loans. On such loans they may lend up to 66⅔ percent of the appraisal value on a 10-year maturity if 40 percent of the principal amount is to be amortized over the life of the loan. As an alternative, they may lend up to 90 percent of the appraised value for a term not longer than 30 years if the loan is secured by an amortized mortgage, deed of trust, or other instrument under the terms of which the installment payments are sufficient to amortize the entire principal of the loan within the period ending on the date of its maturity. Most commercial bank loans on farm mortgages tend to be of the relatively shorter maturities.

Federal Land Banks   The 12 Federal Land Banks, through national farm loan associations, make long-term mortgage loans to farmers and ranchers. As of the end of 1975, the amount of farm mortgages held by Federal Land Banks was slightly more than $16.5 billion.

Such loans are limited to 65 percent of the normal value of the security when used for agricultural purposes. Only those who derive the principal part of their income from farming operations are eligible for Land Bank loans. Such persons may obtain loans to purchase land for agricultural purposes; to make improvements in the form of buildings or otherwise; to refinance debts at least two years old; and to provide funds for long-term agricultural purposes.

Land Bank loans may be made for periods of from 5 to 40 years. Appraisals are made by experienced Land Bank appraisers. All such loans must be collateralized by first mortgages. In addition, each borrower must purchase stock in the Land Bank which makes the loan equal to 5 percent of the amount of the loan. This, too, is held as collateral to protect the loan. Finally, the national farm loan association which recommends the loan must endorse the note given by the borrower.

Interest rates on Land Bank loans are conservative. Farmers obtaining loans from this source are required to pay interest at rates based on the cost of money in the investment market and the cost of operations.

Servicing of Land Bank Loans. Land Bank loans are serviced through the national farm loan associations. When the borrower gets into financial difficulty, forbearance is exercised whenever the borrower is deemed to have a reasonable opportunity to catch up on his obligations. Deferments, extensions, and suspended-payment plans have been developed for this purpose. Loans are sometimes recast and a new plan of amortization is set up. When foreclosure has been necessary, deficiency judgments have not been enforced for amounts greater than the difference between the fair value of the property and the amount of investment shown on the books of the lender. As soon as full recovery is realized, any additional claims are voluntarily released, provided there is no evidence of bad faith on the part of the borrower.

Farmers Home Administration

In 1946, Congress set up the Farmers Home Administration (FmHA) to insure or guarantee private loans or to lend appropriated funds to farmers unable to obtain financial assistance from any other source. Since that time the agency has grown and its functions have expanded to include many areas of rural real estate financing. Currently, rural people may look to the FmHA to help purchase or operate farms, provide new employment and business opportunities, buy homes, and improve the environment or general community living standards. Some loans are strictly for individuals and their families. The concept of "individual" may, however, extend to agriculture-related partnerships and corporations. Other loans are made only to groups, such as associations, partnerships, corporations, or public bodies. The purposes may be nonprofit or for profit subject to limitations.

By classification, the principal types of loans for individuals, as broadly defined, are:

Farm ownership loans.	Farm operating—youth loans.
Rural housing loans.	Farm emergency loans.
Soil and water loans.	Business and industial loan guaranties.
Recreation loans.	

Loan programs for groups include:

Rental and cooperative housing loans.
Rural housing site development loans.
Self-help technical assistance grants.
Loans for community facilities.

Indian land acquisition loans.
Grazing association loans.
Rural conservation and development and watershed loans.
Irrigation and drainage loans.

A common requirement, as indicated above, is that the applicant is unable to obtain credit on reasonable terms elsewhere. The agency's function is to provide a supplemental source of credit, augmenting the efforts of private lenders rather than competing with them. Furthermore, under most of the FmHA programs the borrowers are required to refinance with commercial credit conventionally when they become able to do so.

In most programs the credit may be provided alternatively in the form of an insured loan from a private lender or a direct FmHA loan. Because of the limited appropriation of government funds, loans made under the insurance operation greatly predominate over the direct loans. In either case, the credit arrangements are generous when the FmHA assists the borrower, and he often ends up with better terms than could be obtained from a private lender alone if he had been able to meet ordinary credit standards.

Of the numerous loan programs listed, the most significant are those for farm ownership, rural housing, business and industrial purposes, and rental and cooperative housing. These programs are therefore described in greater detail.

Farm Ownership Loans   Insured and direct farm ownership loans are made to help farmers and ranchers acquire and operate family farms. Operations, however, may include establishment and operation of non-farm enterprises to supplement farm income. The enterprise must be located or headquartered on the borrower's farm, but the operations may be so widely variant as to include a repair shop, service station, grocery store, sporting goods store, beauty or barber shop, cabinet shop, or other viable business.

Who May Borrow.   To be eligible, the loan applicant must:

1. Be a U.S. citizen of legal age.
2. Have sufficient farm experience and training to assure reasonable prospects of success. If the loan is for a nonfarm enterprise, the same standard is applied for that activity, although he need not have personally operated this type of business previously.
3. Be of good character.
4. Be unable to obtain credit from other sources on reasonable terms.

Terms and Security.   The rate on these loans is conservative, with maturities not to exceed 40 years. The maximum FmHA real estate loan is $100,000, with the total real estate debt against the security limited to $225,000, or the market value of the farm, whichever is less. Farm ownership loans must be secured by a mortgage on land owned or purchased by the borrower. The borrower is expected to refinance the unpaid balance due on his loan as soon as he is able to do so on reasonable terms from another lender.

Rural Housing Loans The objective of rural housing loans is to assist eligible individual rural residents, farmers, and senior citizens to obtain adequate housing. Funds from these loans may be used to buy, build, repair, improve, or relocate homes and to buy minimum adequate sites.

Who May Borrow. To be eligible, the borrower must:

1. Be a U.S. citizen or permanent resident of good character.
2. Be of moderate or low income without adequate housing; or be a farm owner without adequate housing for his family or his tenant, share croppers, farm laborers, or farm manager.
3. Have sufficient income prospects to meet a reasonable projection of expenses and loan repayment requirements.
4. Be unable to obtain credit elsewhere.
5. Seek housing located in rural areas, open country, towns, villages, and places without more than 20,000 population that are rural in character and not associated with an urban area.

Terms and Security. Loans may be up to 100 percent of FmHA appraised value. Interest rates are established by the FmHA. An interest credit may be granted on loans to low-income families that may reduce the effective rate to the borrower to as low as 1 percent. Co-signers may be used and the repayment period may extend up to 33 years. Loans may be made on owned land or on leased land where the lease is for a sufficient term. On loans for regular housing purposes, the lease should be for at least 50 years. Repair loans are generally approved if the term of the lease is at least one and one half times the repayment period of the loan.

Business and Industrial Loan Guaranties In the interest of broadening the economic bases of rural areas and towns up to 50,000 population, the FmHA guarantees business and industrial loans made by private lenders on real estate and other security. Such loans may be used for the acquisition, improvement, or control of rural businesses or industries.

Who May Borrow. These loan guaranties from the FmHA are available to individuals, cooperatives, corporations, partnerships, Indian tribal groups, municipalities, counties, and other state political subdivisions. The borrower must first meet the credit tests of the private lender and its credit worthiness is then reviewed by the FmHA.

Terms and Security. Since the loans are made by a private lender, the interest rates and maturities are negotiated, within limits, by the borrower and the lender. The FmHA then guarantees up to 90 percent of the loan for a fee. This fee is ½ percent if the initial maturity date is

1 year or less. For a guaranty on business or industrial, operating, and production-type emergency loans the fee is 1 percent for each three-year period or part thereof. Mortgage security on real estate and other assets satisfactory to both the lender and the FmHA is required.

Rental and Cooperative Housing Loans   Another objective of the FmHA is to increase the amount of available and adequate rental and cooperatively-owned housing designed and constructed for occupancy by low- and moderate-income families and senior citizens. There is, in particular, a serious shortage of good rental housing in rural areas and small towns. To help reduce this shortage, the FmHA assists individuals and both nonprofit and profit organizations in financing new rental units or bringing existing properties up to standard.

To qualify for FmHA assistance, the applicant for a loan must establish that three conditions exist:

1. There must be a need for rental housing in the area.
2. The housing contemplated fits the needs of prospective tenants from the standpoint of design, location, and cost.
3. Good management of the project will be provided.

To answer the questions posed by the requirements listed above, the FmHA looks at:

1. Economic conditions and trends in the community.
2. Estimate of number of houses or apartments in the area currently for rent.
3. Characteristics of available rental housing, such as location, quality and size of units, type of building, age of structure, vacancy rate, reasons for vacancies, and rental levels.
4. Characteristics of the eligible occupants, such as single or couples, male or female, size and composition of family, and number of senior citizens and nonsenior citizens.
5. Income and financial condition of the people in the area who would be eligible to occupy the housing as planned.
6. Present living arrangements of eligible occupants in the area and the extent to which inadequate housing is associated with health or financial conditions.
7. Estimate of the number of eligible occupants who are willing and financially able to occupy the proposed housing.
8. Financial responsibility and managerial competency of the applicant.
9. Architectural planning.
10. Site selection.
11. Financial planning.

Financial Planning.   Since the financial arrangements are of great concern to potential organizers of a rural rental project, the terms, limitations, and inducements are discussed in greater detail. An example is also presented.

Terms and Security.   Interest rates are set in accordance with current market conditions and can be obtained by calling a local FmHA office. Borrowers agreeing to rent to low-income tenants may receive interest credits to reduce the effective rate to as low as 1 percent. Although the government will require that the loan be secured adequately, the loan-to-value ratio may run as high as 95 percent. Furthermore, only 2 percent of the remaining 5 percent equity requirements must be deposited in cash as initial operating expense. The other 3 percent may be earned as architectural or legal fees, or by performance of other services, such as engineering, etc. An additional advantage to the applicant may be granted in appropriate cases in the form of a waiver of individual personal liability. In this instance, the government looks exclusively to the project value for recovery of the loan balance. Where FmHA administrators approve limited profit partnerships, this form, in particular, can be profitably used despite a limitation of 8 percent return on equity investment. An attractive tax shelter is provided the investor in the depreciation deductible by the partners in such a venture. Corporations are generally less popular because the operating losses generated by the depreciation cannot be passed through the corporate entity and the prescribed return allowable to a stockholder has been found to be inadequate.

To induce more construction of this type of housing, the FmHA underwrites rent concessions to low-income tenants who occupy the units. The tenant is required to pay only a basic rental adjusted for possible overage determined by his monthly family income. This basic rental is determined by the amount required to operate the project with payments of principal and interest on the loan amortized over 40 or 50 years with interest at 1 percent per annum. Senior citizen projects have a 50-year amortization; others have 40 years. In determining overage, any tenant is required to pay as rent whichever is the higher of (1) the basic monthly rental or (2) 25 percent of the tenant's adjusted family income where utilities are furnished or 20 percent of the tenant's adjusted family income where utilities are not included in the rent.

The market rental for the project is determined on the basis of operating the project with payments of principal and interest which the borrower is obligated to pay under the terms of the promissory note. The difference between the rental collectible at market rates and that determined under the concession rules becomes the interest credit allowed by the FmHA.

Computation of Interest Credit.   A hypothetical example may contribute to a better understanding of the application of the interest credit to a real situation. In this case, assume a $100,000 loan at 7¼ percent for 50 years for rural rental housing. The project contains five 1-bedroom units and five 2-bedroom units.

Budgets—Schedule I

Budget for Market Rent	*Budget for Basic Rent*
Operation and maintenance expenses, vacancy and contingency allowances, reserve and return allowable on investors' equity ....$ 4,524	Operation and maintenance expenses, vacancy and contingency allowances, reserve and return allowable on investors' equity ....$ 4,524

Loan repayment at 7¼ percent interest ($100,000 × 0.07476)   7,476
   Annual requirement $12,000
	Loan repayment at 1 percent interest ($100,000 × .02551) 2,551
	   Annual requirement ....$ 7,075

$12,000 ÷ 12 = $1,000 monthly requirement
   Market rent for
      2-bedroom units = $106
      1-bedroom units =   94
($106 × 5) + ($94 × 5) = $1,000 monthly income
	$7,075 ÷ 12 = $590 monthly requirement
	Basic rent for
	   2-bedroom units = $65
	   1-bedroom units = $53
	($65 × 5) + ($53 × 5) = $590 monthly income

Calculation of Overage—Schedule II

Apt. No.	Type	Occupant	Basic Monthly Rental	Market Monthly Rental	25 Percent of Adjusted Monthly Family Income	Tenant's Monthly Rental Payment	Overage
1..............	1-Br.	Jones	$ 53	$ 94	$ 52	$ 53	$ 0
2..............	1-Br.	Smith	53	94	60	60	7
3..............	1-Br.	Brown	53	94	75	75	22
4..............	1-Br.	Wilson	53	94	45	53	0
5..............	1-Br.	Bryant	53	94	48	53	0
6..............	2-Br.	Font	65	106	75	75	10
7..............	2-Br.	Doe	65	106	60	65	0
8..............	2-Br.	(Vacant)	65	106	50	65	0
9..............	2-Br.	Jackson	65	106	80	80	15
10..............	2-Br.	Morales	65	106	55	65	0
	Total		$590	$1,000	$600	$644	$54

Interest Credit Calculation—Schedule III

1. Annual payment by borrower at 7¼% interest (Schedule I) $7,476
2. Annual payment by borrower at 1% interest (Schedule I) $2,551
   Overage ($54 × 12 — per Schedule II) 648
   Annual basic rental adjusted for overage 3,199
   Annual interest credit allowed by FmHA $4,277

Volume of Farm Debt   The farm mortgage debt at the end of 1975 was $49.9 billion. This amount is up from $4.8 billion, ten times since the end of 1945. The relative importance of various loan sources at the end of 1975 is shown in Exhibit 22–1. The great significance of federal agencies and individuals to rural credit is readily apparent.

EXHIBIT 22–1

Distribution of Farm Mortgage Loans by Principal Lenders as of December 31, 1975 (in $ billion)

Type of Lender	Amount	Percentage
Commercial banks	$ 6.4	13.1
Life insurance companies	6.8	13.9
Federal and related agencies	17.6	36.0
Individuals and others	18.1	37.0
Total	$48.9	100.0

Source: Federal Reserve Bulletin, March 1976, p. A42.

Although a large portion of farm mortgages are in support of the farming business, there is a new thrust under way toward living in rural communities. The Farmers Home Administration is becoming an increasingly important agency to help fulfill the housing demands created by the new population flow.

QUESTIONS

1.   What are the common sources of farm capital?

2.   Why are partnership and leasing arrangements relatively common in financing farm operations?

3.   What are the chief purposes of farm mortgages and how should mortgage terms be arranged to fulfill these purposes?

4.   Discuss the applicability of the following provisions in a farm mortgage: (*a*) amortization; (*b*) prepayment privileges; and (*c*) sinking fund for future benefits.

5.   What criteria should be used in appraisals for farm loans?

6.   Why are individuals the principal source of mortgage loan funds utilized in financing farms?

7.   Discuss the commercial bank as a source of funds for financing farm real estate?

8.   What has been the experience of life insurance companies as investors in farm mortgages?

9.   Under what conditions may a farmer borrow funds through the Federal Land Bank System?

10.   How does the Farmers Home Administration offer financial assistance to farmers in buying farms? To nonfarming owners?

11. With the recent population trend toward the rural areas, do you see any special opportunities for the developer or investor to work with the FmHA to their mutual advantage?

CASE PROBLEM

The FmHA is contemplating a $100,000 loan at 8% for 40 years for rural rental housing. All income requirements to cover annual expenses of operation and maintenance, allowances, reserves and return to investors were estimated at $6,014. Compute the market and basic rental requirements for eight 1-bedroom units. If the tenants' total monthly overage for the first year should be $60, what would be the FmHA interest credit? Assume that the appropriate constants for a 40-year loan are: at 8%, 0.08386 and at 1%, 0.03046.

Selected References

Selected References

SPECIALIZED BOOKS AND BOOKLETS

Part I: Instruments Used in Real Estate Finance: Legal and Financial Characteristics

Bohon, Davis T. *Complete Guide to Profitable Real Estate Leasing.* Englewood Cliffs, N.J.: Prentice-Hall, Inc., 1969.

Colbleigh, I. U. *All about Investing in Real Estate Securities.* New York: Weybright and Talley, Inc., 1971.

Friedman, M. R. *Friedman on Leases.* New York: Practicing Law Institute, 1974.

Grange, William J., and Woodbury, T. C. *Manual of Real Estate Law and Procedures.* New York: The Ronald Press Co., 1967.

Hebard, Edna L., and Meisel, Gerald S. *Principles of Real Estate Law.* Cambridge, Mass.: Schenkman Publishing Co., 1967.

Kratovil, Robert. *Modern Mortgage Law and Practice.* Englewood Cliffs, N.J.: Prentice-Hall, Inc., 1972.

————. *Modern Real Estate Documentation.* Englewood Cliffs, N.J.: Prentice-Hall, Inc., 1975.

————. *Real Estate Law.* Englewood Cliffs, N.J.: Prentice-Hall, Inc., 1974.

Lusk, Harold F. *The Law of the Real Estate Business.* Homewood, Ill.: Richard D. Irwin, Inc., 1975.

McMichael, Stanley L., and O'Keefe, Paul T. *Leases: Percentage, Short and Long Term.* Englewood Cliffs, N.J.: Prentice-Hall, Inc., 1974.

Thompson, George W. *The Law of Real Property.* Vols. 1–12. Indianapolis, Ind.: The Bobbs-Merrill Co., Inc., 1941 (with later supplements).

Tiffany, Herbert Thorndike. *The Law of Real Property.* Vols. 1–6. Chicago: Callaghan & Co., 1939 (with later supplements).

Part II: Risk and Return Analysis and Financing Techniques

Bagby, Joseph R.   *Real Estate Financing Desk Book.* Englewood Cliffs, N.J.: Institute for Business Planning, Inc., 1975.

Beaton, William R.   *Real Estate Finance.* Englewood Cliffs, N.J.: Prentice-Hall, Inc., 1975.

_____.   *Real Estate Investment.* Englewood Cliffs, N.J.: Prentice-Hall, Inc., 1971.

Candilis, Wray O.   *Variable Rate Mortgage Plans.* Washington, D.C.: The American Bankers Association, 1971.

Clurman, David, and Hebard, Edna L.   *Condominiums and Cooperatives.* New York: Wiley-Interscience, 1970.

Cooper, James R.   *Real Estate Investment Analysis.* Lexington, Mass.: Lexington Books, D. C. Heath & Co., 1974.

David, Philip   *Urban Land Development.* Homewood, Ill.: Richard D. Irwin, Inc., 1970. A casebook.

Downs, J. C., Jr.   *Principles of Real Estate Management.* Chicago: Institute of Real Estate Management, 1970.

Graaskamp, J. A.   *A Guide to Feasibility Analysis.* Chicago: Society of Real Estate Appraisers, 1970.

Kahn, Sanders A., and Case, Frederick E.   *Real Estate Appraisal and Investment.* New York: The Ronald Press Co., 1976.

Kinnard, William N., Jr.   *Income Property Valuation.* Lexington, Mass.: Lexington Books, D. C. Heath & Co., 1971.

_____.   *Industrial Real Estate.* Washington, D.C.: Socitey of Industrial Realtors of the National Association of Real Estate Boards, 1967.

McMichael, Stanley L., and O'Keefe, Paul T.   *How to Finance Real Estate.* Englewood Cliffs, N.J.: Prentice-Hall, Inc., 1967.

Maisel, Serman J., and Roulac, Stephen E.   *Real Estate Investment and Finance.* New York: McGraw-Hill Book Co., Inc., 1976.

Messner, Stephen D., Schreiber, Irving, and Lyon, Victor L.   *Marketing Investment Real Estate: Finance Taxation Techniques.* Chicago: Realtors National Marketing Institute, 1975.

Mossburg, Lewis G., Jr.   *Real Estate Syndicate Offerings, Law and Practice.* San Francisco: Real Estate Syndication Digest, 1974.

Price, I.   *Buying Country Property: Pitfalls and Pleasures.* New York: Harper and Row, Inc., 1972.

Ring, Alfred A.   *The Valuation of Real Estate.* Englewood Cliffs, N.J.: Prentice-Hall, Inc., 1970.

Robinson, Gerald J.   *Federal Income Taxation of Real Estate.* Boston, Mass.: Warren, Gorham & Lamont, Inc., 1974.

Roulac, S. E. *Real Estate Syndicate Digest.* San Francisco: Real Estate Syndicators Digest, Inc., 1972.

————. *Real Estate Venture Analysis 1974.* New York: Practicing Law Institute, 1974.

Seldin, Maury, and Swesnik, Richard H. *Real Estate Investment Strategy.* New York: Wiley-Interscience, 1970.

Wendt, Paul F. *Real Estate Appraisal: Review and Outlook.* Athens: U. of Georgia Press, 1974.

————, and Cerf, Alan R. *Real Estate Investment Analysis and Taxation.* New York: McGraw-Hill Book Co., 1969.

Weston, J. F., and Brigham, E. F. *Essentials of Managerial Finance.* Hinsdale, Ill.: Dryden Press, 1974.

Willis, A. B. *Willis on Partnership Taxation.* New York: McGraw-Hill Book Co., 1971.

Part III: Sources of Real Estate Credit

American Bankers Association. *Mortgage Banker Handbook.* New York, 1963.

Bryant, Willis R. *Mortgage Lending Fundamentals and Practices.* New York: McGraw-Hill Book Co., Inc., 1962.

Campbell, Kenneth D. *Mortgage Trusts: Lenders with a Plus.* New York: Audit Publications, Inc., 1969.

Federal Reserve Bank of Boston. *New Mortgage Designs for Stable Housing in an Inflationary Environment.* Conference Series no. 14, Boston, 1975.

Financial Institute Monographs. Prepared for the Commission on Money and Credit:

> *The Commercial Banking Industry* (The American Bankers Association).
>
> *The Consumer Finance Industry* (National Consumer Finance Association).
>
> *Life Insurance Companies as Financial Institutions* (Life Insurance Institute of America).
>
> *Mortgage Companies: Their Place in the Financial Structure* (Miles Colean, for the Mortgage Bankers Association of America).
>
> *Mutual Savings Banking: Basic Characteristics and Role in the National Economy* (National Association of Mutual Savings Banks).
>
> *Property and Casualty Insurance Companies: Their Role as Financial Intermediaries* (American Insurance Alliance; Association of Casualty and Surety Companies; and National Board of Fire Underwriters).
>
> *The Savings and Loan Business: Its Purposes, Functions, and Economic Justification* (Leon T. Kendall, for the United States League of Savings Associations).

These monographs were published by Prentice-Hall, Inc., Englewood Cliffs, N.J., 1962.

Friend, I., et al. *Study of the Savings and Loan Industry.* Vols 1–4. Washington, D.C.: Federal Home Loan Bank Board, 1969.

Gramlich, E. M., and Jaffee, D. M. (eds.) *Savings Deposits, Mortgages and Housing: Studies from the FRB-MIT-Penn Model.* Lexington, Mass.: Lexington Books, 1972.

Guttentag, Jack M., and Beck, Morris. *New Series on Home Mortgage Fields since 1951.* New York: National Bureau of Economic Research, Columbia University Press, 1970.

Jacobs, D. P., Farwell, L. C., and Neave, E. H. *Financial Institutions.* Homewood, Ill.: Richard D. Irwin, Inc., 1972.

Klaman, Saul B. *The Postwar Rise of Mortgage Companies.* New York: National Bureau of Economic Research, Inc., 1959.

Kroos, Herman E., and Blyn, Martin R. *A History of Financial Intermediaries.* New York: Random House, 1971.

Mortgage Guarantee Insurance Corporation. *MGIC Fact Book.* Milwaukee, Wisc., 1975.

Office of Economic Research, Federal Home Loan Bank Board. *A Financial Institution for the Future (An Examination of the Restructuring of the Savings and Loan Industry).* Washington, D.C.: Federal Home Loan Bank Board, 1975.

Pease, Robert H., and Kerwood, Lewis O. *Mortgage Banking.* New York: McGraw-Hill Book Co., Inc., 1965.

Robinson, Roland I. *The Management of Bank Funds.* New York: McGraw-Hill Book Co., Inc., 1962.

Silber, W. L. *Portfolio Behavior of Financial Institutions.* New York: Holt, Rinehart and Winston, 1970.

Spolan, Harmon S. *Banker's Handbook of Federal Aids to Financing.* Boston, Mass.: Warren, Gorham & Lamont, Inc., 1974 (with 1976 supplement by the staff editors of the Banking Law Journal).

Starr, Roger. *Housing and the Money Market.* New York: Basic Books, Inc., 1975.

Wiedemer, John P. *Real Estate Finance.* Reston, Va.: Reston Publishing Company, Inc., 1974.

U.S. Commission on Financial Structure and Regulation. *Report* (Hunt Commission). Washington, D.C. 1971.

Part IV: Government and Real Estate Finance (including rural housing)

Aaron, Henry J. *Shelter and Subsidies: Who Benefits from Federal Housing Policies?* Washington, D.C.: The Brookings Institution, 1972.

Board of Governors of the Federal Reserve System. *Ways to Moderate Fluctuations in Housing Construction.* Washington, D.C., 1972.

Downs, Anthony. *Federal Housing Subsidies: How Are They Working?* Lexington, Mass.: Lexington Books, 1973.

Fisher, Ernest. *Housing Markets and Congressional Goals.* New York: Praeger Publishers, 1975.

Harrison, Bennett. *Urban Economic Development: Suburbanization, Minority Opportunity, and the Condition of the Central City.* Washington, D.C.: The Urban Institute, 1974.

Institute for Contemporary Studies. *Government Credit Allocation: Where Do We Go from Here?* San Francisco, Calif., 1975.

Nelson, Aaron G., and Murray, William G. *Agricultural Finance.* Ames, Iowa State University Press, 1967.

Netzer, Dick. *Economics and Urban Problems: Diagnoses and Prescriptions.* New York: Basic Books, Inc., 1974.

Schafer, Robert. *The Suburbanization of Multifamily Housing.* Lexington, Mass.: Lexington Books, D. C. Heath & Co., 1974.

Solomon, Arthur P. *Housing the Urban Poor: A Critical Evaluation of Federal Housing Policy.* Cambridge, Mass.: The MIT Press, 1974.

Swackhamer, Gene L., and Doll, Raymond J. *Financing Modern Agriculture.* Kansas City, Mo.: Research Department, Federal Reserve Bank of Kansas City, 1969.

U.S. Department of Housing and Urban Development. *Housing in the Seventies.* Washington, D.C., 1974.

U.S. Department of Housing and Urban Development. *Abandoned Housing Research: A Compendium.* Washington, D.C.: U.S. Government Printing Office (HUD–RT–32), 1973.

GENERAL REFERENCE WORKS ON PRINCIPLES AND PRACTICE

Case, Frederick E. *Real Estate.* New York: Allyn and Bacon, Inc., 1962.

Casey, William J. *Real Estate Desk Book.* Englewood Cliffs, N.J.: Institute for Business Planning, Inc., 1974.

Ficek, Edmund F., Henderson, Thomas P., and Johnson, Ross H. *Real Estate Principles and Practices.* Columbus, Ohio: Charles E. Merrill Publishing Co., 1976.

Hoagland, Henry E. *Real Estate Principles.* New York: McGraw-Hill Book Co., Inc., 1955.

Ratcliff, Richard U. *Real Estate Analysis.* New York: McGraw-Hill Book Co., Inc., 1961.

Ring, Alfred A. *Real Estate Principles and Practices.* Englewood Cliffs, N.J.: Prentice-Hall, Inc., 1972.

Smith, Halbert C., Tschappat, Carl J., and Racster, Ronald L. *Real Estate and Urban Development.* Homewood, Ill.: Richard D. Irwin, Inc., 1973.

Unger, Maurice A. *Real Estate.* Cincinnati: South-Western Publishing Co., 1974.

Weimer, Arthur M., Hoyt, Homer, and Bloom, George F. *Real Estate.* New York: The Ronald Press Co., 1972.

PUBLICATIONS IN PERIODICALS

Alberts, William. "Business Cycles, Residential Construction Cycles, and the Mortgage Market," *Journal of Political Economy* (June 1962), pp 263–87.

Aronsohn, Alan J. B. "The Real Estate Limited Partnership and Other Joint Ventures," *Real Estate Review* (Spring 1971), pp. 43–49.

Bleck, Erick K. "Real Estate Investments and Rates of Return," *The Appraisal Journal* (October 1973), pp. 535–47.

Bradley, Eugene. "A Sectorial Econometric Study of the Postwar Residential Housing Market," *Journal of Political Economy* (April 1967), pp. 274–78.

Brueggeman, William B. "Federal Housing Subsidies: Conceptual Issues and Benefit Patterns," *Journal of Economics and Business* (Winter 1975), pp. 141–49.

————, and Baesel, Jerome B. "The Mechanics of Variable Rate Mortgages and Implications for Home Ownership as an Inflation Hedge," *Appraisal Journal* (April 1976), pp. 236–46.

Chesborough, Lawell D. "Do Participation Loans Pay Off?" *Real Estate Review* (Summer 1974), pp. 95–100.

Clark, William Dennison. "Leverage: Magnificent Mover of Real Estate," *Real Estate Review* (Winter 1972), pp. 8–13.

Cooper, James R., and Pyhrr, Stephan A. "Forecasting the Rates of Return on an Apartment Investment: A Case Study," *The Appraisal Journal* (July 1973), pp. 312–37.

Dasso, Jerome J., Kinnard, William N., Jr., and Messner, Stephen D. "Lender Participation Financing: Applications of Sensitivity and Investment Analysis," *The Real Estate Appraiser* (July–August 1971).

Duffy, Robert E., Jr. "The Real Estate Settlement Procedures Act of 1974," *Real Estate Review* (Winter 1976), pp. 86–93.

Etka, Donald D. "Shopping Center Leasing," *Journal Property Management*, vol. 30, no. 3 (May–June 1965), pp. 136–39.

Fass, Peter M. "The Regulated World of the Real Estate Syndicates," *Real Estate Review* (Winter 1972), pp. 52–56.

Ferebee, Ann, and Vrchota, Janet. "PUD: A Promise with Problems," *Real Estate Review* (Fall 1974), pp. 87–90.

Fitzhugh, Gilbert W. "The Life Insurance Companies' Urban Investment Program," *The Mortgage Banker* (June 1968), pp. 18–24.

Friedman, H. C. "Real Estate Investment and Portfolio Theory," *Journal of Financial and Quantitative Analysis* (March 1971), pp. 861–74.

Goldberg, Alfred M. "How HUD Handles Its Problem Construction Loans," *Real Estate Review* (Winter 1976), pp. 45–48.

Graham, D. H. "Shopping Centers: Financing, Appraisal, and Management," *Journal of Property Management*, vol. 31, no. 3 (May–June 1966), pp. 115 ff.

Grebler, Leo. "The New System of Residential Mortgage Finance," *The Appraisal Journal* (July 1972), pp. 434–48.

Guttentag, Jack. "Mortgage Warehousing," *Journal of Finance,* vol. 12, no. 4 (December 1957), pp. 438–50.

————. "The Short Cycle in Residential Construction: 1946–59," *American Economic Review* (June 1961), pp. 275–98.

Halper, Emanuel M. "What Is a New Net Net Net Lease?" *Real Estate Review* (Winter 1974), pp. 9–14.

Halperin, Jerome Y., and Brenner, Michael J. "Opportunities under the New Section 8 Housing Program," *Real Estate Review* (Spring 1976), pp. 67–75.

Harrington, Phlip N. "Freddie Mac: Big Man in Mortgages," *Real Estate Review* (Winter 1974), pp. 102–4.

Haverkampf, Peter T. "The Pension Trusts Move into Real Estate–Slowly," *Real Estate Review* (Spring 1974), pp. 126–29.

Hemmer, Edgar H. "How a Computer 'Thinks' about Real Estate," *Real Estate Review* (Winter 1975), pp. 113–23.

Higginbottom, Elzie. "Fulfilling Nonprofit Housing Goals with Limited Dividend Partnerships," *The Mortgage Banker* (November 1970), pp. 76–80.

Hines, Mary Alice. "The REIT Shakeout in 1974," *Real Estate Review* (Winter 1975), pp. 56–59.

Hunter, Oakley. "Fannie Mae Prepares for a New Role in Conventional Mortgage Markets," *Banking* (October 1971), pp. 66–70.

Jacobs, Steven, and Kozuch, James R. "Is There a Future for a Mortgage Futures Market?" *Real Estate Review* (Spring 1975), pp. 109–13.

Johnstone, Quintin. "Title Insurance," *The Yale Law Journal,* vol. 66, no. 4 (February 1957), pp. 492–524.

Jones, Oliver. "Private Secondary Market Facilities," *The Journal of Finance,* vol. 23, no. 2 (May 1968), pp, 359–66.

Kaplan, Mortimer. "Recent Institutional Arrangements in Mortgage Lending," *Journal of Finance,* vol. 13, no. 2 (May 1958), pp. 188–200.

Kempner, Paul S. "Investments in Single-Tenant Net Leased Properties," *Real Estate Review* (Summer 1974), pp. 131–34.

Kozuch, James R., and Shank, Andrew G. "Management of Funds Is Key to Successful Condo Conversions," *Mortgage Banker* (November 1974), pp. 5–12.

Lieder, Arnold. "How to Wrap around a Mortgage," *Real Estate Review* (Winter 1975), pp. 29–34.

Leverett, E. J., Jr. "Lease Guarantee Program," *Journal of Property Management,* vol. 33, no. 2 (March–April 1968), pp. 88–91.

Levin, Michael R. "Financing the Commercial Condominium," *Real Estate Review* (Winter 1975), pp. 71–77.

Levy, Daniel S. "ABC's of Shopping Center Leases," *Real Estate Review* (Spring 1971), pp. 12–16.

McKillop, Hart. "Title Insurance," *University of Florida Law Review,* vol. 8, no. 4 (Winter 1955), pp. 447–64.

McMullen, William H., Jr. "Truth in Selling: The Interstate Land Sales Full Disclosure Act of 1968," *Real Estate Review* (Spring 1971), pp. 94–98.

Maisel, Sherman J. "Some Relationships between Assets and Liabilities of Thrift Institutions," *The Journal of Finance,* vol. 23, no. 2 (May 1968), pp. 367–78.

Martin, Wendell H. "Tax Shelter and the Real Estate Analyst," *The Appraisal Journal* (January 1975), pp. 17–28.

Meltzer, Allan H. "Credit Availability and Economic Decisions: Some Evidence from the Mortgage and Housing Markets," *Journal of Finance* (June 1974), pp. 763–77.

Messner, Stephen D., and Findlay, M. Chapman III. "Real Estate Investment Analysis: IRR versus FMRR," *The Real Estate Appraiser* (July–August 1975).

Opperman, John C. "Lender-Developer Participation," *The Mortgage Banker* (September 1968), pp. 30–35, 38.

Parisse, Alan J. "How Not to Analyze a Syndication," *Real Estate Review* (Winter 1974), pp. 89–96.

Pellat, P. G. K. "The Analysis of Real Estate Investments under Uncertainty," *Journal of Finance,* vol. 27, no. 2 (May 1972), pp. 459–71.

Penner, R. G., and Silber, W. I. "The Interaction between Federal Credit Programs and the Impact on the Allocation of Credit," *American Economic Review* (December 1973), pp. 838–52.

Pyhrr, S. A. "A Computer Simulation Model to Measure the Risk in Real Estate Investment," *The Real Estate Appraiser* (May–June 1973).

Rams, Edwin M. "Investment Mechanics vs. Investment Analysis," *The Appraisal Journal* (January 1974), pp. 62–65.

Reiling, William S. "A Program for Joint Ventures," *The Mortgage Banker* (August 1971), pp. 24, 36–42.

Ricks, R. Bruce. "Imputed Equity Returns on Real Estate Financed with Life Insurance Company Loans," *Journal of Finance* (December 1969), pp. 921–37.

Roberts, Paul E. "Working Out the Construction Mortgage Loan," *Real Estate Review* (Summer 1975), pp. 50–57.

Rose, Cornelius C., Jr. "Equity Participations," *The Mortgage Banker* (June 1968), pp. 44–47.

Roulac, Stephen E. "Life Cycle of a Real Estate Investment," *Real Estate Review* (Fall 1974), pp. 113–17.

Schulkin, Peter A. "Construction Lending at Large Commercial Banks," *Real Estate Review* (Spring 1971), pp. 54–60.

Schwind, Robert L. "Land Trusts—A Real Estate Syndication Device," *Trusts and Estates* (July 1962), pp. 650–52.

Shenkel, William M. "Residential Net Ground Leases," *Journal of Property Management,* vol. 29, no. 4 (March and April 1964), pp. 180–93.

Sillcocks, H. Jackson. "Financial Sense in Real Estate Sales and Leasebacks," *Real Estate Review* (Spring 1975), pp. 89–95.

Smith, Lawrence. "A Sectorial Econometric Study of the Postwar Residential Housing Market: An Opposite View," *Journal of Political Economy,* (March/April 1970), pp. 284–89.

Sonnenblick, Jack E. "Shopping Center Financing," *Journal of Property Management,* vol. 30, no. 6 (November–December 1965), pp. 303–6.

Spiezio, Nicholas J. "The Housing and Urban Development Act of 1970," *The Mortgage Banker* (February 1971), pp. 12–19.

Stansell, Stanley R., and Millar, James A. "How Variable-Rate Mortgages Would Affect Lenders," *Real Estate Review* (Winter 1976), pp. 116–18.

Starr, John O. "Lease Guarantee Insurance," *The Appraisal Journal* (April 1972), pp. 175–87.

Stefaniak, Norbert J. "Management Policies of Real Estate Investment Trusts," *Journal of Property Management,* vol. 22, no. 2 (March–April 1968), pp. 63–67.

Stevenson, Eric. "A Commitment Made and Kept: The (Life Insurance Companies') Urban Investment Program," *The Mortgage Banker* (May 1970), pp. 18–27.

Taylor, Harold S. "The REITs Are Sorting Themselves Out," *Real Estate Review* (Spring 1974), pp. 102–5.

"The GNMA Mortgaged-Backed Security," a special issue of *The Mortgage Banker* (May 1971) covering this topic.

"The Real Estate and Mortgage Investment Trust," a special issue of *The Mortgage Banker* (September 1970) covering this topic.

Thorne, Oakleigh J. "Real Estate Financial Analysis–The State of the Art," *The Appraisal Journal* (January 1974), pp. 7–37.

Troxel, Jay C. "Rates: Capitalization and Interest," *The Appraisal Journal* (January 1975), pp. 7–16.

Tucker, Donald P. "The Variable-Rate Graduated-Payment Mortgage," *Real Estate Review* (Spring 1975), pp. 71–80.

Vitt, Lois A., and Berstein, Joel H. "Convertible Mortgages: New Financing Tool?" *Real Estate Review* (Spring 1976), pp. 33–37.

von Furstenberg, George M. "Default Risk on FHA-Insured Home Mortgages as a Function of the Terms of Financing, a Quantitative Analysis," *Journal of Finance* (June 1969), pp. 455–65.

von Furstenberg, George M., and Green, R. Jeffrey. "Home Mortgage Delinquencies: A Cohort Analysis," *Journal of Finance* (December 1974), pp. 1545–48.

Waldron, William D. "Participatory Investment Reviewed," *The Mortgage Banker* (August 1971), pp. 44–49.

Weil, S. Douglas. "Land Leasebacks Move Up Fast as Financing Technique," *Real Estate Review* (Winter 1972), pp. 65–71.

Wendt, Paul F., and Wong, S. N. "Investment Performance: Common Stock, versus Apartment Houses," *Journal of Finance* (December 1965), pp. 633–46.

Wiggin, Charles E. "Doing Business in the Secondary Market," *Real Estate Review* (Summer 1975), pp. 84–95.

Williams, Marvin. "Financing Shopping Centers with Tax-Free Funds," *Real Estate Review* (Winter 1976), pp. 67–71.

Winger, Alan. "Regional Growth Disparities and the Mortgage Market," *Journal of Finance* (September 1969), pp. 659–62.

SUGGESTED SOURCES FOR CURRENT DEVELOPMENTS

The Appraisal Journal. Published quarterly by the American Institute of Estate Appraisers, 36 So. Wabash Ave., Chicago.

Banking. Published monthly by the American Bankers Association, 5601 Chestnut Street, Philadelphia.

Federal Reserve Bulletin. Published monthly by the Board of Governors of the Federal Reserve System, Washington, D.C.; and Federal Reserve Bulletins published by the various Federal Reserve district banks.

Federal Tax Course. Chicago: Commerce Clearing House, Inc., issued annually.

Federal Tax Course. Prentice-Hall, Inc., issued annually.

Institute for Business Planning, Inc. *Real Estate Investment Planning* (vols. 1 and 2). Englewood Cliffs, N.J., Institute for Business Planning, Inc. (looseleaf service updated).

Journal of Real Estate Law, The. Published quarterly by Warren, Gorham & Lamont, Inc., Boston.

Journal of Real Estate Taxation, The. Published quarterly by Warren, Gorham & Lamont, Inc., Boston.

Life Insurance Fact Book. Published annually by the Institute of Life Insurance, New York.

The Mortgage Banker. Published monthly by the Mortgage Bankers Association of America, Chicago.

Mutual Savings Banking. Published monthly by the National Association of Mutual Savings Banks, New York.

The National Fact Book of Mutual Savings Banking. Published annually by the National Association of Mutual Savings Banks, New York and Washington, D.C.

The National League Journal of Insured Savings Associations. Published monthly by the National League of Insured Savings Associations, Washington, D.C.

Proceedings of the annual conferences on savings and residential financing, sponsored by the United States League of Savings Associations, Chicago and Washington, D.C.

Proceedings of the annual conventions of the Mortgage Bankers Association of America, Chicago.

The Real Estate Analyst. Looseleaf statistical service published by Roy Wenzlick Research Corp., St. Louis.

Real Estate Review. Published quarterly by Warren, Gorham & Lamont, Inc., Boston.

The Residential Appraiser. Published monthly by the Society of Real Estate Appraisers, 7 So. Dearborn St., Chicago.

Savings and Loan Fact Book. Published annually by the United States League of Savings Associations, Chicago and Washington, D.C.

Savings and Loan News. Published monthly, except semimonthly in August, by the United States League of Savings Associations, Chicago and Washington, D.C.

Title News. Published monthly by the American Title Association, Detroit, Michigan.

Various publications of governmental agencies, including particularly the reports of Congressional hearings, annual and special reports of the Federal Home Loan Bank Board and the Department of Housing and Urban Development, releases of the Veterans Administration, and the statistical abstracts of the United States.

appendix
Monthly Compound Interest Tables

YR	MOS	(1) COMPOUND VALUE $1	(2) COMPOUND VALUE $1 PER MO	(3) PRESENT VALUE $1	(4) PRESENT VALUE $1 PER MO	(5) LOAN CONSTANT	(6) BAL 25 YR LOAN	(7) BAL 30 YR LOAN
	1	1.00250	1.00250	0.99751	0.99751	1.00250	.9978	.9983
	2	1.00501	2.00751	0.99502	1.99252	0.50188	.9955	.9966
	3	1.00752	3.01503	0.99254	2.98506	0.33500	.9933	.9948
	4	1.01004	4.02506	0.99006	3.97512	0.25156	.9910	.9931
	5	1.01256	5.03763	0.98759	4.96272	0.20150	.9887	.9914
	6	1.01509	6.05272	0.98513	5.94785	0.16813	.9865	.9896
	7	1.01763	7.07035	0.98267	6.93052	0.14429	.9842	.9879
	8	1.02018	8.09053	0.98022	7.91074	0.12641	.9819	.9862
	9	1.02273	9.11325	0.97778	8.88852	0.11250	.9796	.9844
	10	1.02528	10.13854	0.97534	9.86386	0.10138	.9773	.9826
	11	1.02785	11.16638	0.97291	10.83677	0.09228	.9750	.9809
	12	1.03042	12.19680	0.97048	11.80725	0.08469	.9727	.9791
2	24	1.06176	24.76458	0.94184	23.26598	0.04298	.9446	.9576
3	36	1.09405	37.71461	0.91403	34.38646	0.02908	.9156	.9354
4	48	1.12733	51.05854	0.88705	45.17869	0.02213	.8858	.9126
5	60	1.16162	64.80833	0.86087	55.65236	0.01797	.8551	.8891
6	72	1.19695	78.97634	0.83546	65.81685	0.01519	.8234	.8648
7	84	1.23335	93.57528	0.81080	75.68132	0.01321	.7907	.8398
8	96	1.27087	108.61826	0.78686	85.25460	0.01173	.7571	.8141
9	108	1.30952	124.11878	0.76364	94.54530	0.01058	.7224	.7875
10	120	1.34935	140.09077	0.74110	103.56175	0.00966	.6867	.7602
11	132	1.39040	156.54857	0.71922	112.31205	0.00890	.6499	.7320
12	144	1.43269	173.50694	0.69799	120.80406	0.00828	.6119	.7030
13	156	1.47626	190.98112	0.67739	129.04541	0.00775	.5729	.6731
14	168	1.52116	208.98679	0.65739	137.04348	0.00730	.5326	.6423
15	180	1.56743	227.54012	0.63799	144.80547	0.00691	.4911	.6105
16	192	1.61511	246.65777	0.61915	152.33833	0.00656	.4483	.5778
17	204	1.66423	266.35690	0.60088	159.64684	0.00626	.4043	.5440
18	216	1.71485	286.65520	0.58314	166.74356	0.00600	.3589	.5093
19	228	1.76701	307.57089	0.56593	173.62885	0.00576	.3121	.4735
20	240	1.82075	329.12275	0.54922	180.31091	0.00555	.2639	.4366
21	252	1.87613	351.33014	0.53301	186.79572	0.00535	.2142	.3986
22	264	1.93320	374.21298	0.51728	193.08911	0.00518	.1630	.3594
23	276	1.99200	397.79182	0.50201	199.19673	0.00502	.1103	.3191
24	288	2.05259	422.08784	0.48719	205.12407	0.00488	.0560	.2775
25	300	2.11502	447.12284	0.47281	210.87644	0.00474	.0	.2346
26	312	2.17935	472.91931	0.45885	216.45902	0.00462	.0	.1905
27	324	2.24564	499.50040	0.44531	221.87681	0.00451	.0	.1449
28	336	2.31394	526.88998	0.43216	227.13467	0.00440	.0	.0981
29	348	2.38432	555.11264	0.41941	232.23733	0.00431	.0	.0498
30	360	2.45684	584.19373	0.40703	237.18937	0.00422	.0	.0
31	372	2.53157	614.15934	0.39501	241.99524	0.00413	.0	.0
32	384	2.60857	645.03638	0.38335	246.65924	0.00405	.0	.0
33	396	2.68791	676.85257	0.37204	251.18557	0.00398	.0	.0
34	408	2.76967	709.63649	0.36105	255.57830	0.00391	.0	.0
35	420	2.85391	743.41756	0.35040	259.84136	0.00385	.0	.0
36	432	2.94071	778.22612	0.34005	263.97858	0.00379	.0	.0
37	444	3.03016	814.09341	0.33002	267.99368	0.00373	.0	.0
38	456	3.12232	851.05164	0.32027	271.89025	0.00368	.0	.0
39	468	3.21729	889.13399	0.31082	275.67181	0.00363	.0	.0
40	480	3.31515	928.37465	0.30165	279.34175	0.00358	.0	.0

YR	MOS	(1) COMPOUND VALUE $1	(2) COMPOUND VALUE $1 PER MO	(3) PRESENT VALUE $1	(4) PRESENT VALUE $1 PER MO	(5) LOAN CONSTANT	(6) BAL 25 YR LOAN	(7) BAL 30 YR LOAN
	1	1.00333	1.00333	0.99668	0.99668	1.00333	.9981	.9986
	2	1.00668	2.01001	0.99337	1.99004	0.50250	.9961	.9971
	3	1.01003	3.02004	0.99007	2.98011	0.33556	.9941	.9957
	4	1.01340	4.03344	0.98678	3.96689	0.25209	.9922	.9942
	5	1.01678	5.05022	0.98350	4.95039	0.20200	.9902	.9927
	6	1.02017	6.07039	0.98023	5.93062	0.16862	.9882	.9913
	7	1.02357	7.09396	0.97697	6.90759	0.14477	.9862	.9898
	8	1.02698	8.12094	0.97373	7.88132	0.12688	.9843	.9883
	9	1.03040	9.15134	0.97049	8.85181	0.11297	.9823	.9869
	10	1.03384	10.18518	0.96727	9.81908	0.10184	.9803	.9854
	11	1.03728	11.22246	0.96406	10.78314	0.09274	.9782	.9839
	12	1.04074	12.26321	0.96085	11.74399	0.08515	.9762	.9824
2	24	1.08314	25.02603	0.92324	23.02825	0.04342	.9515	.9641
3	36	1.12727	38.30883	0.88710	33.87076	0.02952	.9257	.9450
4	48	1.17320	52.13280	0.85237	44.28883	0.02258	.8989	.9251
5	60	1.22100	66.51998	0.81900	54.29907	0.01842	.8710	.9045
6	72	1.27074	81.49331	0.78694	63.91743	0.01565	.8420	.8830
7	84	1.32251	97.07667	0.75614	73.15927	0.01367	.8118	.8606
8	96	1.37640	113.29493	0.72654	82.03933	0.01219	.7804	.8373
9	108	1.43247	130.17395	0.69809	90.57176	0.01104	.7476	.8131
10	120	1.49083	147.74064	0.67077	98.77017	0.01012	.7136	.7878
11	132	1.55157	166.02302	0.64451	106.64764	0.00938	.6781	.7616
12	144	1.61478	185.05026	0.61928	114.21674	0.00876	.6413	.7343
13	156	1.68057	204.85270	0.59503	121.48953	0.00823	.6029	.7058
14	168	1.74904	225.46192	0.57174	128.47762	0.00778	.5629	.6762
15	180	1.82030	246.91079	0.54936	135.19214	0.00740	.5213	.6454
16	192	1.89446	269.23352	0.52785	141.64382	0.00706	.4781	.6134
17	204	1.97165	292.46571	0.50719	147.84293	0.00676	.4330	.5800
18	216	2.05197	316.64442	0.48734	153.79937	0.00650	.3861	.5453
19	228	2.13558	341.80821	0.46826	159.52263	0.00627	.3374	.5091
20	240	2.22258	367.99721	0.44993	165.02185	0.00606	.2866	.4715
21	252	2.31313	395.25319	0.43231	170.30579	0.00587	.2338	.4324
22	264	2.40737	423.61961	0.41539	175.38289	0.00570	.1788	.3916
23	276	2.50545	453.14173	0.39913	180.26123	0.00555	.1215	.3493
24	288	2.60753	483.86663	0.38350	184.94860	0.00541	.0620	.3051
25	300	2.71377	515.84331	0.36849	189.45247	0.00528	.0	.2592
26	312	2.82433	549.12277	0.35407	193.78004	0.00516	.0	.2114
27	324	2.93940	583.75808	0.34021	197.93819	0.00505	.0	.1617
28	336	3.05915	619.80449	0.32689	201.93357	0.00495	.0	.1099
29	348	3.18379	657.31948	0.31409	205.77254	0.00486	.0	.0560
30	360	3.31350	696.36290	0.30180	209.46123	0.00477	.0	.0
31	372	3.44849	736.99700	0.28998	213.00552	0.00469	.0	.0
32	384	3.58899	779.28660	0.27863	216.41106	0.00462	.0	.0
33	396	3.73521	823.29914	0.26772	219.68329	0.00455	.0	.0
34	408	3.88739	869.10482	0.25724	222.82742	0.00449	.0	.0
35	420	4.04577	916.77670	0.24717	225.84846	0.00443	.0	.0
36	432	4.21060	966.39080	0.23750	228.75125	0.00437	.0	.0
37	444	4.38215	1018.02626	0.22820	231.54040	0.00432	.0	.0
38	456	4.56068	1071.76542	0.21927	234.22036	0.00427	.0	.0
39	468	4.74649	1127.69400	0.21068	236.79541	0.00422	.0	.0
40	480	4.93987	1185.90120	0.20243	239.26966	0.00418	.0	.0

INTEREST RATE = 5.00%

YR	MOS	(1) COMPOUND VALUE $1	(2) COMPOUND VALUE $1 PER MO	(3) PRESENT VALUE $1	(4) PRESENT VALUE $1 PER MO	(5) LOAN CONSTANT	(6) BAL 25 YR LOAN	(7) BAL 30 YR LOAN
	1	1.00417	1.00417	0.99585	0.99585	1.00417	.9983	.9988
	2	1.00835	2.01252	0.99172	1.98757	0.50313	.9966	.9976
	3	1.01255	3.02507	0.98760	2.97517	0.33611	.9949	.9964
	4	1.01677	4.04184	0.98351	3.95868	0.25261	.9932	.9952
	5	1.02101	5.06285	0.97942	4.93810	0.20251	.9915	.9939
	6	1.02526	6.08811	0.97536	5.91346	0.16911	.9898	.9927
	7	1.02953	7.11764	0.97131	6.88478	0.14525	.9881	.9915
	8	1.03382	8.15147	0.96728	7.85206	0.12736	.9864	.9902
	9	1.03813	9.18960	0.96327	8.81533	0.11344	.9846	.9890
	10	1.04246	10.23206	0.95927	9.77460	0.10231	.9829 • .9878	
	11	1.04680	11.27886	0.95529	10.72989	0.09320	.9811	.9865
	12	1.05116	12.33002	0.95133	11.68122	0.08561	.9794	.9852
2	24	1.10494	25.29086	0.90503	22.79390	0.04387	.9577	.9697
3	36	1.16147	38.91481	0.86098	33.36570	0.02997	.9349	.9534
4	48	1.22090	53.23578	0.81907	43.42295	0.02303	.9110	.9363
5	60	1.28336	68.28944	0.77921	52.99070	0.01887	.8858	.9183
6	72	1.34902	84.11328	0.74128	62.09277	0.01610	.8593	.8993
7	84	1.41804	100.74669	0.70520	70.75183	0.01413	.8315	.8794
8	96	1.49059	118.23110	0.67088	78.98944	0.01266	.8023	.8585
9	108	1.56685	136.61004	0.63822	86.82610	0.01152	.7715	.8365
10	120	1.64701	155.92929	0.60716	94.28135	0.01061	.7392	.8134
11	132	1.73127	176.23694	0.57761	101.37373	0.00986	.7053	.7891
12	144	1.81985	197.58358	0.54950	108.12091	0.00925	.6696	.7636
13	156	1.91296	220.02235	0.52275	114.53970	0.00873	.6321	.7367
14	168	2.01083	243.60912	0.49731	120.64607	0.00829	.5926	.7085
15	180	2.11370	268.40265	0.47310	126.45524	0.00791	.5511	.6788
16	192	2.22185	294.46465	0.45008	131.98166	0.00758	.5076	.6476
17	204	2.33552	321.86004	0.42817	137.23910	0.00729	.4617	.6149
18	216	2.45501	350.65703	0.40733	142.24066	0.00703	.4136	.5804
19	228	2.58061	380.92732	0.38751	146.99877	0.00680	.3630	.5442
20	240	2.71264	412.74631	0.36864	151.52531	0.00660	.3098	.5061
21	252	2.85142	446.19321	0.35070	155.83152	0.00642	.2538	.4661
22	264	2.99731	481.35132	0.33363	159.92815	0.00625	.1950	.4240
23	276	3.15066	518.30818	0.31739	163.82539	0.00610	.1332	.3798
24	288	3.31185	557.15583	0.30195	167.53294	0.00597	.0683	.3333
25	300	3.48129	597.99099	0.28725	171.06004	0.00585	.0	.2844
26	312	3.65940	640.91536	0.27327	174.41547	0.00573	.0	.2331
27	324	3.84662	686.03583	0.25997	177.60758	0.00563	.0	.1791
28	336	4.04342	733.46474	0.24732	180.64433	0.00554	.0	.1223
29	348	4.25029	783.32020	0.23528	183.53327	0.00545	.0	.0627
30	360	4.46774	835.72637	0.22383	186.28161	0.00537	.0	.0
31	372	4.69632	890.81373	0.21293	188.89617	0.00529	.0	.0
32	384	4.93660	948.71947	0.20257	191.38349	0.00523	.0	.0
33	396	5.18916	1009.58778	0.19271	193.74974	0.00516	.0	.0
34	408	5.45465	1073.57022	0.18333	196.00082	0.00510	.0	.0
35	420	5.73372	1140.82613	0.17441	198.14233	0.00505	.0	.0
36	432	6.02707	1211.52297	0.16592	200.17962	0.00500	.0	.0
37	444	6.33542	1285.83681	0.15784	202.11775	0.00495	.0	.0
38	456	6.65955	1363.95267	0.15016	203.96154	0.00490	.0	.0
39	468	7.00027	1446.06510	0.14285	205.71560	0.00486	.0	.0
40	480	7.35842	1532.37855	0.13590	207.38428	0.00482	.0	.0

INTEREST RATE = 6.00%

YR	MOS	(1) COMPOUND VALUE $1	(2) COMPOUND VALUE $1 PER MO	(3) PRESENT VALUE $1	(4) PRESENT VALUE $1 PER MO	(5) LOAN CONSTANT	(6) BAL 25 YR LOAN	(7) BAL 30 YR LOAN
	1	1.00500	1.00500	0.99502	0.99502	1.00500	.9986	.9990
	2	1.01003	2.01503	0.99007	1.98510	0.50375	.9971	.9980
	3	1.01508	3.03010	0.98515	2.97025	0.33667	.9956	.9970
	4	1.02015	4.05025	0.98025	3.95050	0.25313	.9942	.9960
	5	1.02525	5.07550	0.97537	4.92587	0.20301	.9927	.9950
	6	1.03038	6.10588	0.97052	5.89638	0.16960	.9912	.9940
	7	1.03553	7.14141	0.96569	6.86207	0.14573	.9897	.9929
	8	1.04071	8.18212	0.96089	7.82296	0.12783	.9883	.9919
	9	1.04591	9.22803	0.95610	8.77906	0.11391	.9867	.9909
	10	1.05114	10.27917	0.95135	9.73041	0.10277	.9852	.9898
	11	1.05640	11.33556	0.94661	10.67703	0.09366	.9837	.9888
	12	1.06168	12.39724	0.94191	11.61893	0.08607	.9822	.9877
2	24	1.12716	25.55912	0.88719	22.56286	0.04432	.9633	.9747
3	36	1.19668	39.53279	0.83564	32.87101	0.03042	.9432	.9608
4	48	1.27049	54.36832	0.78710	42.58032	0.02349	.9219	.9461
5	60	1.34885	70.11888	0.74137	51.72556	0.01933	.8993	.9305
6	72	1.43204	86.84090	0.69830	60.33951	0.01657	.8753	.9140
7	84	1.52037	104.59430	0.65773	68.45304	0.01461	.8498	.8964
8	96	1.61414	123.44268	0.61952	76.09521	0.01314	.8228	.8777
9	108	1.71370	143.45360	0.58353	83.29342	0.01201	.7940	.8579
10	120	1.81940	164.69874	0.54963	90.07345	0.01110	.7635	.8368
11	132	1.93161	187.25424	0.51770	96.45959	0.01037	.7311	.8145
12	144	2.05075	211.20091	0.48763	102.47474	0.00976	.6967	.7908
13	156	2.17724	236.62456	0.45930	108.14044	0.00925	.6602	.7656
14	168	2.31152	263.61629	0.43262	113.47698	0.00881	.6215	.7389
15	180	2.45409	292.27280	0.40748	118.50351	0.00844	.5803	.7105
16	192	2.60546	322.69679	0.38381	123.23802	0.00811	.5366	.6803
17	204	2.76616	354.99726	0.36151	127.69748	0.00783	.4903	.6483
18	216	2.93677	389.28996	0.34051	131.89787	0.00758	.4410	.6144
19	228	3.11790	425.69775	0.32073	135.85424	0.00736	.3887	.5783
20	240	3.31020	464.35110	0.30210	139.58076	0.00716	.3332	.5400
21	252	3.51437	505.38849	0.28455	143.09080	0.00699	.2743	.4994
22	264	3.73113	548.95699	0.26802	146.39692	0.00683	.2118	.4562
23	276	3.96126	595.21270	0.25245	149.51097	0.00669	.1453	.4104
24	288	4.20558	644.32135	0.23778	152.44411	0.00656	.0748	.3617
25	300	4.46497	696.45892	0.22397	155.20686	0.00644	.0	.3101
26	312	4.74036	751.81223	0.21095	157.80910	0.00634	.0	.2553
27	324	5.03273	810.57960	0.19870	160.26016	0.00624	.0	.1970
28	336	5.34314	872.97161	0.18716	162.56883	0.00615	.0	.1352
29	348	5.67270	939.21183	0.17628	164.74338	0.00607	.0	.0696
30	360	6.02258	1009.53760	0.16604	166.79160	0.00600	.0	.0
31	372	6.39403	1084.20091	0.15640	168.72083	0.00593	.0	.0
32	384	6.78840	1163.46929	0.14731	170.53799	0.00586	.0	.0
33	396	7.20710	1247.62677	0.13875	172.24957	0.00581	.0	.0
34	408	7.65162	1336.97490	0.13069	173.86172	0.00575	.0	.0
35	420	8.12355	1431.83382	0.12310	175.38021	0.00570	.0	.0
36	432	8.62459	1532.54344	0.11595	176.81049	0.00566	.0	.0
37	444	9.15654	1639.46460	0.10921	178.15768	0.00561	.0	.0
38	456	9.72130	1752.98043	0.10287	179.42660	0.00557	.0	.0
39	468	10.32088	1873.49767	0.09689	180.62180	0.00554	.0	.0
40	480	10.95745	2001.44814	0.09126	181.74757	0.00550	.0	.0

INTEREST RATE = 6.50%

YR	MOS	(1) COMPOUND VALUE $1	(2) COMPOUND VALUE $1 PER MO	(3) PRESENT VALUE $1	(4) PRESENT VALUE $1 PER MO	(5) LOAN CONSTANT	(6) BAL 25 YR LOAN	(7) BAL 30 YR LOAN
	1	1.00542	1.00542	0.99461	0.99461	1.00542	.9987	.9991
	2	1.01086	2.01628	0.98925	1.98387	0.50407	.9973	.9982
	3	1.01634	3.03262	0.98392	2.96779	0.33695	.9960	.9973
	4	1.02184	4.05446	0.97862	3.94641	0.25339	.9946	.9964
	5	1.02738	5.08184	0.97335	4.91977	0.20326	.9932	.9954
	6	1.03294	6.11478	0.96811	5.88787	0.16984	.9919	.9945
	7	1.03854	7.15332	0.96289	6.85076	0.14597	.9905	.9936
	8	1.04416	8.19749	0.95770	7.80847	0.12807	.9891	.9926
	9	1.04982	9.24730	0.95254	8.76101	0.11414	.9877	.9917
	10	1.05551	10.30281	0.94741	9.70843	0.10300	.9863	.9907
	11	1.06122	11.36403	0.94231	10.65073	0.09389	.9849	.9898
	12	1.06697	12.43101	0.93723	11.58797	0.08630	.9835	.9888
2	24	1.13843	25.69454	0.87840	22.44858	0.04455	.9659	.9769
3	36	1.21467	39.84636	0.82327	32.62749	0.03065	.9471	.9642
4	48	1.29602	54.94595	0.77159	42.16749	0.02371	.9270	.9506
5	60	1.38282	71.05679	0.72316	51.10868	0.01957	.9056	.9361
6	72	1.47543	88.24660	0.67777	59.48865	0.01681	.8828	.9206
7	84	1.57424	106.58764	0.63523	67.34262	0.01485	.8584	.9042
8	96	1.67967	126.15702	0.59536	74.70361	0.01339	.8324	.8866
9	108	1.79216	147.03699	0.55799	81.60257	0.01225	.8047	.8678
10	120	1.91218	169.31534	0.52296	88.06850	0.01135	.7751	.8478
11	132	2.04025	193.08571	0.49014	94.12857	0.01062	.7435	.8264
12	144	2.17689	218.44802	0.45937	99.80826	0.01002	.7098	.8036
13	156	2.32268	245.50889	0.43054	105.13144	0.00951	.6739	.7792
14	168	2.47823	274.38208	0.40351	110.12050	0.00908	.6355	.7533
15	180	2.64420	305.18897	0.37819	114.79641	0.00871	.5946	.7256
16	192	2.82129	338.05904	0.35445	119.17881	0.00839	.5510	.6960
17	204	3.01023	373.13049	0.33220	123.28615	0.00811	.5044	.6645
18	216	3.21184	410.55073	0.31135	127.13567	0.00787	.4547	.6308
19	228	3.42694	450.47708	0.29181	130.74356	0.00765	.4016	.5949
20	240	3.65645	493.07737	0.27349	134.12500	0.00746	.3451	.5566
21	252	3.90133	538.53068	0.25632	137.29419	0.00728	.2847	.5158
22	264	4.16260	587.02808	0.24023	140.26445	0.00713	.2203	.4721
23	276	4.44138	638.77345	0.22516	143.04827	0.00699	.1515	.4256
24	288	4.73883	693.98429	0.21102	145.65736	0.00687	.0782	.3760
25	300	5.05620	752.89271	0.19778	148.10269	0.00675	.0	.3230
26	312	5.39482	815.74634	0.18536	150.39452	0.00665	.0	.2665
27	324	5.75612	882.80938	0.17373	152.54250	0.00656	.0	.2062
28	336	6.14162	954.36377	0.16282	154.55566	0.00647	.0	.1418
29	348	6.55294	1030.71028	0.15260	156.44245	0.00639	.0	.0732
30	360	6.99180	1112.16986	0.14302	158.21081	0.00632	.0	.0
31	372	7.46005	1199.08495	0.13405	159.86818	0.00626	.0	.0
32	384	7.95966	1291.82089	0.12563	161.42151	0.00619	.0	.0
33	396	8.49274	1390.76753	0.11775	162.87735	0.00614	.0	.0
34	408	9.06151	1496.34081	0.11036	164.24180	0.00609	.0	.0
35	420	9.66838	1608.98453	0.10343	165.52061	0.00604	.0	.0
36	432	10.31589	1729.17221	0.09694	166.71916	0.00600	.0	.0
37	444	11.00676	1857.40908	0.09085	167.84247	0.00596	.0	.0
38	456	11.74391	1994.23421	0.08515	168.89527	0.00592	.0	.0
39	468	12.53042	2140.22277	0.07981	169.88199	0.00589	.0	.0
40	480	13.36960	2295.98846	0.07480	170.80678	0.00585	.0	.0

YR	MOS	(1) COMPOUND VALUE $1	(2) COMPOUND VALUE $1 PER MO	(3) PRESENT VALUE $1	(4) PRESENT VALUE $1 PER MO	(5) LOAN CONSTANT	(6) BAL 25 YR LOAN	(7) BAL 30 YR LOAN
	1	1.00583	1.00583	0.99420	0.99420	1.00583	.9988	.9992
	2	1.01170	2.01753	0.98843	1.98263	0.50438	.9975	.9984
	3	1.01760	3.03514	0.98270	2.96534	0.33723	.9963	.9975
	4	1.02354	4.05867	0.97700	3.94234	0.25366	.9950	.9967
	5	1.02951	5.08818	0.97134	4.91368	0.20351	.9938	.9959
	6	1.03551	6.12370	0.96570	5.87938	0.17009	.9925	.9950
	7	1.04155	7.16525	0.96010	6.83948	0.14621	.9912	.9942
	8	1.04763	8.21288	0.95453	7.79402	0.12830	.9899	.9933
	9	1.05374	9.26663	0.94900	8.74302	0.11438	.9886	.9924
	10	1.05989	10.32651	0.94350	9.68651	0.10324	.9873	.9916
	11	1.06607	11.39259	0.93802	10.62454	0.09412	.9860	.9907
	12	1.07229	12.46488	0.93258	11.55712	0.08653	.9847	.9898
2	24	1.14981	25.83084	0.86971	22.33510	0.04477	.9683	.9789
3	36	1.23293	40.16303	0.81108	32.38646	0.03088	.9507	.9673
4	48	1.32205	55.53129	0.75640	41.76020	0.02395	.9318	.9547
5	60	1.41763	72.01053	0.70540	50.50199	0.01980	.9116	.9413
6	72	1.52011	89.68105	0.65785	58.65444	0.01705	.8899	.9269
7	84	1.62999	108.62897	0.61350	66.25728	0.01509	.8667	.9115
8	96	1.74783	128.94665	0.57214	73.34757	0.01363	.8417	.8949
9	108	1.87418	150.73309	0.53357	79.95985	0.01251	.8150	.8772
10	120	2.00966	174.09447	0.49760	86.12635	0.01161	.7863	.8581
11	132	2.15494	199.14465	0.46405	91.87713	0.01088	.7556	.8377
12	144	2.31072	226.00570	0.43277	97.24021	0.01028	.7226	.8158
13	156	2.47776	254.80855	0.40359	102.24173	0.00978	.6873	.7923
14	168	2.65688	285.69356	0.37638	106.90607	0.00935	.6494	.7672
15	180	2.84895	318.81124	0.35101	111.25595	0.00899	.6087	.7402
16	192	3.05490	354.32301	0.32734	115.31258	0.00867	.5651	.7112
17	204	3.27574	392.40192	0.30527	119.09573	0.00840	.5184	.6802
18	216	3.51254	433.23356	0.28469	122.62382	0.00816	.4683	.6469
19	228	3.76646	477.01693	0.26550	125.91407	0.00794	.4145	.6112
20	240	4.03874	523.96539	0.24760	128.98250	0.00775	.3569	.5730
21	252	4.33070	574.30777	0.23091	131.84407	0.00758	.2951	.5319
22	264	4.64377	628.28940	0.21534	134.51272	0.00743	.2289	.4880
23	276	4.97946	666.17336	0.20082	137.00145	0.00730	.1578	.4408
24	288	5.33943	748.24177	0.18729	139.32241	0.00718	.0816	.3902
25	300	5.72542	814.79710	0.17466	141.48690	0.00707	.0	.3360
26	312	6.13931	886.16372	0.16288	143.50546	0.00697	.0	.2778
27	324	6.58312	962.68944	0.15190	145.38794	0.00688	.0	.2154
28	336	7.05901	1044.74721	0.14166	147.14351	0.00680	.0	.1485
29	348	7.56931	1132.73695	0.13211	148.78072	0.00672	.0	.0768
30	360	8.11650	1227.80747	0.12321	150.30756	0.00665	.0	.0
31	372	8.70324	1328.25859	0.11490	151.73146	0.00659	.0	.0
32	384	9.33240	1436.74339	0.10715	153.05937	0.00653	.0	.0
33	396	10.00704	1553.07056	0.09993	154.29776	0.00648	.0	.0
34	408	10.73045	1677.80703	0.09319	155.45266	0.00643	.0	.0
35	420	11.50615	1811.56071	0.08691	156.52970	0.00639	.0	.0
36	432	12.33793	1954.98345	0.08105	157.53413	0.00635	.0	.0
37	444	13.22984	2108.77423	0.07559	158.47084	0.00631	.0	.0
38	456	14.18623	2273.68257	0.07049	159.34441	0.00628	.0	.0
39	468	15.21175	2450.51214	0.06574	160.15908	0.00624	.0	.0
40	480	16.31141	2640.12473	0.06131	160.91883	0.00621	.0	.0

INTEREST RATE = 7.25%

YR	MOS	(1) COMPOUND VALUE $1	(2) COMPOUND VALUE $1 PER MO	(3) PRESENT VALUE $1	(4) PRESENT VALUE $1 PER MO	(5) LOAN CONSTANT	(6) BAL 25 YR LOAN	(7) BAL 30 YR LOAN
	1	1.00604	1.00604	0.99399	0.99399	1.00604	.9988	.9992
	2	1.01212	2.01816	0.98803	1.98202	0.50454	.9976	.9984
	3	1.01823	3.03640	0.98209	2.96411	0.33737	.9964	.9976
	4	1.02439	4.06078	0.97619	3.94031	0.25379	.9952	.9969
	5	1.03058	5.09136	0.97033	4.91064	0.20364	.9940	.9961
	6	1.03680	6.12816	0.96450	5.87514	0.17021	.9928	.9952
	7	1.04307	7.17123	0.95871	6.83385	0.14633	.9915	.9944
	8	1.04937	8.22059	0.95295	7.78681	0.12842	.9903	.9936
	9	1.05571	9.27630	0.94723	8.73404	0.11449	.9891	.9928
	10	1.06209	10.33839	0.94154	9.67558	0.10335	.9878	.9920
	11	1.06850	11.40689	0.93589	10.61147	0.09424	.9865	.9912
	12	1.07496	12.48185	0.93027	11.54174	0.08664	.9853	.9903
2	24	1.15554	25.89932	0.86540	22.27866	0.04489	.9695	.9799
3	36	1.24215	40.32253	0.80505	32.26688	0.03099	.9524	.9687
4	48	1.33526	55.82689	0.74892	41.55861	0.02406	.9342	.9567
5	60	1.43535	72.49343	0.69669	50.20241	0.01992	.9145	.9438
6	72	1.54294	90.40926	0.64811	58.24347	0.01717	.8934	.9299
7	84	1.65860	109.66803	0.60292	65.72381	0.01522	.8707	.9150
8	96	1.78292	130.37041	0.56088	72.68254	0.01376	.8463	.8989
9	108	1.91657	152.62461	0.52177	79.15603	0.01263	.8200	.8816
10	120	2.06023	176.54693	0.48538	85.17812	0.01174	.7918	.8631
11	132	2.21466	202.26244	0.45154	90.78027	0.01102	.7615	.8432
12	144	2.38067	229.90455	0.42005	95.99178	0.01042	.7289	.8217
13	156	2.55912	259.62071	0.39076	100.83989	0.00992	.6938	.7987
14	168	2.75095	291.56329	0.36351	105.34992	0.00949	.6562	.7739
15	180	2.95716	325.90023	0.33816	109.54547	0.00913	.6157	.7473
16	192	3.17882	362.81100	0.31458	113.44846	0.00881	.5721	.7187
17	204	3.41710	402.48854	0.29265	117.07928	0.00854	.5253	.6879
18	216	3.67324	445.14025	0.27224	120.45693	0.00830	.4750	.6548
19	228	3.94858	490.98905	0.25326	123.59904	0.00809	.4210	.6193
20	240	4.24456	540.27460	0.23560	126.52206	0.00790	.3628	.5810
21	252	4.56272	593.25451	0.21917	129.24124	0.00774	.3004	.5400
22	264	4.90473	650.20571	0.20388	131.77082	0.00759	.2332	.4958
23	276	5.27239	711.42587	0.18967	134.12400	0.00746	.1610	.4483
24	288	5.66759	777.23499	0.17644	136.31309	0.00734	.0834	.3973
25	300	6.09243	847.97705	0.16414	138.34954	0.00723	.0	.3424
26	312	6.54911	924.02182	0.15269	140.24398	0.00713	.0	.2835
27	324	7.04002	1005.76677	0.14205	142.00631	0.00704	.0	.2201
28	336	7.56772	1093.63918	0.13214	143.64576	0.00696	.0	.1519
29	348	8.13499	1188.09836	0.12293	145.17089	0.00689	.0	.0787
30	360	8.74477	1289.63803	0.11435	146.58967	0.00682	.0	.0
31	372	9.40026	1398.78895	0.10638	147.90951	0.00676	.0	.0
32	384	10.10489	1516.12164	0.09896	149.13732	0.00671	.0	.0
33	396	10.86234	1642.24938	0.09206	150.27951	0.00665	.0	.0
34	408	11.67656	1777.83145	0.08564	151.34206	0.00661	.0	.0
35	420	12.55182	1923.57651	0.07967	152.33051	0.00656	.0	.0
36	432	13.49268	2080.24638	0.07411	153.25004	0.00653	.0	.0
37	444	14.50407	2248.65995	0.06895	154.10545	0.00649	.0	.0
38	456	15.59127	2429.69752	0.06414	154.90121	0.00646	.0	.0
39	468	16.75996	2624.30535	0.05967	155.64148	0.00643	.0	.0
40	480	18.01626	2833.50066	0.05551	156.33013	0.00640	.0	.0

INTEREST RATE =   7.50%

YR	MOS	(1) COMPOUND VALUE $1	(2) COMPOUND VALUE $1 PER MO	(3) PRESENT VALUE $1	(4) PRESENT VALUE $1 PER MO	(5) LOAN CONSTANT	(6) BAL 25 YR LOAN	(7) BAL 30 YR LOAN
	1	1.00625	1.00625	0.99379	0.99379	1.00625	.9989	.9993
	2	1.01254	2.01879	0.98762	1.98140	0.50469	.9977	.9985
	3	1.01887	3.03766	0.98148	2.96289	0.33751	.9966	.9978
	4	1.02524	4.06289	0.97539	3.93827	0.25392	.9954	.9970
	5	1.03164	5.09454	0.96933	4.90760	0.20377	.9942	.9962
	6	1.03809	6.13263	0.96331	5.87091	0.17033	.9931	.9955
	7	1.04458	7.17721	0.95732	6.82823	0.14645	.9919	.9947
	8	1.05111	8.22831	0.95138	7.77961	0.12854	.9907	.9939
	9	1.05768	9.28599	0.94547	8.72508	0.11461	.9895	.9932
	10	1.06429	10.35028	0.93960	9.66467	0.10347	.9883	.9924
	11	1.07094	11.42122	0.93376	10.59843	0.09435	.9871	.9916
	12	1.07763	12.49885	0.92796	11.52639	0.08676	.9858	.9908
2	24	1.16129	25.96802	0.86111	22.22242	0.04500	.9706	.9808
3	36	1.25145	40.48283	0.79908	32.14791	0.03111	.9541	.9701
4	48	1.34860	56.12446	0.74151	41.35837	0.02418	.9364	.9586
5	60	1.45329	72.98040	0.68809	49.90531	0.02004	.9173	.9462
6	72	1.56612	91.14491	0.63852	57.83652	0.01729	.8967	.9328
7	84	1.68770	110.71957	0.59252	65.19637	0.01534	.8746	.9183
8	96	1.81872	131.81387	0.54984	72.02602	0.01368	.8507	.9028
9	108	1.95991	154.54577	0.51023	78.36366	0.01276	.8249	.8860
10	120	2.11206	179.04241	0.47347	84.24474	0.01187	.7972	.8679
11	132	2.27603	205.44078	0.43936	89.70214	0.01115	.7673	.8485
12	144	2.45272	233.88853	0.40771	94.76640	0.01055	.7350	.8275
13	156	2.64314	264.54475	0.37834	99.46582	0.01005	.7003	.8049
14	168	2.84833	297.58090	0.35108	103.82670	0.00963	.6629	.7805
15	180	3.06945	333.18173	0.32579	107.87342	0.00927	.6225	.7543
16	192	3.30774	371.54634	0.30232	111.62862	0.00896	.5791	.7260
17	204	3.56453	412.88929	0.28054	115.11329	0.00869	.5322	.6955
18	216	3.84125	457.44181	0.26033	118.34692	0.00845	.4818	.6626
19	228	4.13946	505.45305	0.24158	121.34761	0.00824	.4274	.6272
20	240	4.46082	557.19153	0.22417	124.13212	0.00806	.3688	.5890
21	252	4.80712	612.94661	0.20802	126.71604	0.00789	.3056	.5479
22	264	5.18031	673.03009	0.19304	129.11382	0.00775	.2375	.5036
23	276	5.58247	737.77802	0.17913	131.33886	0.00761	.1642	.4558
24	288	6.01585	807.55249	0.16623	133.40360	0.00750	.0851	.4044
25	300	6.48288	882.74374	0.15425	135.31960	0.00739	.0	.3489
26	312	6.98616	963.77227	0.14314	137.09758	0.00729	.0	.2891
27	324	7.52852	1051.09127	0.13283	138.74747	0.00721	.0	.2247
28	336	8.11298	1145.18906	0.12326	140.27850	0.00713	.0	.1553
29	348	8.74281	1246.59191	0.11438	141.69923	0.00706	.0	.0805
30	360	9.42153	1355.86693	0.10614	143.01762	0.00699	.0	.0
31	372	10.15295	1473.62525	0.09849	144.24103	0.00693	.0	.0
32	384	10.94115	1600.52545	0.09140	145.37630	0.00688	.0	.0
33	396	11.79054	1737.27725	0.08481	146.42979	0.00683	.0	.0
34	408	12.70587	1884.64544	0.07870	147.40739	0.00678	.0	.0
35	420	13.69226	2043.45421	0.07303	148.31456	0.00674	.0	.0
36	432	14.75523	2214.59172	0.06777	149.15637	0.00670	.0	.0
37	444	15.90071	2399.01507	0.06289	149.93755	0.00667	.0	.0
38	456	17.13513	2597.75569	0.05836	150.66244	0.00664	.0	.0
39	468	18.46537	2811.92506	0.05416	151.33512	0.00661	.0	.0
40	480	19.89889	3042.72096	0.05025	151.95934	0.00658	.0	.0

INTEREST RATE = 7.75%

YR	MOS	(1) COMPOUND VALUE $1	(2) COMPOUND VALUE $1 PER MO	(3) PRESENT VALUE $1	(4) PRESENT VALUE $1 PER MO	(5) LOAN CONSTANT	(6) BAL 25 YR LOAN	(7) BAL 30 YR LOAN
	1	1.00646	1.00646	0.99358	0.99358	1.00646	.9989	.9993
	2	1.01296	2.01942	0.98721	1.98079	0.50485	.9978	.9986
	3	1.01950	3.03892	0.98087	2.96166	0.33765	.9967	.9979
	4	1.02608	4.06500	0.97458	3.93624	0.25405	.9956	.9971
	5	1.03271	5.09771	0.96832	4.90457	0.20389	.9945	.9964
	6	1.03938	6.13709	0.96211	5.86668	0.17045	.9933	.9957
	7	1.04609	7.18319	0.95594	6.82261	0.14657	.9922	.9950
	8	1.05285	8.23604	0.94980	7.77242	0.12866	.9910	.9942
	9	1.05965	9.29569	0.94371	8.71613	0.11473	.9899	.9935
	10	1.06649	10.36218	0.93765	9.65378	0.10359	.9887	.9927
	11	1.07338	11.43556	0.93164	10.58541	0.09447	.9876	.9920
	12	1.08031	12.51587	0.92566	11.51107	0.08687	.9864	.9912
2	24	1.16708	26.03694	0.85684	22.16638	0.04511	.9717	.9817
3	36	1.26081	40.64391	0.79314	32.02955	0.03122	.9558	.9715
4	48	1.36207	56.42402	0.73418	41.15947	0.02430	.9386	.9604
5	60	1.47146	73.47148	0.67960	49.61065	0.02016	.9201	.9485
6	72	1.58964	91.88807	0.62907	57.43355	0.01741	.9000	.9356
7	84	1.71730	111.78375	0.58231	64.67488	0.01546	.8784	.9216
8	96	1.85523	133.27731	0.53902	71.37787	0.01401	.8550	.9065
9	108	2.00422	156.49708	0.49895	77.58254	0.01289	.8297	.8902
10	120	2.16519	181.58171	0.46185	83.32595	0.01200	.8024	.8727
11	132	2.33908	208.68095	0.42752	88.64237	0.01128	.7730	.8536
12	144	2.52694	237.95662	0.39574	93.56356	0.01069	.7411	.8331
13	156	2.72989	269.58350	0.36632	98.11890	0.01019	.7067	.8109
14	168	2.94913	303.75043	0.33908	102.33558	0.00977	.6695	.7870
15	180	3.18599	340.66141	0.31387	106.23879	0.00941	.6294	.7611
16	192	3.44186	380.53683	0.29054	109.85182	0.00910	.5860	.7331
17	204	3.71829	423.61475	0.26894	113.19625	0.00883	.5391	.7029
18	216	4.01692	470.15240	0.24895	116.29205	0.00860	.4885	.6703
19	228	4.33953	520.42762	0.23044	119.15770	0.00839	.4338	.6350
20	240	4.68805	574.74059	0.21331	121.81030	0.00821	.3747	.5969
21	252	5.06456	633.41561	0.19745	124.26571	0.00805	.3109	.5558
22	264	5.47131	696.80299	0.18277	126.53858	0.00790	.2419	.5113
23	276	5.91073	765.28120	0.16918	128.64248	0.00777	.1674	.4633
24	288	6.38543	839.25910	0.15661	130.58997	0.00766	.0869	.4114
25	300	6.89827	919.17838	0.14496	132.39267	0.00755	.0	.3554
26	312	7.45229	1005.51623	0.13419	134.06136	0.00746	.0	.2948
27	324	8.05080	1098.78812	0.12421	135.60600	0.00737	.0	.2294
28	336	8.69739	1199.55096	0.11498	137.03580	0.00730	.0	.1587
29	348	9.39590	1308.40637	0.10643	138.35931	0.00723	.0	.0824
30	360	10.15051	1426.00428	0.09852	139.58443	0.00716	.0	.0
31	372	10.96573	1553.04683	0.09119	140.71847	0.00711	.0	.0
32	384	11.84642	1690.29255	0.08441	141.76820	0.00705	.0	.0
33	396	12.79784	1838.56088	0.07814	142.73989	0.00701	.0	.0
34	408	13.82568	1998.73709	0.07233	143.63934	0.00696	.0	.0
35	420	14.93606	2171.77753	0.06695	144.47193	0.00692	.0	.0
36	432	16.13562	2358.71536	0.06197	145.24262	0.00689	.0	.0
37	444	17.43152	2560.66673	0.05737	145.95601	0.00685	.0	.0
38	456	18.83150	2778.83742	0.05310	146.61637	0.00682	.0	.0
39	468	20.34391	3014.53006	0.04915	147.22764	0.00679	.0	.0
40	480	21.97779	3269.15187	0.04550	147.79346	0.00677	.0	.0

INTEREST RATE = 8.00%

YR	MOS	(1) COMPOUND VALUE $1	(2) COMPOUND VALUE $1 PER MO	(3) PRESENT VALUE $1	(4) PRESENT VALUE $1 PER MO	(5) LOAN CONSTANT	(6) BAL 25 YR LOAN	(7) BAL 30 YR LOAN
	1	1.00667	1.00667	0.99338	0.99338	1.00667	.9989	.9993
	2	1.01338	2.02004	0.98680	1.98018	0.50501	.9979	.9987
	3	1.02013	3.04018	0.98026	2.96044	0.33779	.9968	.9980
	4	1.02693	4.06711	0.97377	3.93421	0.25418	.9958	.9973
	5	1.03378	5.10089	0.96732	4.90153	0.20402	.9947	.9966
	6	1.04067	6.14157	0.96092	5.86245	0.17058	.9936	.9959
	7	1.04761	7.18918	0.95455	6.81700	0.14669	.9925	.9952
	8	1.05459	8.24377	0.94823	7.76524	0.12878	.9914	.9945
	9	1.06163	9.30540	0.94195	8.70719	0.11485	.9903	.9938
	10	1.06870	10.37410	0.93571	9.64290	0.10370	.9892	.9931
	11	1.07583	11.44993	0.92952	10.57242	0.09459	.9880	.9924
	12	1.08300	12.53293	0.92336	11.49578	0.08699	.9869	.9916
2	24	1.17289	26.10608	0.85260	22.11054	0.04523	.9727	.9826
3	36	1.27024	40.80580	0.78725	31.91180	0.03134	.9574	.9728
4	48	1.37567	56.72558	0.72692	40.96191	0.02441	.9407	.9622
5	60	1.48985	73.96670	0.67121	49.31843	0.02028	.9227	.9507
6	72	1.61350	92.63883	0.61977	57.03452	0.01753	.9032	.9382
7	84	1.74742	112.86073	0.57227	64.15926	0.01559	.8821	.9248
8	96	1.89246	134.76104	0.52841	70.73797	0.01414	.8592	.9102
9	108	2.04953	158.47907	0.48792	76.81249	0.01302	.8345	.8944
10	120	2.21964	184.16567	0.45052	82.42148	0.01213	.8076	.8772
11	132	2.40387	211.98426	0.41600	87.60060	0.01142	.7786	.8587
12	144	2.60339	242.11177	0.38411	92.38280	0.01082	.7471	.8386
13	156	2.81947	274.73986	0.35468	96.79849	0.01033	.7130	.8169
14	168	3.05348	310.07605	0.32749	100.87578	0.00991	.6761	.7933
15	180	3.30692	348.34514	0.30240	104.64059	0.00956	.6361	.7678
16	192	3.58139	389.79054	0.27922	108.11687	0.00925	.5928	.7402
17	204	3.87865	434.67589	0.25782	111.32673	0.00898	.5459	.7103
18	216	4.20057	483.28670	0.23806	114.29059	0.00875	.4952	.6778
19	228	4.54922	535.93218	0.21982	117.02731	0.00855	.4402	.6428
20	240	4.92680	592.94721	0.20297	119.55429	0.00836	.3806	.6048
21	252	5.33572	654.69446	0.18742	121.88760	0.00820	.3161	.5636
22	264	5.77859	721.56670	0.17305	124.04209	0.00806	.2463	.5190
23	276	6.25821	793.98931	0.15979	126.03147	0.00793	.1706	.4707
24	288	6.77764	872.42295	0.14754	127.86838	0.00782	.0887	.4185
25	300	7.34018	957.36655	0.13624	129.56451	0.00772	.0	.3618
26	312	7.94941	1049.36043	0.12580	131.13066	0.00763	.0	.3005
27	324	8.60920	1148.98975	0.11615	132.57678	0.00754	.0	.2341
28	336	9.32376	1256.88825	0.10725	133.91207	0.00747	.0	.1622
29	348	10.09763	1373.74228	0.09903	135.14502	0.00740	.0	.0843
30	360	10.93573	1500.29514	0.09144	136.28348	0.00734	.0	.0
31	372	11.84339	1637.35182	0.08444	137.33470	0.00728	.0	.0
32	384	12.82638	1785.78413	0.07796	138.30535	0.00723	.0	.0
33	396	13.89097	1946.53626	0.07199	139.20161	0.00718	.0	.0
34	408	15.04391	2120.63073	0.06647	140.02918	0.00714	.0	.0
35	420	16.29255	2309.17496	0.06138	140.79333	0.00710	.0	.0
36	432	17.64482	2513.36826	0.05667	141.49891	0.00707	.0	.0
37	444	19.10933	2734.50951	0.05233	142.15042	0.00703	.0	.0
38	456	20.69540	2974.00538	0.04832	142.75200	0.00701	.0	.0
39	468	22.41311	3233.37928	0.04462	143.30748	0.00698	.0	.0
40	480	24.27338	3514.28108	0.04120	143.82038	0.00695	.0	.0

INTEREST RATE = 8.25%

YR	MOS	(1) COMPOUND VALUE $1	(2) COMPOUND VALUE $1 PER MO	(3) PRESENT VALUE $1	(4) PRESENT VALUE $1 PER MO	(5) LOAN CONSTANT	(6) BAL 25 YR LOAN	(7) BAL 30 YR LOAN
	1	1.00688	1.00688	0.99317	0.99317	1.00688	.9990	.9994
	2	1.01380	2.02067	0.98639	1.97956	0.50516	.9980	.9987
	3	1.02077	3.04144	0.97966	2.95922	0.33793	.9970	.9981
	4	1.02778	4.06922	0.97297	3.93218	0.25431	.9959	.9974
	5	1.03485	5.10408	0.96632	4.89851	0.20414	.9949	.9968
	6	1.04197	6.14604	0.95972	5.85823	0.17070	.9938	.9961
	7	1.04913	7.19517	0.95317	6.81140	0.14681	.9928	.9954
	8	1.05634	8.25151	0.94666	7.75807	0.12890	.9917	.9948
	9	1.06360	9.31512	0.94020	8.69827	0.11497	.9907	.9941
	10	1.07092	10.38603	0.93378	9.63204	0.10382	.9896	.9934
	11	1.07828	11.46431	0.92740	10.55945	0.09470	.9885	.9927
	12	1.08569	12.55000	0.92107	11.48052	0.08710	.9874	.9921
2	24	1.17873	26.17544	0.84837	22.05490	0.04534	.9738	.9834
3	36	1.27974	40.96848	0.78141	31.79466	0.03145	.9589	.9741
4	48	1.38940	57.02916	0.71974	40.76567	0.02453	.9428	.9639
5	60	1.50846	74.46611	0.66293	49.02861	0.02040	.9253	.9528
6	72	1.63772	93.39727	0.61060	56.63938	0.01766	.9064	.9408
7	84	1.77806	113.95069	0.56241	63.64943	0.01571	.8857	.9278
8	96	1.93043	136.26537	0.51802	70.10619	0.01426	.8634	.9137
9	108	2.09585	160.49224	0.47713	76.05333	0.01315	.8391	.8984
10	120	2.27545	186.79517	0.43947	81.53107	0.01227	.8127	.8817
11	132	2.47044	215.35205	0.40479	86.57646	0.01155	.7841	.8636
12	144	2.68213	246.35603	0.37284	91.22362	0.01096	.7530	.8440
13	156	2.91197	280.01681	0.34341	95.50399	0.01047	.7192	.8226
14	168	3.16150	316.56205	0.31631	99.44652	0.01006	.6826	.7995
15	180	3.43242	356.23893	0.29134	103.07786	0.00970	.6428	.7744
16	192	3.72655	399.31581	0.26834	106.42259	0.00940	.5996	.7471
17	204	4.04589	446.08404	0.24716	109.50333	0.00913	.5527	.7175
18	216	4.39259	496.85994	0.22766	112.34091	0.00890	.5018	.6853
19	228	4.76900	551.98693	0.20969	114.95452	0.00870	.4465	.6504
20	240	5.17766	611.83787	0.19314	117.36184	0.00852	.3865	.6125
21	252	5.62135	676.81757	0.17789	119.57916	0.00836	.3214	.5713
22	264	6.10305	747.36552	0.16385	121.62147	0.00822	.2506	.5266
23	276	6.62604	823.95887	0.15092	123.50258	0.00810	.1739	.4781
24	288	7.19384	907.11567	0.13901	125.23521	0.00798	.0905	.4255
25	300	7.81029	997.39835	0.12804	126.83109	0.00788	.0	.3683
26	312	8.47957	1095.41755	0.11793	128.30102	0.00779	.0	.3062
27	324	9.20621	1201.83622	0.10862	129.65492	0.00771	.0	.2388
28	336	9.99511	1317.37414	0.10005	130.90196	0.00764	.0	.1656
29	348	10.85161	1442.81275	0.09215	132.05057	0.00757	.0	.0862
30	360	11.78151	1579.00046	0.08488	133.10853	0.00751	.0	.0
31	372	12.79109	1726.85839	0.07818	134.08298	0.00746	.0	.0
32	384	13.88718	1887.38658	0.07201	134.98052	0.00741	.0	.0
33	396	15.07721	2061.67077	0.06633	135.80722	0.00736	.0	.0
34	408	16.36920	2250.88975	0.06109	136.56867	0.00732	.0	.0
35	420	17.77192	2456.32330	0.05627	137.27002	0.00728	.0	.0
36	432	19.29483	2679.36090	0.05183	137.91601	0.00725	.0	.0
37	444	20.94824	2921.51106	0.04774	138.51102	0.00722	.0	.0
38	456	22.74334	3184.41159	0.04397	139.05906	0.00719	.0	.0
39	468	24.69227	3469.84063	0.04050	139.56384	0.00717	.0	.0
40	480	26.80820	3779.72869	0.03730	140.02879	0.00714	.0	.0

INTEREST RATE = 8.50%

YR	MOS	(1) COMPOUND VALUE $1	(2) COMPOUND VALUE $1 PER MO	(3) PRESENT VALUE $1	(4) PRESENT VALUE $1 PER MO	(5) LOAN CONSTANT	(6) BAL 25 YR LOAN	(7) BAL 30 YR LOAN
	1	1.00708	1.00708	0.99297	0.99297	1.00708	.9990	.9994
	2	1.01422	2.02130	0.98598	1.97895	0.50532	.9981	.9988
	3	1.02140	3.04270	0.97905	2.95800	0.33807	.9971	.9982
	4	1.02864	4.07134	0.97216	3.93016	0.25444	.9961	.9976
	5	1.03592	5.10726	0.96532	4.89548	0.20427	.9951	.9969
	6	1.04326	6.15052	0.95853	5.85402	0.17082	.9941	.9963
	7	1.05065	7.20117	0.95179	6.80581	0.14693	.9931	.9957
	8	1.05809	8.25926	0.94510	7.75090	0.12902	.9921	.9950
	9	1.06559	9.32485	0.93845	8.68936	0.11508	.9910	.9944
	10	1.07313	10.39798	0.93185	9.62120	0.10394	.9900	.9937
	11	1.08074	11.47872	0.92530	10.54650	0.09482	.9890	.9931
	12	1.08839	12.56711	0.91879	11.46529	0.08722	.9879	.9924
2	24	1.18459	26.24503	0.84417	21.99945	0.04546	.9747	.9842
3	36	1.28930	41.13196	0.77561	31.67811	0.03157	.9604	.9753
4	48	1.40326	57.33476	0.71262	40.57074	0.02465	.9448	.9655
5	60	1.52730	74.96974	0.65475	48.74118	0.02052	.9279	.9549
6	72	1.66230	94.16349	0.60158	56.24808	0.01778	.9094	.9434
7	84	1.80923	115.05379	0.55272	63.14532	0.01584	.8893	.9308
8	96	1.96915	137.79061	0.50783	69.48242	0.01439	.8674	.9171
9	108	2.14321	162.53715	0.46659	75.30487	0.01328	.8436	.9022
10	120	2.33265	189.47106	0.42870	80.65447	0.01240	.8177	.8860
11	132	2.53883	218.78569	0.39388	85.56961	0.01169	.7895	.8684
12	144	2.76324	250.69146	0.36189	90.08558	0.01110	.7588	.8492
13	156	3.00749	285.41741	0.33250	94.23479	0.01061	.7254	.8283
14	168	3.27332	323.21282	0.30550	98.04704	0.01020	.6890	.8056
15	180	3.56265	364.34900	0.28069	101.54969	0.00985	.6494	.7808
16	192	3.87756	409.12125	0.25789	104.76788	0.00954	.6064	.7539
17	204	4.22030	457.85095	0.23695	107.72471	0.00928	.5595	.7246
18	216	4.59334	510.88792	0.21771	110.44141	0.00905	.5084	.6927
19	228	4.99935	568.61287	0.20003	112.93748	0.00885	.4529	.6579
20	240	5.44124	631.44018	0.18378	115.23083	0.00868	.3924	.6201
21	252	5.92220	699.82086	0.16886	117.33794	0.00852	.3267	.5790
22	264	6.44567	774.24576	0.15514	119.27393	0.00838	.2550	.5342
23	276	7.01541	855.24915	0.14254	121.05269	0.00826	.1771	.4855
24	288	7.63550	943.41251	0.13097	122.66809	0.00815	.0923	.4325
25	300	8.31041	1039.36870	0.12033	124.18856	0.00805	.0	.3747
26	312	9.04498	1143.80655	0.11056	125.56819	0.00796	.0	.3119
27	324	9.84447	1257.47575	0.10158	126.83578	0.00788	.0	.2435
28	336	10.71463	1381.19227	0.09333	128.00042	0.00781	.0	.1691
29	348	11.66171	1515.84421	0.08575	129.07048	0.00775	.0	.0881
30	360	12.69250	1662.39816	0.07879	130.05363	0.00769	.0	.0
31	372	13.81440	1821.90615	0.07239	130.95695	0.00764	.0	.0
32	384	15.03547	1995.51318	0.06651	131.78690	0.00759	.0	.0
33	396	16.36447	2184.46551	0.06111	132.54945	0.00754	.0	.0
34	408	17.81094	2390.11949	0.05615	133.25007	0.00750	.0	.0
35	420	19.38526	2613.95142	0.05159	133.89379	0.00747	.0	.0
36	432	21.09874	2857.56806	0.04740	134.48523	0.00744	.0	.0
37	444	22.96368	3122.71819	0.04355	135.02864	0.00741	.0	.0
38	456	24.99346	3411.30519	0.04001	135.52792	0.00738	.0	.0
39	468	27.20265	3725.40064	0.03676	135.98665	0.00735	.0	.0
40	480	29.60712	4067.25928	0.03378	136.40813	0.00733	.0	.0

INTEREST RATE = 8.75%

YR	MOS	(1) COMPOUND VALUE $1	(2) COMPOUND VALUE $1 PER MO	(3) PRESENT VALUE $1	(4) PRESENT VALUE $1 PER MO	(5) LOAN CONSTANT	(6) BAL 25 YR LOAN	(7) BAL 30 YR LOAN
	1	1.00729	1.00729	0.99276	0.99276	1.00729	.9991	.9994
	2	1.01464	2.02193	0.98557	1.97834	0.50548	.9981	.9988
	3	1.02203	3.04396	0.97844	2.95678	0.33821	.9972	.9983
	4	1.02949	4.07345	0.97136	3.92813	0.25457	.9962	.9977
	5	1.03699	5.11044	0.96433	4.89246	0.20440	.9953	.9971
	6	1.04456	6.15500	0.95735	5.84980	0.17095	.9943	.9965
	7	1.05217	7.20717	0.95042	6.80022	0.14705	.9933	.9959
	8	1.05984	8.26702	0.94354	7.74375	0.12914	.9924	.9953
	9	1.06757	9.33459	0.93670	8.68046	0.11520	.9914	.9947
	10	1.07536	10.40994	0.92992	9.61038	0.10405	.9904	.9941
	11	1.08320	11.49314	0.92319	10.53358	0.09493	.9894	.9934
	12	1.09110	12.58424	0.91651	11.45009	0.08734	.9884	.9928
2	24	1.19049	26.31485	0.83999	21.94420	0.04557	.9757	.9850
3	36	1.29894	41.29626	0.76986	31.56216	0.03168	.9619	.9764
4	48	1.41727	57.64241	0.70558	40.37712	0.02477	.9468	.9671
5	60	1.54637	75.47763	0.64667	48.45611	0.02064	.9303	.9569
6	72	1.68724	94.93756	0.59268	55.86058	0.01790	.9124	.9458
7	84	1.84094	116.17021	0.54320	62.64686	0.01596	.8928	.9336
8	96	2.00864	139.33707	0.49785	68.86654	0.01452	.8714	.9204
9	108	2.19162	164.61433	0.45628	74.56695	0.01341	.8480	.9060
10	120	2.39127	192.19425	0.41819	79.79142	0.01253	.8226	.8902
11	132	2.60911	222.28658	0.38327	84.57970	0.01182	.7948	.8730
12	144	2.84679	255.12019	0.35127	88.96821	0.01124	.7645	.8543
13	156	3.10612	290.94481	0.32195	92.99032	0.01075	.7314	.8338
14	168	3.38907	330.03290	0.29507	96.67663	0.01034	.6954	.8115
15	180	3.69780	372.68176	0.27043	100.05516	0.00999	.6560	.7871
16	192	4.03465	419.21575	0.24785	103.15162	0.00969	.6130	.7605
17	204	4.40219	469.98879	0.22716	105.98955	0.00943	.5662	.7315
18	216	4.80322	525.38704	0.20819	108.59055	0.00921	.5150	.6999
19	228	5.24077	585.83184	0.19081	110.97439	0.00901	.4592	.6654
20	240	5.71818	651.78291	0.17488	113.15920	0.00884	.3983	.6277
21	252	6.23908	723.74184	0.16028	115.16160	0.00868	.3319	.5866
22	264	6.80744	802.25593	0.14690	116.99682	0.00855	.2594	.5417
23	276	7.42757	887.92233	0.13463	118.67881	0.00843	.1804	.4928
24	288	8.10419	981.39258	0.12339	120.22038	0.00832	.0941	.4394
25	300	8.84244	1083.37758	0.11309	121.63324	0.00822	.0	.3812
26	312	9.64795	1194.65299	0.10365	122.92814	0.00813	.0	.3176
27	324	10.52684	1316.06512	0.09500	124.11493	0.00806	.0	.2482
28	336	11.48579	1448.53738	0.08706	125.20263	0.00799	.0	.1726
29	348	12.53210	1593.07732	0.07980	126.19952	0.00792	.0	.0900
30	360	13.67372	1750.78424	0.07313	127.11318	0.00787	.0	.0
31	372	14.91934	1922.85761	0.06703	127.95056	0.00782	.0	.0
32	384	16.27843	2110.60613	0.06143	128.71803	0.00777	.0	.0
33	396	17.76133	2315.45777	0.05630	129.42142	0.00773	.0	.0
34	408	19.37931	2538.97053	0.05160	130.06608	0.00769	.0	.0
35	420	21.14468	2782.84436	0.04729	130.65692	0.00765	.0	.0
36	432	23.07088	3048.93409	0.04334	131.19843	0.00762	.0	.0
37	444	25.17254	3339.26348	0.03973	131.69473	0.00759	.0	.0
38	456	27.46565	3656.04066	0.03641	132.14960	0.00757	.0	.0
39	468	29.96766	4001.67491	0.03337	132.56648	0.00754	.0	.0
40	480	32.69758	4378.79501	0.03058	132.94857	0.00752	.0	.0

INTEREST RATE = 9.00%

YR	MOS	(1) COMPOUND VALUE $1	(2) COMPOUND VALUE $1 PER MO	(3) PRESENT VALUE $1	(4) PRESENT VALUE $1 PER MO	(5) LOAN CONSTANT	(6) BAL 25 YR LOAN	(7) BAL 30 YR LOAN
	1	1.00750	1.00750	0.99256	0.99256	1.00750	.9991	.9995
	2	1.01506	2.02256	0.98517	1.97772	0.50563	.9982	.9989
	3	1.02267	3.04523	0.97783	2.95556	0.33835	.9973	.9983
	4	1.03034	4.07556	0.97055	3.92611	0.25471	.9964	.9978
	5	1.03807	5.11363	0.96333	4.88944	0.20452	.9955	.9972
	6	1.04585	6.15948	0.95616	5.84560	0.17107	.9945	.9967
	7	1.05370	7.21318	0.94904	6.79464	0.14717	.9936	.9961
	8	1.06160	8.27478	0.94198	7.73661	0.12926	.9927	.9955
	9	1.06956	9.34434	0.93496	8.67158	0.11532	.9917	.9949
	10	1.07758	10.42192	0.92800	9.59958	0.10417	.9908	.9943
	11	1.08566	11.50759	0.92109	10.52067	0.09505	.9898	.9938
	12	1.09381	12.60139	0.91424	11.43491	0.08745	.9888	.9932
2	24	1.19641	26.38488	0.83583	21.88914	0.04568	.9766	.9857
3	36	1.30865	41.46136	0.76415	31.44680	0.03180	.9633	.9775
4	48	1.43141	57.95212	0.69861	40.18478	0.02489	.9487	.9686
5	60	1.56568	75.98982	0.63870	48.17337	0.02076	.9327	.9588
6	72	1.71255	95.71958	0.58392	55.47685	0.01803	.9153	.9481
7	84	1.87320	117.30013	0.53385	62.15396	0.01609	.8961	.9364
8	96	2.04892	140.90508	0.48806	68.25844	0.01465	.8752	.9236
9	108	2.24112	166.72435	0.44620	73.83938	0.01354	.8524	.9096
10	120	2.45136	194.96563	0.40794	78.94169	0.01267	.8274	.8943
11	132	2.68131	225.85615	0.37295	83.60642	0.01196	.8000	.8775
12	144	2.93284	259.64440	0.34097	87.87109	0.01138	.7701	.8592
13	156	3.20796	296.60223	0.31172	91.77001	0.01090	.7374	.8392
14	168	3.50889	337.02696	0.28499	95.33456	0.01049	.7016	.8173
15	180	3.83804	381.24381	0.26055	98.59340	0.01014	.6625	.7933
16	192	4.19808	429.60850	0.23820	101.57276	0.00985	.6196	.7671
17	204	4.59189	482.51013	0.21778	104.29661	0.00959	.5728	.7384
18	216	5.02264	540.37430	0.19910	106.78685	0.00936	.5216	.7070
19	228	5.49380	603.66653	0.18202	109.06353	0.00917	.4655	.6727
20	240	6.00915	672.89601	0.16641	111.14495	0.00900	.4042	.6351
21	252	6.57285	748.61969	0.15214	113.04786	0.00885	.3372	.5941
22	264	7.18943	831.44677	0.13909	114.78758	0.00871	.2639	.5492
23	276	7.86385	922.04360	0.12716	116.37810	0.00859	.1836	.5001
24	288	8.60153	1021.13905	0.11626	117.83221	0.00849	.0959	.4463
25	300	9.40841	1129.53032	0.10629	119.16161	0.00839	.0	.3876
26	312	10.29099	1248.08945	0.09717	120.37701	0.00831	.0	.3233
27	324	11.25635	1377.77024	0.08884	121.48816	0.00823	.0	.2530
28	336	12.31228	1519.61598	0.08122	122.50403	0.00816	.0	.1760
29	348	13.46725	1674.76783	0.07425	123.43277	0.00810	.0	.0919
30	360	14.73058	1844.47400	0.06789	124.28186	0.00805	.0	.0
31	372	16.11241	2030.09977	0.06206	125.05813	0.00800	.0	.0
32	384	17.62386	2233.13853	0.05674	125.76782	0.00795	.0	.0
33	396	19.27710	2455.22371	0.05188	126.41665	0.00791	.0	.0
34	408	21.08542	2698.14202	0.04743	127.00984	0.00787	.0	.0
35	420	23.06338	2963.84774	0.04336	127.55215	0.00784	.0	.0
36	432	25.22689	3254.47849	0.03964	128.04796	0.00781	.0	.0
37	444	27.59334	3572.37241	0.03624	128.50124	0.00778	.0	.0
38	456	30.18179	3920.08697	0.03313	128.91565	0.00776	.0	.0
39	468	33.01305	4300.41955	0.03029	129.29452	0.00773	.0	.0
40	480	36.10990	4716.42996	0.02769	129.64089	0.00771	.0	.0

INTEREST RATE = 9.25%

YR	MOS	(1) COMPOUND VALUE $1	(2) COMPOUND VALUE $1 PER MO	(3) PRESENT VALUE $1	(4) PRESENT VALUE $1 PER MO	(5) LOAN CONSTANT	(6) BAL 25 YR LOAN	(7) BAL 30 YR LOAN
	1	1.00771	1.00771	0.99235	0.99235	1.00771	.9991	.9995
	2	1.01548	2.02318	0.98476	1.97711	0.50579	.9983	.9990
	3	1.02330	3.04649	0.97723	2.95434	0.33849	.9974	.9984
	4	1.03119	4.07768	0.96975	3.92409	0.25484	.9965	.9979
	5	1.03914	5.11682	0.96233	4.88642	0.20465	.9957	.9974
	6	1.04715	6.16397	0.95497	5.84140	0.17119	.9948	.9968
	7	1.05522	7.21919	0.94767	6.78906	0.14730	.9939	.9963
	8	1.06336	8.28255	0.94042	7.72948	0.12937	.9930	.9957
	9	1.07155	9.35410	0.93322	8.66271	0.11544	.9921	.9952
	10	1.07981	10.43392	0.92609	9.58879	0.10429	.9911	.9946
	11	1.08814	11.52205	0.91900	10.50779	0.09517	.9902	.9941
	12	1.09652	12.61858	0.91197	11.41977	0.08757	.9893	.9935
2	24	1.20237	26.45515	0.83169	21.83428	0.04580	.9775	.9864
3	36	1.31842	41.62729	0.75848	31.33204	0.03192	.9647	.9786
4	48	1.44568	58.26390	0.69172	39.99373	0.02500	.9505	.9700
5	60	1.58523	76.50635	0.63083	47.89295	0.02088	.9350	.9606
6	72	1.73824	96.50963	0.57530	55.09683	0.01815	.9181	.9503
7	84	1.90602	118.44372	0.52465	61.66657	0.01622	.8994	.9391
8	96	2.09000	142.49497	0.47847	67.65799	0.01478	.8790	.9267
9	108	2.29173	168.86776	0.43635	73.12200	0.01368	.8566	.9131
10	120	2.51294	197.78615	0.39794	78.10503	0.01280	.8321	.8982
11	132	2.75550	229.49586	0.36291	82.64942	0.01210	.8052	.8819
12	144	3.02147	264.26633	0.33096	86.79377	0.01152	.7756	.8640
13	156	3.31312	302.39299	0.30183	90.57331	0.01104	.7433	.8444
14	168	3.63291	344.19979	0.27526	94.02015	0.01064	.7078	.8229
15	180	3.98357	390.04195	0.25103	97.16357	0.01029	.6689	.7993
16	192	4.36809	440.30900	0.22893	100.03028	0.01000	.6262	.7735
17	204	4.78971	495.42802	0.20878	102.64464	0.00974	.5794	.7451
18	216	5.25203	555.86736	0.19040	105.02887	0.00952	.5281	.7140
19	228	5.75898	622.14056	0.17364	107.20322	0.00933	.4718	.6799
20	240	6.31486	694.81072	0.15836	109.18617	0.00916	.4101	.6425
21	252	6.92440	774.49531	0.14442	110.99457	0.00901	.3425	.6015
22	264	7.59277	861.87138	0.13170	112.64377	0.00888	.2683	.5566
23	276	8.32566	957.68136	0.12011	114.14780	0.00876	.1869	.5073
24	288	9.12929	1062.73931	0.10954	115.51944	0.00866	.0977	.4532
25	300	10.01048	1177.93789	0.09990	116.77033	0.00856	.0	.3939
26	312	10.97674	1304.25591	0.09110	117.91111	0.00848	.0	.3290
27	324	12.03626	1442.76668	0.08308	118.95147	0.00841	.0	.2577
28	336	13.19804	1594.64708	0.07577	119.90025	0.00834	.0	.1795
29	348	14.47197	1761.18760	0.06910	120.76552	0.00828	.0	.0939
30	360	15.86887	1943.80330	0.06302	121.55461	0.00823	.0	.0
31	372	17.40060	2144.04583	0.05747	122.27424	0.00818	.0	.0
32	384	19.08018	2363.61660	0.05241	122.93053	0.00813	.0	.0
33	396	20.92187	2604.38125	0.04780	123.52905	0.00810	.0	.0
34	408	22.94134	2868.38550	0.04359	124.07487	0.00806	.0	.0
35	420	25.15573	3157.87254	0.03975	124.57266	0.00803	.0	.0
36	432	27.58387	3475.30206	0.03625	125.02662	0.00800	.0	.0
37	444	30.24638	3823.37120	0.03306	125.44062	0.00797	.0	.0
38	456	33.16588	4205.03742	0.03015	125.81818	0.00795	.0	.0
39	468	36.36719	4623.54364	0.02750	126.16250	0.00793	.0	.0
40	480	39.87751	5082.44581	0.02508	126.47651	0.00791	.0	.0

INTEREST RATE = 9.50%

YR	MOS	(1) COMPOUND VALUE $1	(2) COMPOUND VALUE $1 PER MO	(3) PRESENT VALUE $1	(4) PRESENT VALUE $1 PER MO	(5) LOAN CONSTANT	(6) BAL 25 YR LOAN	(7) BAL 30 YR LOAN
	1	1.00792	1.00792	0.99215	0.99215	1.00792	.9992	.9995
	2	1.01590	2.02381	0.98435	1.97650	0.50595	.9984	.9990
	3	1.02394	3.04775	0.97662	2.95312	0.33863	.9975	.9985
	4	1.03204	4.07980	0.96895	3.92207	0.25497	.9967	.9980
	5	1.04022	5.12001	0.96134	4.88341	0.20477	.9958	.9975
	6	1.04845	6.16846	0.95379	5.83720	0.17132	.9950	.9970
	7	1.05675	7.22521	0.94630	6.78349	0.14742	.9941	.9965
	8	1.06512	8.29033	0.93886	7.72236	0.12949	.9933	.9960
	9	1.07355	9.36388	0.93149	8.65385	0.11556	.9924	.9954
	10	1.08205	10.44592	0.92417	9.57802	0.10441	.9915	.9949
	11	1.09061	11.53654	0.91691	10.49494	0.09528	.9906	.9944
	12	1.09925	12.63579	0.90971	11.40465	0.08768	.9897	.9938
2	24	1.20835	26.52564	0.82758	21.77961	0.04591	.9784	.9871
3	36	1.32827	41.79403	0.75286	31.21785	0.03203	.9660	.9796
4	48	1.46010	58.57777	0.68489	39.80395	0.02512	.9523	.9714
5	60	1.60501	77.02726	0.62305	47.61482	0.02100	.9373	.9624
6	72	1.76430	97.30781	0.56680	54.72049	0.01827	.9208	.9525
7	84	1.93941	119.60116	0.51562	61.18460	0.01634	.9027	.9416
8	96	2.13189	144.10707	0.46907	67.06509	0.01491	.8827	.9297
9	108	2.34347	171.04514	0.42672	72.41464	0.01381	.8608	.9165
10	120	2.57606	200.65674	0.38819	77.28121	0.01294	.8367	.9021
11	132	2.83172	233.20722	0.35314	81.70838	0.01224	.8102	.8862
12	144	3.11276	268.98825	0.32126	85.73584	0.01166	.7811	.8687
13	156	3.42170	308.32047	0.29225	89.39968	0.01119	.7491	.8495
14	168	3.76129	351.55632	0.26587	92.73272	0.01078	.7139	.8284
15	180	4.13459	399.08322	0.24186	95.76483	0.01044	.6752	.8052
16	192	4.54494	451.32704	0.22002	98.52317	0.01015	.6327	.7797
17	204	4.99602	508.75595	0.20016	101.03248	0.00990	.5859	.7517
18	216	5.49186	571.88453	0.18209	103.31523	0.00968	.5345	.7209
19	228	6.03691	641.27847	0.16565	105.39188	0.00949	.4781	.6870
20	240	6.63606	717.55959	0.15069	107.28103	0.00932	.4160	.6498
21	252	7.29467	801.41143	0.13709	108.99962	0.00917	.3477	.6089
22	264	8.01865	893.58536	0.12471	110.56304	0.00904	.2727	.5639
23	276	8.81448	994.90733	0.11345	111.98530	0.00893	.1902	.5144
24	288	9.68930	1106.28527	0.10321	113.27916	0.00883	.0996	.4601
25	300	10.65094	1228.71719	0.09389	114.45619	0.00874	.0	.4003
26	312	11.70802	1363.30018	0.08541	115.52696	0.00866	.0	.3346
27	324	12.87001	1511.24022	0.07770	116.50104	0.00858	.0	.2624
28	336	14.14733	1673.86294	0.07068	117.38719	0.00852	.0	.1831
29	348	15.55142	1852.62557	0.06430	118.19332	0.00846	.0	.0958
30	360	17.09486	2049.12996	0.05850	118.92667	0.00841	.0	.0
31	372	18.79148	2265.13694	0.05322	119.59381	0.00836	.0	.0
32	384	20.65649	2502.58209	0.04841	120.20072	0.00832	.0	.0
33	396	22.70660	2763.59310	0.04404	120.75283	0.00828	.0	.0
34	408	24.96018	3050.50882	0.04006	121.25509	0.00825	.0	.0
35	420	27.43741	3365.90023	0.03645	121.71200	0.00822	.0	.0
36	432	30.16051	3712.59347	0.03316	122.12766	0.00819	.0	.0
37	444	33.15387	4093.69518	0.03016	122.50579	0.00816	.0	.0
38	456	36.44431	4512.62032	0.02744	122.84979	0.00814	.0	.0
39	468	40.06132	4973.12276	0.02496	123.16272	0.00812	.0	.0
40	480	44.03731	5479.32895	0.02271	123.44740	0.00810	.0	.0

INTEREST RATE = 9.75%

YR	MOS	(1) COMPOUND VALUE $1	(2) COMPOUND VALUE $1 PER MO	(3) PRESENT VALUE $1	(4) PRESENT VALUE $1 PER MO	(5) LOAN CONSTANT	(6) BAL 25 YR LOAN	(7) BAL 30 YR LOAN
	1	1.00813	1.00813	0.99194	0.99194	1.00812	.9992	.9995
	2	1.01632	2.02444	0.98395	1.97589	0.50610	.9984	.9991
	3	1.02457	3.04901	0.97602	2.95190	0.33876	.9976	.9986
	4	1.03290	4.08191	0.96815	3.92005	0.25510	.9968	.9981
	5	1.04129	5.12320	0.96035	4.88040	0.20490	.9960	.9976
	6	1.04975	6.17295	0.95261	5.83300	0.17144	.9952	.9971
	7	1.05828	7.23124	0.94493	6.77793	0.14754	.9944	.9967
	8	1.06688	8.29811	0.93731	7.71525	0.12961	.9935	.9962
	9	1.07555	9.37366	0.92976	8.64501	0.11567	.9927	.9957
	10	1.08429	10.45795	0.92227	9.56727	0.10452	.9918	.9952
	11	1.09310	11.55104	0.91483	10.48211	0.09540	.9910	.9947
	12	1.10198	12.65302	0.90746	11.38957	0.08780	.9901	.9941
2	24	1.21435	26.59636	0.82348	21.72514	0.04603	.9793	.9877
3	36	1.33819	41.96160	0.74728	31.10425	0.03215	.9673	.9806
4	48	1.47466	58.89375	0.67812	39.61543	0.02524	.9541	.9727
5	60	1.62504	77.55259	0.61537	47.33897	0.02112	.9395	.9641
6	72	1.79075	98.11421	0.55842	54.34778	0.01840	.9235	.9546
7	84	1.97337	120.77264	0.50675	60.70799	0.01647	.9058	.9441
8	96	2.17461	145.74172	0.45985	66.47962	0.01504	.8863	.9325
9	108	2.39637	173.25707	0.41730	71.71715	0.01394	.8648	.9198
10	120	2.64074	203.57836	0.37868	76.46999	0.01308	.8412	.9058
11	132	2.91004	236.99174	0.34364	80.78301	0.01238	.8151	.8903
12	144	3.20680	273.81252	0.31184	84.69690	0.01181	.7864	.8733
13	156	3.53382	314.38818	0.28298	88.24859	0.01133	.7548	.8545
14	168	3.89419	359.10163	0.25679	91.47161	0.01093	.7199	.8338
15	180	4.29130	408.37483	0.23303	94.39637	0.01059	.6814	.8110
16	192	4.72892	462.67278	0.21146	97.05048	0.01030	.6391	.7859
17	204	5.21116	522.50788	0.19190	99.45897	0.01005	.5924	.7582
18	216	5.74258	588.44480	0.17414	101.64458	0.00984	.5410	.7276
19	228	6.32819	661.10579	0.15802	103.62793	0.00965	.4843	.6940
20	240	6.97352	741.17653	0.14340	105.42775	0.00949	.4218	.6570
21	252	7.68466	829.41267	0.13013	107.06100	0.00934	.3530	.6161
22	264	8.46833	926.46689	0.11809	108.54312	0.00921	.2771	.5711
23	276	9.33190	1033.79678	0.10716	109.88808	0.00910	.1936	.5215
24	288	10.28354	1151.87352	0.09724	111.10858	0.00900	.1014	.4669
25	300	11.33223	1281.99140	0.08824	112.21613	0.00891	.0	.4067
26	312	12.48786	1425.37833	0.08008	113.22119	0.00883	.0	.3403
27	324	13.76134	1583.38747	0.07267	114.13324	0.00876	.0	.2672
28	336	15.16468	1757.50994	0.06594	114.96089	0.00870	.0	.1866
29	348	16.71113	1949.38893	0.05984	115.71195	0.00864	.0	.0978
30	360	18.41529	2160.83521	0.05430	116.39350	0.00859	.0	.0
31	372	20.29323	2393.84419	0.04928	117.01199	0.00855	.0	.0
32	384	22.36267	2650.61478	0.04472	117.57324	0.00851	.0	.0
33	396	24.64316	2933.57013	0.04058	118.08255	0.00847	.0	.0
34	408	27.15620	3245.38047	0.03682	118.54473	0.00844	.0	.0
35	420	29.92551	3588.98836	0.03342	118.96414	0.00841	.0	.0
36	432	32.97723	3967.63642	0.03032	119.34474	0.00838	.0	.0
37	444	36.34016	4384.89797	0.02752	119.69011	0.00835	.0	.0
38	456	40.04602	4844.71068	0.02497	120.00353	0.00833	.0	.0
39	468	44.12981	5351.41382	0.02266	120.28794	0.00831	.0	.0
40	480	48.63004	5909.78913	0.02056	120.54603	0.00830	.0	.0

YR	MOS	(1) COMPOUND VALUE $1	(2) COMPOUND VALUE $1 PER MO	(3) PRESENT VALUE $1	(4) PRESENT VALUE $1 PER MO	(5) LOAN CONSTANT	(6) BAL 25 YR LOAN	(7) BAL 30 YR LOAN
	1	1.00833	1.00833	0.99174	0.99174	1.00833	.9992	.9996
	2	1.01674	2.02507	0.98354	1.97527	0.50626	.9985	.9991
	3	1.02521	3.05028	0.97541	2.95069	0.33890	.9977	.9987
	4	1.03375	4.08403	0.96735	3.91804	0.25523	.9969	.9982
	5	1.04237	5.12640	0.95935	4.87739	0.20503	.9962	.9978
	6	1.05105	6.17745	0.95143	5.82882	0.17156	.9954	.9973
	7	1.05981	7.23726	0.94356	6.77238	0.14766	.9946	.9968
	8	1.06864	8.30591	0.93577	7.70815	0.12973	.9938	.9964
	9	1.07755	9.38346	0.92803	8.63618	0.11579	.9930	.9959
	10	1.08653	10.46999	0.92036	9.55654	0.10464	.9922	.9954
	11	1.09558	11.56557	0.91276	10.46930	0.09552	.9914	.9949
	12	1.10471	12.67028	0.90521	11.37451	0.08792	.9905	.9944
2	24	1.22039	26.66731	0.81941	21.67085	0.04614	.9801	.9883
3	36	1.34818	42.13000	0.74174	30.99123	0.03227	.9685	.9815
4	48	1.48935	59.21185	0.67143	39.42816	0.02536	.9557	.9740
5	60	1.64531	78.08238	0.60779	47.06537	0.02125	.9416	.9657
6	72	1.81759	98.92891	0.55018	53.97866	0.01853	.9261	.9566
7	84	2.00792	121.95834	0.49803	60.23666	0.01660	.9088	.9465
8	96	2.21818	147.39925	0.45082	65.90149	0.01517	.8898	.9353
9	108	2.45045	175.50416	0.40809	71.02935	0.01408	.8688	.9230
10	120	2.70704	206.55202	0.36941	75.67116	0.01322	.8456	.9094
11	132	2.99050	240.85100	0.33439	79.87298	0.01252	.8200	.8943
12	144	3.30365	278.74152	0.30270	83.67652	0.01195	.7916	.8777
13	156	3.64958	320.59968	0.27400	87.11954	0.01148	.7604	.8593
14	168	4.03174	366.64094	0.24803	90.23620	0.01108	.7258	.8390
15	180	4.45392	417.92426	0.22452	93.05743	0.01075	.6876	.8166
16	192	4.92030	474.35667	0.20324	95.61125	0.01046	.6454	.7919
17	204	5.43552	536.69829	0.18397	97.92300	0.01021	.5988	.7645
18	216	6.00469	605.56790	0.16654	100.01563	0.01000	.5473	.7343
19	228	6.63346	681.64905	0.15075	101.90990	0.00981	.4905	.7009
20	240	7.32807	765.69689	0.13646	103.62461	0.00965	.4276	.6640
21	252	8.09542	858.54564	0.12353	105.17679	0.00951	.3582	.6233
22	264	8.94311	961.11687	0.11182	106.58185	0.00938	.2816	.5783
23	276	9.87958	1074.42864	0.10122	107.85372	0.00927	.1969	.5286
24	288	10.91410	1199.60564	0.09162	109.00504	0.00917	.1033	.4736
25	300	12.05694	1337.89031	0.08294	110.04722	0.00909	.0	.4130
26	312	13.31946	1490.65518	0.07508	110.99062	0.00901	.0	.3459
27	324	14.71419	1659.41654	0.06796	111.84460	0.00894	.0	.2719
28	336	16.25495	1845.84941	0.06152	112.61763	0.00888	.0	.1901
29	348	17.95706	2051.80425	0.05569	113.31738	0.00882	.0	.0997
30	360	19.83740	2279.32524	0.05041	113.95081	0.00878	.0	.0
31	372	21.91463	2530.67065	0.04563	114.52420	0.00873	.0	.0
32	384	24.20938	2808.33522	0.04131	115.04324	0.00869	.0	.0
33	396	26.74442	3115.07489	0.03739	115.51307	0.00866	.0	.0
34	408	29.54491	3453.93421	0.03385	115.93838	0.00863	.0	.0
35	420	32.63865	3828.27653	0.03064	116.32337	0.00860	.0	.0
36	432	36.05634	4241.81738	0.02773	116.67187	0.00857	.0	.0
37	444	39.83191	4698.66136	0.02511	116.98733	0.00855	.0	.0
38	456	44.00283	5203.34288	0.02273	117.27289	0.00853	.0	.0
39	468	48.61050	5760.87114	0.02057	117.53139	0.00851	.0	.0
40	480	53.70066	6376.77990	0.01862	117.76538	0.00849	.0	.0

INTEREST RATE = 10.25%

YR	MOS	(1) COMPOUND VALUE $1	(2) COMPOUND VALUE $1 PER MO	(3) PRESENT VALUE $1	(4) PRESENT VALUE $1 PER MO	(5) LOAN CONSTANT	(6) BAL 25 YR LOAN	(7) BAL 30 YR LOAN
	1	1.00854	1.00854	0.99153	0.99153	1.00854	.9993	.9996
	2	1.01716	2.02570	0.98313	1.97466	0.50642	.9985	.9992
	3	1.02584	3.05154	0.97481	2.94947	0.33904	.9978	.9987
	4	1.03461	4.08615	0.96655	3.91602	0.25536	.9971	.9983
	5	1.04344	5.12959	0.95836	4.87439	0.20515	.9963	.9979
	6	1.05236	6.18195	0.95025	5.82463	0.17168	.9956	.9974
	7	1.06135	7.24330	0.94220	6.76683	0.14778	.9948	.9970
	8	1.07041	8.31371	0.93422	7.70105	0.12985	.9940	.9965
	9	1.07955	9.39326	0.92631	8.62736	0.11591	.9933	.9961
	10	1.08878	10.48204	0.91846	9.54582	0.10476	.9925	.9956
	11	1.09808	11.58011	0.91068	10.45651	0.09563	.9917	.9952
	12	1.10746	12.68757	0.90297	11.35948	0.08803	.9909	.9947
2	24	1.22646	26.73848	0.81536	21.61676	0.04626	.9809	.9889
3	36	1.35825	42.29924	0.73624	30.97879	0.03238	.9697	.9824
4	48	1.50420	59.53208	0.66481	39.24713	0.02548	.9574	.9752
5	60	1.66583	78.61668	0.60030	46.79399	0.02137	.9437	.9673
6	72	1.84483	99.75201	0.54205	53.61310	0.01865	.9286	.9585
7	84	2.04307	123.15845	0.48946	59.77056	0.01673	.9118	.9488
8	96	2.26261	149.08002	0.44197	65.33057	0.01531	.8932	.9380
9	108	2.50574	177.78701	0.39908	70.35110	0.01421	.8727	.9261
10	120	2.77499	209.57870	0.36036	74.88449	0.01335	.8499	.9128
11	132	3.07318	244.78658	0.32540	78.97801	0.01266	.8247	.8982
12	144	3.40341	283.77773	0.29382	82.67434	0.01210	.7968	.8820
13	156	3.76912	326.95867	0.26531	86.01202	0.01163	.7659	.8640
14	168	4.17413	374.77963	0.23957	89.02585	0.01123	.7316	.8442
15	180	4.62266	427.73919	0.21633	91.74725	0.01090	.6937	.8221
16	192	5.11939	486.38954	0.19534	94.20459	0.01062	.6517	.7977
17	204	5.66950	551.34216	0.17638	96.42350	0.01037	.6052	.7707
18	216	6.27871	623.27428	0.15927	98.42712	0.01016	.5537	.7408
19	228	6.95339	702.93587	0.14381	100.23632	0.00998	.4966	.7077
20	240	7.70057	791.15751	0.12986	101.86998	0.00982	.4335	.6710
21	252	8.52804	888.85902	0.11726	103.34513	0.00968	.3635	.6304
22	264	9.44442	997.05905	0.10588	104.67715	0.00955	.2860	.5854
23	276	10.45927	1116.88574	0.09561	105.87992	0.00944	.2002	.5355
24	288	11.58317	1249.58842	0.08633	106.96598	0.00935	.1052	.4804
25	300	12.82784	1396.55069	0.07796	107.94667	0.00926	.0	.4193
26	312	14.20626	1559.30480	0.07039	108.83221	0.00919	.0	.3516
27	324	15.73279	1739.54768	0.06356	109.63182	0.00912	.0	.2766
28	336	17.42336	1939.15859	0.05739	110.35384	0.00906	.0	.1936
29	348	19.29559	2160.21871	0.05183	111.00581	0.00901	.0	.1017
30	360	21.36900	2405.03288	0.04680	111.59452	0.00896	.0	.0
31	372	23.66521	2676.15359	0.04226	112.12611	0.00892	.0	.0
32	384	26.20816	2976.40761	0.03816	112.60611	0.00888	.0	.0
33	396	29.02436	3308.92547	0.03445	113.03955	0.00885	.0	.0
34	408	32.14318	3677.17409	0.03111	113.43092	0.00882	.0	.0
35	420	35.59713	4084.99290	0.02809	113.78433	0.00879	.0	.0
36	432	39.42222	4536.63395	0.02537	114.10344	0.00876	.0	.0
37	444	43.65835	5036.80614	0.02291	114.39159	0.00874	.0	.0
38	456	48.34966	5590.72441	0.02068	114.65178	0.00872	.0	.0
39	468	53.54508	6204.16405	0.01868	114.88672	0.00870	.0	.0
40	480	59.29877	6883.52092	0.01686	115.09887	0.00869	.0	.0

INTEREST RATE = 10.50%

YR	MOS	(1) COMPOUND VALUE $1	(2) COMPOUND VALUE $1 PER MO	(3) PRESENT VALUE $1	(4) PRESENT VALUE $1 PER MO	(5) LOAN CONSTANT	(6) BAL 25 YR LOAN	(7) BAL 30 YR LOAN
	1	1.00875	1.00875	0.99133	0.99133	1.00875	.9993	.9996
	2	1.01758	2.02633	0.98273	1.97405	0.50657	.9986	.9992
	3	1.02648	3.05281	0.97420	2.94826	0.33918	.9979	.9988
	4	1.03546	4.08827	0.96575	3.91401	0.25549	.9972	.9984
	5	1.04452	5.13279	0.95738	4.87138	0.20528	.9965	.9980
	6	1.05366	6.18645	0.94907	5.82045	0.17181	.9958	.9976
	7	1.06288	7.24934	0.94084	6.76129	0.14790	.9950	.9971
	8	1.07218	8.32152	0.93268	7.69397	0.12997	.9943	.9967
	9	1.08156	9.40308	0.92459	8.61856	0.11603	.9936	.9963
	10	1.09103	10.49411	0.91657	9.53513	0.10488	.9928	.9959
	11	1.10057	11.59468	0.90862	10.44374	0.09575	.9920	.9954
	12	1.11020	12.70488	0.90074	11.34448	0.08815	.9913	.9950
2	24	1.23255	26.80989	0.81132	21.56286	0.04638	.9816	.9894
3	36	1.36838	42.46932	0.73079	30.76692	0.03250	.9709	.9833
4	48	1.51918	59.85446	0.65825	39.05734	0.02560	.9589	.9764
5	60	1.68660	79.15552	0.59291	46.52482	0.02149	.9457	.9688
6	72	1.87247	100.58361	0.53405	53.25105	0.01878	.9310	.9604
7	84	2.07883	124.37315	0.48104	59.30961	0.01686	.9147	.9510
8	96	2.30792	150.78439	0.43329	64.76677	0.01544	.8966	.9406
9	108	2.56226	180.10623	0.39028	69.68223	0.01435	.8765	.9290
10	120	2.84463	212.65944	0.35154	74.10975	0.01349	.8541	.9162
11	132	3.15812	248.80013	0.31664	78.09779	0.01280	.8294	.9020
12	144	3.50615	288.92364	0.28521	81.68995	0.01224	.8018	.8862
13	156	3.89254	333.46891	0.25690	84.92554	0.01178	.7713	.8686
14	168	4.32151	382.92322	0.23140	87.83996	0.01138	.7374	.8491
15	180	4.79776	437.82756	0.20843	90.46507	0.01105	.6997	.8275
16	192	5.32649	498.78255	0.18774	92.82961	0.01077	.6579	.8035
17	204	5.91349	566.45499	0.16910	94.95943	0.01053	.6115	.7768
18	216	6.56517	641.58517	0.15232	96.87784	0.01032	.5600	.7472
19	228	7.28868	724.99495	0.13720	98.60582	0.01014	.5028	.7144
20	240	8.09192	817.59677	0.12358	100.16227	0.00998	.4392	.6779
21	252	8.98367	920.40364	0.11131	101.56422	0.00985	.3687	.6374
22	264	9.97371	1034.54018	0.10026	102.82701	0.00973	.2904	.5924
23	276	11.07284	1161.25496	0.09031	103.96445	0.00962	.2035	.5425
24	288	12.29311	1301.93414	0.08135	104.98898	0.00952	.1070	.4870
25	300	13.64785	1458.11666	0.07327	105.91181	0.00944	.0	.4255
26	312	15.15189	1631.51103	0.06600	106.74304	0.00937	.0	.3572
27	324	16.82168	1824.01405	0.05945	107.49175	0.00930	.0	.2813
28	336	18.67549	2037.73157	0.05355	108.16615	0.00925	.0	.1971
29	348	20.73359	2275.00150	0.04823	108.77360	0.00919	.0	.1037
30	360	23.01851	2538.41940	0.04344	109.32076	0.00915	.0	.0
31	372	25.55523	2830.86685	0.03913	109.81360	0.00911	.0	.0
32	384	28.37150	3155.54302	0.03525	110.25752	0.00907	.0	.0
33	396	31.49814	3515.99963	0.03175	110.65737	0.00904	.0	.0
34	408	34.96934	3916.17980	0.02860	111.01754	0.00901	.0	.0
35	420	38.82308	4360.46120	0.02576	111.34195	0.00898	.0	.0
36	432	43.10152	4853.70394	0.02320	111.63416	0.00896	.0	.0
37	444	47.85146	5401.30374	0.02090	111.89736	0.00894	.0	.0
38	456	53.12485	6009.25092	0.01882	112.13444	0.00892	.0	.0
39	468	58.97939	6684.19597	0.01696	112.34798	0.00890	.0	.0
40	480	65.47913	7433.52230	0.01527	112.54033	0.00889	.0	.0

YR	MOS	(1) COMPOUND VALUE $1	(2) COMPOUND VALUE $1 PER MO	(3) PRESENT VALUE $1	(4) PRESENT VALUE $1 PER MO	(5) LOAN CONSTANT	(6) BAL 25 YR LOAN	(7) BAL 30 YR LOAN
	1	1.00896	1.00896	0.99112	0.99112	1.00896	.9993	.9996
	2	1.01800	2.02696	0.98232	1.97344	0.50673	.9987	.9992
	3	1.02712	3.05407	0.97360	2.94704	0.33932	.9980	.9989
	4	1.03632	4.09039	0.96495	3.91200	0.25562	.9973	.9985
	5	1.04560	5.13599	0.95639	4.86838	0.20541	.9966	.9981
	6	1.05497	6.19096	0.94790	5.81628	0.17193	.9959	.9977
	7	1.06442	7.25538	0.93948	6.75576	0.14802	.9952	.9973
	8	1.07395	8.32933	0.93114	7.68690	0.13009	.9945	.9969
	9	1.08358	9.41291	0.92287	8.60977	0.11615	.9938	.9965
	10	1.09328	10.50619	0.91468	9.52444	0.10499	.9931	.9961
	11	1.10308	11.60927	0.90656	10.43100	0.09587	.9924	.9957
	12	1.11296	12.72223	0.89851	11.32951	0.08827	.9916	.9953
2	24	1.23868	26.88153	0.80731	21.50914	0.04649	.9823	.9900
3	36	1.37859	42.64023	0.72538	30.65561	0.03262	.9720	.9841
4	48	1.53432	60.17901	0.65176	38.87377	0.02572	.9605	.9775
5	60	1.70763	79.69894	0.58561	46.25785	0.02162	.9477	.9703
6	72	1.90052	101.42380	0.52617	52.89248	0.01891	.9334	.9621
7	84	2.11520	125.60265	0.47277	58.85375	0.01699	.9175	.9531
8	96	2.35413	152.51270	0.42479	64.20998	0.01557	.8998	.9431
9	108	2.62005	182.46246	0.38167	69.02259	0.01449	.8802	.9319
10	120	2.91600	215.79528	0.34294	73.34675	0.01363	.8583	.9195
11	132	3.24539	252.89331	0.30813	77.23204	0.01295	.8339	.9056
12	144	3.61198	294.18186	0.27686	80.72300	0.01239	.8068	.8902
13	156	4.01998	340.13428	0.24876	83.85964	0.01192	.7766	.8731
14	168	4.47407	391.27740	0.22351	86.67794	0.01154	.7430	.8540
15	180	4.97945	448.19754	0.20083	89.21020	0.01121	.7056	.8327
16	192	5.54192	511.54726	0.18044	91.48545	0.01093	.6640	.8091
17	204	6.16793	582.05285	0.16213	93.52978	0.01069	.6177	.7828
18	216	6.86464	660.52260	0.14567	95.36662	0.01049	.5662	.7535
19	228	7.64006	747.85615	0.13089	97.01703	0.01031	.5088	.7209
20	240	8.50307	845.05471	0.11760	98.49994	0.01015	.4450	.6846
21	252	9.46356	953.23263	0.10567	99.83234	0.01002	.3740	.6443
22	264	10.53254	1073.63012	0.09494	101.02952	0.00990	.2949	.5993
23	276	11.72228	1207.62746	0.08531	102.10518	0.00979	.2069	.5493
24	288	13.04640	1356.76088	0.07665	103.07168	0.00970	.1089	.4937
25	300	14.52010	1522.74011	0.06887	103.94008	0.00962	.0	.4317
26	312	16.16026	1707.46803	0.06188	104.72034	0.00955	.0	.3628
27	324	17.98569	1913.06245	0.05560	105.42141	0.00949	.0	.2861
28	336	20.01731	2141.88040	0.04996	106.05133	0.00943	.0	.2007
29	348	22.27843	2396.54517	0.04489	106.61732	0.00938	.0	.1056
30	360	24.79496	2679.97636	0.04033	107.12586	0.00933	.0	.0
31	372	27.59575	2995.42338	0.03624	107.58279	0.00930	.0	.0
32	384	30.71291	3346.50267	0.03256	107.99334	0.00926	.0	.0
33	396	34.18218	3737.23917	0.02926	108.36222	0.00923	.0	.0
34	408	38.04333	4172.11249	0.02629	108.69367	0.00920	.0	.0
35	420	42.34063	4656.10824	0.02362	108.99147	0.00918	.0	.0
36	432	47.12334	5194.77518	0.02122	109.25905	0.00915	.0	.0
37	444	52.44630	5794.28887	0.01907	109.49948	0.00913	.0	.0
38	456	58.37053	6461.52243	0.01713	109.71550	0.00911	.0	.0
39	468	64.96394	7204.12537	0.01539	109.90959	0.00910	.0	.0
40	480	72.30214	8030.61125	0.01383	110.08399	0.00908	.0	.0

INTEREST RATE = 11.00%

YR	MOS	(1) COMPOUND VALUE $1	(2) COMPOUND VALUE $1 PER MO	(3) PRESENT VALUE $1	(4) PRESENT VALUE $1 PER MO	(5) LOAN CONSTANT	(6) BAL 25 YR LOAN	(7) BAL 30 YR LOAN
	1	1.00917	1.00917	0.99092	0.99092	1.00917	.9994	.9996
	2	1.01842	2.02758	0.98192	1.97283	0.50689	.9987	.9993
	3	1.02775	3.05534	0.97300	2.94583	0.33946	.9981	.9989
	4	1.03717	4.09251	0.96416	3.90999	0.25576	.9974	.9986
	5	1.04668	5.13919	0.95540	4.86539	0.20553	.9968	.9982
	6	1.05628	6.19547	0.94672	5.81211	0.17205	.9961	.9978
	7	1.06596	7.26143	0.93812	6.75023	0.14814	.9954	.9974
	8	1.07573	8.33716	0.92960	7.67983	0.13021	.9948	.9971
	9	1.08559	9.42275	0.92116	8.60099	0.11627	.9941	.9967
	10	1.09554	10.51829	0.91279	9.51378	0.10511	.9934	.9963
	11	1.10558	11.62387	0.90450	10.41828	0.09599	.9927	.9959
	12	1.11572	12.73959	0.89628	11.31456	0.08838	.9920	.9955
2	24	1.24483	26.95340	0.80332	21.45562	0.04661	.9831	.9905
3	36	1.38888	42.81200	0.72001	30.54487	0.03274	.9731	.9849
4	48	1.54960	60.50575	0.64533	38.69142	0.02585	.9620	.9786
5	60	1.72892	80.24700	0.57840	45.99303	0.02174	.9495	.9716
6	72	1.92898	102.27268	0.51841	52.53734	0.01903	.9357	.9639
7	84	2.15220	126.84714	0.46464	58.40290	0.01712	.9202	.9552
8	96	2.40125	154.26534	0.41645	63.66010	0.01571	.9030	.9455
9	108	2.67912	184.85633	0.37326	68.37204	0.01463	.8838	.9347
10	120	2.98915	218.98729	0.33454	72.59527	0.01377	.8623	.9226
11	132	3.33505	257.06783	0.29985	76.38048	0.01309	.8384	.9092
12	144	3.72098	299.55501	0.26875	79.77311	0.01254	.8117	.8941
13	156	4.15157	346.95876	0.24087	82.81385	0.01208	.7818	.8774
14	168	4.63198	399.84802	0.21589	85.53923	0.01169	.7486	.8587
15	180	5.16799	458.85755	0.19350	87.98193	0.01137	.7115	.8378
16	192	5.76602	524.69561	0.17343	90.17129	0.01109	.6701	.8146
17	204	6.43326	598.15236	0.15544	92.13357	0.01085	.6239	.7886
18	216	7.17771	680.10945	0.13932	93.89233	0.01065	.5724	.7597
19	228	8.00830	771.55051	0.12487	95.46868	0.01047	.5149	.7274
20	240	8.93501	873.57303	0.11192	96.88153	0.01032	.4507	.6913
21	252	9.96896	987.40148	0.10031	98.14785	0.01019	.3792	.6511
22	264	11.12256	1114.40201	0.08991	99.28283	0.01007	.2993	.6062
23	276	12.40965	1256.09891	0.08058	100.30009	0.00997	.2102	.5561
24	288	13.84568	1414.19280	0.07222	101.21185	0.00988	.1108	.5003
25	300	15.44789	1590.58113	0.06473	102.02904	0.00980	.0	.4379
26	312	17.23550	1787.38092	0.05802	102.76147	0.00973	.0	.3684
27	324	19.22997	2006.95415	0.05200	103.41794	0.00967	.0	.2908
28	336	21.45524	2251.93613	0.04661	104.00632	0.00961	.0	.2042
29	348	23.93802	2525.26715	0.04177	104.53368	0.00957	.0	.1076
30	360	26.70810	2830.22771	0.03744	105.00634	0.00952	.0	.0
31	372	29.79873	3170.47795	0.03356	105.42998	0.00948	.0	.0
32	384	33.24700	3550.10156	0.03008	105.80968	0.00945	.0	.0
33	396	37.09430	3973.65476	0.02696	106.14999	0.00942	.0	.0
34	408	41.38681	4446.22105	0.02416	106.45502	0.00939	.0	.0
35	420	46.17605	4973.47216	0.02166	106.72840	0.00937	.0	.0
36	432	51.51949	5561.73615	0.01941	106.97343	0.00935	.0	.0
37	444	57.48126	6218.07336	0.01740	107.19305	0.00933	.0	.0
38	456	64.13292	6950.36115	0.01559	107.38989	0.00931	.0	.0
39	468	71.55431	7767.38843	0.01398	107.56631	0.00930	.0	.0
40	480	79.83449	8678.96116	0.01253	107.72444	0.00928	.0	.0

INTEREST RATE = 11.25%

YR	MOS	(1) COMPOUND VALUE $1	(2) COMPOUND VALUE $1 PER MO	(3) PRESENT VALUE $1	(4) PRESENT VALUE $1 PER MO	(5) LOAN CONSTANT	(6) BAL 25 YR LOAN	(7) BAL 30 YR LOAN
	1	1.00938	1.00938	0.99071	0.99071	1.00937	.9994	.9997
	2	1.01884	2.02821	0.98151	1.97222	0.50704	.9988	.9993
	3	1.02839	3.05660	0.97239	2.94462	0.33960	.9982	.9990
	4	1.03803	4.09463	0.96336	3.90798	0.25589	.9975	.9986
	5	1.04776	5.14240	0.95441	4.86239	0.20566	.9969	.9983
	6	1.05759	6.19998	0.94555	5.80794	0.17218	.9963	.9979
	7	1.06750	7.26748	0.93677	6.74471	0.14826	.9956	.9976
	8	1.07751	8.34499	0.92807	7.67278	0.13033	.9950	.9972
	9	1.08761	9.43260	0.91945	8.59223	0.11638	.9943	.9968
	10	1.09781	10.53040	0.91091	9.50314	0.10523	.9937	.9965
	11	1.10810	11.63850	0.90245	10.40558	0.09610	.9930	.9961
	12	1.11849	12.75699	0.89407	11.29965	0.08850	.9923	.9957
2	24	1.25101	27.02550	0.79935	21.40228	0.04672	.9837	.9910
3	36	1.39924	42.98462	0.71467	30.43470	0.03286	.9741	.9856
4	48	1.56503	60.83468	0.63897	38.51027	0.02597	.9634	.9796
5	60	1.75046	80.79972	0.57128	45.73036	0.02187	.9514	.9730
6	72	1.95787	103.13034	0.51076	52.18560	0.01916	.9379	.9655
7	84	2.18985	128.10682	0.45665	57.95701	0.01725	.9229	.9571
8	96	2.44931	156.04266	0.40828	63.11703	0.01584	.9061	.9478
9	108	2.73952	187.28851	0.36503	67.73043	0.01476	.8873	.9373
10	120	3.06412	222.23655	0.32636	71.85511	0.01392	.8663	.9257
11	132	3.42717	261.32544	0.29179	75.54284	0.01324	.8427	.9126
12	144	3.83324	305.04581	0.26088	78.83992	0.01268	.8164	.8980
13	156	4.28743	353.94644	0.23324	81.78772	0.01223	.7870	.8816
14	168	4.79543	408.64110	0.20853	84.42325	0.01185	.7541	.8633
15	180	5.36362	469.81631	0.18644	86.77959	0.01152	.7173	.8428
16	192	5.99913	538.23992	0.16669	88.88631	0.01125	.6761	.8199
17	204	6.70995	614.77076	0.14903	90.76986	0.01102	.6300	.7943
18	216	7.50498	700.36944	0.13324	92.45387	0.01082	.5785	.7657
19	228	8.39421	796.11035	0.11913	93.95949	0.01064	.5209	.7337
20	240	9.38881	903.19521	0.10651	95.30562	0.01049	.4565	.6979
21	252	10.50125	1022.96813	0.09523	96.50914	0.01036	.3844	.6578
22	264	11.74550	1156.93245	0.08514	97.58517	0.01025	.3038	.6130
23	276	13.13718	1306.76966	0.07612	98.54721	0.01015	.2136	.5628
24	288	14.69375	1474.36047	0.06806	99.40734	0.01006	.1127	.5068
25	300	16.43475	1661.80844	0.06085	100.17635	0.00998	.0	.4441
26	312	18.38204	1871.46635	0.05440	100.86389	0.00991	.0	.3739
27	324	20.56005	2105.96578	0.04864	101.47860	0.00985	.0	.2955
28	336	22.99613	2368.25009	0.04349	102.02820	0.00980	.0	.2078
29	348	25.72085	2661.61140	0.03888	102.51957	0.00975	.0	.1096
30	360	28.76841	2989.73190	0.03476	102.95889	0.00971	.0	.0
31	372	32.17706	3356.73006	0.03108	103.35167	0.00968	.0	.0
32	384	35.98959	3767.21235	0.02779	103.70284	0.00964	.0	.0
33	396	40.25385	4226.33101	0.02484	104.01681	0.00961	.0	.0
34	408	45.02336	4739.84878	0.02221	104.29752	0.00959	.0	.0
35	420	50.35800	5314.21118	0.01986	104.54849	0.00956	.0	.0
36	432	56.32471	5956.62745	0.01775	104.77288	0.00954	.0	.0
37	444	62.99840	6675.16101	0.01587	104.97349	0.00953	.0	.0
38	456	70.46282	7478.83069	0.01419	105.15286	0.00951	.0	.0
39	468	78.81168	8377.72393	0.01269	105.31322	0.00950	.0	.0
40	480	88.14975	9383.12337	0.01134	105.45660	0.00948	.0	.0

INTEREST RATE = 11.50%

YR	MOS	(1) COMPOUND VALUE $1	(2) COMPOUND VALUE $1 PER MO	(3) PRESENT VALUE $1	(4) PRESENT VALUE $1 PER MO	(5) LOAN CONSTANT	(6) BAL 25 YR LOAN	(7) BAL 30 YR LOAN
	1	1.00958	1.00958	0.99051	0.99051	1.00958	.9994	.9997
	2	1.01926	2.02884	0.98111	1.97161	0.50720	.9988	.9994
	3	1.02903	3.05787	0.97179	2.94341	0.33974	.9982	.9990
	4	1.03889	4.09676	0.96257	3.90597	0.25602	.9976	.9987
	5	1.04884	5.14560	0.95343	4.85940	0.20579	.9970	.9984
	6	1.05890	6.20450	0.94438	5.80378	0.17230	.9964	.9980
	7	1.06904	7.27354	0.93542	6.73920	0.14839	.9958	.9977
	8	1.07929	8.35283	0.92654	7.66574	0.13045	.9952	.9974
	9	1.08963	9.44246	0.91774	8.58348	0.11650	.9946	.9970
	10	1.10007	10.54253	0.90903	9.49251	0.10535	.9939	.9967
	11	1.11062	11.65315	0.90040	10.39291	0.09622	.9933	.9963
	12	1.12126	12.77441	0.89185	11.28476	0.08862	.9926	.9960
2	24	1.25722	27.09783	0.79540	21.34913	0.04684	.9844	.9914
3	36	1.40967	43.15810	0.70938	30.32508	0.03298	.9751	.9863
4	48	1.58061	61.16583	0.63267	38.33032	0.02609	.9648	.9806
5	60	1.77227	81.35716	0.56425	45.46982	0.02199	.9531	.9742
6	72	1.98718	103.99688	0.50323	51.83722	0.01929	.9401	.9671
7	84	2.22814	129.38188	0.44880	57.51602	0.01739	.9255	.9590
8	96	2.49832	157.84505	0.40027	62.58067	0.01598	.9091	.9500
9	108	2.80127	189.75964	0.35698	67.09761	0.01490	.9907	.9399
10	120	3.14095	225.54417	0.31838	71.12606	0.01406	.8701	.9286
11	132	3.52182	265.66791	0.28394	74.71885	0.01338	.8470	.9159
12	144	3.94887	310.65703	0.25324	77.92309	0.01283	.8211	.9016
13	156	4.42771	361.10150	0.22585	80.78081	0.01238	.7920	.8857
14	168	4.96461	417.66283	0.20143	83.32948	0.01200	.7595	.8678
15	180	5.56661	481.08275	0.17964	85.60252	0.01168	.7230	.8477
16	192	6.24162	552.19293	0.16021	87.62974	0.01141	.6820	.8252
17	204	6.99847	631.92588	0.14289	89.43773	0.01119	.6361	.7999
18	216	7.84710	721.32719	0.12744	91.05019	0.01098	.5846	.7716
19	228	8.79863	821.56925	0.11365	92.48827	0.01081	.5269	.7399
20	240	9.86555	933.96659	0.10136	93.77083	0.01066	.4621	.7043
21	252	11.06184	1059.99315	0.09040	94.91469	0.01054	.3896	.6644
22	264	12.40319	1201.30161	0.08062	95.93484	0.01042	.3082	.6197
23	276	13.90720	1359.74504	0.07191	96.84467	0.01033	.2169	.5695
24	288	15.59357	1537.40122	0.06413	97.65610	0.01024	.1146	.5133
25	300	17.48444	1736.59986	0.05719	98.37978	0.01016	.0	.4502
26	312	19.60459	1959.95319	0.05101	99.02520	0.01010	.0	.3795
27	324	21.98183	2210.39020	0.04549	99.60081	0.01004	.0	.3002
28	336	24.64733	2491.19503	0.04057	100.11418	0.00999	.0	.2113
29	348	27.63605	2806.05007	0.03618	100.57203	0.00994	.0	.1116
30	360	30.98718	3159.08422	0.03227	100.98037	0.00990	.0	.0
31	372	34.74466	3554.92704	0.02878	101.34454	0.00987	.0	.0
32	384	38.95778	3998.76951	0.02567	101.66933	0.00984	.0	.0
33	396	43.68177	4496.43201	0.02289	101.95900	0.00981	.0	.0
34	408	48.97859	5054.44073	0.02042	102.21734	0.00978	.0	.0
35	420	54.91771	5680.11321	0.01821	102.44774	0.00976	.0	.0
36	432	61.57699	6381.65432	0.01624	102.65323	0.00974	.0	.0
37	444	69.04377	7168.26382	0.01448	102.83649	0.00972	.0	.0
38	456	77.41598	8050.25707	0.01292	102.99993	0.00971	.0	.0
39	468	86.80338	9039.20022	0.01152	103.14570	0.00970	.0	.0
40	480	97.32910	10148.06195	0.01027	103.27570	0.00968	.0	.0

INTEREST RATE = 11.75%

YR	MOS	(1) COMPOUND VALUE $1	(2) COMPOUND VALUE $1 PER MO	(3) PRESENT VALUE $1	(4) PRESENT VALUE $1 PER MO	(5) LOAN CONSTANT	(6) BAL 25 YR LOAN	(7) BAL 30 YR LOAN
	1	1.00979	1.00979	0.99030	0.99030	1.00979	.9994	.9997
	2	1.01968	2.02947	0.98070	1.97100	0.50736	.9989	.9994
	3	1.02966	3.05913	0.97119	2.94219	0.33988	.9983	.9991
	4	1.03975	4.09888	0.96177	3.90397	0.25615	.9977	.9988
	5	1.04993	5.14881	0.95245	4.85642	0.20591	.9972	.9985
	6	1.06021	6.20901	0.94321	5.79963	0.17242	.9966	.9981
	7	1.07059	7.27960	0.93407	6.73369	0.14851	.9960	.9978
	8	1.08107	8.36067	0.92501	7.65870	0.13057	.9954	.9975
	9	1.09166	9.45233	0.91604	8.57474	0.11662	.9948	.9972
	10	1.10235	10.55468	0.90716	9.48190	0.10546	.9942	.9968
	11	1.11314	11.66782	0.89836	10.38026	0.09634	.9936	.9965
	12	1.12404	12.79185	0.88965	11.26991	0.08873	.9930	.9962
2	24	1.26346	27.17040	0.79147	21.29616	0.04696	.9850	.9919
3	36	1.42018	43.33244	0.70413	30.21601	0.03310	.9761	.9870
4	48	1.59634	61.49921	0.62643	38.15155	0.02621	.9661	.9816
5	60	1.79435	81.91936	0.55731	45.21139	0.02212	.9549	.9755
6	72	2.01692	104.87241	0.49581	51.49216	0.01942	.9422	.9686
7	84	2.26709	130.67254	0.44109	57.07985	0.01752	.9280	.9609
8	96	2.54830	159.67289	0.39242	62.05093	0.01612	.9120	.9522
9	108	2.86439	192.27041	0.34911	66.47344	0.01504	.8941	.9424
10	120	3.21969	228.91130	0.31059	70.40792	0.01420	.8739	.9314
11	132	3.61906	270.09708	0.27632	73.90823	0.01353	.8512	.9191
12	144	4.06796	316.39151	0.24582	77.02228	0.01298	.8257	.9052
13	156	4.57255	368.42826	0.21870	79.79269	0.01253	.7970	.8896
14	168	5.13972	426.91960	0.19456	82.25738	0.01216	.7648	.8721
15	180	5.77725	492.66614	0.17309	84.45009	0.01184	.7286	.8524
16	192	6.49385	566.56782	0.15399	86.40083	0.01157	.6878	.8303
17	204	7.29934	649.63619	0.13700	88.13630	0.01135	.6421	.8054
18	216	8.20474	743.00827	0.12188	89.68026	0.01115	.5906	.7774
19	228	9.22245	847.96215	0.10843	91.05385	0.01098	.5328	.7460
20	240	10.36639	965.93439	0.09647	92.27585	0.01084	.4678	.7107
21	252	11.65223	1098.53980	0.08582	93.36301	0.01071	.3947	.6709
22	264	13.09756	1247.59345	0.07635	94.33020	0.01060	.3126	.6263
23	276	14.72217	1415.13558	0.06792	95.19066	0.01051	.2203	.5761
24	288	16.54830	1603.45946	0.06043	95.95616	0.01042	.1165	.5197
25	300	18.60093	1815.14285	0.05376	96.63719	0.01035	.0	.4563
26	312	20.90817	2053.08324	0.04783	97.24307	0.01028	.0	.3850
27	324	23.50160	2320.53753	0.04255	97.78209	0.01023	.0	.3049
28	336	26.41672	2621.16658	0.03785	98.26163	0.01018	.0	.2148
29	348	29.69342	2959.08537	0.03368	98.68825	0.01013	.0	.1136
30	360	33.37656	3338.91926	0.02996	99.06779	0.01009	.0	.0
31	372	37.51656	3765.86739	0.02665	99.40545	0.01006	.0	.0
32	384	42.17008	4245.77374	0.02371	99.70585	0.01003	.0	.0
33	396	47.40081	4785.20720	0.02110	99.97310	0.01000	.0	.0
34	408	53.28036	5391.55146	0.01877	100.21085	0.00998	.0	.0
35	420	59.88921	6073.10607	0.01670	100.42238	0.00996	.0	.0
36	432	67.31780	6839.20004	0.01485	100.61056	0.00994	.0	.0
37	444	75.66784	7700.31956	0.01322	100.77797	0.00992	.0	.0
38	456	85.05360	8668.25150	0.01176	100.92691	0.00991	.0	.0
39	468	95.60357	9756.24477	0.01046	101.05941	0.00990	.0	.0
40	480	107.46214	10979.19165	0.00931	101.17729	0.00988	.0	.0

INTEREST RATE = 12.00%

YR	MOS	(1) COMPOUND VALUE $1	(2) COMPOUND VALUE $1 PER MO	(3) PRESENT VALUE $1	(4) PRESENT VALUE $1 PER MO	(5) LOAN CONSTANT	(6) BAL 25 YR LOAN	(7) BAL 30 YR LOAN
	1	1.01000	1.01000	0.99010	0.99010	1.01000	.9995	.9997
	2	1.02010	2.03010	0.98030	1.97039	0.50751	.9989	.9994
	3	1.03030	3.06040	0.97059	2.94098	0.34002	.9984	.9991
	4	1.04060	4.10101	0.96098	3.90197	0.25628	.9978	.9988
	5	1.05101	5.15202	0.95147	4.85343	0.20604	.9973	.9985
	6	1.06152	6.21354	0.94205	5.79548	0.17255	.9967	.9982
	7	1.07214	7.28567	0.93272	6.72819	0.14863	.9962	.9979
	8	1.08286	8.36853	0.92348	7.65168	0.13069	.9956	.9976
	9	1.09369	9.46221	0.91434	8.56602	0.11674	.9950	.9973
	10	1.10462	10.56684	0.90529	9.47130	0.10558	.9944	.9970
	11	1.11567	11.68250	0.89632	10.36763	0.09645	.9938	.9967
	12	1.12683	12.80933	0.88745	11.25508	0.08885	.9932	.9964
2	24	1.26973	27.24320	0.78757	21.24339	0.04707	.9856	.9923
3	36	1.43077	43.50765	0.69892	30.10750	0.03321	.9771	.9877
4	48	1.61223	61.83483	0.62026	37.97396	0.02633	.9674	.9825
5	60	1.81670	82.48637	0.55045	44.95504	0.02224	.9565	.9766
6	72	2.04710	105.75703	0.48850	51.15039	0.01955	.9443	.9700
7	84	2.30672	131.97900	0.43352	56.64845	0.01765	.9304	.9626
8	96	2.59927	161.52656	0.38472	61.52770	0.01625	.9149	.9542
9	108	2.92893	194.82150	0.34142	65.85779	0.01518	.8973	.9448
10	120	3.30039	232.33907	0.30299	69.70052	0.01435	.8776	.9342
11	132	3.71896	274.61481	0.26889	73.11075	0.01368	.8553	.9222
12	144	4.19062	322.25217	0.23863	76.13715	0.01313	.8302	.9087
13	156	4.72209	375.93114	0.21177	78.82293	0.01269	.8019	.8935
14	168	5.32097	436.41794	0.18794	81.20643	0.01231	.7700	.8763
15	180	5.99580	504.57599	0.16678	83.32166	0.01200	.7341	.8570
16	192	6.75622	581.37818	0.14801	85.19882	0.01174	.6936	.8353
17	204	7.61308	667.92081	0.13135	86.86470	0.01151	.6480	.8107
18	216	8.57861	765.43922	0.11657	88.34309	0.01132	.5966	.7831
19	228	9.66659	875.32539	0.10345	89.65508	0.01115	.5387	.7520
20	240	10.89255	999.14789	0.09181	90.81941	0.01101	.4734	.7169
21	252	12.27400	1138.67418	0.08147	91.85269	0.01089	.3999	.6774
22	264	13.83065	1295.89589	0.07230	92.76968	0.01078	.3170	.6328
23	276	15.58472	1473.05725	0.06417	93.58345	0.01069	.2237	.5826
24	288	17.56126	1672.68710	0.05694	94.30564	0.01060	.1185	.5261
25	300	19.78847	1897.63502	0.05053	94.94654	0.01053	.0	.4623
26	312	22.29814	2151.11196	0.04485	95.51531	0.01047	.0	.3905
27	324	25.12610	2436.73612	0.03980	96.02007	0.01041	.0	.3096
28	336	28.31272	2758.58458	0.03532	96.46801	0.01037	.0	.2184
29	348	31.90348	3121.25147	0.03134	96.86554	0.01032	.0	.1156
30	360	35.94964	3529.91360	0.02782	97.21832	0.01029	.0	.0
31	372	40.50895	3990.40432	0.02469	97.53140	0.01025	.0	.0
32	384	45.64650	4509.29678	0.02191	97.80924	0.01022	.0	.0
33	396	51.43562	5093.99780	0.01944	98.05581	0.01020	.0	.0
34	408	57.95894	5752.85354	0.01725	98.27463	0.01018	.0	.0
35	420	65.30959	6495.26868	0.01531	98.46882	0.01016	.0	.0
36	432	73.59248	7331.84064	0.01359	98.64116	0.01014	.0	.0
37	444	82.92585	8274.51086	0.01206	98.79410	0.01012	.0	.0
38	456	93.44292	9336.73525	0.01070	98.92982	0.01011	.0	.0
39	468	105.29382	10533.67629	0.00950	99.05027	0.01010	.0	.0
40	480	118.64771	11882.41940	0.00843	99.15716	0.01008	.0	.0

INTEREST RATE = 12.25%

YR	MOS	(1) COMPOUND VALUE $1	(2) COMPOUND VALUE $1 PER MO	(3) PRESENT VALUE $1	(4) PRESENT VALUE $1 PER MO	(5) LOAN CONSTANT	(6) BAL 25 YR LOAN	(7) BAL 30 YR LOAN
	1	1.01021	1.01021	0.98989	0.98989	1.01021	.9995	.9997
	2	1.02052	2.03073	0.97989	1.96979	0.50767	.9990	.9995
	3	1.03094	3.06167	0.96999	2.93978	0.34016	.9985	.9992
	4	1.04146	4.10313	0.96019	3.89996	0.25641	.9979	.9989
	5	1.05209	5.15523	0.95048	4.85045	0.20617	.9974	.9986
	6	1.06283	6.21806	0.94088	5.79133	0.17267	.9969	.9983
	7	1.07368	7.29174	0.93137	6.72270	0.14875	.9963	.9980
	8	1.08464	8.37639	0.92196	7.64466	0.13081	.9958	.9978
	9	1.09572	9.47211	0.91264	8.55731	0.11686	.9952	.9975
	10	1.10690	10.57901	0.90342	9.46073	0.10570	.9947	.9972
	11	1.11820	11.69721	0.89429	10.35502	0.09657	.9941	.9969
	12	1.12962	12.82683	0.88526	11.24028	0.08897	.9935	.9966
2	24	1.27604	27.31624	0.78368	21.19079	0.04719	.9862	.9927
3	36	1.44143	43.68373	0.69375	29.99954	0.03333	.9780	.9883
4	48	1.62827	62.17272	0.61415	37.79754	0.02646	.9687	.9833
5	60	1.83932	83.05822	0.54368	44.70075	0.02237	.9581	.9777
6	72	2.07773	106.65083	0.48130	50.81186	0.01968	.9462	.9714
7	84	2.34703	133.30146	0.42607	56.22176	0.01779	.9328	.9643
8	96	2.65125	163.40648	0.37718	61.01090	0.01639	.9176	.9562
9	108	2.99490	197.41362	0.33390	65.25051	0.01533	.9005	.9471
10	120	3.38309	235.82868	0.29559	69.00365	0.01449	.8811	.9368
11	132	3.82160	279.22300	0.26167	72.32614	0.01383	.8593	.9252
12	144	4.31694	328.24198	0.23165	75.26739	0.01329	.8346	.9120
13	156	4.87649	383.61467	0.20507	77.87114	0.01284	.8067	.8972
14	168	5.50857	446.16462	0.18154	80.17614	0.01247	.7751	.8805
15	180	6.22258	516.82214	0.16071	82.21664	0.01216	.7395	.8615
16	192	7.02913	596.63809	0.14227	84.02301	0.01190	.6993	.8401
17	204	7.94023	686.79957	0.12594	85.62211	0.01168	.6538	.8160
18	216	8.96942	788.64755	0.11149	87.03772	0.01149	.6025	.7887
19	228	10.13202	903.69680	0.09870	88.29090	0.01133	.5445	.7579
20	240	11.44530	1033.65843	0.08737	89.40028	0.01119	.4790	.7230
21	252	12.92881	1180.46534	0.07735	90.38236	0.01106	.4050	.6837
22	264	14.60461	1346.30097	0.06847	91.25176	0.01096	.3215	.6393
23	276	16.49762	1533.63178	0.06061	92.02140	0.01087	.2270	.5891
24	288	18.63600	1745.24392	0.05366	92.70273	0.01079	.1204	.5324
25	300	21.05155	1984.28467	0.04750	93.30588	0.01072	.0	.4683
26	312	23.78019	2254.30925	0.04205	93.83982	0.01066	.0	.3960
27	324	26.86252	2559.33370	0.03723	94.31249	0.01060	.0	.3142
28	336	30.34437	2903.89462	0.03296	94.73093	0.01056	.0	.2219
29	348	34.27752	3293.11662	0.02917	95.10135	0.01052	.0	.1176
30	360	38.72049	3732.78855	0.02583	95.42927	0.01048	.0	.0
31	372	43.73933	4229.44959	0.02286	95.71956	0.01045	.0	.0
32	384	49.40871	4790.48653	0.02024	95.97655	0.01042	.0	.0
33	396	55.81294	5424.24360	0.01792	96.20404	0.01039	.0	.0
34	408	63.04726	6140.14659	0.01586	96.40543	0.01037	.0	.0
35	420	71.21928	6948.84304	0.01404	96.58372	0.01035	.0	.0
36	432	80.45054	7862.36060	0.01243	96.74154	0.01034	.0	.0
37	444	90.87833	8894.28589	0.01100	96.88126	0.01032	.0	.0
38	456	102.65773	10059.96662	0.00974	97.00495	0.01031	.0	.0
39	468	115.96396	11376.73981	0.00862	97.11444	0.01030	.0	.0
40	480	130.99490	12864.18967	0.00763	97.21137	0.01029	.0	.0

INTEREST RATE = 12.50%

YR	MOS	(1) COMPOUND VALUE $1	(2) COMPOUND VALUE $1 PER MO	(3) PRESENT VALUE $1	(4) PRESENT VALUE $1 PER MO	(5) LOAN CONSTANT	(6) BAL 25 YR LOAN	(7) BAL 30 YR LOAN
	1	1.01042	1.01042	0.98969	0.98969	1.01042	.9995	.9997
	2	1.02094	2.03136	0.97949	1.96918	0.50783	.9990	.9995
	3	1.03158	3.06294	0.96939	2.93857	0.34030	.9985	.9992
	4	1.04232	4.10526	0.95940	3.89796	0.25654	.9980	.9990
	5	1.05318	5.15844	0.94951	4.84747	0.20629	.9975	.9987
	6	1.06415	6.22259	0.93972	5.78719	0.17280	.9970	.9984
	7	1.07524	7.29782	0.93003	6.71722	0.14887	.9965	.9982
	8	1.08644	8.38426	0.92044	7.63766	0.13093	.9960	.9979
	9	1.09775	9.48201	0.91095	8.54861	0.11698	.9954	.9976
	10	1.10919	10.59120	0.90156	9.45017	0.10582	.9949	.9973
	11	1.12074	11.71194	0.89227	10.34244	0.09669	.9944	.9970
	12	1.13242	12.84436	0.88307	11.22550	0.08908	.9938	.9967
2	24	1.28237	27.38951	0.77981	21.13838	0.04731	.9868	.9931
3	36	1.45217	43.86068	0.68862	29.89212	0.03345	.9789	.9889
4	48	1.64446	62.51289	0.60810	37.62227	0.02658	.9699	.9842
5	60	1.86222	83.63496	0.53699	44.44852	0.02250	.9597	.9788
6	72	2.10880	107.55393	0.47420	50.47655	0.01981	.9482	.9728
7	84	2.38804	134.64015	0.41875	55.79971	0.01792	.9351	.9659
8	96	2.70426	165.31302	0.36979	60.50043	0.01653	.9203	.9581
9	108	3.06235	200.04747	0.32655	64.65147	0.01547	.9036	.9493
10	120	3.46785	239.38133	0.28836	68.31713	0.01464	.8846	.9394
11	132	3.92705	283.92361	0.25464	71.55415	0.01398	.8632	.9281
12	144	4.44705	334.36401	0.22487	74.41266	0.01344	.8389	.9153
13	156	5.03591	391.48352	0.19857	76.93692	0.01300	.8113	.9008
14	168	5.70275	456.16658	0.17535	79.16601	0.01263	.7802	.8844
15	180	6.45788	529.41471	0.15485	81.13444	0.01233	.7449	.8659
16	192	7.31301	612.36207	0.13674	82.87271	0.01207	.7049	.8449
17	204	8.28137	706.29299	0.12075	84.40771	0.01185	.6596	.8211
18	216	9.37796	812.66187	0.10663	85.76322	0.01166	.6084	.7941
19	228	10.61975	933.11569	0.09416	86.96023	0.01150	.5503	.7636
20	240	12.02597	1069.51954	0.08315	88.01727	0.01136	.4846	.7291
21	252	13.61841	1223.98544	0.07343	88.95071	0.01124	.4102	.6899
22	264	15.42170	1398.90510	0.06484	89.77500	0.01114	.3259	.6456
23	276	17.46378	1596.98694	0.05726	90.50290	0.01105	.2304	.5954
24	288	19.77627	1821.29799	0.05057	91.14569	0.01097	.1223	.5386
25	300	22.39496	2075.31142	0.04465	91.71332	0.01090	.0	.4743
26	312	25.36042	2362.96030	0.03943	92.21457	0.01084	.0	.4014
27	324	28.71854	2688.69851	0.03482	92.65721	0.01079	.0	.3189
28	336	32.52134	3057.56969	0.03075	93.04809	0.01075	.0	.2254
29	348	36.82768	3475.28533	0.02715	93.39326	0.01071	.0	.1196
30	360	41.70426	3948.31322	0.02398	93.69807	0.01067	.0	.0
31	372	47.22657	4483.97759	0.02117	93.96724	0.01064	.0	.0
32	384	53.48013	5090.57252	0.01870	94.20493	0.01062	.0	.0
33	396	60.56176	5777.49035	0.01651	94.41483	0.01059	.0	.0
34	408	68.58110	6555.36712	0.01458	94.60019	0.01057	.0	.0
35	420	77.66234	7436.24726	0.01288	94.76387	0.01055	.0	.0
36	432	87.94608	8433.77006	0.01137	94.90842	0.01054	.0	.0
37	444	99.59155	9563.38088	0.01004	95.03606	0.01052	.0	.0
38	456	112.77907	10842.57030	0.00887	95.14877	0.01051	.0	.0
39	468	127.71283	12291.14492	0.00783	95.24831	0.01050	.0	.0
40	480	144.62406	13931.53406	0.00691	95.33620	0.01049	.0	.0

INTEREST RATE = 12.75%

YR	MOS	(1)COMPOUNDVALUE $1	(2)COMPOUNDVALUE $1PER MO	(3)PRESENTVALUE $1	(4)PRESENTVALUE $1PER MO	(5)LOANCONSTANT	(6)BAL25 YRLOAN	(7)BAL30 YRLOAN
	1	1.01063	1.01063	0.98949	0.98949	1.01062	.9995	.9998
	2	1.02136	2.03199	0.97908	1.96857	0.50798	.9991	.9995
	3	1.03221	3.06420	0.96879	2.93736	0.34044	.9986	.9993
	4	1.04318	4.10739	0.95861	3.89597	0.25668	.9981	.9990
	5	1.05427	5.16165	0.94853	4.84449	0.20642	.9976	.9988
	6	1.06547	6.22712	0.93856	5.78305	0.17292	.9971	.9985
	7	1.07679	7.30391	0.92869	6.71174	0.14899	.9966	.9983
	8	1.08823	8.39214	0.91892	7.63066	0.13105	.9961	.9980
	9	1.09979	9.49193	0.90926	8.53992	0.11710	.9956	.9977
	10	1.11148	10.60340	0.89970	9.43963	0.10594	.9951	.9975
	11	1.12329	11.72669	0.89025	10.32987	0.09681	.9946	.9972
	12	1.13522	12.86191	0.88089	11.21076	0.08920	.9941	.9969
2	24	1.28873	27.46302	0.77596	21.08615	0.04742	.9873	.9934
3	36	1.46299	44.03851	0.68353	29.78525	0.03357	.9797	.9895
4	48	1.66082	62.85536	0.60211	37.44816	0.02670	.9710	.9850
5	60	1.88539	84.21664	0.53039	44.19831	0.02263	.9612	.9798
6	72	2.14034	108.46642	0.46722	50.14441	0.01994	.9500	.9740
7	84	2.42976	135.99527	0.41156	55.38225	0.01806	.9374	.9674
8	96	2.75831	167.24661	0.36254	59.99619	0.01667	.9230	.9600
9	108	3.13130	202.72379	0.31936	64.06055	0.01561	.9066	.9515
10	120	3.55471	242.99823	0.28132	67.64078	0.01478	.8881	.9418
11	132	4.03538	288.71862	0.24781	70.79455	0.01413	.8670	.9309
12	144	4.58105	340.62138	0.21829	73.57266	0.01359	.8431	.9184
13	156	5.20051	399.54248	0.19229	76.01987	0.01315	.8159	.9043
14	168	5.90373	466.43095	0.16938	78.17557	0.01279	.7851	.8883
15	180	6.70203	542.36416	0.14921	80.07450	0.01249	.7501	.8701
16	192	7.60829	628.56514	0.13144	81.74724	0.01223	.7104	.8495
17	204	8.63709	726.42230	0.11578	83.22073	0.01202	.6654	.8261
18	216	9.80501	837.51182	0.10199	84.51871	0.01183	.6142	.7995
19	228	11.13085	963.62298	0.08984	85.66208	0.01167	.5561	.7693
20	240	12.63598	1106.78703	0.07914	86.66926	0.01154	.4901	.7350
21	252	14.34463	1269.30988	0.06971	87.55646	0.01142	.4153	.6961
22	264	16.28433	1453.80924	0.06141	88.33799	0.01132	.3303	.6519
23	276	18.48631	1663.25680	0.05409	89.02643	0.01123	.2338	.6018
24	288	20.98605	1901.02609	0.04765	89.63287	0.01116	.1242	.5448
25	300	23.82381	2170.94679	0.04197	90.16707	0.01109	.0	.4802
26	312	27.04529	2477.36647	0.03698	90.63764	0.01103	.0	.4068
27	324	30.70238	2825.22054	0.03257	91.05216	0.01098	.0	.3235
28	336	34.85399	3220.11182	0.02869	91.41730	0.01094	.0	.2290
29	348	39.56698	3668.40072	0.02527	91.73895	0.01090	.0	.1216
30	360	44.91727	4177.30773	0.02226	92.02228	0.01087	.0	.0
31	372	50.99103	4755.02969	0.01961	92.27187	0.01084	.0	.0
32	384	57.88610	5410.87184	0.01728	92.49173	0.01081	.0	.0
33	396	65.71352	6155.39767	0.01522	92.68540	0.01079	.0	.0
34	408	74.59937	7000.59909	0.01340	92.85600	0.01077	.0	.0
35	420	84.68678	7960.08955	0.01181	93.00628	0.01075	.0	.0
36	432	96.13822	9049.32335	0.01040	93.13866	0.01074	.0	.0
37	444	109.13813	10285.84451	0.00916	93.25527	0.01072	.0	.0
38	456	123.89590	11689.56940	0.00807	93.35799	0.01071	.0	.0
39	468	140.64924	13283.10748	0.00711	93.44847	0.01070	.0	.0
40	480	159.66798	15092.12549	0.00626	93.52818	0.01069	.0	.0

INTEREST RATE = 13.00%

YR	MOS	(1) COMPOUND VALUE $1	(2) COMPOUND VALUE $1 PER MO	(3) PRESENT VALUE $1	(4) PRESENT VALUE $1 PER MO	(5) LOAN CONSTANT	(6) BAL 25 YR LOAN	(7) BAL 30 YR LOAN
	1	1.01083	1.01083	0.98928	0.98928	1.01083	.9996	.9998
	2	1.02178	2.03262	0.97868	1.96796	0.50814	.9991	.9995
	3	1.03285	3.06547	0.96819	2.93615	0.34058	.9987	.9993
	4	1.04404	4.10951	0.95782	3.89397	0.25681	.9982	.9991
	5	1.05535	5.16487	0.94755	4.84152	0.20655	.9977	.9988
	6	1.06679	6.23165	0.93740	5.77891	0.17304	.9973	.9986
	7	1.07834	7.31000	0.92735	6.70626	0.14911	.9968	.9983
	8	1.09002	8.40002	0.91741	7.62367	0.13117	.9963	.9981
	9	1.10183	9.50185	0.90758	8.53125	0.11722	.9958	.9979
	10	1.11377	10.61562	0.89785	9.42910	0.10605	.9953	.9976
	11	1.12584	11.74146	0.88823	10.31733	0.09692	.9948	.9973
	12	1.13803	12.87949	0.87871	11.19604	0.08932	.9943	.9971
2	24	1.29512	27.53677	0.77213	21.03411	0.04754	.9879	.9938
3	36	1.47389	44.21723	0.67848	29.67892	0.03369	.9805	.9900
4	48	1.67733	63.20014	0.59619	37.27519	0.02683	.9722	.9857
5	60	1.90886	84.80331	0.52387	43.95011	0.02275	.9627	.9808
6	72	2.17234	109.38841	0.46033	49.81542	0.02007	.9518	.9752
7	84	2.47219	137.36705	0.40450	54.96933	0.01819	.9395	.9689
8	96	2.81344	169.20766	0.35544	59.49811	0.01681	.9255	.9617
9	108	3.20178	205.44331	0.31233	63.47760	0.01575	.9095	.9535
10	120	3.64373	246.68065	0.27444	66.97441	0.01493	.8914	.9442
11	132	4.14669	293.61008	0.24116	70.04710	0.01428	.8707	.9336
12	144	4.71906	347.01730	0.21191	72.74710	0.01375	.8472	.9215
13	156	5.37045	407.79645	0.18620	75.11961	0.01331	.8204	.9077
14	168	6.11174	476.96510	0.16362	77.20436	0.01295	.7900	.8921
15	180	6.95536	555.68127	0.14377	79.03625	0.01265	.7553	.8743
16	192	7.91543	645.26282	0.12634	80.64595	0.01240	.7159	.8540
17	204	9.00802	747.20954	0.11101	82.06040	0.01219	.6710	.8309
18	216	10.25142	863.22822	0.09755	83.30330	0.01200	.6199	.8047
19	228	11.66644	995.26124	0.08572	84.39545	0.01185	.5618	.7748
20	240	13.27679	1145.51911	0.07532	85.35513	0.01172	.4956	.7408
21	252	15.10942	1316.51744	0.06618	86.19840	0.01160	.4203	.7021
22	264	17.19501	1511.11910	0.05816	86.93940	0.01150	.3347	.6581
23	276	19.56848	1732.58211	0.05110	87.59052	0.01142	.2371	.6080
24	288	22.26957	1984.61420	0.04490	88.16267	0.01134	.1262	.5510
25	300	25.34349	2271.43491	0.03946	88.66542	0.01128	.0	.4861
26	312	28.84171	2597.84620	0.03467	89.10719	0.01122	.0	.4122
27	324	32.82281	2969.31284	0.03047	89.49538	0.01117	.0	.3282
28	336	37.35342	3392.05394	0.02677	89.83649	0.01113	.0	.2325
29	348	42.50941	3873.14705	0.02352	90.13622	0.01109	.0	.1237
30	360	48.37709	4420.64663	0.02067	90.39960	0.01106	.0	.0
31	372	55.05469	5043.71893	0.01816	90.63103	0.01103	.0	.0
32	384	62.65403	5752.79545	0.01596	90.83439	0.01101	.0	.0
33	396	71.30232	6559.74756	0.01402	91.01309	0.01099	.0	.0
34	408	81.14436	7478.08527	0.01232	91.17011	0.01097	.0	.0
35	420	92.34492	8523.18341	0.01083	91.30809	0.01095	.0	.0
36	432	105.09151	9712.53904	0.00952	91.42933	0.01094	.0	.0
37	444	119.59755	11066.06437	0.00836	91.53587	0.01092	.0	.0
38	456	136.10590	12606.42015	0.00735	91.62948	0.01091	.0	.0
39	468	154.89294	14359.39507	0.00646	91.71174	0.01090	.0	.0
40	480	176.27319	16354.33746	0.00567	91.78402	0.01090	.0	.0

		(1) COMPOUND VALUE $1	(2) COMPOUND VALUE $1 PER MO	(3) PRESENT VALUE $1	(4) PRESENT VALUE $1 PER MO	(5) LOAN CONSTANT	(6) BAL 25 YR LOAN	(7) BAL 30 YR LOAN
YR	MOS							
	1	1.01125	1.01125	0.98888	0.98888	1.01125	.9996	.9998
	2	1.02263	2.03388	0.97787	1.96675	0.50845	.9992	.9996
	3	1.03413	3.06801	0.96700	2.93374	0.34086	.9988	.9994
	4	1.04577	4.11377	0.95624	3.68998	0.25707	.9983	.9992
	5	1.05753	5.17130	0.94560	4.83558	0.20680	.9979	.9990
	6	1.06943	6.24073	0.93508	5.77066	0.17329	.9975	.9987
	7	1.08146	7.32219	0.92468	6.69534	0.14936	.9971	.9985
	8	1.09362	8.41581	0.91439	7.60973	0.13141	.9966	.9983
	9	1.10593	9.52174	0.90422	8.51395	0.11745	.9962	.9981
	10	1.11837	10.64011	0.89416	9.40811	0.10629	.9957	.9979
	11	1.13095	11.77106	0.88421	10.29232	0.09716	.9953	.9976
	12	1.14367	12.91474	0.87437	11.16669	0.08955	.9948	.9974
2	24	1.30799	27.68499	0.76453	20.93057	0.04778	.9889	.9944
3	36	1.49592	44.57735	0.66849	29.46785	0.03394	.9821	.9910
4	48	1.71084	63.89671	0.58451	36.93264	0.02708	.9743	.9871
5	60	1.95665	85.99177	0.51108	43.45965	0.02301	.9654	.9826
6	72	2.23777	111.26133	0.44687	49.16671	0.02034	.9553	.9775
7	84	2.55927	140.16147	0.39074	54.15682	0.01846	.9437	.9717
8	96	2.92698	173.21383	0.34165	58.52005	0.01709	.9304	.9650
9	108	3.34751	211.01496	0.29873	62.33514	0.01604	.9152	.9574
10	120	3.82846	254.24716	0.26120	65.67097	0.01523	.8978	.9487
11	132	4.37851	303.69071	0.22839	68.58772	0.01458	.8779	.9387
12	144	5.00759	360.23804	0.19970	71.13806	0.01406	.8552	.9273
13	156	5.72706	424.90977	0.17461	73.36801	0.01363	.8292	.9142
14	168	6.54989	498.87318	0.15267	75.31783	0.01328	.7995	.8993
15	180	7.49094	583.46324	0.13349	77.02270	0.01298	.7655	.8822
16	192	8.56719	680.20672	0.11672	78.51339	0.01274	.7266	.8627
17	204	9.79808	790.84978	0.10206	79.81681	0.01253	.6821	.8403
18	216	11.20582	917.38941	0.08924	80.95649	0.01235	.6312	.8148
19	228	12.81580	1062.10956	0.07803	81.95300	0.01220	.5731	.7856
20	240	14.65711	1227.62228	0.06823	82.82432	0.01207	.5065	.7521
21	252	16.76296	1416.91496	0.05966	83.58619	0.01196	.4304	.7139
22	264	19.17137	1633.40416	0.05216	84.25234	0.01187	.3434	.6702
23	276	21.92580	1880.99732	0.04561	84.83481	0.01179	.2439	.6202
24	288	25.07598	2164.16329	0.03988	85.34410	0.01172	.1301	.5631
25	300	28.67876	2488.01296	0.03487	85.78942	0.01166	.0	.4977
26	312	32.79916	2858.39156	0.03049	86.17879	0.01160	.0	.4229
27	324	37.51157	3281.98410	0.02666	86.51924	0.01156	.0	.3374
28	336	42.90102	3766.43606	0.02331	86.81693	0.01152	.0	.2396
29	348	49.06480	4320.49138	0.02038	87.07722	0.01148	.0	.1277
30	360	56.11416	4954.15028	0.01782	87.30481	0.01145	.0	.0
31	372	64.17633	5678.84978	0.01558	87.50381	0.01143	.0	.0
32	384	73.39682	6507.67006	0.01362	87.67781	0.01141	.0	.0
33	396	83.94207	7455.57063	0.01191	87.82995	0.01139	.0	.0
34	408	96.00240	8539.66029	0.01042	87.96298	0.01137	.0	.0
35	420	109.79549	9779.50592	0.00911	88.07930	0.01135	.0	.0
36	432	125.57030	11197.48567	0.00796	88.18100	0.01134	.0	.0
37	444	143.61154	12819.19286	0.00696	88.26993	0.01133	.0	.0
38	456	164.24484	14673.89793	0.00609	88.34769	0.01132	.0	.0
39	468	187.84263	16795.07670	0.00532	88.41567	0.01131	.0	.0
40	480	214.83081	19221.01464	0.00465	88.47512	0.01130	.0	.0

INTEREST RATE = 14.00%

YR	MOS	(1) COMPOUND VALUE $1	(2) COMPOUND VALUE $1 PER MO	(3) PRESENT VALUE $1	(4) PRESENT VALUE $1 PER MO	(5) LOAN CONSTANT	(6) BAL 25 YR LOAN	(7) BAL 30 YR LOAN
	1	1.01167	1.01167	0.98847	0.98847	1.01167	.9996	.9998
	2	1.02347	2.03514	0.97707	1.96554	0.50877	.9993	.9996
	3	1.03541	3.07055	0.96580	2.93134	0.34114	.9989	.9994
	4	1.04749	4.11804	0.95466	3.88600	0.25733	.9985	.9993
	5	1.05971	5.17775	0.94365	4.82965	0.20705	.9981	.9991
	6	1.07207	6.24982	0.93277	5.76243	0.17354	.9977	.9989
	7	1.08458	7.33440	0.92201	6.68444	0.14960	.9973	.9987
	8	1.09723	8.43164	0.91138	7.59582	0.13165	.9969	.9985
	9	1.11004	9.54167	0.90087	8.49669	0.11769	.9965	.9983
	10	1.12299	10.66466	0.89048	9.38718	0.10653	.9961	.9981
	11	1.13609	11.80075	0.88021	10.26739	0.09740	.9957	.9979
	12	1.14934	12.95009	0.87006	11.13745	0.08979	.9953	.9977
2	24	1.32099	27.83417	0.75701	20.82774	0.04801	.9898	.9950
3	36	1.51827	44.94107	0.65865	29.25890	0.03418	.9835	.9919
4	48	1.74501	64.60274	0.57306	36.59454	0.02733	.9763	.9884
5	60	2.00561	87.20073	0.49860	42.97701	0.02327	.9680	.9843
6	72	2.30513	113.17356	0.43381	48.53017	0.02061	.9585	.9796
7	84	2.64938	143.02521	0.37745	53.36176	0.01874	.9476	.9743
8	96	3.04505	177.33497	0.32840	57.56555	0.01737	.9350	.9681
9	108	3.49980	216.76863	0.28573	61.22311	0.01633	.9205	.9610
10	120	4.02247	262.09138	0.24860	64.40542	0.01553	.9039	.9528
11	132	4.62319	314.18272	0.21630	67.17423	0.01489	.8848	.9434
12	144	5.31363	374.05350	0.18820	69.58326	0.01437	.8628	.9327
13	156	6.10718	442.86549	0.16374	71.67928	0.01395	.8376	.9203
14	168	7.01924	521.95401	0.14247	73.50294	0.01360	.8086	.9060
15	180	8.06751	612.85376	0.12395	75.08965	0.01332	.7753	.8897
16	192	9.27232	717.32867	0.10785	76.47018	0.01308	.7369	.8709
17	204	10.65707	837.40608	0.09383	77.67133	0.01287	.6929	.8493
18	216	12.24862	975.41609	0.08164	78.71641	0.01270	.6423	.8244
19	228	14.07785	1134.03679	0.07103	79.62569	0.01256	.5841	.7959
20	240	16.18027	1316.34623	0.06180	80.41682	0.01244	.5173	.7631
21	252	18.59666	1525.88213	0.05377	81.10516	0.01233	.4404	.7253
22	264	21.37393	1766.71054	0.04679	81.70405	0.01224	.3521	.6820
23	276	24.56595	2043.50476	0.04071	82.22513	0.01216	.2506	.6322
24	288	28.23468	2361.63599	0.03542	82.67850	0.01210	.1340	.5749
25	300	32.45131	2727.27758	0.03082	83.07296	0.01204	.0	.5091
26	312	37.29765	3147.52483	0.02681	83.41616	0.01199	.0	.4334
27	324	42.86776	3630.53265	0.02333	83.71477	0.01195	.0	.3465
28	336	49.26971	4185.67384	0.02030	83.97458	0.01191	.0	.2466
29	348	56.62775	4823.72094	0.01766	84.20063	0.01188	.0	.1317
30	360	65.08466	5557.05529	0.01536	84.39731	0.01185	.0	.0
31	372	74.80453	6399.90727	0.01337	84.56844	0.01182	.0	.0
32	384	85.97599	7368.63248	0.01163	84.71732	0.01180	.0	.0
33	396	98.81582	8482.02907	0.01012	84.84686	0.01179	.0	.0
34	408	113.57317	9761.70256	0.00880	84.95957	0.01177	.0	.0
35	420	130.53442	11232.48509	0.00766	85.05764	0.01176	.0	.0
36	432	150.02870	12922.91726	0.00667	85.14296	0.01174	.0	.0
37	444	172.43429	14865.80200	0.00580	85.21719	0.01173	.0	.0
38	456	198.18597	17098.84107	0.00505	85.28178	0.01173	.0	.0
39	468	227.78347	19665.36673	0.00439	85.33798	0.01172	.0	.0
40	480	261.80111	22615.18253	0.00382	85.38688	0.01171	.0	.0

YR	MOS	(1) COMPOUND VALUE $1	(2) COMPOUND VALUE $1 PER MO	(3) PRESENT VALUE $1	(4) PRESENT VALUE $1 PER MO	(5) LOAN CONSTANT	(6) BAL 25 YR LOAN	(7) BAL 30 YR LOAN
	1	1.01208	1.01208	0.98806	0.98806	1.01208	.9997	.9998
	2	1.02431	2.03640	0.97626	1.96433	0.50908	.9993	.9997
	3	1.03669	3.07309	0.96461	2.92893	0.34142	.9990	.9995
	4	1.04922	4.12230	0.95309	3.88203	0.25760	.9986	.9993
	5	1.06189	5.18420	0.94171	4.82374	0.20731	.9983	.9992
	6	1.07473	6.25892	0.93047	5.75421	0.17379	.9979	.9990
	7	1.08771	7.34663	0.91936	6.67357	0.14984	.9975	.9988
	8	1.10086	8.44749	0.90838	7.58195	0.13189	.9972	.9986
	9	1.11416	9.56165	0.89754	8.47949	0.11793	.9968	.9985
	10	1.12762	10.68927	0.88682	9.36632	0.10677	.9964	.9983
	11	1.14125	11.83051	0.87624	10.24255	0.09763	.9960	.9981
	12	1.15504	12.98555	0.86577	11.10833	0.09002	.9957	.9979
2	24	1.33411	27.98431	0.74957	20.72563	0.04825	.9906	.9955
3	36	1.54094	45.30842	0.64895	29.05205	0.03442	.9849	.9927
4	48	1.77984	65.31837	0.56185	36.26085	0.02758	.9782	.9895
5	60	2.05578	88.43058	0.48643	42.50204	0.02353	.9704	.9858
6	72	2.37450	115.12599	0.42114	47.90550	0.02087	.9615	.9815
7	84	2.74263	145.96013	0.36461	52.58369	0.01902	.9512	.9766
8	96	3.16783	181.57466	0.31567	56.63393	0.01766	.9393	.9709
9	108	3.65896	222.71070	0.27330	60.14054	0.01663	.9255	.9643
10	120	4.22623	270.22428	0.23662	63.17646	0.01583	.9097	.9567
11	132	4.88144	325.10414	0.20486	65.80489	0.01520	.8913	.9479
12	144	5.63824	388.49232	0.17736	68.08051	0.01469	.8701	.9377
13	156	6.51236	461.70791	0.15355	70.05069	0.01428	.8456	.9260
14	168	7.52201	546.27451	0.13294	71.75642	0.01394	.8174	.9124
15	180	8.68819	643.95192	0.11510	73.23320	0.01366	.7847	.8967
16	192	10.03516	756.77277	0.09965	74.51175	0.01342	.7470	.8787
17	204	11.59097	887.08485	0.08627	75.61869	0.01322	.7034	.8578
18	216	13.38798	1037.59991	0.07469	76.57705	0.01306	.6531	.8336
19	228	15.46359	1211.45012	0.06467	77.40678	0.01292	.5950	.8058
20	240	17.86099	1412.25326	0.05599	78.12513	0.01280	.5279	.7736
21	252	20.63007	1644.18799	0.04847	78.74706	0.01270	.4503	.7364
22	264	23.82847	1912.08080	0.04197	79.28552	0.01261	.3608	.6934
23	276	27.52272	2221.50646	0.03633	79.75169	0.01254	.2573	.6438
24	288	31.78971	2578.90404	0.03146	80.15530	0.01248	.1379	.5865
25	300	36.71824	2991.71087	0.02723	80.50473	0.01242	.0	.5203
26	312	42.41087	3468.51736	0.02358	80.80726	0.01238	.0	.4439
27	324	48.98605	4019.24571	0.02041	81.06918	0.01234	.0	.3556
28	336	56.58062	4655.35642	0.01767	81.29595	0.01230	.0	.2536
29	348	65.35262	5390.08678	0.01530	81.49227	0.01227	.0	.1358
30	360	75.48459	6238.72631	0.01325	81.66225	0.01225	.0	.0
31	372	87.18737	7218.93497	0.01147	81.80941	0.01222	.0	.0
32	384	100.70449	8351.11063	0.00993	81.93682	0.01220	.0	.0
33	396	116.31724	9658.81353	0.00860	82.04712	0.01219	.0	.0
34	408	134.35053	11169.25661	0.00744	82.14262	0.01217	.0	.0
35	420	155.17961	12913.87176	0.00644	82.22531	0.01216	.0	.0
36	432	179.23794	14928.96393	0.00558	82.29689	0.01215	.0	.0
37	444	207.02615	17256.46662	0.00483	82.35886	0.01214	.0	.0
38	456	239.12252	19944.81451	0.00418	82.41252	0.01213	.0	.0
39	468	276.19497	23049.95135	0.00362	82.45898	0.01213	.0	.0
40	480	319.01495	26636.49416	0.00313	82.49919	0.01212	.0	.0

INTEREST RATE = 15.00%

YR	MOS	(1) COMPOUND VALUE $1	(2) COMPOUND VALUE $1 PER MO	(3) PRESENT VALUE $1	(4) PRESENT VALUE $1 PER MO	(5) LOAN CONSTANT	(6) BAL 25 YR LOAN	(7) BAL 30 YR LOAN
	1	1.01250	1.01250	0.98765	0.98765	1.01250	.9997	.9999
	2	1.02516	2.03766	0.97546	1.96312	0.50939	.9994	.9997
	3	1.03797	3.07563	0.96342	2.92653	0.34170	.9991	.9996
	4	1.05095	4.12657	0.95152	3.87806	0.25786	.9987	.9994
	5	1.06408	5.19065	0.93978	4.81783	0.20756	.9984	.9993
	6	1.07738	6.26804	0.92817	5.74601	0.17403	.9981	.9991
	7	1.09085	7.35889	0.91672	6.66273	0.15009	.9978	.9989
	8	1.10449	8.46337	0.90540	7.56812	0.13213	.9974	.9988
	9	1.11829	9.58167	0.89422	8.46234	0.11817	.9971	.9986
	10	1.13227	10.71394	0.88318	9.34553	0.10700	.9967	.9985
	11	1.14642	11.86036	0.87228	10.21780	0.09787	.9964	.9983
	12	1.16075	13.02112	0.86151	11.07931	0.09026	.9960	.9981
2	24	1.34735	28.13544	0.74220	20.62423	0.04849	.9914	.9960
3	36	1.56394	45.67945	0.63941	28.84727	0.03467	.9861	.9935
4	48	1.81535	66.04374	0.55086	35.93148	0.02783	.9799	.9906
5	60	2.10718	89.68169	0.47457	42.03459	0.02379	.9727	.9872
6	72	2.44592	117.11954	0.40884	47.29247	0.02115	.9643	.9833
7	84	2.83911	148.96815	0.35222	51.82218	0.01930	.9546	.9787
8	96	3.29551	185.93657	0.30344	55.72457	0.01795	.9434	.9735
9	108	3.82528	228.84783	0.26142	59.08651	0.01692	.9303	.9673
10	120	4.44021	278.65727	0.22521	61.98284	0.01613	.9151	.9602
11	132	5.15400	336.47380	0.19402	64.47806	0.01551	.8975	.9520
12	144	5.98253	403.58459	0.16715	66.62772	0.01501	.8771	.9424
13	156	6.94424	481.48376	0.14400	68.47966	0.01460	.8534	.9313
14	168	8.06056	571.90556	0.12406	70.07513	0.01427	.8258	.9184
15	180	9.35633	676.86307	0.10688	71.44964	0.01400	.7939	.9034
16	192	10.86041	798.69299	0.09208	72.63379	0.01377	.7568	.8860
17	204	12.60627	940.10760	0.07933	73.65394	0.01358	.7137	.8658
18	216	14.63278	1104.25526	0.06834	74.53282	0.01342	.6637	.8424
19	228	16.98507	1294.79040	0.05888	75.28997	0.01328	.6057	.8152
20	240	19.71549	1515.95491	0.05072	75.94227	0.01317	.5383	.7837
21	252	22.88485	1772.67263	0.04370	76.50423	0.01307	.4601	.7470
22	264	26.56369	2070.65887	0.03765	76.98836	0.01299	.3694	.7045
23	276	30.83392	2416.54774	0.03243	77.40545	0.01292	.2640	.6551
24	288	35.79061	2818.03982	0.02794	77.76477	0.01286	.1418	.5978
25	300	41.54412	3284.07356	0.02407	78.07433	0.01281	.0	.5313
26	312	48.22252	3825.02432	0.02074	78.34102	0.01276	.0	.4541
27	324	55.97451	4452.93537	0.01787	78.57077	0.01273	.0	.3645
28	336	64.97266	5181.78595	0.01539	78.76871	0.01270	.0	.2605
29	348	75.41731	6027.80255	0.01326	78.93923	0.01267	.0	.1398
30	360	87.54099	7009.82013	0.01142	79.08614	0.01264	.0	.0
31	372	101.61360	8149.70148	0.00984	79.21270	0.01262	.0	.0
32	384	117.94844	9472.82390	0.00848	79.32173	0.01261	.0	.0
33	396	136.90919	11008.64422	0.00730	79.41567	0.01259	.0	.0
34	408	158.91795	12791.35459	0.00629	79.49659	0.01258	.0	.0
35	420	184.46473	14860.64371	0.00542	79.56631	0.01257	.0	.0
36	432	214.11827	17262.58039	0.00467	79.62637	0.01256	.0	.0
37	444	248.53875	20050.63923	0.00402	79.67811	0.01255	.0	.0
38	456	288.49248	23286.89112	0.00347	79.72269	0.01254	.0	.0
39	468	334.86895	27043.38511	0.00299	79.76109	0.01254	.0	.0
40	480	388.70064	31403.75247	0.00257	79.79418	0.01253	.0	.0

INTEREST RATE = 16.00%

YR	MOS	(1) COMPOUND VALUE $1	(2) COMPOUND VALUE $1 PER MO	(3) PRESENT VALUE $1	(4) PRESENT VALUE $1 PER MO	(5) LOAN CONSTANT	(6) BAL 25 YR LOAN	(7) BAL 30 YR LOAN
	1	1.01333	1.01333	0.98684	0.98684	1.01333	.9997	.9999
	2	1.02684	2.04018	0.97386	1.96070	0.51002	.9995	.9998
	3	1.04054	3.08071	0.96104	2.92174	0.34226	.9992	.9997
	4	1.05441	4.13512	0.94840	3.87014	0.25839	.9990	.9995
	5	1.06847	5.20359	0.93592	4.80606	0.20807	.9987	.9994
	6	1.08271	6.28631	0.92360	5.72966	0.17453	.9984	.9993
	7	1.09715	7.38346	0.91145	6.64112	0.15058	.9981	.9992
	8	1.11178	8.49524	0.89946	7.54057	0.13262	.9979	.9990
	9	1.12660	9.62184	0.88762	8.42820	0.11865	.9976	.9989
	10	1.14162	10.76346	0.87594	9.30414	0.10748	.9973	.9988
	11	1.15685	11.92031	0.86442	10.16856	0.09834	.9970	.9987
	12	1.17227	13.09258	0.85305	11.02161	0.09073	.9967	.9985
2	24	1.37422	28.44063	0.72769	20.42354	0.04896	.9928	.9968
3	36	1.61096	46.43270	0.62075	28.44381	0.03516	.9883	.9948
4	48	1.88848	67.52428	0.52953	35.28546	0.02834	.9830	.9924
5	60	2.21381	92.24932	0.45171	41.12170	0.02432	.9767	.9896
6	72	2.59518	121.23377	0.38533	46.10028	0.02169	.9694	.9863
7	84	3.04226	155.21139	0.32870	50.34723	0.01986	.9608	.9825
8	96	3.56635	195.04235	0.28040	53.97007	0.01853	.9508	.9780
9	108	4.18072	241.73504	0.23919	57.06052	0.01753	.9390	.9727
10	120	4.90094	296.47150	0.20404	59.69681	0.01675	.9252	.9666
11	132	5.74523	360.63747	0.17406	61.94569	0.01614	.9090	.9593
12	144	6.73497	435.85735	0.14848	63.86408	0.01566	.8901	.9508
13	156	7.89520	524.03542	0.12666	65.50056	0.01527	.8678	.9409
14	168	9.25532	627.40400	0.10805	66.89654	0.01495	.8417	.9292
15	180	10.84974	748.57997	0.09217	68.08739	0.01469	.8112	.9156
16	192	12.71883	890.63101	0.07862	69.10323	0.01447	.7753	.8996
17	204	14.90991	1057.15331	0.06707	69.96978	0.01429	.7333	.8808
18	216	17.47845	1252.36253	0.05721	70.70900	0.01414	.6841	.8588
19	228	20.48948	1481.20060	0.04881	71.33958	0.01402	.6264	.8329
20	240	24.01922	1749.46078	0.04163	71.87750	0.01391	.5587	.8027
21	252	28.15703	2063.93436	0.03552	72.33636	0.01382	.4794	.7672
22	264	33.00766	2432.58256	0.03030	72.72780	0.01375	.3864	.7256
23	276	38.69392	2864.73807	0.02584	73.06171	0.01369	.2774	.6769
24	288	45.35975	3371.34135	0.02205	73.34655	0.01363	.1496	.6198
25	300	53.17391	3965.21758	0.01881	73.58953	0.01359	.0	.5528
26	312	62.33423	4661.40135	0.01604	73.79680	0.01355	.0	.4743
27	324	73.07259	5477.51724	0.01369	73.97362	0.01352	.0	.3822
28	336	85.66087	6434.22607	0.01167	74.12445	0.01349	.0	.2743
29	348	100.41773	7555.74789	0.00996	74.25311	0.01347	.0	.1478
30	360	117.71678	8870.47516	0.00849	74.36287	0.01345	.0	.0
31	372	137.99594	10411.69155	0.00725	74.45650	0.01343	.0	.0
32	384	161.76861	12218.41451	0.00618	74.53637	0.01342	.0	.0
33	396	189.63662	14336.38307	0.00527	74.60450	0.01340	.0	.0
34	408	222.30547	16819.21575	0.00450	74.66262	0.01339	.0	.0
35	420	260.60221	19729.76799	0.00384	74.71220	0.01338	.0	.0
36	432	305.49635	23141.72338	0.00327	74.75449	0.01338	.0	.0
37	444	358.12445	27141.45904	0.00279	74.79057	0.01337	.0	.0
38	456	419.81884	31830.23234	0.00238	74.82135	0.01337	.0	.0
39	468	492.14136	37326.74434	0.00203	74.84760	0.01336	.0	.0
40	480	576.92295	43770.14483	0.00173	74.86999	0.01336	.0	.0

INTEREST RATE = 17.00%

YR	MOS	(1) COMPOUND VALUE $1	(2) COMPOUND VALUE $1 PER MO	(3) PRESENT VALUE $1	(4) PRESENT VALUE $1 PER MO	(5) LOAN CONSTANT	(6) BAL 25 YR LOAN	(7) BAL 30 YR LOAN
	1	1.01417	1.01417	0.98603	0.98603	1.01417	.9998	.9999
	2	1.02853	2.04270	0.97226	1.95829	0.51065	.9996	.9998
	3	1.04310	3.08581	0.95868	2.91696	0.34282	.9994	.9997
	4	1.05788	4.14369	0.94528	3.86225	0.25892	.9991	.9996
	5	1.07287	5.21656	0.93208	4.79433	0.20858	.9989	.9995
	6	1.08807	6.30462	0.91906	5.71339	0.17503	.9987	.9994
	7	1.10348	7.40811	0.90622	6.61961	0.15107	.9985	.9993
	8	1.11911	8.52722	0.89356	7.51318	0.13310	.9982	.9992
	9	1.13497	9.66219	0.88108	8.39426	0.11913	.9980	.9991
	10	1.15105	10.81324	0.86877	9.26303	0.10796	.9977	.9990
	11	1.16735	11.98059	0.85664	10.11967	0.09882	.9975	.9989
	12	1.18389	13.16448	0.84467	10.96434	0.09120	.9973	.9988
2	24	1.40160	28.74981	0.71347	20.22561	0.04944	.9940	.9974
3	36	1.65934	47.20114	0.60265	28.04834	0.03565	.9902	.9958
4	48	1.96448	69.04553	0.50904	34.65599	0.02886	.9856	.9939
5	60	2.32573	94.90691	0.42997	40.23728	0.02485	.9802	.9916
6	72	2.75342	125.52400	0.36319	44.95163	0.02225	.9738	.9888
7	84	3.25975	161.77130	0.30677	48.93372	0.02044	.9663	.9856
8	96	3.85919	204.68419	0.25912	52.29728	0.01912	.9573	.9818
9	108	4.56886	255.48840	0.21887	55.13838	0.01814	.9468	.9773
10	120	5.40904	315.63509	0.18488	57.53817	0.01738	.9342	.9719
11	132	6.40371	386.84226	0.15616	59.56522	0.01679	.9194	.9656
12	144	7.58130	471.14383	0.13190	61.27740	0.01632	.9018	.9581
13	156	8.97544	570.94777	0.11142	62.72363	0.01594	.8810	.9493
14	168	10.62595	689.10482	0.09411	63.94523	0.01564	.8564	.9388
15	180	12.57997	828.98998	0.07949	64.97707	0.01539	.8272	.9263
16	192	14.89333	994.59886	0.06714	65.84864	0.01519	.7927	.9116
17	204	17.63209	1190.66184	0.05671	66.58483	0.01502	.7519	.8942
18	216	20.87448	1422.77919	0.04791	67.20667	0.01488	.7035	.8735
19	228	24.71313	1697.58099	0.04046	67.73193	0.01476	.6462	.8491
20	240	29.25767	2022.91657	0.03418	68.17559	0.01467	.5784	.8202
21	252	34.63791	2408.07867	0.02887	68.55034	0.01459	.4982	.7860
22	264	41.00754	2864.06889	0.02439	68.86688	0.01452	.4031	.7454
23	276	48.54848	3403.91194	0.02060	69.13426	0.01446	.2906	.6975
24	288	57.47615	4043.02766	0.01740	69.36010	0.01442	.1574	.6407
25	300	68.04553	4799.67147	0.01470	69.55086	0.01438	.0	.5734
26	312	80.55854	5695.45582	0.01241	69.71200	0.01434	.0	.4938
27	324	95.37259	6755.96749	0.01049	69.84810	0.01432	.0	.3995
28	336	112.91082	8011.49849	0.00886	69.96306	0.01429	.0	.2880
29	348	133.67419	9497.91125	0.00748	70.06017	0.01427	.0	.1558
30	360	158.25577	11257.66301	0.00632	70.14219	0.01426	.0	.0
31	372	187.35769	13341.01856	0.00534	70.21147	0.01424	.0	.0
32	384	221.81122	15807.48595	0.00451	70.26999	0.01423	.0	.0
33	396	262.60047	18727.51628	0.00381	70.31943	0.01422	.0	.0
34	408	310.89052	22184.51602	0.00322	70.36118	0.01421	.0	.0
35	420	368.06072	26277.22941	0.00272	70.39645	0.01421	.0	.0
36	432	435.74404	31122.55893	0.00229	70.42624	0.01420	.0	.0
37	444	515.87376	36858.90444	0.00194	70.45140	0.01419	.0	.0
38	456	610.73867	43650.11642	0.00164	70.47265	0.01419	.0	.0
39	468	723.04846	51690.17608	0.00138	70.49060	0.01419	.0	.0
40	480	856.01109	61208.73617	0.00117	70.50577	0.01418	.0	.0

YR	MOS	(1) COMPOUND VALUE $1	(2) COMPOUND VALUE $1 PER MO	(3) PRESENT VALUE $1	(4) PRESENT VALUE $1 PER MO	(5) LOAN CONSTANT	(6) BAL 25 YR LOAN	(7) BAL 30 YR LOAN
	1	1.01500	1.01500	0.98522	0.98522	1.01500	.9998	.9999
	2	1.03023	2.04523	0.97066	1.95588	0.51128	.9996	.9999
	3	1.04568	3.09090	0.95632	2.91220	0.34338	.9995	.9998
	4	1.06136	4.15227	0.94218	3.85438	0.25944	.9993	.9997
	5	1.07728	5.22955	0.92826	4.78264	0.20909	.9991	.9996
	6	1.09344	6.32299	0.91454	5.69719	0.17553	.9989	.9996
	7	1.10984	7.43284	0.90103	6.59821	0.15156	.9987	.9995
	8	1.12649	8.55933	0.88771	7.48592	0.13358	.9985	.9994
	9	1.14339	9.70272	0.87459	8.36052	0.11961	.9983	.9993
	10	1.16054	10.86326	0.86167	9.22218	0.10843	.9981	.9992
	11	1.17795	12.04121	0.84893	10.07112	0.09929	.9979	.9992
	12	1.19562	13.23683	0.83639	10.40750	0.09168	.9977	.9991
2	24	1.42950	29.06302	0.69954	20.03040	0.04992	.9950	.9980
3	36	1.70914	47.98511	0.58509	27.66068	0.03615	.9918	.9966
4	48	2.04348	70.60870	0.48936	34.04255	0.02937	.9879	.9951
5	60	2.44322	97.65787	0.40930	39.38027	0.02539	.9832	.9932
6	72	2.92116	129.99835	0.34233	43.84466	0.02281	.9777	.9909
7	84	3.49259	168.66522	0.28632	47.57863	0.02102	.9710	.9882
8	96	4.17580	214.69603	0.23947	50.70167	0.01972	.9631	.9850
9	108	4.99267	270.17043	0.20029	53.31375	0.01876	.9536	.9811
10	120	5.96932	336.25751	0.16752	55.49845	0.01802	.9422	.9765
11	132	7.13703	415.27241	0.14011	57.32571	0.01744	.9287	.9710
12	144	8.53316	509.74407	0.11719	58.85401	0.01699	.9124	.9644
13	156	10.20241	622.69610	0.09802	60.13226	0.01663	.8930	.9565
14	168	12.19818	757.74360	0.08198	61.20137	0.01634	.8698	.9471
15	180	14.58437	919.20885	0.06857	62.09556	0.01610	.8421	.9358
16	192	17.43733	1112.25963	0.05735	62.84345	0.01591	.8089	.9223
17	204	20.84839	1343.07465	0.04797	63.46897	0.01576	.7693	.9062
18	216	24.92672	1619.04128	0.04012	63.99216	0.01563	.7219	.8869
19	228	29.80284	1948.99199	0.03355	64.42974	0.01552	.6652	.8639
20	240	35.63281	2343.48706	0.02806	64.79573	0.01543	.5975	.8363
21	252	42.60324	2815.15254	0.02347	65.10184	0.01536	.5164	.8033
22	264	50.93721	3379.08435	0.01963	65.35786	0.01530	.4196	.7640
23	276	60.90145	4053.33146	0.01642	65.57200	0.01525	.3038	.7169
24	288	72.81488	4859.47356	0.01373	65.75110	0.01521	.1653	.6605
25	300	87.05879	5823.31171	0.01149	65.90090	0.01517	.0	.5932
26	312	104.08907	6975.69410	0.00961	66.02618	0.01515	.0	.5127
27	324	124.45079	8353.50342	0.00804	66.13097	0.01512	.0	.4165
28	336	148.79562	10000.83728	0.00672	66.21862	0.01510	.0	.3014
29	348	177.90275	11970.41957	0.00562	66.29193	0.01508	.0	.1638
30	360	212.70376	14325.28794	0.00470	66.35324	0.01507	.0	.0
31	372	254.31248	17140.81134	0.00393	66.40452	0.01506	.0	.0
32	384	304.06062	20507.10227	0.00329	66.44741	0.01505	.0	.0
33	396	363.54040	24531.90086	0.00275	66.48328	0.01504	.0	.0
34	408	434.65551	29344.02318	0.00230	66.51328	0.01503	.0	.0
35	420	519.68202	35097.48404	0.00192	66.53838	0.01503	.0	.0
36	432	621.34126	41976.42638	0.00161	66.55937	0.01502	.0	.0
37	444	742.88690	50201.01480	0.00135	66.57692	0.01502	.0	.0
38	456	888.20908	60034.48214	0.00113	66.59160	0.01502	.0	.0
39	468	1061.95891	71791.55434	0.00094	66.60388	0.01501	.0	.0
40	480	1269.69737	85848.52346	0.00079	66.61416	0.01501	.0	.0

INTEREST RATE = 19.00%

YR	MOS	(1) COMPOUND VALUE $1	(2) COMPOUND VALUE $1 PER MO	(3) PRESENT VALUE $1	(4) PRESENT VALUE $1 PER MO	(5) LOAN CONSTANT	(6) BAL 25 YR LOAN	(7) BAL 30 YR LOAN
	1	1.01583	1.01583	0.98441	0.98441	1.01583	.9999	.9999
	2	1.03192	2.04775	0.96907	1.95348	0.51191	.9997	.9999
	3	1.04826	3.09601	0.95397	2.90745	0.34394	.9996	.9998
	4	1.06485	4.16086	0.93910	3.84654	0.25997	.9994	.9998
	5	1.08171	5.24257	0.92446	4.77100	0.20960	.9993	.9997
	6	1.09884	6.34141	0.91005	5.68105	0.17602	.9991	.9997
	7	1.11624	7.45765	0.89587	6.57692	0.15205	.9989	.9996
	8	1.13391	8.59157	0.88190	7.45882	0.13407	.9988	.9995
	9	1.15187	9.74343	0.86816	8.32698	0.12009	.9986	.9995
	10	1.17010	10.91354	0.85462	9.18160	0.10891	.9985	.9994
	11	1.18863	12.10217	0.84130	10.02291	0.09977	.9983	.9993
	12	1.20745	13.30962	0.82819	10.85110	0.09216	.9981	.9993
2	24	1.45794	29.38033	0.68590	19.83788	0.05041	.9958	.9984
3	36	1.76039	48.78493	0.56806	27.28065	0.03666	.9931	.9973
4	48	2.12558	72.21503	0.47046	33.44468	0.02990	.9898	.9960
5	60	2.56654	100.50573	0.38963	38.54968	0.02594	.9858	.9945
6	72	3.09897	134.66537	0.32269	42.77759	0.02338	.9810	.9926
7	84	3.74185	175.91145	0.26725	46.27911	0.02161	.9751	.9904
8	96	4.51810	225.71407	0.22133	49.17904	0.02033	.9681	.9876
9	108	5.45539	285.84830	0.18331	51.58073	0.01939	.9596	.9843
10	120	6.58711	358.45743	0.15181	53.56979	0.01867	.9494	.9804
11	132	7.95362	446.12940	0.12573	55.21711	0.01811	.9370	.9756
12	144	9.60360	551.98901	0.10413	56.58141	0.01767	.9220	.9698
13	156	11.59588	679.80930	0.08624	57.71131	0.01733	.9040	.9628
14	168	14.00146	834.14603	0.07142	58.64708	0.01705	.8822	.9543
15	180	16.90607	1020.50007	0.05915	59.42208	0.01683	.8558	.9441
16	192	20.41325	1245.51345	0.04899	60.06393	0.01665	.8240	.9318
17	204	24.64800	1517.20607	0.04057	60.59550	0.01650	.7857	.9169
18	216	29.76125	1845.26160	0.03360	61.03574	0.01638	.7393	.8989
19	228	35.93526	2241.37257	0.02783	61.40034	0.01629	.6833	.8772
20	240	43.39006	2719.65715	0.02305	61.70231	0.01621	.6158	.8510
21	252	52.39137	3297.16235	0.01909	61.95239	0.01614	.5342	.8194
22	264	63.26002	3994.47157	0.01581	62.15950	0.01609	.4357	.7812
23	276	76.38337	4836.43829	0.01309	62.33104	0.01604	.3167	.7351
24	288	92.22917	5853.07184	0.01084	62.47310	0.01601	.1731	.6794
25	300	111.36221	7080.60702	0.00898	62.59075	0.01598	.0	.6122
26	312	134.46441	8562.79561	0.00744	62.68819	0.01595	.0	.5310
27	324	162.35918	10352.46568	0.00616	62.76889	0.01593	.0	.4330
28	336	196.04076	12513.40459	0.00510	62.83572	0.01591	.0	.3146
29	348	236.70961	15122.63243	0.00422	62.89107	0.01590	.0	.1717
30	360	285.81525	18273.14717	0.00350	62.93692	0.01589	.0	.0
31	372	345.10791	22077.23933	0.00290	62.97488	0.01588	.0	.0
32	384	416.70089	26670.49418	0.00240	63.00632	0.01587	.0	.0
33	396	503.14590	32216.62432	0.00199	63.03236	0.01586	.0	.0
34	408	607.52401	38913.30467	0.00165	63.05393	0.01586	.0	.0
35	420	733.55548	46999.21801	0.00136	63.07179	0.01585	.0	.0
36	432	885.73229	56762.56210	0.00113	63.08658	0.01585	.0	.0
37	444	1069.47833	68551.32163	0.00094	63.09884	0.01585	.0	.0
38	456	1291.34267	82785.67103	0.00077	63.10898	0.01585	.0	.0
39	468	1559.23299	99972.95037	0.00064	63.11738	0.01584	.0	.0
40	480	1882.69743	120725.74788	0.00053	63.12434	0.01584	.0	.0

YR	MOS	(1) COMPOUND VALUE $1	(2) COMPOUND VALUE $1 PER MO	(3) PRESENT VALUE $1	(4) PRESENT VALUE $1 PER MO	(5) LOAN CONSTANT	(6) BAL 25 YR LOAN	(7) BAL 30 YR LOAN
	1	1.01667	1.01667	0.98361	0.98361	1.01667	.9999	*****
	2	1.03361	2.05028	0.96748	1.95109	0.51253	.9998	.9999
	3	1.05084	3.10112	0.95162	2.90271	0.34451	.9996	.9999
	4	1.06835	4.16947	0.93602	3.83873	0.26050	.9995	.9998
	5	1.08616	5.25563	0.92068	4.75941	0.21011	.9994	.9998
	6	1.10426	6.35989	0.90558	5.66499	0.17652	.9993	.9997
	7	1.12266	7.48255	0.89074	6.55573	0.15254	.9991	.9997
	8	1.14138	8.62393	0.87614	7.43186	0.13456	.9990	.9996
	9	1.16040	9.78433	0.86177	8.29364	0.12057	.9989	.9996
	10	1.17974	10.96406	0.84765	9.14128	0.10939	.9987	.9995
	11	1.19940	12.16347	0.83375	9.97503	0.10025	.9986	.9995
	12	1.21939	13.38286	0.82008	10.79511	0.09263	.9984	.9994
2	24	1.48691	29.70179	0.67253	19.64798	0.05090	.9966	.9987
3	36	1.81313	49.60096	0.55153	26.90806	0.03716	.9942	.9979
4	48	2.21092	73.86582	0.45230	32.86191	0.03043	.9914	.9968
5	60	2.69597	103.45418	0.37092	37.74456	0.02649	.9880	.9956
6	72	3.28744	139.53396	0.30419	41.74873	0.02395	.9838	.9940
7	84	4.00868	183.52932	0.24946	45.03247	0.02221	.9787	.9921
8	96	4.88815	237.17687	0.20458	47.72540	0.02095	.9725	.9898
9	108	5.96056	302.59422	0.16777	49.93383	0.02003	.9649	.9870
10	120	7.26825	382.36355	0.13758	51.74492	0.01933	.9557	.9836
11	132	8.86284	479.63355	0.11283	53.23016	0.01879	.9444	.9794
12	144	10.80727	598.24373	0.09253	54.44818	0.01837	.9306	.9744
13	156	13.17829	742.87593	0.07588	55.44705	0.01804	.9139	.9682
14	168	16.06949	919.23913	0.06223	56.26621	0.01777	.8934	.9606
15	180	19.59500	1134.29486	0.05103	56.93799	0.01756	.8685	.9514
16	192	23.89396	1396.53189	0.04185	57.48890	0.01739	.8380	.9402
17	204	29.13609	1716.30138	0.03432	57.94069	0.01726	.8010	.9264
18	216	35.52829	2106.22545	0.02815	58.31120	0.01715	.7557	.9097
19	228	43.32287	2581.69538	0.02308	58.61505	0.01706	.7006	.8894
20	240	52.82753	3161.47918	0.01893	58.86422	0.01699	.6334	.8645
21	252	64.41741	3868.46236	0.01552	59.06857	0.01693	.5514	.8342
22	264	78.55002	4730.55136	0.01273	59.23615	0.01688	.4514	.7973
23	276	95.78319	5781.77499	0.01044	59.37358	0.01684	.3295	.7522
24	288	116.79717	7063.62770	0.00856	59.48628	0.01681	.1908	.6973
25	300	142.42143	8626.70747	0.00702	59.57871	0.01678	.0	.6303
26	312	173.66742	10532.71299	0.00576	59.65451	0.01676	.0	.5486
27	324	211.76851	12856.87913	0.00472	59.71667	0.01675	.0	.4490
28	336	258.22863	15690.94658	0.00387	59.76764	0.01673	.0	.3275
29	348	314.88168	19146.78316	0.00318	59.80945	0.01672	.0	.1794
30	360	383.96392	23360.79945	0.00260	59.84373	0.01671	.0	.0
31	372	468.20218	28499.33333	0.00214	59.87185	0.01670	.0	.0
32	384	570.92156	34765.21571	0.00175	59.89490	0.01670	.0	.0
33	396	696.17665	42405.77679	0.00144	59.91381	0.01669	.0	.0
34	408	848.91160	51722.60881	0.00118	59.92932	0.01669	.0	.0
35	420	1035.15524	63083.47068	0.00097	59.94203	0.01668	.0	.0
36	432	1262.25906	76936.80431	0.00079	59.95246	0.01668	.0	.0
37	444	1539.18744	93829.43576	0.00065	59.96101	0.01668	.0	.0
38	456	1876.87144	114428.15988	0.00053	59.96803	0.01668	.0	.0
39	468	2288.64029	139546.06032	0.00044	59.97378	0.01667	.0	.0
40	480	2790.74755	170174.60408	0.00036	59.97850	0.01667	.0	.0

Index

Index

631

Q–R

*This book has been set in 10 and 9 point
Caledonia, leaded 2 points. Part and chapter
numbers are in 24 point (large) Helvetica
Medium. Part titles are in 24 point (small)
Helvetica and chapter titles are in 18 point
Helvetica. The size of the type page is 27
by 45½ picas.*